TRIAL PRACTICE SERIES

Successful Trial Techniques of Expert Practitioners

Robert V. Wells, J.D., Ph. D.
Wells and Wells
Kansas City, Kansas

SHEPARD'S/McGRAW-HILL, INC.
P.O. Box 1235
Colorado Springs, Colorado 80901

McGRAW-HILL INFORMATION SERVICES COMPANY
New York • St. Louis • San Francisco • Auckland • Bogotá • Caracas
Colorado Springs • Hamburg • Lisbon • London • Madrid • Mexico • Milan
Montreal • New Delhi • Oklahoma City • Panama • Paris • San Juan
São Paulo • Singapore • Sydney • Tokyo • Toronto

12345678910 SHHA 897654321098

Library of Congress Cataloging-in-Publication Data

Wells, Robert V., 1946-
  Successful trial techniques of expert practitioners / Robert V. Wells.
      p.   cm. — (Trial practice series)
  Includes index.
  ISBN 0-07-172103-7
  1. Trial practice—United States.   2. Forensic oratory.
I. Title. II. Series.
KF8915.W486   1988
347.73'7—dc19
[347.3077]
                                            88-39418
                                               CIP

ISBN0-07-172103-7

The sponsoring editor for this book was Bradley Abramson and the editor was Joan Goldsmith.

Shepard's Trial Practice Series

I dedicate this book with love and affection to Connie and our four kids.

To Jeffrey and Matthew for reshaping my life.

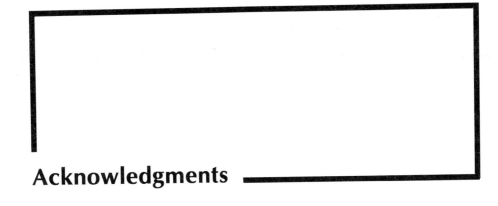

Acknowledgments

I would like to acknowledge those people who assisted and supported this work. First, I would like to thank Karlyn Kohrs Campbell for her encouragement and help in formulating the initial study that was the basis for this work. She helped me to develop the discipline I needed to make the transition from lawyer to author. Her way of approaching her work will always be a standard for me in approaching mine.

I would like to thank Wil Linkugel, Donn Parson, and Thomas Beisecker, professors, for encouraging my efforts in legal communication.

I would like to express my appreciation to my parents, Sam and Mary Wells, who provided support throughout my scholastic career. My father, as law partner, helped to keep my law practice alive while I obtained my Ph.D.

I thank my friend, Gerard, whose encouragement gave me the impetus I needed to return to school and take a new path within the field of law.

Finally, I would like to thank the lawyers who took time out from their busy schedules to respond to my request for transcripts.

Preface

In attempting to learn and understand trial technique, lawyers are faced with the confusing problem of where to start. The American legal system has produced a distinguished group of civil trial lawyers who have captured the imagination and respect of the general public and their colleagues. We know them as charismatic, witty, and intelligent. While this perception promotes their status as mythic figures in the American legal system, it does little to further our understanding of trial technique. A review of writings by lawyers on trial technique reveals varying approaches to trial technique based on the individual styles and personalities of the individual lawyers. The writings of social science researchers provide theories based on what "what ought to work," but many times these theories either have not been tested, or do not work when tested.

The purpose of this book is to provide insight into the trial technique of successful trial practitioners. As well as providing an overview of those psychological and communication concepts that come to bear on the trial process, this book examines the trial practices of some of America's most successful trial lawyers. A structure for successful trial technique is identified, explored, and analyzed. This structure for successful trial technique may be used as a starting guide by inexperienced lawyers and as a checklist for those experienced lawyers who wish to ensure that they are doing all that they can for their clients.

Contents

Summary

Detailed

3   Lawyer Credibility

6 Opening Statement

7 Direct Examination

1

Understanding Successful Trial Techniques

§1.01   Introduction

The American legal system has produced a distinguished group of civil trial lawyers who have captured the imagination and respect of the general public, as well as of their colleagues. We know them as charismatic, witty, and intelligent. While this perception promotes their status as mythic figures in the American legal system, it does little to further our understanding of legal argumentation or technique. Students in law school are taught how to understand and recognize legal theory, how to reason inductively, and how to argue logically, but they spend little time comparing transcripts of actual jury trials in order to see what successful trial lawyers do in presenting their cases.[1] Similarly, communication scholars have ignored comparative studies of successful

---

[1] See I. Goldstein, Trial Techniques (1935) and A. Julien, Opening Statements (1980) as examples of trial technique texts or handbooks. While these texts provide insightful examples and suggestions about how lawsuits should be tried, they provide no comparative analysis of actual trial rhetoric.

trial lawyers. Experimentalists have conducted mock jury studies,[2] persuasion scholars have attempted to make predictions about the effectiveness of persuasive techniques based on persuasion literature,[3] and rhetoricians have studied individual lawyers intensively.[4] Although these studies are valuable, they fail to provide explanations of why successful lawyers are, as a group, successful. The approaches are unsatisfactory because they cannot simulate the trial setting, they analyze arguments apart from the context in which they occur, and they fail to analyze the techniques of successful lawyers as a group. Therefore, a new approach to the study of legal rhetoric is needed.

Mock jury research has demonstrated that jurors decide cases on the basis of many factors other than evidence and reasoning, such as the socioeconomic status and attractiveness of the litigants, and the socioeconomic status and educational level of the jurors.[5] Mitchell and Byrne have demonstrated that authoritarian jurors favor litigants perceived as similar to themselves.[6] Kaplan and Miller have demonstrated that, as the facts of the case become more ambiguous, the effect of juror bias on the jury's decision increases.[7] From these studies, it can be argued that it is the situation that determines which factors will come into play. It seems appropriate to assume that, as a class, successful lawyers are successful not solely because of their innate charm or their ability to formulate logical arguments, but because they have the same understanding and capabilities with respect to the rhetorical situation as do other classes of successful speakers, such as politicians and religious leaders. Thus, a methodological approach is called for which takes into account situational factors and the lawyers' responses to them. A comparative analysis provides this approach.

This book is divided into two parts. Part One contains an overview of the communication process and how these concepts relate to jury trials (Chapter 1), an analysis of lawyer credibility and why jurors find one side of the case more believable than the other (Chapter 2), and an analysis of the psychological aspects of jury selection (Chapter 3). Part Two contains a comparative study of the trial transcripts of successful trial lawyers, which discloses a common structure for successful trial technique.

---

[2] See Gerbase, Zuckerman & Reis, *Justice Needs a New Blindfold: A Review of Mock Jury Research,* 84 Psychological Bull 323-45 (1977), for a description of various types of mock jury research.

[3] For example, see P. Taylor, R. Buchanan & D. Strawn, Communication Strategies for Trial Attorneys (1984).

[4] For an example of this approach, see E. Southerland, Principles of Criminology (1966); Attorney for the Damned (A. Weinberg ed 1957).

[5] Gerbase, Zuckerman & Reis, *supra* note 2.

[6] Mitchell & Byrne, *The Defendant's Dilemma: Effects of Juror's Attitude and Authoritarianism on Judicial Decisions,* 25 J Personality & Soc Psychology, 123-129 (1973).

[7] Kaplan & Miller, *Reducing the Effects of Juror Bias,* 36 J Personality & Soc Psychology, 1443-45 (1978).

§1.02 Survey of the Literature

A selected review of the literature on trial technique is useful at this point to illuminate the approaches to understanding trial technique that have been undertaken. The literature on trial technique may be roughly divided into two categories: writings by lawyers based on their own personal trial experiences, and writings by social scientists based on persuasion theory or mock jury research.

Trial technique literature by lawyers is best illustrated by the work of Irving Goldstein,[8] Alfred Julien,[9] Melvin Belli,[10] Melvin Block,[11] Leonard Decof,[12] David M. Harney,[13] and Thomas Mauet.[14] *Trial Technique,* by Goldstein, was for many years the prototypical trial technique text by a lawyer for lawyers. Goldstein covers each aspect of a civil jury trial by discussing his personal analysis of proper practice and procedure, followed by illustrations from actual trials. For example, on opening statements, Goldstein presents his personal views under headings such as "in general," "purpose," "failure to make a good opening statement," "testing opening statement," and "overstatement and exaggeration."[15] In some instances, illustrations, such as what to say to the jury in a final argument when opposing counsel has committed the error of exaggeration in an opening statement, are provided.[16] At the end of the chapter, Goldstein provides various specimens of opening statements taken from actual cases.

In the preface to *Opening Statements,* Julien states his belief that there is no recognized method of trial technique; rather, there are many methods.[17] He compares teaching trial technique to "listening to one's next-door office neighbor who needs some help in formulating his or her ideas and theories about an oncoming trial."[18] In such cases, "in talking to an older acquaintance or associate, ideas are honed and the oncoming trial can be analyzed."[19] Consistent with this view of formulating trial technique, Julien treats opening statements by setting out his own precepts, followed by excerpts from his own cases.

In *Modern Trials,* Melvin Belli implies that his book on trial technique is, to an extent, autobiographical.[20] Indeed, much of the book presents his personal

---

[8] I. Goldstein, Trial Techniques (1935).

[9] A. Julien, Opening Statements (1980).

[10] M. Belli, Modern Trials (2d ed 1982).

[11] The Art of Summation (M. Block ed 1968).

[12] L. Decof, Art of Advocacy: Opening Statement (1984).

[13] D. Harney, Medical Malpractice (1987).

[14] T. Mauet, *Fundamentals of Trial Techniques* (1980).

[15] I. Goldstein, *supra* note 8, at 201-11.

[16] *Id* 211.

[17] A. Julien, *supra* note 9, at vii.

[18] *Id.*

[19] *Id.*

[20] M. Belli, *supra* note 10, at xxii.

views on trial technique, followed by excerpts from his own cases or those of other well-known trial lawyers.

In the *Art of Advocacy: Opening Statement,* Leonard Decof states:

> The trial of a case is a highly specialized, highly sophisticated affair, even when the facts are most mundane. It requires a great deal of many qualities, a great many skills. It demands creativity. It should never be a casual exercise. . . .The things the trial lawyer needs to know had traditionally never been a part of the law school education.[21]

With respect to trial technique and the excerpts set out in his book, Decof notes that "the techniques and content are extremely subjective, and will vary widely with the nature, personality, and experience of the lawyer."[22] In discussing opening statements, Decof presents his personal views, based on his experiences, followed by actual opening statements, followed by his analysis of what each attorney is attempting to accomplish in each case.

Melvin Block, in *The Art of Summation,* presents a series of actual closing statements by various well-known, successful lawyers.[23] Each case is used to illustrate how a particularly difficult problem was resolved. For example, a closing statement by James Dempsey is presented to illustrate how the attorney surmounted the problem of proving and recovering damages for the death of a young child at a time when the prevailing public attitude held that small children were a liability rather than an asset.[24] No commentary on, or analysis of, the closing statements is provided.

David Harney provides a specialized analysis of medical negligence cases based on his own experience. Although the text is specialized, Harney provides an excellent analysis of how the trial lawyer should present his or her case.

With respect to trial work, Thomas Mauet asserts that "there is no 'right way' to try cases, or 'authority' on trial techniques."[25] Thus, in *Fundamentals of Trial Techniques,* Mauet presents his personal perception of standard trial techniques followed by examples from actual trials, with the specific reservation that there are various approaches to trial work and that "the examples set forth in the text are not the only way of accomplishing the particular task involved."[26]

Other illustrative trial texts are *Fundamentals of Criminal Advocacy,* by F. Lee Bailey and Henry Rothblatt,[27] *The Anatomy of a Personal Injury Lawsuit* series by

---

[21] L. Decof, *supra* note 12, at vii.

[22] *Id* ix.

[23] M. Block, *supra* note 11.

[24] *Id* 167.

[25] T. Mauet, *supra* note 14, at xi.

[26] *Id.*

[27] F. Bailey & H. Rothblatt, Fundamentals of Criminal Advocacy (1974).

the Association of Trial Lawyers of America,[28] and *Closing Argument, the Act and the Law* by Jacob Stein.[29] In all of these texts, the lawyers treat their subjects by presenting their personal axioms for proper trial techniques, followed by selected illustrative excerpts from actual trials.

There have been many articles written by lawyers dealing with specific aspects of trial practice. Some of the illustrative articles are worth noting. Scott Baldwin outlines good practice for effective cross-examination, based on his personal experience and success.[30] He discusses such matters as how to determine whether to cross-examine a witness and how to control a difficult witness. John Cleary traces case law regulating closing arguments and provides examples of strategies drawn from his personal experiences.[31] In one section, he suggests that the trial lawyer may benefit from contrasting himself or herself with the opposing attorney. William Colson outlines his personal beliefs about closing argument, followed by stories about his career and a transcript of one of his actual closings.[32] Richard Crawford sets out his personal views on the importance of closing argument.[33] He argues that juries make up their minds prior to deliberation and, in fact, often decide cases after the opening statement. Based on this assumption, Crawford suggests that opening statements at best will decide the case, and at least will provide a framework through which the jury will see the trial unfold. Francis Hare examines strategies for arguing monetary damages in the closing argument.[34] He deals with such topics as "placing a price on human life and disability" and the use of argument by analogy. Russ Herman provides an analysis of direct examination of lay witnesses.[35] He discusses how to frame questions and provides tips for handling witnesses. Joseph Karcher uses his personal experiences to provide the framework for his theory of closing argument.[36] He discusses the law with respect to closing argument and details a strategy for choosing between single and split final arguments. C. T. Fitzpatrick uses his experience as a lawyer and a juror to provide insight as to how a better defense could be prepared.[37] Weyman Lundquist advocates the use of education in opening statements.[38] He argues that since a jury does not know how the trial will progress, the lawyer

---

[28] See The Anatomy of a Personal Injury Lawsuit (J. Norton ed 2d ed 1981) as an example of this series.

[29] J. Stein, Closing Argument: The Act and the Law (1969).

[30] Baldwin, *Cross-examination,* July 1987 Trial Mag 76-81.

[31] Cleary, *The Final Argument in a Criminal Case,* 27 Prac Law 39-53 (1981).

[32] Colson, *Final Argument,* 36 Miss LJ 500-04 (1964-5).

[33] Crawford, *Opening Statement for the Defense in Criminal Cases,* Spring 1982 Litigation at 26-29.

[34] Hare, *The Importance of Argument in Tort Cases: Observations of a Plaintiff's Lawyer,* "33 Ala Law 187-195 (1972).

[35] Herman, *Direct Examination of Lay Witnesses,* Feb. 1988 Trial Mag 77-79.

[36] Karcher, *The Closing Argument,* 15 Prac Law 49-67 (1969).

[37] Fitzpatrick, *A Lawyer's Impression of Jury Duty, or Who Would Leave a Lawyer on a Jury?* 71 Ill BJ 702-05 (1983).

[38] Lundquist, *Advocacy in Opening Statements,* Spring 1982 Litigation at 23-25.

who attempts to educate the jury will be given a high credibility rating. John P. Miller draws upon his personal experiences in advocating a fact-oriented alternative, as opposed to the storytelling perspective, for opening statements and closing arguments.[39] Peter Perlman outlines the human factors involved in trying jury trials.[40] He discusses such topics as how to elicit honest information on voir dire, primacy effect in opening statements, and how to speak in a way that will create an atmosphere of trust.

It is of note that most of these lawyers express the opinion that there is no right or wrong way to try lawsuits, and that approaches to trial technique will vary with the lawyer. Further, the trial texts examine trial excerpts apart from the contexts in which they occur, as isolated acts, without appreciation of recurring situations across time. There is no comparative analysis of the actual trial techniques of successful lawyers in order to determine if there are similar trial techniques used by these lawyers as a response to recurring situations.

The trial technique literature of communication and psychology scholars follows the same pattern. Raymond Buchanan takes a functional approach to the discussion of opening statements and closing arguments.[41] He characterizes the stated goal of the opening statement as informational and distinguishes that goal from operational or persuasive goals. He argues that jurors should be treated as the "common man" and that lawyers should address the jurors as they would a group of PTA members. Michael Colley attempts to adapt concepts from persuasion theory to a discussion of opening statements.[42] William Costospoulas examines social psychology research and relates it to the various persuasive aspects of a trial.[43] He discusses the impact on the trial of variables such as source credibility, recency and primacy effects, and emotional appeals. The author attempts to integrate these factors and provide strategies for dealing with opening statements, direct examination, cross-examination, and closing arguments. Robert Lawson applies research findings from the social sciences to the courtroom setting.[44] For example, the literature with respect to inoculation theory is reviewed, and its applicability to the jury trial is discussed. Don Peters discusses the importance of participatory persuasion in opening statements and closing arguments.[45] The use of analogies, vivid language, and visual aids, and the exploitation of the jurors' visual impressions

---

[39] Miller, *Opening and Closing Statements from the Viewpoint of the Plaintiff's Lawyer,* 10 Prac Law 87-94 (1964).

[40] Perlman, *The Key to Trial Psychology,* Sept. 1987 Trial Mag 91-93.

[41] R. Buchanan, *Opening Statements and Closing Arguments: A Response from the Communication Perspective,* in Communication Strategies in the Practice of Lawyering 449-60 (R. Matlon & R. Crawford (eds 1983).

[42] Colley, *The Opening Statement: Structure, Issues, Techniques,* July 1982 Trial 53-57.

[43] Costospoulas, *Commentaries: Persuasion in the Courtroom,* 10 Duq L R 384-409 (1972).

[44] Lawson, *Experimental Research on the Organization of Persuasive Arguments: An Application to Courtroom Communications,* 1970 Law & Soc Order 579-608.

[45] Don Peters, *Participatory Persuasion: Strategies and Research Needs in Opening Statements and Closing Arguments,* in Communication Strategies in the Practice of Lawyering, *supra* note 41, at 401-23.

are stressed. Donald Vinson provides a comprehensive analysis of the psychology of jury trials.[46] He discusses such matters as juror attitudes, how jurors see and hear, how jurors fix blame, juror bias, communication strategy, psychological strategies in voir dire, juror selection strategy, opening statement strategy, and juror research. Robert Wells uses social science literature and his own studies of jurors' mental impressions as the basis for predicting how jurors will arrive at lawyer credibility assessments.[47] He argues that an understanding of how jurors form credibility assessments will allow the trial lawyer to predict and control these assessments throughout the trial.

W. Lance Bennett suggests that the construction of plausible story lines gives jurors the necessary structure and information by which to form judgments.[48] He provides numerous examples and describes the process by which jurors evaluate evidence presented in story form and argues that the best lawyers are the best storytellers. Bennett also describes and explains the uses of rhetorical devices to improve the usefulness of evidence for jurors.[49] He argues that the impact of evidence can be improved through the use of three separate devices—definitional tactics, connecting the evidence, and establishing the credibility of evidence. Examples from actual cases are used to support his arguments. Vivian Dicks, using the Bennett articles as a starting point, analyzes the defense and prosecution strategies in the trial of Angela Davis.[50] Ruth McGaffey reviews research relating to jury selection and persuasive voir dire strategies, and makes some suggestions with respect to effective voir dire tactics.[51]

Phillip Taylor, Raymond Buchanan, and David Strawn suggest communication strategies for use at all stages in the trial process.[52] Their suggestions are based on insights gained from jury research and on theoretical application of persuasion research. Walter Jordan reviews jury selection strategies from social science research and suggests a list of *dos* and *don'ts* that facilitate making a favorable impression on the jury.[53]

With respect to mock jury research, Gerald Miller, *et al* review assumptions made in simulation jury studies and outline requirements for valid, generaliz-

---

[46] D. Vinson, Jury Trials: The Psychology of Winning Strategy (1986).

[47] Wells, *Lawyer Credibility*, July 1985 Trial Mag 69-72.

[48] W. Lance Bennett, *Storytelling in Criminal Trials: A Model of Social Judgment*, 64 QJ Speech 1-22 (1978).

[49] Bennett, *Rhetorical Transformations of Evidence in Criminal Trials: Creating Grounds for Legal Argument*, 65 QJ Speech, 311-23 (1979).

[50] Dicks, *Courtroom Rhetorical Strategies: Forensic and Deliberative Perspectives*, QJ Speech 178-92 (1981).

[51] R. McGaffey, *Communication Strategies and Research Needs in Selecting Juries*, in Communication Strategies in the Practice of Lawyering, *supra* note 41, at 250-73.

[52] P. Taylor, R. Buchanan & D. Strawn, Communication Strategies for Trial Attorneys (1984).

[53] W. Jordan, Jury Selection (Shepard's/McGraw-Hill, 1980).

able mock jury studies.[54] Thomas Pscynski and Lawrence Wrightsman analyze the effect of the length of the opening statement on the trial outcome and conclude that if one statement is brief and the other statement is detailed, the detailed statement will meet with more success.[55] Wrightsman, *et al* examine the effect of overstated promises in opening statements on trial outcomes, and conclude that it is strategically wise to overstate the case.[56] They argue that opening statements create cognitive schemata that influence jurors' processing and interpretations of evidence throughout the trial. Thus, by making the strongest and most extensive opening statement possible, the attorney provides a favorable framework that jurors will use to interpret subsequent evidence. Janet Sigal, *et al* analyze presentation style and conclude that aggressive assertive styles for defense lawyers obtained more *not guilty* verdicts in criminal cases.[57] They concluded that the aggressive assertive style was perceived as stereotypically appropriate for defense lawyers in criminal cases. Bonnie Erickson, *et al* study juror credibility assessments with respect to "powerful" and "powerless" speaking styles, and conclude that speakers using a "powerful" style that contains fewer hedges and qualifications are judged to be more credible than are speakers using a "powerless" speaking style.[58] They suggest that the "powerful" style leads to listeners' concluding that the communicator believes the statements being made to be true, and that the "powerful" style is viewed as a more straightforward communication of information.

The trial technique literature from the social science field consists mainly of discussions of how persuasion theory ought to be applied in a courtroom setting, with some reliance on conclusions based on mock jury research. While theorists use excerpts from actual jury trials to support their claims, there is no use of comparative studies to generate a structure for successful trial technique. Thus, there appears to be no extant research that uses a comparative analysis of complete trial transcripts in order to generate a common structure for successful trial technique.

§1.03   Scope of the Study and Method for Study

The above review of the literature discloses that lawyers provide varying approaches to trial techniques based on their individual styles and personalities. Social science researchers and theorists provide theories based on what

---

[54] Miller, Frontes, Boster, & Sunnafrank, *Methodological Issues in Legal Communication Research: What Can the Trial Simulation Tell Us?* 50 Comm Monographs, 33-46 (1983).

[55] Psczynski & Wrightsman, *The Effects of Opening Statements on Mock Jurors' Verdicts in a Simulated Criminal Trial,* 11 J Applied Soc Psychology 301-13 (1981).

[56] Psczynski, Greenberg, Mack & Wrightsman, *Opening Statements in a Jury Trial: The Effect of Promising More Than the Evidence Can Show,* 11 J Applied Soc Psychology 434-44 (1981).

[57] Sigal, Braden-Maguire, Hayden & Mosley, *The Effect of Presentation Style and Sex of Lawyer on Decision Making Behavior,* 22 Psychology 13 (1985).

[58] Erickson, Lind, Johnson & Barr, *Speech Style and Impression Formation in a Court Setting: The Effects of 'Powerful' and 'Powerless' Speech,* 14 J Experimental Soc Psychology 266-79 (1978).

"ought to be," what occurs in isolated cases, or how mock jurors respond to simulated trials. While these studies are certainly enlightening, they provide limited insight into why certain lawyers enjoy greater success than others. Further, they do not begin to tell the student of trial technique which approach to take in learning how to become a successful trial lawyer. A new approach is, therefore, called for in the study of trial practice. This book provides such an approach.

It is assumed that as a class of speakers and persuaders, successful lawyers are successful because they have the same understanding and capabilities with respect to the rhetorical situation as do other classes of speakers. It is further assumed that successful trial lawyers are successful because they respond in similar ways to recurring trial situations. Given these assumptions, a methodological approach is called for which takes into account situational factors, and the lawyers' response to the situational factors. A comparative analysis provides this approach.

This book consists of a comparative analysis of the trial transcripts of successful trial lawyers. It is not limited to one aspect of the trial, as are many studies, but covers voir dire, opening statements, direct examination, cross-examination, and closing statements. This comparative study generates a structure for successful trial technique that both explains the success of certain lawyers and provides guidance to students of trial practice.

In doing a comparative analysis of trial transcripts of successful lawyers, it is first assumed that, while each trial may involve different parties and different sets of facts, each trial has similar issues and similar demands made upon the trial lawyers in their efforts to obtain a favorable verdict. Once this assumption is made, the trial transcripts can be studied in an effort to determine whether the successful lawyers are doing similar things in trying their cases. These common elements may be considered a structure for successful trial technique.

It is acknowledged here that most successful lawyers are charismatic and are probably able to use their intuition and instincts in ways that account to an extent for their success. While it is hoped that all of us as trial lawyers have within us the potential to be charismatic and intuitively powerful, as are these successful trial lawyers, this book makes no effort to analyze or explain these intangible factors. However, there are, no doubt, other predictable, describable things that successful lawyers do in order to be successful that can be understood and learned by those who wish to learn them. This book seeks to identify those things that all successful trial lawyers do in winning their cases. These common techniques may be called a structure for successful trial technique and may at least be used as a starting point for those lawyers beginning their careers and those who are attempting to tap that great potential that rests within them. It may also be used as a point of comparison which those of us who have been practicing for many years can use in order to determine whether we are doing all that we can do in order to establish and maintain winning ways. It goes beyond assertions of how strategies "ought" to work to illuminate what actually works.

§1.04   Material for Analysis

In selecting the transcripts for this study, several criteria were used. The first criterion was that the lawyers selected be successful lawyers as determined by their peers. The second criterion was that the presentations selected be taken from successful cases, determined by the result obtained from the jury with respect to the problem presented in the specific case. The third criterion was that the cases selected be models of good trial practice as determined by the lawyers themselves.

The trial presentations selected were made by Scott Baldwin, Victor Bergman, Melvin Block, William Colson, Phillip Corboy, Robert Gibbons, Herman Glaser, Robert Habush, Peter Perlman, Leonard Ring, Gerry Spence, and Lantz Welch. All of these lawyers have consistently achieved good results in their jury cases and are considered to be successful lawyers by their peers. All have been frequent lecturers at trial lawyer seminars on various aspects of jury trial work.

Scott Baldwin

Scott Baldwin has been a successful trial lawyer for many years and is so recognized by his peers.[59] He is a past president of the Texas Trial Lawyers Association, a member of the Inner Circle of Advocates, a Fellow of the International Society of Barristers, a Fellow of the International Academy of Trial Lawyers, and is currently president of the Association of Trial Lawyers of America.[60] Baldwin has represented plaintiffs from all over the world in complex litigation involving products ranging from asbestos to atom bombs.[61] His "31-year track record as a lawyer has demonstrated that no claim is too complex, nor any defendant too powerful, to deter his instigating, and winning, a lawsuit."[62] He has consistently achieved success as a trial lawyer, obtaining large verdicts in difficult cases. Baldwin was primarily responsible for obtaining one of the largest recoveries in a product liability case involving asbestos, when, acting as lead counsel, he and a handful of other plaintiffs' lawyers filed the first lawsuit on behalf of injured asbestos workers in 1978 and settled the claims for $20 million two years later.[63]

Two of Mr. Baldwin's trial transcripts were selected for use in this study. The first case is *Foster v Ford Motor Company*, in which the plaintiff was severely injured while operating a Ford tractor.[64] A bale of hay fell off a front-end loader on the tractor, landing on the plaintiff and causing crippling injuries. The plaintiff filed suit under the Texas product liability law, alleging that the tractor was unreasonably dangerous in its design in that its front-end loading system

---

[59] V Martindale-Hubbell Law Directory 1160, 3070B (1985).

[60] *ATLA's National Officers,* Sept. 1984 Trial 22.

[61] Fortune, *Profile: Scott Baldwin—No Ordinary Small Town Lawyer,* Winter 1985 Litigation News at 23.

[62] *Id.*

[63] *Id.*

[64] *Foster v Ford Motor Co,* 616 F2d 1304 (5th Cir 1980).

allowed it to lift loads of up to 1,500 pounds over the operator's head without providing any protection to the operator. The defendant contended that it was not liable, because the plaintiff was using a customized device not manufactured by Ford for the front-end system, and, therefore, it was not liable for injuries caused by this device. The defendant also argued that safety options were available for use with the tractor that would have protected the plaintiff, and that since the plaintiff failed to buy or use the optional devices, the plaintiff's injuries were due to his own negligence. The plaintiff countered by arguing that the use of customized devices was foreseeable by Ford in its design and manufacture of the tractor, and that the plaintiff was not aware of optional safety devices. The plaintiff suffered a crippling injury and alleged that he would be confined to a wheelchair for the rest of his life, with loss of bodily function. The *Foster* case was a difficult case to win, because the plaintiff was taking on one of America's largest and oldest corporations. Further, it was uncontroverted that the tractor accident happened because the plaintiff had improvised and used an accessory not manufactured or sold by the defendant Ford, thus allowing the defendant to assert that the accident was not foreseeable. The jury returned a verdict of $2,500,000.

In the *Foster* transcript, voir dire and opening statements were not transcribed, and, therefore, a voir dire and opening statement from a similar case with similar issues was requested from Mr. Baldwin. He could not locate any transcripts in which his voir dire was transcribed and, therefore, could not submit a voir dire for study. Mr. Baldwin submitted his opening statement from the case of *Branch v Liebherr Crane, Inc,* which was a product liability case with issues similar to those in the *Foster* case.[65] In *Branch,* the plaintiff was a crane operator who fell 27 stories to his death when the large crane he was operating collapsed. The plaintiff's widow and family filed suit under the Texas product liability law against the manufacturers and assemblers of the crane, alleging improper design and assembly of the crane. The plaintiffs claimed damages for the death of the decedent, lost wages that the decedent would have earned, loss of services, loss of care, guidance, and nurturing, pain and suffering of the survivors, and pain and suffering of decedent while falling to his death. The case was difficult because it involved multiple defendants and because it involved complex proof as to the cause of the crane collapse. The jury returned a substantial verdict for the plaintiffs.

Victor Bergman

Victor Bergman has had tremendous success in recent years with difficult cases. He submitted three cases for study that resulted in verdicts in excess of $1 million for each case. In the medical negligence case of *Olsen v Humana,* in which a child was born brain damaged due to complications from labor and delivery, he obtained a $15 million verdict, of which a substantial portion was for punitive damages, that sent shock waves throughout the national medical

---

[65] Branch v Liebherr Crane, Inc, No M-79-4-CA (ED Tex Oct 22-31, 1980).

community.[66] The *Olsen* case involved allegations of failure to monitor the child and allowing the child to become oxygen-deprived. Of significance in the *Olsen* case was an enormously successful claim against the defendant doctors and hospital for punitive damages. *Johnson v Colt Industries* involved the negligent design and malfunction of a Colt .45 handgun.[67] The *Johnson* case was understandably difficult because Bergman challenged a handgun design that had been in existence for many years. Nevertheless, Bergman not only obtained a verdict, but also obtained a substantial punitive damage verdict. Further, the damage claim was based on the plaintiff's loss of sexual potency. The plaintiff was a "macho" type man, a solid citizen, and a very good husband and lover who suffered an erectile impotence as a result of his gunshot wound. This condition changed his image of himself, his personality, and had an impact upon his marital and family relationships. It is of note that while the gunshot wound was clear, the causal connection between the wound and the impotency was not absolutely subject to objective proof. The jury returned a verdict of $500,000 for Mr. Johnson, $500,000 to Mrs. Johnson for damage to the marital relationship, and $1.25 million in punitive damages.

Morrison v Hanson, involved the failure to timely diagnose Hodgkin's disease, resulting in the loss of the chance to obtain timely treatment and cure.[68] This case was understandably difficult because of the problematic nature of the treatment and cure for cancer. There was no way the plaintiff could conclusively prove that she could have been cured had the disease been timely diagnosed. Nevertheless, Bergman obtained a verdict in excess of $1 million.

Melvin Block

Melvin Block was certainly one of the great lawyers of his time. He was a past president of the New York State Trial Lawyers Association, past vice-president of the Association of Trial Lawyers of American, a member of the Inner Circle of Advocates, Roscoe Pound Foundation, International Academy of Trial Lawyers, International Society of Barristers, and the author of articles on trial practice.[69] During his career, he was involved in many important cases. *Micallef v Miehle Co* overruled *Campo v Scofield* and established manufacturer's liability for patent and obvious defects.[70] In *Hall v DuPont,* Block established industry-wide liability in product liability cases where the specific manufacturer of the product cannot be identified.[71] In *Baird v Day & Zimmerman, Inc,* which involved an exploding howitzer shell, Block established the right of servicemen to recover for defective products.[72] Mr. Block submitted the transcript of

---

[66] Olsen v Humana, Inc, No 107480 (Kan Johnson County Dist Ct Oct 1984).

[67] Johnson v Colt Indus Operating Corp, No 82-1390 (D Kan Jan 1985).

[68] Morrison v Hanson, No 86C281 (Kan Johnson County Dist Ct April 20, 1987).

[69] IV Martindale-Hubbell Law Directory 418, 1006B (1985).

[70] 39 NY2d 376 348 NE2d 571 (1976).

[71] 345 F Supp 353 (EDNY 1972).

[72] No 71 Civ 3205 (SDNY 1975); Burns v Day & Zimmerman, Inc, No 71 Civ 3205 (SDNY 1975).

Baird v Day & Zimmerman, Inc for study. The case involved the injury and death of two servicemen in Vietnam who were injured when a defective shell exploded in a howitzer. The case was difficult because there was little investigation done to determine the cause of the malfunction, and the manufacturer offered proof of human error as opposed to manufacturing defect. The case resulted in substantial verdicts for both plaintiffs.

Bill Colson

Bill Colson is a past president of the Association of Trial Lawyers of America, a Fellow of the American College of Trial Lawyers, a member of the Inner Circle of Advocates, and is recognized as a successful trial lawyer by his peers.[73] In 1967, Colson obtained a $1.5 million verdict in a medical malpractice case that was the first million dollar jury verdict in the state of Florida, the first million dollar malpractice award in the United States, the largest verdict for a woman in the United States, and one of the first five verdicts in the United States for over $1 million.[74] In 1975, Colson obtained the first successful jury verdict involving the Pinto automobile in the sum of $3 million, which was the largest jury verdict in Florida to that date.[75]

Mr. Colson submitted the voir dire from a medical negligence case in which a child was born brain damaged due to complications during labor and cesarean delivery.[76] The alleged injuries were spastic quadriparesis and brain damage due to lack of oxygen during labor and birth. The plaintiffs contended that the defendant physicians were negligent in failing to monitor the child and in allowing the child to be deprived of oxygen during labor and delivery. The defendants contended that the child's condition either developed during pregnancy through no fault of their own, or was a genetic defect over which they had no control. The case was a difficult one because the plaintiff's injuries resembled conditions found in children born with birth defects, and it was difficult to prove that the conditions were caused by negligence as opposed to some preexisting defect. Further, the child was born in a breech position, which also made it possible for the defendants to claim that the injuries were caused by conditions out of their control. Mr. Colson obtained a substantial recovery for the plaintiffs.

Phillip Corboy

Phillip Corboy is a past president of the Illinois Trial Lawyers Association, past president of the Chicago Bar Association, a fellow of the International Academy of Trial Lawyers, a fellow of the American College of Trial Lawyers, a fellow of the American Bar Foundation, a past editor of the *ATLA Law Journal,*

---

[73] II Martindale-Hubbell Law Directory 363, 1119B (1985).

[74] Holl v Talcott, 224 So 2d 420 (Fla Dist Ct App 3d 1967).

[75] Havlick v Ford Motor Co, 351 So 2d 1050 (Fla Dist Ct App 1977); Cert denied 358 So 2d 130 (1978).

[76] Willison v Fischer, No 80-239 (Fla 17th Cir Ct Sept 1981); this transcript was obtained and is available through the office of Bill Colson.

and is recognized as a successful trial lawyer by his peers.[77] He has authored over 40 articles on the practice of law and is a regularly featured speaker at trial lawyer seminars and institutes.[78] He has a reputation as a skilled trial lawyer to whom other lawyers and judges go for advice on personal injury cases.[79] His Chicago-based law firm has been called the "Phillip Corboy University College of Law" because of the many top trial lawyers who have graduated from it.[80] He is widely recognized as one of the nation's foremost and innovative trial lawyers.[81] Corboy has obtained many million dollar verdicts and is known as one of the best in the business at getting the most from his cases.[82] As stated by Joseph Tybor of the *National Law Journal*, Corboy is a trial lawyer *par excellence* who "almost every day handles matters other personal injury lawyers would drool to get once in a lifetime."[83]

Mr. Corboy submitted the case of *Block v Jarvis*, which involved a personal injury claim arising out of an automobile collision.[84] The plaintiff was a young law professor at the time he sustained his injuries, and as a result of the collision, he became a spastic quadraplegic in a locked-in syndrome. The plaintiff had a functioning brain, but was paralyzed from the eyes down and could only communicate through his eyes. Corboy alleged that the plaintiff would have a normal life expectancy, but would require constant medical attention for the rest of his life. The defendants alleged that the collision was due in part to the negligence of the plaintiff, and that the plaintiff would have a reduced life expectancy and would not require medical attention for as many years as claimed by the plaintiff. The case was difficult because Corboy was required to prove that the plaintiff would have a normal life expectancy. Further, the medical expenses of keeping the plaintiff alive for a normal life expectancy involved an astronomical sum of money, and Corboy was faced with convincing the jury that such a sum was necessary, fair, and reasonable. Corboy obtained a verdict of $9,332,000, which at the time was the second largest verdict ever for a personal injury case in the state of Illinois.[85]

Robert Gibbons

Robert Gibbons is a past director of the Texas Trial Lawyers Association, a member of the board of governors and a member of the Executive Committee for the Association of Trial Lawyers of America, a diplomate of the American Board of Trial Advocates, a member of the International Academy of Trial Law-

---

[77] II Martindale-Hubbell Law Directory 793, 2418B-2419B (1985).

[78] *Id* 2419B.

[79] *Power,* Natl LJ, Apr 15, 1985, at 23.

[80] *Id.*

[81] *Corboy to Succeed Lundquist,* Litigation News, July, 1979, at 3.

[82] Tybor, *Windy City Wizard,* Natl LJ, July 21, 1980, at 1, 24.

[83] *Id.*

[84] No. 82 L 3713 (Ill Cir Ct Cook County Feb 1984); this transcript was obtained and is available through the office of Phillip Corboy.

[85] Kaplan, *On & Off the Record,* Nat LJ, Feb 27, 1984), at 2.

yers, International Association of Barristers, and is certified as a Trial Advocate by the National Board of Trial Advocates.[86] Mr. Gibbons has a track record of handling and winning difficult cases, and has obtained several million dollar verdicts. He submitted the case of *Wahl v McDonnell Douglas* for study.[87] The case involved the death of an United States Air Force pilot who was killed when his plane malfunctioned and crashed. The pilot was able to eject from his plane, but was then killed due to the negligent design of the ejection seat. The lawsuit was filed against the manufacturer of the plane and the manufacturer of the ejection seat. This case was a difficult case to try because the cause of the malfunction of the plane was not clear and because the defendants attempted to blame the crash on pilot error. Gibbons alleged that the flight controls were defective in design in that they permitted foreign objects to get into the "white area" and jam the flight controls, requiring an ejection with an ejection seat that was defective in design in that it permitted the pilot to twist and turn in the air, snapping his neck and severing his spinal cord when the parachute opened. The widow and son were awarded $1.5 million in compensatory damages and $2 million in punitive damages, with the damages being allocated 60 per cent against the ejection seat manufacturer and 40 per cent against the aircraft manufacturer.

Herman Glaser

Herman Glaser has been active in the Association of Trial Lawyers of America as chairman of the Tort Section, Continuing Legal Education, and Basic Trial Advocacy Program, is a past president of the New York State Trial Lawyers Association, has authored numerous articles on trial tactics and torts, and has lectured nationally on trial tactics, products liability, and medical malpractice. Mr. Glaser submitted the case of *Lewis v Cavalli*, which involves the performance of an unnecessary hysterectomy and oopherectomy upon the plaintiff, which resulted in premature menopause and other physical and mental damages.[88] The plaintiff predicated her lawsuit on the issues of medical malpractice and lack of informed consent. The lawsuit was difficult in that the defendants produced several experts to testify that the surgery was justified, and that, in any event, the surgery did not cause the plaintiff's damages. The result was unique in that jury returned a verdict for the plaintiff in an amount of $1,490,000 on the issue of lack of informed consent, and found for the defendant on the issue of malpractice.

Robert Habush

Robert Habush is a past president of the Wisconsin Academy of Trial Lawyers, past president of the Association of Trial Lawyers of America, a fellow of the Inner Circle of Advocates, International Academy of Trial Lawyers, International Society of Barristers, author of numerous publications on trial

---

[86] VI Martindale-Hubbell Law Directory 707, 2085B (1988).

[87] No. A-80-CA-214 (US Dist Ct, Western Dist Texas, Austin Div, Dec 1981).

[88] No 15866/78 (S Ct of NY, County of Bronx, March 1984).

advocacy, and frequent lecturer on trial advocacy.[89] Mr. Habush submitted the case of *Schulz v Bituminous Casualty Corp,* which involved catastrophic injuries sustained by a dock worker due to the negligent design of a forklift.[90] In *Schulz,* the injuries were clear and convincing, but liability was a problem. The plaintiff was operating a forklift and was in the process of removing some material from a truck that was backed up to a dock. The truck apparently rolled away from the dock and caused the forklift and the plaintiff to fall off the dock, at which time the plaintiff suffered a severe spinal injury. The plaintiff sued the owner of the truck, alleging that it should have secured the wheels so that the truck could not have rolled away from the dock; the manufacturer of the forklift, alleging that the forklift was improperly designed in that it did not have adequate rear crash bar protection; and the designer of the dock, alleging that the dock was improperly designed. Habush claimed that the injuries were caused not only because of the negligence of the truck company in failing to secure their truck at the dock, but also because of the negligence of the manufacturer of the forklift in improperly designing the forklift by failing to supply rear crash bars, which allowed a portion of the dock to protrude into an unprotected area of the cab of the forklift and crush the plaintiff's spine. The manufacturer of the forklift attempted to place blame on the plaintiff and other dock workers and produced experts to prove that the plaintiff's injuries were caused by the fall, which was not caused by the manufacturer of the forklift. The jury assessed 7.5 per cent of blame on the plaintiff, 7.5 per cent of blame on the dock designer, 42.5 per cent of blame on the truck company, and 42.5 per cent of blame on the manufacturer of the forklift, and returned a money verdict in the amount of $1.5 million.

Peter Perlman

Peter Perlman is a past president of the Association of Trial Lawyers of America, past president of the Kentucky Association of Trial Attorneys, a member of the Inner Circle of Advocates, International Academy of Trial Lawyers, American Board of Trial Advocates, a fellow of the Roscoe Pound Foundation, and is the author of many articles on trial technique.[91] Perlman is a noted trial advocate who has obtained several verdicts in excess of one million dollars.[92] He specializes in product liability and medical malpractice cases. The case submitted for study was the case of *Shackleford v Joy Manufacturing Co,* in which the plaintiff coal miner was pinned by a runaway boom from a continuous mining machine.[93] The case was difficult in that the cause of the malfunction was not clear and the plaintiff had to overcome defense witnesses who blamed the cause of the malfunction on other parties. The plaintiff lost the sight in one eye, his

---

[89] VII Martindale-Hubbell Law Directory 424, 1236B (1988).

[90] No 561-607 (Wis Cir Ct Milwaukee County Nov 1986).

[91] III Martindale-Hubbell Law Directory 695, 1830B (1988).

[92] Perkins v Kings Daughters Memorial Hosp, No 83-CI-0482 (Ky Franklin Cir Ct Aug 1984) ($2,530,000); *Riffe v International Harvester,* No 78-CI-197 (Ky Martin Cir Ct Jul 1981) ($2,103,835).

[93] No 82-9 (ED Ky Dec 1984).

sense of taste and smell, and suffers epileptic seizures. The jury returned a verdict for the plaintiff in the amount of $1,821,353.

Leonard Ring

Leonard Ring is a past president of the Association of Trial Lawyers of America, past president of the Illinois Trial Lawyers Association, a member of the Roscoe Pound American Trial Lawyers Foundation, a Fellow of the International Society of Barristers, the International Academy of Trial Lawyers, and the American College of Trial Lawyers, and is recognized by his peers as a successful trial lawyer.[94] He has authored many articles dealing with trial technique, and is presently the editor of *Trial Diplomacy Journal*.[95] Mr. Ring has earned a reputation as one of Chicago's premier attorneys, and has made a career out of confounding the experts.[96] He has successfully handled many million dollar lawsuits and cases which have produced new law.[97] He successfully challenged the constitutionality of the Illinois no-fault law,[98] the constitutionality of the Illinois law allowing the state legislature to investigate judicial misconduct,[99] and established strict liability in product liability cases in Illinios.[100] Mr. Ring is an expert in product liability litigation, and was co-chairman of the plaintiffs' legal team in the 1980 MGM-Grand Hotel Las Vegas fire case, which was ultimately settled for approximately $150,000,000.[101] He is considered an indefatigable attorney with a sharp legal mind, and has been described by his well-known colleague, Phil Corboy, as being "as competent and as capable a plaintiff's lawyer as any in the country."[102]

Mr. Ring submitted the case of *Smith v Verson Allsteel Press Co*, which was tried in 1977 and involved a 19-year-old plaintiff who had both of his hands crushed in a brake press machine.[103] This case was difficult to prove because the machine in question was approximately 35 years old at the time of the injury and had had numerous modifications, thus allowing the defendant manufacturer to contend that the injury was due to the modifications made by the plaintiff's employer. The case was further complicated because of several material inconsistencies in the plaintiff's prior deposition testimony. Mr. Ring obtained a verdict of $800,000.

---

[94] II Martindale-Hubbell Law Directory 877, 2687B (1985).

[95] II Martindale-Hubbell Law Directory 2687B (1985).

[96] Ranii, *Confounding the Experts: Leonard Ring's Low-Key Appeal*, Nat LJ, Dec 27, 1982, at 14.

[97] *Id.*

[98] Grace v Howlett, 51 Ill.2d 478, 283 NE2d 474 (1972).

[99] Cusack v Howlett, 44 Ill.2d 233, 254 NE2d 506 (1969).

[100] Suvada v White Motor Co, 32 Ill.2d 612, 210 NE2d 182 (1965).

[101] Ranii, *supra* note 96.

[102] *Id.*

[103] No 72 L 17132 (Ill Cir Ct Cook County March 1977); this transcript was obtained and is available through the office of Leonard Ring.

Gerry Spence

Gerry Spence has long been recognized as a successful trial lawyer.[104] In 1981, he had a record of not losing a jury case in 12 years, even though he had regularly been opposed by polished lawyers who represented powerful corporations.[105] He established a track record of obtaining huge verdicts in difficult cases. His more controversial cases include a $10.5 million award in the *Silkwood v Kerr-McGee* case, in which Karen Silkwood was contaminated by plutonium radiation while employed by the Kerr-McGee Corporation, a $26.6 million verdict in the *Pring v Penthouse Magazine* case, in which a Miss Wyoming was libeled by *Penthouse Magazine,* and a $52 million verdict in the case of *Central Ice Cream Co v McDonald's Corp,* in which the plaintiff won a breach of contract claim against the McDonald's Corporation.[106] With reference to his courtroom technique, a former partner and current Wyoming Supreme Court Chief Justice has stated: "He comes off as so real that jurors can trust him. They have to decide which side to be on, and if he wants to be your friend, you can barely resist him."[107]

The case of *Silkwood v Kerr-McGee Corp* was selected for study.[108] The plaintiff, Karen Silkwood, was a young woman who had been engaged in union activities to force Kerr-McGee to provide better protection to employees from plutonium radiation poisoning, and to keep the union from being decertified. At a time when her union activities were escalating, Karen Silkwood was contaminated with plutonium particles that had been placed in a urine contamintion testing kit given to her by Kerr-McGee for use at home. Upon examination, it was determined that Karen Silkwood's body was so polluted with plutonium that she would certainly have developed and died of cancer. Nine days after receiving this information, Karen Silkwood mysteriously died in an automobile collision. Mr. Spence brought suit on behalf of the heirs of Karen Silkwood for actual and punitive damages. The case was extremely difficult because it was impossible to prove exactly how, why, and by whom the plaintiff was contaminated, because Karen Silkwood's damages consisted of her knowledge for nine days prior to her death that she would develop cancer, because Karen Silkwood led a somewhat deviant lifestyle, and because the defendant Kerr-McGee was one of the most powerful and respected corporations in America at the time. Mr. Spence received a verdict of $10.5 million.

Lantz Welch

Lantz Welch is a past president of the Kansas City Bar Association and is

---

[104] George Gold, *Gerry Spence,* 67 ABA J 48 (Nov 1981).

[105] Beach & Woodbury, *Fastest Gun in the West,* 117 Time 48 (Mar 1981).

[106] Gupla, *Interview with Gerry Spence,* 11 Barrister 59 (Winter 1984).

[107] Beach & Woodbury, *supra* note 105, at 48.

[108] No 76-0888 (WD Okla March 1979); a copy of this transcript was obtained and is available through the office of Don Icard.

recognized by his peers as a successful trial lawyer.[109] He has obtained many million dollar verdicts and recently received national attention from his successful handling of *Firestone v Hyatt Corp*, in which he obtained a verdict in excess of $15 million for his client, who was injured in the collapse of the Kansas City Hyatt Hotel.[110] Mr. Welch submitted the case of *Cooper v General Standard, Inc*, in which the plaintiff, Robert Cooper, was injured in an automobile collision caused by the negligence of the defendant, *General Standard, Inc*[111] The plaintiff claimed personal injury damages, and the plaintiff's wife, Ruth Cooper, brought suit for loss of consortium as a result of her husband's injuries. The defendant denied that it was negligent, and denied the nature and extent of the plaintifff's injuries. The case was difficult in that the largest part of the plaintiffs' claims for damages involved pain and suffering for Mr. Cooper and loss of consortium for Mrs. Cooper, both of which are abstract, subjective items of damages. Welch was faced with presenting these elements of damages in ways that the jury could appreciate and understand. Both plaintiffs were awarded a verdict, with the wife receiving one of the largest verdicts in the state of Missouri for loss of consortium.

§1.05   The Rhetorical Problem: Common Problems Facing All Trial Lawyers in All Jury Trials

Although every civil suit is unique, they will all contain common problems that the lawyers must overcome in order to win their cases. By identifying these common problems all attorneys representing plaintiffs in civil suits before juries face at various stages, it is then possible to identify the ways that highly successful attorneys overcome these obstacles to obtain verdicts for the plaintiff, including sizable awards for damages.

The rhetorical problem is a framework developed to describe in general terms the range of problems speakers face in achieving goals with audiences. Lawyers, like all speakers, confront these general problems; however, these general problems take on specific forms in the kinds of suits that are the subject of this study.

In analyzing the trial transcripts, common rhetorical problems were identifiable. During the entire trial, each side of the case presented competing and conflicting views of reality. Each side presented its version of the facts and the law, and each side asserted that its version was the "correct" version. Ultimately the jury was called on to resolve this conflict. Thus, the overall rhetorical problem was to persuade the jury that the plaintiff's version of the facts was the correct version.

In voir dire, the lawyers were faced with the problem of discovering juror background information and attitudes so that a favorable jury could be

---

109 III Martindale-Hubbell Law Directory 1174 (1985).

110 No CV81-16451 (Mo Cir Ct Jackson County 1983).

111 No CV80-4202 (Mo Cir Ct Jackson County April 1982); a copy of this transcript was obtained and is available through the office of Lantz Welch.

selected. Jurors, like most people, are reticent to admit prejudice, and, therefore, the lawyers had to conduct their voir dire in such a way as to coax the jurors into openly admitting their biases.

In persuading the jury that their version of reality was the "correct" version, the lawyers were also faced with the problem of presenting the case in such a way that the mass of evidence was made meaningful to the jurors. Each side called witnesses and cross-examined the other side's witnesses, and, in all cases, the evidence involved some complex expert testimony. The lawyers had to integrate and present the evidence in such a way that the jurors did not become confused or misled in hearing and deciding the case. The lawyers had to create a schema to guide the process by which jurors formed impressions of the plaintiffs, the defendants, and the attorneys representing them.

Each side of the case claimed that its witnesses were credible, while the other side's witnesses were not. Since the jurors did not know the lawyers, litigants, or witnesses involved in the case, the credibility of each was at issue. Therefore, the lawyers had to demonstrate to the jury that their witnesses were believable.

In order to win, the lawyers had to prove that the defendants were negligent, and that the plaintiffs had suffered injuries and damages. Negligence, pain, and suffering are abstract, subjective concepts, and the outcome of the cases depended on the ability of the lawyers to present the evidence and arguments in such a way that the jury could appreciate and understand these abstract, subjective concepts.

Finally, although the jury was instructed by the court that their purpose was to do justice and to render a fair and impartial verdict, this definition of purpose was vague. The concepts of justice, fairness, and impartiality were open to interpretation, and the way the concepts were interpreted would determine the outcome of the case. Therefore, the lawyers were faced with defining and refining jury purpose.

Although these problems were present throughout the trial, their prominence differed in each segment of the trial. The ostensible purpose of voir dire is to get at juror attitudes and beliefs so that meaningful jury selection can occur. Although the lawyers were engaged in that, they were also involved in resolving the competing views of reality. If there is any validity to primacy theory, it can be argued that first impressions will affect the process by which jurors form impressions throughout the trial.[112] Thus, while probing juror background and attitudes, the lawyers had to begin the process of resolving the competing claims of reality and credibility, proving their cases, and shaping jury purpose. Since the ostensible purpose of voir dire was to discover juror background information and attitudes, and since this segment of the trial was prescribed and limited by the court, the persuasive maneuvers had to be handled subtly.

In the opening statement, each lawyer had to lay out the schema that would guide jurors in forming impressions throughout the trial. Here the lawyers

---

[112] For an example of recency theory applied to the practice of law, see Costospoulas, *Commentaries: Persuasion in the Courtroom*, 10 Duq L Rev 384 (1972).

were faced with the problem of previewing the trial, and putting the case together in such a way that the subsequent evidence would be meaningful.

In direct examination, the lawyers were involved in proving their cases and establishing the credibility of their witnesses. In some cases the witnesses were lay witnesses, not used to presenting themselves before groups of people, and the lawyers had to pattern their questioning in a way that allowed the witnesses to get all of the important information to the jurors. With any of the witnesses, a wrong slip could have been fatal to the case, and, therefore, the lawyers had to pattern their questions in a way that allowed the lawyers to maintain control of the witnesses' testimony.

In cross-examination, the lawyers were faced with the defendant's witnesses who had presented the competing view of reality. In order to win their cases, the lawyers had to controvert either the credibility or the testimony of these witnesses.

In their closing arguments, the lawyers were faced with the problem of integrating the evidence and law into a coherent whole. In order to win their cases, they had to create meaning for the evidence, present abstract concepts such as negligence, pain, and suffering in such a way that the jury could appreciate and understand them, and shape jury purpose.

§1.06   The Solution to the Rhetorical Problem: A Structure for Successful Trial Technique

This book demonstrates that successful plaintiffs' lawyers approached and surmounted the rhetorical problems inherent in civil jury trials in similar ways. These common responses to the rhetorical problems may be viewed as a structure for successful trial technique.

In voir dire, in addition to gathering basic information about jurors and their attitudes, they (1) set the tone for the trial, (2) introduced concepts and evidence and conditioned the jurors for things to follow in the trial, (3) obtained public commitments from jurors favorable to their cases, (4) used language that created connotations favorable to their clients, their witnesses, and other relevant facets of their case, (5) rehearsed the arguments they would use in the trial, (6) refuted opposition arguments, (7) enhanced their credibility, and (8) created jury purpose. The period of voir dire became a preview of the entire trial, preparing jurors for what would follow and creating an atmosphere highly favorable to the plaintiff's case.

In the opening statement, the lawyers used a narrative structure to create the cognitive schemata that would influence impressions the jurors formed. The case was transformed into a story through the use of language and themes, to make the events come alive and to present the plaintiffs as heroes and the defendants as villains. Within this storytelling structure, the lawyers also developed themes that organized the evidence and claims of liability, set a serious tone, defined jury purpose, specified their bases of authority, introduced key concepts and key pieces of evidence, enhanced credibility, laid out the central arguments in their cases, and refuted the central contentions of the defendant.

Direct examination was used to present facts in support of the story line, personalize the plaintiffs, provide technical information, and enhance the credibility of the witnesses. The questions asked of all these witnesses were simple and direct, using everyday language. The lawyers controlled the testimony of all of the witnesses by the use of narrow questions calling for specific answers.

Cross-examination was used to achieve three purposes: (1) to destroy the credibility of the witness, (2) to controvert arguments or facts presented previously by the witness or by the defense, and (3) to elicit facts in support of the plaintiff's case. The basic strategies used in the questioning were designed to control all aspects of the witnesses' testimony. The lawyers controlled the testimony of the witnesses during cross-examination by the use of leading questions or the use of narrow questions calling for specific answers.

In closing statements, the lawyers utilized a narrative structure that integrated the evidence, created jury purpose, and created meaning through the use of themes and the strategic use of language.

§1.07   Conclusion

In Part I of what follows, I will discuss communication and psychology as it relates to trial technique. This overview will allow for a better understanding of the analysis that will follow in Part II. Part II contains a comparative analysis of trial transcripts of successful lawyers. As will be demonstrated, there is a common structure that successful trial attorneys follow in trying their cases.

2

The Process of Communication and Impression Formation

§2.01 Introduction

All jury trials may be characterized as a process of communication and impression formation. Both sides of the case, through the use of communication, present opposing views of reality to jurors, who are then asked to decide which view of reality is the "correct" or "just" view of reality. For example, in a product liability case, the plaintiff claims a defective product caused serious injury, while the defense claims that the negligent use of a safe product caused

23

the injury. The final decision that jurors make about these conflicting views of reality will depend upon the impressions they form of the lawyers, litigants, witnesses, facts, and laws involved in the case. As will be demonstrated in the following chapters, successful lawyers are successful because they are good communicators and are skillful in shaping these juror impressions. In order to better understand the analysis of successful trial technique, an overview of the communication and impression formation process will be presented in this chapter.

§2.02 Communication and Symbols

Humans approach the world with a desire to create order.[1] Since the world is a confusing place, humans create order through communication. Things are placed in categories, and symbols are attached to these categories of things. When all things have symbols that refer to them, humans can then order and organize these symbols and bring order to the world. Thus, rather than a confusing jumble of things, there are humans, animals, minerals, liquids, etc. Time and space are controlled with the creation of symbol systems that account for hours, miles, etc. In the legal system, people who bring lawsuits become plaintiffs, and people who defend lawsuits become defendants. As the world becomes more orderly, it becomes less confusing.

§2.03 The Meaning of Symbols Resides in People

As legal communicators, one of the most important things we must always remember is that the meaning of symbols does not reside in symbols, but in people; that is, symbols are arbitrary, and in themselves have no meaning.[2] A "lawyer" could just as easily be called a "saint," but by agreement, we refer to lawyers with the symbol, "lawyer." Once the symbol is attached to the thing, humans then interpret the thing and provide the meaning for the symbol. Thus, the meaning of symbols is the interpretation that individuals give to them.[3] For example, to some people, lawyers are the protectors of society, champions of justice, and pillars of the legal system. To others, lawyers are slick, fast-talking shysters. As lawyers trying jury trials, we must always be aware that each juror will provide his or her own interpretation for the symbols used in the trial. One juror may interpret plaintiffs as good, deserving people who have been wronged, while another juror may interpret plaintiffs as greedy people who will cause their insurance rates to go up. One juror may see a personal injury claim as a way to adjust interests in society, while another may see it as a threat to the business system. The fact that jurors will assign different

---

[1] J. Delia & D. Swanson, The Nature of Human Communication, Modcom: Modules in Speech Communication 13 (1976).

[2] *Id.* 4.

[3] *Id* 4.

meanings to the various elements of the trial means that jurors will have differing attitudes toward the various elements of the trial.

Once aware of the fact that each juror will have differing attitudes toward the various elements of the trial, the skillful trial lawyer must use voir dire to discover each juror's attitudes toward the important aspects of the case so as to select the jurors most inclined to form a favorable impression of his or her case. Once jurors are selected, the skillful trial lawyer will then communicate in such a way as to shape juror meaning, and hence, shape juror impressions.

§2.04 Meaning is Open

The fact that meaning resides in people means that meaning is open; that is, since meaning resides in people, each juror will provide his or her own meaning for symbols and things. Just as fingerprints are different, the interpretations that each person provides for things are different. Thus, meaning is open and always subject to interpretation. A cigar may be interpreted by one person as a foul pollutant, and by another person as an aromatic experience. Lawyers must remember that one juror will view medical malpractice suits as beneficial to medical consumers, while others will view them as harmful to the medical system.

Awareness of the fact that meaning is open becomes even more important when dealing with abstract concepts such as "justice," "negligence," and "pain and suffering." These concepts do not exist in concrete form that we can see directly or quantify precisely. Jurors will all have different meanings, which may be vague and hazy, for these legal concepts. To one juror, "justice" is compensating the plaintiff, while to another juror, "justice" is not damaging a doctor's reputation.

To the less skillful lawyer, the fact that meaning is open may produce confusion and anxiety. However, to the skillful lawyer, the fact that meaning is open may be used as an advantage. Rather than passively accepting the meanings for the trial as already determined or set, the skillful lawyer takes an active role in shaping meanings, attitudes, and impressions. The skillful lawyer uses his or her communication skills to create meaning for the jurors and for the trial. For example, rather than being merely a plaintiff, the lawyer's client may be characterized as an innocent victim who has in some way been deprived of his or her dignity or who has been deprived of some basic human right as a result of the defendant's improper conduct. When a working man has been crippled, he may be characterized as having been deprived of his ability to work and support himself, and, therefore, as having been stripped of his dignity. The trial, and finally, the verdict, become a way in which the jury may make the injured victim whole and restore the plaintiff's dignity. For example, a verdict for the plaintiff will allow the plaintiff to support himself and to lead a productive life in society. A verdict for the parents of a deceased child will provide a decent burial for the child and will insure a lasting final memory of the child.

Skillful lawyers create meaning for litigants, opposing lawyers, trial strategies, legal concepts, and elements of the trial process. By creating this meaning, skillful lawyers shape jurors' impressions and, hence, their verdicts.

§2.05   The Sources of Meaning

In order to create meaning, we must understand the factors that give rise to meaning. Meaning is based on two factors, personal construct systems and context.

Personal Construct Systems

As noted earlier, because the world is confusing, humans approach the world with a desire to create order. One of the ways humans order the world is through a system of personal constructs.[4] In growing up, through perception or communication with other people, humans develop systems of interpretation or understanding of things known as personal constructs. These constructs are based on people's experience with things in the world. For example, based on a person's experience with lawsuits, he or she develops constructs about lawsuits and the legal system. If a person's mother was injured and had to file a lawsuit in order to recover damages to pay her medical bills and compensate her for lost wages, that person will form an understanding of civil lawsuits as being a means to compensate deserving victims of negligence. On the other hand, if a person's father had his business bankrupted by a large civil judgment, that person will form an understanding of civil lawsuits as being abusive means for greedy people to damage respectable businessmen. Thus, our constructs are based to a large extent on our past experiences.

When humans approach new and different experiences, they provide meaning to these experiences based on their personal construct systems. In the same way, when jurors enter the jury system, their personal constructs provide meaning to the persons and things involved in the jury process. For example, in an automobile negligence case, a juror who has never driven an automobile may view an automobile as a dangerous instrumentality that must be handled with great care. Jurors who have never driven motorcycles generally feel that motorcycles are dangerous instrumentalities, and that motorcycle drivers who are injured get what they deserve. Jurors whose parents have had negative experiences with lawyers view lawyers with distrust. Jurors who have respected doctors as relatives view medical negligence cases with disdain. Jurors who have seen their loved ones damaged by the negligence of another and then helped in some way by the legal system view civil lawsuits as a positive way to remedy wrongs committed by negligent parties.

Thus, lawyers must always be aware that jurors will bring their personal constructs to the jury process, and that these constructs will determine the meanings that they will give to people, things, and concepts involved in the trial. This knowledge can be used in two very important ways to shape juror impressions. First, voir dire must be used to discover juror constructs. By discovering juror constructs, predictions can be made about how jurors will view the case, and, hence, how they will decide the case. Ways of discovering juror constructs will be discussed in Chapter 4. At this point, suffice it to say that if we can discover juror constructs on voir dire, we can use that information to predict how

---

[4] *Id* 14.

they will decide the case, and, thus, can make meaningful decisions about peremptory challenges and challenges for cause. Recently, I tried a damage suit arising out of a dispute with respect to an employment contract. I probed all jurors about whether they had been employed on the management side or the labor side of business. For those employees who had been employed on the management side of business, I probed for experiences with employee-employer disputes. I then questioned all jurors who had been involved in management disputes about their ability to be fair and impartial. One juror readily admitted that he had a dispute pending at work and that he felt he would be unable to keep this out of his mind, and, therefore, asked if he could be excused.

Once jurors are selected, a knowledge of their constructs will allow the lawyer to make meaningful choices about how evidence and strategies will affect them. A housewife who relies on her factory worker husband for support will be receptive to an argument to the effect that manufacturers of machines must attempt to foresee and protect against hazards to machine users.

Context

In addition to being based upon personal constructs, meaning is also created by the context in which communication occurs. When humans encounter new experiences, the meaning provided by their personal constructs depends on the context in which the experience occurs. More simply stated, meanings are context-dependent.[5] When humans engage in new experiences, they bring their constructs with them and provide meaning based on their constructs. However, each time a person experiences something new, the context of the experience determines how the construct will be applied, and in some situations will alter or refine the meaning of the construct. For example, the statement "I love you," is ambiguous when stated in the abstract, without reference to context. In each context in which that statement is made, the statement means something different. If it is said by a father to a child, it means one thing; if it is said by a wife to a husband, it means another thing; and if it is said by a man to a woman he has known for only two hours in a bar on Saturday night at midnight after he has had many drinks, it means something altogether different. A person with negative personal constructs of lawyers could have those understandings modified, if placed in a situation in which he or she encountered an honest, sensitive lawyer. The new context of the honest lawyer would create new meaning and modify the personal constructs.

Thus, humans create context and meaning through communication. When people meet they have constructs about the world. For example, suppose that two people meet in the morning and that they have both just read an article in the newspaper about a person who has received a verdict of $1 million against a soft drink company because the bottle cap prematurely released and blew off the bottle into the person's eye, causing blindness in that eye. They then engage in communication about this verdict, and through this communi-

---

[5] Cronen, Pearce, & Harris, *The Coordinated Management of Meaning: A Theory of Communication,* in Human Communication Theory: Comparative Essays 71 (F. Dance ed 1982).

cation they create context and meaning for the trial. The first person thinks that the verdict appeared to be excessive and that this was bad for business. However, the second person informs the first person that she knew the lawyer involved in the case and was aware that the soft drink company in question had been knowingly making defective bottles over the past five years and that some 5,000 people had been injured from prematurely released bottle caps. She further informs her friend that a simple warning on the bottle to point the bottle away from the user's face would have prevented most, if not all, of the injuries, but that the manufacturer had refused to place the warnings on the bottles for fear of losing profits to the competition, and that the bulk of the verdict was for punitive damages for knowingly causing injuries. This explanation places the trial and the verdict in a different context and creates a new meaning of the trial for the first person. Thus, context shapes meaning already existing by virtue of our constructs, and in many cases alters and refines our constructs.

§2.06 Creating Meaning for the Trial

The fact that meaning is context-dependent has important implications for the trial lawyer. Many aspects of the trial situation are unfamiliar to jurors. They don't know anything about the law, the facts, the litigants, the lawyers, or the trial process. Their understanding of these aspects of the trial process is vague. Lawyers may use communication to create context for the jurors with respect to these aspects of the trial, and, thus, create meaning for the trial. By creating meaning, the lawyer will be shaping juror impressions. In fact, much of the trial process is simply creating context and meaning. By taking an active role in creating context, the lawyer can control meaning and ultimately juror impression formation.

In order to create meaning, lawyers must be aware of the various elements of the trial of which the jurors will be forming understandings that will be crucial to forming ultimate verdict decisions. Some of these elements of the trial are the nature of the civil process, juror purpose, assessments of the credibility and personas of the lawyers and litigants, the facts of the case, and the law of the case. The trial lawyer may begin creating meaning for these elements of the trial in voir dire and will continue throughout the trial.

§2.07 —Juror Purpose

Jurors are uncertain of their roles and functions as jurors. They are told by the judge that they will decide the case and that they must do justice, but these are vague and poorly defined roles. If left to their own interpretations, jurors would probably form differing ideas about the nature of their role and function as jurors. However, the role and function that jurors adopt will determine the type of verdict that they render. If they feel that they are simply to behave as computers or accountants, they will probably return small judgments based solely on economic losses. If they view themselves as protectors of the status quo, they will render conservative verdicts. However, if they feel that they are to be agents of change with the responsibility of preserving the rights of the individual, they will render liberal verdicts.

Lawyers must have a sense of the purpose that they wish to have their jury adopt, and must take an active role in creating the meaning for jury purpose by creating context. The obvious basic role for the jury is to evaluate the case and return a verdict for the plaintiff. The lawyer can sow the seed for this purpose at the outset of the trial in voir dire by telling the jury that he or she will be asking them to evaluate this case and return a verdict for the plaintiff and by then asking if they all agree that they will return a verdict for the plaintiff if it is justified by the evidence.

Other possibilities for juror function are to be champions of justice, protectors of society, protectors of the plaintiff's dignity, judges of credibility, and agents of reintegration. One way to create purpose as the champions of justice is by the following questioning to an individual juror on voir dire:

> LAWYER: Mr. Smith, our society is based on our constitution, which guarantees a right to a fair and impartial trial. Do you understand that in our system of justice, that for the system to work properly, that justice must be done in all cases, including this case?
>
> JUROR: Yes.
>
> LAWYER: Do you understand that if individual jurors and juries decide not to follow the law and decide not to do justice, our system fails?
>
> JUROR: Yes.
>
> LAWYER: Can you tell us that you will follow the law and do justice in this case? Any problem in playing by these ground rules?
>
> JUROR: No.

This line of questioning creates a context for trial and the juror's role in the trial. Jurors who adopt this function will be less inclined to rule against a plaintiff simply because they feel sorry for the defendant or because they are worried about the impact of their verdict on a doctor's reputation. This theme should be carried throughout the trial. Moe Levine once told a jury in closing, "This is a very important case. A great principle is involved here aside from the case itself. The principle is whether the little people haven't the same rights in law that the big people do."[6]

As will be noted in the next chapter, credibility assessments form a major role in the trial. Therefore, jurors should be told throughout the trial that they will be called on to evaluate credibility. They should be told in voir dire and opening that, as the plaintiff's lawyer, you will take issue with the factual accounts given by the defendant's witnesses and that they will have to determine who is telling the truth. Voir dire commitments may be obtained to the effect that jurors will be willing to examine the witnesses' motives for testifying and will be willing to determing who is telling the truth.

---

[6] M. Levine, *A Subway Death Case*, in The Art of Summation 186 (M. Block ed 1964).

Jurors may be placed in the role of the protectors of the plaintiff's dignity. They may be told that the plaintiff, due to the negligence of the defendant, has been injured and prevented from working and from being self-sufficient, and has, therefore, been stripped of dignity, and that a verdict providing full compensation for this loss will allow the plaintiff to lead a productive life, and, therefore, will restore his or her dignity. In his closing argument in a case in which he was representing an injured cleaning woman many years ago, Melvin Block argued as follows:

> Now, Katherine Tompkins has been working since fifteen years of age as a domestic. At the time of the accident and at the time of this occurrence she was 39. For a period of twenty-four years she was working consistently, with brief times off here and there, as a domestic. She has given you the names and as near as she can recollect, the addresses of the various hotels and the persons by whom she was employed; and all through this she never averaged higher than $40.00 a week, a dollar an hour plus meals. This was her lot in life and she accepted it. She believed she would be making the same $40.00 a week plus meals at the time of her last room she would clean. You saw her. She can't bend, she can't walk straight, she can't get down under the furniture and clean and dust, she can't stand up on her toes to get rid of the dirt in out-of-the-way places. What is she to do, this woman, ruined in the prime of life, whose position as a domestic mind you, gave her dignity, and who is now unable to scrub a floor, a position which meant so much to her; mind you, a person living on $40.00 a week for the rest of her life. Let us assume that she was to work to the age of sixty-five. At $40.00 a week for twenty-six years, let's say roughly it comes out to $2000 a year; for the next 26 years it would be $52,000. We're not talking about inflation, we're not talking about meals, we're not talking about the fact that a dollar is less than the minimum wage paid in this City and State and many parts of the country. This is all she asks, this is what was taken away from her.
>
> But what of herself? That is only the out-of-pocket expense the money that would have been rightfully due her, which has been taken away by the City through its wrongdoing. What is she herself to do? How is she to live? How is she to exist? How is her house to be taken care of? With what pain does she do things that she is able to do? She has told you about the many things, from basic necessities of life to the myriad things that she must do in passing 24 hours of the day. You have lived. She is now 44. Is this injury disabling? Does it not go to the very essence and existence of a person? What is she to do? Get a girl? She was the girl, and I do not say that in a derogatory manner. She knows that the only time that she would have been in a courtroom before would be if she were lucky enough to pass a Civil Service test; and her education has not been that far advanced to take one; or if she were lucky enough to have a politician appoint her to this great, big political plum of cleaning the floors of the Courthouse. She is a person who would probably meet you only if you had someone in like her to clean your floor.

. . . .

I ask, in behalf of Katherine Tompkins, for a verdict at your hands in the sum of $175,000 without apology, without lawyer's talk, straight on the level, as we have been talking all along. Do not demean her. I asked certain questions when I questioned you on the voir dire during your selection. I asked one or two questions on a certain subject and I said I would not refer to it, and I do not feel that I have to again. All I say is, don't demean her as a human being. I ask for her what I would ask for anyone. This is the here and now for Katherine Thompkins. She has waited five years. The burden is no longer mine. You cannot consign her to ask Heaven what has been denied her here on earth. It is yours to do justice, and no one else. For Katherine Tompkins and myself, God bless you in your deliberation.[7]

The jurors should be cast as agents of reintegration. The plaintiff has been injured and damaged by the defendant and has been deprived of something, such as the ability to work, which has separated the plaintiff in some way from society. One of the jury's functions will be to render a verdict that will in some way reintegrate the plaintiff back into society. A verdict compensating plaintiff for lost working capacity will allow the plaintiff to carry on a productive life. Jurors should be cast as helpers to the plaintiff. The plaintiff's future must be placed in the jurors' hands, with a verdict for the plaintiff being the means to a decent, fair, or proper future. For example, in arguing the need for a verdict in favor of the plaintiffs for the death of their child, James Dempsey told the jury:

This is their only day in court, ladies and gentlemen. They can't come back next month or next year or any other day in the future, before any other court and jury for redress in this case.

This is their only opportunity. See that they get an ample and adequate six figure award for the loss of this boy.

I leave that question with you. Mr. and Mrs. Marianiello and their future, with respect to the loss of their boy, Carmine, I leave in your capable hands. From you they will get adequate and ample justice, sufficient for the rest of their days. May I thank you on their behalf and mine for your manifest attention and consideration.[8]

In arguing a wrongful death case, Moe Levine suggests that a verdict for the surviving heirs will give the decedent a proper burial:

This man is gone. He will not be talked about in a public place ever again, I hope. Let us put him to rest finally, forever. But, only with a verdict under the law, without any inflammation, without any prejudice, with-

---

[7] M. Block, *Malpractice in X-Ray Diagnosis*, in *id* 249-51.

[8] J. Dempsey, *The Death of a Five Year Old Boy*, in *id* 175.

out any feelings of hatred, which don't belong in this case; but under the law. You twelve judges without robes, and that's what you are, will have to make your decision on that basis.[9]

§2.08 —Persona and Credibility

Lawyers must create meaning for the personas and credibility of the various actors in the trial; that is, the lawyers must use communication to create desirable images for themselves, their clients, and witnesses, and undesirable images for their opponents, when appropriate. When jurors come to the jury process, as a rule they will not know any of the actors in the trial, and the passive lawyer risks being categorized with all the other stereotypes that the jurors hold about lawyers. The same holds true with respect to the litigants and witnesses. Thus, as lawyers, we must work to create meaning in the minds of the jurors for ourselves, our clients, and our witnesses. As will be discussed later, credibility is something that is developed during the trial, and lawyers must work to develop credibility.

Lawyers should always adopt the role of the champion of justice, and should always align themselves with justice. This creates a positive persona and creates credibility. This may be accomplished by always asking for justice, and defining justice as a verdict for the plaintiff. Moe Levine once told the jury in closing:

> Can you stand upon ivory towers and look down upon these little people and say they are so far beneath us that we will not consider their rights? Or instead of that, will you do what you have dedicated yourselves to do, by agreeing to serve as jurors, to say to yourselves that there is no class, there is no creed, there is no color, there is only the principle of abstract justice to which we are dedicated. . . . When I prayed for my own strength and eloquence, I prayed for yours, because that which is required of you here is to apply the law strictly, without permitting any of these extraneous matters about which passion was raised to interfere with your judg-ment. . . . No censure of anyone, please! Simply desire to do justice. . . . I knew at the beginning that we would come to the time when we had to discuss abstract principles—justice, truth, live, life—these. . . . This man is gone. . . . Let us put him to rest finally, forever. But, only with a verdict under the law, without any inflammation, without any prejudice, without any feelings of hatred, which don't belong in this case, but under the law. . . . So please render a verdict that will permit you to leave the courtroom with a feeling that you have participated in the administration of justice and that the verdict is one of which you can be proud.[10]

The defense lawyers, when appropriate, should be cast as attempting to subvert justice, and their bad personas should be juxtaposed with the good personas of the plaintiff's lawyers. If the defense lawyers make claims not supported

---

[9] M. Levine, *supra* note 6, at 189.
[10] M. Levine, *A Subway Death Case*, in The Art of Summation 187-192 (M. Block ed 1964).

by the evidence, attempt to withhold evidence, or treat the plaintiff rudely, they should be exposed as trying to subvert justice. Thus, the plaintiff's lawyer becomes the champion of justice and the guide to the truth, while the defendant's lawyer becomes the subverter of justice. In the same way, lawyers must create a positive image for their clients. In his case involving the death of a child, James Dempsey develops a negative image for the defendants and their lawyers:

> Now think of that! Think of that. The attorney representing the defendants here in this case served a paper, in which he said this little boy lost his life through his own negligence. Here's a child, playing in his own back yard. . . . It is a defense in the case that is concocted and conceived in the mind of a lawyer in an effort to deprive these parents of their just due or to put a stigma upon the memory of the child, who lost his life, by saying it happened because it was his fault.[11]

Moe Levine creates a negative image for the defendant by pointing out how one of the defendant's employees took his time walking to the aid of the deceased, who laid on the train tracks, unconscious, while a train approached, when he tells the jury:

> The station agent is told a man is lying on the tracks. He knows the schedule of trains. He knows they are coming. Does he rush to the tracks to stop the train? Not this man. This man first closed up his booth—this of course was to avoid the pilfering of the tokens and the change. This is the first step—he locked the booth up. This of course, presuming that somebody was lurking there waiting for him to leave for a moment or two, so they could rush in and steal everything and be off.
>
> Never mind that. Here was knowledge brought home to the station agent of a man in dire peril, facing death. He waited to close the booth. You might excuse that. You might say he is an old time railroad man. Maybe he is chargeable with the tokens and the money. He doesn't want to have to make good for a possible loss, so he closes the booth.
>
> He got a flashlight, fine. But he walked to the tracks! He walked! Doesn't that stagger your imagination? He knows that a man is lying on the tracks. He knows a train is coming. He walks to the tracks.[12]

In referring to the defense attorney's remarks about the character of the deceased, Levine states:

> The children had a right to their father. They had a right to their father. The arrogance of the defendant's counsel to talk about what kind of parental care and guidance did they lose! How dare they say that? What

---

[11] J. Dempsey, *The Death of a Five Year Old Boy*, in *id* 169.

[12] M. Levine, *supra* note 10, at 179-80.

does he know about it? Does he think now that they are better off with no father? What does he know about the tenderness and gentleness and kindliness of this man? What does he know about him at all?[13]

§2.09   —The Facts and the Law

The facts of the case are not facts with universal meaning. Lawyers must always be aware that, due to their personal constructs, the jurors will, if left to their own interpretations, all view the facts differently. Plaintiffs' lawyers must take an active role in creating context and meaning for the facts of the case.

The same is true for the legal principles applicable to the case. As noted earlier, since these principles are abstract concepts, they will not have universal meanings, and each juror will have a vague and differing understanding of their meaning. The plaintiff's lawyer must create meaning for these concepts. For example, to some jurors, negligence may mean only active, conscious acts, and therefore, the lawyer must create the understanding that negligence also includes passive, unconscious omissions as well.

Since the creation of meaning is so important to the trial, the next sections will be devoted to a review of communication strategies that may be used to create meaning.

§2.10   Strategies for the Creation of Meaning

Successful trial strategy must be geared toward the creation of meaning. In the typical trial situation, the lawyers have a short period of time to prevail upon an uninformed jury. Strategies that will help accomplish this task are the use of a narrative or storytelling structure, storytelling themes, labels, figurative language, and common sense appeals.

§2.11   —Storytelling or Narrative Structure

In the typical trial, uninformed jurors are bombarded with an overwhelming mass of facts and legal concepts, and are then asked to form a decision. In order to be successful, the lawyer must integrate this mass of information into a coherent whole that can be easily understood by the jurors. This is best accomplished by using a storytelling or narrative structure. With a narrative structure, the lawyers become storytellers, presenting human dramas to the jury.

The storytelling structure is effective for several reasons. First, stories organize information in ways that help the jurors perform interpretive operations.[14] A storytelling structure helps the jurors locate the central action of the trial. Jurors may have various concerns about the legal system and the trial. One juror may be concerned about the damage to the plaintiff, while another juror

---

[13] *Id* 189.

[14] Bennett, *Storytelling in Criminal Trials: A Model of Social Judgment*, 61 QJ Speech 5 (1978).

may be concerned with the impact of a large verdict on the defendant. The storytelling structure may be used to create the central focus of the action for the jurors. For example, for the plaintiff, the central action is the negligence of the defendant and the damage to the plaintiff.

The storytelling structure provides inferences that the jurors will need to make in order to render a verdict. When the facts unfold, there will be various elements of the story that will require interpretive inferences in order for a decision to be reached. The storytelling structure provides these inferences. For example, in a product liability case, the plaintiff seeks punitive damages for willful and wanton negligence. The plaintiff proves that over a period of years the product in question has injured thousands of people, and that these injuries could have been avoided with a simple warning on the product, but that the manufacturer failed to provide the warning. The plaintiff also demonstrates that competition is keen between the defendants and its rivals in the field. The chairman of the board of the defendant corporation testifies that neither he nor the board of directors had any intention of injuring the plaintiff or any other consumer with their product, and that no other producers of the product in the field used or use warning labels, and, therefore, that the defendant is simply following industry standards. With the use of a narrative structure, the plaintiff can draw inferences from the evidence which tells a story of corporate greed in which a group of greedy corporations are competing for consumer dollars and are unwilling to place a simple warning on a package for fear of losing profits to a rival company. The narrative structure is used to draw inferences that are not specifically made by the witnesses on the witness stand.

Finally, the storytelling structure adds drama and emotion to the trial. Clarence Darrow once said, "Jurymen seldom convict a person they like, or acquit one they dislike. The main work of the trial lawyer is to make a jury like his client, or at least to feel sympathy for him. Facts regarding the crime are relatively unimportant."[15] The storytelling structure is one of the ways to create sympathy and liking for the client. In the same way that an author or playwright evokes sadness or joy in the reader or audience, the skillful trial lawyer evokes sympathy and indignation in the jury. Clients are not simply plaintiffs bringing product liability claims, but must be cast as real life people with feelings, hopes, and dreams that become affected by the acts of the defendants. For example, using this type of structure, Moe Levine presented the case of a deceased alcoholic who became drunk and passed out on railroad tracks and was killed by a train. The defendant maligned the character of the deceased and Levine skillfully used a storytelling structure to rehabilitate the image of the decedent:

> You heard about it. There was no concealment. She loved him, she said. She had a right to. Women are strange about their emotional reactions to the men with whom they live. They love the ones less likely to be loved, and dislike the ones they should love. These are the vagaries of women's reactions. She had three children with him. She knew his weaknesses. I

---

[15] E. Southerland, Principles of Criminology 442 (1966).

could see within this a form of mother complex. He was the weak one and she the strong one. She had to keep the home together. . . . You have felt yourselves on occasion in the scheme of eternity, that even the smallest sparrow doesn't fall without his passing being marked, and William Stevenson was a very small sparrow indeed. He was, in all probability, as unimportant a man as you will ever meet in your life, except that he forms a part of a little group. You know that he wasn't bad. You heard nothing bad about him. If he perpetrated crimes you would have heard about them. You heard nothing bad. You heard of weakness. You heard of no evil.

He might have reformed from these weaknesses with a wife who was tolerant and understanding enough to keep pressing him to remain as part of this family group.

He was removed from it needlessly. This is the basis for the request for damages. . . . This is not a case for a token verdict. This verdict must compensate according to law for the deprivation to a woman of her husband whom she wanted. Never mind whether you think she should have. She had a right to want him. This was her Man. *As he was, weak, she wanted him.* She was deprived of him, and if she was deprived of him under such circumstances as the law says, it gives her actionable rights, and then she must be compensated.

. . . .

Did he play with his children? Did he take them to church with him? When they had problems did he answer their problems? He was growing up. He was growing up. Remember that for three years he had not been away from home.

He had flitted about. Women attracted him and he attracted them. He was weak. He was a child, yet he was growing up. He had reached 39, and he had these three children whom you've seen and I'm sure, if he had lived, he would have been proud of. He was growing up and he might have matured had he lived. In any event they had a right to his being there to comfort them, and to guide them. They had a right not to have to say to other children, "I have no daddy."

. . . .

You must say what loss this represents to the children, and how it should be compromised. They don't know anything about his weakness. To them he was just a big, strong, happy, laughing daddy.[16]

The storytelling structure allows the lawyer to present background information about the plaintiff such that the jury is able to get to know and like him or her. The jury is allowed, through the story, to experience that plaintiff's trials and tribulations.

---

[16] M. Levine, *A Subway Death Case*, in The Art of Summation 185-91 (M. Block ed 1964).

§2.12 —Themes

The plaintiff's story is made up of various themes that state and prove the case. The storytelling structure integrates these themes. Some themes are more appropriately dealt with in opening and some in closing. The themes will simply be outlined in this section, and will be explained in detail and illustrated in Part II.

An obvious theme is that the defendant was negligent. Within this theme, the plaintiff's claims of liability are detailed. A related theme is that, due to the defendant's negligence, the plaintiff suffered permanent injuries and damages. Within this theme, causal connection and the nature and extent of damages are developed.

That the plaintiff has been wronged by the defendant's acts and that the jury must or can act to rectify this wrong is an important theme. The jury must be convinced that the plaintiff has been separated from or deprived of some right or ability, and that the jury by its verdict can rectify this wrong.

A theme that develops credibility is that the plaintiff was a good or noble person and that the defendant behaved improperly. In this theme, the good and bad characters of the parties are developed and the plaintiff's goodness is juxtaposed against the defendant's badness.

An important theme for creating meaning for the nature of the case is that the issues in the case are simple. A jury will be hesitant to assess fault and large damages in a case that it feels it does not understand. Thus, the lawyer must convince the jury that, in the final analysis, the issues are simple and the jury is competent to hear and decide the case.

The pursuit of justice is a theme that the plaintiff must always try to develop. The jury is told by the judge that its function is to render justice, and, therefore, the lawyer must convince the jury that the plaintiff's case embodies and is consistent with the pursuit of justice. Ultimately a verdict for the plaintiff must be conceptualized as the rendering of justice. For example, in concluding his closing statement, Moe Levine equates a verdict for the plaintiffs as the rendering of justice when he states:

> Nothing will ever replace him, and so within the framework of $100,000, award a sum that will adequately compensate them for the loss of this little man. Yours will be the final determination. Please render a verdict based upon the law. . . . So please render a verdict that will permit you to leave this courtroom with a feeling that you have participated in the administration of justice and that the verdict is one of which you can be proud. Thank you very much.[17]

Jury purpose is an important theme. As noted above, jury purpose is important in that a jury will render a verdict based upon its understanding of its purpose. If a jury views its purpose as maintaining the status quo, it will react one way, while if it views its purpose as effecting change, it will react in an entirely

---

[17] M. Levine, *A Subway Death Case,* in The Art of Summation 191-92 (M. Block ed 1964).

different way. Thus, an important theme will be jury purpose. Important jury purposes for the plaintiff will be to judge the evidence, to judge the parties and their actions, to render justice, to return money damages, and to rectify wrongs. In developing jury purpose in a wrongful death case, James Dempsey told the jury:

> Actually the sole function of this jury, in this case, ladies and gentlemen, is perhaps the greatest distinction that can be afforded any jury anywhere, to sit in judgment as to the pecuniary loss to the parents for the death of their child.[18]

§2.13 —Use of Words and Labels

Language affects the way people perceive reality;[19] that is, the way we react to the word by which things are labeled can affect the way we react to the things themselves.[20] For example, a department store manager in an experimental mood once placed identical piles of high quality linen handkerchiefs in two separate piles on opposite ends of a counter. He labeled one pile with a sign that read, "Fine Irish Linen-50 cents," and he labeled the other pile with a sign that read, "Nose Rags-3 for 25 cents." The "Irish linens" outsold the "nose rags" five to one.[21] Thus, the symbol people attach to a thing will affect the meaning people give to the thing.

An understanding and appreciation of the impact of language on perception can provide a powerful tool to the trial lawyer. As lawyers, we can affect juror perception by our selection of the labels and words we use to describe our clients and our cases. Labels and words may be used strategically to pin certain positive or negative associations on processes, persons, or things by calling them a certain name.[22] Labels and words may be used to provoke emotions, attitudes, and beliefs in the minds of the jurors. The lawyer must never walk into court and tell the jury in voir dire that they are going to hear a "product liability case in which the plaintiff was injured." The lawyer must package the case by deliberately selecting labels that will provide the appropriate positive impact. Plaintiffs must never be referred to as plaintiffs, but by name or by some other label that creates a favorable image. The plaintiff becomes an "innocent victim" and a deceased child is referred to as a "little boy." The defendant, on the other hand, is always the "defendant" and its acts are always "wrongful," "negligent," "irresponsible," etc. The jury's role is not simply to render a verdict, but rather, its role becomes a "great responsibility."

---

[18] J. Dempsey, *The Death of a Five Year Old Boy*, in *id* 173.

[19] B. Whorf, *The Name of the Situation as Affecting Behavior, in The Relation of Habitual Thought and Behavior to Language,* in Language, Culture, and Personality: Essays in Memory of Edward Sapir 75-77 (L. Spier, A. Hallowell, and S. Newman eds 1941).

[20] W. Haney, Communication and Interpersonal Relations 494-95 (1979).

[21] *Id* 494.

[22] K. Campbell, The Rhetorical Act 27 (1982).

In the introduction of his closing argument, in which the defense attorney has made a joke, Mel Block illustrates the power of using labels when he states:

> Neither will I tell you jokes such as concerning "two Irishmen having a cup of coffee," nor will I dance a little jig for you to show you the mobility of the leg, and believe me, I will take second to none when it comes to having a sense of humor; but I will not profane this house of the law with a cheap, elementary tactic known to every freshman law student: —that is, to divert the jury from the sober and serious task at hand— that is your decision whether the time is here and now, for retribution against the City of New York in the form of compensatory money damages for the plaintiff Katherine Tompkins, or your decision that she has no reason to be here. I sincerely hope and pray that the vaudeville act of Mr. _____ was as obvious to you in its intent and purpose as it was to me. At the expense of a cripple he wanted to cripple her case by telling you a few tawdry jokes so as to divert you—so as for you to be in such a frame of humorous mind as to reject her claim; so that the atmosphere of this courtroom would be that of a gay and hilarious nightclub routine having no place for the legitimate business of evaluating a severe, serious and permanent destruction of a human being's future happiness and life. And let me say this at the outset: If he has, and I am quite sure he has not succeeded in purpose, then not only will Katherine Tompkins not have that which the law provides her when she has been wrongly maimed and disabled in the form of compensation, but also she will not have enough to pay a Mr. _____ to dance a jig for her and tell her a few jokes in the confines of whatever home she has in the future to assuage her pain and distract her mind from her awful, lonely and bleak existence.[23]

By carefully selecting labels and words, the lawyer can shape juror impressions.

§2.14 —Use of Figurative Language

Another important and powerful communication tool available to the trial lawyer is the use of figurative language. Figurative language consists of the use of examples, analogies, metaphors, and allusions to create meaning and support their arguments. Figurative language involves the use of imaginative comparisons between things, events, and persons that are not obviously alike at all, but that resemble each other in some way.[24] Figurative language is powerful because it grasps and defines the intangible qualities of experience[25] and because it illustrates and holds the listener's attention. As such, it can be used to explain or illustrate difficult laws and concepts such as negligence, justice,

[23] M. Block, *Malpractice in X-Ray Diagnosis*, in the Art of Summation 242 (M. Block ed 1964).
[24] Campbell, The Rhetorical Act 32 (1982).
[25] *Id* 261.

and pain and suffering. Further, figurative language contains compacted lines of argument that invite inductive and deductive leaps. After first presenting facts and arguments in straightforward terms, lawyers may use figurative language to move to higher levels of analysis.

An example is "a case or an instance, real or hypothetical, detailed or undetailed, used to illustrate an idea or to prove that a particular kind of event has happened or could happen."[26] It is the presentation of a single instance of a phenomenon in order to illustrate or support an argument. Examples are important and powerful because they illustrate ideas, contain compacted lines of argument, and because they invite identification and prompt inferential leaps from a single example to a generalization. For example, in his closing argument in a medical malpractice case, Mel Block attempts to convince the jury that the defendant hospital was negligent because in diagnosing the plaintiff's hip injury, it took only a one-angle view of the hip with x-rays and therefore failed to find a fracture which was present. As a result of this failure, the plaintiff was allowed to leave the hospital and as a result of walking on the hip, developed crippling arthritis. In arguing that the doctors were negligent for failing to take several x-ray views of the hip, he used two examples which dramatically proved his point:

> I told you that I don't think I had to call a doctor in this case, and here is why: The care they gave Katherine Tomkins was less than they would give in selecting a five-cent apple. When you and I buy an apple from a fruit peddler or in a fruit store, do we plunk down the nickel right away and accept or grab any apple? No, we turn it around and we look at it at all angles and from perspectives and make sure it doesn't have a bad portion or a blemish or a rotten part that is visible. Only a nickel; we make a bad purchase, we can buy another one for another nickel. In a hip joint, you can't get another hip, you can't make whole that which is crippled. And yet, they only took an A-P view, which you know is a front to back view. They couldn't tell whether it was cracked on the side or cracked at an angle. And yet this is what they try to tell you is the proper thing to do. Proper for a hip, improper for an apple?
>
> You go into a store to buy a suit, or a jacket, or a coat. You stand before three-way mirrors, and looking into it becomes a complete hall of mirrors, each mirror reflecting the images in the other mirrors. I remember when for a few bucks I would purchase a suit with two pairs of pants, and judging from what clothes cost these days the price was cheap and inexpensive indeed. But yet I would turn and turn and turn to make sure that each crease, each seam was in place; that there were no bulges or puffs. I didn't expect the suit to make me an Adonis, and I didn't expect to look like a movie star. Why I looked was to see that what I was paying for at least was presentable. And I turned and the tailor would come over and would look. And perhaps a relative along with me would look, and if we made a mistake we could always bring the suit back for an alteration; we could

---

[26] *Id* 174.

always buy another suit. Not so with a hip, ladies and gentlemen. And yet they say taking one view of a hip is proper. Proper for a hip, improper for a suit? I ask you.[27]

This example illustrates and supports his argument that the hospital failed to conduct a proper x-ray examination. It further invites inductive and deductive leaps in that the examples invite the jurors to inductively arrive at the generalization that whenever inspecting something for flaws and defects, more than one view of the article should be examined. The examples then invite the jurors to move from this generalization deductively to the conclusion that since the doctors failed to inspect more than one view or angle, they certainly conducted an inadequate inspection and were, therefore, negligent.

Analogies are "likenings or comparisons between things, processes, persons, or events."[28] By use of analogies, the lawyer can present a situation familiar to the juror, which helps the jury to form generalizations about certain situations that can then be applied to the unfamiliar situation that is involved in the trial. For example, in Mel Block's malpractice case involving the failure to properly read x-rays, Block argues that the doctors were negligent in that they attempted to read a wet x-ray plate. In providing support for this argument, he points out that one of the doctors testified that attempting to read a wet x-ray plate was like "riding a car in a rainstorm without the windshield wipers working."[29] The analogous situation of riding an automobile in a rainstorm is familiar to jurors and allows them to easily grasp and understand the situation of attempting to read a wet x-ray plate.

Metaphors are figures of speech that function like examples and analogies in that they connect what is known and familiar with what is unknown and unfamiliar.[30] They reflect attitudes and evaluate. For example, Mel Block uses the metaphor of a prison in describing how his client is limited by the arthritis that has developed as a result of the negligence of the defendant when he tells the jury:

> She still has to live 24 hours a day, and all that is in pain now. She is as much entombed and encased in a prison of bone as any inmate of any penitentiary or prison is.

Allusions are references to historical events, literature, mythology, or some other source of cultural wisdom.[31] Humans store knowledge in their minds that is linked to some historical, mythological, cultural, or literary event or reference. When the speaker alludes to this event or reference, the allusion calls up the stored knowledge, which can be used to support the argument being

---

[27] M. Block, *Malpractice in X-Ray Diagnosis,* in The Art of Summation 245-46 (M. Block ed 1964).

[28] Campbell, *supra* note 24, at 183.

[29] M. Block, *supra* note 27, at 245.

[30] Campbell, *supra* note 24, at 262.

[31] *Id* 33.

made. Like analogies, allusions allow the listeners to generalize from a familiar situation to a new and unfamiliar situation. For example, in his medical malpractice case, Mel Block was arguing that the hospital in question was negligent in that it allowed the plaintiff to leave the hospital and walk about on a broken hip, which resulted in permanent damage. In supporting that argument, he alluded to the Boy Scouts in order to provide support for his argument when he stated:

> Now, you and I have learned very young, as every Boy Scout knows, that you don't move a person with a fractured bone. Why? Because it gets better, because it stays the same? No, of course not. Because it gets worse, it deteriorates and disintegrates; and that is what happened here.

At this point Block has won over any juror who subscribes to this Boy Scout belief.

§2.15 —Common Sense Arguments

Common sense arguments are some of the most persuasive arguments because they rely on shared knowledge; that is, as humans, we have stored knowledge called common sense, knowledge that is based on what we as humans all know or feel to be true about the world. It is called common sense because we assume that all others share these beliefs or understandings. In actuality, common sense knowledge is based on each individual's personal experience. Thus, it is persuasive, because if a speaker makes an argument that we know to be true based on our personal experience, we will support the argument, but if the argument goes against our personal experience, we will reject it. Common sense arguments will be explained in greater detail in Chapter 3, and, therefore, suffice it to say at this point that in creating meaning for the trial, common sense appeals operate to link arguments to the shared knowledge that jurors hold to be true, thus creating favorable juror impressions.

§2.16 Nonverbal Communication

The nonverbal communication that goes on in and out of the courtroom is just as important as the verbal communication. Jurors will form impressions about the lawyers, litigants, and witnesses based on their observations of the nonverbal communication. Therefore, the lawyer must give consideration to what is being communicated nonverbally, and he or she should keep in mind that juror impressions can be shaped by nonverbal communication.

§2.17 —Dress

Jurors will form impressions about lawyers, litigants, and witnesses based on their dress. As will be demonstrated in Chapter 3, jurors have role expectations about the people involved in jury trials. They will expect the lawyers, litigants, and witnesses to dress in certain appropriate ways. The parties to the lawsuit will be expected to dress in a way that demonstrates respect for the jury process. If jurors perceive that the plaintiff is dressing in a way that shows a lack of respect or seriousness for the jury process, then the jurors will probably not take the plaintiff's claim seriously. Therefore, clients should be counseled to dress in appropriate ways for the trial proceeding. They should not overdress or dress in a way that is clearly out of character for their situation, because this will cause them to feel out of place and uncomfortable and may cause them to send nonverbal signals to the jury that may be interpreted as deceptiveness.

Counsel clients and witnesses not to wear loud clothing that will detract attention from the focus of the trial. They should not wear excessive or gaudy jewelry or makeup. Beware of pins, labels, or other paraphernalia that link the wearer with a particular group or philosophy. This is not to say that they should not be worn, but the lawyer should be aware of who he or she is winning or losing by wearing such labels. An appearance of sloppiness should be avoided.

The rule of thumb is that the dress should fit the situation. A garage mechanic called away from his job to testify would be accepted in a pair of greasy overalls. However, a garage mechanic as plaintiff should wear the type of clothing he would wear when going to church or on other serious occasions.

§2.18 —Nonverbal Behavior in and out of the Courtroom

The jurors will observe the lawyers and litigants throughout the trial. Over the course of several days, it will be apparent whether the husband and wife plaintiffs truly love each other or are simply putting on a show for the jury. It will also be apparent whether or not the lawyer really believes in and cares about his clients or whether he or she is simply putting on a dog and pony show for the jury. If the jurors perceive that the lawyer does not like or does not care about the clients, they will have difficulty getting emotionally involved in the case themselves. Clients should be carefully counseled prior to trial about the importance of their nonverbal behavior during the trial.

The jurors will also be looking at the lawyers and litigants outside of the courtroom. Jurors will take note of the lawyers who fight in the courtroom, but laugh and joke during breaks. In the same way, the jurors will take note of the plaintiff who looks sad or serious in the courtroom, but changes demeanor outside of the courtroom. The rule of thumb here is consistency. The behavior outside the courtroom should be consistent with the behavior inside the courtroom in order for the jurors to feel that the lawyers and litigants are presenting themselves in an honest and straightforward way.

§2.19 —Eye Contact

Eye contact is one of the most important elements of nonverbal communication. The failure on the part of witnesses to make eye contact will result in the jurors perceiving the witnesses as being deceptive. Therefore, you must insist that your clients and witnesses make eye contact with the jurors. If they find making eye contact difficult, it should be practiced in your office prior to trial. Clients must be told that their failure to make eye contact will hurt their case. Tell clients that the jury will be made up of people like them who are anxious to hear their story and who should be considered as friends. If they are nervous, questions can be asked, such as, "Have you ever testified before?" and "Are you nervous?" in order to diffuse the nervousness. When one side of the case presents witnesses who make eye contact and the other side of the case presents witnesses who do not make eye contact, the jury will tend to find the witnesses who made eye contact more credible than the witnesses who did not.

§2.20   Conclusion

Communication affects perception. Thus, lawyers can affect the way the jurors perceive the trial by the way they communicate with the jurors. The successful lawyer will be the lawyer who understands this fundamental aspect of communication and takes an active role in shaping juror impressions.

3

Lawyer Credibility

§3.01 Introduction

Credibility assessments made by jurors about lawyers, litigants, and witnesses are crucial elements in any jury trial. Most jury trials involve ambiguous factual situations in that the facts are in dispute by the parties. The jurors who are selected to hear the case are, as a rule, unfamiliar with the lawyers, litigants, facts, and law involved in the case. Each side of the case presents a conflicting view of the "reality" of the case, and the jury is called upon to make a decision as to which is the "correct" reality. In so doing, the jury must decide which position is more credible. Thus, an understanding of how jurors form credibility assessments will be an invaluable tool to the trial lawyer. The purpose of this chapter is to review the process by which jurors form credibility assessments.

§3.02   The Constructivist Nature of Credibility Assessments

Credibility assessments are an aspect of the process by which humans form impressions of others.[1] As human perceivers, we construct or create the world in which we live. Our understanding of others is always in terms of images and impressions.[2] Since we cannot directly perceive another's intentions, inner qualities, or attitudes, we construct an "impression" of the actions, qualities, or attitudes of the other by interpreting the other's appearance and behavior.[3] As an example of this constructivist process, different people construct different perceptions or impressions of a cigar. To one person, a cigar is an aromatic experience, while to another, it is a foul pollutant. In the same manner, jurors construct credibility impressions of lawyers, litigants, and witnesses.

§3.03   The General Dimensions of Credibility

Because humans are socialized within common cultures and use shared languages, they have shared or generalized constructions of reality.[4] Americans have generalized constructions of reality that differ from other cultures. Thus, due to the socialization process, general dimensions for credibility assessment exist across the American population. Studies have identified these general dimensions of credibility. American jurors can be expected to form credibility assessments about lawyers, litigants, or witnesses based on the extent to which they appear to exhibit the general dimensions of *expertness*, *trustworthiness*, and *dynamism*.

§3.04   Experts—Lawyers

The dimension of expertness is the extent to which the lawyer appears to

---

[1] Delia, *A Constructivist Analysis of the Concept of Credibility*, 62 QJ Speech, 361, 366 (1976).

[2] *Id* 367.

[3] *Id* 367; Delia, O'Keefe & O'Keefe, *The Constructivist Approach to Communication*, in Human Communication Theory 147, 151 (F. Dance ed 1982).

[4] Delia, *A Constructivist Analysis of the Concept of Credibility*, 62 QJ Speech 361, 369 (1976); Delia, O'Keefe & O'Keefe, *The Constructivist Approach to Communication*, in Human Communication Theory 158 (F. Dance ed 1982).

be competent,[5] intelligent, authoritative, trained, experienced, skilled, informed,[6] professional,[7] and a source of valid information.[8] Therefore, to establish expertness, lawyers must demonstrate general intelligence and ability; training, experience, and qualifications with respect to the practice of law; and accuracy and validity as sources of information. Lawyers can demonstrate intelligence and ability by doing all of their homework and by appearing knowledgeable about all aspects of each case. In a civil case, lawyers can demonstrate expertness by explaining the plaintiff's medical condition to the jury and by conversing knowledgeably with doctors on direct and cross-examination. Conversely, lawyers' inability to explain concepts or to pronounce words correctly will result in low judgments of expertness.

Lawyers who know trial practice and procedure demonstrate legal qualifications and training. Conversely, those who are continually corrected or reprimanded by the court for improper courtroom practice will be perceived as incompetent. Lawyers who show they have thought out all aspects of the case and are prepared for any contingencies that arise will be perceived as expert. Lawyers who appear to "know what they are talking about" will be viewed as accurate and valid sources of information.

Competency will also be based on lawyers' ability to deal with both positive and negative aspects of their cases. In a study in which jurors were interviewed about their perceptions of lawyer credibility, the plaintiff's lawyer continually did not acknowledge weaknesses in his case during the opening statement and in direct examination of his witnesses.[9] The defense lawyer brought out these weaknesses in his opening statement and on cross-examination.

For example, the plaintiff's lawyer did not acknowledge in his opening statement that the plaintiff told the police officer at the accident scene that he was not hurt and that after the collision, he went to a party and did not seek medical attention until the next day. These developments are common after automobile collisions and could have been explained. The plaintiff's lawyer ignored these facts, however, and allowed the defendant to present the "real" story. As a group, the jurors perceived the plaintiff's lawyer as incompetent, saying he was either stupid or unprepared. Several acknowledged that these facts were not unusual and could have been explained and that, by failing to do so, the plaintiff's lawyer hurt his case.

Lawyers, witnesses, and litigants will also be judged competent and expert

---

[5] McCroskey & Young, *Ethos and Credibility: The Constraint and Its Measurement After Three Decades,* 32 Cent States Speech J 33 (1981).

[6] Berlo, Lemert & Mertz, *Dimensions for Evaluating the Acceptability of Message Sources,* 33 Pub Opinion Q 563, 575 (1969-70).

[7] Schweitzer & Ginzberg, *Factors of Communicator Credibility,* in Problems in Social Psychology 94 (C. Backman & P. Secord ed 1966).

[8] C. Hovland, I. Janis & H. Kelley, Communication and Persuasion 20 (1953).

[9] *See* jury study, §§3.14-3.20.

to the extent that they fulfill the jurors' expectations of their roles.[10] Just as theatergoers have expectations of actors and actresses in a play, jurors have role expectations of participants in a trial. Jurors have expectations about what a lawyer should look like and how a lawyer should behave. The judge lawyers who look the part and who appear knowledgeable about courtroom etiquette and practice as competent; they judge lawyers who violate their role expectations as low in credibility.

Jurors also have expectations about the proper role of plaintiffs and defendants. They expect plaintiffs to behave consistently with what they are asking for. For example, in a medical malpractice case, the plaintiff was judged low in credibility because she was shown not to have followed doctor's orders and not to have done everything she could have to protect her own health. In a hunting injury case where the plaintiff was suing a gun manufacturer for negligence in the design of a rifle safety catch, jurors perceived the plaintiff as low in credibility because he did not follow accepted safety rules. A plaintiff claiming damages for pain and suffering was judged low in credibility because he took passes from the hospital during the time period that he claimed to be in pain.

§3.05   —Expertness—Witnesses

Lawyers can establish or destroy witness credibility using the standards of expertness. The credibility of expert witnesses is established in part by bringing out their education, training, and experience on direct examination. In this regard, it should be noted that training in many cases is considered just as important as education in establishing expertness.[11] An expert witness's credibility can be destroyed on cross-examination by demonstrating that he or she does not have the necessary education, training, or skill upon which to base an opinion.

The credibility of experts can be established by demonstrating that they did the necessary groundwork and took into account all relevant factors in arriving at opinions. Their credibility can be damaged by showing that they did not do their homework. For example, a doctor's credibility may be destroyed if the lawyer can show that the doctor reached an opinion before conducting tests or viewing important medical records.

§3.06   —Expertness—Choice

Choices lawyers and litigants make are crucial determinants of credibility.[12] Jurors will view choices as intentional and will take the lawyer's choices into consideration when determining expertness. Lawyers who take charge and

---

[10] *See id.*

[11] Sennett, Hagen, & Harvey, *Credibility of Sources of Information About Drugs to Heroin Addicts,* 37 J Applied Soc Psychology 1239-42 (1975).

[12] O. Walter, Speaking to Inform and Persuade 128 (1982).

actively make strategic decisions throughout the trial will be viewed as competent, while those who passively react indecisively to the other side will be perceived as incompetent.

§3.07   —Trustworthiness—Lawyers

The dimension of trustworthiness is the extent to which lawyers appear to be honest, just, open-minded, friendly,[13] well-mannered, warm,[14] fair, loyal to listeners, and reliable sources of information.[15] They may appear warm, friendly, and well-mannered by being polite and by recognizing the rights and feelings of others. At all stages of the trial, lawyers should treat jurors, witnesses, and opposing litigants with respect.

On voir dire, lawyers should be polite and friendly to all the jurors regardless of their predispositions. All jurors should be treated as equally important.

Lawyers should not abuse witnesses on the stand. They should remember that people have feelings, and whenever possible, take these into consideration. This is not to say that lawyers should hide anger or contempt for a witness or litigant who has lied or attempted to subvert justice. In fact, such a display, when justified, adds to credibility by demonstrating the lawyer's commitment to the client and to the pursuit of justice. Lawyers, however, must never go to the extreme of browbeating witnesses who are captives on the witness stand.

Lawyers can demonstrate open-mindedness and fairness by being even-handed in voir dire questioning. Jurors had more respect for lawyers who treated favorable and unfavorable prospective jurors equally during voir dire than for those who did not.[16] Typically, if a prospective juror acknowledges a connection with an opposing litigant or attorney, this juror is questioned thoroughly about the connection and possible prejudice. Jurors gave higher credibility assessments to lawyers who asked the same probing set of questions to favorable and unfavorable jurors alike than those who summarily questioned and accepted the fairness of favorable jurors.

Lawyers will be judged trustworthy if they are perceived as reliable sources of information. This means that lawyers, litigants, or witnesses must present evidence honestly. Those lawyers who appear to be just another salesperson will generally be judged low in credibility.

§3.08   —Trustworthiness—Loyalty to Listeners

The most important aspect of trustworthiness is loyalty to listeners, or a lawyer's desire not only to further his or her client's interest, but to do good for

---

[13] Berlo, Lemert & Mertz, *Dimensions for Evaluating the Acceptability of Message Sources,* 33 Pub Opinion Q 563, 574-75 (1969-70).

[14] Schweitzer & Ginzberg, *Factors of Communicator Credibility,* in Problems in Social Psychology 98 (C. Backman & P. Secord eds 1966).

[15] C. Hovland, I. Janis & H. Kelley Communication and Persuasion 23-24, 34 (1953).

[16] See jury study, §§3.14-3.20.

the sake of the jury. Usually, in opening the case and in the jury instructions, the judge will tell jurors that their function is to reach a fair and impartial verdict. Jurors want to do that. Thus, they feel deceived if they perceive that a lawyer is trying to keep evidence from them in order to obtain an unjust decision.

Lawyers may trigger this aspect of trustworthiness by telling the jury in the opening statement, "I am going to get all the evidence before you so that you can reach a fair and just decision."

Jurors may view continuous objections to the admission of evidence as a lawyer's attempt to keep evidence from them.[17] Therefore, lawyers should use motions in limine to obtain rulings on the admission of evidence out of the hearing of the jury.

By demonstrating that opponents are intentionally trying to withhold evidence, a lawyer can convince a jury that the opponents are untrustworthy. How choice comes into play can be seen in the use of police reports in automobile accident cases. Generally, these reports contain elements unfavorable to both sides. For example, a report may contain a plaintiff's statement to a police officer denying injury immediately after the accident. It may also include an inadmissible conclusion of the officer that the defendant's negligence caused the collision. Typically, the defense will try to have the officer on cross-examination read the plaintiff's statement denying injury. At this point, the plaintiff's lawyer may offer the entire report into evidence so that the jury can read it for themselves. Defense counsel will then be forced to object to keep the damaging conclusion out of evidence. The court will sustain the objection, but the jurors will see the defense lawyer as choosing to withhold evidence from them.

§3.09   —Trustworthiness—Witnesses

A witness's trustworthiness may be destroyed by demonstrating that the witness is biased, prejudiced, or has a motive for testifying. Thus, if it can be shown on cross-examination that a witness has an interest in the outcome of the case, he or she will be judged low in credibility. In-house or "company" experts in product liability cases are subject to the suggestion that their jobs depend on their testimony. Doctors in medical malpractice cases can be expect to be motivated by a desire to prevent malpractice verdicts. Committees that set industry standards for safety are many times made up of "company" employees and are open to the suggestion that they will set standards that serve the interests of the companies involved, as opposed to consumers. By showing that the witness is just another "used car salesman" out to say or do anything to further a "sale," his or her credibility can be destroyed.

A witness's credibility may be destroyed by demonstrating that he or she is withholding relevant information or opinions, and, thus, is not loyal to the jury's interest in rendering justice. The expert who withholds or attempts to conceal results or tests of studies that support contrary opinions will be seen as low in credibility.

---

[17] See jury study, §§3.14-3.20.

A witness who renders rigid opinions and refuses to change those opinions when the facts change will be seen as untrustworthy. For example, all expert witnesses base their opinions on a set of assumed facts. The witness may be asked if his or her opinion would change if a different set of facts were assumed. If the witness says "no", he or she will be seen as untrustworthy in that he or she is simply a paid witness offering the same opinion no matter what the facts demonstrate. If the witness agrees that his or her opinion would change if the relevant facts changed, the witness may then be given a different set of assumptions and asked if that changes the opinion. If he or she says "yes" the lawyer may then establish favorable opinions. If the witness says "no," new facts will not change the opinion, he or she will be seen as offering opinions not based on the facts and will be seen as untrustworthy.

Witnesses may be shown to be untrustworthy if it can be demonstrated that they have taken inconsistent positions at prior times or if inconsistencies can be shown within their testimony. In order to be perceived as reliable, witnesses must be consistent over time.

§3.10   Dynamism

This dimension includes such characteristics as being aggressive rather than meek, emphatic rather than hesitant, bold rather than timid, active rather than passive, and energetic rather than tired.[18] Dynamism is an intensifier, so if the lawyer, litigant, or witness is perceived as expert or trustworthy, these perceptions will be intensified if the jury also seems them as dynamic.

Dynamism can be developed in two ways. First, if lawyers take cases they believe in and use themes they feel strongly about, they tend to be dynamic. Lawyers who become protectors of the little guy or watchdogs against big business will tend to be more dynamic than those who are trying just another case. Second, lawyers can develop and hone their trial skills until trying jury cases becomes almost second nature. A good analogy is that of the basketball player. The more the player practices and the more the acts of dribbling and shooting become second nature, the easier it is to race down the court and do an over-the-head slam dunk. The lawyer who practices until he or she becomes comfortable with being in the courtroom may then concentrate on developing a dynamic style and presentation.

§3.11   Individual Dimensions of Credibility

Jurors will also have individual dimensions for assessing credibility. Because jurors have different educational and social backgrounds, they have different

---

[18] Berlo, Lemert & Mertz, *Dimensions for Evaluating the acceptability of message sources*, 33 Pub Opinion Q 563, 574 (1969-70).

perceptions of reality,[19] and they can be expected to have different dimensions or constructs for assessing credibility.

How can lawyers discover these dimensions? As a rule, the individual dimensions will be consistent with the individual backgrounds of the jurors. People are attracted to people they perceive as similar to themselves.[20] so it can be predicted that they will attribute credibility to those they perceive as similar to themselves.

Credibility studies support this prediction. Minorities assessed politicians who espoused minority rights as more credible than those who did not.[21] Gays assessed gay therapists as more credible than heterosexual ones.[22] Drug counselors experienced with drugs were rated as more credible by addicts than counselors with no drug experience,[23] and speakers who presented messages listeners disagreed with were rated lower in credibility than those who presented messages listeners agreed with.[24]

Predictably, jurors will tend to assess credibility to those who are perceived as sharing similar philosophies, backgrounds, or goals. Thus, lawyers should use voir dire to find out as much as possible about the jurors' educations, socio-economic backgrounds, attitudes, and beliefs, and then highlight those aspects of the client's personal profile that are most similar to the jurors'. In the opening statement, for example, a lawyer might say to a jury: "The evidence will demonstrate that the plaintiff is just like most of you. He grew up in this area, is married, has a family, and has worked for a living all his life." In trying a case, a lawyer should select themes consistent with the backgrounds of jurors.

§3.12   Delivery and Style

The style and delivery of the lawyer will be a partial determinant of credibility. "Non arrogant" communication has been found to be more trustworthy and more believable than "arrogant" communication.[25] Stylistic dimensions such as listenability, human interest, and vocabulary diversity were determi-

---

[19] Delia, *Constructivism and the Study of Human Communication,* 63 Q J Speech 66, 70 (1977); F. Epting, Personal Construct Counseling and Psychotherapy 37-40 (1984).

[20] D. Byrne, The Attraction Paradigm (1971); Wetzler & Insko, *The Similarity Attraction Relationship,* 18 J Experimental Soc Psychology 245 (1982).

[21] R. Emry, Methodological Study: Public Figure Credibility (Dissertation, University of Kansas, 1976).

[22] Atkinson, Brady & Casas, *Sexual Preference Similarity, Attitude Similarity and Perceived Counselor Credibility and Attractiveness,* 28 J Counseling Psychology 504 (1981).

[23] Sinnet, Hagen & Harvey, *Credibility of Sources of Information About Drugs to Heroin Addicts,* 37 Psychological Rep 1239 (1975).

[24] Jurma, *Evaluations of Credibility of the Source of a Message,* 49 Psychological Rep 778 (1981).

[25] R. Lajoy, *The Effects of Arrogance and Expertise on the Communication of Physicians and Auto Repairment,* 36 Dissertation Abstracts 5264B (University of Connecticut 1976).

nants of expertness, trustworthiness, and dynamism.[26] Low lexical diversity has been found to reduce credibility assessments.[27] Listeners used lexical diversity to judge a speaker's intellectual and communicative abilities as well as emotional state of mind and social status. Listeners have expectations with respect to speaking situations. In formal situations, people expect high lexical diversity and when expectations are violated in the formal situation, perceivers assigned low credibility to the speaker. It can be predicted that jurors will expect lawyers to have high lexical diversity, and if they do not, jurors will assess low credibility.

Studies indicate that a speaking style characterized by frequent use of linguistic features such as hedges, hesitation forms, and questioning intonations will be perceived as "powerless," while a speaking style characterized by a lack of use of these features will be viewed as "powerful."[28] Thus, lawyers should avoid language that hesitates, questions, or hedges. For example, in the opening statement, lawyers should never say things such as "we hope to prove" or "we will try to prove," but rather, they should simply say, "we will prove," or "our evidence will demonstrate." In closing, the lawyers should never say, "I hope we have established our case to your satisfaction," but rather, they should say "we have established all elements of our case."

Studies have documented that speakers whose nonverbal communication was synchronized appropriately with their verbal communication were judged higher in credibility than speakers who were not synchronized.[29] Synchronicity of verbal with nonverbal communication was found to affect the dimensions of believability and dynamism. Thus, if a person has nonverbal twitches or idiosyncrasies that are not in synch with verbal delivery, he or she will be judged low in credibility. Lawyers should be aware of their own nonverbal style, and should counsel witnesses when it appears that their nonverbal behavior will detract from their verbal message.

A lack of eye contact by a speaker will result in low credibility assessments.[30] Lawyers and witnesses must make eye contact with the judge and jury when they speak. While it cannot be said that making eye contact will win the case, it can definitely be said that failure to make eye contact will lose the case.

---

[26] T. Carbone, *Stylistic Variables as Related to Source Credibility Perceptions, A Content Analysis Approach,* 34 Dissertation Abstracts 4457A (University of California at Los Angeles 1974).

[27] Bradac, Konsley & Davies, *Two Studies of the Effects of Linguistic Diversity Upon Judgments of Communicator Attributes and Message Effectiveness,* 43 Speech Monographs 70-79 (1976).

[28] Erickson, Lind, Johnson & Barr, *Speech Style and Impression Formation in a Court Setting: The Effects of "Powerful" and "Powerless" Speech,* 14 J Experimental Soc Psychology 266-79 (1976).

[29] S. Beebe, *Effects of Eye Contact, Posture and Vocal Inflection Upon Comprehension and Credibility,* Dissertation Abstracts, 5436A (University of Missouri 1977); Woodall & Burgoon, *The Effects of Nonverbal Synchronicity on Message Comprehension and Persuasiveness,* 5 Nonverbal Behavior 207-23 (1981).

[30] Hensley & Doob, *The Effect of Looking Behavior on Perceptions of a Communicator's Credibility,* 8 J Applied Soc Psychology 136-44 (1978).

§3.13   Common Sense Arguments

As noted in §2.17 as illustrated in §3.20, common sense arguments are some of the most credible arguments because they rely on shared knowledge. If an argument coincides with a common sense belief of the juror, he or she will obviously find it compelling, while if the argument conflicts with common sense beliefs, it will be given low credibility. This will be illustrated in §3.20.

§3.14   Jury Studies on Credibility

As noted previously, a civil jury trial may be conceptualized as an issue of credibility. As a rule, the jurors selected to hear the case are unfamiliar with the lawyers, litigants, facts, and law involved in the case. In the typical trial, the facts are in dispute, and many times there is no objective evidence to verify the claims of either side of the controversy. Each side of the lawsuit presents a conflicting view of the "reality" or "facts" of the case, and the jury must decide which is the "correct" reality. For example, in the standard inter-section automobile collision case, two drivers enter the intersection from different streets at a right angle and collide, and each driver claims to have had the green light. Often there are no independent witnesses to determine objectively who had the green light, and the only evidence is each party's word against the other. In deciding the case, the jurors must decide which version is more credible. Thus, an understanding of how jurors form credibility assessments is invaluable to the trial lawyer.

This research was designed to study the processes by which jurors determine credibility, and to ascertain whether these processes are consistent with communication research on credibility assessment. In the previous sections, I have reviewed the literature on source credibility in order to determine the correct theoretical conceptualizations of the formation of credibility assessments. In what follows, I will describe and report the results of a study in which actual jurors were contacted and interviewed with respect to the factors that accounted for their jury verdicts.[31] Finally, the study will be discussed with respect to its implications for understanding juror credibility assessments, and with respect to its implications for a general conceptualization of source credibility.

§3.15   —Method

Four jury cases were selected for study. In each case, the trial reached a final jury decision. All cases were civil negligence cases in which a plaintiff was suing a defendant alleging personal injury damages as a result of the defendant's negligence. In all cases, the plaintiff and defendant provided testimony, and in all cases, expert testimony was used. A list of the names of the jurors was obtained from the court file for each case, and each court file was reviewed

---

[31] See jury study, §§3.14-3.20.

by the researcher in order to provide an understanding of the issues of the cases and the claims of the parties.

Jurors were contacted individually by phone by the researcher. The researcher advised each juror that the researcher was conducting research on the jury system in order to better understand the factors affecting jury decisions. The jurors were then asked a series of questions about their jury experience.

§3.16 —Case One

Case One was a product liability case in which the plaintiff was suing the manufacturer of a hunting rifle. The plaintiff alleged that while hunting, he climbed a tree with the loaded rifle, and while climbing down, fell, causing the rifle to fire and shoot plaintiff in the arm. The plaintiff alleged that he had the safety catch for the gun in the "on" position and that the gun was defective in that it should have had a better or different safety device. Plaintiff admitted that he had been drinking alcohol before the incident. Plaintiff claimed serious personal injury to his right arm, and his wife claimed loss of consortium, alleging that they could no longer enjoy sexual relations. The evidence indicated that a child was born to plaintiff more than a year after the accident. The jury assessed greater than 50 per cent negligence (68 per cent) on the plaintiff, and therefore, the defendant prevailed and the plaintiff received no recovery.

An interesting development in this case was that the plaintiff's attorney in voir dire identified all jurors with hunting experience and then left these jurors on the jury panel. The implication is that the plaintiff's attorney apparently felt that hunters would be favorable jurors for the plaintiff hunter. However, the hunters were overwhelmingly against the plaintiff. The responses of the hunters fell into three categories. First, several hunters indicated that they felt plaintiff was negligent because his actions violated the jurors' personal experiences and beliefs about guns and proper gun handling. Several of the hunters said they had hunting or military experience and that they didn't feel that it was right to mix alcohol and guns and that they "knew you didn't climb up and down from a tree with a loaded gun." Several jurors felt that based on their experience with guns, the accident could not have happened as the plaintiff said it did. Several jurors also commented that "you don't climb a tree with a loaded gun when it is wet." Secondly, many of the hunters felt that the plaintiff violated what "we all know" about gun safety. Several jurors went beyond their personal experience to what they thought all hunters knew to be true as common sense. One juror stated that one of the "Ten Commandments of Hunting" was that "you don't climb out of a tree with a loaded gun." One juror said that he taught gun safety and that the plaintiff violated safety standards that "all good hunters knew." Finally, many of the hunters expressed the belief that the plaintiff had been in the military, had had a lot of gun training, and that he knew better than to do what he did. Thus, the hunters felt that the plaintiff went against what he himself knew to be good gun safety. Several jurors even noted that it was foolish for the plaintiff to leave hunters on the jury, since the plaintiff had violated good gun safety practice. Several jurors expressed, "I can't believe he left me on the jury panel."

Several jurors were skeptical of the plaintiff's reason for not unloading his gun when descending. Plaintiff testified that he didn't unload the gun because that might have scared the deer away. Several jurors remarked that, based on their personal experiences, the noise made descending from the tree would have scared the deer away anyway, and therefore, they found his story unbelievable.

Based on the plaintiff's failure to exercise common sense, many jurors described him as careless and haphazard. Several jurors volunteered that drinking and hunting hurt the plaintiff's credibility. A couple of jurors indicated that if the plaintiff had not been drinking, they would have voted in his favor.

With respect to damages, most jurors thought that the plaintiffs were asking for too much money, and they seemed offended by the wife's claim for loss of consortium. Plaintiff and his wife claimed that the injury to his arm prevented them from enjoying sexual relations. Several jurors remarked that the wife became pregnant during this time, so obviously they could have sexual relations. Several jurors remarked that they were offended by this and thought that it shouldn't have been injected into the trial.

The consensus was that considering the plaintiff's drinking and bad judgment, he was asking for way too much money—$750,000. Several jurors noted that the evidence indicated that the plaintiff's arm was still broken and needed to be reset, but that the plaintiff had not done this. They commented that "obviously the plaintiff would be in pain if his arm was broken" and they noted "how can I give him money for pain and suffering if he wouldn't do what he needed to do to stop the pain?" Plaintiff also claimed that he was unable to work since the injury. Several jurors commented that they knew people with only one arm who could work, and, therefore, based on their experience, didn't believe plaintiff about his damages.

With respect to the drinking, plaintiff was unable to say with certainty how many drinks he had had prior to the injury. Several jurors responded to this by noting that if he can't or won't tell how much he had to drink, then he must have been drunk. There seemed to be an expectation that he should have known and been able to tell the facts.

Each side of the case called expert witnesses. Plaintiff's experts were more along the line of gun collectors, while the defendant's experts were gun manufacturers. The jurors felt that since the defendant's experts had actual experience with manufacturing, they were more knowledgeable and more effective as witnesses. Several jurors commented that the plaintiff's experts speculated, whereas the defendant's experts talked about actual gun specifications. Several jurors commented that the plaintiff's experts didn't seem to be aware of all conditions existing at the time of the injury. Several jurors commented that they knew as much about guns as did the plaintiff's experts. Several jurors noted that plaintiff's expert testimony violated what they knew about guns.

With respect to the lawyers, the jury perceived the defense lawyer as more formal, even-tempered, and calm. Several jurors said that they couldn't say why, but that the defense lawyer appeared more formal and they liked that.

Several jurors thought the plaintiff's lawyer was too forward. Several said they felt that he badgered them on voir dire by repeating the same questions. These same jurors said that the plaintiff's lawyer kept pounding the same points over and over again and seemed to go too far. The defense lawyer, by comparison, "made his points and sat down." Several said that the defense lawyer seemed more professional. The defense lawyer was characterized as more technical, more in touch with reality and the facts, and more knowledgeable, whereas the plaintiff's lawyer was described as more folksy, more subjective, and at times hotheaded. Two jurors commented that the plaintiff's lawyer got mad a couple of times and didn't say what he meant. Several jurors stated that the plaintiff's lawyer continually went too far and offended people.

§3.17 —Case Two

Case Two involved a rear-end automobile collision in which the plaintiff claimed that the defendant's negligence caused the accident by rearending plaintiff's vehicle. As a result of the defendant's negligence, plaintiff sought $30,000 in damages for a soft tissue neck and back injury, claiming $2,548.70 for medical bills, and the rest for pain and suffering. During the trial, several inconsistencies in the plaintiff's testimony were brought out by the defense. After the accident, at the scene, when asked by the police officer if he was injured, the plaintiff stated, "No." Plaintiff did not seek medical attention the night of the accident. Plaintiff was in the hospital for 11 days shortly after the accident, and at the trial, the plaintiff claimed to have been in great pain during his hospital stay. However, the hospital records and nurses' notes did not reflect any complaints by the plaintiff of pain during his stay. Further, the records disclosed that the plaintiff had taken several 24-hour hospital leave passes during his hospital stay. Plaintiff's wife testified that she visited plaintiff in the hospital on several days and verified that he was suffering. However, the records disclosed that the plaintiff had taken his leave passes from the hospital on the days his wife claimed to have visited him. Plaintiff's doctor testified that he saw plaintiff in the hospital every day for 11 days. The records again disclosed plaintiff was not in the hospital on several of those 11 days because of his 24-hour passes. The plaintiff's attorney made no attempt in the opening statement or direct examination to address any of these inconsistencies, and they were all brought out by the defendant on cross-examination or during the defendant's portion of the case. The jury assessed 30 per cent of the negligence on plaintiff, 70 per cent on defendant, and awarded the plaintiff $5,000. The plaintiff, therefore, recovered $3,500.

The jurors were almost unanimous in their observations. Overall, the jurors felt that the plaintiff and his lawyer did a sloppy job on their case. They perceived the plaintiff's lawyer as shoddy and sloppy and observed that he had not done his homework. They felt that he wasn't aware of what was in the court records or hospital records. The defense lawyer, on the other hand, was perceived as sharp, professional, aggressive, and to the point. They felt that the defense lawyer was thorough and had done his homework. They were impressed with his attention to detail and his use of the nurses' notes to refute the plaintiff's claims of pain and suffering.

With respect to the plaintiff, there were several common observations about his behavior. On the level of facts presented, the testimony of the plaintiff and his witnesses was inconsistent, and therefore, not believable. Plaintiff was claiming a serious injury, but told the police officer he wasn't hurt and went on to play cards with friends after the accident rather than seeking medical treatment or going home. Plaintiff claimed that he was hurt so badly that he had to be hospitalized for 11 days and was in great pain during that time. However, the nurses' notes showed no complaints of pain, and plaintiff took several 24-hour "passes out" during his hospital stay. Plaintiff's wife claimed to have visited him in the hospital on the days he was not there. All jurors felt that the plaintiff's evidence was inconsistent, contradictory, and confusing, and hence, not believable. All jurors felt that the plaintiff and his wife should have done their homework better so as to avoid needless discrepancies in their testimony. Further, plaintiff had been injured previously, but did not tell the jury about this. The plaintiff and his attorney allowed the defense to bring this out on cross-examination.

On another level, plaintiff failed in his role as an injured plaintiff. All jurors felt that the plaintiff simply did not act as a person would act if he were seriously injured. He didn't tell the police he was hurt, went on to play cards, didn't seek medical attention, left the hospital, and made no complaints of pain to the nurses. The jurors expressed that, "if he was really hurt" or "when people are really hurt," they would behave in certain expected ways. Thus, the jurors had expectations about how injured people should behave, and the plaintiff, by his conduct, violated these expectations.

Along the same line, the plaintiff's case seemed to violate the jurors' personal experience and what "we all know" about the injured people. The jurors continually commented that they personally knew injured people and this plaintiff did not appear to behave like the injured people they knew. Several jurors commented that the plaintiff did not look injured when he moved around in the courthouse. Several jurors said that they had been around people with back injuries, and that this man did not behave like the people they knew. Several jurors commented, "We all know that if he was really injured, he would have gone to the emergency room."

As a tactical matter, the jurors were amazed that the plaintiff's lawyer did not bring out some of these discrepancies in the opening statement and deal with them directly. For example, two jurors commented that it is not uncommon for people to be in shock and not feel pain immediately after an accident, and that this could have been explained away by plaintiff's attorney. He could have said that the man felt pain but hoped it would go away. But neither the plaintiff nor his lawyer mentioned these facts. When all of these discrepancies were brought out by the defendant, it made the plaintiff appear to be a liar. Several jurors indicated that if the plaintiff's lawyer had forewarned, acknowledged, and explained the discrepancies first, the jury probably would have accepted them. They felt that the plaintiff should have admitted the weaknesses in his case.

The plaintiff's expert witness was viewed unfavorably because he testified that he saw the plaintiff in the hospital on days the plaintiff was not there. The jury did not know what to make of this discrepancy and reacted by discounting what the doctor had to say. They perceived the doctor as the type who, "if any patient said they were hurt, would give them time of from work." Finally, the doctor read verbatim from his records and reports, which led jurors to believe that he had no actual or independent knowledge of the case.

Based on the inconsistencies in the plaintiff's case, the jury felt that $30,000 was an excessive demand, and many were "turned off" by this figure.

With respect to the lawyers, the jurors were favorably impressed by the defendant's lawyer. They were impressed by his use of the records and depositions to refute the plaintiff's claims. They thought he was aggressive and to the point. They all felt he had "done his homework." They saw the plaintiff's lawyer as either stupid and unaware of the facts, aware of the facts and incompetent, or dishonest in presenting them the way he did. They felt that he didn't prove what he promised in opening statement.

Several jurors expressed the feeling that they felt "ripped off" by the plaintiff in that he was dishonest and wasted their time as jurors. They commented that if the plaintiff and his lawyer had done their homework, they would have received more money.

§3.18 —Case Three

Case Three was a medical malpractice case. The plaintiff contracted Crohn's disease either before or during her pregnancy and, as a result, required a premature cesarean delivery in which her baby died. She was found after the operation to have a perforated bowel which required a resection. The plaintiff brought a negligence action on behalf of herself and a wrongful death action for the deceased child. The plaintiff alleged that her doctor was negligent in failing to properly diagnose and treat the disease and in not referring the plaintiff to other physicians. Plaintiff asked for $1,000,000. The jury found the defendant doctor to be negligent, but found that the negligence did not contribute to plaintiff's injuries and damages. The defendant had contended that the disease plaintiff contracted was something that was genetically determined and that she had the disease before pregnancy, and therefore, there would have been nothing he could have done to prevent the damages.

Most of the jurors were swayed by the conduct of the plaintiff. The plaintiff testified that she was sick and that the doctor should have diagnosed her illness. However, there was evidence presented that the plaintiff failed to go to some of her doctor appointments while she was pregnant and feeling very sick. She skipped a couple of doctor appointments at this time because, according to her testimony, she was ill and because she could not get a ride to the doctor's office. All of the jurors had problems with this testimony or behavior. Several of the women stated that they had been pregnant, and if they were feeling as if something were wrong, they would find a ride to the doctor's office, no matter what. Thus, the plaintiff seemed to violate the common sense experience of the mothers on the jury. The men also felt that this behavior violated "what we all know." They expressed, "We all know that when you are pregnant, you have to take care of yourself and go to the doctor and report illnesses and complications." Thus, the plaintiff's conduct violated common sense experience and knowledge, and as a result, she was judged adversely. Several jurors said, "If I was as sick as she claimed to be, I would have handled myself differently."

The plaintiff also failed to follow the doctor's advice. When in the hospital, the plaintiff was told not to flush her toilet so that stool samples could be examined. However, the nurses' notes and plaintiff's testimony disclosed that the plaintiff always flushed her stool, thus preventing the doctor from diagnosing her problem. Thus, plaintiff was perceived to have failed in her role as patient. Patients are expected to follow doctors' orders and to cooperate. The plaintiff violated this expectation, and the jury viewed her as an incompetent patient, expectant mother, and plaintiff. Several jurors commented that "we all know you are supposed to follow the doctor's orders," in explaining why they had problems believing the plaintiff's claims.

The jurors noted that while the plaintiff testified on the witness stand about how she was obviously sick while in the hospital prior to the birth, the hospital records did not reflect any complaints of pain or suffering. They found this inconsistency to be determinative of the issue of credibility.

With respect to the plaintiff's demeanor in the courtroom, many jurors noted that the plaintiff came across as angry, vengeful, and unstable. She cried at inappropriate times. Plaintiff's husband also was perceived as vengeful. Several jurors felt that the plaintiff was mad and hurt and that she wanted to hurt the doctor. The jurors perceived the plaintiff to be out for revenge rather than fair compensation. Many jurors felt that the plaintiff and her family members went too far in their emotional displays. Several jurors noted that there appeared to be an inconsistency in that the family wasn't around at the time of the disease but was in court at the trial acting "like this was the end of the world." Plaintiff's emotional displays and demeanor led several jurors to speculate that she was unstable psychologically and that this emotional state may have been why she got into trouble with her pregnancy.

The plaintiff's expert witness was a physician from San Francisco who spent most of his time testifying for plaintiffs in malpractice cases. The jury seemed to disregard his testimony, since he was not a local physician and because he appeared to be a paid professional or hired gun. Several jurors said he seemed self-righteous. Others said he looked real calm and collected on direct examination but tense on cross-examination. Several jurors stated that he seemed to be slapping the defendant doctor's wrist, and the jury didn't like this. The defense doctors were given higher credibility since they were local and were "just doctors."

With respect to the defendant's lawyer, the jury perceived him as prepared, professional, and even-tempered. He appeared to have the same demeanor when examining plaintiff or defense witnesses. Several jurors stated that he just kept plugging along. The plaintiff's lawyer was described by several jurors as a "little mean," sarcastic, and vengeful. They stated that he was pleasant and polite to plaintiff's witnesses, but sarcastic and mean to defense witnesses. It was noted by several witnesses that he smirked whenever he made a point, while the defendant's lawyer seemed more "professional." The jury also noted that the plaintiff's lawyer appeared to be tricky and to try to ask tricky questions, whereas the defendant's lawyer was straightforward. They noted that the defendant's lawyer always went right to the point and didn't hesitate to jump in immediately to clear up discrepancies.

§3.19   —Case Four

Case Four was a medical malpractice case. Plaintiff had cerebral palsy and went in for surgery to try to correct a problem with her leg. In surgery, the plaintiff's doctor allowed other doctors to conduct the operation, which was improperly done. Plaintiff sued the defendant, alleging improper procedure, failure to inform, and failure to supervise residents. As a result of the defendant's negligence, plaintiff alleged permanent nerve damage to her leg. Plaintiff received a verdict of $1,250,000. The facts in the case seemed pretty clear-cut, and the defendant doctor apparently admitted plaintiff's claims to an extent.

The juror comments in this case focused on the lawyers and the defendant doctor. All the jurors felt that the plaintiff's lawyer was well prepared. He used hospital records and depositions to point out discrepancies and inconsistencies. The jurors commented that he had done his homework. He was described as energetic and positive. The jurors were particularly impressed with the plaintiff's lawyer's cross-examination of witnesses. He always had records or depositions at hand to make his points and demonstrate inconsistencies. The defense lawyer was perceived as not being thorough or well prepared.

With respect to the defendant doctor, many jurors noted that he seemed "tentative," "puzzled," "not definite," and "not confident." This gave the jury the impression that he did not know what he was talking about or did not believe or mean what he was saying. Several jurors said that at times the doctor could not remember the names of the other doctors in the operating room, and this made him appear to be unprepared. In contrast, the plaintiff's expert was described as more knowledgeable and "fresher." He appeared prepared and had no discrepancies in his testimony. He was described as confident and certain.

The jurors were less talkative in this case, which led to the assumption that the facts were more clear-cut, and the main issue was simply a matter of how much money to award in damages. In this case, the plaintiff was described as making a sympathetic and emotional appeal, but the jurors said this did not bother them. She was described as sympathetic.

§3.20   —Results of Juror Study

This study appears to support the literature with respect to credibility assessments. The jurors appeared to make general assessments of credibility based on expertness, trustworthiness, and dynamism, and they appeared to apply these general dimensions in idiosyncratic ways to form their individual assessments of credibility based on their personal construct systems.

On a general level, the jurors all expressed perceptions that clearly fit within the dimensions of expertness and trustworthiness. The lawyers, litigants, and witnesses who did their homework, were prepared, appeared confident, and were sources of valid information were perceived as credible, while those who were unprepared, tentative, and were sources of incorrect or inconsistent information were perceived as low in credibility. Lawyers, litigants, and witnesses who appeared as fair, even-tempered, and sources of reliable information were perceived as trustworthy, while those who appeared driven by motives other than fairness, who appeared as mean or uneven-tempered, and who were unreliable sources of information were perceived as low in credibility.

Two important gauges for judging credibility based on the general dimensions emerged from the study. The first is consistency. Inconsistent behavior on the part of lawyers, witnesses, and litigants resulted in low assessments of expertness and trustworthiness., while consistent behavior promoted high assessments of expertness and trustworthiness. When the testimony of the wife and doctor were inconsistent with the testimony of the car wreck victim, the jury rendered low trustworthiness assessments across the board. The jury determined that the plaintiff and his wife were fabricating their claims, and that the doctor was the type who would excuse anyone who claimed to be in pain from work. Jurors were distrustful of family members who were absent at the hospital through all of the plaintiff mother's medical problems, but who were at the trial acting as if it were "the end of the world." The jury was offended when the hunter and his wife claimed that they could no longer enjoy sex due to the injury, yet the wife had become pregnant after the injury. The jurors were distrustful of lawyers and witnesses who behaved one way on direct examination and a different way on cross-examination. When inconsistencies arose, the jurors assumed either that the parties were lying, and, therefore, were untrustworthy, or had failed to do their homework, and therefore, were incompetent.

It is also obvious from the study that if it becomes clear that inconsistencies in the plaintiff's case are going to arise during the trial, it is absolutely essential that the plaintiff's lawyer acknowledge and explain the inconsistencies before the defense lawyer has the opportunity to expose them as "lies" or "incompetence." The plaintiff's acknowledgement of inconsistencies may be seen as a sign of trust and competence, but a failure to acknowledge inconsistencies will certainly result in perceptions of untrustworthiness or incompetence.

The second gauge for judging credibility assessments using the general dimensions is role expectation. It is clear that the jurors had role expectations of lawyers, witnesses, and litigants, and a violation of the role expectations resulted in low assessments of trustworthiness and expertness. The jurors expected plaintiffs to be able to tell their story clearly. When the hunter could not state clearly how many beers he had consumed prior to the gun accident, they assumed he was lying and was really drunk. Since the plaintiffs were bringing claims of negligence against other parties, there appeared to be an expectation that the plaintiffs behave in an appropriate nonnegligent manner. A hunter was expected to follow good hunting practices, and a sick pregnant woman was expected to keep her doctor appointments and follow the doctor's directions. Plaintiffs making injury claims were expected to act like injured people. The car wreck victim was expected to seek medical care, stay in the hospital, and report pain and suffering. The defendant doctor was expected to appear confident and definite in explaining his actions in the operating room. When he appeared tentative, he was viewed as incompetent. It can be predicted that jurors will have role expectations of all of the parties to the lawsuit, and violations of these role expectations will result in low credibility assessments.

This study sheds some additional light on the extent to which credibility assessments are based on personal experiences and common sense experiences. The jurors applied the general dimensions of expertness and trustworthiness in two idiosyncratic ways, based on their own personal experiences, or based on common sense experiences. In deciding whether litigants, witnesses, or lawyers were trustworthy, jurors compared their behavior with their own personal experiences. In judging the hunter's claim that he could not work at all because of his damaged arm, jurors used their own experiences with people who had completely lost arms and continued to work in order to determine that his claim was not believable. In judging the pregnant woman's claims, the women drew on their own experiences with pregnancy to determine whether the claims were credible. Thus, it can be predicted that jurors will judge claims based on their own experiences and will have a tendency to be distrustful of claims that are not consistent with personal experiences.

Even more powerful than personal experiences are common experiences or common sense beliefs. Jurors move from personal experiences to common experiences, common sense beliefs, or what the jurors believe that all people know to be true as gauges for credibility assessments. Claims that are consistent with common sense beliefs and common experiences will be judged high in credibility, while claims that are inconsistent with common sense beliefs and common experiences will be judged low in credibility. Several jurors reported that they disbelieved claims because they were contrary to what "we all know." The hunter was judged low in credibility because he violated what all hunters knew to be the proper way to hunt and handle a gun. In judging the car wreck victim's claims of pain and injury, the jurors reported that "we all know" that if you really believe you are injured or if you are really in pain, you will go to a hospital immediately, and since the plaintiff did not, his claims were disbelieved. The jurors "all knew" that if the pregnant woman really thought she had a problem, she would have gone to the doctor and would not have skipped her doctor appointments. Thus, jurors can be expected to determine the general dimensions of credibility based on how the claims correspond with their personal experiences or their perceptions of common experiences or common sense beliefs.

4 Profiling Jurors for Systematic Jury Selection

§4.01 Introduction

There are two basic aspects of systematic jury selection. One part is the questioning process which, as demonstrated in Chapter 5, consists of (1) gathering basic information about jurors and their attitudes, (2) setting the tone for the trial, (3) introducing concepts and evidence and conditioning the jurors for things to follow in the trial, (4) obtaining public commitments from jurors favorable to the case, (5) using language that creates connotations for clients, witnesses, and other relevant facts of the case, (6) rehearsing the arguments that will be used in the trial, (7) refuting opposition arguments, (8) enhancing credibility, and (9) creating jury purpose.

The second part is profiling desirable and undesirable jurors. In order to have a comprehensive jury selection, lawyers must profile jurors, because the questioning process is meaningless if lawyers do not have some idea of the types of jurors and the types of juror information they are looking for.

Profiling desirable and undesirable jurors is more frequently becoming a task performed by experts with backgrounds in communication or psychology. Experts spend great amounts of time studying the psychological literature and conducting experiments in order to determine how certain types of jurors can be expected to vote in certain cases. Their predictions are very accurate and valuable. However, in many jury cases, this type of investment in an expert is not merited, or the lawyer and the client simply don't have the money to allocate for this expense. In those cases in which the lawyer can afford to hire a consultant, the lawyer, who has a much better understanding of the case and the jury process, must still be able to guide and evaluate the consultant's suggestions. Therefore, the trial attorney must have some strategy for profiling jurors.

At first glance, the process of profiling jurors seems overwhelming. Experts use a range of methods such as examining racial, ethnic, and socioeconomic backgrounds, identifying personality types, examining the color of juror clothing, and studying nonverbal responses. All of these have merit, and the best method is one that incorporates all theories. The following are simple strategies that can be used for profiling jurors.

§4.02   Identifying the Issues upon which Profiling Jurors will be Based

In order to decide what jurors will be good or bad jurors, the trial lawyer must first determine what socioeconomic and psychological issues are involved in the case. Once the issues involved in the case are fully identified and understood, it is then possible to gather information, and based on that information, to predict the stance jurors will take toward those issues.

For example, in a product liability case, the following are a few of the possible social and psychological issues:

1. The right of consumers to be protected against dangerous products
2. The right of consumers to be fully instructed on the use of products
3. The right of consumers to be fully warned of any dangers inherent in the use of products
4. The effect of product liability cases on the ability of a business to function
5. The extent to which manufacturers and business owners must insure the safety of consumers

In a medical malpractice action, the following are a few of the possible social and psychological issues:

1. The right of patients to be protected against improper and negligent medical procedures
2. The right of patients to be fully advised and informed by doctors
3. The effect of medical malpractice claims on the ability of hospitals and doctors to function
4. Whether doctors and hospitals should be given special legal rights
5. Whether doctors and hospitals should be subjected to legal claims
6. Whether lawyers and jurors are capable of judging doctors
7. Whether doctors and hospitals should always place the welfare of patients above other considerations, such as operating costs
8. Whether hospitals should be held accountable for the mistakes of their employees

In any case involving personal injuries, pain and suffering, and economic loss, the following are a few of the issues that may arise:

1. The nature and extent of injury
2. Whether people should be compensated for pain and suffering
3. The impact of an injury to one family member on other family members
4. The economic impact of an injury on the family unit
5. Even though the law provides that the negligent party must respond in damages, whether the negligent party should pay all of these damages if they are astronomical
6. Whether mental and physical pain and suffering exist and can be measured
7. Which party should bear the responsibility for injuries caused by negligence

Other general issues applicable to all personal injury cases are:

1. Whether people should be allowed to file lawsuits for personal injury damages
2. Whether people should be allowed to challenge the existing system through lawsuits
3. Whether injuries are competent to judge business operations, doctors, hospitals, etc.

Once these issues are identified, the lawyer, prior to trial, may begin to develop profiles of jurors that can be expected to be good and bad plaintiff's jurors. Once these profiles are developed, voir dire may be use to gather information to identify which jurors fit in the desired profiles. Juror information may be further used to determine how jurors will vote on the various issues involved.

§4.03 Developing Juror Profiles Prior to Trial

Once you have identified the various issues that may arise in the trial, you may being profiling jurors. Profiles can be developed using four basic principles: 1) people tend to be attracted to people they view as being similar to themselves; 2) jurors' attitudes, beliefs, and opinions will be a product of their backgrounds and upbringing; 3) jurors will decide cases based on what is salient or important in their lives; and 4) certain personality types will tend to vote in predictable ways. In the following sections, use of these principles to profile jurors will be examined and illustrated.

§4.04 Profiling Jurors on the Basis of the Similarity Factor

Psychological studies have demonstrated that people tend to be attracted to others perceived as being similar to themselves.[1] Thus, jurors can be expected to be attracted to and favor those litigants they perceive as being similar to themselves. Based upon this assumption, it can be predicted that good plaintiff's jurors would be jurors who perceive themselves to be similar to the plaintiff and dissimilar to the defendant. Using this theory, the trial lawyer begins by becoming familiar with the background of the parties to the lawsuit. On voir dire, demographic information is gathered in order to determine how the jurors are similar or dissimilar to the parties.

The following is a list of questions that should be asked of all jurors in order to determine similarity:

1. Marital status
2. Family status (children)
3. Education
4. Occupation
5. Employment history
6. Residence history
7. Activities and organizations
8. Prior jury experience
9. Prior involvement in personal injury litigation

This list is not exhaustive, and questions would need to be added to account for specific aspects of each case.

---

[1] D. Byrne, The Attraction Paradigm (1971); Wetzler & Insko, *The Similarity Attraction Relationship,* 18 Experimental Soc Psychology 245 (1982).

In gathering this information, the lawyer should also inquire about close family members. It could be assumed that jurors' attitudes would, in part, be a product of the attitudes of their close relatives, and, therefore, this information should be gathered with respect to close family relatives as well as the jurors themselves.

After this information is elicited, it can be predicted that those jurors whose background, upbringing, and attitudes are similar to those of the plaintiff will be favorable jurors for the plaintiff, and that those jurors who are similar to the defendant will be unfavorable jurors for the plaintiff.

§4.05   Profiling Jurors on the Basis of Juror Background

Psychological studies generally indicate that human attitudes are, to an extent, a product of background and upbringing.[2] More specifically, in studies this author has conducted in which jurors were interviewed, it became apparent that jurors' attitudes and opinions about the issues in the trial were based on their own personal experiences. For example, in deciding whether litigants, witnesses, or lawyers were trustworthy and whether claims were valid, jurors compared the litigants' behavior with their own personal experiences. As demonstrated in the juror studies in §§3.14-3.20, when judging a plaintiff's claim that he could not work at all because of his damaged arm, jurors used their own experiences with people with damaged arms who continued to work, and determined that the plaintiff's claim was not believable. In judging a pregnant woman's claims, women jurors drew on their own experiences with pregnancy to determine whether the claims were believable. Thus, it can be predicted that jurors will judge claims based on their own background and experiences and will have a tendency to be distrustful of claims that are not consistent with personal experiences.

Juror background information has a twofold use for profiling jurors. First, once the issues in the trial are identified prior to trial, general predictions may then be made that certain people with certain backgrounds will have certain types of attitudes about the issues, and these predictions may be used as the basis for juror profiles. Secondly, during voir dire, lawyers must discover juror background information in order to determine which jurors fall within the designated profiles, and further to determine whether additional new profiles are identified.

§4.06   —Use of Background Information to Develop Profiles Prior to Trial

Prior to trial, lawyers may predict that people with certain general backgrounds will be favorable or unfavorable jurors. For example, in a product liability case, a possible issue identified above is consumer rights versus business

---

[2] Delia, *Constructivism and the Study of Human Communication,* 63 QJ Speech 66, 70 (1977).

profitability. It is easy to predict that factory workers will be good plaintiff's jurors because they will be concerned with product safety because their health, and, hence, their ability to earn a living, will depend upon it. Housewife spouses of factory workers will also make good plaintiff's jurors because they will be concerned with their husband's safety, that will in turn be dependent upon product safety. Conversely, a business owner or executive will be concerned with the ability of a business to function profitably, and will see product injuries as simply the cost of doing business, and will make a bad plaintiff's juror and a good defendant's juror. While these predictions may seem obvious, more subtle predictions can be made, such as the fact that a single woman with children might make a good plaintiff's juror in a medical malpractice case, because she is used to living on a limited budget, is used to examining and comparing services and goods based on quality and costs, and is used to resolving family disputes. This type of person can be expected to be willing and able to examine the standard of care provided by a physician. On the other hand, a housewife whose husband makes all of her decisions for her may not feel capable of judging a doctor's actions, and might make a bad plaintiff's juror in a medical malpractice action.

Once all possibilities have been exhausted for the types of jurors sought in terms of background, some fairly specific juror profiles should have been developed.

§4.07 —Use of Voir Dire Background Information

In voir dire, background information on the jurors must be discovered so that a determination may be made as to whether jurors fall within the favorable or unfavorable profiles.

In voir dire, lawyers must also be open-minded and quick on their feet in order to identify other profiles that may develop based on the background information that arises. For example, when questioning jurors about product safety, if a farmer is encountered who begins to suggest that product malfunctions and injuries are just a way of life and are not something that one should be compensated for, the lawyer should recognize this as a new profile category. In this case, it can be predicted that this farmer may be a bad plaintiff's juror because farmers as a rule view product malfunctions and injuries as a way of life, and do not feel that people should always be compensated for injuries caused by defective products.

As a further example, in the case of an employee suing his or her employer, jurors should be thoroughly questioned about their experiences with labor unions, management and labor disputes, and negotiations. Not only will jurors have been on one side or the other, they will have positive or negative feelings about their experiences. Their personal experiences about their positions will determine whether they are desirable or undesirable jurors. Jurors who have never been involved personally in unions or management activities should be asked about their close relatives, and could be asked which side they would take if they had a chance.

In determining the value of a personal experience or common sense belief, it is not so much that jurors have had similar experiences, but rather, that their personal experiences support the claims you are making. For example, in the case involving the injured hunter, recall that, several hunters on the jury panel voted against the plaintiff hunter's claim against a gun manufacturer for a defective gun because, in the jurors' view, the plaintiff had violated several of the "commandments" for safe hunting. They were undesirable jurors because the plaintiff's claims were inconsistent with their personal experiences.

§4.08   —Juror Background—Pain and Suffering

Personal experience can be critical in the area of compensation for injuries and pain and suffering. People who have been around loved ones who have suffered from disabling and painful injuries or illnesses will be a lot more sympathetic to plaintiffs than people who have not had that experience. People who function in occupations that are involved with numbers and computers can be expected to be less sympathetic to plaintiffs than jurors who work around people. For example, accountants tend to return low verdicts for pain and suffering. Doctors and nurses tend to be bad plaintiff's jurors because they see pain and suffering as a way of life and are less likely to feel that someone should be compensated for pain and suffering.

Even more powerful than personal experiences are common sense beliefs. Jurors generalize personal experiences into common sense beliefs, which are what the jurors perceive all people know to be true, as gauges for credibility assessments. In other words, it is one thing for jurors to believe that something is true based on their personal experience, and it is another thing if the jurors feel that all other people share this belief. These common sense beliefs will shape jurors' perceptions of whether something is believable. Claims that are consistent with common sense beliefs and common experiences will be judged high in credibility, while claims that are inconsistent with common sense beliefs and common experiences will be judged low in credibility. Several jurors reported that they disbelieved claims because they were contrary to what "we all know." As noted in §§3.14-3.20, in judging a car wreck victim's claims of pain and injury, the jurors reported that "we all know" that if you really believe you are injured or if you are really in pain, you will go to a hospital immediately, and since the plaintiff did not, his claims were disbelieved. The jurors "all knew" that if the pregnant woman really thought she had a problem, she would have gone to the doctor and would not have skipped her doctor appointments. Thus, jurors can be expected to determine believability based on how the claims of the parties correspond with their personal experiences or their perceptions of common experiences or common sense beliefs.

Thus, prior to voir dire, lawyers should prepare profiles based on what types of juror experiences would create common sense beliefs that would then cause jurors to be good or bad jurors. Then, during voir dire, when questioning jurors, questions should be asked that discover those personal and common sense experiences the jurors hold that are relevant to the case. Then those jurors should be selected whose personal experiences and common sense beliefs are consistent with the types of claims being made. Further, since the pretrial profiles may not have been exhaustive, in gathering information, lawyers should be determining whether additional profiles are identified that will be good or bad for the issues in the case.

§4.09 Profiling Jurors Based on What is Important or Salient in Their Lives

It can be predicted that jurors will decide cases based on what is salient or important in their lives; that is, all jurors will have things going on currently in their lives that will cause them to have certain attitudes about the issues in the case or will cause them to take a certain psychological stance toward the case. For example, a manufacturer of consumer products is concerned with the costs and profits, and, therefore, would view a product liability claim as a threat to survival. A person who has children and is supporting a household will view the ability to earn a living as a survival issue, whereas a college student being supported by his or her parents may not view earning a living as such an important issue. Thus, in using this principle, the lawyer must first isolate the psychological and social issues involved in the case and then must gather information about jurors that will help determine each juror's stance toward those issues. In any injury claim, there is the issue of the continued ability of the plaintiff to earn a living. In product liability cases, there are the issues of consumer protection versus the ability of a business to function. Accountants, bankers, businessmen, and persons who are support personnel for business tend to make good defense jurors, while laborers, housewives, students, and teachers tend to make good plaintiff's jurors. Teachers tend to be good jurors for plaintiffs in product liability claims because they are aware of the need for proper supervision, education, and protection for certain elements of society.

The difference between profiling jurors based on background and profiling jurors based on what is important in their lives is that in dealing with background, the trial lawyer should attempt to look at the jurors' lifelong backgrounds and their family backgrounds in order to determine their general philosophical leanings. In profiling jurors based on what is important in their lives, lawyers are looking at what is of immediate importance in their lives at the time of the trial.

§4.10 Profiling Jurors on the Basis of Personality Types

It can be predicted that jurors with certain personality types will tend to vote in predictable ways on the issues of the trial. Psychologists and sociologists have always known that certain personality types behave in predictable ways, and this knowledge has formed the basis for psychotherapy. This knowledge may also form the basis for predicting how jurors will vote on the issues of a trial. The problem is that there are many personality types, and the lawyer does not possess the knowledge necessary to identify them and does not have the time to acquire the knowledge. While experts are available with this knowledge, they are expensive, and lawyers cannot always afford them.

However, lawyers need not ignore this basis for profiling jurors. There is one clearly identifiable basic personality type that can be consistently expected to take a uniform approach to the underlying issues of almost any lawsuit. By understanding this one personality type, the trial lawyer can gain great insight into how jurors can be expected to decide issues in civil trials.

§4.11 The Authoritarian Personality

During the course of the trial, each side uses various persuasive techniques in order to get the jury to form the desired impression. In deciding how to present information and which persuasive techniques to use, it is crucial that the lawyers know as much as possible about how jurors process information. One approach to understanding how jurors process information is the authoritarian personality structure. It is generally agreed that each person's personality structure can be located somewhere on a continuum between authoritarianism and antiauthoritarianism. It is further agreed that this personality structure variable can account for some aspects of information processing behavior and that authoritarians process information differently than nonauthoritarians. Thus, understanding this personality structure can be extremely helpful to lawyers engaged in the jury process because, among other things, the authoritarian juror will process information and hold attitudes different from those held by antiauthoritarian jurors.

In what follows, the authoritarian personality will be described, and it will be explained why identifying this personality is important for profiling jurors. For those who wish to fully understand the nature of the authoritarian personality, a complete analysis is contained in the following section.[3]

§4.12 —Background of the Authoritarian Personality

One of the first to describe the authoritarian personality was Fromm.[4] Fromm noted that the feature common to all authoritarian thinking is the conviction that life is determined by forces outside of the person's own self, interests, and wishes. Fromm saw the authoritarian as willing to give oneself up for the sake of others.

In 1943, Maslow described the submissive authoritarian in terms of masochism, avoidance of responsibility for one's own fate, and compulsive concern

---

[3] The review of the early background research on the authoritarian personality is indebted to D. Crary, Dogmatism, Yielding, and Comprehension, Thesis, Kansas University (1974).

[4] E. Fromm, Escape From Freedom (1941).

for order.[5] Maslow also discussed authoritarian dominance and noted that some authoritarians were motivated to exert dominance over others, justified by the need for order.

As a result of Nazism, a group of researchers investigated whether there was a personality characteristic or group of characteristics which would predispose people toward intolerant, authoritarian behavior. This research resulted in the publication of *The Authoritarian Personality* in 1950.[6] Among the hypothetical components of authoritarianism which the researchers pieced together from interviews with anti-Semitic subjects were conventionalism (value placed on customary mores), authoritarian aggression, authoritarian submission, superstition, stereotyping, and power and toughness (preoccupation with a strength-weakness dimension). Authoritarianism was seen as contributing to certain behavior and is viewed as both fixed and flexible; that is, it is an enduring feature of personality structure, but it represents one end of the continuum along which people may be seen as located relative to others.

Methodologically, Adorno, Frenkel-Bronswick, Levinson, and Sanford used questionnaires to discuss the ranges of responses relevant to anti-Semitism. From these interviews and Thematic Aperception tests, they developed the F scale which attempted to measure fascist tendencies, the E or ethnocentrism scale to measure anti-semitism, and the PEC or politic-economic-conservatism scale.

In 1960, Milton Rokeach published the *Open and Closed Mind,* which built on and extended the idea of authoritarianism.[7] As opposed to Adorno, *et al,* who dealt only with authoritarianism as being on the right end of the ideological continuum, Rokeach conceived of authoritarianism as a part of one's personality structure, distinct from ideological content, and thus, discoverable in persons of all ranges of politics or other ideology. Rokeach developed a personality model based on authoritarianism which could explain a wide range of human behavior. Central to this theory were belief structures. Rokeach called his personality structure dogmatism and viewed dogmatism and authoritarianism as a structural feature of personality. Rokeach viewed dogmatism and authoritarianism as equivalent, so long as dogmatism is not used to indicate authoritarianism of only the right.

Central to Rokeach's theory are the terms belief and belief-disbelief systems, which are defined as an organization of verbal and nonverbal implicit and explicit beliefs, sets, or expectancies. The belief-disbelief system includes, on the one hand, a system of beliefs that one accepts, and, on the other, a series of systems that one rejects. For example, a Catholic has one set of beliefs he or she accepts while rejecting several others. The belief system represents all the beliefs, sets, expectancies, or hypotheses, conscious and unconscious, that a person at a given time accepts as true of the world he or she lives in. The

[5] Maslow, *The Authoritarian Character Structure,* 18 J Soc Psychology, Bulletin of the Society For the Psychological Study of Social Issues 401-11 (1943).

[6] T. Adorno, E. Frenkle-Brunswick, D. Levinson & R. Sanford, The Authoritarian Personality (1950).

[7] M. Rokeach, The Open And Closed Mind 14 (1960).

disbelief system is composed of a series of subsystems rather than a single one, and contains all the disbeliefs, sets, expectancies, conscious and unconscious, that, to one degree or another, a person at a given time rejects as false.

In these psychological systems, the parts may be interrelated without necessarily being logically interrelated. In fact, according to Rokeach, the parts of the system are isolated or segregated from each other, and it is this isolation or segregation of parts which describes their relationship and makes possible certain predictions about behavior. The belief-disbelief system is an organization of parts that may not be logically interrelated.

Belief systems are organized along several dimensions. The first dimension is the organization along the belief-disbelief dimension. As discussed above, beliefs are organized into two interdependent parts: a belief system and a disbelief system. The disbelief system is further conceived as being composed of several disbelief systems, which vary in degree of similarity to the belief system. The belief-disbelief dimension is assumed to have several properties. Two of the most important are isolation and differentiation. Belief systems are characterized by isolation. To the extent that beliefs are intrinsically related and that we are reluctant to see them as related, the beliefs are isolated from each other. This isolation indicates the coexistence of logically contradictory beliefs within the belief system. This is the psychological mechanism known as compartmentalization. Thus, a person believes in freedom for all, but also believes that certain groups should be restricted.

This isolation of beliefs further means that the authoritarian will tend to accentuate differences and minimize similarities between belief and disbelief systems. Thus, an authoritarian Catholic denies that communism and Catholicism have any similarities and insists that they are totally different; an authoritarian American denies that there is any similarity between the United States and Russia and insists that they are totally different. Such accentuations of differences are viewed as attempts to ward off a threat to the validity of one's own system and are possible only if the systems are structurally isolated.

Isolation of beliefs indicates the perception of irrelevance. A person asserts that the similarities between communism and Catholicism are irrelevant, which points to a state of isolation between belief and disbelief systems. It is designed to ward off contradiction, and thus, to maintain intact one's own system.

Finally, isolation indicates denial of contradiction. Contradictory facts are outright denied.

Belief-disbelief systems are also characterized by differentiation. Belief-disbelief systems may vary in their degrees of differentiation or articulation or richness of detail. Differentiation indicates relative amounts of knowledge possessed. Most people have more information, ideas, and interpretations consistent with their belief system than with their disbelief system. Thus, the belief system is generally more differentiated than any one of the disbelief subsystems. In some cases, this discrepancy is great, in others, less. This discrepancy in knowledge may be taken as an index of the relative degree of differentiation of the belief as compared with the disbelief system. There will, furthermore, be discrepancies in the amount of knowledge about disbelief subsystems, and hence, there will be discrepancies in knowledge or varying degrees of differentiation among parts of the disbelief subsystem.

Differentiation indicates the perception of similarity between adjacent disbelief subsystems. There will be varying degrees of differentiation within the disbelief system. An American may see Nazism and communism as the same or different.

Beliefs are also organized along a central-peripheral dimension. The central region represents the person's primitive beliefs and refers to all the beliefs a person has about the nature of the physical world he lives in, the nature of the self, and the generalized other. The primitive beliefs that were formed early in life are not questioned and are unstated. It is out of the primitive beliefs that the total belief-disbelief system grows. Primitive beliefs cover such beliefs as whether the world is a friendly or unfriendly place and beliefs about self-worth. These beliefs also include beliefs about whether everyone else shares certain beliefs. Intermediate and peripheral beliefs emerge from primitive beliefs.

The intermediate region of beliefs represents the beliefs a person has in and about the nature of authority and the people who line up with authority, on whom he or she depends to help form a picture of the world he or she lives in. Such beliefs are concerned with the nature of the positive and negative authority to be depended on to map out the world. Authorities are the intermediaries to whom we turn for information to supplement what we can get for ourselves. Authority is any source we look to for information about the universe, or to check out information we already possess. People differ in the kind of authority they depend on for information. People vary in their ideas about the nature of authority. People range from a tentative reliance on authority to an arbitrary, absolute reliance on authority. Some people tentatively believe in God, whereas others believe absolutely in God and use the Bible to totally govern their lives. These authority beliefs tell us where to look to determine what is true or false about the world. The intermediate region also contains beliefs about people who have beliefs. We have beliefs about people based upon how they line up with our authority beliefs.

The peripheral region represents the beliefs derived from authority. Within this region are beliefs and disbeliefs emanating from positive or negative authority beliefs. Information coming to the individual is screened through the primitive and authority beliefs. It is rejected or altered to "fit" these beliefs. The information that is left after this process is filed in the person's world outlook in the peripheral belief system as a belief or disbelief.

Finally, the belief-disbelief systems are organized along a time perspective. A time perspective refers to the person's beliefs about the past, present, and future and the manner in which they are related to each other. Time perspectives range from narrow to broad. A broad time perspective is one in which the person's past, present, and future are all represented within the belief-disbelief system, and the person sees them as related to each other. A narrow time perspective is one in which the person overemphasizes or fixates on the past, or the present, or the future, without appreciating the continuity and the connections that exist among them. Thus, persons with a completely past, present, or future-oriented time perspective are equally narrow in their time perspective.

Rokeach then describes the closed mind. First, with respect to its organization along the belief-disbelief continuum, in the closed mind the magnitude of rejection of disbelief systems is relatively high at each point along the disbelief continuum; there is isolation of parts within and between belief and disbelief systems; there is relatively great discrepancy in the degree of differentiation between belief and disbelief systems; and there is relatively little differentiation within the disbelief system. With respect to the organization along the central-peripheral dimension, the specific content of primitive beliefs (central region) is to the effect that the world is a threatening world; the formal content of beliefs about authority and about people who hold to systems of authority (intermediate region) is to the effect that authority is absolute and that people are to be accepted and rejected according to their agreement or disagreement with such authority; and the structure of beliefs and disbeliefs perceived to emanate from authority (peripheral region) is such that its substructures are in relative isolation with each other. Finally, with respect to organization along the time perspective dimension, there is a relatively narrow, future-oriented time perspective. This personality structure is seen as protecting the individual from threats to his cognitive structure from a seemingly threatening world.

Rokeach developed the D and E scales and argued that these scales measured generalized authoritarianism not bound to the left or right. Later researchers confirmed this. In 1968, Hanson found significant correlations between dogmatism and authoritarianism, and his findings support the contention that dogmatism is ideologically unbound authoritarianism.[8] Barker found that Rokeach's E scale was a measure of authoritarianism of the right and left.[9] Ray found that when measured by a behavior inventory, authoritarianism is uncorrelated with political vote, ideology, or working class.[10]

§4.13   —Importance of Identifying the Authoritarian Personality When Profiling Jurors

The authoritarian personality processes information differently and holds different attitudes than does the nonauthoritarian personality, and therefore, it is essential that these personality types be identified and understood in profiling jurors. Some of the important differences in information processing and attitudes for the authoritarian personality are as follows.

First, with respect to the belief-disbelief dimension, the authoritarian will reject all information that conflicts with previously held beliefs. This is sup-

---

[8] Hanson, *Dogmatism and Authoritarianism*, 76 J Soc Psychology, 89-95 (1968).

[9] Barker, *Authoritarianism of the Political Right, Center, and Left*, 19 J Soc Issues 63-74 (1963).

[10] Ray, *Half of All Authoritarians Are Left Wing: A Reply to Eysenk and Stone*, 4 Pol Psychology, 139-43 (1971).

ported by Jacoby, who found authoritarians less willing to accept innovative products than were nonauthoritarians.[11] Sexton found that authoritarians have high intolerance for opposing beliefs and, as a rule, will reject opposing beliefs.[12] Thus, authoritarian jurors will be expected to reject any facts, evidence, or arguments that conflict with their already held beliefs.

Due to the isolation among, within, and between the belief and disbelief systems, the authoritarian can hold logically contradictory beliefs. The authoritarian can support democracy but advocate the suppression of the liberal left as being a threat to democracy. Milford, *et al* found that authoritarians tended to hold irrational and illogical beliefs.[13] Thus, logical arguments will not be compelling arguments for authoritarians. If contradictions are confronted, the authoritarian will deny the contradiction. Thus, authoritarian jurors can be expected to claim to believe in the American system of justice on one hand, but feel that individuals should not be allowed to challenge the system with lawsuits.

Authoritarians accentuate differences and minimize similarities between the belief and disbelief systems. The similarities between belief and disbelief systems are seen as irrelevant. For example, as mentioned above, the Catholic will assert that Catholicism and communism have nothing in common and are completely different, when in reality there are many similarities. Authoritarian jurors can be expected to view persons with different backgrounds and belief systems as totally different, even though they may share common ground. Thus, authoritarians tend to see things as black and white, and will not see subtle distinctions. If they are predisposed against something to begin with, they will most likely stay that way.

Further, there is a relatively great discrepancy in the degree of differentiation between belief and disbelief systems. Thus, the authoritarian will know a lot about what she or he believes in, and little about what she or he disbelieves. There will be fine differentiation among beliefs and very little differentiation within the disbelief subsystems. Thus, the authoritarian religious person will know a lot about his or her own church, but all other religions will be undifferentiated and lumped together as heathen. This promotes stereotyping. The authoritarian Caucasian will finely differentiate between Caucasians, while all other races will be undifferentiated and lumped together as foreigners. This leads to stereotypes such as "all black people are the same." As an example, this hypothesis of Rokeach and Adorno, *et al* is supported by the research of Rubovits and Maehr, who found that highly dogmatic white teachers discriminated between gifted and nongifted white students, but lumped all black stu-

---

[11] Jacoby, *Multiple-Indicant Approach for Studying New Product Adopters*, 54 J Applied Psychology 384-88 (1971).

[12] Sexton, *Alienation, Dogmatism, and Related Personality Characteristics*, 39 J Clinical Psychology 80 (1983).

[13] Tobacyk & Milford, *Criterion Validity for Ellis' Irrational Beliefs: Dogmatism and Uncritical Inferences*, 38 J Clinical Psychology 605 (1982).

dents together and failed to discriminate between gifted and nongifted blacks.[14] Jain, *et al* also found evidence to support the hypothesis that authoritarians failed to differentiate as much as nonauthoritarians.[15] Thus, authoritarian jurors can be expected to engage in stereotyping. If the authoritarian juror perceives the plaintiff to be different from himself or herself, the plaintiff will be stereotyped in a negative way, and the plaintiff's case will be rejected.

With respect to the organization along the central-peripheral dimension, due to the content of primitive beliefs, the world is perceived as a threatening world.[16] It could be hypothesized here that authoritarians would be subject to fear appeals and that a particularly salient fear appeal could be one in which it is asserted that outside forces are threatening to destroy the established order. Hitler used this type of approach in mobilizing Germany. Thus, information with fear appeals could be particularly compelling to authoritarians. Authoritarian jurors could be expected to view plaintiffs as being threats to the established order of things and would make bad jurors in medical malpractice and product liability cases.

Authoritarians feel that authority is absolute and that people are to be accepted and rejected according to their agreement or disagreement with such authority. Authority is the source to whom humans look for information about the universe or to check out information they already possess. Authoritarians have different ideas about the nature of authority. The authoritarian has an arbitrary, absolute reliance on authority. Thus, there will be on religion, one political party, or one cause, and this authority will be the sole source of confirmation for all information having to do with this issue. What is important here is the fact that the authoritarian places arbitrary, absolute reliance on this authority.[17] Thus, authoritarian jurors will tend to place an absolute reliance on authority and will be unwilling to challenge the existing authority. They will judge others by the authorities that they hold.

Further, authoritarians accept and reject others according to their agreement or disagreement with the authority they hold as important. The authoritarian evaluates people according to the authorities and belief systems they line up with. To the authoritarian, others are seen as faithful and unfaithful, law-abiding or subversive, friendly or unfriendly, based on how they line up with the authority accepted by the authoritarian. Those who disagree are rejected as enemies, and harsh attitudes are taken toward the renegade. Thus, authoritarians accept or reject people and accept or reject information coming from people based on how the people line up with authority. This hypothesis is supported by Bray and Noble, who found in mock jury research that authoritarians who viewed the state as a place of authority found in favor of the state in crimi-

---

[14] Rubovits & Maehr, *Pygmalion Black and White*, 25 J Personality & Soc Psychology 210-18 (1973).

[15] Malherta, Jain & Pension, *Extremity of Judgment and Personality Variables: Two Empirical Investigations*, 20 J Soc Psychology, 111-18 (1983).

[16] Sexton, *supra* note 12.

[17] K. Rigby, *Acceptance of Authority and Directness As Indicators of Authoritarianism: A New Framework*, 122 J Soc Psychology 171-80 (1984); Sexton, *supra* note 12.

nal cases more often than nonauthoritarians and imposed more severe sentences than did nonauthoritarians.[18] Werner, *et al* found that authoritarians were pro-state and anti-defendant regardless of the evidence or jury instructions.[19] Thus, acceptance or rejection was in part determined by how the litigants lined up with authority (state). This hypothesis is also supported by the research of Mitchell and Bryne, who found that, in mock jury situations, authoritarians found in favor of those litigants perceived as similar to themselves more often than did nonauthoritarians.[20] These results suggest that authoritarians view those litigants perceived as similar as holding similar authority beliefs, and therefore, accept these people and their position based on this link to the "accepted authority." Thus, authoritarian jurors will reject others who appear to differ in their recognition of authority. Going further, it can be generally predicted that authoritarians will tend to side with the defendants in civil cases, while antiauthoritarians will tend to side with the plaintiffs.

With respect to the peripheral belief region, the authoritarian accepts or rejects information based on whether it emanates from an intermediate authority belief or central belief. This hypothesis is important for two reasons. First, it suggests that nonauthoritarians will accept new information based on its merits and will adjust his or her belief system to account for the new information. However, the authoritarian will reject new information that conflicts with his or her existing belief structure, regardless of the validity of the information. The authoritarian will resist any change in his or her central and intermediate beliefs. Secondly, the hypothesis indicates that the authoritarians will uncritically accept new information which emanates from a highly authoritarian source, and an authoritarian will be highly susceptable to a change in beliefs if the suggestion or information comes from a highly authoritarian source. Rokeach's theory suggests that the closed-minded person will be expected to change more easily than the open-minded subject if the information is linked to a highly authoritative source. Rokeach call this a "party line" change. This view stems from the fact that since the authoritarian relies heavily on authority, he or she is a "party line" thinker and accepts uncritically beliefs suggested by highly authoritarian sources. Since the authoritarian's peripheral beliefs are isolated, newly assimilated beliefs are not logically related, but are accepted based on recommendation by positive authority figures and sources. These beliefs are held uncritically, resulting in inconsistencies among beliefs within the belief system. Thus, in the jury setting, the authoritarian can be expected to accept new information and change if the information comes from a person judged to line up with the accepted authority. Thus, authoritarian jurors will readily accept information and arguments presented by authority figures. In

---

[18] Bray & Noble, *Authoritarianism and Decisions of Mock Jury Bias and Group Polarization*, 36 J Personality & Soc Psychology 1424-30 (1978).

[19] Werner & Kagehiro, *Conviction Process and the Authoritarian Juror: Inability to Disregard Information or Attitudinal Bias*, 67 J Applied Psychology, 629-36 (1982).

[20] Mitchell & Byrne, *The Defendant's Dilemma: Effects of Juror's Attitude and Authoritarianism on Judicial Decisions*, 35 J Personality & Soc Psychology 123-29 (1973).

product liability cases, they can be expected to accept any position advanced by the in-house experts, and in medical malpractice actions, they can be expected to accept any position advanced by the defense doctors.

§4.14 —The Authoritarian Juror—Plaintiff versus Defendant

The authoritarian juror will generally make a good defendant's juror, while the nonauthoritarian juror will make a good plaintiff's juror. The authoritarian juror will look toward the system as the repository of knowledge, wisdom, and authority, and will view anyone who challenges the system as a threat to the well-being of the system. Product liability actions, malpractice actions, actions against the government, and actions against businesses will, as a rule, be viewed as endangering the established order. Authoritarians will not tolerate inferiors questioning superiors. The issues will not be viewed as a question of right and wrong, but rather as a question of maintaining the chain of command. Authoritarians will favorably receive the party line witnesses and will reject those witnesses who question the established order of things.

§4.15 Profiling the Authoritarian Juror

Identifying the authoritarian personality is not as easy as it seems, because some authoritarians are not easily recognizable. However, there are some obvious guidelines. For example, high ranking business officials, religious leaders, law enforcement personnel, career government employees, political leaders, and military leaders can be identified as potential authoritarians because they are in positions in which the authority from above is viewed as absolute. Career employees in the lower levels of government and the military may be authoritarians because they have spent their lives dedicated to the chain of command concept. Doctors and many medical personnel are strongly committed to a system that relies on an authoritarian chain of command from the doctors to the lower levels, and hence, many of these people may be authoritarians. People with great wealth may be interested in preserving the system, while some people with little wealth may be interested in challenging the system. Generally, authoritarians will be people who place absolute reliance on authority. People who exist within systems that place absolute reliance on authority and who can be expected to adhere to this authority should be scrutinized as potential authoritarian jurors.

These people can be identified by questions that inquire into the responsibilities of systems to be held accountable for their acts. Jurors should be asked about how they feel about lawsuits against doctors, corporations, the government, etc. Jurors should be asked whether doctors, corporations, the government, etc., should be held accountable for negligence. Jurors should be asked about how they feel about patients questioning doctors and employees questioning their superiors. Jurors should be asked whether certain groups, i.e. the state, doctors and other professional groups, and businesses should receive special treatment from the courts. Jurors may be questioned about whether the "system knows what is best for an individual."

All people in positions such as those mentioned above are not necessarily authoritarians, but they should at least be scrutinized in order to determine if they are authoritarians and whether they would be good or bad for a particular side of the case. This is not to say that authoritarians are bad people; they are not. All that can be said about them is that they rely on certain authorities more than others and will be less likely to accept certain appeals than will other types of people.

§4.16   General Juror Profile Information

Using all of the above information, it is possible to construct general profiles about whether jurors will be good jurors for plaintiffs. It should be noted that, in a sense, profiling jurors is stereotyping. However, stereotyping is not necessarily bad, as long as it is understood that generalizations are being made to develop general categories, and that at the trial, the lawyer will have to make a value judgment as to whether the generalization holds up. For example, rural dwellers tend to make better defense jurors in many cases. However, in today's times, for example, with the farm system collapsing, many farmers may be questioning the system when they wouldn't have ten years ago. Further, a rural dweller may have had a personal experience with a loved one's being injured that may pull them out of the generalized profile. The lawyer must be able to put all of the information together to judge whether the profiles are holding up or whether jurors are representative members of the profile. However, with these reservations in mind, profiles can be extremely useful in thinking about who to select as jurors.

The following are examples of the types of generalizations that can be made in profiling jurors. Authoritarians will make good defendant's jurors, and non-authoritarians will make good plaintiff's jurors. Therefore, those people identified above as potential authoritarians, such as high ranking business officials, religious leaders, law enforcement personnel, career government employees, political leaders, military leaders, medical personnel, and people with great wealth can be expected to make bad plaintiff's jurors.

Jurors who appear to be overpowering or dominating because of their wealth, prestige, power, education, or position in life should be avoided unless they clearly favor your position. These people can be expected to attempt to exert influence over the rest of the jurors during deliberations, and therefore, they should be avoided unless it is certain that they will be favorable jurors. Persons who have specific knowledge about the case, such as medical personnel in a medical negligence case, fall into this category as well. These witnesses will be accorded special importance due to their knowledge and thus can be expected to sway other jurors. Therefore, they should be avoided unless they are clearly in favor of the plaintiff's position.

Generally, minority groups have been predicted to be good plaintiff's jurors, probably because they will be less authoritarian than other groups. Since they, as minorities, have had to break into a system, they might be more inclined to side with a plaintiff than with a defendant.

In terms of occupation, the unemployed, students, laborers, service workers, social workers, teachers, artists, musicians, carpenters, mechanics, salespersons, office workers, union workers, actors, writers, urban housewives, and craftspersons would tend to make better plaintiff's jurors than managers, accountants, engineers, military personnel, medical personnel, suburban housewives, government workers, bankers, business leaders, and insurance company employees.

In terms of political preference, in light of the above material on the authoritarian personality, it could be predicted that straight-ticket Republicans would make better defendant's jurors, while Independents and Democrats would make better plaintiff's jurors.

In a medical malpractice action, good plaintiff's jurors would be young (especially under 35), because younger adults tend to be more questioning of the medical profession. They tend to ask for more information and expect to be allowed to share in the decision-making process regarding health care. Educated jurors would be good for the plaintiff in medical malpractice actions because they would be able to understand and sort through the many considerations involved. Single females with family responsibilities (divorced or widowed) would make good plaintiff's jurors in medical negligence cases because they must make family decisions and recognize that they may have to rely on the judgment of others. People under treatment for chronic, debilitating medical conditions will make bad plaintiff's jurors because they will tend to be fatalistic about what can be done to preserve, promote, and improve a person's medical condition. Authoritarians will be for the defendant and against the plaintiff.

People knowledgeable about consumers' rights and patients' rights would make good plaintiff's jurors in medical malpractice and product liability actions.

§4.17   Conclusion

Profiling jurors is absolutely necessary in order to have systematic jury selection. The above strategies can help provide such a jury selection process. In using these strategies, the lawyer must always keep in mind that in profiling jurors, generalizations are being made that may not always hold up. Thus, the lawyer must always be alert and aware of the jurors who will be exceptions to the rule. However, with this in mind, lawyers may use these strategies to identify desired jurors.

5

Voir Dire

§5.01 Introduction

Contrary to trial texts describing voir dire as a time in which lawyers gather background information about jurors in order to eliminate those biased against their clients or themselves, in what follows I shall demonstrate that highly successful lawyers for the plaintiff in civil suits "do everything."[1] In addition to gathering basic information about jurors and their attitudes, they (1) set the tone for the trial, (2) introduce concepts and evidence and condition the jurors for things to follow in the trial, (3) obtain public commitments from jurors favorable to their cases, (4) use language that places their clients, their witnesses, and other relevant facets of their case in a favorable light, (5) rehearse the arguments they will use in the trial, (6) refute opposition arguments, (7) enhance their credibility, and (8) create jury purpose. In other words, the period of voir dire becomes a preview of the entire trial, preparing jurors for what will follow and creating an atmosphere highly favorable to the plaintiff's case.

The voir dires examined were those of Bill Colson, Phil Corboy, Gerry Spence, Lantz Welch, Victor Bergman, and Robert Habush. Victor Bergman submitted two voir dires for study. The first involved a case of medical negligence in which a child was born brain-damaged due to complications from labor and delivery. The case involved allegations of failure to monitor the child and allowing the child to become oxygen-deprived. The second case was also a medical malpractice action which involved the failure to timely diagnose Hodgkin's disease, resulting in the loss of the chance to obtain timely treatment. The Colson voir dire also involved a medical malpractice action in which a child was born brain-damaged due to complications during labor and cesarean delivery. This case also involved allegations of failure to monitor the child and of allowing the child to become oxygen-deprived during labor and delivery. The Corboy voir dire involved an automobile collision which left the plaintiff a spastic quadraplegic with locked-in syndrome. The Spence voir dire involved the trial of *Silkwood v Kerr-McGee*,[2] in which it was alleged that Karen Silkwood was negligently contaminated with plutonium. The Welch voir dire involved claims for damages and loss of consortium by a husband and wife stemming from an automobile collision. The Habush voir dire involved injuries caused in an industrial accident involving a forklift.

§5.02 Lawyers' Introductions

In each case, the lawyers introduced themselves and their clients to the jury. Gerry Spence presented a colorful introduction when he stated:

> Thank you, your Honor. Ladies and gentlemen of the jury, the court told you my name is Gerry Spence. I'm from Wyoming. And, I did come in

---

[1] For examples of traditional and modern trial text descriptions of voir dire, see respectively, H. Kuvin, Trial Handbook 4 (1965); and T. Mauet, Fundamentals of Trial Techniques 31 (1980).

[2] No. 76-0888 (WD Okla, March 1979).

to help my friend Bill Silkwood to try this case. I saw a sign in the YMCA today, where I ate lunch, a big sign and board saying, 'We speak Western,'—'we' meaning the YMCA, and they do, and I do, and I hope you do.

In making his introduction, Lantz Welch stated:

Thank you, your Honor. May it please His Honor, Judge Meyers, ladies and gentlemen of this prospective jury panel, because that's what you are at this point, my name is Lantz Welch, and Spencer Miller is seated here at my right, and I represent the plaintiffs who have brought this lawsuit which you will hear. The plaintiffs are the parties who bring the litigation. The defendants are those who defend the litigation. This is a personal injury suit to recover the losses suffered by Mr. and Mrs. Robert Cooper, Robert and Ruth Cooper, and there was a head-on collision wherein Mr. Cooper was severely injured in the crash, and about a year and a half after the crash, the Coopers found it necessary to retain our firm and asked us to bring a lawsuit for them, which we did, to recover their losses for medical expenses, loss of income, pain and suffering, and so forth.

In one case, Bergman gave a very brief and concise introduction:

Good morning, ladies and gentlemen. I was introduced before, and I'll introduce myself again. My name is Victor Bergman, and I'm pleased to be representing the Olsens in this case.

In another case, Bergman gave a detailed introduction for both himself and his clients:

I introduced myself a minute ago. I'll give you my name again. It is Victor Bergman. I represent the Morrison family, or at least most of the Morrison family in this case. Specifically, the principal plaintiff is a sixteen-year-old girl named Shanna Morrison. Her parents have separate claims, Mrs. Judith Morrison and Mr. Ken Morrison. That is who I represent. We are the people who are making the claim in this case, called the plaintiffs.

As I said before, Shanna Morrison and her father Ken are not here this morning. We regret that, but Shanna is presently finishing up some evaluation down at M.D. Anderson Hospital in Houston, Texas. Her father Ken is with her.

Hopefully to assist you in maybe finding out whether Shanna is somebody that you recognize or know and also so you don't get the wrong mental word picture of Shanna or what she looks like, we have got some photographs here.

§5.03   Explanation of the Purpose of Voir Dire

When permitted by the court, the lawyers told the jury the function of voir dire and how they intended to conduct their questioning. Bill Colson explained voir dire by stating:

> If it please the Court, ladies and gentlemen, what I intend to do here with the limited time that we have is to try to find out if there might be anything that I know about this lawsuit and what is going to happen with these witnesses here that you obviously can't know about and see, for instance, that you might know a witness or there might be something in your past experience that might have something to do with the courthouse, with hospitals, with doctors, with births, and things such as that.
>
> But my plan of proceeding, so that I may move as quickly as I can, would be to go down the row and for just a little while ask you a few questions, and only you individually can answer. And let me give you an example of what I am going to ask. I would like to know, of course, whether you are married, if you have children, what is your occupation, where are you from and other things that you have done during your adult life. But I have to do that individually. And when I finish that, then I'll be asking you some questions about you, as a group, to just see, for instance, as a group I can save time, have any of you ever been in a courthouse in some litigation like we are standing here, that type of question.
>
> And then from that I'm going to go to some general questions as a group again and see if the type of case that we are concerned with here, where you have heard a little bit from the judge, whether or not in your experience if those of you that have had children and have had any sort of experience and so forth where the mother while she was pregnant had any events and so forth.
>
> And from there I'm going to go to asking you about this type of baby who has this type of result and if you know anything about that.
>
> So, if you will kind of relax, but be thinking about that. And that's where I'll come later on and ask you those questions, not to pry because I'm trying to be nosy, but really to protect everyone in this courtroom that you are not embarrassed later.

Lantz Welch, in explaining his approach to voir dire, stated:

> This portion of the trial, for those of you who have served, bear with me. This is the portion of the trial wherein the lawyers are allowed to ask you questions and is a very important portion of the trial. Those of you who have served before, you will have heard a lot of these questions, because they get to be pretty standard. Lawyers find that they ask the same questions, but have different jury panels as years go along, so you who have been here before, please be patient with us. Also, some of these questions you may feel get to be a little too personal, and if that occurs and you feel that I am being too inquisitive about something, just tell me, and I'll back off. I'm trying to ask questions that I think are relevant to the

issues that will come up in this case, and the facts and some of your feel-ings—by the way, we're going to be asking you about your feelings and your opinions, and we all have opinions and feelings. You don't come into this courtroom with just a vacuum in your head. It's not a crime, it's not bad to have an opinion about something. What is bad is not to be willing to share that opinion with the proper questions asked of you, so we'll be seeking some of your opinions and feelings about things that we think can bear upon your deliberations in this case. And this is, of course, taking us, we hope, to the desired end of this fair and impartial jury for both sides.

Robert Habush told the jurors:

Members of the jury, Judge Doherty was very thorough, but I have some questions I would like to address to all of you as a group, and then, I am going to talk to some of you individually.

Again, as the judge indicated, we are not trying to be nosy, but we have a very short period of time that we have to try to get to know you, and it's a very important case to both sides, and so we would like to spend some time asking some additional questions of you. And most of the ques-tions I will ask will just require you to raise your hand, if you have some-thing to say about it, I will try to write it down as fast as I can and get back to you individually when I have a chance to talk with you.

I am going to be asking some questions of you which will ask you to discuss with us some experiences you may have had; and when I do so, I would like you to broaden the scope of people who are involved in these questions to your spouse, if any, your parents, your children, adult mem-bers of your household, brothers, or sisters, or other close relatives, or a close friend, in other words, people in your universe who might have either influenced you or you them with respect to personal experiences; and you will see more of why that is important as I am asking you ques-tions. But when I am asking you about experiences or attitudes of some-one close to you, if it's a relative as I have described or otherwise, indicate that experience as well as for me.

Bergman described his method of voir dire as follows:

I think just to give you some indication of where we're going there's five sets of lawyers. I go first, and I'll probably be asking you many, many questions that we'll all want to ask you. So I in a sense carry the laboring oar, and I'll probably be up here a significant longer time than anyone else for that reason. I think, as we go down the line, the questions will tend to get shorter and shorter, but the purpose for all of us is the same, and that is, we all want to start out with a group of twelve people and two alternates, who are going to be completely fair and impartial.

One of the things that I want to do is explore with you, ladies and gen-tlemen, some of the preconceived notions that you might have as we start out in this case. There are things that come up in a case, as the evidence unfolds, that you need to know, at least certain types of issues that you need to know about, because you may find at some point in the case that you have a very strong opinion or feeling or emotional reaction to certain things that will come out during the trial, and that is the intent and design of some of my questions and I hope that you can expect—accept them in the spirit in which they're offered. I want to explore with you your feelings about the issues in this case that you might be confronted with and some of the things that you're going to be—going to have to do in this case as we go along.

In another case, Bergman described the purpose of voir dire as follows:

It is our hope that both Ken and Shanna will be here Wednesday or Thursday. The purpose of this process, I know that you have been told, the purpose specifically of my questions is to determine whether there is anything in your make-up, in your background, in your experience that might cause you to have difficulty being a fair and impartial juror. That is what all of my questions are designed to do.

There are some things that are thrown at you during the course of a trial that you didn't know were coming. Sometimes some people come into the courtroom as witnesses that you didn't know would be there. We don't want you to be in a situation on down the line during the trial, or particularly during the deliberations, where all of a sudden you are confronted with a problem. The idea here is that you folks won't be.

I would hope that as I ask these questions and I know that Mr. Saunders does too—that you really be candid. Reach down inside of yourself. It may be that we are asking you things that you never thought about before, never been asked to consider before. So as you are thinking about them, if you think that maybe you are a person who on a particular point might be sensitive, might have a problem being fair and impartial, just please raise your hand and at least let's discuss it.

§5.04   Gathering Demographic and Background Information about Jurors

Most trial texts agree that one of the main purposes of jury selection is to learn about jurors' background so that peremptory challenges can be intelligently exercised.[3] The theory behind this approach is that people's attitudes are the product of their social background, education, and experiences in life.[4] These lawyers have accepted this theory and systematically gathered background information about the jurors. They appeared to look for two types of background information. First, they collected general background information that could have been expected to give them an idea of the jurors' general atti-

---

[3] T. Mauet, Fundamentals of Trial Techniques 31 (1980).
[4] Id 32.

tudes toward life, social issues, and legal issues. For example, jurors' social, educational, or occupational backgrounds could lead to inferences about whether a juror's orientation would be liberal or conservative, establishment or anti-establishment, or for the plaintiff or the defendant. Second, they gathered information about experiences that related specifically to participants or issues involved in the case.

§5.05 —General Background Information

In all cases examined, either the judge or the plaintiff's lawyer gathered the following general background information from jurors:

1. Marital status
2. Family status (children)
3. Education
4. Occupation
5. Employment history
6. Residence history
7. Activities and organizations
8. Prior jury experience
9. Prior involvement in personal injury litigation

In gathering this information, the lawyers also inquired about close family members. It could be assumed that jurors' attitudes would, in part, be a product of the attitudes of their close relatives, and therefore, these lawyers gathered much of this information with respect to close family relatives as well as the jurors themselves. For example, almost all jurors were asked for the occupational histories of their spouses. As noted above, Robert Habush told the jurors that when answering voir dire questions about experiences, he wanted them to answer with respect to not only themselves, but also their friends and relatives.

§5.06 —Information Relevant to Participants in the Case or Specific Issues in the Case

The lawyers all inquired about any relationship to any of the participants in the trial. Such relationships could be expected to imply juror bias for or against the participants. Jurors were also asked about their knowledge of the facts of the case. Thus, all jurors were asked whether they:

1. Knew the lawyers or members of their firms
2. Knew the parties or their family members or employees
3. Knew the witnesses
4. Knew the facts of the case
5. Had been exposed to pretrial publicity

The lawyers then inquired about experiences related to the specific issues involved in the case. This specific background information could be used to make inferences about juror attitudes with respect to specific issues of the trial.

In the *Silkwood* case, it was expected that Karen Silkwood's role as a union activist would be injected into the trial. Therefore, Spence asked jurors whether they or members of their families had ever belonged to a union. He further asked whether any jurors or members of their families had had any experience dealing with unions as members of management. Plutonium contamination of the plaintiff was an issue in the case, and therefore, the jurors were asked whether they had any knowledge of or experience with plutonium or knowledge of plutonium as a cause of leukemia. Since the plaintiffs contended that Karen Silkwood's contamination gave her knowledge of the fact that she would develop cancer, the jurors were asked whether they had had any personal experience with cancer in their lives or in the lives of their family members.

Since Robert Habush's case involved an injury caused by a forklift in a warehouse, he asked all jurors whether they had ever worked in a warehouse, whether they had ever operated forklifts, and whether they had ever witnessed any injuries caused by forklifts in these situations. He asked jurors about their experiences with the specific types of forklifts involved in the case. For example, in examining one juror, he asked:

> HABUSH: First of all, has anybody either here or as I have defined it for you ever worked in a warehouse?
>   Okay, that's Mr. Shawver?
> JUROR: Yes.
>
> . . . .
>
> HABUSH: What warehouse?
> JUROR: Allen Bradley.
> HABUSH: And in connection with your duties there, did you operate any forklift trucks or other industrial machinery?
> JUROR: Yes, I did.
> HABUSH: Do you remember if you ever operated any forklift trucks which were manufactured by Yale or Eaton?
> JUROR: I don't remember the manufacturer.
> HABUSH: What kind of forklift truck did you operate?
> JUROR: An electric forklift truck used for—I don't know what kind of terminology you would call it, but just a standard forklift. It was a stand-on model too.
> HABUSH: That was my next question.
> JUROR: It was a stand-up.
> HABUSH: Stand-up?
> JUROR: Yes.

HABUSH: Where you stand up behind the machine as you are operating it?

JUROR: Yes.

HABUSH: What type of goods were you loading or unloading?

JUROR: Coiled steel, steel for die-stamping.

HABUSH: When is the last time you operated one of those machines?

JUROR: Well, presently in my job I do now, I use a small forklift sit-down model to unload, bring off from trucks.

HABUSH: Have you ever had an incident in which the forklift tipped over or fell off the dock?

JUROR: No.

HABUSH: Have you ever had any experience where you were struck by another vehicle or something else that you bumped into with the forklift?

JUROR: No.

HABUSH: Thank you, sir.

In trying an automobile collision case, Corboy asked jurors to specify the type of automobile driven by themselves, their spouses, and, in some cases, by their parents or children. From this information, inferences could be made about jurors' attitudes toward automobiles and automobile safety. Jurors were asked whether they had ever been involved in an automobile accident before, and whether they had ever been injured in an automobile accident.

Since Colson's and Bergman's cases involved allegations of medical malpractice during a cesarean birth delivery, including failure to properly monitor the fetus, oxygen deprivation, and resulting brain damage, they asked all women jurors about their own pregnancies, in some cases the pregnancies of their daughters, their delivery room experiences, their experiences with fetal monitoring devices and practices, and their experiences with brain damaged children. For example, at one point in voir dire, Victor Bergman asked:

BERGMAN: Without getting into very much detail at all, I want to tell you a little bit more about the nature of this case. It happened at Suburban. There will be evidence in the case on subjects of female anatomy, labor and delivery. It might tend to get graphic at some points in time. There will be evidence about forceps deliveries, the resuscitation of depressed infants. Brent needed to be resuscitated in this instance. . . .

. . . . .

Is there anyone who has had an experience in their own life or in the life of a close relative or close friend that might parallel the kind of situation that I've just outlined, where as a result of labor and delivery and birth, there have been any of those things that have happened, forceps delivery or resuscitated infant, that sort of thing?

Okay, I'll want to explore a little more with you all, your experiences with regard to the birth of your children and that sort of thing. I think that will be very pertinent in this case. I want to take a couple of minutes to go around and maybe not all of you, I think most of you, I'm going to have a few questions that I want to go through.

. . . .

BERGMAN: Did you have any problems of any kind in connection with any of your pregnancies or birth of any of your children?

JUROR: My first child was a forceps delivery, but she's fine. Everything is okay.

. . . .

BERGMAN: Do you know whether it was a—what we call a "low forceps" or a "mid forceps"?

JUROR: Low.

BERGMAN: Low forceps. All right, was there any monitoring done in connection with your pregnancy that you were aware of?

JUROR: No.

BERGMAN: What that offered to you or discussed with you?

JUROR: I don't believe so.

BERGMAN: Are you familiar with fetal heart monitoring?

JUROR: Yes.

BERGMAN: How did you become familiar with it?

JUROR: Well, just during, you know, classes, you know, parent classes, and my doctor was like—he's been in the business fifty years, and he just didn't think it was best for all of those things.

With another juror, Bergman asked:

BERGMAN: When you delivered your children, were there any complications that you can recall that came up?

JUROR: Two boys were lower forceps.

BERGMAN: Did any of the children need to be resuscitated? In other words, were they born blue or anything like that?

JUROR: No.

With respect to anesthetic, Bergman asked:

BERGMAN: Okay. Was there any kind of anesthetic used?

JUROR: She had a spinal block on the first child, and I think a local on the second child.

BERGMAN: Are you familiar with the term, "paracervical block?"

JUROR: No.

BERGMAN: Okay. That doesn't ring a bell in terms of what was done? Did your wife or either of your children have any effects from any of the anesthetic that you can recall?

JUROR: None.

Since Bergman's case concerning the misdiagnosis of cancer involved a young girl who was dying, he asked all jurors whether they had experienced the loss of a child.

All lawyers asked whether the jurors had any special training in subjects that were involved in the trial. Colson asked jurors whether they had had any training in medicine, nursing, economics, and engineering. Welch asked whether any of the jurors were trained in medicine or law. Since Bergman was dealing with damages to a young child that would continue throughout the child's life, he asked jurors whether they had had any experiences with projecting life expectancies.

Since all cases were injury cases, jurors were asked about injuries sustained by themselves and their family members, and their experience with injuries similar to those suffered by their clients. Habush asked jurors whether they or any of their relatives or friends had experienced injury while working with industrial machinery. Habush's client had suffered paralysis as a result of his injury, and therefore, all jurors were asked:

> Is there anyone on the panel sitting here in the courtroom or again who has a close relative or friend who suffers from any degree of paralysis either paraplegia, quadraplegia, or other substantial paralysis as a result of any injury or illness?

§5.07   —Strategies for Getting at Background Information

Whenever possible, the lawyers asked open-ended questions to the jurors. As a matter of strategy, open-ended questions allow jurors to select what is relevant to them and to elaborate rather than give a narrow answer restricted by the lawyer's question. Corboy asked a juror, "And would you just narratively give me your educational background, please?" Colson asked, "Okay. And in talking about your adult life, other things that you might have done, tell us some of those that would be of interest to us, please." When seeking to discover family history, Colson asked, "And would you tell us about your family please?"

If jurors indicated something in their background that was particularly relevant to the case, the area was probed thoroughly. For example, when Colson found any juror who had worked around a hospital in any capacity, he probed thoroughly for facts that would give him some idea of their predispositions toward hospitals. When a juror indicated that she was an Licensed Practical Nurse, Colson questioned her this way:

COLSON: And may I ask you about your LPN? How long have you done that?

JUROR: For about 10 years.

COLSON: And would you tell us where please, ma'am?

JUROR: I graduated from Sheridan Vocational School, Hollywood.

COLSON: And with whom have you worked? In other words, tell us, you know, is it hospital settings or home settings or what?

JUROR: Private duty. I work for the American Homemakers.

COLSON: And they provide the services that have been asked for? I mean, they give you your assignments?

JUROR: Yes.

COLSON: And then do you have an LPN in your home work? Do you have something that you specialize in?

JUROR: No, whatever care the patient needs.

COLSON: Do you take care of mothers that have just had babies?

JUROR: Yes.

COLSON: When they first get home from the hospital?

JUROR: Humn, humn.

COLSON: And you act as—taking care of the babies from a nursery standpoint?

JUROR: Yes.

COLSON: And do you take care of the mother if any problems happen there; is that correct?

JUROR: Right.

. . . .

COLSON: Now, what about in going back in your other years? Have you worked at the same percentage of the time or have you worked more?

JUROR: No, before I became an LPN, I was a nurse's assistant.

COLSON: Tell me about that.

JUROR: Well, I worked at Broward General.

. . . .

COLSON: Okay, and may I ask you then during that time at Broward did you have one area of the hospital that you worked in more than others?

JUROR: Yes.

COLSON: What was that?

JUROR: Surgical.

COLSON: And would that include cesarean sections?

JUROR: Yes.

COLSON: And did you actually assist at the operations as—

JUROR: No.

COLSON: What would you do?

JUROR: This was after the surgery.

COLSON: I see, in the recovery room?

JUROR: No, after, after everything.

.   .   .   .

COLSON: But, would you try to help me because you know what we're dealing with here. It is the subject of pregnant women. We're dealing with cesarean sections. We're dealing with birth. We're dealing with a brain damaged child. All right. If you will, just take those areas. How much time—and obviously the next question is how much exposure and experience have you had in these particular fields?

JUROR: Quite a bit. I've had quite a bit with all of it. We're assigned to all kinds of babies, you know, from surgery to retardation, all of it.

When Bergman found a juror who worked in a company that might be subject to malpractice claims, he probed thoroughly:

BERGMAN: You're with Bayvet?

JUROR: That's correct.

BERGMAN::   Is that over on 63rd Street?

JUROR: In Shawnee, yes.

BERGMAN: Yeah, a blue building over there?

JUROR: That's correct.

BERGMAN::   And you've described what you do a little bit, but what is the nature of your work with Bayvet?

JUROR: Well, of course, Bayvet researches, manufactures, and markets animal health care products. We're the second largest in this business in the United States. My job is toxicology and governmental affairs and I evaluate the safety of our products. I handle product complaints, whether they be associated with animal safety of the party that's applying or using our products.

BERGMAN: When you say "you"—go ahead.

JUROR: And I also handle our affairs with the Food and Drug Administration and the Environmental Protection Agency in gaining approval so we may market these products.

BERGMAN: Does that require you to dig into the Federal Register and regulations and things like that?

JUROR: Yes. I'm quite involved in that area.

BERGMAN: And you say you're involved in consumer complaints?

JUROR: That's correct.

BERGMAN: What kind of complaints does your company get, just generally?

JUROR: Well, with the volume of products we well, of course, the human complaints might be somebody spilling the product, a child consuming the product, accidentally, these type of complaints, and invariably, most of my contacts are in an Emergency Room, a physican who might call, wants to know about our product and seek advice and of course I do have consulting physicians which I may refer him to, also.

BERGMAN: You have local consulting physicians?

JUROR: That is correct.

BERGMAN: Who are they?

JUROR: Dr. John Doull, at the University of Kansas Medical Center, is my consulting physician on toxicology.

BERGMAN: Okay. Do you get involved in consumer claims after they are in that acute stage of somebody feeling like they've been poisoned or whatever?

JUROR: There have been rare occasions. I certainly—I do the research as far as providing our corporate attorneys with information on how to deal with these situations, and that is about the extent of my involvement.

BERGMAN: Do you have in-house corporate attorneys, or is it a local firm?

JUROR: We are a division of the Miles Laboratory. So our corporate attorneys are in Elkhart, Indiana.

BERGMAN: Are there local attorneys who would handle some of these things, too?

JUROR: We always go to the corporate level.

BERGMAN: Have you been involved in any lawsuits arising out of the use of any of the products of your company?

JUROR: As far as an expert witness or anything of this nature?

BERGMAN: In any way.

JUROR: No, I have not directly other than doing research, and you know, evaluating risk assessments, such as this, and of course, I do that for the federal government in, you know, attempting to get approval for our products, too.

BERGMAN: The reason I ask that in reading the law, I noticed that there seems to be growing concern about animal products as they may kind of translate through the food chain and into the human body and I'm sure you're tuned right into that, the whole controversy—

JUROR: Yes, I am.

THE COURT: Is this pertinent?

BERGMAN: I hope it is.

THE COURT: I hope it is, too. I fail to see it, but maybe it is. Proceed.

BERGMAN: Well, the reason I ask is, it's the whole subject of litigation, you know, the Olsens are here, making a claim because they feel that it's a legitimate claim, and it's going to be defended because they feel it's to be defended. Have you been in any way influenced in your judgment about litigation by your own experiences, what's going on in your own industry, that sort of thing?

JUROR: Okay. One other area that I must mention to you, I have done—as far as the American Veterinary Medical Association is concerned, they have a group, malpractice insurance trust, and there have been a few occasions in the eleven years I've been with Bayvet that they've called upon me to seek advice in that area, too. Now those are direct—there have already have been litigations ongoing as far as veterinarians' malpractice suits, and once in a while involving our company's products indirectly or directly, so I have had that more of an involvement with the actual malpractice world, and when I was in veterinary practice, of course, I, like all veterinarians, maintained malpractice insurance for obvious reasons, so I would want that to be know too.

BERGMAN: Okay. I appreciate that, and I'm going to ask you a couple of questions about it. With that background, I mean with all that experience that you've had, really on sort of the medical side of it and the side that may be challenged by the people who, we think they've been injured, do you feel that you can be completely fair and impartial in this case and give the Olsens, you know, start them out even rather than starting out having to be shown more by them than you otherwise might?

JUROR: I must be completely honest with you. There are very—there are many, very substantiated cases, I feel, and there are many frivolous cases in my mind that get brought to the stage where I have to get involved, and in all candidness, I probably have somewhat of a negative outlook on malpractice cases.

BERGMAN: We have started out that way in your case?

JUROR: Yes, I'm sorry, I am, at this time.

BERGMAN: Your honor, for that, I would challenge for cause.

THE COURT: You may step down, Doctor.

§5.08   Discovering Juror Attitudes and Beliefs

As the lawyers gathered information that could be used to form inferences, they also directly questioned jurors about their attitudes and beliefs about the various aspects of the trial. The attitudes discussed may be categorized into general attitudes about generalized aspects of the case, and specific attitudes about specific aspects of the case.

§5.09   —Attitudes about General Aspects of the Case

The lawyers examined those attitudes that jurors brought with them to the courthouse about life and the legal system in general.

Jurors were asked, in one form or another, whether they had any preconceived notions about the legal system, whether they had any philosophical or religious beliefs that would prevent them from sitting in judgment of others, whether they would be able to confine their deliberations to the facts presented in the case, whether they would be able to follow the law given to them by the judge, whether they could base their judgment on reason rather than sympathy, whether they would be willing to consider damages such as pain, suffering, and disability, and whether they would have any hesitancy in rendering a substantial verdict if the evidence justified it.

Colson asked the jurors whether they had any philosophical or religious beliefs or attitudes which would make it difficult for them to sit in judgment of others, and whether they would have any problems following the law given to them by the judge. He asked:

> Does anyone, generally, in lawsuits, now, let's get off the subject of just involving doctors and hospitals, but generally is there any one that has in your personal lives a philosophy or a religion in which you would say, "I don't want to be a part of a process down at the courthouse in which I have to listen to the evidence and in which this judge will tell me to judge somebody else and in which I have to look at a serious problem for both sides and serious amounts of damages in the future when this particular child will be over 73 years." Is there anyone that has any religious problems with that? Any philosophical problems that they follow the law as it is in the State for everybody that his Honor will give it to you? Is there any problem about that if Judge Farrington tells you to do it, that you can follow it if he says to do it?
>
> I can count on that?
>
> . . . .
>
> Do you know of any reason that you couldn't let this case be tried?
>
> His Honor asked you this at the beginning. I don't mean to repeat, but having heard what I told you now, a lot of questions, you know, do you, brand new, have any reason why you couldn't let the chips fall where they may and bring in what the Judge will tell you your job is as far as to fill out the verdict and turn that problem back to the Judge and let him handle it from there on, what happens after that is up to the Judge, any of you have any reason now that you shouldn't do that? Couldn't do that? Hesitate to do that?

With respect to their attitudes about the jury system, Colson asked all jurors:

> I would like to assume, first of all, that you all believe in the jury system. . . . But I asume you believe in the jury system, that if you can't handle something and there is a problem outside the courtroom, you bring it to the courtroom in front of a judge and let the people in the community decide it as a jury. Is that all right with everybody?

When Spence encountered a juror who had worked at a defense firm that represented primarily insurance companies, he questioned her thoroughly about her attitudes toward people who bring lawsuits:

SPENCE: Mrs. _____ were you, you know, everytime I find people that are working for lawyers I get spooky.

JUROR: I appreciate your feeling.

SPENCE: You expected that, didn't you?

JUROR: Yes.

SPENCE: Now, I have people that work for me in Wyoming that are legal assistants,—and that is what you say you were?

JUROR: Yes.

SPENCE: And, because, you know, they develop philosophies, because they are exposed to philosophies of the office, and attitudes that they just start to develop because of the kind of cases that he finds himself involved in, and they get—they're very loyal people—and they get behind me, you know, and sometimes maybe they shouldn't be behind, but they are behind me, and that is the way you are, isn't it, with your boss when you were working for them.

JUROR: Well, I tried.

SPENCE: Well, what kind of cases did that law firm handle mostly, from the standpoint of trial work?

JUROR: Mostly—Well, cases go by case load.

SPENCE: Yes; mostly.

JUROR: Mostly. It mostly is defense cases.

SPENCE: So, would it be fair to say that they were a firm that mostly represented people who were being sued?

JUROR: Correct.

SPENCE: And, so they were a firm that was mostly doing cases, like these people over here (indicating), isn't that right?

JUROR: Well, percentage-wise; yes.

SPENCE: That's why I'm getting spooky, because of the kind of cases—I don't represent anybody but people—I just don't represent anybody but people, and nobody in my firm does. I don't represent any banks, or any corporations, or anything like that. Did most of the people— strike "people"—did most of the clients that your law firm represented, were most of those corporations and insurance companies?

JUROR: Well, we were representative customers of insurance companies.

SPENCE: In other words, the insurance company was the one that actually paid the bill?

JUROR: Correct. Generally.

SPENCE: And, there's a philosophy that developed in a firm like that—they are called "defense firms" aren't they?

JUROR: Certainly.

SPENCE: And, they are hired by large corporations, and insurance companies, and their philosophy gets sort of—well, that people that sue in the courts like my client, well, you defend those cases, right?

JUROR: Right.

SPENCE: And, you kind of develop an attitude after awhile, don't you, about people that bring lawsuits?

.   .   .   .

SPENCE: If you knw that your effort, on behalf of your law firm, would result in depriving a person of his right to recover, did that ever bother you?

JUROR: I don't go with the word "deprive."

SPENCE: That is what I thought. You know, I want to ask you a question. If we were sitting over there in Bill Silkwood's chair, representing his three grandchildren, would you feel comfortable with the jury made up of six legal assistants who have worked for defense law firms?

JUROR: I think not.

.   .   .   .

SPENCE: Would there be any other reason other than balance? You know, we've got to get a unanimous verdict here. So one, you know, one may be enough, one person that holds out could be enough to deprive my client of a verdict, and if I were representing you, would you feel comfortable as one of the persons on the jury who has worked for a defense law firm, whoworked for large corporations, who go against cases of this kind as a matter of habit, would you feel comfortable about that?

.   .   .   .

SPENCE: The more I got to thinking about this, the more I got kind of scared about you sitting on this jury—just to be honest, and that is the way you would like me to be, wouldn't you?

JUROR: Certainly.

SPENCE: The reason I'm concerned about it, and anxious about it, and feel it right about here (indicating) is because you've said that you have worked for a defense firm, and you say that you know some of these fellows over here at the defense table—and you don't know me.

.   .   .   .

SPENCE: And, you have said that you would—you might feel a little uneasy if you were sitting in Mr. Silkwood's chair and there was a juror with that kind of knowledge and that kind of background sitting on your case, and so I want to ask you just straight: Don't you feel that under the circumstances, that you and I have shared with each other, that the fair thing in this case would be for another juror to take your spot?

JUROR: I guess you have to do what you think is fair to your client, and disregard my feelings about it.

With respect to the willingness of a juror to follow the law, Corboy asked:

By the way, is this lawsuit, the Judge at the end of the case is going to tell you what the law is. Now, a lot of people including lawyers have ideas about the law which are not accurate. That's why we have to have a judge tell us what the law is. He is going to tell you what the law is. Will you follow his instructions as we must whether you agree with them or not?

Corboy asked all jurors about their disposition toward returning a substantial verdict for the plaintiff. After questioning a juror about his willingness to return a verdict with respect to his specific damage claims for pain, suffering, disability, medical expense, lost wages, and disfigurement, Corboy focused in on a willingness to return a substantial verdict:

CORBOY: And after that is all over, sir, and I say this categorically straightforward to you and I will look you eyeball to eyeball, if you find out, after you have heard all of the evidence and heard all of the law, that my client is entitled to as much as $25 million or $30 million or perhaps, even more than that, would you have any hesitancy in signing such a verdict?

JUROR: No, I wouldn't.

On the matter of juror willingness to return a substantial verdict, Spence asked:

Now, the Judge talked about ten and a half million dollars, and whether that shocked anybody, and some people it shocked a little bit to start with—and it is a lot of money—and when you get into the jury room you're going to have the power of "writing a check" for anything up to eleven and a half million dollars—ten million dollars punitive, and a million and a half actual. How many of you would be afraid to use that power, if you felt it was justified under the law and the facts of the case—anybody that would be afraid of that? I don't think any of us have written a check that big. Would any of you be afraid to do that—because you're going to be called upon to do that—and I'm going to ask you, at the conclusion of the case to do that. Any of you be afraid to do that if you felt it was just?

With respect to juror attitudes about the jury system, Habush asked:

Is there anybody who doesn't believe in the right of citizens to present a case in front of a jury like yourselves in personal injuries, feels that they shouldn't come to court and have a jury trial like this, anyone feel that way? If so, please raise your hand.

Does anyone feel if a person has a legitimate injury and they feel that they would like to have it tried by a jury such as yourself because they believe they were hurt due to someone else's fault or defective product that they shouldn't do that? Does anyone feel that people shouldn't do it if they have a legitimate injury and feel that it was caused by some else's fault or defective product?

Bergman asked all jurors about their prior jury experiences and then asked them how those experiences affected their attitudes toward the jury system. For example, he asked:

BERGMAN: Was there anything about that experience that left you with any feeling that there's something wrong with the jury system or that you liked the jury system.

JUROR: I like the jury system.

. . . .

BERGMAN: Was there anything about that experience or any of your experiences, probably not, you're probably an expert by now, that leaves you with the feeling that this is not the appropriate way to resolve disputes?

JUROR: Oh, no, this is the way.

In another case, after a juror had expressed a negative attitude about large settlements and verdicts, Bergman questioned jurors about their general attitudes toward large verdicts and their effects on insurance premiums:

BERGMAN: There has been a considerable amount of advertising, public relations, commercials, pamphlets in doctors' offices, editorials or letters to the editor. I noticed that there was one yesterday. I want to make this a question to all of you. This is a veryimportant question in this case. Is there anybody who feels that if you sit in a medical malpractice case and return a verdict that somehow that is going to cause your own premiums to go up or going to cause you any embarrassment with any of your neighbors or anybody who has just developed an opinion that there is something wrong with big settlements as applied to medical malpractice cases. And there could not be a more important serious issue that I would want to ask all of you about.

. . . .

I mean we have respect, most of us—I do—for the medical profession, which sometimes is hard to overcome. And then you add to that this notion that, should they be sued, and what does that all mean. I'm not going to argue with anybody about it. I would like for all of you to think about it for a minute and tell me whether you think you have any of those feelings and whether you think that in the course of the deliberations in this case they might surface and make it really difficult for you to really be fair and impartial and not compromise a verdict.

JUROR: I'm concerned about awards on architectural claims. I pay a lot of money for insurance every year. I know that a lot of the claims that are made against the architects sometimes are frivolous and given huge amounts of money. That concerns me every time that I write my check for my insurance.

BERGMAN: On your mind a lot?

JUROR: Right.

BERGMAN: Do you think that would cause you to hesitate to return a verdict against another professional or do you think—let me give you some examples of the ways that I think that this can come up, where you can go back and tell your partners or associates that you have just returned a very large verdict, if you think that it was warranted, or just give you any difficulty in deliberating in this case, whether that feeling that you have would somehow work its way into your view of the case and your deliberations in the case.

JUROR: I think that I would try to be impartial, but it is a very big concern of my professional now and me personally, the amounts given.

BERGMAN: Okay. Do you think that we would start off with you with a heavier burden, in other words, you would really have to be convinced more than you would be if this were maybe an automobile type case or a commercial case or a criminal case?

JUROR: I would have to say yes.

Bergman: Okay. You'd be a little more skeptical about the claim?

JUROR: Uh-huh.

BERGMAN: I would ask Mr. Holloway be excused.

. . . .

THE COURT: Mr. Holloway, you understand issues of architectural malpractice have nothing to do with this.

JUROR: I understand that.

The Court: Are you still telling me that you feel that you could not be a fair and impartial juror in this particular case just because it is a professional malpractice case.

JUROR: The only thing that concerns me in my profession are the amounts that are awarded.

THE COURT: I will excuse you.

§5.10 —Attitudes about Specific Aspects of the Case

When the lawyers discovered jurors who had specific experiences that might have given rise to attitudes about specific aspects of the case, these attitudes were probed. When Colson encountered a woman who had done volunteer work for hospitals for 20 years, he inquired about her ability to judge a hospital for malpractice. He asked:

My other client that is not mentioned here, although His Honor mentioned him, but she is not here, she is a little four-year-old baby girl. Do you feel that you will have any problem if you sit as a juror, the fact that you did volunteer work, which we all applaud you for, but that you have been around hospitals and around doctors all of your twenty years, is that going to be a problem to Karin Willison, the little four-year-old?

In probing the attitudes of a teacher's aide for retarded children, Colson asked:

COLSON: All right. Now, you obviously have a lot of advanced knowledge going into this case. And without getting into the details, I could tell you that although Karin has many problems of not being able to move, things like that, that you will hear details of later, that she has a very high IQ, her mental faculties. And she will need an opportunity, I think is a better word, for problems in education and things like that. And you have a lot of experience in that.

JUROR: Yes, I do.

COLSON: And do you, ma'am, have any problems, do you think, sitting here on this jury? Would Karin have a problem?

JUROR: No.

COLSON: With you being here would the hospitals or the doctors have a problem with you?

JUROR: No, I don't think so.

COLSON: On these issues where you could realize what would have to be if we are entitled to a verdict and you turn to the problems of her future, can you listen to the evidence here and have any problem with that? Do you feel one way or the other?

JUROR: No, I won't have any problem at all.

COLSON: Do you have any idea to start with as to for instance, that a child such as this should only be in one place, or it's all solved, or are you willing to listen to the evidence on this?

When Colson found a juror who had a medical doctor for a brother, he asked:

Do you feel, ma'am, again, the questions I have to ask you, you have been around hospitals and your brother, is that a problem here if you had to tell your brother after this case that you found against the osteopathic hospital, the osteopathic physicians in favor of a girl who was born on a particular day, would that give you any hesitation at all?

When Bergman encountered jurors who had themselves been in the defendant hospital or who had had relatives in the defendant hospital, he questioned them about their attitudes toward the defendant and asked whether their experiences would affect their ability to render a verdict against the hospital:

BERGMAN: Just a few other questions, was there anything about the experience that you personally had or that your son had over at Suburban which caused you to come away with a feeling about the institution that would perhaps make you more inclindes to favor them or disfavor them in this case?

JUROR: I can't think of any complaint in this case.

BERGMAN: Okay. In the case of your son?

JUROR: Yes.

BERGMAN: My question really is, do you, as a result of your son's hospitalization there, feel that you might have some feeling about Suburban that would make it difficult for you—if you thought the evidence warranted it—to return a verdict against the hospital.

JUROR: I don't think so.

When encouraging a juror who was a patient of one of the defendant's partners, Bergman asked:

BERGMAN: Okay. I'll just ask you whether the fact that you go to see Dr. Powers might make it difficult for you to be as objective as you might otherwise be in this case since he's a partner of Dr. Younglove's?

JUROR: No.

BERGMAN: Do you feel that during the course of this trial, you might be going to see Dr. Powers?

JUROR: It's possible.

BERGMAN: Okay. And if you do, you'd—you don't think that would be a problem for you?

JUROR: No.

With respect to the graphic nature of medical malpractice actions and the ability of jurors to listen to the evidence about labor and delivery, Bergman asked:

There will be evidence in the case on subjects of female anatomy, labor and delivery. It might tend to get graphic at some points in time. There will be evidence about forceps deliveries, the resuscitation of depressed infants. Brent needed to be resuscitated in this instance, and also some really—some evidence that might upset one or more of you about the sequence of events since Brent's birth, the nature of his birth, the nature of his injury, that sort of thing. Is there anybody who, you know, just has a weak stomach or cannot—feels that they might have difficulty sitting through this case and keeping your mind open and your mind focused on the evidence if these kinds of subjects come up? It tends to happen sometimes in malpractice cases. Lawyers and judges have had experiences, where people have just keeled over in the courtroom. We don't want that to happen to anyone, but I ask that, and I ask you to think about that, and if anyone feels that they might have a problem that might cause them to shut it off or keep it out because they don't want to hear it, would you please raise your hand.

Jurors were asked about their specific attitudes toward factual matters that would arise in the case. Since Karen Silkwood was a union activist, involved in whistleblowing activities against Kerr-McGee, Spence questioned all jurors about their activities toward unions:

> SPENCE: Karen Silkwood was a member of a union. This Court has asked you about that. But, I kind of would like to know what your feelings are about a union. Some of you belong to a union, may like a union or may not. Some of you may be employers and have had experience with unions from the other side. So, could I just ask you about what your attitude is with respect to a union . . .

Anticipating evidence that Karen Silkwood had a somewhat deviant lifestyle, Spence questioned all jurors about how they felt about people such as Karen Silkwood who had a "different" lifestyle. He questioned as follows:

> SPENCE: You know, your Honor talked a little bit with you folks about "life style." We all have different life styles—we all go to different churches—or we don't go to church at all—we all have ideas about marriage—some of our younger people have ideas about marriage that aren't shared by the older folks—some of my kids have ideas that I have a little trouble with. Does anybody have the same problems that I just suggested? Do any of you have any trouble with the ideas of the younger generation—any of you that would feel, those of you that feel sort of like that, any of you feel that the younger generation isn't entitled to the same protection of the law as we are, even if we don't agree with their moral code?
>
> It's an important question, and I'm not getting a response, and it is scaring me a little bit. Is there anybody here—let me strike that. Let me put it this other way around: If it were shown to you that Karen Silkwood had a different moral system that you and me, would that affect your judgment at all as to her rights under the law? Would it? Okay. You said it wouldn't, Mrs. _____, and I believe you. Would it for you Mrs. _____?

With respect to evidence, Corboy told the jurors that he would bring in witnesses who would testify about what the plaintiff was like before the injury, and asked whether they would consider such testimony in rendering a verdict:

> And in this lawsuit, there will be many witnesses who knew Dr. Block's son Randy before this occurrence and friends of his son. I assure you we are not bringing any of his enemies in. We are not bringing anybody in to say he was a bad guy. We are bringing in people who knew him, who swam with him, played tennis with him, went to school with him, studied with him, did all of those things that young people do. And we will bring in a couple of his lady friends. Will you listen to all of that testimony and decide what his past was like compared to what his present is concerning all of these elements of damages?

Bergman advised the jurors that the plaintiff was a lawyer and asked jurors about this fact:

> . . . and does anybody have any difficulty with the fact that Bob Olsen is a lawyer, somehow, you think that might enter into your thinking in this case in any way at all? Can all of you put that fact aside and treat Bob just like any other citizen who might be in court with a lawsuit?

When encountering jurors with certain birthing experiences, Bergman questioned them about how their experiences in giving birth might affect their ability to be objective as jurors. He asked:

> BERGMAN: Was the outcome okay?
>
> JUROR: Yeah, it was fine.
>
> BERGMAN: You had a healthy baby?
>
> JUROR: Yeah.
>
> BERGMAN: Is there anything about that experience, knowing that this is a case involving the Olsens' experience in connection with the delivery of Brent, that you feel might cause you to substitute what happened with you to what happened—for what happened to them and make it difficult for you to be fair and objective to both sides, to all sides, in this case?
>
> JUROR: I don't believe so.

In those cases where a particular legal concept or law was involved, the lawyers questioned jurors about attitudes toward the law. In the case where the plaintiff was attempting to hold a corporation liable for the acts of its employee, Welch asked the jurors:

> Now, corporations can act only through their employees and officers who attempt to make money or improve the position of the corporation. The employees of a corporation can also make mistakes for which a corporation may be held liable. Do any of you hold a quarrel with the proposition that holds a corporation liable?

Spence discussed juror attitudes toward the concept of strict liability in tort:

> Now, there is a basic proposition of law that his honor has already mentioned to you—that has something to do with the escape of a dangerous substance—in which he said that—he hasn't ruled on that—but that if there is a dangerous substance, and it escapes and hurts somebody else, the party who had control of that substance may be liable—may have to pay in damages whether or not they were at fault, whether or not they were negligent. That is called negligence—that is called liability without fault—or the legal term is called strict liability. It is well-known in the law. We see it involved all the time in nitroglycerin cases, like where dangerous substances are brought in to an area and it escapes and hurts

somebody else. Now, is there anybody here that would be unwilling to find and to follow that rule of law if the facts support it? And, if this Honor gives you that information. Anybody?

You see, the other side of it is a lot of us think, "Well, if they didn't violate a law or didn't violate—if they weren't negligent, or if—you know—they were careful or tried to do things right they shouldn't have to pay," but his Honor may instruct that they may have to pay even if they were careful, if it got loose and hurt somebody. Would that strike any of you as being unfair?

Would any of you go into the jury room and say: "Well, you know Mr. Spence didn't show there was any negligence, and therefore we're not, you know, and they showed they were careful, and therefore we can't find for Mr. Silkwood and his grandchildren." Would you all be able to follow the instruction of the Court that says you don't have to prove any negligence?

You may not have to prove—or if they prove that they are careful, it may not be a defense—if they had a dangerous substance and it escaped and hurt somebody, they may have to pay whether they were careful or not—could you all follow that rule—any of you that wouldn't?

In exploring jurors' attitudes about malpractice claims and judging doctors, Bergman asked:

Is there anyone who has a feeling deep down of such respect or such admiration for the medical profession as a whole for all the good that it does that it might make it difficult for you to sit here and listen to evidence and actually pass judgment on the conduct of a hospital and on the conduct of doctors? Is there anybody here that has any hesitation or any feeling at all that that might be a problem for you? I assume from the no response that everyone is willing to do that then.

With respect to the concept of professional negligence, Colson asked all jurors:

You have heard His Honor use the word professional negligence. And that is the correct word. And that is the subject that this lawsuit is about, both as to the hospital and to the doctors. I would like to ask if any of you have any feelings, I want to go very slowly on this, I have been trying to rush, but I want to go very slowly here, do any of you have any problems at all that if a mistake is made by a hospital and it results in an injury to someone or a mistake is made by doctors and results in an injury to someone, is there any problem about bringing a lawsuit, a claim for that by the mere fact that they are in a profession of osteopathy, which is a fine profession, osteopathic hospital, which is a fine hospital, you know, hospitals are wonderful, we all love hospitals, but is that a problem with any of you that you feel that Karin should not be in here with her parents and for her day in court to ask you to listen to what we are going to say on her behalf? Does anybody have any problem with that?

In all cases, the lawyers questioned the jurors about their attitudes toward their claims for damages, and their predispositions toward those claims. Corboy questioned jurors about their attitudes toward returning a verdict for pain, suffering, disability, medical expense, and lost wages:

> CORBOY: This is a lawsuit in which my client is seeking damages under the law for pain and suffering. If you find, under all of the law and under all of the evidence, that he is entitled to compensation for pain and suffering, will you sign the verdict for pain and suffering?
>
> JUROR: Yes, I will.
>
> CORBOY: In addition to it not being a cause of action for sympathy, it is a cause of action for disability. Now that means lack of ability to do things. He cannot walk. He cannot talk. He cannot do that sort of thing. If you find, under all the law and under all of the evidence, that he is entitled to compensation for disability, will you sign such a verdict for disability and allot a specific amount of money for that?
>
> JUROR: Yes I will.
>
> CORBOY: If you find, after you hear all of the law and all of the evidence that my client is entitled to compensation for disfigurement and you find that he is disfigured, will you have any hesitancy in signing a verdict for disfigurement?
>
> JUROR: No.
>
> CORBOY: And if, after you have heard all of the law and evidence you find that there has been a very large sum of money expended on behalf of his medical care up to date and that that sum of money is, under the law and under the evidence, related to this accident, this collision, will you have any hesitancy in signing a verdict for that past medical expense?
>
> JUROR: No, I wouldn't.
>
> CORBOY: If you find that he is entitled to future medical expense, whatever that medical expense might be, no matter how many millions of dollars it might be to supply him with the necessary medical care and medical provisions that are needed, will you sign such a verdict?
>
> JUROR: Yes I will.
>
> CORBOY: If you find, after you have heard all of the evidence, that he is entitled to loss of earnings not only since August 23, 1981, but loss of earnings into the future based upon what you find he would have earned into the future, will you have any hesitancy in signing such a verdict?
>
> JUROR: No.

Karen Silkwood died in a car wreck nine days after finding out that she had been exposed to plutonium contamination and would, in all probability, contract lung cancer as a result. Therefore, the plaintiff's claim for actual damages

consisted of nine days of emotional pain and suffering due to the knowledge
of impending lung cancer.

Spence questioned the jurors about their attitudes toward this element of
damage:

> SPENCE: All right. Now, his Honor talked a little bit about damages
> in this case. I want to ask a general question of you about damages
> because in part, damages will be based upon some allegations and
> proofs that the plaintiffs give relative to nine days of suffering, and
> terror, and panic, fear of death—those are the bases of the damages
> for her—and proof that she was injured in a very serious frightening
> way. Now, she died nine days after the damage commenced, so we are
> talking about, in part, nine days of her life. And, the claim is for a mil-
> lion and a half dollars of actual damages for that pain, terror, and fear.
> I want to know if there is anybody here who believes, in their heart,
> that no matter what it was like, what terror there was, what it was like
> for nine days is [not] worth a million and half dollars. Does anybody
> come to that conclusion? Bill Silkwood doesn't set the amount. That
> is the amount that I have asked for my client, on behalf of my client,
> based upon my judgment. Pretty soon six of you will have to make your
> judgment. Are there any of you that feel prejudiced against my client
> and his three grandchildren, for whom this case is brought, because
> his lawyer had the audacity to ask for a million and a half dollars for
> those nine days?
>
> . . . .
>
> SPENCE: I'm concerned about that issue, and I want to know if any of
> you feel any sort of resentment, or distrust, for my client Bill Silkwood,
> because I have asked for a million and a half dollars involving nine
> days of her life?

After introducing the damages his clients will claim, Bergman probed juror
attitudes with respect to these claims:

> Is there anybody on the panel having heard that description and having
> heard that number who has a view that $10,000,000 is just plain too much
> money for anybody in this case, no matter what the evidence? I ask you
> to really dig down and search your feelings on this . . . I was asking you
> about the amount that I mentioned, the $10,000,000, and let me say pre-
> liminarily and I think most of you probably know this already, it's your
> function and your function alone as a jury to determine the amount of
> damages that are fair and reasonable in a particular case, and there are
> really two things that I want to ask you.
>
> First of all, does anybody have a reaction based upon the amount that
> I just gave you, $10,000,000, that might enter into your thinking in this
> case, make it difficult for you to hear the case, or do you have any view
> about that amount alone in the abstract as being just simply unreachable
> or too much, no matter what the evidence. Anybody have any feelings

about that? So everybody can start out with an open mind on the amount
of damages and is willing to do that job.

In another case, with respect to damages for pain and suffering, Bergman
questioned the jury about their willingness and ability to place a value on pain
and suffering:

> BERGMAN: Let me depart from the individual questions to the panel
> as a whole. On the subject of damages, you know that there are people
> that just hold the view, and I am not here to argue with the view, that
> you just can't put a value on some of these things that I have men-
> tioned—pain, suffering, mental anguish, emotional distress—and who
> would not be prepared to do that, would have difficulty with that?
>
>   Is there anybody on the panel who has that idea, who feels that way,
> that you just can't put a value on it or that it doesn't matter because
> it doesn't help the situation and therefore you'd be reluctant to do it
> even though there might be evidence to support it? Anybody on the
> back row feel that way? Mrs. _____?
>
> JUROR: You know. I mentioed that before.
>
> BERGMAN: Uh-huh.
>
> JUROR: I feel like, you know, how do you decide, okay, this patient,
> you know, went through this much, so much pain, a hundred million
> dollars for that, you know. I feel like it's very difficult to put an amount
> on, you know, I'm not saying that I don't have sympathy one way or
> another, because as I said, I have seen both sides of the coin. But I
> feel that that is rather a difficult decision to try to put some dollar
> amount because whatever dollar amount on that you put on is not
> going to alleviate the suffering that that family or that particular patient
> or the doctor or whoever went through, you know.
>
> BERGMAN: Mrs. _____, when we get to the end of the trial, if we
> are at that point and you are on the jury, are you going to be hesitant
> or unwilling to assign a monetary value to Shanna Morrison's pain and
> suffering and mental anguish?
>
> Juror: If the evidence proved that a dollar amount should be given to
> the plaintiff, I would have no problem with that. I just—I think in my
> own mind that I would have a hard time deciding what dollar amount
> to put on it.
>
> BERGMAN: There are other things like the medical expenses, but we
> are not . . . talking about anything that has come out of anybody's
> pocket. I'm talking about the intangible kinds of human losses. I think
> you'll be instructed that the law says that they are compensable. It is
> up to the jury to decide how much. What I'm asking is, "Are you going
> to be able to assign a value to those things?"
>
> JUROR: I suppose with some instruction, according to what the law
> says, that would help, I suppose. But I still feel like I'd have a hard

time trying to decide in my own mind whether a million or five million or ten million would be an adequate amount.

BERGMAN: You have expressed there may be a number of issues where you would have a hard time in this. I'm not—

JUROR: I'm just trying to be honest with you. As I said, I would try to keep an open mind and listen to both sides of it. Being in the medical profession and knowing how things go and how things operate you know, it is—it is difficult, but I would try to stay open-minded about it. I'm just giving you this.

BERGMAN: I would appreciate that you would try to do that. Let me put it to you straight. Can you be fair, can you give me any assurance that you can be fair and impartial to my clients?

JUROR: I would try my best.

After introducing the concept of punitive damages, Bergman asked jurors about their attitudes toward awarding punitive damages:

My question is, is there anything about the concept of punitive damages that makes you feel uncomfortable, makes you unwilling to consider as we start out this case? Everybody willing to consider punitives if asked to by the Court?

Habush outlined what the evidence would be with respect to damages and then questioned the jurors about their attitudes toward such damages:

HABUSH: Again assuming the evidence is as I have described it, is there anyone who feels that they could not sit on such a case, and judge such a case, and award damages in such a case? Is there anyone who comes to this jury and has in their mind a set amount above which they would never agree to award a verdict regardless of the evidence, that they have a predetermined feeling before they hear the evidence of what kind of damages they would be willing to award?

JUROR: I think I might have, I think I would have a feeling that there might be a certain sum beyond which I would not go.

HABUSH: I think everyone probably feels that way, Mrs. _____. I was just wondering if you would be able to fairly sit and listen to the evidence and not prejudge it.

JUROR: Oh, yes, I think I could do that fairly as long as it's—as long— you know, I think I could do that.

HABUSH: Having that in mind what I have just told you of the damages that I expect the evidence to show totals up close to $800,000 without regard to pain and suffering, is there anyone on this panel who would be unable to award damages in excess of a million dollars if the evidence justified it, if the evidence justified it?

§5.11 —Strategies for Getting at Juror Attitudes and Beliefs

Each lawyer had a strategy for convincing the jurors that they should be honest in their voir dire responses with respect to admitting bias and prejudice. On those occasions when permitted by the court, in their introductions, the lawyers commented on the importance of answering honestly. For example, immediately after introducing himself and explaining the nature of voir dire, Gerry Spence stated:

> You know, we have heard the word " prejudice" and I'm prejudiced about the word " prejudice" because I don't want to tell anyone that I'm prejudiced. And, I just wonder if anybody else is prejudiced against the word "prejudice." Anyone have a sense of that? By that I mean we are not supposed to be prejudiced—and I don't want to admit to doing anything that I'm not supposed to do—so it is pretty hard for me to say I'm prejudiced, but on the other hand anybody that has any opinion about anything, that has any sense or any brains about any thought or thinking in his life has an opinion about it and, therefore, if you've got an opinion I guess that makes you, you would have a prejudice one way or the other. For example, if you have eaten an apple, I guess you might have an opinion about the apple. And, you might be prejudiced either for or against it. And, that is the way the law means to use that word—not in the derogatory fashion.
>
> The biggest crime that could be committed in this courtroom today would be for somebody who really has an opinion about something—and we all have to have opinions if we've got any brains to think with—to have an opinion about something and not be willing to say it because they were sort of prejudiced against admitting their prejudice. So, with that thought in mind—and I'm sure counsel for the defense shares that with me—and I know the court does, I want to ask you some questions about that, if I might.

Similarly, in an effort to convince the jurors to answer questions honestly, Lantz Welch stated:

> I'm trying to ask questions that I think are relevant to the issues that will come up in this case, and the facts and some of your feelings—by the way, we're going to be asking you about your feelings and your opinions, and we all have opinions and feelings. You don't come into this courtroom with just a vacuum in your head. It's not a crime, it's not bad to have an opinion about something. What is bad is not to be willing to share that opinion with the proper questions asked of you, so we'll be seeking some of your opinions and feelings about things that we think can bear upon your deliberations in this case. And this is, of course, taking us, we hope, to the desired end of this fair and impartial jury for both sides. . . . It's important to both sides of this case for you to think over your answers

to these questions very carefully, because—and here is part of the trial, we could spend this time together and an unintentional oversight on your part or misstatement or failure to follow a question could lead to our trying this case for three or four days and because of the problems that I'm mentioning now, the verdict might have to be set aside. But it's a very significant portion of the trial.

In his introduction, Bergman told the jurors:

There are some things that are thrown at you during the course of a trial that you didn't know were coming. Sometimes some people come into the courtroom as witnesses that you didn't know would be there. We don't want you to be in a situation on down the line during the trial, or particularly during the deliberations, where all of a sudden you are confronted with a problem. The idea here is that you folks won't be.

During the course of their questioning, the lawyers asked the witnesses, point blank, whether their attitudes would create problems. For example, Habush asked all jurors:

I believe the judge asked you this question generally, but I will ask it again. Is there anyone for any reason whatsoever from anyone who has influenced you, or anything you have read, or heard, or seen, or believed, that would be uncomfortable sitting on this case; or I guess the best way to put it is—if you were the plaintiff would you feel comfortable with you as a juror?

In many cases the lawyers asked the jurors to comment on their suitability as jurors by asking them to put themselves in the plaintiff's position. In this way the jurors were forced to evaluate themselves, such as when Spence encountered the woman who had worked for a defense firm which represented primarily insurance companies.

SPENCE: You know, we've got to get a unanimous verdict here. So one, you know, one may be enough, one person, that holds out could be enough to deprive my client of a verdict, and if I were representing you, would you feel comfortable as one of the persons on the jury who has worked for a defense law firm, who worked for large corporations, who go against cases of this kind as a matter of habit, would you feel comfortable about that?

When Bergman encountered a juror whose son had clerked with one of the defendant's law firms while in law school and who was expecting to take a job with the firm, he asked the juror whether he would want a juror such as himself if he were in the plaintiff's position:

BERGMAN: Anybody who is part of the twenty know any of these people?

JUROR: I don't know any of those, but my son will start for them May 18th, and is already working for the firm. He is not—he is employed—

BERGMAN: In what capacity?

JUROR: He is finishing law school and he has been working there for a year.

BERGMAN: Do you think my client ought to worry about that?

JUROR: I don't know.

BERGMAN: Your son could well have an interest of sorts.

JUROR: He may have done some work on this case. He has been there a year. I don't have any idea. I don't talk to my son about his—

BERGMAN: I don't know. I can't make that judgment.

BERGMAN: Well, you are the only one—

JUROR: I don't talk to my son about his law practice or his cases.

BERGMAN: Do you think that when you get back to the jury room that, knowing that your son is going to start with this firm in a couple of weeks, if you felt that the evidence warranted it, that you might be reluctant to return a verdict or compromise an amount? In some way would that relationship compromise my client? Do you think that might happen?

JUROR: I can't—I can't say myself. I think that I'm fairly impartial. But I think that the person that is bringing the case might have an insecurity about that because, of course, I would be for the firm that my son is working for.

BERGMAN: Yeah. I know that my mother would be for mine.

JUROR: I'm for my son. I mean you would have to make the judgment. I'm a fairly impartial person, but—

BERGMAN: I believe you are. Everybody tries to be. The question is whether there is something about the parties or the line-up in a case that gets you more personally involved in it that you would be as just a neutral, detached and objective person. When I hear that somebody's son is going to be on the low end of the totem pole in Mr. Saunders' firm, you know, one of the questions that is usually asked—I think that, Mr. Saunders, I have heard him ask it—if you were sitting here as one of the parties, would you want a juror sitting there hearing your case with your frame of mind or your relationship to the case?

JUROR: No.

BERGMAN: With that, Your Honor, I would ask that this juror be excused for cause.

THE COURT: Very well.

In other instances, jurors were asked whether their attitudes caused them to place a greater burden of proof on the plaintiff. For example, when encoun-

tering a juror who went to one of the defendant doctors for his personal physician, Bergman questioned as follows:

BERGMAN: You heard who all of the parties are?

JUROR: I do know Dr. Houston and Dr. Layle. They are my doctors.

BERGMAN: So you go to the same office where Dr. Hanson practices.

JUROR: Regularly.

BERGMAN: Have you seen Dr. Hanson there on occasion?

JUROR: I have seen him, yes.

BERGMAN: How long have you been going there?

JUROR: Probably ten years.

BERGMAN: And you intend to go back?

JUROR: Oh, yes.

BERGMAN: As the need arises?

JUROR: Oh, yes.

BERGMAN: Do you think that service on this jury might put you in a
position where you feel like you might have to compromise somewhere, either on who your doctors are, or as to my clients and their
claims.

JUROR: Mo.

BERGMAN: Do you think that you could be completely fair and impartial in this case?

JUROR: Yes.

BERGMAN: Do you think that if you felt that it was warranted by the
evidence that you could return a verdict against Dr. Hanson and also
this Mid-America Medical Consultants which includes your two
doctors?

Juror: Yes.

BERGMAN: Thank you, sir. Let me ask that one more way. Do you
think, the way that I asked Mr. _____, do you think that the plaintiffs
in this case are going to start with a little bit heavier burden of convincing you than they would otherwise if Dr. Layle and Dr. Houston were
not your physicians?

JUROR: That's a tough question. I think that it probably would have
a bearing, yes.

BERGMAN: Do you think that you would need a little more evidence?

JUROR: Yes, I would.

BERGMAN: A little more convincing than you would need if you didn't
have this relationship?

JUROR: Yes.

BERGMAN: Your Honor, with that, I would ask that Mr. _____ be excused for cause.

THE COURT: Very well.

With another juror, Bergman asked:

We wouldn't be starting out with any heavier burden on the part of the claimant in this case than we would with you, than we would presumably with anybody else.

In many instances, the lawyers got at juror attitudes by framing questions that forced jurors to take a stand on an issue in a way that clearly disclosed their attitudes. Questions were formulated which conceptualized attitudes for or against some issue and which required a yes or no answer. Corboy skillfully used this strategy. Corboy's case involved a totally paralyzed man with a normal projected life expectancy who would require constant medical attention for the rest of his life. Corboy would present evidence by medical experts to the effect that the plaintiff would require millions of dollars of medical treatment throughout his lifetime. It could be expected that the plaintiff's concern was that some jurors might have a tendency to place a cap on the amount of recovery they would allow, or that they would be shocked by a request of $20 million for medical expenses. In order to get at this attitude, he asked the question of all jurors individually, "Do you believe in the phrase that life is sacred?" Those who answered the question in the positive could be expected to form the attitude that the plaintiff's life should be sustained at any cost, and therefore, plaintiff should be given a verdict for an amount that would cover the expenses necessary to sustain his life.

Spence skillfully used the same strategy. After having difficulty in getting the jurors to express clear attitudes toward union involvement, Spence formulated a question about unions, requiring a "yes" or "no" answer, which conceptualized attitudes for or against union involvement.

SPENCE: Is there anybody here, all things being equal, assuming that you had, you know, a union that was alright, that did something for the employees, and you had a chance to either be on the union or not, is there anybody here—just how would you choose to be? If it was all, you know, it was a good union, did something for its employees, but you had a choice to be on the union side, to be a part of that union and join it, or not to join it, which would you go? And, I will start with you, Mrs. _____, how would you go?

This type of question forced the jurors to take a stand one way or the other on the question of unions. For example, one juror responded, "All things being equal, and being a good union, I would not join the union." Another juror stated, "Well, all things being equal, and I have the right to choose whether I wanted to be in a union or not a union, if I felt it was a good union, I would join it." At the very least, this type of question encouraged jurors to explain their position. One juror responded:

JUROR: I'm not sure—I'm not sure.

SPENCE: Is there some reason why you are not sure? Is there something going on there that we could share with each other?

JUROR: yes. I just had an experience with United Farm Workers Union.

SPENCE: Was it an unpleasant experience?

JUROR: Oh, yes. It was tear gas that had been thrown, and it was, yes, an unpleasant experience.

SPENCE: You wouldn't want to join a union like that, would you?

JUROR: No, I wouldn't. No. But, I think it was a good thing before Chavez got in it, or they would still be making a dollar an hour.

SPENCE: You see the reason I'm asking this question about the union is because Karen Silkwood was a member of a union, and there are allegations in the case that her involvement in the union had something to do with the problem that came up. That is, Kerr-McGee makes allegations that are related to the union—

JUROR: She belonged to a union?

Spence: She belonged to a union.

JUROR: Well, no, I don't agree with that. Just because she worked for a union.

SPENCE: Well, they are trying to say things about that that I'm not permitted to talk about right now.

JUROR: I don't know that much about it. My husband belongs to a union.

SPENCE: You see what is going to happen here is eventually you may have to decide whether Kerr-McGee's position is correct, and their allegations against Karen Silkwood, and what she was involved in, in her union activities, or whether Karen Silkwood's activity is correct. And, of course, she's dead and her lips are sealed, and she can't say, but there will be people to testify here, as best they can, whether her position is correct. And, of course, Mr. Silkwood wants me to find out if any of you, because of your experience, would feel that maybe—well, you could lean one way or the other because of your own personal experience.

JUROR: Well, then, I have a personal experience at home. My husband belongs to a union, which is the postal union.

SPENCE: Does he think that is all right?

JUROR: And, I think it is all right. Yes, I do. I certainly do, yes.

Bergman skillfully questioned jurors in a way that forced them to admit their prejudices. He patiently established so many areas that gave rise to potential bias that the jurors were forced to admit that they would not make good jurors. He did not question their integrity, but rather simply elicited so many areas of involvement with the issues of the case that the jurors were forced to admit their bias. Bergman pressed the jurors on the question of whether they, because of their particular backgrounds and attitudes, would demand a higher burden of proof for the plaintiffs than would other jurors. In the case of a woman whose husband was connected with the medical profession, he questioned as follows:

BERGMAN: Mrs _____, I'm going to follow up on a couple of things the Judge asked you because there initially seemed to be some hesitancy in your response and I'm going to say, candor is what we want. We want to know what your real feelings are, and everybody is going to appreciate that. You made the comment that your husband is with the company that is in the medical instruments industry. What company is that?

JUROR: Greb X-ray.

BERGMAN: Greb?

JUROR: Greb X-ray.

BERGMAN: How long has he been with that company?

JUROR: Eight years.

BERGMAN: Does he have a territory that would include Humana Hospital?

JUROR: He does not call on Humana. He calls on the building, the medical building, next to Humana. It's the Suburban Medical Building.

BERGMAN: That includes the offices of several of the Defendants in the case?

JUROR: Yes.

BERGMAN: Dr. Jouvenat, Dr. Rubin, and you've heard the ones. Let me ask you this: Do you feel you will be under any additional pressure in this case in connection with your deliberations, not only on the question of who might be liable, but on the questions of what the damages would be, knowing that your husband has got to go to those same offices and, you know, try to sell his product in a competitive market? Is that going to be a problem for you? This is very important to the Plaintiffs in this case to know.

JUROR: No, I wouldn't—I would hope it certainly wouldn't affect his business, no, and I would not assume that it would.

BERGMAN: Well, my question really is, whether it's going to affect you.

JUROR: Okay.

BERGMAN: And not his business. Whether, even the thought of that, or the concern about that, that might develop, at any point during the trial—

JUROR: No.

BERGMAN: Might be a problem for you.

JUROR: No, I would not be concerned about that.

BERGMAN: Okay. On the other point that you talked about, the question of your high opinion of Humana, have you been there at all?

JUROR: No, I have met several of the doctors, socially, and one of my friends has stayed there, and I thought it was a very nice hospital.

BERGMAN: In connection with your husband's business, do you have occasion to entertain doctors, be out socially with them?

JUROR: We have been invited by medical doctors to weddings, Christmas parties, and such.

BERGMAN: Do you feel that—have you met any of these doctors?

JUROR: No, I don't think so.

Bergman: What type of X-ray equipment does your husband sell, or what does his company manufacture?

JUROR: They don't manufacture. They are a distributor for Picker. They sell anything to deal with X-ray basically. They have several subsidiaries. They cover everything from film to this new magnetic stuff, which I'm not sure about.

BERGMAN: I don't mean to dwell on this, but you're—the hesitancy in your initial responses is what concerned me. Are we going to start out in this case—are the Plaintiffs going to start out with you, perhaps, whether you want to be that way or not, with a higher burden to convince you that Humana may have done something wrong than we might start out with if we are some other hospital or some other type of case?

JUROR: No. I hope to keep an open mind.

BERGMAN: That's the part that concerns me, is, I don't want to go into this case on a hope, that your mind—will be open. I want to be sure that everybody's mind—and I know you'll try— I'm not questioning your integrity, but there are certain types of cases that for any number of reasons a particular person probably shouldn't serve on and from the whole gamut of your responses, the contacts you have with the doctors, your opinion of the hospital, how your husband's business is tied in with that industry and these very medical groups that are involved here, do you feel that you would be an appropriate person to serve on this jury, where we could be assured that we're not going to run into one of those hurdles or blocks somewhere down the line?

JUROR: I believe there will probably be someone else who might be able to have more of a clear slate on the subject rather than I can.

THE COURT: I'm going to excuse this panelist. You may step down.

BERGMAN: Thank you very much. I appreciate your candor.

With an insurance adjuster, Bergman used the same patient, skillful approach:

BERGMAN: Mr. _____.

JUROR: Yes, sir.

BERGMAN: Okay. You have three children?

JUROR: Yes, sir.

BERGMAN: And what are their ages?

JUROR: Twenty-nine, twenty-two, and nineteen.

BERGMAN: Do you have any grandchildren?

Juror: No.

BERGMAN: Okay. Were you present for the delivery of any of your children?

JUROR: No.

Bergman: Where were they delivered?

JUROR: All in Portland, Oregon.

BERGMAN: Were there any other pregnancies that your wife had that didn't result in a child?

JUROR: No.

BERGMAN: Are your children all in good health?

JUROR: Yes.

BERGMAN: Were any of them in need of any special resuscitation or special care early in life?

JUROR: No.

BERGMAN: You are with Atlas Mutual Insurance Company?

JUROR: Yes, sir.

BERGMAN: And what is your function in the company?

JUROR: I'm corporate secretary.

BERGMAN: Your function on a corporate staff level?

JUROR: Yes, sir.

BERGMAN: Is this their home base?

JUROR: Kansas City, Missouri.

BERGMAN: And what type of lines of insurance do they get into?

JUROR: Personally, I'm in the property end. I'm secretary, but I do extensive travel and field production work. I'm in charge of claims and all the other routine things that go into the insurance business.

BERGMAN: What other lines of coverage are they into other than the property that you're into?

JUROR: Automobile, substandard automobile.

BERGMAN: Do they get into any professional insurance of any kind?

JUROR: No.

BERGMAN: Let me ask you this, and I'm sort of struggling with this a minute ago, being in that industry, the insurance industry, there's opinions about litigation, and very strong opinions, sometimes about litigation.

JUROR: Yes, sir.

BERGMAN: And whether it's a good thing or a bad thing, whether verdicts are too high, too low, et cetera. Having been with the insurance
industry, have you developed any views of your own that might make
it difficult for you to be completely fair and impartial when there are
people here who are seeking compensation for some injuries?

JUROR: I don't know that I have anything in concrete, but on a given
case, yes, I think there have been some unfair awards made.

BERGMAN: Are you thinking of any types of awards in particular?

JUROR: This would be in the property line, where something is
destroyed by a hazard, a fire, or a theft and the amount claimed for
that particular loss. I think there's a tendency oftentimes to go for all
you can get, and I have to take the conservative point of view and try
to think; I like to see a claim paid for not one penny less or one penny
more than is just, and that's a very difficult thing to establish.

BERGMAN: I'm going to get into this a little more in a little while, but
there was—this is a different breed of claim than a property claim.

JUROR: Surely.

BERGMAN: We're talking about this case about various types of damages, some of which are not tangible. Some of which, are intangible,
pain, suffering, disability, that sort of thing.

JUROR: Surely.

BERGMAN: Do you get into the adjustment of any of those kinds of
claims or—

JUROR: We don't write that type of insurance, so, no.

BERGMAN: Do you have any preconceived notions or opinions about
whether or not those kinds of claims ought to be made? In other words,
whether monetary compensation should be paid for intangible kinds
of losses?

JUROR: I think it should be paid if it is proven beyond doubt that someone is liable for that particular injury, arriving at the amount is a very
difficult problem.

BERGMAN: Is that a process that you feel you can get into on a very
objective basis in light of the fact that you've got to go back to the office
and face your company? Might it be difficult for you to put yourself
in that position?

JUROR: Yes, it possibly would be.

BERGMAN: Do you feel that if you were in the position of the Plaintiff
in this case that you would be concerned about you, in other words,
about your state of mind as we start this case?

JUROR: I think they might because of the industry that I'm in, although
I'm an honest person, I think. Yet, I think there'd be doubt in the mind
because of the business I'm in.

BERGMAN: I'm not asking you to read our minds and I'm not questioning your integrity. I appreciate your honesty because this is exactly what this process is about. What I'm really asking is whether there is reason to be concerned on the part of the Plaintiffs that you might have a reaction in this case, where there's going to be a very sizable claim made, and a lot of it for intangible types of things, where you might find it more difficult than maybe someone who doesn't have your background to look at it objectively.

JUROR: Yes, I think the answer would be yes, I would find it somewhat difficult.

BERGMAN: All right, I appreciate your honesty. Your Honor, I would challenge for cause.

THE COURT: We'll excuse this panelist.

§5.12   Setting the Tone for the Trial

The lawyers used voir dire to begin setting the tone for the trial. For each lawyer, the tone was serious, yet personal. It is obvious that these lawyers saw their cases as important events for themselves and their clients. They presented their cases as the life and death struggles of their clients. The lawyers viewed the jury selection process and the function of the jury seriously. If the lawyers wanted the jury to take their claims for damages seriously, then the lawyers themselves had to behave in a serious manner. For example, while explaining the purpose of voir dire, Spence told the jury of the importance of the case:

> I need to ask you a few questions about some things that his Honor has given us, on both sides, a chance to ask about, and to get acquainted with you just a little bit. It is an important case, ladies and gentlemen, and I hope that you would understand that if I were representing you, you would want me to find out as much as possible about these people who are going to have the control of your very important case. I think you would want me to find out about these people if I were representing you, and I hope you will be patient with me if I ask the questions about that.

Spence further gave the case a tone of importance and significance when he asked a juror, "Do you recognize that the case may have some extraordinary importance?" When the juror replied that she did, Spence continued, by stating, "And, that it may be a case that could change the course of not only the law but the country." Finally, in this regard, he asked, "Would you like to take part in something that is as important as this case?"

In making his introduction, Habush told the jury, "Again, as the judge indicated, we are not trying to be nosy, but we have a very short period of time that we have to try to get to know you; and it's a very important case to both sides . . ."

Bergman set a serious tone for the trial when he asked jurors whether they had strong enough stomachs to sit through a medical malpractice case with issues such as his. Later, when encountering a juror whose wife was a nurse, he again set a serious tone when he questioned about bias in the following manner:

> There's an issue that I want to discuss with you because it is a serious issue in the case and that is, there is a very serious contention being made that the nurses in this instance were negligent, and I'm going to call several of these nurses as witnesses, and may—it may appear to you that we're being tough with them or whatever, but since your wife is a nurse, I'm wondering whether you would have a tendency to identify with those nurses and perhaps, you know penalize me if you think I'm getting too zealous on behalf of my clients, that sort of thing. Do you think we could get into that kind of situation?

At all phases of voir dire, Bergman emphasized the serious nature of his questioning. At one point he told a juror that "this is going to be an emotional case." In asking jurors about their ability to place a value on the plaintiff's losses, he told jurors that "this is a very serious question in this case because it is a sad case." In asking a juror whether his decision would be influenced by the fact that his wife worked for a doctor and might be embarrassed at work if her husband returned a plaintiff's verdict, he stated, "But this is a very serious question. Your wife will have to work?"

In questioning a juror about a commitment not to discuss the case with her husband who had a background in entomology, Corboy set a serious tone for the trial when he referred to the sacredness of jury duty:

> Now, I certainly am not entitled nor is the defendant entitled to any opportunity to form barriers in the married lives of jurors. We are not expected nor are you expected to live in a vacuum; but you can appreciate and the Court, I think, has told you the sacredness of jury duty and how, as an officer of this Court, which you may shortly become, that it is your responsibility to find the facts in this case, not your husband's?

Colson set a serious tone when questioning jurors about their ability to find fault with the doctors and return a verdict for the plaintiffs. He asked:

> . . . would that cause any of you to say, "No, I don't want to serve on anything that's that serious or that tragic." Would that be a problem to you, Ma'am?

At the same time, these lawyers were friendly and personal in their interaction with the jury. They related to the jurors as people. The voir dire was one of the few places in the trial in which they engaged in humor with the jurors and the court. While the judge was questioning the jurors about whether they had a regular course of exercise or physical fitness, Spence introduced humor when he cautioned, "Don't ask that of counsel, your honor." Spence's introduction to the jury was very friendly and personal when he told them that he spoke "Western" and hoped they did too, and when a juror noted that she had three girls, one married, and two about to be married, and that two at once was a horrendous situation, Colson responded, "Particularly when you are paying for the wedding."

§5.13 Introducing Concepts and Evidence: Conditioning the Jury

While probing juror attitudes and gaining juror commitments, the lawyers also introduced evidence, issues, concepts, and procedures that would arise in the trial. In order to discuss a juror's attitude toward a jury instruction, legal concept, defense, or piece of evidence, the lawyers explained or described the matter in question. By introducing and explaining the matter in issue, the lawyers conditioned the jurors to things that would transpire later in the trial.

The lawyers introduced the facts of the case and concepts that would arise in the trial whenever possible. In asking jurors if they were familiar with his case, Welch presented the facts:

> I'd like to see if you are acquainted with the accident that brings us here today. On September 29, 1978, almost three and a half years ago, at about 7:45 a.m., Mr. Cooper was eastbound on 23rd Street going up the hill just east of 435. That would be 23rd that would take you on toward Independence. He was traveling just under the speed limit of 55 at that time. The defendant, Raymond A. Hawk, was driving a company van owned by General Standard Company. He was traveling at about the same speed coming in the westbound lane. So my client is going up the hill and he's coming down the hill. . . . There was a big concrete medial strip between them. Somehow the van got over the medial strip on our side of the road and hit us head-on. Now these are the facts of the accident. My first question, then, is, did any of you all happen to have witnessed the accident, any of you come along later, any of you read any account of it in the newspaper or see any TV coverage, or have any facts in your mind from any source whatsoever about this accident?

When discussing a juror's truck driving experience, Habush introduced the concept of "chocking truck tires" when he questioned as follows:

> HABUSH: Have you delivered at warehouses?
>
> JUROR: No, I don't. I haul scrap.
>
> HABUSH: Scrap. Are you familiar with the procedure of chocking the tires on trucks?
>
> JUROR: Yes.
>
> HABUSH: Have you done that?
>
> JUROR: Yes.
>
> HABUSH: Chocking, just for the benefit of the other jurors, is a wedge, something you put under the tires to keep it from rolling; is that correct?

Bergman introduced the facts of his case involving the failure to diagnose Hodgkin's disease in the following way:

> I want to tell you a little bit about the facts of the case without arguing the case. On September 6th, 1983, Shanna Morrison went to Dr. Hanson. Her mother brought her, complaining of an enlarged lymph node under her arm pit. She had been fatigued over the summer and the spring before that. She had been bitten by a cat over the summer.
>
> Dr. Hanson is a specialist in internal medicine, hematology and oncology. He made the diagnosis of something called cat scratch fever. It turned out that diagnosis was wrong.
>
> The following year, 1984, about five months later, the correct diagnosis was made of Hodgkin's disease, which is a form of cancer. Following that, in February of 1984, Shanna went down to M.D. Anderson Hospital in Houston, Texas, where she has been treated ever since. She has been through a variety of different kinds of treatment that you will hear about—chemotherapy, radiation, bone marrow transplants—and it appears that the treatment has failed to cure her.
>
> We really don't know what the future holds for Shanna. You know, the doctors don't have much more to offer her. That is her situation and that is the skeletal outline of the facts of the case.
>
> The claim in the case is that Dr. Hanson was negligent in failing to do a proper work-up and making the diagnosis of cat scratch disease, failing to make the diagnosis of Hodgkin's disease.

Upon discovering a juror who was a teacher, Corboy used the opportunity to interject additional facts about his client:

> In any event, I think Randy—that's what John Randolf Block's name is; they call him Randy—went to the University of Illinois down state for one summer. He went to Princeton University. And during the summertime, he went to what is called Northern Illinois in DeKalb one summer. And he went to the University of Illinois another summer and then went to the University of Chicago Law School.
>
> So there is a similarity of your backgrounds; also, that he is a teacher. And he teaches at DePaul. He is not teaching right now. He is incapacitated; but, in any event, does that teacher background in any way prevent you from giving the defendants the kind of trial they are entitled to in this lawsuit?

Knowing that the defense would attempt to characterize Karen Silkwood as a union agitator, Spence introduced the jury to the fact that her union activities would be an issue in the case. Spence also forewarned the jury that the defendant would seek to show that Karen Silkwood had a different type of lifestyle than the jurors, and conditioned the jurors to the idea that she was entitled to the same rights under the law as people with other lifestyles.

While discussing a juror's mother's experience with keeping medical records as a registered nurse, Colson introduced the issue of whether the plaintiff's medical records were accurately kept:

COLSON: Does she handle charts as a secretary?

JUROR: Yes, sir, I think so.

COLSON: So that she's working with charts day in and day out?

JUROR: Yes, sir.

COLSON: That's important in this case, whether or not charts were kept properly and so forth. Do you have any personal knowledge of that?

Bergman used his questions with respect to jurors' birthing experiences to introduce many of the medical terms that would be important in the trial. For example, since the appropriateness of fetal monitoring was an issue in the case, most jurors were asked about the role of fetal monitoring in their own personal experiences. This continual reference to fetal monitoring stressed its importance. An example of the questions is as follows:

BERGMAN: One of the things I was going to ask later on is about childbirth situations. This case arises out of a Labor and Delivery Room incident, and involved in the case was some electronic fetal monitoring. Was there fetal monitoring done with regard to your wife's case? Juror: Yes, there was an internal fetal monitor.

In the same fashion, Bergman introduced such concepts as "resuscitation," "paracervical block," and "marcaine."

When the lawyers questioned jurors about their attitudes toward the damage claims as set out above, they introduced the elements of damages that would be involved in the case. Habush introduced his damage claims as follows:

Members of the jury, I believe that the evidence is going to show that Roger Schulz, age 49, as a result of this incident is a paraplegic and paralyzed, and that he has experienced paralysis, loss of bowel functions, loss of bladder functions, loss of sexual functions, and will be so disabled for the rest of his life.

I believe the evidence will show that there has been incurred $88,000 in past medical expenses, $150,000 in lost income, that it's expected over $200,000 in future medical expenses, and it's expected over $200,000 in lost income in the future.

We believe that we will show that he is experiencing constant pain as a result of these injuries, assuming the evidence is as I have described it.

Again assuming the evidence is as I have described it, is there anyone who feels that they could not sit on such a case, and judge such a case, and award damages in such a case?

When probing juror attitudes toward the plaintiffs' elements of damage, Bergman introduced their claims for damages:

> I want to be sure that everybody understands what the claims are that are being made in this case. There is a claim in the case for Brent Olsen for his personal injuries, and that falls into two general categories. One category would be described generally as "tangible damages," things like medical bills, future medical bills, cost of care, that sort of thing. Another category is the "intangible damages," things such as pain and suffering, disability, disfigurement, both for the past five years and then on into the future. There's one claim being made today for all the damages that will ever be, ever can be made arising out of this incident.
>
> There's a separate claim in the case for Teri Olsen, Brent's mother, in a variety of categories of damages. Her own physical injury, her emotional distress, that sort of thing, and there's a third category of damages called—that may or may not be in the case by the time it's submitted to you—called "punitive damages," and there's a claim being made for punitive damages against the physicians, not all the physicians, against Dr. Younglove, and against Humana, and the Judge will instruct you at the appropriate time if and when that claim is submitted to you.
>
> The claim that we're making on behalf of Brent because of the magnitude of what we consider to be his injuries is $10,000,000, and that's a claim for everything that's happened to him the past five years and everything that will happen to him for the rest of his life, and I mention that number and I mention all this background because I've got a few more questions that I want to ask you and then I'll try to conclude.

While discussing juror attitudes toward returning a verdict for damage elements such as pain and suffering, disability, disfigurement, past and future medical expense, and past and future wage loss, Corboy was familiarizing the jury with the elements of damage in the case:

> My client in this lawsuit is seeking damages for various elements that he expects to prove, intends to prove in this lawsuit. One of those elements of damage that he expects or intends to prove is that called pain and suffering. If my client under the law is entitled to pain and suffering, compensation for it, will you sign such a verdict?
>
> . . . .
>
> And then the other elements I believe will be loss of income and loss of future income and medical expenses and future medical expenses, all right sir?

Spence explained to the jury that the plaintiff's actual damages would be based on the claims that she spent nine days of "suffering, and terror, and panic, fear of death . . . and proof that she was injured in a very serious frightening way." He told the jury that the claim was for $1,500,000 for that pain, terror, and fear.

Under the pretext of asking jurors about their experiences with respect to the types of injuries and damages sustained by the plaintiff, Welch explained the nature of his client's disability, introduced concepts that would be used in the trial to describe this disability, and conditioned the jury to the evidence to come:

> Now, I'm going to ask you a little bit about your knowledge of the injuries suffered by my client, so I can find out a little bit about your experiences in your families. Following this collision, aside from the lacerations and all these things, there was a condition known as a herniated disc. It was at two different levels in his cervical spine up in his neck. It brought about two separate spinal surgeries called laminectomies, or discectomies. It's called various things, but the operation where a doctor goes in through the front of the throat, back into the cervical spine and removes the disc that exists between the vertebrae. He did this two times, and each time he also went to the iliac crest—that's the crest of the hip here—went in there, took a certain type of drill they use, takes the bones out, puts that in, and did what is called . . . a fusion. So there were two laminectomies and two fusions. With that information, have you or any members of your immediate family ever been subjected to such surgeries, whether they be in the neck area or the low back?

While questioning a juror about his experiences with quadriparesis, Colson introduced elements of his clients damages:

> COLSON: Does anyone, even though this is technically called quadri-paresis, as distinguished from quadriplegic—plegic means that you can't move anything and paresis means that there's a tightness or spas-ticity or inability, but you have no control over it, and then it changes on you. But you have still no ability to use these limbs to amount to anything, I mean, but do any of you have any knowledge of that subject at all? Does paraplegia mean anything to you or have you been exposed to that part of things medically . . . have you had any exposure to that? I don't mean seeing someone in the gift shop, but I'm talking about actually on the floor where you worked for any period of time.
>
> JUROR: No.
>
> COLSON: How about in the subject of being around any sort of birth brain damage? Now, I'm going to use birth brain damage and change it to another phrase that is sometimes used with it that you might hear during this trial, CP, there are CP children and there are—how many of them are caused at birth, I'm not here to discuss, you will hear about that at trial, but does the whole subject of cerebral palsy, are any of you affected by that in your families? Any of your close intimate friends whatsoever?

Similarly, when the lawyers probed attitudes about substantial verdicts, they conditioned the jury to the fact that the cases would involve substantial injuries and damages. Colson introduced a juror to the idea that his case might involve a substantial verdict in the following way:

> COLSON: Do you know of any reason in your personal philosophy or in your personal religion that you could not handle the elements of damages if you did determine that she was entitled to a verdict?
>
> JUROR: No.
>
> COLSON: Do you know of any reason that if those elements of damages added up because of her life expectancy and because of the care needed for her to a very substantial sum of money, would that in and of itself give you any problem?
>
> JUROR: No.

Bergman conditions the jury to the idea that his case is a substantial case when he probes juror attitudes about the size of the plaintiff's claims:

> Okay. Let me throw this out to the panel too. The claim in this case on behalf of Judy and Shanna and Ken Morrison, we'll be asking at the conclusion of the evidence for you to return a verdict of $5 million. That is a substantial amount of money. Is there anybody who, hearing that amount alone, feels that there is no case, no matter what the evidence, that they could return a verdict in that amount, that the amount is just more than you are prepared to deal with? As we get into the case, do you feel that way, Mr. _____?

The lawyers introduced legal concepts, procedures, and jury instructions that would be crucial to their case. Spence introduced the concept of "preponderance of evidence" and conditioned the jury to the fact that the case was a civil case for money as opposed to a criminal case:

> Of course, the Judge has already told you something that you understand in criminal cases, that you have to prove everything beyond a reasonable doubt, and that is the American system, and that is the right thing to do in a criminal case. In a civil case it is different. Nobody's going to jail. Nobody in Kerr-McGee is going to jail. Nobody is charging them with any crime. This is a lawsuit for money, and the bottom dollar, or bottom line is "dollars" in this case, because that is the only kind of justice we can get. We can't bring her back. We can't give her these days back and give her peace. We can't overdo or undo the things that have been done. All we can do is get a verdict in dollars. That is all the law is able to do. That is all we ask for, is justice. Now, in this case we have to prove our case first to you by a preponderance of the evidence—and the Judge says that is an adjusting of the scales—that isn't proof beyond a reasonable doubt like in a criminal case where a man's life is at stake—but you have to just tip the scales. If you weigh up all the evidence on both sides, which is the most believable case, Karen Silkwood's case or Kerr-McGee's case? Would any of you hold Karen Silkwood-or my friend, my client, Bill Silk-

wood, to a higher proof than that before you would return a verdict? In other words, if we tip the scales which makes the evidence preponderate, if we tip the scales in our favor, will you return a verdict, a full uncompromised verdict in this case? Will you? And, even if it takes the courage to write a check for eleven and a half million dollars—and that is full justice—will you do that?

Habush conditioned the jurors to the duties of a manufacturer and the failure of the defendant to meet those duties when he asked:

> Is there anyone who believes on this panel that they wouldn't be able to follow the judge's instructions at the end of the case that a manufacturer owes a duty to design, produce, and sell a product that is reasonably safe for users? (No response)
>
> And if the evidence does show that the manufacturer, Eaton Corporation, did, in fact, fail to properly design its forklift truck, is there anyone if the evidence does show that that could not render a verdict against them?

With respect to the burden of proof, after discovering a juror who had previously served on a criminal jury, Colson stated:

COLSON: That was a criminal case?

JUROR: Well, yes, it was a criminal case.

COLSON: I'm talking about opposed to a civil case where it's two private parties, this is where a government is involved for somebody allegedly drunken driving. Is that about what it was?

JUROR: Yes.

COLSON: You would have heard some law there about things that the law is not the same in criminal cases as they are here. And only one person is going to give you that, and he is sitting right there. And that's the only place it will come from. Can you set what that experience was aside and just forget what you may have heard that you proved beyond a reasonable doubt, because there are different rules here, and just forget it here. Can I count on that?

While discovering juror attitudes toward corporate responsibility under the law, Welch introduced corporate negligence responsibility:

WELCH: Along with the rights of a citizen, this corporation has certain duties, the same duties as any other citizen. Do any of you feel that simply because the defendant, General Standard, is a corporation, that they should be treated better or in some way differently than any other citizen?

JURORS: (No response).

WELCH: I assume from your silence, none of you have that feeling. Now, corporations can act only through their employees and officers

who attempt to make money or improve the position of the corporation. The employees of a corporation can also make mistakes for which
a corporation may be held liable. Do any of you hold a quarrel with
the proposition that holds a corporation liable?

. . . .

The question before you now is whether any of you have a quarrel with
the proposition of law or any present state of mind that would cause you
not to follow this law if it was given to you that a corporation is liable
for the negligent acts of its employees who are acting within the scope
of the accident. Any of you quarrel with that basic concept of law? Any
of you hold not to follow the law if given by the court?

On the subject of the standard of care required of doctors and hospitals,
Colson introduced the notion that the jurors must judge the case by the standard of care in effect at the time of the occurrence in question rather than the
standard of care in effect at the time of juror birth experiences.

Both Spence and Bergman introduced and explained the concept of punitive
damages.

§5.14   Obtaining Juror Commitment on Relevant Issues

After discovering juror attitudes, these lawyers obtained commitments from
the jurors that their attitudes would not prevent them from acting as fair and
impartial jurors. One of the corollaries of Festinger's Dissonance Theory is
that public commitment leads to behavior change.[5] The theory suggests that
if a person makes a voluntary public commitment toward a position, then that
person will pattern his or her behavior to conform to the position in order to
avoid dissonance due to inconsistency. It could be predicted that if jurors make
a voluntary public commitment not to let something affect their deliberations,
they will be under pressure to conform to this commitment in the jury room
in the presence of other jurors. Therefore, whenever possible, the lawyers
obtained public commitments from the jurors favorable to their cases.

After the detailed questioning of the juror who had worked for a defense
firm set out above, Spence asked:

SPENCE: But, I'm concerned about your feelings, because you're going
to be the one, if you stay on the case, that decides my client's case,
and so I asked you the straight question, and I want you to be just as
honest with me as I have been with you.

JUROR: If I didn't think I would be fair, I could say anything that would
get me off the jury, but, I—

SPENCE: Would there be the tiniest doubt in your mind about that?

---

[5] L. Festinger, A Theory of Cognitive Dissonance 84-97, 122 (1957); J. Brehm & A.
Cohen, Explorations in Cognitive Dissonance 8 (1962).

JUROR: Nope.

SPENCE: Not even the tiniest?

JUROR: Not even the tiniest.

SPENCE: And, I don't even need to worry about that tonight when I go home and try to get a little sleep?

JUROR: You may worry, but I don't think you need to.

SPENCE: I don't need to. You're going to be absolutely fair to my client?

JUROR: I'm going to try to be.

SPENCE: And, you can assure us of that?

JUROR: Yes, sir.

. . . .

SPENCE: All, right. Well, if you're satisfied, and I have your assurance, I can't ask for anything more, can I? If you are a member of this jury, and you are in the jury room, and you start to argue the case, will you call to your mind and your attention, your own personal attention, the assurances that you have given me?

JUROR: Certainly.

After telling the jurors that Karen Silkwood may have had a different moral system than some of the jurors, and after exploring attitudes toward different lifestyles, Spence obtained a commitment from the jurors to treat her the same under the law as someone with a more acceptable lifestyle:

SPENCE: Would every one of you give her the same rights, and her children the same rights, under the law as you would as if she was the Blessed Mother? Would you? Would you, sir?

JUROR: I would; yes, sir.

While discussing the burden of proof, Spence obtained a commitment from the jurors to find in favor of his clients if they met the preponderance of the evidence burden of proof.

After discovering a juror whose husband handled safety and workmen's compensation insurance claims for his corporate employer, Welch asked:

If it turns out that you are selected for this case and your husband has become so jaded after hearing all this, would you promise not to talk to him about those things and confine yourself to the evidence in this case?

In discussing the concept of professional negligence, Colson obtained commitments from the jurors that they agreed with the concept of professional responsibility. He stated:

You realize that this is only for what happened that day, it has nothing to do with their reputations or their licenses or any other thing. We are just here to try this event, this day, not before, or after, but just that event.

And is that all right with everybody? Does anybody have any hesitation with that at all? Any feelings that their field should not live up to whatever their standards are, that their rules are, their regulations are, that if they make a mistake that they be responsible? Is that all right with everybody? Can we count on you, you, you, you, you, you?

Colson asked all jurors whether they would have any problems following the judge's jury instructions. After the jurors as a group indicated that they would have none, he asked, "I can count on that?"

In discussing the jury's willingness to return a substantial money verdict, Colson asked:

Do you have any reason that if the evidence should add up because of the years involved to a very substantial sum of money and just the medical care should add up to just substantial sums of money, would the mere fact that it's a substantial sum, would that in and of itself cause you to say, well, I can't handle that. I won't do that, I won't be on this jury, I can't look that in the eye. Or are you willing to listen to the evidence and to consider it and if it does because of the evidence show that we are right and they are wrong and it then shows that to fully compensate under the law of Florida that there is a very substantial sum of money, are you willing to look that in the eye and to award such damages as you in your heart feel is the correct thing to do? Are you willing to do that, sir? Are you willing? You? You? You? You?

Since many of the jurors had had birthing experiences that had occurred many years before his case, he obtained a commitment from all jurors that they would follow the standards for delivery procedures in effect at the time of the plaintiff's delivery, as opposed to the standards in effect at the time of the jurors' delivery experiences.

Corboy obtained commitments that the jurors would return a verdict for each element of damage, if the plaintiff was entitled to it:

CORBOY: In this lawsuit my client will be seeking damages for the pain and suffering that he has experienced to date and the pain and suffering in the future. Will you sign such a verdict if he is entitled to it?

JUROR: Yes.

CORBOY: In this lawsuit my client is seeking damages in terms of money for the disability he has incurred. Will you sign a verdict?

JUROR: Yes.

CORBOY: The same with that which I call loss of earnings, both past and future?

JUROR: Yes.

CORBOY: Medical expenses in the future?

JUROR: Yes.

Later, he went further, and obtained a commitment from the juror that she would return a verdict for each element of damage that the plaintiff was entitled to, no matter what the amount:

CORBOY: The next responsibility will be to determine how many dollars he would be entitled to, his past medical expense and his future medical expenses and his caretaking expenses and his computer expenses and all of that sort of thing?

JUROR: Yes, sir.

CORBOY: Would you sign such a verdict?

JUROR: Yes, sir.

CORBOY: No matter what the amount is?

JUROR: Yes.

CORBOY: The dollars, the amount of dollars you have heard here, not to be restricted in any way as a commitment or in any way affecting your judgment, but at the same time you are not—I think one of the questions I would like to ask you is if you find that he is entitled to "X" number of dollars, no matter what it is, will you sign a verdict?

JUROR: Yes.

. . . .

CORBOY: If you find that he is entitled to future medical expense, whatever that medical expense might be, no matter how many millions of dollars it might be to supply him with the necessary medical care and medical provisions that are needed, will you sign such a verdict?

Juror: Yes, I will.

Corboy obtained a commitment from a juror to give both sides a fair trial when he asked:

CORBOY: Is there anything you can think of which would prevent you from giving everybody in this lawsuit a fair trial?

JUROR: No.

CORBOY: Will you do that?

JUROR: Yes.

In the case of a juror who was acquainted with a possible witness, Bergman obtained a commitment that this acquaintance would not affect his ability to fairly hear the evidence:

BERGMAN: Would it cause you to tend to believe what he says over what someone else says simply because he might have been your family doctor and did a good job for you?

JUROR: I wouldn't believe so.

BERGMAN: Okay: You would be willing to put that aside and listen to it on the basis of the evidence in the case?

JUROR: Yes, I would.

With respect to a juror who had been a patient in the defendant hospital, Bergman asked:

BERGMAN: Okay. I'll ask you the same question; I've asked it a few times now. Are you going to be able to set aside your own experience and decide this case with regard to the hospital on its merits?

JUROR: That's correct.

When discussing juror attitudes toward the large amount of the plaintiffs' claims, Bergman obtained commitments that the jurors would be open-minded and that they would be willing to consider a large verdict:

BERGMAN: Well, I guess that the only question is, can you start out open-minded without a preconceived notion that the amount that is being asked in this case is just plain too much, without having that amount cause you to be very skeptical?

JUROR: No, I think that I can put that aside.

BERGMAN: You could?

JUROR: Yes.

BERGMAN: All right. Thank you. There were a couple of other hands up. I'm sorry. I don't remember. Mrs. _____?

JUROR: Yes. I have the same opinion as the lady who just spoke. I want to ask, does the jury have to give the amount that you are asking for or can it give what it was is justified?

BERGMAN: I believe that you'll be told that the amount of your verdict is solely within the discretion of the jury.

JUROR: Uh-huh.

BERGMAN: That it is not an all or nothing. You listen to the evidence, you make your decision. We make our recommendations as attorneys as to what we think is appropriate. But I just want you to know up front that that is what we'll be asking you for. You are not bound by it.

JUROR: Uh-huh.

BERGMAN: What I'm concerned about is that the amount isn't—I don't like to wait until the end of the trial to tell you, because it does offend some people. That is fine. Everybody had their own views. That is what this is all about. But, having heard the amount, all that I want to know is whether that shocks you or whether that is something that is even outside of the realm of your capacity to do so, even before you hear the evidence.

JUROR: Well, it startled me, but if the jury can evaluate and decide on the amount that it feels is justified, that makes a difference to me.

BERGMAN: Okay. In other words, if you don't have to listen, if you can disregard what I say, which you can, absolutely.

JUROR: Yes.

BERGMAN: All right. But on my question, do you think that there is a circumstance that would arise out of this case that could cause you to feel that a verdict in that amount would be appropriate, or do you just rule it out and figure that you will decide it later on with the other members of the jury?

JUROR: Well, I would just have to hear the evidence.

BERGMAN: You'll be open-minded on that.

JUROR: Yes.

BERGMAN: Okay. Thank you.

In questioning jurors about placing a value on pain and suffering, Bergman obtained commitments that jurors would consider this element of damage:

BERGMAN: What I want to know is, if the Court instructs you—let me put this question to you, Mrs. _____—if the Court instructs you that the law says that those are the things that a jury should assign a monetary value to, do you have any preconceived idea of your own or opinion of your own about whether—some people feel, it doesn't matter, that was expressed here, that it won't help the situation—would you have any problem assigning a monetary value to these kind of things if that is what the law says that you should do?

JUROR: If it was proven to me that there was a neglect, then I would have no problems.

BERGMAN: All right. Thank you.

With another juror whose husband was a hospital administrator, Bergman asked:

BERGMAN: Well, for example, would you hesitate at all to return a substantial verdict if you thought it was warranted by the evidence?

JUROR: No.

With respect to a juror who had worked at a hospital, Bergman obtained a commitment that the juror could return a verdict against the defendant doctors if justified:

Do you feel that you can be entirely fair and impartial, and if you feel that the evidence warrants it, you could return a verdict against a physician?

With respect to a juror who had a daughter who was a doctor, Bergman asked:

BERGMAN: Do you think that if you felt that the evidence warranted it that you could return a verdict without compromising it and look at your daughter and not have any hesitation with that?

JUROR: I think so.

§5.15   Strategic Use of Language to Create Connotations Favorable to Their Clients and Witnesses

Strategic use of language involves selection of words, terms, and labels that have persuasive impact. These lawyers didn't describe the facts of their cases in neutral ways; rather, they used words that asserted positions and gave authority to these assertions. They used analogies and metaphors in order to transform abstract concepts such as negligence and pain and suffering into concrete ideas that could be easily understood. For these lawyers, the strategic use of language created connotations and meanings favorable to their clients, witnesses, and other relevant facets of their cases.

When introducing the names of his witnesses to the jury, Welch referred to them as "independent" witnesses. When turning to his discussion of the plaintiff's medical treatment, he began by stating, "Now, to Mr. Cooper's quest for relief from his pain and disability." When asking jurors whether they had ever filed personal injury actions, Welch asked whether they were ever "forced" to hire a lawyer to file a lawsuit for personal injury. In asking the jury if they could base their verdict on reason rather than sympathy, he referred to his client as an "injured, disabled person" and his client's damage as "rather extensive loss."

Colson referred to his economics expert as an economist who had "taught economics or has been a professor of economics." When asking jurors about their attitudes about sitting in judgment, he referred to the "serious problem" for both sides, the "serious amounts of damages" sustained by the plaintiff, and "very substantial" sum of money that the jury may have to return as a verdict. When talking to jurors about their experiences with persons with conditions similar to the plaintiff's, he referred to the "catastrophic" condition and the "tragic" health situation.

Corboy referred to the "devastated" condition of his client. In relating the fact that the plaintiff was paralyzed and could communicate only through the muscles in his eyes, Corboy told the jury that his client "lives through his eyes," and that he was a "prisoner in his body." This description portrayed the plaintiff's existence in very concise and chilling terms.

As noted below in **§5.16,** in order to argue that the jury should return a verdict for whatever medical bills were necessary in order to maintain the plaintiff's life, Corboy linked his argument with the idea that "life is sacred" and should be preserved no matter what the cost. In that way, he used words that gave his claims religious and moral overtones that became very compelling to those jurors who held such religious and moral beliefs.

Spence referred to his case as an "important" case, and asked a juror whether she was aware that the case might have "extraordinary importance." As previously noted, he suggested that the case was so important as to change the history of the law and the United States.

In discussing Karen Silkwood's damages, Spence referred to "nine days of suffering, and terror, and panic." He asserted that she was injured in a "very serious frightening way." With reference to juror experience with plutonium,

Spence asked the jury, "How many of you know anything about the dangers of plutonium?" With respect to cancer, Spencer asked the jury whether any of them had had any experience with the "dread disease, cancer."

In explaining punitive damages, Spence used the analogy of punishment to children. As will be noted in §5.16 below, this analogy transformed an abstract concept such as punitive damages into a simple situation that had occurred in many of the jurors' lives. It made the assessment of punitive damages easily understandable.

In the same way, Spence likened the rendering of a multimillion dollar verdict to the writing of a check. Most jurors would view the rendering of a multimillion dollar verdict as an overwhelming and probably scary task. However, by reconceptualizing the rendering of such a verdict to the writing of a check, the process was transformed to something all jurors had done in their lives and was rendered less frightening.

In obtaining juror commitment that they would not discriminate against Karen Silkwood because of her "different" type of lifestyle, Spence asked all jurors whether they would give her the same consideration under the law as if she were the "Blessed Mother." By the use of this language, Spence metaphorically transformed her from a young lady with a "different" lifestyle to the moralistic religious figure. By linking her to the "Blessed Mother," Spence evoked religious and moral images and feelings in the jurors, which were then associated with Karen Silkwood.

In discussing juror attitudes about the jury system, Habush referred to his client's injury as a "legitimate injury." In describing his client's injuries and damages to the jury, rather than simply saying that his client had suffered damage to his bowel, damage to his bladder, and damage to his sexual processes, Habush told the jury that he had experienced a loss of bowel functions, loss of bladder functions, and loss of sexual functions. By characterizing these as losses rather than damages, Habush made it clear that these functions were gone rather than simply damaged, which created a stronger impact on the jury.

In discussing the ability of jurors to render a verdict against the defendant, Bergman referred to a "sizable" verdict, and referred to the case as a "sad" case, an "emotional" case, and a "serious" case. In this way, he was subtly creating the impression that his case was in fact a legitimate case in which a tragedy was created, and that it was in fact a big and important case. Bergman referred to his question about big verdicts and settlements in malpractice claims as a "very serious question." In asking jurors whether they had strong enough stomachs to sit and hear his case, he created a serious atmosphere for the trial. In discussing a juror's experience with children like the plaintiff, Bergman asked whether the juror had had experience with "severely" multi-handicapped children. He referred to his clients' claims as "legitimate" claims.

§5.16   Presenting Arguments

All of these lawyers argued their cases during voir dire. Considerable time has been spent describing how lawyers discovered juror attitudes, obtained juror commitments, introduced facts, concepts, issues, and conditioned the jury. These purposes also functioned as arguments. While the lawyers were discussing various aspects of the trial and performing purposes such as discovering attitudes, they were at the same time rehearsing arguments that would be made throughout the trial.

When Corboy introduced the nature of his client's injuries to the jury, he was also asserting these facts to be true. His description functioned as an argument about the seriousness of his client's injuries:

> Have you ever known of a person with a problem called spastic quadriplegia and locked-in syndrome, which means he cannot walk, he cannot talk, he cannot work his bowels, he cannot work his bladder, he cannot use his hands, cannot use his arms, cannot turn himself, can only communicate with his eyes?
>
> . . . .
>
> In addition to being paralyzed from the waist down, my client is paralyzed, in effect, from the eyes down. Have you ever heard of a person that seriously injured?
>
> . . . .
>
> Have you had any experience or exposure with a person who is a spastic quadriplegic? And by spastic quadriplegic, that means their arms and legs are not only not movable, but they are extended. My client's feet are extended like that. His hands are in that position and clenched. He cannot walk, he cannot talk. He is not able to control his bowel movements, his urinary activities. He eats through his stomach. He cannot swallow. He can move his head a little. He can move his left thumb and, I think, a little bit of his left foot. He, in effect, lives through his eyes, communicates through his eyes. Have you had any experience either firsthand or by reading, knowledge of any kind, concerning a person such as that?

Corboy's questioning about juror attitudes with regard to the concept "life is sacred," noted above, functioned as argument. He was attempting to obtain a verdict for damages that the average juror would find staggering. He surmounted this problem by suggesting that life was sacred and should be preserved no matter what the cost. This argument appealed to religious and moral beliefs. If Corboy could get the jurors to affirm the belief that life was sacred, then it was a small leap to the position that they should then return a verdict for whatever figure the experts said was necessary to sustain the plaintiff, no matter how many millions of dollars it cost. He asked:

CORBOY: With reference to this question of "life is sacred," do you believe that life is sacred?

JUROR: Yes, I do.

CORBOY: Do you believe a person is entitled to the medical care he needs in order to supply him with the nourishment and the medical care to keep him alive?

JUROR: Yes.

With another juror, Corboy asked:

> CORBOY: Okay. Do you have any thoughts or reactions to this phrase that I used with the other people that life is sacred?
>
> JUROR: No.
>
> CORBOY: You have none at all?
>
> JUROR: No.
>
> CORBOY: My point is do you believe life is sacred?
>
> JUROR: Yes.
>
> CORBOY: So you believe a person is entitled to the medical care and medical provisions and entitled to the nurses and the therapists and the doctoring for all of the problems he might have that came from this occurrence?
>
> JUROR: Yes.

Corboy's questioning of the jury with respect to their attitudes about the elements of damage functioned as argument. By asking the jurors about their willingness to return a verdict for these elements, Corboy was asserting that his client was entitled to compensation for these elements. In the same way, his questions about the jurors' willingness to return a substantial verdict functioned as argument:

> In this case, as the Court has indicated to you, we are seeking money damages as a result of an injury suffered from the automobile collision of August 23, 1981. Without going into the details of what my client may or may not be entitled to, if my client is entitled to a very large sum of money, would you have any hesitancy in any way of signing such a verdict?

Welch's questioning of jurors with respect to their experience with the type of injury sustained by the plaintiff functioned as an argument about the nature and extent of disability. He established through the jurors that people don't fully recover from surgeries such as the plaintiff underwent:

> WELCH: So there were to laminectomies and two fusions. With that much information, have you or any members of your immediate family ever been subjected to such surgeries, whether they be in the neck area or the low back?
>
> .   .   .   .
>
> JUROR: Yes, sir. My father.
>
> WELCH: Okay. What sort of condition?
>
> JUROR: He had a spinal—they took some bone out of here and put it in his neck to stabilize it. I'm not sure what, but it was a long surgery due to a severe accident.
>
> WELCH: Do you remember how long ago that was?
>
> JUROR: About four years ago.

WELCH: Has he recovered from that? Was it successful?

JUROR: Partially, but he was partially disabled. He had to quit work.

WELCH: So your father, then, was disabled from work?

JUROR: Yes.

. . . .

WELCH: And did he also, as a result of that surgery to his neck area, have problems down into his arms and hands?

JUROR: Some parts of his body, yeah. I don't know exactly what.

WELCH: Okay. Anything about your father's experience and the similarity of Mr. Cooper's experience from what you know about it so far, anything about that that would make you feel that you cannot be a fair and impartial juror if chosen in this case?

In asking jurors about their experiences with persons with physical problems like the plaintiff's, Colson argued the seriousness of his client's injuries:

Now, we would like to ask you your past experience of something that might be in your particular life, your families, and that is, your past experience having to do with health, with accidents in which regardless of them coming in and having anything to do with litigation whether or not that you might be in a situation in which you have ever been called upon to be a part of—and I'm going to use the word tragedy, without apology here, but a catastrophic type injury, where something was very serious and very permanent and that whether you have in your family any situations that you have had to live with, long illnesses, I know we have all lost people in our—we haven't all, but many of us, and I'm not talking about whether, you know, a loved parent or something like that passed away, but I'm talking about a long situation, a serious situation that might be involved, does anyone have that experience?

In discussing the pregnancies of jurors, Colson argued that the plaintiff's mother had a normal pregnancy:

I have to talk about the subject of bleeding during the first few months, the first two or three months of a pregnancy. Does that ring a bell with anyone? Does anyone have any particular knowledge about that or anyone that didn't have a normal pregnancy, which we claim she did have, of course, I mean our witnesses will say until she got to the hospital that day that she had a normal pregnancy except for getting a cold and things that they knew completely before. Did anybody have any particular problem with pregnancies other than what you have told us.

Colson's questioning of jurors about their own birthing experiences functioned as argument in the sense that many jurors had pregnancies similar to the plaintiff's, but they all delivered normal children. He questioned each juror about the pregnancies of their spouses and relatives, and in almost every case the pregnancies resulted in normal children. The fact that the birthing results for the jurors were normal under conditions similar to the plaintiff's functioned as a subtle argument that there must have been negligence in the plaintiff's case. An example of his questioning is as follows:

COLSON: Why don't we start with you?

JUROR: I had a normal pregnancy, but a breech delivery.

COLSON: And was the breech delivery handled without incident?

JUROR: Yes.

COLSON: And was it handled through a cesarean section?

JUROR: No.

COLSON: It was delivered vaginally?

JUROR: Right.

COLSON: And when was that, please?

JUROR: That was years ago, almost 20.

COLSON: You have no idea or may I ask do you have any idea what caused the baby to be in a breech position?

JUROR: No.

COLSON: The baby was born normally and has lived normally and there was no problem with it?

JUROR: Right.

COLSON: Even though you knew that ahead of time of the delivery, I assume?

JUROR: Ahead of time? No.

COLSON: You did not know it until the actual delivery?

JUROR: Until the actual delivery.

COLSON: And at that time there had not been X-rays taken to show the position of the child? So you had no knowledge of it?

JUROR: Right.

COLSON: But still you had your—the situation where there was no problem with it?

JUROR: Right.

Colson used the same strategy with respect to fetal monitoring. The plaintiffs claimed that the defendants failed to properly monitor the fetus during labor and delivery. Colson discussed each juror's experience with fetal monitoring, and established through the jurors themselves the importance of continuous fetal monitoring through the entire labor process.

In questioning jurors about their attitudes toward the plaintiffs' claims for damages, as set out above, Spence argued the nature and extent of damages. He went on to argue the merit of the plaintiffs' claim of $1.5 million for nine days of suffering:

Do any of you have a sense that the loss of a day of one's life is sort of insignificant? What I'm trying to find out is: Is there anybody here on the jury that says, you know, a day of one's life isn't important—anybody sort of have an idea that their own life is unimportant—anybody have a feeling like that? Some people do. Some people are maybe unaware of the value of our days. Anybody here who wouldn't find a special value in the last nine days of your life, if you knew you were living them right now? Anybody that wouldn't care? Or, anybody wouldn't find them valuable? If I were representing you for the last nine days of your life, would any of you be upset with me if I asked for a million and a half dollars for them?

While asking jurors about their attitudes as to whether lawyers exaggerated their damage claims, Spence argued that he asked only for the amount that his client was entitled to:

SPENCE: Do any of you feel that lawyers always ask twice or three times the amount that they think their client is entitled to? Does anybody think that about lawyers?

JUROR: (Several simultaneously) Sometimes.

SPENCE: Would you make, those of you who think that, make room for the possibility in this case that, after you have heard the testimony, you will agree with the assessment that we have made on behalf of this case—would you make room for that—anybody that wouldn't? Would you make room for the fact that some lawyers don't ask for twice the amount that they want—that they ask for the exact amount to the penny that they believe their client is entitled to?

JUROR: There is always one that will.

SPENCE: Would you make room for the possibility, Mr. _____,— Thank you for your comment.

JUROR: I didn't say you did.

SPENCE: I know. I wish you had. Would you make room for the possibility, Mr. _____, that that is the kind of lawyer I am?

In probing juror attitudes toward the question of punitive damages, Spence set up his argument on how punitive damages should be assessed. He used the analogy of punishment of children to conceptualize how Kerr-McGee should be punished:

Now, punitive damages has something to do with punishment as his Honor said. It wouldn't be fair to punish a large corporation to the same extent that you would punish a paper boy, or your son for not getting home on time, and you dock him ten cents. If he makes fifty cents a week, ten cents is a lot of money to him. Nobody would be shocked by that. That is twenty percent of his income for the week. Twenty percent. So, now, when we start talking about the relationship of a claim for punitive

damages it may be that you may have to take into account what is a sufficient sum to punish a corporation based upon their earnings. You can
see it wouldn't be the same. You wouldn't punish a large corporation the
same as the paper boy, or the paper boy the same as a large corporation
and somehow try to make the punishment fit the individual, because Kerr-
McGee in this case claims that they have the right of an individual—and
the Court says they do have the right—but they also have the responsibility. So, would all of you bear that in mind on the question of punitive
damages? Anybody that wouldn't? Anybody doesn't understand what I
was talking about?

Bergman, like Colson, presented an indirect form of argument by asking all
jurors about their experiences with the births of their children. He asked all
jurors whether their children were born with disabilities and whether they had
any problems with their birthing experiences. The fact that almost all of the
jurors had healthy children functioned as argument that something must have
gone wrong in the plaintiffs' case.

Bergman argued the nature of his case when he continually told the jurors
that it was going to be an emotional case and that it was a "sad case."

Bergman presented an interesting argument on the issue of whether sympathy should enter into their judgment. He knew that his case involving a young
girl with terminal cancer was going to be an emotional, sympathetic case. He
also knew that the court would later instruct the jury that sympathy should not
enter into their decision. In asking a juror about the issue of sympathy, he presented an argument to the effect that human feelings should be a part of their
decision:

BERGMAN: You think that you could hear that like all of the other testimony and weight it on its own merit?

JUROR: Yes. Except that I'm a very emotional person. Sometimes I
just—I don't know. I'm just emotional, just to tell you my feelings.

BERGMAN: I'm emotional too.

JUROR: I'll try my best.

BERGMAN: This is going to be an emotional case.

JUROR: I can see that.

BERGMAN: Do you think that this is a case that you could sit on and—
you know, jurors are always told usually at the end of the trial that sympathy should not enter into your deliberations. I think that is a different
concept from empathy. Sympathy is deciding a case because you feel
sorry for somebody. Empathy is just—

JUROR: Putting yur own

BERGMAN: —the human feeling of understanding the person's situation. Do you think that you could separate those two concepts and keep
sympathy out of it while not hardening your heart? Do you follow what
I'm saying?

JUROR: Yes, sir. I'll try my best.

BERGMAN: On that point, I always get concerned when the juror hears that sympathy should not enter into your deliberations that it is interpreted as having to harden your hearts to people and be very cold-blooded, and I think that is a different concept.

. . . .

BERGMAN: Let me put it another way. Is there anybody who, when they are told that sympathy should not enter into your deliberations, would think that they are supposed to harden their hearts and not look at the human aspects of this case, because one of the things that you are asked to do in a case is place a value on certain kinds of losses. Everybody think that they can keep both of these concepts separate? This is a very serious question in this case because it is a sad case. We don't want to get halfway through the trial and realize that, "I can't do this."

When Bergman encountered a nurse who worked at a hospital in the oncology department, he used her experience to construct an argument in support of his claims, since his case involved the failure to timely diagnose Hodgkin's disease. In order to prove his claim, he had to prove that "staging" was important, in that the disease could be successfully treated if diagnosed in its early stages. When he encountered the nurse with a background in oncology, he used her experience to support his argument:

BERGMAN: You know, one thing that a jury is told is that, on the question of what the standard of care is for a physician's conduct, you are to look to the expert testimony in the case. We'll have expert testimony. Do you think that because you have been there, in the pits, so to speak, doing it yourself or being involved in it that you would have a tendency to substitute your own view of how things should be done for what comes from the witness stand?

JUROR: I would admit that it would be difficult. I would try to keep an open mind by, as I said, having seen both sides of the coin from a patient and family standpoint and also the physician. It depends on which way that the evidence would be, which way I would be swayed.

BERGMAN: You would follow the evidence on that point?

JUROR: I would try.

BERGMAN: What type of—how are you involved in hematology and oncology? What type of patients?

JUROR: We had a wide range of tumors, leukemia, just about any type. It was mostly with adults. The youngest patient that I had was a 17-year-old—a 16-year-old boy.

BERGMAN: Were there any Hodgkin's disease patients?

JUROR: Yes.

BERGMAN: Any of them on an aggressive, prolonged type of basis?

JUROR: Yes. The unit that I worked on was mostly terminal. I have had some patients, and I know of one lady in particular, that I took care of for three or four months before that had Hodgkin's.

BERGMAN: Do you feel that you have any special expertise with regard to survival rates, you know, the data having to do with the treatment and how that relates to the outcome, that sort of thing?

JUROR: I feel that after working with that I would be a very pessimistic person as far as taking the chemotherapy or radiation. In most cases, depending on the cancer, and the stage in which it was caught, usually in the end it doesn't change the difference. It makes the lifestyle of the person a lot more miserable. But I do know also that Hodgkin's has a better cure rate than some types of lymphomas, and other types of tumors.

Habush argued the standard of care for manufacturers when he asked the jurors whether they would be able to follow the judge's instructions that a manufacturer "owes a duty to design, and produce, and sell a product that is reasonably safe for users." He went on to ask whether the jurors would return a verdict against the manufacturer if the evidence demonstrated that the manufacturer "did in fact, fail to properly design its forklift truck."

§5.17   Refuting Argumentts Made by the Defendant

As well as rehearsing the arguments that would be made by the plaintiffs during the trial, the lawyers refuted the arguments that the defendant would make during the trial. When introducing the concept of breech birth, Colson argued that the doctors knew of the breech position well before delivery:

> . . . if the subject of breech birth—and I might stop there and say that there was some mention made today about breech birth. There is no question that the breech had taken place and was well known several days before she went to the hospital. In other words, the breech did not take place that day.

At another point, in regard to the issue of birth defect, Colson argued:

> His Honor mentioned that there had been a defect. The damage we're contending, of course, it wasn't a defect the child was born with like some spot on its skin. This is a—we're contending that this was brain damage that happened that day in labor in that hospital.

In asking about one of the defendant's defenses, Corboy argued his response to the defense:

> CORBOY: Now, you understand that and Mr. Johnson mentioned to one of these other people there may be evidence that this young man's

life expectancy is decreased. And he asked one or two of you if that would offend you as a defense. I think they all answered no. And I take it that would not offend you either?

Juror: No.

CORBOY: You understand, do you not, sir, that if there is such a thing in this case—if there is one—as a decreased life expectancy, it is the result of this accident?

JUROR: Yes.

CORBOY: It is not something he had before the occurrence?

JUROR: Yes.

§5.18   Enhancing Credibility

All of these lawyers made efforts to enhance the credibility of themselves, their clients, and the issues of their cases. Credibility was established by linking themselves or their cases with commonly held values or beliefs of the jurors, by aligning themselves with the judge, the law, or the pursuit of justice, or by presenting themselves in a candid manner. Further, these lawyers began establishing their personas in voir dire. They all became champions of justice and seekers of the truth. In our society, there are strong myths about the system of justice with which jurors have become familiar. Thus, adopting a persona that was aligned with the myths of truth and justice established a common bond with the jurors. At every stage the lawyers advised the jury that they were seeking a fair and impartial jury, and that they wanted justice rather than sympathy. In questioning the jurors about their attitudes, they always asked if the jurors could be fair to both sides of the case. Finally, these lawyers were all personal, respectful, and candid with the jurors.

§5.19   —Linking Themselves with the Common Values of the Jurors

Spence established himself as the common man or the champion of the common man. After he was introduced by the judge, in his first statement to the jury, Spence began to establish his persona. As mentioned previously, he stated:

Thank you, your Honor. Ladies and gentlemen of the jury, the court told you my name is Gerry Spence. I'm from Wyoming. And, I did come in to help my friend Bill Silkwood to try this case. I saw a sign in the YMCA today, where I ate lunch, a big sign and the board saying: We speak Western, and "we" meaning the YMCA, and they do, and I do, and I hope you do.

This case was being tried in Oklahoma, and it could be presumed that many of the jurors would experience commonality with Mr. Spence, who spoke

"Western." By alluding to the fact that he had eaten lunch at the YMCA, Spence identified in socioeconomic terms with the jurors. Rather than eating at a fancy or expensive restaurant, Spence chose to associate with the common man.

Spence also developed his persona as a champion of the rights of people against corporations. As noted above, when talking to the juror he wanted to excuse because of her work with defense firms, Spence stated:

> SPENCE: That's why I'm getting spooky, because of the kind of cases—I don't represent anybody but people—I just don't represent anybody but people, and nobody in my firm does. I don't represent any banks, or any corporations, or anything like that. Did most of the people— strike "people"—did most of the clients that your law firm represented, were most of those corporations and insurance companies?
>
> JUROR: Well, we were representative customers of insurance companies.
>
> SPENCE: In other words, the insurance company was the one that actually paid the bill?
>
> JUROR: Correct. Generally.
>
> SPENCE: And, there's a philosophy that developed in a firm like that— they are called "defense firms" aren't they?
>
> JUROR: Certainly.
>
> SPENCE: And, they are hired by large corporations, and insurance companies, and their philosophy gets sort of—well, that people that sue in the courts, like my client, well, you defend those cases, right?
>
> JUROR: Right.
>
> . . . .
>
> SPENCE: Well, as a matter of fact, the largest corporations, with the most money in the whole world, paid your bills, and that is mainly the insurance companies, isn't that true?

Colson subtly established credibility for his claims of medical negligence by the questioning of all jurors about their own pregnancy experiences. As has been pointed out previously almost every juror who had had an experience with breech birth or cesarean delivery ultimately ended up with a healthy baby. Further, all jurors indicated that they were aware of the importance of fetal monitoring. Thus, Colson linked his case with common sense knowledge of the jurors. By linking his case with what the jurors knew to be true from their own experiences, he bolstered the credibility of his case.

Bergman also used the personal experiences of the jurors to establish the credibility of his claims. By his questioning of all jurors about their birthing experiences, he established by inference that when proper procedures were followed, the jurors or their spouses delivered healthy babies. When questioning the nurse with experience in oncology, he established the credibility of his claim that Hodgkin's disease could be successfully treated by eliciting statements from the nurse that, in her experience, Hodgkin's disease had one of the best cure rates when timely diagnosed. By linking his claims with what the nurse knew to be true from her own experience, he bolstered his credibility.

Bergman many times admitted sharing similar feelings with jurors. As the reader will recall, after one juror stated that she was an emotional person, Bergman told the juror that he was an emotional person as well, and when trying to get the juror with the lawyer son to admit that he could not be fair because his son worked for one of the defendant's law firms, Bergman offered that his mother would probably be for his firm if she were a juror in a case his firm was involved in.

Corboy established credibility for his claim that the plaintiff was entitled to a multimillion dollar verdict by linking his claim to a commonly shared value of the jurors. As noted above, he first obtained commitments from the jurors that they agreed with the phrase "life is sacred" and the concept that "life should be sustained." The idea that life is sacred and should be sustained is a commonly held value with religious overtones. He then suggested that due to the defendant's negligence, the plaintiff had been left a helpless quadriplegic and that it would be necessary for him to have many millions of dollars worth of medical treatment and support in order to sustain his life. The logical implication which followed was that the plaintiff should be given whatever medical care was necessary to sustain him for the rest of his life.

§5.20 —Aligning Themselves with Trust, Justice, the Court, and the Law

In American society, we are saturated with myths about the American system of justice. These lawyers drew upon these myths and aligned their causes with them. Whenever possible, they presented themselves as in pursuit of justice, with the law and the court on their side.

With respect to sympathy and justice, Spence suggested that he and his client were engaged in the pursuit of justice:

> Now, you know, something I want to say to you right now, and that is that I'm not going to ask any of you in this case for any sympathy. I don't want any sympathy, and I don't want any sympathy for Bill Silkwood, nor for the children. That isn't the issue in any way. All I simply want, on behalf of my client, is justice, and a full and adequate and uncompromised verdict—we just want justice—an uncompromised verdict. I don't want sympathy. We just want justice. Is there anybody here that wouldn't be willing to decide the case on those basic ground rules?

At various points in the voir dire, Spence suggested that he and the judge were aligned in interest with respect to the pursuit of justice. In his discussion of the subject of prejudice and the fact that the jurors must be willing to admit their prejudices, Spence statement,

> The biggest crime that could be committed in this courtroom today would be for somebody who really has an opinion about something—and we

all have to have opinions if we've got any brains to think with—to have an opinion about something and not be willing to say it because they were sort of prejudiced against admitting their prejudice. So, with this thought in mind—and I'm sure counsel for the defense shares that with me—and I know the Court does, I want to ask you some questions about that, if I might.

added credibility to his position by suggesting that the court agreed with his position.

Bergman continually stressed to the jurors that he wanted fair and impartial jurors. When asking if the jurors could be fair, he many times couched his questions in terms of being fair to both parties and not just the plaintiff. After acknowledging that the case would be emotional and would evoke sympathy for the plaintiff, Bergman asked jurors if they could be fair toward the defendant. At one point, he challenged and excused a juror who felt that he could not be fair to the defendant because his father had died due to medical malpractice. While some lawyers would have attempted to keep this juror, Bergman established his credibility by excusing the juror, and hence demonstrating his interest in obtaining a fair jury.

§5.21   —Presenting Themselves in an Honest Personal Manner

The lawyers all appeared candid, forthright, personal, and respectful when addressing the jurors.

In a recent interview, Spence stated:

> Magic occurs when you become truthful with the jury. The great truth in the courtroom is not just the words. . . . It has to do with the emotional content of human beings. They know you care. . . . If you don't care about your client, you probably won't get any verdict at all."[6]

These lawyers appeared to follow this philosophy in presenting their voir dire. They all gave the impression that they cared about their clients and believed in what they were doing. For example, in describing his relationship with his client, Spence stated that he came to the trial to "help my friend Bill Silkwood try his case."

The lawyers appeared to be forthright in their approach to the jury. In discussing the nature of prejudice with the jurors and the fact that all people, including the jurors, could be expected to have prejudice, Spence presented his own feelings on the subject, stating that he "didn't want to tell anyone that I'm prejudice. And, I just wonder if anybody else is prejudiced against the word 'prejudice?'" With his honest, straightforward approach, Spence acknowledged his prejudices and invited the jury to do the same. At another point, when addressing the juror Spence viewed as biased because she was formerly

[6] Blodgett, *Stage Fright*, 71 ABAJ, Litigation Today 26 (1985).

employed at a defense law firm, Spence began by telling her that "every time I find people that are working for lawyers I get spooky." He told the juror that he was scared about her sitting on the jury and that when she answered the questions he put to her, he wanted her to be as honest with him as he was with her.

Colson thanked jurors for volunteering information, and acknowledged that it was tough to bring such information up. When discussing juror attitudes toward medical malpractice lawsuits, Colson presented himself as a man of fairness when he acknowledged that the profession of osteopathy was a "fine profession," that the osteopathic hospital was a "fine hospital," and that hospitals were "wonderful" and that "we all love hospitals." Thus, while his client was suing the hospital, Colson was not afraid to admit that doctors and hospitals were worthy professionals and institutions.

At the conclusion of his voir dire, Habush thanked the jurors:

> With that, ladies and gentlmen, I thank you for your patience. I hope I haven't intruded upon your privacy, and thank you for being so honest and candid with me.

Bergman continually shared his feelings with jurors in a way that made him appear honest and straightforward. As noted in Chapter 3, appearing open and honest aids in establishing credibility, and Bergman demonstrated this dimension. When one juror stated that he was a close personal friend of one of the defense lawyers, Bergman stated honestly, "The way you say that scares me." Even though both of his cases involved malpractice claims, Bergman admitted to the jurors that most people, including himself, held doctors in high regard. Thus, even though he was suing doctors, Bergman was able to admit that it was an admirable profession. This created for him the image of a professional bringing a claim he believed in, as opposed to the image of just another salesman willing to say anything to make his case.

Bergman always made a point of thanking jurors for their candor when they admitted that they would have difficulty in being fair.

These lawyers never argued with the court in front of the jury. If the court interrupted and advised the lawyers to do or not do something, as a rule, the lawyers thanked the court and moved on.

§5.22   Establishing Jury Purpose

These lawyers did not accept the jury as constituted by the court, but rather, they took an active role in creating the jury's purpose. The court advised the jury prior to voir dire that its function was to do justice and to render a fair and impartial verdict. However, this is an abstract and undefined purpose. For example, what is a "fair and impartial verdict" and what is "justice?" These lawyers specifically defined the function and purpose of the jury.

When asking the jurors if they understood the nature of a civil case, Spence told them that all they could do was to render a verdict in dollars:

This is a lawsuit for money, and the bottom dollar, or bottom line is "dollars" in this case, because that is the only kind of justice we can get. We can't bring her back. We can't overdo or undo the things that have been done. All we can do is get a verdict in dollars. That is all the law is able to do.

Spence then went further and suggested to the jury their function of "writing a check" for $11.5 million:

Now, the judge talked about ten and a half million dollars, and whether that shocked anybody, and some people it shocked a little bit to start with—and it is a lot of money—and when you get into the jury room you're going to have the power of "writing a check" for anything up to eleven and a half million dollars—ten million dollars punitive, and a million and a half actual. . . . Would any of you be afraid to do that—because you're going to be called upon to do that—and I'm going to ask you, at the conclusion of the case to do that. . . .

In asking jurors about their attitudes toward signing a verdict for the various elements of damages, Corboy told them that their function would be to determine the amount of damages that the plaintiff was entitled to:

CORBOY: You will be called upon essentially as Mr. _____ has pointed out to assess damages in this lawsuit and in assessing damages you will be required to follow the law, follow the evidence. The evidence is completely your responsibility. Your job is to determine what that evidence means, to translate evidence into facts and those facts then are determinative of the role that those facts take in the lawsuit to apply the law to those facts and reach a verdict in this case. After applying that law to those facts, you will probably be required to determine the amount of money my client is entitled to in compensation for his injuries. Is that—there anything about that which in any way will prevent you from satisfying your role in it?

JUROR: No.

At another point, Corboy suggested to the jury that their purpose would be to determine damages:

CORBOY: My client is—as the Court has just pointed out a moment ago, is damaged and he is damaged permanently and he is not going to get any physically better. Excuse me, he is not going to get any neurologically better. This means he is locked in his body and he talks and emotes and communicates with his eyes. In this particular lawsuit, if called upon to serve, you will be called upon eventually to determine damages in this lawsuit. If you determine under the law and under the facts that my client is entitled to dollars and perhaps cents, for pain and suffering, you will be required to sign a verdict and we will have a line for it. It will say "pain and suffering." Will you sign such a verdict

in the amount of money to which he is entitled to, no matter how much
it is?

JUROR: Yes, sir.

. . . .

CORBOY: The next responsibility will be to determine how many dollars he would be entitled to, his past medical expense and his future
medical expenses and his caretaking expenses and his computer
expenses and all of that sort of thing? Would you sign such a verdict?

JUROR: Yes, sir.

CORBOY: No matter what the amount is?

JUROR: Yes.

This was an effective suggestion, because it presupposed the issue of liability.
If successful, Corboy has the jurors considering the amount of damages before
hearing facts on liability.

Welch first told the jury that the plaintiffs didn't want sympathy, because
they had already received that from their friends and at church. He then suggested that the jury's function would be to determine damages:

WELCH: Now, at the close of the case, Judge Meyers is going to give
you a tremendous amount of power, you who are selected. You will
fill out a verdict form that has blanks in it, where you put in a dollar
amount for a jury verdict. . . . But in any event, you will be asked to
fill in a blank and asked to write a sum of money, and it's very much
like writing a personal check, and I'm wondering if any of you have
ever written a personal check for a quarter or a half million dollars,
or sums of that sort.

JURORs: (No response).

WELCH: My question to you is: Would any of you be afraid to use that
kind of power if you felt that it was warranted by the evidence in the
case, the evidence that you heard?

JURORs: (No response).

WELCH: I assume by your silence that none of you would.

Colson told the jury that its function would be to judge whether mistakes
were made by the defendants:

We are here and we are bringing a lawsuit because we are contending
and expect to prove to you that the hospital and the doctors made a mistake that day with this mother and this child. Now, will you be called upon
to sit as a judge. You don't have a black robe, but you will be judging
whether or not mistakes were made that day in this birth. Now, can you
help me with that? Do you fell that either side would have any problem
with you sitting here?

Habush suggested that the purpose of the jurors was to judge the case and award damages when he asked:

> Again assuming the evidence is as I have described it, is there anyone who feels that they could not sit on such a case, and judge such a case, and award damages in such a case?

Habush went on to suggest that the jury's purpose was to award damages in excess of $800,000 when he asked:

> Having in mind what I have just told you of the damages that I expect the evidence to show totals up close to $800,000 without regard to pain and suffering, is there anyone on this panel who would be unable to award damages in excess of a million dollars if the evidence justified it, if the evidence justified it?

Bergman suggested to the jurors that their purpose was to return a money verdict when, immediately after his introduction to the jury, he stated that the purpose of the case was "to obtain monetary compensation." He further reinforced this purpose when he continually asked jurors if their experiences would make it difficult for them to "return a verdict against the hospital." When jurors had connections with doctors and hospitals, Bergman asked if they felt that they would have trouble returning to the hospital after they had returned a verdict against a hospital in this case. As the voir dire progressed, the purpose shifted from returning a verdict against the hospital to returning a substantial verdict for money damages. Bergman told the jury that "damages is what is being sought here." Finally, he told the jurors that their function was to determine damages, and he outlined the various damages that they should return, when he stated:

> I was asking you about the amount that I mentioned, the $10,000,000, and let me say preliminarily and I think most of you probably know this already, it's your function and your function alone as a jury to determine the amount of damages that are fair and reasonable in a particular case, and there are really two things that I want to ask you.
>
> First of all, does anybody have a reaction based upon the amount that I just gave you, $10,000,000, that might enter into your thinking in this case, or do you have any view about that amount alone in the abstract as being just simply unreachable or too much, no matter what the evidence. Anybody have any feelings about that? So everybody can start out with an open mind on the amount of damages and is willing to do that job.
>
> Secondly, getting back to the various elements of the claim that I mentioned to you, I think in the experience of most lawyers, we find sometimes that people have their own views on what ought to be compensable and what shouldn't be. My only question to you is, if you are instructed by the Court that you are to give full and fair compensation on a particular element of damages, are you all willing to do that, even if you don't feel

that that type of thing ought to be compensable and the example would be, pain and suffering or disability. Is everybody willing to do that and follow the instructions of the Court on every element of damages? Okay, nobody is responding, so I assume that you're all willing to do that and we'll rely on that.

Finally, Bergman told the jury that its function was to judge the conduct of the defendant hospital and doctors:

Just one other area that I mentioned briefly, and that is, you may be called on in this case, depending on the view of the Court, to consider the question of punitive damages. Punitive damages are something different from the compensatory damages that I just outlined for you. They're a completely different breed. They require you to sit in judgment of the conduct of a doctor and a corporation.

In his case involving the failure to diagnose cancer, initially Bergman told the jury that there were two aspects to the case:

I don't see that as having—there are two aspects of the case. One is whether you think that there is liability, and the other is the amount of damages.

With respect to determining the amount of damages, Bergman told the jurors that one of their tasks would be to place a value on pain and suffering:

Let me put it to you another way. Is there anybody who, when they are told that sympathy should not enter into your deliberations, would think that they are supposed to harden their hearts and not look at the human aspects of this case, because one of the things that you are asked to do in a case is to place a value on certain kinds of losses.

Later he elaborated on the types of damages they would consider:

Let me ask you this question. This is a question I want to ask the panel as a whole. The whole idea, the only objective—that is probably not true—but the ultimate objective of a civil case is monetary compensation. There will come a time in the trial when the jury will have to deliberate on those two issues, whether there is fault and how much are the damages. I would like to ask everybody whether you are all prepared, if the Court instructs you, to assign a monetary value to things like pain, suffering, mental anguish, emotional distress, the reasonable value of services that a family provides to a child, these kind of things. This is ultimately one of the things that you will all be asked to do.

§5.23 Conclusion

It al times during voir dire, it is clear that these lawyers looked beyond the jury selection process to the trial itself. They used voir dire to begin shaping the impression formation process of the jurors. These lawyers did not take the jury as given, but, rather, they took an active role in using voir dire to shape juror perception and jury purpose. As well as skillfully gathering background information about jurors in order to eliminate those biased against their clients, themselves, or their case, they (1) set the tone for the trial, (2) introduced concepts and evidence and conditioned the jurors for things to follow in the trial, (3) obtained public commitments from jurors favorable to their cases, (4) used language that created connotations favorable to their clients, their witnesses, and other relevant facets of their case, (5) rehearsed the arguments they would use in the trial, (6) refuted opposition arguments, (7) enhanced their credibility, and (8) created jury purpose. By the time voir dire was completed, the lawyers had previewed the entire trial for the jurors and had created a favorable atmosphere for the plaintiff's case.

Appendix 5-1
Voir Dire

THE COURT: Now, Mr. Spence, as the lead counsel for the plaintiff, would you begin your examination, sir.

MR. SPENCE: Thank you, your Honor. Ladies and gentlemen of the jury, the court told you my name is Gerry Spence. I'm from Wyoming. And, I did come in to help my friend Bill Silkwood to try this case. I saw a sign in the YMCA today, where I ate lunch, a big sign and board saying: We speak Western, and "we" meaning the YMCA, and they do, and I do, and I hope you do.

I need to ask you a few questions about some things that his Honor has given us, on both sides, a chance to ask about, and to get acquainted with you just a little bit.

It is an important case, ladies and gentlemen, and I hope that you would understand that if I were representing you you would want me to find out as much as possible about these people who are going to have the control of your very important case. I think you would want me to find out about these people if I were representing you, and I hope you will be patient with me if I ask the questions about that. You know, we have heard the word "prejudice" and I'm prejudiced about the word "prejudice" because I don't want to tell anyone that I'm prejudiced. And, I just wonder if anybody else is prejudiced against the word "prejudice." Anyone have a sense of that? By that I mean we are not suppose to be prejudiced—and I don't want to admit to doing anything that I'm not suppose to do—so it is pretty hard for me to say I'm prejudiced, but on the other hand anybody that has any opinion about anything, that has any sense or any brains about any thought or thinking in his life has an opinion about it and, therefore, if you've got an opinion I guess that makes you, you would have a prejudice one way or the other. For example, if you have eaten an apple, I guess you might have an opinion about the apple. And, you might be prejudiced either for or against it. And, that is the way the law means to use that word—not in the derrogatory fashion.

The biggest crime that could be committed in this courtroom today would be for somebody who really has an opinion about something— and we all have to have opinions if we've got any brains to think with—to have an opinion about something and not be willing to say it because they were sort of prejudiced against admitting their prejudice. So, with that thought in mind—and I'm sure counsel for the defense shares that with me—and I know the Court does, I want to ask you some questions about that, if I might. And, one that comes immediately to mind that may have something to do with your attitude in the case would be this: Karen Silkwood was a member of a union. This Court has asked you about that. But, I kind of would like to know what your feelings are about a union. Some of you belong to a union, and some of you, because you belong to a union, may like a union or may not. Some of you may be employers and have had experience with unions from the other side. So, could I just ask you about what your attitude is with respect to a union—and there is nothing wrong—the only problem would be if you have some experience and still didn't have any attitude, then I would wonder what was wrong.

Mrs. Estus, have you had any experience or any relationship with a union one way or the other?

JUROR ESTUS: Other than my dad belonged to one. He was a railroad man.

MR. SPENCE: How do you feel about unions?

JUROR ESTUS: I think there have to be unions for a working man.

MR. SPENCE: Okay. Now, Mrs. Estus just made an expression of how she feels about a union, and I can cut through a lot of questions by simply asking you how many of you agree with her, with Mrs. Estus? Just raise your hands. Okay. How many of you disagree with that proposition? All right. Mr. Guyer. And, could you tell me, Mr. Guyer, what your attitude is.

JUROR GUYER: It depends on the union. There are good ones, and bad ones.

MR. SPENCE: Thank you, Mr. Guyer. Okay. Would you have any hesitation in belonging to a good union?

JUROR GUYER: No. In most cases people are forced to work in a union.

MR. SPENCE: I said would you have any hesitation yourself in working for or becoming a part of a good union?

JUROR GUYER: Probably not.

THE COURT: Is there some question about that in your mind?

JUROR GUYER: Not if I thought it was a good union.

MR. SPENCE: What, in your mind, would be a good union?

JUROR GUYER: One that does something for you. I worked for a company awhile ago in college, and I worked in a salaried position, but hourly people had a union, and I didn't see any real need to it, and the hourly people wanted to get rid of it, so it apparently didn't do anything for the people.

MR. SPENCE: You feel, Mr. Guyer, that a union should do something for the people that it represents, don't you?

JUROR GUYER: Yes.

MR. SPENCE: How many of you agree with that? How many of you disagree?

How many of you have had experience as employers, or as somebody who supervises labor where there were unions involved? All right, Mr. Long, you have?

JUROR LONG: Yes.

MR. SPENCE: Were you a union member?

JUROR LONG: No. Management did belong to a union.

MR. SPENCE: I made a note here that you have—but you have belonged to a union?

JUROR LONG: Right. I do now.

MR. SPENCE: You do now.

JUROR LONG: I did while I was working, but I was service manager for General Truck Company, and I was the foreman for Trans Con. Trans Con had a union, but management cannot be union. At that time I was not in union.

MR. SPENCE: So you have been on both sides of the fence?

JUROR LONG: Been on both sides of the fence.

MR. SPENCE: Did it feel all right to be on both sides?

JUROR LONG: Sure.

MR. SPENCE: Does it feel all right to be on the union side of the fence now?

JUROR LONG: Yes.

MR. SPENCE: Is there anybody here, all things being equal, assuming that you had, you know, a union that was all right, that did something for the employees, and you had a chance to either be on the union or not, is there anybody here—Just how would you choose to be? I guess that is the question that I want to know. If it was all, you know, it was a good union, did something for its employees, but you had a choice to be on the union side, to be a part of that union and join it, or not to join it, which way would you go? And, I will start with you, Mrs. Estus, how would you go?

JUROR ESTUS: I don't know. I would have to know what the conditions were that, you know, I thought I needed some help on.

MR. SPENCE: Considering all the facts that I gave you, could you make a decision just on that—that it was a good union you would join it, or you didn't have to.

JUROR ESTUS: Before I joined something I've got to know about it. That is all I can say.

MR. SPENCE: I will accept that answer, Mrs. Estus. But, if you could give me sort of how you felt without me—

JUROR ESTUS: If I was making a dollar and a half an hour, and everything had increased in price, and I needed two dollars and a half an hour, then I would probably join the union.

MR. SPENCE: Okay. How about you, Mrs. Gowen?

JUROR GOWEN: If my employer was paying top wages, I would stay out of the union. If he wasn't, I would probably join it.

MR. SPENCE: Okay. Mrs. Fink.

JUROR FINK: I'm not sure—I'm not sure.

MR. SPENCE: Is there some reason why you are not sure? Is there something going on there that we could share with each other?

JUROR FINK: Yes. I just had an experience with United Farm Workers Union.

MR. SPENCE: Was it an unpleasant experience?

JUROR FINK: Oh, yes. It was tear gas that had been thrown, and it was, yes, an unpleasant experience.

MR. SPENCE: You wouldn't want to join a union like that, would you?

JUROR FINK: No, I wouldn't. No. But, I think it was a good thing before Chavez got in it, or they would still be making a dollars an hour.

MR. SPENCE: You see the reason I'm asking this question about the union is because Karen Silkwood was a member of a union, and there are allegations in the case that her involvement in the union had something to do with the problem that came up. That is, Kerr-McGee makes allegations that are related to the union—

JUROR FINK: She belonged to a union?

MR. SPENCE: She belonged to a union.

JUROR FINK: Well, no, I don't agree with that. Just because she worked for a union.

MR. SPENCE: Well, they are trying to say things about that that I'm not permitted to talk about right now.

JUROR FINK: I don't know that much about it. My husband belongs to a union.

MR. SPENCE: You see what is going to happen here is eventually you may have to decide whether Kerr-McGee's position is correct, and their allegations against Karen Silkwood, and what she was involved in, in her union activities, or whether Karen Silkwood's activity is correct. And, of course, she's dead and her lips are sealed, and she can't say, but there will be people to testify here, as best they can, whether her position is correct. And, of course, Mr. Silkwood wants me to find out if any of you, because of your experience, would feel that maybe—well, you could lean one way or the other because of your own personal experience.

JUROR FINK: Well, then, I have a personal experience at home. My husband belongs to a union, which is the postal union.

MR. SPENCE: Does he think that is all right?

JUROR FINK: And, I think it is all right. Yes, I do. I certainly do; yes.

MR. SPENCE: Okay.

JUROR FINK: So, what I'm saying is that I see the good side of it, and the bad side of it.

MR. SPENCE: Well; thank you for being frank with me, Mrs. Fink. And, let me understand—you're saying, in effect, that you have had trouble with the throwing of this tear gas but—

JUROR FINK: No, no. They were not throwing the tear gas. The police were to break it up. That is the way that was.

MR. SPENCE: Now, I don't know whether you were made at the police, or the union.

JUROR FINK: Well, anyhow, when they are burning the fields and houses down there, and the strikers strike, that is too bad.

MR. SPENCE: That is going too far.

JUROR FINK: A little bit, I think. But, what I'm saying is I had the good side of it and the bad side of it.

MR. SPENCE: Okay. Thank you, Mrs. Fink.

Mrs. Henthrorn, how do you feel about unions?

JUROR HENTHORN: All things being equal, and being a good union, I would not join the union.

MR. SPENCE: Now, that is the kind of answer that I was trying to find. I will just write out here on my card here, and that will mean that, and is there any—Mrs. Henthorn, that answers the questions just the way I wanted it presented. I want Mrs. Clark—could you answer the question that way?

JUROR CLARK: Well, all things being equal, and I have the right to choose whether I wanted to be in a union or not a union, if I felt it was a good union, I would join it.

MR. SPENCE: So, I'm going to write down on yours "in" and, I will put a circle around it.

And, how about you, Mrs. Rogstad?

JUROR ROGSTAD: I'm not sure. I might join the union.

MR. SPENCE: I'm going to put "in" and kind of a question mark.

And, Mrs. Roberson?

JUROR ROBERSON: Well, my husband belongs to a union, and as far as I know it is a good union, but there are some things about the union that promoted bad things that happened, but if I could join, yes, I would join.

MR. SPENCE: Okay. So can I put you down as "in?"

JUROR ROBERSON: Yes.

MR. SPENCE: All right. Now, I'm back to Mrs. Guyer, and could you answer that question that way?

JUROR GUYER: No. But, under certain circumstances, you know, I might. I would say just put a question by me.

MR. SPENCE: Okay. Mr. Ford.

JUROR FORD: No union is any better than the people that belong, belongs there, and I feel like a union has its place, and I would join the union.

MR. SPENCE: Okay. Thank you. Mr. Maxwell Hall?

JUROR HALL: I would not join the good union unless there was some clear-cut advantage to me.

MR. SPENCE: Okay. So, I would put you "out" wouldn't I? And, Mr. Akin?

JUROR AKIN: Being a good union, I think I would join the union, but I still think I would—I should have the freedom of choice to join or not join.

MR. SPENCE: That is in my question. If you could choose either way.

JUROR AKIN: I think I would; yes.

MR. SPENCE: Thank you. I will put you down for "in." Mrs. Blan?

JUROR BLAN: Well, it would depend on the circumstances, but I feel like unions are good. If I felt like I needed to join one, I would.

MR. SPENCE: You would?

JUROR BLAN: Yes.

MR. SPENCE: Should I put you "in" or "out"?

JUROR BLAN: Probably "in."

MR. SPENCE: All right. Mr. Royse?

JUROR ROYSE: A good union is, like Mr. Ford says, as good as the people in it. I would join if it were good.

MR. SPENCE: Okay. Thank you. Mrs.—I can't read my writing—

JUROR SANGER: Sanger.

MR. SPENCE: Sanger. I can read it. How about you?

JUROR SANGER: Being basically a non-joiner, if circumstances were equal, I would not be in.

MR. SPENCE: Put you down for "out."

JUROR SANGER: Right.

MR. SPENCE: Now, let's see—I'm down to Mrs. Freeman.

JUROR FREEMAN: I think I would join, if I had a choice of my own.

MR. SPENCE: Okay. Put you down for "in?"

How about you, Mr. Long?

JUROR LONG: Put me "in."

MR. SPENCE: Put you "in."

MR. LONG: Every worker should belong to a union, and work as though he didn't.

MR. SPENCE: Mrs. Isbill?

JUROR ISBILL: If it was a large company I would, but a small one I don't think I would.

MR. SPENCE: So, what in the world am I going to write down for you?

JUROR ISBILL: A question mark, I guess.

JUROR FORD: "in" big and "out" small.

MR. SPENCE: Okay. Who said that?

   Mr. Wood?

JUROR WOOD: I worked for the Civil Service Commission for thirty-two years, but I haven't been union, but I have no problem with the union. We haven't been able to have no union so—you know, I don't know anything about it, to be truthful with you.

MR. SPENCE: Civil Service Commission for thirty-two years.

JUROR WOOD: That is a union to itself.

MR. SPENCE: What?

JUROR WOOD: It is a union in itself.

MR. SPENCE: In itself?

JUROR WOOD: Uh huh. Some fellows.

MR. SPENCE: Should I put you "in" or "out?"

JUROR WOOD: "in", I guess. I'm not opposed to it, but I never belonged to it.

MR. SPENCE: I hear you. Mrs. Gourley?

JUROR GOURLEY: I would join.

MR. SPENCE: I've got you "in." Mrs. Hodges?

JUROR HODGES: I would join, because I belong to a union.

MR. SPENCE: All right. Thank you, your Honor. And, I'm starting to feel better already.

THE COURT: Good. I'm glad your health has improved.

MR. SPENCE: Now, there are a few things that I have noted down here relative to some things that his Honor asked, and I wanted to ask a few questions of you, and I want to start with—I want to start with Mrs. Sanger.

JUROR SANGER: Yes.

MR. SPENCE: Mrs. Sanger, were you, you know, everytime I find people that are working for lawyers I get spooky.

JUROR SANGER: I appreciate your feeling.

MR. SPENCE: You expected that, didn't you?

JUROR SANGER: Yes.

MR. SPENCE: Now, I have people that work for me in Wyoming that are legal assistants,—and that is what you say you were?

JUROR SANGER: Yes.

MR. SPENCE: And, because, you know, they develop philosophies, because they are exposed to philosophies of the office, and attitudes that they just start to develop because of the kind of cases that he find himself involved in, and they get—they're very loyal people—and they get behind me, you know, and sometimes maybe they shouldn't be behind me, but they are behind me—

JUROR SANGER: Yes.

MR. SPENCE: —and that is the way you are, isn't it, with your boss when you were working for them?

JUROR SANGER: Well, I tried.

MR. SPENCE: Well, what kind of cases did that law firm handle mostly, from the standpoint of trial work?

JUROR SANGER: Mostly—well, cases go by case load.

MR. SPENCE: Yes; mostly.

JUROR SANGER: Mostly. It mostly is defense cases.

MR. SPENCE: So, would it be fair to say that they were a firm that mostly represented people who were being sued?

JUROR SANGER: Correct.

MR. SPENCE: And, so they were a firm that was mostly doing cases, like these people over here (indicating), isn't that right?

JUROR SANGER: Well, percentage-wise; yes.

MR. SPENCE: That's why I'm getting spooky, because of the kind of cases—I don't represent anybody but people—I just don't represent anybody but people, and nobody in any firm does. I don't represent any banks, or any corporations, or anything like that. Did most of the people—strike "people"—did most of the clients that your law firm represented, were most of those corporations and insurance companies?

JUROR SANGER: Well, we were representative customers of insurance companies.

MR. SPENCE: In other words, the insurance company was the one that actually paid the bill?

JUROR SANGER: Correct. Generally.

MR. SPENCE: And, there's a philosophy that developed in a firm like that—they are called "defense firms" aren't they?

JUROR SANGER: Certainly.

MR. SPENCE: And, they are hired by large corporations, and insurance companies, and their philosophy gets sort of—well, that people that sue in the courts, like my client, well, you defend those cases, right?

JUROR SANGER: Right.

MR. SPENCE: And, you kind of develop an attitude after awhile, don't you, about people that bring lawsuits?

JUROR SANGER: No. I can't buy that.

MR. SPENCE: You can't buy that?

JUROR SANGER: No.

MR. SPENCE: Well, how did you feel, Mrs. Sanger, how did you feel about the work you were doing there as a legal assistant?

JUROR SANGER: I don't get your question.

MR. SPENCE: I take it that you did some work in gathering evidence?

JUROR SANGER: I did document work.

MR. SPENCE: Did you like the job?

JUROR SANGER: Yes.

MR. SPENCE: If you knew that your effort, on behalf of your law firm, would result in depriving a person of his right to recover, did that ever bother you?

JUROR SANGER: I don't go with the word "deprive."

MR. SPENCE: That is what I thought. You know, I want to ask you a question:

JUROR SANGER: All right.

MR. SPENCE: If you were sitting over there in Bill Silkwood's chair, representing his three grandchildren, would you feel comfortable with the jury made up of six legal assistants who have worked for defense law firms?

JUROR SANGER: I think not.

MR. SPENCE: Why not—why wouldn't you be comfortable?

JUROR SANGER: In the first place it would seem to be a pretty unbalanced jury.

MR. SPENCE: Yes.

JUROR SANGER: I would assume that any—

MR. SPENCE: You wouldn't feel uncomfortable with six school teachers, would you, or six people that work in a cafe?

JUROR SANGER: I might.

MR. SPENCE: You might?

JUROR SANGER: Uh huh.

MR. SPENCE: Would there be any other reason other than the balance? You know, we've got to get a unanimous verdict here. So one, you know, one may be enough, one person, that holds out could be enough to deprive my client of a verdict, and if I were representing you, would you feel comfortable as one of the persons on the jury who has worked for a defense law firm, who worked for large corporations, who go against cases of this kind as a matter of habit, would you feel comfortable about that?

JUROR SANGER: Frankly, I never thought that we—I never felt like we were working for large corporations, though in fact we might have been.

MR. SPENCE: Well, as a matter of fact, the largest corporations, with the most money in the whole world, paid your bills, and that is mainly the insurance companies, isn't that true?

JUROR SANGER: Yes. But, I never thought of "X" company as being a defendant.

MR. SPENCE: Well, if there was a—

MR. FENTON: Your Honor, may we approach the bench?

THE COURT: Come up, gentlemen.
(At the bench.)

[The Court and counsel have a discussion out of the presence of the jury regarding Mr. Spence's references to corporations and insurance companies.]

THE COURT: All right. All the jurors are present. Mr. Spence, sir, you may continue.

MR. SPENCE: Thank you, Judge. I know you want me to finish by 6:00, if I can, and I'm going to try to do that. If I can't, why I'll tell the Judge, but I will try to do it.

THE COURT: All right. I appreciate that. As I said, we need to give the defendants the same amount of time to be fair to both sides. So, that is why I had my law clerk tell you—and that is what I indicated at the bench—that I didn't tell them I would keep them all night. I think that there is considerable disconfiture among the jury, from what I've heard anyhow, and I don't know as I blame them. I will just ask you to be patient here.

MR. SPENCE: Yes, your Honor. And, I do want to say that it is important that we conclude, but it is more important to my client that we satisfy ourselves that we have done our job correctly.

THE COURT: Well, I want you to have that satisfaction, if you can, but I'm the fellow that has the overall responsibility, and I want to feel that both sides have had a fair chance at it.

MR. SPENCE: Now, Mrs. Sanger, you know what we were talking about before the recess. The more I got to thinking about this, the more I got kind of scared about you sitting on this jury—just to be honest with you, and that is the way you would like me to be, wouldn't you?

JUROR SANGER: Certainly.

MR. SPENCE: The reason I'm concerned about it, and anxious about it, and feel it right about here (indicating) is because you've said that you have worked for a defense firm, and you say that you know some of these fellows over here at the defense table,—and you don't know me—

JUROR SANGER: No.

MR. SPENCE: You don't know any of the fellows that I'm associated with?

JUROR SANGER: I know Mr. Ikard, but I don't know that I've ever met him.

MR. SPENCE: You don't know my client?

JUROR SANGER: No.

MR. SPENCE: And, you have said that you would—you might feel a little uneasy if you were sitting in Mr. Silkwood's chair and there was a juror with that kind of knowledge and that kind of background sitting on your case, and so I want to ask you just straight: Don't you feel that under the circumstances, that you and I have shared with each other, that the fair thing in this case would be for another juror to take your spot?

JUROR SANGER: I guess you have to do what you think is fair to your client, and disregard my feelings about it.

MR. SPENCE: But, I'm concerned about your feelings, because you're going to be the one, if you stay on the case, that decides my client's case, and so I asked you the straight question, Mrs. Sanger, and I want you to be just as honest with me as I have been with you.

JUROR SANGER: If I didn't think I would be fair, I could say anything that would get me off the jury, but I—

MR. SPENCE: Would there be the tiniest doubt in your mind about that?

JUROR SANGER: Nope.

MR. SPENCE: Not even the tiniest?

JUROR SANGER: Not even the tiniest.

MR. SPENCE: And, I don't even need to worry about that tonight when I go home and try to get a little sleep?

JUROR SANGER: You may worry, but I don't think you need to.

MR. SPENCE: I don't need to. You're going to be absolutely fair to my client?

JUROR SANGER: I'm going to try to be.

MR. SPENCE: And, you can assure us of that?

JUROR SANGER: Yes, sir.

MR. SPENCE: And, I can rest assured of that?

JUROR SANGER: Yes. I have been on both sides of the fence.

MR. SPENCE: Yes. But, I haven't. You want to be on this jury?

JUROR SANGER: I would think it would be an interesting experience. I don't know that I'm absolutely thrilled to be on the jury that is going to be four to six week's duration, but—

MR. SPENCE: You haven't got anything better to do at home right now, have you?

JUROR SANGER: Make up my income tax, but I guess I can file an extension.

MR. SPENCE: Do you want to be on the case?

JUROR SANGER: Yeah.

THE COURT: Well, really, that is not the area of inquiry. Some of them don't want to be on. They would rather be in Timbuktu.

MR. SPENCE: Well, Judge, that is true. The next question might clear up why I asked it: Is there any other reason that you would like to be on the case, other than the fact that you think it might be interesting?

JUROR SANGER: I hope I would contribute to, you know, the functioning of the legal system. Beyond those two things, that would most basically be it.

MR. SPENCE: Do you recognize that the case may have some extraordinary importance?

JUROR SANGER: I would assume it would; yes.

MR. SPENCE: And, that it may be a case that could change the course of not only the law but the country?

JUROR SANGER: I think there's always that possibility, certainly.

MR. SPENCE: Would that have something to do with your desire to be on the case?

JUROR SANGER: You mean do I want to make law?

MR. SPENCE: Would you like to take part in something that is as important as this case?

JUROR SANGER: Yes, I would, but that wouldn't be a—I would just as soon serve on one that wasn't going to make law.

MR. SPENCE: All right. Well, if you're satisfied, and I have your assurance, I can't ask for anything more, can I? If you are a member of this jury, and you are in the jury room, and you start to argue the case, will you call to your mind and your attention, your own personal attention, the assurances that you have given me?

JUROR SANGER: Certainly.

MR. SPENCE: All right. Now, his Honor talked a little bit about damages in this case. I want to ask a general question of you about damages because in part, in part, damages will be based upon some allegations and proofs that the plaintiff's give relative to nine-days of suffering, and terror, and panic, fear of death—those are the bases of the damages for her—and proof that she was injured in a very serious frightening way.

Now, she died nine days after the damage commenced, so we are talking about, in part, nine days of her life. And, the claim is for a million and a half dollars of actual damages for that pain, terror, and fear. I want to know if there is anybody here who believes, in their heart, that no matter what it was like, what terror there was, what it was like for nine days is worth a million and a half dollars. Does anybody come to that conclusion? Bill Silkwood doesn't set the amount. That is the amount that I have asked for my client, on behalf of my client, based upon my judgment. Pretty soon six of you will have to make your judgment. Are there any of you that feel prejudiced against my client and his three grandchildren, for whom this case is brought, because his lawyer had the audacity to ask for a million and a half dollars for those nine days? Do any of you hold a feeling—now listen—I know you would raise your hand if something was rumbling around in your mind saying "yeah, I ought to answer that." Well, would you answer that, I mean, if that was going on, would you tell me? How many of you would—how many of you wouldn't? Well, how about those that—

JUROR LONG: I misunderstood the question. Would you repeat that?

MR. SPENCE: Since I don't ask very good questions, I'm going to start over again. I'm concerned about that issue, and I want to know if any of you feel any sort of resentment, or distrust, for my client Bill Silkwood, because I have asked for a million and a half dollars involving nine days of her life? Any of you feel that way? Do any of you feel that lawyers—I ought to ask you, Mrs. Sanger,—do any of you feel that lawyers always ask twice or three times the amount that they think their client is entitled to? Does anybody think that about lawyers?
(Reporter's note: Simultaneous response by some jurors: "sometimes")

MR. SPENCE: Would you make, those of you who think that, make room for the possibility in this case that, after you have heard the testimony, you will agree with the assessment that we have made on behalf of this case—would you make room for that—anybody that wouldn't?
(No responses.)

MR. SPENCE: Would you make room for the fact that some lawyers don't ask for twice the amount that they want—that they ask for the exact amount to the penny that they believe their client is entitled to?

JUROR LONG: There is always one that will.

MR. SPENCE: Would you make room for the possibility, Mr. Long,— Thank you for your comment.

JUROR LONG: I didn't say "you" did.

MR. SPENCE: I know. I wish you had. Would you make room for the possibility, Mr. Long, that that is the kind of lawyer I am?

JUROR LONG: I will just have to be honest—I don't have an opinion.

MR. SPENCE: You will just have to find out?

JUROR LONG: I just met you.

MR. SPENCE: That's right. But, you could make room for the possibility that I might be that kind of a person?

JUROR LONG: I could.

MR. SPENCE: Would the rest of you agree with Mr. Long on that subject?

(No responses.)

MR. SPENCE: Now, the Judge talked about ten and a half million dollars, and whether that shocked anybody, and some people it shocked a little bit to start with—and it is a lot of money—and when you get into the jury room you're going to have the power of "writing a check" for anything up to eleven and a half million dollars—ten million dollars punitive, and a million and a half actual. How many of you would be afraid to use that power, if you felt it was justified under the law and the facts of the case—anybody that would be afraid of that? I don't think any of us have written a check that big. Would any of you be afraid to do that—because you're going to be called upon to do that—and I'm going to ask you, at the conclusion of the case to do that. Any of you be afraid to do that, if you felt it was just?

(No responses.)

MR. SPENCE: Now, punitive damages has something to do with punishment as his Honor said. It wouldn't be fair to punish a large corporation to the same extent that you would punish a paper boy, or your son for not getting home on time, and you dock him ten cents. If he makes fifty cents a week, ten cents is a lot of money to him. Nobody would be shocked by that. That is twenty percent of his income for the week. Twenty percent. So, now, when we start talking about the relationship of a claim for punitive damages it may be that you may have to take into account what is a sufficient sum to punish a corporation based upon their earnings. You can see it wouldn't be the same. You wouldn't punish a large corporation the same as the paper boy, or the paper boy the same as a large corporation and somehow try to make the punishment fit the individual, because Kerr-McGee in this case claims they have the right of an individual—and the Court says they do have the right—but they also have the responsibility. So, would all of you bear that in mind on the question of punitive damages? Anybody that wouldn't? Anybody doesn't understand what I was talking about?

(No responses.)

MR. SPENCE: The reason I ask those questions of you together is because the Judge wants me to do that; is that right, your Honor?

THE COURT: That's right.

MR. SPENCE: I would ask you that individually, and chat with you about it individually, but I have been asked to do that. Would you please hold up your hand. It applies to you in some way?

(No responses.)

MR. SPENCE: Do any of you have a sense that the loss of a day of one's life is sort of insignificant? What I'm trying to find out is: Is there anybody here on the jury that says, you know, a day of one's life isn't important—anybody sort of have an idea that their own life is unimportant—

anybody have a feeling like that? Some people do. Some people are maybe unaware of the value of our days. Anybody here who wouldn't find a special value in the last nine days of your life, if you knew you were living them right now? Anybody that wouldn't care? Or, anybody wouldn't find them valuable?

(No responses.)

MR. SPENCE: If I were representing you for the last nine days of your life, would any of you be upset with me if I asked for a million and a half dollars for them?

(No responses.)

MR. FENTON: I don't believe that is a proper question. I believe we will object to that, your Honor.

THE COURT: Well, it has been asked and answered, and there is no response.

MR. SPENCE: I'm skipping over some of these questions, Judge, as I go down the list, in deference to you.

THE COURT: That is very commendable, Mr. Spence. I thought I'd covered the ground pretty good. And, the other counsel are going to have to have an opportunity. And, as I said, this is an area of limited inquiry. I mean, some places they don't allow counsel to inquire. So, I'm doing it in deference to both sides—anything that may help get the best jury, and to give you the opportunity, both sides, to make the choices that you're going to be forced to make here pretty soon.

MR. SPENCE: Thank you, your Honor. Now, you know, something I want to say to you right now, and that is that I'm not going to ask any of you in this case for any sympathy. I don't want any sympathy, and I don't want any sympathy for Bill Silkwood, nor for the children. That isn't the issue in any way. All I simply want, on behalf of my client, is justice, and a full adequate and uncompromised verdict—we just want justice—an uncompromised verdict. I don't want sympathy. We just want justice. Is there anybody here that wouldn't be willing to decide the case on those basic ground rules?

(No responses.)

MR. SPENCE: Now, there is a basic proposition of law that his Honor has already mentioned to you—that has something to do with the escape of a dangerous substance—in which he said that—he hasn't ruled on that—but that if there is a dangerous substance, and it escapes and hurts somebody else, the party who had control of that substance may be liable—may have to pay in damage whether or not they were at fault, whether or not they were negligent. That is called negligence— that is called liability without fault—or the legal terms is called strict liability. It is well-known in the law. We see it involved all the time in nitroglycerin cases, like where dangerous substances are brought into an area and it escapes and hurts somebody else. Now, is there anybody here that would be unwilling to find and to follow that rule of law if the facts support it? And, if his Honor gives you that instruction. Any-body?

(No responses.)

MR. SPENCE: You see, the other side of it is a lot of us think "well, if they didn't violate a law, or didn't violate—if they weren't negligent, or if—you know—they were careful or tried to do things right they shouldn't have to pay," but his Honor may instruct that they may have to pay even if they were careful, if it got loose and hurt somebody. Would that strike any of you as being unfair?

(No responses.)

MR. SPENCE: Would any of you go into the jury room and say: "Well, you know Mr. Spence didn't show there was any negligence, and there-fore we're not you know, and they showed they were careful, and there-fore we can't find for Mr. Silkwood and his grandchildren." Would you all be able to follow the instruction of the Court that says you don't have to prove any negligence?

(No responses.)

MR. SPENCE: You may not have to prove—or, if they prove that they are careful, it may not be a defense—if they had a dangerous substance and it escaped and hurt somebody, they may have to pay whether they were careful or not—could you all follow that rule—any of you that wouldn't?

(No responses.)

MR. SPENCE: How many of you know anything about the dangers of plutonium?

(No responses.)

MR. SPENCE: How many of you have heard about it?

(Reporter's note: Five jurors indicate by raising their hands.)

MR. SPENCE: Have any of you heard about it being a cause of leukemia and cancer?

(Two jurors raise their hands.)

UNIDENTIFIED JUROR: We read about it.

MR. SPENCE: Yes. Have any of you had any personal experience in your life, or any of your family, with that dread disease, cancer?

(Reporter's note: Six jurors raise their hands.)

MR. SPENCE: Have any of you lost a loved one from it?

(Reporter's note: Six jurors raise their hands.)

MR. SPENCE: Could I ask you to hold your hand up for just a minute on that. Would you write down those for me, Art.

Lost a loved one from cancer.

Can the defense counsel see the jurors, likewise?

MR. PAUL: Yes, sir.

MR. SPENCE: Have any of you read the—I think some of you did read this Oklahoma Journal in the last day or two in which the Silkwood case was reported. How many of you did, in the Oklahoma Journal? (Reporter's note: Juror Long raises his hand.)

MR. SPENCE: How many of you take the Oklahoma Journal? (Reporter's note: Juror Long raises his hand.)

MR. SPENCE: I hope that the Oklahoma Journal, that have seen that response, don't feel too badly.

Did you read the statement in the Oklahoma Journal attributed to the attorneys for Kerr-McGee referring to Karen Silkwood as the Queen of the Safety Ball?

MR. PAUL: We would object to that as improper, your Honor.

THE COURT: Sustained. I agree. There might be statements by attorneys on either side.

MR. SPENCE: Have any of you read anything about missing plutonium and the possibility of missing plutonium being in the hands of foreign powers that have been stolen from plants in this country—any of you read about that? (Reporter's note: Jurors indicate by raising hands.)

MR. SPENCE: Any of you read an article in the recent newspaper about that? (Reporter's note: One juror raises hand.)

MR. SPENCE: Thank you. You know, your Honor talked a little bit with you folks about "life style." We all have different life styles—we all go to different churches—or we don't go to church at all—we all have ideas about marriage—some of our younger people have ideas about marriage that aren't shared by the older folks—some of my kids have ideas that I have a little trouble with— Does anybody have the same problems that I just suggested? Do any of you have any trouble with the ideas of the younger generation—any of you that would feel, those of you that feel sort of like that, any of you feel that the younger generation isn't entitled to the same protection of the law as we are, even if we don't agree with their moral code? (No responses.)

MR. SPENCE: It's an important question, and I'm not getting a response, and it is scaring me a little bit. Is there anybody here—let me strike that. Let me put it this other way around: If it were shown to you that Karen Silkwood had a different moral system than you and me, would that affect your judgment at all as to her rights under the law? Would it? Okay. You said it wouldn't, Mrs. Estus, and I believe you. Would it for you, Mrs. Gowen?

JUROR GOWEN: No.

MR. SPENCE: Do you all understand my question? Would it for you, Mrs. Fink?

JUROR FINK: No.

MR. SPENCE: Would everyone of you give her the same rights, and her children the same rights, under the law as you would as if she was the Blessed Mother? Would you? Would you, sir?

JUROR WOOD: I would; yes, sir.

MR. SPENCE: Of course, the Judge has already told you something that you understand in criminal cases, that you have to prove everything beyond a reasonable doubt, and that is the American system, and that is the right thing to do in a criminal case. In a civil case it is different. Nobody's going to jail. Nobody in Kerr-McGee is going to jail. Nobody that works for them is going to jail. Nobody is charging them with any crime. This is a lawsuit for money, and the bottom dollar, or bottom line is "dollars" in this case, because that is the only kind of justice we can get. We can't bring her back. We can't give her these days back and give her peace. We can't overdo or undo the things that have been done. All we can do is get a verdict in dollars. That is all the law is able to do. That is all we ask for, is justice. Now, in this case we have to prove our case first to you by a preponderance of the evidence—and the Judge says that is an adjusting of the scales—that isn't proof beyond a reasonable doubt like in a criminal case where a man's life is at stake— but you have to just tip the scales. If you weigh up all the evidence on both sides, which is the most believable case, Karen Silkwood's case or Kerr-McGee's case? Would any of you hold Karen Silkwood—or, my friend, my client, Bill Silkwood, to a higher proof than that before you would return a verdict? In other words, if we tip the scales which makes the evidence preponderate, if we tip the scales in our favor, will you return a verdict, a full uncompromised verdict in this case? Will you? And, even if it takes the courage to write a check for eleven and a half million dollars—and that is full justice—will you do that? (No responses.)

MR. SPENCE: Judge, how did I do? I'm all through.

6

Opening Statement

§6.01   Introduction

Most trial texts assert that the opening statement is important because it is the first opportunity to tell the jury what the case is about.[1] Social scientists argue that opening statements create cognitive schemata that influence the ways jurors process and interpret evidence throughout the trial.[2] In what follows, I will demonstrate that successful lawyers for the plaintiff develop a narrative or storytelling structure to create the cognitive schemata that guide the perceptions of the jurors throughout the trial. The central element in creating such a framework is transforming the case into a story, through the use of language and themes, to make the events come alive and to present the plaintiffs as heroes and the defendants as villains. In the course of telling the story, the lawyers also develop themes that organize the evidence and claims of liability, set a serious tone, define jury purpose, specify their bases of authority, introduce key concepts and key pieces of evidence, enhance credibility, and lay out the central arguments in their cases and refute the central contentions of the defendant.

The openings examined were those by Scott Baldwin, Victor Bergman, Melvin Block, Bill Colson, Phil Corboy, Robert Gibbons, Herman Glaser, Robert Habush, Peter Perlman, Leonard Ring, Gerry Spence, and Lantz Welch. Scott Baldwin's case involved a product liability claim in which a crane operator fell to his death as a result of a crane collapse. Victor Bergman submitted two openings for study. The first involved a medical malpractice action in which the failure to timely diagnose Hodgkin's disease resulted in the loss of the chance to obtain timely treatment and cure. The second case involved a suit against Colt Industries for the negligent design and malfunction of a Colt .45 handgun. The Block opening involved a product liability claim against the manufacturer of an artillery shell that malfunctioned in a howitzer and injured two soldiers in combat during the Vietnam War. The trial was bifurcated, and, thus, Block presented three openings, one on the issue of liability, and two on the issue of damages. The Colson opening involved a medical malpractice action in which a child was born brain damaged due to complications during labor and cesarean delivery. The case involved allegations of failure to monitor the child and of allowing the child to become oxygen-deprived during labor and delivery. The Corboy voir dire involved an automobile collision which left the plaintiff a spastic quadraplegic with locked-in syndrome. The Gibbons opening involved a product liability claim for the negligent design of an ejection device that resulted in the death of a jet fighter pilot. The Glaser opening was presented in a medical negligence case involving the performance of an unnecessary hysterectomy. The Habush voir dire involved catastrophic injuries caused in an industrial accident involving a forklift. The Perlman opening involved a mining accident in which an automatic mining machine malfunctioned and caused severe injury to a miner. Perlman's trial was bifurcated, and, therefore,

---

[1] T. Mauet, Fundamentals of Trial Techniques 49 (1980).

[2] Pyszczynski, Greenberg, Mack & Wrightsman, *Opening Statements in a Jury Trial: the Effect of Promising More Than the Evidence Can Show*, 11 J Applied Soc Psychology 434-44 (1981).

he presented two openings, one on the issue of liability, and the other on the issue of damages. The Ring voir dire involved the malfunction of a machine brake press machine in which the operator's hands were severely crushed. The Spence opening involved the trial of *Silkwood v Kerr-McGee*,[3] in which it was alleged that Karen Silkwood was negligently contaminated with plutonium. The Welch opening involved claims for damages and loss of consortium by a husband and wife stemming from an automobile collision.

§6.02   Narrative Structure—Introduction

All of the lawyers used a narrative or storytelling structure in presenting their openings. The elements of the structure consisted of an introduction, a body which developed the evidence in the same way that a story or drama develops a plot and story line, and a conclusion. These elements are illustrated below.

All of the openings examined contained an introduction that described either the purpose of the opening statement or the scope of the trial. These lawyers used their introductions strategically to shape the jurors' impressions of what would follow in the trial. The introduction gave the jurors an idea of what to expect in the rest of the statement. For example, Spence described the purpose of his opening statement and invited the jury to become a part of the case:

> Thank you, your Honor. Good morning, ladies and gentlemen: This is the time in the case when we have a chance to get acquainted, both with each other, and with the case of the parties. It is called the opening statement. And, my purpose in making an opening statement is to sort of give you an overview of what the case is going to be like. It is sort of like looking at a picture on the box of a picture puzzle box. The pieces of the puzzle are the pieces of evidence that will come in that you will be called upon to put together. We will try to help you do that. But, the picture on the box is what the puzzle will look like when it is all put together. That is what I'm going to try to do this morning in this very important case that you have been called upon to listen to and to try and become a part of.

Similarly, Ring described the nature of his opening statement:

> If the Court please, Counsel, Mr. Leonard, Mr. Zeilenga, Ladies and Gentlemen of the Jury. At this time, and I know that only one of you has had some jury service, before, but I can tell you that we are, all of us—at this time it is our privilege—that is, the lawyers—to address you and to tell you in what we call our opening statement what the case is about, sort of a bird's-eye view of the evidence that will follow in the hope that it will help you follow the evidence as it comes in—some of it will be technical—and give you a picture, so to speak, of what you will hear.

---

[3] No. 76-0888 (WD Okla, March 1979).

Scott Baldwin skillfully used language to create a favorable impression of his case:

> Ladies and gentlemen of the Jury, as I have told you, I am Scott Baldwin, and I represent the plaintiffs in this case, and I'm going to tell you what we expect to prove.
>
> This case is one that involves what I determine the tragic and needless death of Kenneth Branch, as he was the operator of a crane that you know by now fell in Dallas, when he was working on One Dallas Centre. He was lifting two yards of cement, as he had done many times before, and importantly, the two yards of cement that he was lifting was well within the capacity of this crane. Suddenly and with no forewarning the crane collapsed. It crashed some twenty-seven stories below carrying Mr. Branch to his death. He made a noble effort to escape, but he didn't have time. That was denied him, and he went down with the crane and was killed in the wreckage of the super structure, if you please, of the crane, and leaves surviving his widow and three children, who are here before you today.

In his first opening, Melvin Block described the scope of the trial:

> May it please the Court, Mr. Justice Canella, Mr. Brumbelow, Mr. Cox, Ladies and Gentlemen of the jury. No doubt you are wondering what brings you here from your various walks of life, from your trades, your occupations, your professions, your crafts. Well, it all comes about, it all emanates out of a tragic war and this is a tragic occurrence in that war.

In his second opening, Block described the function of opening statement and told the jurors what their function would be:

> May it please the Court, Judge Canella; Mr. Robert, my associate; ladies and gentlemen of the jury. At this time, as his Honor has told you, it is my privilege to open and give you an outline of what the proof will be in behalf of my client, Dorman Baird, the gentleman sitting at the outer point of that bench over there.
>
> Now, your function is a very important one. You are here to evaluate damages so that Mr. Baird gets full and adequate compensation for each and every injury he sustained and for the other damages such as loss of earning capacity and loss of earnings that the law allows.

In his third opening, Block described the scope of the trial, the purpose of opening statement, told the jury that the opening statement was not evidence, and made a commitment that what he said in opening would be supported by the evidence:

> May it please the Court, Judge Cannella, Mr. Brumbelow, Mr. Finkelstein, Mr. Roberts, Ms. Forewoman, ladies and gentlemen of the jury. We are about to embark upon a very important and responsible aspect,

the second phase of this trial, to assess the damages which were done to the survivors of Wendell Burns. Now in order to ascertain what that damage is, we must understand who Wendell Burns was, from whence he came, the type of life and upbringing he had, his character, his habits, his mode of life, who were the people he associated with, what sort of guy he was until his untimely death.

What I tell you now is not evidence. No lawyer's words are evidence. The evidence solely comes from the witness stand, from the documents and other exhibits that may be allowed in evidence; but I make this bond to you: what I tell you now, the evidence will bear out as to the sterling type of person Wendell Burns was; and the type of life he led; and the enormous damage done to his survivors because of his untimely and unwarranted death.

Lantz Welch described the nature of opening statement:

May it please the Court, ladies and gentlemen of this jury, you are now a cohesive, sworn-together jury. This portion of the trial is known as opening statement. Its purpose, its design is so that you might better understand the overall view of what has occurred to the parties in this lawsuit. Its necessity is based on the fact that it's very hard for a trial lawyer to control evidence as to when it will arrive and witnesses show up. Sometimes they show up a day late, and so forth.

It may be, as you hear this evidence, it will come in topsy-turvy sometimes. It's hoped that through our opening statement to you we can just chronologically tell you what's happened, and I'm going to tell you what's happened to Bob Cooper.

Bergman began his opening in his gun case telling the jury that his case was about his clients' damages. This opening presupposed liability and immediately placed the jury's focus on damages:

Good morning, ladies and gentlemen. As I said yesterday, my name is Victor Bergman and I represent the plaintiffs in this case, Paul and Jannie Johnson, who are from Junction City, Kansas.

This is a very serious and substantial case arising out of a gunshot wound that occurred to Paul Johnson on July 3, 1981. The case is really about the impact on the lives of Paul and Jannie that arose as a consequence of his injury.

In his medical negligence case, Bergman outlined the issues in the trial:

May it please the Court, ladies and gentlemen. For Shanna and Ken and Judy Morrison, this day has been a long time in coming. I know that Shanna and Ken are really regretful that they can't be here for the start of the trial, but, as I said, I'm pretty confident that they'll be here later in the week.

I personally am honored to be able to be the Morrisons' representative and to be able to tell you what has happened to them, what has happened to Shanna.

In this case you are going to hear evidence about what it means to be thirteen years old and to be told that you have a form of cancer called Hodgkin's disease. You are going to hear what it means to find out that Hodgkin's disease is very treatable if it is diagnosed early enough, if you don't let it get too far out of hand, but that your case was so extensive by the time that it was diagnosed that treatment has failed.

The trial of this case is going to take some time, as you have been told. The issues are medical issues, but they are really not too complicated. The issues, as they boil down, are as follows: Was Dr. Hanson negligent in failing to do a biopsy on this enlarged node which would hve definitely made the diagnosis of Hodgkin's disease? Did the delay in the diagnosis from September of 1983 to February of 1984 decrease Shanna Morrison's chance to be cured of the disease? In other words, what was the consequence of that passage of time to Shanna?

The third issue is what is the full nature and full extent of Shanna Morrison's injuries and damages and Judy Morrison's injuries and damages and Ken Morrison's injuries and damages? Finally, what monetary value is this community, in the form of this jury, going to put on these damages?

The opening statement is my opportunity to tell you what we believe the facts and the evidence to be that you will hear from the witness stand. As Mr. Saunders said, we have a pretty good idea of what people are going to say because we have taken a lot of depositions and interviewed a lot of people, so we know pretty well.

Perlman began his opening by explaining the purpose of opening and by telling the jurors what they would be learning about:

Thank you, Your Honor. May it please the Court, Counsel, Ladies and Gentlemen of the jury. A few minutes ago, you were on the prospective panel of jurors, and now you are on the jury that has been selected to try this case. As the lawyers in this case, it's our obligation to tell you what the case is about and what the facts are that you will be hearing from the witnesses that testify from the witness stand.

As you have already learned from the comments of the Court, this is a case in which Henry Shackleford suffered a major head injury, including the loss of his left eye, while he was an employee of the Golden Glow Mining Company on May 15th of 1981. We'll learn in this case about Henry Shackleford, who was a coal miner. We'll also learn about a continuous mining machine, a Joy 15-CM continuous mining machine.

Robert Gibbons began his opening forcefully and with the strategic use of language to create impact and meaning. He introduced the parties and explained the contentions, issues, and jury's role in the trial:

May it please the Court, ladies and gentlemen of the jury, and members of the defense: ladies and gentlemen, we are here today on behalf of the widow, Dianne Wahl, and minor son, Billy, to find out why Captain Harry Wahl died needlessly in the service of his country approximately 2 years ago right now. Thus your job is going to be to determine why, among other things, he had to bail out or eject from a crippled A10 fighter plane manufactured by one of the Defendants, Republic Fairchild in this case. Your job will also be to determine why, when it was necessary for him to eject, that his spinal cord was severed in his neck during the parachute opening.

Your job is also going to be to determine why, or if you will whether or not Captain Wahl's needless death, was caused or contributed to by the defective design of this airplane so that the flight controls became jammed. And then whether or not the ejection seat that was in there to save his life, and that is the purpose of an ejection seat, whether or not it was defectively designed in that during the process of the ejection, at chute opening or immediately prior thereto, his neck was literally yanked out of the socket, or whether they were both defectively designed products. And that is our contention in this case.

Now, this lawsuit then is brought against the Defendants, Republic Fairchild who manufactured, designed and manufactured, and actually sold the A10 fighter plane, as it had been known, the Thunderbolt 2, to one of its customers among others, the United States Air Force, and whether or not it was an unreasonably risky airplane as far as flight control jams or ejections were concerned. And it has also been brought against McDonnell-Douglas Corporation who was the designer and manufacturer of the ESCAPAC 1E9 ejection seat on the grounds that it was defectively designed because it is inherently dangerous and unstable, and mispositions the pilot, to set him up literally, even though he ejects within the design envelope, to have serious neck injuries and/or death.

Robert Habush presented an intricate introduction in which he introduced the jury to several concepts involved in the case:

May it please the Court, Mr. Daily, Mr. Gonring, Mr. Johnson, may it please you, Members of the Jury.

As indicated during the jury selection, I'm Bob Habush and I represent, with Catherine Tully, Mr. and Mrs. Schulz. They will be here in a little while, and as I get into my opening statement, you will understand why they are not here right now.

We all have our opinions of court cases, sometimes shaped by television and what—what we see or read about them so let me just, as a preliminary, remind you that this is a civil case. This is not a criminal prosecution. Nobody's licenses or ability to practice business is at stake. No one is going to jail. Guilty or not guilty is not an issue.

More importantly, as the person representing the injured party, we don't have to prove intent.

The Court will instruct you at the end of the case that this is a negligence case, a products liability case, and he will define for you, I believe, the law with respect to that. We're talking about carelessness, not intent to do harm to anybody.

Moreover, unlike the old District Attorney in Perry Mason, Hamilton Berger, I don't have to prove anything to you beyond a reasonable doubt which is a criminal prosecutor's burden. But, rather, by the greater weight of the credible evidence.

If you have two scales of justice and one party's evidence seems to weigh with more persuasive power, that will be sufficient for us to have met our obligation to you.

Whereas, clearly, I have the burden to prove people at fault who I suggest to you are at fault, whereas it's clearly true, I have the burden to prove the extent of the damages to Mr. and Mr. Schulz, it is equally true that the defense attorneys have the burden to prove anyone else at fault, and if that's what they suggest, then that shifts the ball so-to-speak—it goes into their court.

After a lawsuit is started a great deal of work goes into it, some of which you will hear and see and some of which you won't.

There is a lot of deposition-taking. You will be hearing from time to time—reading from depositions. They are—they are hearings that are taken in front of court reporters like Mary here. The people are sworn under oath, and they end up in little books, the questions and the answers and from time to time the lawyers will remind witnesses of what they said at these depositions, and portions of these depositions will be read to you as evidence.

An awful lot of what we call discovery has gone on, so Mr. Daily, myself and Mr. Johnson have a rough idea of what has happened up to now, but as you will see and as we always experience, things don't always go as planned in the courtroom and although we hoped that things would be logically presented to you step by step like a story, sometimes things get out of joint and witnesses are taken out of order and, hopefully, by the—by the end of the case, we will have the puzzle all back together again so we can go from A to Z like a story.

You are, Members of the Jury, representatives of the community and competent to sit on this case, and competent to, as the Court has just instructed you, judge the credibility of the witnesses and evaluate the evidence and, of course, follow the law.

You will be hearing from a number of experts. Experts will be determined by the Court to be competent to give you opinion testimony, what they think, but you can take it or leave it, and you can accept or reject expert opinions if you don't buy it.

The experts which you will hear are all competent, well-qualified prestigious people for both sides, and you will hear and realize that experts can differ in their opinions about how things happen and still be honest and still have integrity.

I suggest you to be very suspicious of any attorney who suggests that because he or she doesn't agree with an expert, that means the expert is dishonest.

The opening statement is—well, it's kind of like my table of contents to you. I want to outline what I think this case is going to look like as the evidence unfolds.

And as the Court indicated to you a few moments ago, what I say is not evidence. What Mr. Daily says is not evidence. What Mr. Johnson says is not evidence, but what the witnesses say will be, what documents you see, what photographs you see will be.

At the end of the case, we all will have a chance to stand up again and address you like this, and at that time we will review what did come into evidence, and at that time you will be able to see whether or not we have kept our bargain with you, that is did Bob Habush really prove what he said he was going to prove on Tuesday morning, did Mr. Daily, did Mr. Johnson?

And although the case may take two weeks, it's not going to be that long that we all won't remember what was said this morning, and if you do, we are going to have daily copy, that is, transcripts to remind each other of what we said we proved.

So we will keep a good accounting on each other as to what the proof looks like.

§6.03 —Body of the Opening Statement

The bodies of these opening statements were all developed as narratives. W. Lance Bennett has suggested that storytelling is the most common form of discourse used to provide accounts of social behavior and human events, and that storytelling, as applied to trials, may operate to isolate the central action of the story, establish relations between the action and the surrounding situational elements in the story, and it facilitates evaluating the possible interpretations of the action.[4] These openings confirmed his suggestion. In order to present their complex cases in a simple, coherent, and logical form, the lawyers became storytellers. The stories all had at least three parts. First, the lawyers provided the background of the case and described the parties and things involved in the lawsuit; second, the lawyers described how the injury occurred; and third, the lawyers discussed the nature and extent of the damages. In some instances the lawyers digressed or varied the order of presentation. In some cases the lawyers included a description of the defendant with a description of how the injury occurred. However, these three elements of the story were clearly identifiable in all openings.

Corboy outlined the three elements of his story line in his introduction:

---

[4] Bennett, *Storytelling in Criminal Trials: a Model of Social Judgment,* 64 QJ Speech 1-22 (1978).

> May it please the Court, Mr. Johnson, Mr. Jarvis, Dr. Block, Ms. Zanios, the fellow officers of the Court, this is the history and the life that you are going to see unravelled in the next several days of John Randolph Block. This is a story like most stories with a middle and with an end.
>
> This is a story that began February of 1953. When it was at its birth because that was the date, the month and the year that John Randolph Block was born.
>
> The middle of the story is the stature and the status and the posture his life had risen to by the 23rd day of August, 1981, a Sunday afternoon.
>
> The end of the story is as what is known as the present. Why do I say the end, because the evidence in this case is going to show that John Randolph Block is a prisoner, he is in internal carceration [sic] within the confines of his body.

In the first part of his story, Corboy introduced facts and evidence about his client's life before the accident. His life history was summarized in story form from his birth until the date of the automobile collision. Corboy's client had been seriously injured, and his story was one of a happy, healthy man who had had his life radically altered by a catastrophic injury. Therefore, the first part of the story told about how healthy the plaintiff was before the injury. Corboy concluded the first part of the story by relating how, just prior to the collision, the plaintiff and his grandmother went out for dinner:

> He came out to dinner on the Sunday afternoon, and Edward saw him. Edward was the last person of the family to see him before this occurrence. Fourteen-year-old Edward will tell you that Randy was smiling, again he was up, he was happy, and emotionally stable and everything was fine.

The second part of Corboy's story concerned background facts about the defendant and the occurrence causing the injury. The facts about the defendant could have been included in part one, but obviously, Corboy chose to devote the first section of his story to presenting the active, healthy, good plaintiff. He chose to merge the facts about the defendant with the facts about how the collision occurred, which strategically placed the defendant squarely within the tragic act. Part two began with a brief explanation of corporations and how they functioned, followed by a description of the defendant corporation. The driver of the defendant's vehicle, the vehicle in question, and the facts surrounding how and why the defendant driver reached the scene of the collision were described. Corboy then described the facts of the collision, concentrating on the negligent actions of the defendant. The last section of Corboy's story concerned the injuries and damages to the plaintiff which resulted from the defendant's negligence. The plaintiff suffered catastrophic injuries that radically changed his life. Corboy painstakingly outlined the evidence of the plaintiff's injuries. Through the story, the jury was able to experience the plaintiff's misfortune. The plaintiff's medical treatment and rehabilitation were detailed. Evidence was then developed to show the plaintiff's damages and future needs.

The plaintiff had suffered severe permanent injuries that had changed his life, had lost income and would lose income in the future, and would require constant medical attention.

Habush used language that gave his opening a storytelling flavor. He began his factual statement by stating, "Now, the case before you, is unfortunately, is not an uncommon case." Habush developed the background facts about the plaintiff as one would develop background facts for a character in a story. In discussing the day of the injury, Habush stated, "And this day, as fate would have it, was his first day on the job at the produce warehouse."

Instead of laying out the facts of his medical negligence case in a detached manner, Bergman presented them in the same way that a storyteller would, providing drama and impact. He began by telling the jury: "In this case you are going to hear evidence about what it means to be thirteen years old and to be told that you have a form of cancer called Hodgkin's disease." Bergman developed the plaintiff's character as a bright, attractive, loving, and popular girl with a loving family. In the first part of the story the family was described. In telling the story of the family, it was stressed that the mother had always taken great pains to see that her daughter had the best medical care possible so that she could live a healthy life. In the second part of the story, the plaintiff's efforts to have her condition diagnosed and treated were outlined. In this part of the story, it was stressed that the plaintiff made every effort to have the disease successfully treated, while the defendant doctor failed to exert the minimum effort and skill required to diagnose the condition. In the final part of the story, the plaintiff's damages, pain, and suffering were described. The story became the tragic story of a family, who despite their best efforts to obtain adequate medical treatment, received inadequate care and as a result suffered grave consequences.

Spence began his story by giving the jury an overview of what the case was about. In the first part of the story, Spence outlined his evidence about the nature and dangers of plutonium, Karen Silkwood and her efforts on the part of the union at Kerr-McGee to protect her fellow workers and the public from plutonium contamination, and Kerr-McGee's responsibilities with respect to plutonium. In the second part of the story, Spence told the jury about the bad actions of the defendant Kerr-McGee in its efforts to defeat the union, discredit Karen Silkwood, and avoid its responsibilities with respect to the production of plutonium. In the last part of his story, Spence outlined his claims for damages on behalf of the plaintiff.

Ring began his story with background information about the plaintiff and the machine in question. He went into great detail in describing the machine and how it works. In the second part of his story, Ring described how the machine malfunctioned and crushed the plaintiff's finger. He introduced the background information about the defendant manufacturer of the machine in question, along with a further history of the machine, its alterations, and how parts were ordered for the machine from the defendant. He outlined his claims of how and why the machine malfunctioned. In the third part of the story, Ring outlined the plaintiff's injuries and damages.

Welch began his story by presenting background information about the plaintiff. In the second part of the story, Welch described the defendant's work with the liquor company and the facts about how the collision occurred. In the last section of his opening, Welch outlined the plaintiff's injuries and damages. He graphically described the disc surgery, resulting disability, and pain and suffering to the jury.

Scott Baldwin began with a brief summary of the facts of the occurrence. He then introduced and identified the various defendant manufacturers of the crane in question, followed by a description of the crane and how it operated. The second part of his story consisted of an outline of how the crane was defective and why it collapsed. In the third part of his story, he explained the loss to the plaintiff's family and the pain and suffering of the plaintiff while he was falling to his death.

Block's use of language made his storytelling structure evident. He began his opening on liability by telling the jury that his case emanated out of a "tragic war" and that it was a "tragic occurrence." He went on to tell the story of two American soldiers "doing their duty as good soldiers." He developed their characters as actors in a play, telling the jury that in order to understand what the damage was they would have to understand who the plaintiff was, "from whence he came, the type of life and upbringing he had, his character, his habits, his mode of life, who were the people he associated with, what sort of guy he was."

§6.04 —Conclusion of Statement

The conclusions of the openings were short and to-the-point statements either summarizing the facts, expressing confidence about their cases, or suggesting a verdict for the plaintiff. Welch summarized his case and expressed confidence in the jury's decision:

> So as a result of this head-on collision you will see unfold here in a several-day trial, a picture of a couple who chose to live their life in a quiet, unassuming way, which has been altered for them by a careless motorist, and if that evidence is produced as I'm satisfied it will be, I'm going to return and ask for a very substantial verdict. Thank you very much.

In Block's first opening, he expressed confidence in the fact that his statements to the jury would be corroborated by the evidence, and expressed confidence that they would reach a just decision:

> At the end of the case I will have another opportunity to speak to you and show you where my statements were actually corroborated by the proof, by the documents and I think you will have no problem with a just decision in this case.

In his second opening, Block asked for a verdict for the plaintiff and summarized his damage claims:

At the end of the case when I address you again, you will be asked to compensate him for each and every injury, and as I say to you, we are going to add them up because justice means meaningful full justice. Each and every injury, and that's why I say that this case involves damages of the highest, the most highest magnitude.

He will never work again as long as he lives. He has had a tenth grade education, comes from Boaz, Alabama, and the damages to his earning capacity and his lost earnings in themselves are monumental and when you add them to the grievous physical and mental damages, you can readily see that we are dealing in very, very serious figures.

So pay attention to each and every word said by the witnesses, by the doctors, and do justice as you would have justice done for anyone who seeks a claim.

In Block's last opening, the storytelling flavor was evident:

My words are not evidence. You will see by the end of the case, a full panorama, a full panoply. You will get the sense of the person Wendell Burns was, and you will get a full sense of the void that he has left with all whom he was associated.

Now, this case is almost like a cold bookkeeping operation. There is no other way, unfortunately. We don't have an eye-for-an-eye concept. We have to listen carefully to each item of loss that these people sustained, because at the end of the case, in his charge to you, Judge Cannella will tell you what you must compensate for if you find from the evidence that such compensation is warranted; so it's an important case. Pay attention.

It's a family who is coming here on fault that's already established against the defendant, and they are entitled to each and every item of damage, no matter how large; because the law says that if the defendant casts a person into great damage, they must compensate accordingly dollar for dollar.

At the end of the case, we will have a chance, when you have heard the evidence, to more or less put against and compare, with my opening statement, what has been proven.

Meanwhile, I'd like to thank you for your present attention; and I am sure, at the end of the case I will thank you again for your rapt attention during the whole trial. Thank you.

In the conclusion of his opening, Spence argued the credibility of his evidence and told the jury what he would ask for at the end of the case:

And, so, we expect the evidence to be, from our standpoint, in summary, the evidence of the facts, evidence that we can prove that we believe is credible from the world's experts. And, you will not hear from me an insinuation or a suggestion that isn't supported, ladies and gentlemen, by honest, competent evidence in this case. And, maybe it will be the conclusion, after it is all over, that it's better to pay, for Kerr-McGee to pay the eleven million dollars, than it is to tell you what the facts are and where the forty pounds are, and how it got away.

And, it will be based, then, your Honor, and ladies and gentlemen of the jury, on these facts that we are going to ask you for a million and half dollars for those three children, to represent the last nine days of Karen Silkwood's life, and ten million dollars to stop forever this conduct by that industry, and others, forever. Thank you very much.

Corboy concluded his opening by drawing the jury into his client's story:

Ladies and gentlemen, that is the type of testimony you will hear during the remaining portion of this trial. It is the type of testimony that will supply you with the middle of this young man's life. It will supply you with the testimony that will supply you with the evidence of what happens during the rest of this young man's life.

Perlman closed his opening on liability by summarizing his facts and claims:

The facts will be that this, this event, this tragedy was caused by a machine that failed because it was unsafe and dangerous. The proof will be that the boom switch had a mechanical failure; that the pump motor signal was on, but the wiring sent out a signal to the boom. The design had a built-in propensity to fail in the environment it was in. It was not sealed, it was not airtight, it was defective. It had no adequate override whereby the operator could bring the boom back. There was no warning to anybody that this could happen or that, in this design of this machine, if there is a short within the system, that this kind of thing could happen.

In conclusion, the evidence will be that there are many hazards in coal mining. Henry Shackleford had the right to expect a safe product in the coal mining environment. He didn't get one. And as a result of that, he suffered injuries. And Joy has not taken the responsibility for those. And that's the reason we are here. Thank you.

Gibbons reconceptualized his claims into plain and simple language the jury could understand:

And in the interest of time we might omit to call one or more, if it would be somewhat repetitious or overlapping with others, and we have been encouraged to move as fast as we can, and we want to do that, and at the same time still give our clients their day in Court. But your job throughout the next week is a most important one. We are going to be talking in terms of technical things which I never dreamed in my life, or in my most vivid imagination that I would have even the know-how to pronounce the words, but it really boils down to be quite a simple thing, and that is that this airplane was defectively designed, and we will prove that because it allowed the flight controls to jam which necessitated ejection by an inherently unstable seat which in effect severed the spinal cord of Captain Wahl, when the seat was advertised to save your life. And although any ejection is a risky business, we expect to offer expert evidence that it doesn't have to be. It is like a fireman's safety net, like a fire extinguisher or any, any product that presupposes that an emergency has already occurred, but once that emergency occurs the customer, in this instance the United States Air Force officer, has a right to have a product designed that is not unreasonably risky or unreasonably dangerous, particularly one they knew was that way.

Thank you very much, Your Honor.

Habush summarized his damages and told the jury that he would return in closing to determine whether he had substantiated his claims, and told the jury that he would then ask for a verdict for the plaintiffs:

In short, members of the Jury, I think you are going to see and listen to a terrific guy who has made a tremendous adjustment to a serious injury. But, you will hear evidence that the couple has suffered a terrible loss.

The doctor will tell you and will testify that there is no more serious injury than a spinal cord injury, but, at the end of the case, I will stand up again with you and will discuss the evidence and see whether or not I've proven my case of defect against their machine, the cause of the accident, and at that time will discuss again what has been presented to you in terms of his injuries and his damages. And at that time I will ask you to award a fair and adequate sum to both Roger and Beverly.

I want to thank you for being so attentive. I want to thank you for listening to me. I look forward to the opportunity at the end of the case to discuss this case with you again.

Thank you.

Bergman summarized his claims and expressed confidence that the theories supporting his claims were basic:

I think that when you have heard the evidence in this case, there really isn't going to be any doubt at all that some of these things are just always considered basic: If you are considering cancer, you do a biopsy; if you don't do that, that is negligence; if you let cancer progress from minimal to extensive, that jeopardizes a person's chances for recovery. As a result of those things, I think you will find that Dr. Hanson is liable for the damage that has been done to Shanna and Judy and Ken Morrison and that you will find a verdict for the plaintiff in this case. Thank you.

§6.05   Strategic Use of Language

Perelman and Olbrechts-Tyteca assert that presence is an essential element of argumentation.[5] Presence is:

---

[5] Perelman & L. Olbrechts-Tyteca, The New Rhetoric 117 (1969).

to make present, by verbgal magic alone, what is actually absent but what he [sic] considered to be important to his argument or, by making them more present, to enhance the value of some of the elements of which one has actually been made conscious.[6]

A good story involves the listener and has dramatic impact. This is accomplished by creating presence. These lawyers were all involved in creating presence through the strategic use of language in order to give life to their stories. The strategic use of language involves the "selection of terms and labels for their appropriateness and impact."[7] Through the strategic use of language, these lawyers made their clients into real people, brought events of the past vividly into the here and now, made abstract concepts concrete, and ingeniously managed to argue their cases while telling a story.

§6.06 —Personalizing the Parties

Clarence Darrow once said:

> Jurymen seldom convict a person they like or acquit one they dislike. The main work of the trial lawyer is to make a jury like his [sic] client, or at least feel sympathy for him; facts regarding the crime are relatively unimportant.[8]

The lawyers accomplished this by personalizing the plaintiffs and defendants in the lawsuit. They were presented so that they became real people with feelings, hopes, and motives.

Corboy used language to create an image of the plaintiff before the injury. Corboy's client had been rendered a helpless quadriplegic, and therefore, Corboy's story became the story of a bright, energetic, active, multitalented, happy, popular person who had been tragically robbed of his life. Therefore, the first part of the story told about how healthy and vibrant the plaintiff had been before the tragedy befell him. Corboy related numerous instances in his client's life which illustrated his active, happy, productive life. He presented the good side of the plaintiff's life before the collision. He told of buddies and girlfriends, school activities, sports activities, creative pursuits, employment successes, and future goals and ambitions. He related antecdotes that gave the jury a glimpse into his personality and his life before the collision. He spoke of his warmth, courage, generosity, humor, and individuality. He described his favorite activities, such as making spicy chili. By the time the first part of the story was completed, the jury had a clear picture of who and what the plaintiff was before the collision. As with any good story, the jurors were allowed to enter into the life of the plaintiff, gain a sense of its quality, and begin to feel sadness and pity for the tragedy that came into his life. Corboy described Randy Block as:

---

[6] *Id.*

[7] K. Campbell, The Rhetorical Act 32 (1982).

[8] E. Southerland, Principles of Criminology 442 (1966).

a well rounded man . . . a very, very good person . . . warm and generous with everything that he had including his time. . . . He did not get a letter, he wasn't good enough but . . . his friends on the swimming team learned that . . . he had a lot of guts, determination, fortitude, attitudes and characteristics of his personality which are today holding him in good stead. . . . He was a social person. . . . He had determination. He had guts, and had courage and he was an individual. . . . His well-rounded personality again came forth. . . . He became known as a very, very vibrant person . . . a mature person. . . . He was a loyal friend. He was honest. He was a compassionate . . . an excellent teacher . . . very conscientious . . . John Randolph Block as he traveled north on that afternoon was a 28-year-old loving, capable, competent, giving, articulate, intelligent human being.

Spence was a master at dramatizing the issues. In describing the purpose of his case and Karen Silkwood's activities, Spence told the jury that the case would ultimately be about the "survival of the American people and it is about preventing, ladies and gentlemen, the dastardly escape of plutonium particles ever again." Thus, the *Silkwood* case became a story about the struggles of Karen Silkwood in her effort to keep America safe. The plaintiff was personalized as someone the jury could identify with as a real person as opposed to a plaintiff presenting a claim. He told the jury that "the case is a true story," and that Karen Silkwood was "trying to make her life count for something." He stated that "like many young women do when they fall in love—she fell in love and married," and became a mother who had "three beautiful children." After her divorce, which was "tragic to her," she was "on her own, alone in the world." In introducing the surviving plaintiffs, he referred to Karen Silkwood's "three little" children. Karen Silkwood's father was introduced as the administrator for the Silkwood children, and therefore, an "officer of the court."

Welch used language to personalize the plaintiffs. Bob and Ruth Cooper were "high school sweethearts." The plaintiff performed his job as a crane operator with a "great amount of pride" and did it with a "great amount of consistency." The plaintiff had an "enviable record" at work. During his convalescence and rehabilitation from the injury in question, the plaintiff was a "very determined man." In his conclusion, Welch told the jury that the plaintiff and his wife, prior to the collision, had tried to live their lives in a "quiet, unassuming way, which has been altered for them by a careless motorist. . . ."

Baldwin told the jury about his client's "noble" effort to escape the falling crane. He told the jury that after his death, he left his "widow and children." In further personalizing the plaintiff, he stated:

Mr. Branch was a young man just starting out on his career . . . he was a good operator . . . a dependable worker . . . he made good money. . . . He worked a lot of overtime, and had he worked out his life expectancy— had he been allowed or accorded the privilege, except for this unnecessary death, he would have earned more than a million dollars.

Block personalized the plaintiffs as follows:

> Among the battery of six men with Wendell Burns, who is no longer with us, and Dorman Baird, the gentleman you met yesterday who is seated in the first row. They were manning a 105-millimeter howitzer and they were experienced men. They had been trained in it and they had been firing rounds for six, seven months prior to this occurrence as a team, as buddies to each other, taking care of each other's welfare and making sure that they did the right thing.

With respect to the plaintiff Burns, Block stated:

> Wendell Burns, when he met his death, was not quite 21 years of age. He was born in the state of Washington, he was reared in the state of Washington, he went to school in the state of Washington. He came from a decent family, what would be called a God-fearing family, a religious family; and he went to high school in Wapato, Washington.
> . . . .
> When Wendell Burns went out of high school, he intended to go to college, and to take up either a program that would make him ultimately a mechanical engineer, or an electrical engineer.
> Shortly after getting out of high school, he married Doris, and Doris Burns, whom he had known for one year, as she subsequently became to be known. And prior to attending college, he worked for a short while with the Wapato Fruit Co., operating a fork lift. It was sort of an interim job, pending his induction into the Service on July 13, 1968. His son Stacy was subsequently born on March 27, 1969.
> . . . .
> Wendell Burns had the character, and it was known—and we will bring people in from his home town—of a hard-working fellow. He was the type of kid who was a band leader, ran a little band of four people, and they played weekends, after school. He worked as a fork lift driver in this fruit factory. He is the type of kid who tied up, chopped, and delivered cord wood to make money. . . . In the service, we'll have members here from his gun crew to tell you the type of fellow he was. He was a fellow who was old beyond his years. He was a fellow they could rely on. He was the gunner, and they looked to him for guidance. They came to him with their problems in the field, and he was a person who, if they got into trouble, he was sort of a psuedo-chaplain, more or less, as they explained it. He would straighten it out or attempt to straighten it out.

With respect to Dorman Baird, Block told the jury:

> Dorman Baird was born as a farm boy in Alabama on March 7, 1947. His father was a farmer. He lived with his family on a farm. That's all he knew except for a couple of jobs prior to going into the Service where he worked for approximately six months for a gas station doing odd jobs, mechanical jobs, and for a mobile home contractor. . . . The one bright spot that has

happened to him is that his childhood sweetheart Barbara has stood by him. They were going together since she was 13 and he was 15 and they were married despite all this, maybe in spite of it, in 1971.

Robert Habush personalized his client as follows:

Prior to 1981, Members of the Jury, Roger Schulz was healthy, happy, was a terrific worker, terrific husband and a terrific father. He loved sports. He was very physically active. He loved working around the house. He loved working with his hands. He was well liked by his friends and co-workers, and well loved by his wife and children.

Prior to discussing the impact of damages, Glaser brought his client to life as a person:

We have a woman 47, that's rather young, good health. I told you about her occupation, married life, happy life at home, living with her husband who operated a limousine service, two children, I think one was—let's see, her husband, she was 47, her husband Julian was 54, and she had two daughters, Beverly about 26, and Andrea, about 24, they're sitting, the two daughters with her. Great happy family life, good community worker as well, loving wife and loving, enjoying it, enjoying her job and enjoying her household, enjoying the community. Great, good emotional happy state, and independent completely. Great pride.

Gibbons presented his clients' deceased husband and father in a way that brought him to life so that the jurors could fully understand the loss created by his death:

. . . he was a healthy, young, approximately 34-year-old United States Air Force officer who was planning on making a 20-year career out of the Air Force and to finishing that career. The evidence will also show that back when he was 17 years old he married his 17-year-old sweetheart, Dianne, that he then joined the United States Air Force as an enlisted man and that he was chosen by the United States Air Force to go to college. He was one of the chosen few. And that he did indeed go to college after serving several years as an enlisted man, and he graduated with the highest honors at Oklahoma State University through the Air Force program. He graduated as an electrical engineer. He was then sent to Officers' Training School, and you will find again that he was a distinguished graduate of Officers' Training School in San Antonio, Lackland Air Force base in approximately 1970. You will also hear evidence that this man, Harry Wahl, Captain Harry Wahl, had flown over 2000 hours of flying time. You will hear evidence that he had 535 actual combat hours of flying in Vietnamese war zone. You will also hear evidence that he was awarded with our nation's air medal with 7 oak leaf clusters for his service in the Vietnamese war zone, or Viet Nam as it was known. You will also hear evidence that he attended some 18 different United States Air Force schools to become a very skilled pilot in all respects. You will also hear evidence that even though he continued his career as an officer that Captain Harry Wahl attended night school and took extensive courses, and shortly before his tragic death he received a Master's of Business Administration Degree from Northern Colorado University, that he was looking forward to serving out his 20 years' retirement to go into the business world. And as a matter of fact on this very assignment in which he was killed, he had been sent to Davis Monthan Air Force Base, the evidence will show he was given his choice of many different assignments and that he actually put in on a United States Air Force document that he wanted this particular assignment because he thought it was in the best interest of his minor son to be close to him and his wife. And that was put in official documents that will be in evidence in this case, in July of 1979, as to why he wanted this particular assignment, to be close to his wife and son.

In order to convince the jury that the plaintiffs suffered a loss when the young daughter was deprived of the opportunity of a timely cure for her cancer, Bergman personalized the plaintiff and her parents:

> I want to tell you a little bit about the Morrison family since that is who is involved here. Ken and Judy Morrison met, I think, while they were both at the public beach at Lake Quivira back in 1956. He was eighteen years old and she was fifteen years old. Ken told me that the first time that he met Judy that he knew that she would be his wife. And four years later, when they were both out of high school—I think that Ken graduated from Argentine High School; Judy from Turner High School—they were married in '60.
>
> It has been a solid marriage for the past twenty-six years and is still a solid marriage. Four years later—excuse me—eight years later they were blessed with the birth of their first child, daughter Kenda, who is now eighteen years old and recently graduated from Northwest High School. Two years after that, July 22nd, 1970, Shanna was born.
>
> Ken Morrison has been employed by AT&T or one of its various divisions for the past, I think, thirty-one years. He has worked hard. He has done well. Since Shanna has become ill he has changed positions in his job. He has had a difficult time fulfilling the requirements of his job in the last three or four years, but he is still solid in the company.
>
> The Morrisons have lived in the same home in Shawnee for twenty years. It is the only house that either of their children have ever known. Before her illness, Shanna was a normal, happy child, thirteen years old. She did average in school although she never really pushed herself too hard, she never had to work too hard. She had planned, and there was no doubt, just because of the way that they were raised, she had planned to go to college.
>
> She was friendly, outgoing, fairly popular. She had a lot of good friends. Her social life was very important to her, as any 13-year-old girl, particularly with her friends. She hadn't really gotten to the point where she was doing much dating of boys.

Shanna was blessed with natural beauty. I want to show you a couple of photographs that we will have in evidence of Shanna in the year that she became ill. A naturally gorgeous girl. Somehow she always had an inferiority complex about that and made a lot of effort to look good. She still does. In fact, the photograph that you saw earlier, Shanna, when she knows that she is going to be photographed, she tries to put on her best face. This is a wig that she is wearing because she doesn't have any hair now. She hasn't had any hair for about three years.

Shanna was blessed with a constitution that allowed her to function normally on five or six hours of sleep a night. She was a pretty good athlete. She liked water skiing, she was going out for cheerleading, she was a good swimmer. She was just a normal, active person, child.

In his case involving the defective design of a handgun, Bergman also brought his clients to life for the jury by bringing out background facts and information:

Now, I want to get a little deeper into the problem and the reason why this gun is inherently dangerous but first I think you need to know a little about Paul Johnson's circumstances and some of his background leading up to his injury.

Paul was born December 1, 1946 in Parsons, Kansas. He grew up in Augusta, Kansas, about twelve miles from Wichita. He is now 38 years old. He graduated from high school in Augusta in 1964, went to college for a little bit less than a year and the day after his 19th birthday, enrolled in the Air Force. He spent over three years in the Air Force. He did a tour of duty in Korea, he spent 13 months in Viet Nam, in heavy combat. He was in an engineers' unit building bridges, towns, whatever needed to be built, in combat zones. He was there for the Tet offensive. And even through all that experience, other than—I think Paul got a shrapnel wound to the knee, which is certainly not, you couldn't consider that as an accident because of what he was doing, he has never been involved in any other accident or injury that could be called an accidental-type injury.

By the time Paul was discharged from the Air Force, honorably, in 1969, he had reached the rank of sergeant. He received the Air Force Commendation Medal for Meritorious Service which is an individual honor, not a group honor. And he also got a citation as a small arms expert in the service. . . .

I want to talk about Jannie a little bit because she is very much a part of this case, at least their relationship. Paul met Jannie at Randolph Air Force Base in San Antonio in the fall of 1968, shortly after he got back from Viet Nam. He was 22 and she was 18. She was at the base with a couple of friends. She had given them a ride over there and when Paul saw Jannie, he asked her out on the spot. He had a tremendous attraction, or she had a tremendous attraction for him. She turned him down but shortly after that they got together. It wasn't too long before they got married. They had a nice big wedding on February 2, 1969.

§6.07   —Proving Damages

Translating pain, suffering, and damages into words the jury will understand is a difficult rhetorical problem. It is one thing to tell a jury that a person's life has been changed or that a person is in pain, but it is another thing to put it in terms that the jury can feel and comprehend. The jury could not see the plaintiffs' deaths or pain and suffering, and, therefore, the lawyers had to describe them in ways that made them "present, by verbal magic alone."[9] Since the opening was the beginning of the case, and the jury had not heard any evidence, these lawyers did not treat damages as comprehensively or as intensively as they would in closing. However, in the openings, the outlines for their strategic use of language to prove damages emerged. Each lawyer described his client's injuries and damages, and then strategically used language to highlight the loss. In most cases, the lawyers juxtaposed or compared images of their clients before the injury to images of their clients after their injuries. As noted above in §6.06, the lawyers at some point in their openings personalized their clients and created images of happy, healthy, productive people prior to their injuries. The lawyers then juxtaposed these positive images with the negative post-injury images of broken, crippled, and suffering plaintiffs.

Welch, in explaining the nature of a herniated disc, used the analogy of a jelly doughnut:

> You're going to learn that these vertebral bodies are separated by discs. They are like little doughnuts filled with jelly. That's the best thing I've ever heard a doctor call it. If there is enough injury, those discs can be crushed and the substance squirts out. When that happens the victim feels shocks down the arms, they feel numbness, they lose control over certain parts of their bodies . . .

In describing the plaintiff's disc surgery, Welch used everyday language rather than medical terms, to describe the procedure:

> This neurosurgeon then . . . went in through the throat. They open up the throat and take all your vocal cords and move everything aside, went clear back to the spine and operated on that C6. . . . Now, in the first surgery they cut him open on his hip, and on the top of your hip bone you feel here is called the iliac crest. . . . They go in with a drill and they take a plug out. Then they take the plug of bone and go in through this opening after they take the disc out and hammer it in. That's called a fusion.

Spence told the jury that the case was about Karen Silkwood's "suffering," her "terrors in the night for nine days before her death," and her "suffering, how she lived through the panic of these nine days, how she spent some of those periods in stark terror." He told them:

---

[9] C. Perleman & L. Olbrechts-Tyteca. The New Rhetoric 117 (1969).

The evidence will show that had Karen Silkwood lived she would not have likely died, but that she would have actually, absolutely died . . . the father of plutonium who worked hand-in-hand with the man who discovered it will take the stand and will tell you that Karen Silkwood had cancer, had cancer in her lungs the day she died, on the day she was exposed. . . . She had called her mother, and her sister, crying. . . . That she was afraid for her life, and afraid for her safety. That she was being— and she complained to her family—she was being intentionally contaminated. She called Dr. Abrahamson, the man, the expert . . . to talk to him about her exposure. She was so frightened, so concerned, so terror-stricken . . . that she was in agony from the terror of dying from cancer . . . and intentional contamination of her body by this dreaded substance.

Corboy first outlined many instances of the plaintiff's happy active life and his healthy body. He then used words to suggest the loss of this happy, healthy, active life. He began his opening by telling the jury that "John Randolph Block is a prisoner, he is in internal carceration [sic] within the confines of his body." With respect to his condition, Corboy stated:

It was determined shortly that there was a possibility that this young man was not brain dead, was not in a perpetual coma, was not in a vegetative state. It was determined by early encephalograms that he was possibly in what is called a locked-in syndrome. A locked-in syndrome is a fancy way of saying he is locked in his body, his eyes are open and his brain is working. He knows what is going on, he knows what is going on outside of the body he is in. He is five feet ten inches of no ability to move, no ability to talk because that is part of the locked-in syndrome. That means you are a spastic quadriplegic, paralyzed for practical purposes from the eyes down but he can only see and communicate through his eyes. . . . This lifeless body for the next almost a month was just that except he could use his eyes. . . . He can't talk, he can't swallow. He can't indicate what he wants. He can't scream. If something happens to him in the middle of the night, somebody has got to be there. He cannot do anything on his own except blink his eyes.

Corboy illustrated the catastrophic injuries and damages the plaintiff had suffered by graphically describing the many surgical procedures the plaintiff had needed to sustain his life. He outlined the many procedures of which the following are examples:

A ventriculocisternostomy which was a two-hour operation or a little short of two hours is a very fancy way of saying they burnt a hole in his head, they took a catheter or a tube and they put the tube in his head hoping it would release the pressure that had been caused by what was now known as a closed head injury he was put on a foley catheter. A foley catheter is nothing more and nothing less than a tube through the genital area of the man's body up through the genital area between his legs up into the bladder so that the urine can come out of the bladder. . . . In addition to that, it was determined that he should have a nasogastric tube. A naso-gastric tube is a tube going up through the nasal opening back through the esophagus down into the stomach, and that's how he was given nutri-ents eventually. . . . They decided to perform a tenotomy. A tenotomy is where you cut the tendons. They decided he was never going to walk again so the tenotomies were performed on May 5th of 1982, and the operation was done by a Dr. Laros who cut the tendons both from the hips and behind the knees so that Randy could have extended legs rather than contracted legs.

In order to demonstrate what the wife had lost, Baldwin used examples:

In addition to that, there is the element of loss of services that Mrs. Branch is entitled to damages for. What's it worth to have a husband around the house. The little things that he may do, like repairing a screen, painting the house.

The examples of household chores that most husbands routinely perform pro-vided concrete illustrations of the plaintiff's losses. In describing the pain and suffering that the plaintiff suffered while falling to his death with the crane, Baldwin stated:

He went down with that and inside the super structure of that crane know-ing he was going to his certain death, and that took a horrible long amount of time. Now that's conscious pain and suffering, and we're seeking dam-ages for that.

Glaser was particularly adept at using analogies and juxtapositioning in order to describe the plaintiff's damages. In order to demonstrate damage, Glaser first painted a glowing picture of the happy plaintiff before her unnecessary surgery. He then juxtaposed this happy plaintiff with the miserable plaintiff after surgery. At the same time he used analogies to illustrate her situation. His comparison of his client to a castrated male was particularly forceful and dramatic. He presented her damages as follows:

Now, what are the damages in this case? We have a woman 47, that's rather young, good health. I told you about her occupation, married life, happy life at home, living with her husband who operated a limousine service, two children, I think one was—let's see, her husband, she was 47, her husband Julian was 54, and she had two daughters, Beverly about 26, and Andrea, about 24, they're sitting, the two daughters with her. Great happy family life, good community worker as well, loving wife and loving, enjoying it, enjoying her job and enjoying her household, enjoying the community. Great, good emotional happy state, and independent completely. Great pride.

Now, what happens? Her whole life changes after the removal, unneces-sarily, of these organs. Told you about eighty to one hundred doctors and about ten hospitalizations, these are their specific damages, plus a lot of pain and suffering, all kinds of tests, about $80,000, I think for medical. Loss of earnings, she was making—she was working at that job for about eleven years, or different jobs for the City and the Board of Education for about ten years, and at the time of the unnecessary hysterectomy, she was earning approximately $12,500 a year.

It is our contention that the injuries are permanent. It's now six, seven years, she still has the same complaints. She'll have them for the rest of her life, so at a loss of earnings, you've got 47, oh, about twenty years, about, that's roughly $250,000 by shear—just multiplication, simple arithmetic, that's about $250,000, yes, but that is the smallest item in this case. Those two items going to about $330,000 a year, that's the smallest. The main item is what we legal writers call general damages, and that's personal injuries and pain and suffering, past, present and future.

Well, what's the personal injury? They're separate items. Personal injuries, and then the pain and suffering. What's the personal injuries? Well, they took her womb away. Some women at 40 want children, or forty and over, want children. And still have children at the age of 47 years of age. They took all her reproductive organs away from her, they took out her tubes, those tubes, they took those ovaries away that produce the eggs that become fertilized in the womb. They in effect castrated her. Taking away the ovaries of a woman is like taking away the testicles of a man— forgive me—.

Well, what about the pain and suffering, the other item of damages? From right after the hysterectomy to today, she has severe pains all over her body. She has severe pain in her abdomen, she has flushes, which by the way, is a typical menopausal symptom, we'll talk a little more about that in a few minutes, she has a severe rash, and you'll see this in the hospital records, a rash all over the body, and with severe itching. A very painful condition. You'll hear her describe how she feels when she has that itch all over the body, wanting to jump out of her skin. She has blurred vision. You may wonder what does the blurred vision got to do with these organs, and I'm going to tell you about the mechanism in a minute. What has a rash got to do with that? She has dizziness, severe dizziness and headaches, all borne out, by the way, not just through her mouth or her lips, but right in the record.

She has swollen and painful joints, she has weakness and exhaustion constantly. She has severe pain in the back area, in the arm, in the leg. She has pain all over her body. And you'll see this document in the hospital record, not just her statement alone. And she has severe melancholy, another word for depression. And I talk about depression, not in the social sense, but depression in the sick sense where there's no motivation in life, where life means very little, almost nothing. She'll tell you how she feels.

In describing the surviving plaintiff's injuries, Block used graphic language to make the damages comprehendible to the jury. He stated:

His left leg was hanging by a string, fragments went into his scrotum, tearing his left testicle, having the testicle extrude and hang down, all the bones in the toes of his right foot were broken, he had a perforation of the right tympanic membrane in the ear, resulting in a high frequency neurosensory hearing loss, he lost procreative power, both in the fact that his sperm count is low but even if his sperm count was adequate, his psychic damage and the damage done to his scrotum and his testicle left his mind so scarred that he cannot achieve an erection to insert it into his wife.

He had burns of his face, head, neck and chest area. He had fragment wounds over his upper extremities, he had a deep scar in the remaining foot, in the right thigh, he had a wound in his right forearm that was open and draining, he had an evulsion fracture of the foot; he was in shock because of blood loss, he had a concussion and post-concussion syndrome.

Now, it took me probably no longer than two, three minutes to say that, but Dorman Baird, you will see, will suffer from the effects of this for the rest of his life, and remember this happened to him when he was 22 years of age.

Also, as part of the damage, he suffers from nightmares, where he relives the incident, where he sees his buddy, the dead gunner, where he sees the other injured people, and he wakes up literally screaming.

From there he was taken to a hospital in Japan and from there he was taken to a hospital in Fort Gordon, Georgia, where he spent six months, where the wounds were draining pus and blood, where he was given blood to stay alive because he was in a state of shock, where he was given painkillers. . . . Dorman Baird is 100% disabled according to the Veterans Administration and the Army. He still has to take painkillers, he has to wear a prosthesis.

Prior to the injury he was an active person in sports, played softball, football, went roller skating, hunting, horseback riding.

But, since his mental and physical castration and since these injuries he doesn't partake of anything worthwhile other than once in awhile talking to the boys down by the gas station or going fishing. He can't sit for any length of time, he can't stand for any length of time, he can't walk for any length of time, without feeling deep and hurtful pain.

· · · · ·

Today he is depressed, he feels pain in the remaining stump and there is a strange phenomenon that the doctors will tell you about, phantom pain, where you actually feel hurt and pain in the missing limb.

He has dizziness, headaches, difficulty in concentrating, feels nauseous, constant ringing in the ears, has pain in the other leg where the fractures have deformed the toes of his leg and we will show you that he is unemployable.

In describing the effect of the death of Wendell Burns, Block stated:

Now, to the old, death comes really, let's face it, as a fair visitor. To the young, it's really a savage intruder; and it does not affect the person who dies, alone; it affects a whole family.

In developing the plaintiff's gunshot injuries, Bergman first went to great lengths to create a pre-injury image of a happy, active, productive plaintiff as set out in §6.06 above. For example, he ended that narration of facts that personalized the plaintiff in a positive way by stating:

And they have had a very happy, very satisfactory life in Junction City. They have a place in the country about three miles out of town, right near where the Line Creek and the Smokey Hill River intersect. It's right at the end of their property. It is a very nice spot and Paul and his family enjoy it there. They have two boys, Chris and Nik, who are 14 and 10 years old, both of whom are good students, fine athletes. Paul is a talented musician. He plays guitar, banjo, bass. He has written some three to four hundred songs in his life. And that used to be because it is no more. And Paul and Jannie will explain why it is that somehow Paul has completely lost his interest in music, musical things; in fact social type things.

Bergman then contrasted the image of the happy plaintiff with that of a depressed and damaged post-injury plaintiff. He provides jury impact by describing the plaintiff's reluctance to discuss his impotence with friends and family members:

The important thing about the pathway of the bullet, though is that it passed through an area where there are some microscopic nerves and blood vessels that control erection. And there is medical evidence of damage to those nerves and blood vessels and the medical opinion of the doctors who treated Paul is unanimous without any uncertainty at all that the gunshot wound caused the impotence.

. . . .

Paul followed Dr. Fieldstone's advice and refrained from exertion for about three months. And on October 2, 1981, he went back to see Dr. Fieldstone, the wound was healing, and he was, those restrictions were essentially lifted. In the period between October of 1981 and 1982, Paul and Jannie made five or six attempts at having sexual relations. And each attempt resulted in terrible tension, depression, anxiety, frustration, because Paul could not maintain an erection, and they had had no problems in the history of their marriage. The reality of that situation is something that Paul had then and still has now, difficulty in accepting. As I said, the bullet passed through certain structures that are, you know, the path of the bullet is very consistent with the nature of the injury. And Dr. Fieldstone did what he could and then sent Paul to K.U. Medical Center to see a man named Dr. John Weigel who specializes in this kind of problem for a more definitive evaluation. Dr. Weigel put Paul through a very comprehensive battery of tests, consultations, et cetera, and he was, among other things, trying to figure out whether Paul's problem was organic as they call it, meaning physical, or psychogenic, meaning psychological. You can be impotent for psychological reasons. And Dr. Weigel found that there was a substantial amount of evidence to establish an organic problem and virtually no evidence at all to suggest a psychological problem, which will be the suggestion of the defense.

The effect of Paul's injury on himself, and on Jannie, is really what this case is all about. As a consequence of Paul's injury, there has been an impact on many, many important aspects of the Johnsons' lives, not just their ability to engage in sexual relations. Paul doesn't get involved in family decisions as he used to, for some reason. Jannie doesn't have a husband to accompany her to the many, many activities that she is involved in. She doesn't have Paul to consult with as she used to. He doesn't fulfill the same role in the family unit. You learn that Paul is so uptight about what has happened to him that he hasn't discussed it with anybody. His parents don't know. His brothers don't know. The only people who know are medical people, people who know of necessity. I think the only friend of Paul's who knows is a fellow named Ron McKenzie who was with the reserve and because he was with the reserve got involved in this case, his deposition was taken, and in connection with the taking of his deposition and all those events, he learned of Paul's problem. But Paul has kept it completely bottled up inside. Even Paul and Jannie have never been able to have the frank discussion about the problem. It is difficult for them to talk about it. And when it comes time for them to testify in this case, at my request, because I want them to be as uninhibited as they can be, when Paul testifies I am going to have Jannie out and when Jannie testifies I am going to have Paul out.

Habush began his presentation of damages by first presenting a positive image of the plaintiff before the injury. He then contrasted this with the defendant's state after the injury. Finally, he described the plaintiff's heroic efforts to rehabilitate himself from his injury. Since his client had been rendered a paraplegic by the injury, Habush described those unpleasant day-to-day things that a paraplegic must deal with that a healthy person takes for granted or does not even think about. By describing these unpleasant problems in graphic detail, Habush painted a picture that allowed the jury to truly grasp the extent of the plaintiff's damages:

> He dropped out of high school in the 11th grade and joined the Army. He was in the Army for three years, serving overseas in Germany.
>
> He worked steady at Kohl's, as I indicated, for 21 years as a receiver and unloader and as an order selector.
>
> At the time of this incident in 1981 he was earning around $30,000 a year and he put in as much overtime as he could. He's married to Bev eighteen years today, will be 19 years in January. It's a second marriage for both of them.
>
> With Bev, they have had two children Brian, age 18 and Colleen, age 16. In addition to that, he has raised and was the father to Beverly's chil-

dren from her first marriage, Debbie who is now age 25 and Dean. He is man who is now age 23. Bev works as a librarian at the Germantown library.

Prior to 1981, Members of the Jury, Roger Schulz was healthy, happy, was a terrific worker, terrific husband and a terrific father. He loved sports. He was very physically active. He loved working around the house. He loved working with his hands. He was well liked by his friends and co-workers, and well loved by his wife and children.

On June 8, 1981, because as we will indicate, of the absence of a rear pipe, his spine was crushed. His vertebraes were crushed, and although the defendants may attempt to show that he hurt his back and was paralyzed by falling down on the dock with his rear end, eyewitnesses and doctors will tell you that's not how it happened. If it happened that way, the injury would look different.

But on this day, his spine was crushed and when that happened, he became paralyzed from the waist down.

He can't walk or move his legs. His ability to feel or have normal bladder functioning is gone forever. His bowel functioning is gone forever. He can't feel when he has to go to the bathroom. Doesn't know when he goes to the bathroom. For bladder control he has to put a catheter into himself into his bladder to drain into a bag he wears on his leg. This has to be changed every two weeks and he has to irrigate it twice a day.

For his bowels, he has to every other day put suppositories up himself, stimulate his rectum and wait two to three hours for bowel movements to occur. That's where he was this morning. If it's not done he gets an impacted bowel. In the accident he fractured multiple ribs which have subsequently healed. He experienced a reflux or a flow back into his kidneys and that's required the indwelling, the catheter to be worn full time.

The doctors will tell that spinal cord injured people are subject to skin breakdowns because they can't feel anything and they can't know when their skin becomes irritated and a threat of blisters, infections because of the indwelling catheter, and the doctors will tell you that Roger is experiencing, and he will tell you, constant pain in one of his legs and in the back area where he had his operation, constant, unremitting, always-there pain.

You will hear that after the injury he was taken to County Hospital emergency and then Froedert Hospital, and then VA Hospital, that he spent about four months in hospitals, that while he was in the hospital that he had an operation that fused his spine and stabilized his spine.

He will tell you that when he was at VA Hospital he was taught how to use a wheelchair, how to use braces, was even taught how to drive a van. He will discuss with you, as will Bev, their worry, their anxiety, and the pain and the fright that he felt during this period of time when he realized that he was paralyzed and would be paralyzed for life.

They will tell you their concerns for each other and his concern that Beverly would leave him because of this accident. I can assure you that their marriage is never more solid, that they love each other more than they did before, and that there is nothing that's going to happen with respect to this marriage.

That when he went home he was taken care of and has been taken care of by Bev, that he has learned to take care of himself, that he can dress himself, feed himself. As a matter of fact, he does the housework and helps Beverly at home.

And as he rehabilitated himself he became a chauffeur and drove the kids back and forth to school and did the work around the house. He will tell you what he can do and what he can't do.

You will hear evidence, however, that there have been very rough times, that he has had bowel movements in bed, accidents in his clothes, that he's had difficulty with architectural restrictions that wheelchair people experience in restaurants and going out.

You will hear evidence, Members of the Jury, that he had a tough time getting his act together, that it took him some years to adjust to this disability. But that he has made as good an adjustment as the doctors could hope for. That he does go out with Beverly socially, that he's now joined—joined a bowling league for paraplegics, that he even joined a baseball league for wheelchair people. That in addition to working about the house, he does volunteer work. He goes down and volunteers and repairs wheel chairs for other wheelchair operators.

He will tell you and she will tell you that, of course, as the doctors explained to you, they haven't been able to have normal sexual relations since this accident since he is unable due to the spinal cord injury to have an erection and have normal intercourse.

You will hear, Members of the Jury, that there has been no, I repeat no alteration of affection and support from the children to him and from him to the children. And you will hear from him that he's anxious to start earning some money, and that his stepson who will testify here named Dean, he is a man in 1981, coincidentally the month of his injury, started a cabinetmaking business and that Dean has done so well that he's now ready to expand his business and presently has plans to make his cabinetmaking shop accessible to Roger,—wheelchair accessible and have machines that he can operate, and space that he can operate in. And Roger has done some work for him up to now doing cabinetwork and repair work. And that he will begin employment with Dean, doing cabinetwork for Dean, as much as he can physically take, and it's hoped that he will be able to work as many as 20 hours a week and that Dean will pay him a wage for that.

In short, Members of the Jury, I think you are going to see and listen to a terrific guy who has made a tremendous adjustment to a serious injury. But, you will hear evidence that the couple has suffered a terrible loss.

In his cancer case, Bergman described the reaction of the father to the news that his daughter had cancer, described the progression of the disease due to a lack of timely diagnosis, and the effects of the chemotherapy treatment:

In any event, after a series of appointments, Shanna was finally admitted to St. Luke's by Dr. Koontz. The biopsy was done on February 2nd. And to the Morrisons' absolute shock and absolute surprise, Judy Morrison was told, "Your daughter has cancer. It is Hodgkin's."

Ken Morrison says when he heard that news it was like a knife had been stuck right in his midsection, and he has not been able to get rid of the feeling of that knife in his midsection for over three years.

. . . .

When Dr. Sullivan first saw Shanna, she was taken aback by the extent of the visible tumors that were bulging out of Shanna. This is a person who had seen literally hundreds of Hodgkin's patients. The axillary mass had grown from four centimeters to twelve centimeters. The superclavicular nodes had gone from little one-and-three-centimeter nodes to taking up from the bottom of her ear, filling up this area down to the clavicle.

The masses at the back of the head were there. There was a second mass at the back of the head. They were in the abdomen, in the pelvis, and the inguinal area, just every place where you can have lymph nodes enlarged, which is just the Hodgkin's cancer cells replacing the normal cells in the lymphatic system. Every place that you could have them, she had them.

. . . .

Dr. Sullivan undertook to treat Shanna. She started with chemotherapy on February 23rd, 1984. That is a combination of killer chemicals that they put into somebody's body to get rid of the cancer cells. But the mass, the literal mass of the tumor load in Shanna's body did not allow for successful treatment with that chemotherapy, so Dr. Sullivan pretty quickly changed direction and gave her an even more potent, even more lethal combination of chemicals, more chemotherapy. The attack, in essence, was escalated. More weapons were being used against this disease.

Shanna lost her hair and she vomited continuously. I'm talking continuous vomiting for twelve to fourteen hours as a consequence of these chemicals. There are a lot of other horrible side effects that you will hear about.

After four months of this chemotherapy regimen, a Dr. Lillian Fuller was brought into the case. Dr. Fuller is a radiotherapist, a specialist in the use of radiation to treat cancer. Among other things, Dr. Fuller is a general oncologist as well. She manages cancer patients, pediatric and adult.

Dr. Fuller took Shanna through a sequence of bombarding her with the radiation between June and November of 1984 on over a hundred occasions. She had to subject herself for this radiation treatment. You will hear about the horrible side effects of radiation. Shanna developed a series of painful infections. She began to have pulsating, unremitting headaches. She developed shingles, which is the herpes zoster virus on her rear end, just horrible red, ugly, open sores which are the complications and the side effects of the treatment that she was getting.

Finally, in early December, the Morrisons thought that they had it licked. They thought that Shanna may be in remission. She did a CT scan. They were doing the tests to kind of verify that when they got the first of what became a series of bad news. There were some suspicious lesions found on the CT scan in the liver. This led to further tests and finally the catastrophic news that the Hodgkin's disease was in the liver. It had escaped from the lymphatic system. So they were back to where they started, maybe even worse, because now the armamentarium, the tools and the weapons that are available to fight cancer, had mostly been used. Now they had to start with experimental protocols, drugs that were investigational drugs.

They used a drug called VP16. At first they put it right into Shanna's liver, but the pathway for that died. So they couldn't get it right into the liver anymore and they began to give her systemic infusions of VP16. On forty-eight separate occasions Shanna submitted to VP16 treatments.

You pay a very high price in side effects, complications, when you start using these kinds of lethal toxic drugs. She developed a severe pain in her liver. She developed lesions like hives on her arms and legs and various other parts of her body. Her feet swelled up and hurt so badly that they had to be rubbed five, six or seven times a day by family members or nurses, or whoever was there. Now Shanna's feet can't be touched. You can't go near her feet they are so painful.

Shanna's headaches got so bad that virtually on a daily basis her left arm would go numb.

And then finally in May of 1986, it was decided that Shanna just could not tolerate any more of this VP16. The only thing left was a bone marrow transplant. You are going to hear about a bone marrow transplant, going into the bubble, which is called the protective environment, which is an experience that is very difficult to describe in words. I am really not adequate and I won't try to describe it for you. You will hear about it, where you go in and you have even more super potent drugs put into your body to destroy your bone marrow, to wipe it out. They had already taken some marrow out of Shanna, and they put it back in. It is just an awful, painful, horrible experience.

The bone marrow transplant was ultimately a failure, just like the other treatment had been, and this roller coaster ride continued. There was more evidence of disease, this time some spots in the lungs. Shanna developed things like hemorrhagic cystitis. She just started bleeding. There would be blood in the urine. She would just start bleeding. It was extremely painful.

In February of 1987, the physicians on the adult service at M.D. Anderson Hospital where Shanna had been transferred for the bone marrow transplant began to develop new experimental combinations of drugs that hadn't been used before to try to combat this Hodgkin's disease. The cycle of treatment, the complications, the side effects and the life-threatening developments continued. And the efforts continue.

You know, Shanna has now been diagnosed for 1,783 days. She spent 461 days at or in a hospital. To date, the medical expenses are right around $300,000.00, medical and related expenses. She has had ten major surgeries—I define that as having to go under a general anesthetic—plus a lot of other painful procedures that you will hear about.

§6.08   Themes

In his article on storytelling, Bennett argues that storytelling is a good form of discourse for a trial because it organizes information in ways that help the listener to perform interpretive functions.[10] One of the ways a story may organize information is through the use of themes. Themes link narrative and argument to show the role of human action in producing the particular plot. These stories don't just happen, but they are caused by the actions of the parties. All of the openings had clearly identifiable common themes that organized the evidence that was presented in the case.

§6.09   —The Defendant Was Negligent—Claims of Liability

The first theme was that the defendant was negligent. The lawyers stated their claims of liability against the defendant and outlined the evidence supporting those claims. Thus, within the general theme that the defendant was negligent were subthemes consisting of the claims of liability against the defendant.

Ring's case was based on negligence. He described the 100-ton press and how it worked. He then explained how a tension spring, the brake spring, broke, causing the machine to come down and crush the plaintiff's hands. He then outlined the claims of liability:

> And the evidence will show that the very designing of this press was not proper because they should have, in its original manufacture, used a compression, not a tension spring. . . . And the evidence will show, on the part of the plaintiff at least, that there . . . was a defect or condition. The reason it broke was a condition that was created in the course of manufacture of the particular spring.

Spence enumerated many claims of negligence against the defendant. His general claims were for negligence, strict liability in tort, and gross and wanton negligence. In the early part of his opening statement, he summarized part of his claims:

> The evidence will be about the insidious and agonizing death that people suffer from that dread disease, and the attitudes of the company rela-

---

[10] Bennett, *Storytelling in Criminal Trials: a Model of Social Judgment,* 64 QJ Speech 1 (1978).

tive to that danger. And, all of the evidence in the case from the plaintiff's side, as it is presented against the defendant, will show that it was the legal and lawful responsibility of Kerr-McGee to make that place where they lived safe, to make that place where they worked safe, and to keep control of the plutonium that they had in their possession so that it couldn't escape into Karen Silkwood—or hundreds of Karen Silkwoods— and her brothers and people like her. It was their plutonium, the evidence will show. That is, it didn't belong to them, but it was in their plant, they had the control of it, it was their position of power, their control, their responsibility, and the evidence in the case is going to show you—I don't think there is going to be any question but what the first witness in the case will show you that Kerr-McGee violated that responsibility, and that it was they who permitted the terror—that we will describe—to happen to her. And, it was they who let her be placed in a position where she would, had she lived, died of cancer.

They were negligent, ladies and gentlemen of the jury, and the evidence will show that not only they were negligent, but that there were some other things that they were that become the key words in this trial, and you will hear them from the Court relative to punitive damages. For ten million dollars they were grossly negligent. That means more than ordinary negligence. It is more than just running through a stop sign and running over a little girl—it is running through the stop sign, not at twenty-five miles an hour but at fifty miles an hour. They were more than grossly negligent. They were willfully and wantonly—those are the key words under law—negligent. Willful negligence, unlawful, wanton negligence, which is more than running through a stop sign at fifty miles an hour—it is running through the stop sign at fifty miles an hour with a blindfold on. Negligence so great that it is tantamount, ladies and gentlemen, to not caring about the health and the safety and the welfare and the future of the employees who contributed their lives to the profit-seeking undertaking of Kerr-McGee.

Spence went on to enumerate many acts on the part of Kerr-McGee that supported his claims of liability. He outlined many instances of the escape of plutonium contamination due to the negligence of Kerr-McGee, and instances which illustrated the careless and wanton attitude of Kerr-McGee regarding how it responded to the contamination. He described Karen Silkwood's attempts to inform her union of these problems and the efforts on the part of Kerr-McGee to stop her. He outlined how Karen Silkwood was contaminated in the plant, and finally how her urine kit was spiked with plutonium, giving her a fatal dose of contamination.

Welch's case was based on negligence. He told the jury how the defendant driver got up in the morning, after three hours of sleep, got into his van, fell asleep at the wheel, crossed over the median strip, and ran into the vehicle occupied by the plaintiff. He tells about how the plaintiff tried to turn away from the van, but that at the last minute, the defendant swerved again into the plaintiff's vehicle.

Corboy claimed negligence against the defendant in the operation of his automobile. He described how the defendant driver, unfamiliar with the area in which he was driving, placed a map in his lap or on the steering wheel, and drove up to and through the intersection in question while looking at the map instead of the road. He explained that there was a "stop ahead" sign placed some 433 feet before the intersection that the defendant failed to see because he was looking at the map.

Baldwin's case rested on claims of negligence and strict liability in tort in the construction and assembly of the crane. He first explained the responsibility of each defendant in the manufacture and construction of the crane, and then turned to a summary of his claims of negligence. He stated:

> Now, the law as it applies in this case we say is the law of strict liability, and that is a product that is unreasonably dangerous, is defective, and if that is a producing cause of the accident, then the defendant is responsible in damages. We say the law of strict liability is that a product can be defective in this instance for more than one reason. It can be defective in design, which we allege it is, and I'll go more in detail in a moment. And it can be defective by reason of the fact that it does not have a proper warning, which you will hear more about in a moment.
>
> So then we say that the major areas of defect—there are more than this, but I'm just going to cover the major ones with you—are as I alluded to previously. The design of the crane is simply under strength. I think that you like I was will be surprised, if not alarmed to find out that this crane is so frail with design as to have absolutely no safety margin. That if an operator lifts a load like this one, well within the capacity, and for one reason or another lets that load slip six inches or even less and suddenly puts the brake on, that the crane will collapse. Now that's by design. It's hard for me to believe, but that's the testimony of their engineer.

After detailing his claims for negligence, Perlman summarized as follows:

> The facts will be this, this tragedy was caused by a machine that failed because it was unsafe and dangerous. The proof will be that the boom switch had a mechanical failure; that the pump motor signal was on, but the wiring sent out a signal to the boom. The design had a built-in propensity to fail in the environment it was in. It was not sealed, it was not airtight, it was defective. It had no adequate override whereby the operator could bring the boom back. There was no warning to anybody that this could happen or that, in this design of this machine, if there was a short within the system, that this kind of thing could happen.

Habush outlined his many claims of liability against the various defendants:

> Clearly, the evidence will show, Members of the Jury, that the truck rolled away and we believe the evidence will convince you that the truck had not been properly secured, that the driver of the truck had not blocked or chocked the tires of his truck as he is required to do, and which

signs in the docking area instructed to be done. That, clearly, the truck driver did not have his emergency break on or have the truck in gear or any combination of these things, because if he had, the truck wouldn't have rolled away.

. . . .

And the—and the experts will tell you, Members of the Jury,—If you look at this man, you can see how his back is exposed. And they will tell you that on this particular forklift, which is called a stand-up, as you see the operator standing up while he is operating it, that he had absolutely no protection for his back, none.

. . . .

And when Roger fell, and when the fork truck went backwards, it was this area which curves in that the eye witnesses will tell you they saw the dock come into the forklift, actually intrude right into the operator's compartment and crush his spine. Right in this area. Where it curves in.

. . . .

We will show you, Members of the Jury, that the Eaton Corporation did recognize that rear protection was inadequate on this machine, and that it needed improvement, and, in fact, did ultimately respond.

. . . .

Some of the pretrial depositions of my experts has indicated that they weren't satisfied with the design of the dock plate, that metal plate I showed you that goes up and down, and it should have had a safety stop to avert this particular incident.

In addition to that, you will hear some criticism of the designer of the dock itself, suggesting that it should have been on a different angle which would have prevented the truck from rolling away if it wasn't chocked properly.

After detailing the individual claims, Habush summarized the claims as follows:

And so, Members of the Jury, before I go into the damages discussion with you, I'm satisfied that at the end of the case when I stand up here and talk to you again, the evidence will have proven to you and will prove that although, certainly, the driver of the Pre-pac truck was at fault for not securing this truck, that had this forklift truck been designed with proper operator protection, we wouldn't be here today, and that Roger would have sustained some minor injuries but not the serious paralyzing injuries he sustained.

Block outlined his claims of liability as follows:

How did that come about? It came about because of a defect in the base of the projectile shell which was set off by the propellant, which is below it in the cartridge casing. . . . First, let us describe what this 105 millimeter shell is all about. It has a cartridge at the bottom. In that cartridge case there are bags of powder. On the top of the cartridge case is what is called the projectile. There is propellant powder, as I say, in the cartridge case and there is also an explosive charge in the upper portion called the projectile. That projectile bottom has to be intact and has to be perfect, has to be free from defects, has to be free from breaks because what could happen is, if the propellant in that bottom portion gets hot or cooks, it can, if the bottom of that upper portion of the projectile, the base of the projectile is not intact, you could have a flame from the heating of that bottom portion which would work itself way into that crack or the defect of the projectile and cause an explosion within the cannon and that is precisely what happened here as you will hear from the evidence and from the expert testimony.

Why are we suing Day and Zimmermann? Because Day and Zimmermann, and I don't want to trespass on Judge Canella's province, but in order to give you this outline, Day and Zimmermann, as an assembler, has certain duties, rights and obligations under the law and they are responsible to those for whom this product is intended, namely the servicemen in the field to make that product free from defects because if there is the defect, then what I just narrated will transpire as it did. Knowing that, the law casts upon them a burden to make a defect-free product. Also, the law casts upon them a second burden, to use reasonable care in the assemblage.

Now, we are suing on two bases. One we are saying that under the law if they assemble this product with a defect in it, and if that defect was a cause of this accident, regardless of whether they use the best care in the world, as long as that product had a defect in it when it left their hands and that defect was a cause of the tragedy that befell these men, they are responsible, and on the second ground we are saying that they did not use reasonable care in the fabrication, in the testing, and in the packaging and shipping of their product.

§6.10 —That Due to Defendant's Negligence Plaintiff Suffered Serious Permanent Injuries and Damages

The next major theme was that due to the defendant's negligence, the plaintiff suffered serious permanent injuries and damages. The subthemes were the various injuries and damages that the plaintiffs had suffered. In each case the lawyers itemized the damages suffered by the plaintiffs as a result of the negligence of the defendants. The lawyers laid the foundation for the damage claims by first presenting the good and healthy aspects of the plaintiffs' lives prior to the injuries. The lawyers then proceeded to describe the injuries and demonstrate how they had changed and limited the lives of the plaintiffs and their families. Pain and suffering was an important subtheme here. The lawyers relied on the strategic use of language to present the injuries and damages in such a way that the jurors could understand what had occurred and empathize with the plaintiffs.

§6.11 —That Plaintiff Was a Good or Noble Person and Defendant Behaved Improperly

All of these plaintiffs were presented as good or noble people. In most cases this theme was juxtaposed with the theme that the defendants had behaved improperly. These lawyers seemed to act on the notion that good stories have heroes and villains, and therefore, the plaintiffs became the heroes and the defendants became the villains. This theme enhanced the personalization of the parties, and as was done in personalizing the parties as set out in **§6.06,** language was used strategically to create the good and bad personas inherent in these themes.

Scott Baldwin stated that his client made a "noble" effort to escape the falling crane. In discussing damages, he told the jury:

> I think by the time that this case is over, you're going to agree with this statement, that nobody as to this date, and nobody is going to say anything bad about Mr. Branch. He was a good operator. He was a dependable worker. He made good money.

With respect to the defendants, Baldwin suggested that they acted "irresponsibly." The plaintiff's death was called "needless," suggesting that the defendants could have prevented it. Baldwin told the jury that one of the defendants put the crane together wrong when "they ought to have known better."

Corboy presented numerous examples demonstrating the plaintiff's good character. He stated:

> By the time he got to college he was known as a very, very good person, he had no hesitancy to give money to people, he had no hesitancy to become close to people, no hesitancy in being warm and generous with everything that he had including his time but he had a lot of guts, determination, fortitude, attitudes and characteristics of his personality which are today holding him in good stead. . . . He was a social person. . . . He had determination. He had guts, and had courage and he was an individual. . . . His well-rounded personality again came forth. . . . He became known as a very, very vibrant person. . . . He was a loyal friend. He was honest. He was compassionate.

In demonstrating the bad actions of the defendant driver, Corboy described how he carelessly drove through the intersection into the plaintiff's vehicle, without looking, while he was reading a map placed in his lap. He pointed out the inconsistent statements made by the defendant driver with respect to how the collision occurred, suggesting that the defendant was untruthful. At one point the driver said he was going through the intersection slowly, while in his deposition he stated that he was going 45 to 50 miles per hour.

Welch told the jury about the pride with which the plaintiff performed his job, and about his enviable work record. In the 18 years that the plaintiff had worked, he missed no time from work except for a period of time when he had a leg injury. At other times, the plaintiff suffered injuries, but lost no time from work. During his convalescence and rehabilitation from the injury in question, the plaintiff was a "very determined man." Welch presented the defendant as being untruthful by pointing out that the defendant gave inconsistent statements after the collision in an effort to avoid liability. He juxtaposed the goodness of the plaintiff and the badness of the defendant when he concluded his opening by telling the jury that they would hear the story of the "unassuming" plaintiffs whose lives had been altered by a "careless" motorist.

The juxtaposition of the goodness of Karen Silkwood and the evil of Kerr-McGee was highlighted in the early part of Spence's opening when he stated:

> Now this case is principally about a human being. It is about a woman, a young woman, who you will be relieved to discover wasn't perfect, and who, you may be shocked to discover, didn't view things the way many human beings do, who had a perhaps different lifestyle than many. But, the bottom line about Karen Silkwood was that she was a very ordinary woman. And by "ordinary" I don't mean "common," I mean she was a plain, ordinary human being like you and me. And, the case is about her suffering, and the facts in the case will be about her suffering, and the facts in the case will be about her terrors in the night for nine days before her death. And, the case is about her daytime life as an employee at Kerr-McGee, where they attempted in those last nine days, the evidence I believe will show, to discredit her and to make her into something that she was not in the eyes of her fellow employers and her fellow employees.
>
> Now, that attempt to somehow change Karen Silkwood from an ordinary person like you and me into something that she was not, the evidence will be in this case, has not stopped to this moment, and the minute I sit down you will see that effort being continued on the part of the defendant in this case.

Spence spent a great deal of time outlining how Karen Silkwood dedicated herself to helping the public and her fellow workers discover the truth about the bad actions of Kerr-McGee. Her efforts were directed toward making America a safer place to live:

> This is perhaps where the case really began, and I want to tell you now where the case factually really began. It really began in an attempt by Karen Silkwood herself, in 1974, to aid the public to discover the truth about this giant corporation and this work that was being undertaken by it. It was her effort and her dedication to expose to the public about the death and danger to the employees of Kerr-McGee. . . . She was one, from the beginning, the evidence will be, who even as a child, as a young child the age of her oldest daughter, was wanting to do something reasonable and meaningful with her life. She was characterized, by people who knew her, as a very nice person who wanted to be right about everything . . .

Spence enumerated the many instances in which the defendant allowed Kerr-McGee employees and the public to be contaminated with plutonium in total disregard of their safety, and how the defendant refused to take any corrective measures. He pointed out how they doctored the x-rays of the plutonium storage cases in order to conceal contamination leakage. Spence explained how after Karen Silkwood went to the Atomic Energy Commission to report the abuses being committed by Kerr-McGee, rather than tightening up their security, or making it safer, Kerr-McGee brought in a lie detector and began questioning employees about union officials and Karen Silkwood in an effort to intimidate employees into keeping quiet. He pointed out how Kerr-McGee officials claimed under oath in their depositions that they didn't know what Karen Silkwood was doing, when the evidence proved that not only did they know what she was doing, but they were discussing her activities in their board meetings and in their daily meetings.

In his case involving the failure to diagnose cancer, Bergman carefully developed the plaintiffs as a family of happy, caring people. The daughter was described as "friendly, outgoing, fairly popular. She had a lot of friends." He then noted how the plaintiff's mother was a devoted mother who had taken great pains over the years to see that her daughter had good medical care so that she would lead a healthy life. In developing the mother's good efforts to keep her children healthy, Bergman stated:

> Judy Morrison has always been a devoted mother. And the strength of her devotion has been demonstrated, as you will find out, for the last three years. Judy has always been interested and involved with her daughters, always known what her daughters are doing, how they are feeling. She was active with them at school. Shanna's friends always seemed to be over at her house. Judy made the home a place where her friends were welcome. That is where she seemed to hang out.
>
> Judy didn't overindulge her children. If anything, I think that she feels guilty today that maybe she was too strict with Shanna at times. That is just a natural feeling that you would have when your child is considered to be terminally ill. But there is one area where Judy Morrison was always meticulous and where there is absolutely no room to fault her or for her to fault herself, and that has to do with the medical care for her children. If something wasn't right with Kenda or Shanna, they went to the doctor. There was no hesitation about it. There was no doubt about it. Not only do they go to the doctor, but they went to the best possible doctor Judy Morrison could find for whatever the problem seemed to be.
>
> Shanna had a little curvature of the spine that many youngsters have, called scoliosis. Judy took her to an orthopedist, Dr. Kozikiwski, I think who was discussed this morning.
>
> Shanna developed a problem with some warts growing on her fingers. Judy took her to a doctor knowledgeable about that.
>
> Shanna opened up a gash in her left knee and had a scar. Judy took her to a plastic surgeon to get the scar revised so that it would go away. Dr. Carl Saffo was that plastic surgeon.
>
> If Shanna had ordinary infections or colds or runny noses, whatever it would be, she went to Dr. Korasco, the family pediatrician.

Probably the best evidence of just how meticulous that Judy was about her child's medical care is the stack of medical records that exists for an otherwise fairly normal, healthy child. She had no major problems, no major illnesses; and yet when we go back and get all of the medical records, it is quite a stack. And I think that is testimony to how meticulous and careful that Judy Morrison has always been about her children's health.

Bergman then went on to document how Shanna and her mother attempted to get appropriate treatment and diagnosis of the Hodgkin's disease. He noted how Shanna's mother went to the effort to get Shanna's emergency records relating to her cat scratch and bring them to the defendant oncologist so that he would have her past history. He noted how the plaintiff followed all medical advice and sought medical doctors to have her condition diagnosed and treated. He noted how the plaintiff's mother always gave the doctor all the information she had on Shanna when they went to see the doctor. He described how the plaintiff's mother brought the plaintiff back to the defendant doctor before her scheduled visit because the plaintiff was worse and the mother wished to express her concern for her daughter's health. Finally, Bergman detailed the family's trials and tribulations with respect to Shanna's chemotherapy treatment. The family sacrificed in order to be at the daughter's side, and the daughter painfully endured, without complaint, whatever treatment her doctors prescribed in an effort to get well. With respect to the family's efforts to fight the disease, Bergman stated:

> Judy Morrison had been with her every day. You will hear about the hundreds and the thousands of hours of care that Shanna has gotten from her family; that every night that she was in the hospital, a family member was there with her, the hospital encourages that; what Judy has been through. But they are fighters, and I think that even defense counsel will say and agree that heroic effort has been made to save Shanna's life.

In short, the plaintiffs were described as good, courageous people who did everything in their power to have the plaintiff's condition diagnosed and treated.

This image was then juxtaposed and compared with the negative image of the defendant doctor. Bergman noted that on their first visit the doctor wrote in the chart the diagnosis of "cat scratch fever," but did not tell the plaintiffs that that was his diagnosis. At other points, the doctor noted that the plaintiff thought her enlarged lymph node was decreasing in size, while the doctor noted in the chart that it was the same size. Bergman then noted the mother's attempts to obtain an evaluation of the condition and the doctor's failure to provide the same:

> On that visit, Dr. Hanson told the Morrisons that he had seen other cat scratch cases, that he did some reading on it, and he was sure that this was cat scratch fever, so there would be no need to do a biopsy. Judy said, "But this node is kind of enlarged and painful for Shanna." She had

some swelling above the breast. "Can you go in there with a needle and maybe draw out some fluid?" And he said, "Oh, no, Mrs. Morrison. That is how people used to die from cat scratch disease," which is not true.

I asked Dr. Hanson at his deposition, "What medical literature were you referring to when you told the Morrisons that you had gone to the books and read up on cat scratch disease?" And he told me that he had looked at Cecil's Textbook of Medicine, which is a book that he had in his office which has a chapter on cat scratch disease. Obviously, I went to look to see what Cecil's Textbook of Medicine has to say about cat scratch disease. Actually the name—he called it cat scratch fever—actually the disease is called cat scratch disease.

I have got an enlarged section, not the whole excerpt from Cecil's Textbook of Medicine, and I have it here to show you. This is by a doctor called Margoleth out of Cecil's Textbook of Medicine, 1982 edition, which would have been the current edition at the time. This talks about how you make the—there is a section in the article on diagnosis. It talks about regional lymphadenopathy two weeks after cat contact, and especially if a primary inoculation papule or pustule follows a scratch, it suggests cat scratch disease. Three of the four following manifestations would confirm the diagnosis in a typical case, whereas all four would be necessary in an atypical case. There are four things, a little checklist that the doctor can go through to make the diagnosis. Let me go back. Let's figure out if we need three or four of them.

. . . .

Developing two weeks after cat contact. That is the key right there, developing two weeks after cat contact, not twelve hours or twenty-four hours. Because the bacteria, the little organism that is considered to cause cat scratch disease, has to multiply at the site of the cat contact. It takes some time to do that and make its way to the lymph node, and then cause the enlargement. That takes some time. In the literature, there is no report of enlargement of lymph nodes in cat scratch disease less than three days after the cat bite, especially if a primary inoculation papule or pustule follows the scratch. Dr. Hanson didn't even ask about that. That is a characteristic little scab on the area of the cat bite which, had he asked about, he would have learned did not exist, never happened. But he didn't ask about it. Even though it said right in his book.

So this is an atypical case, not to mention the supraclavicular nodes which are the flashing light for the malignancy. But what would he have had to do to establish the diagnosis? A history of animal contact is number one. That existed. And an enlarged node. Frankly those are the only things that existed. The second thing is a supperation of sterile pus from the node or laboratory results excluding other etiologic possibilities. In other words, you take some pus out of the node, which is what Judy had asked to be done, and put it under a microscope, and there are characteristics of cat scratch disease. Then you do other blood work and you start ruling out things like mononucleosis and toxicomycosis and a whole list of other things that should be ruled out that could account for these symptoms.

The third thing is a possible—excuse me, a positive skin test result to cat scratch antigen. You will hear quite a bit about cat scratch antigen. This is a list like the tuberculum in a tuberculosis test. You inject a little of the cat scratch antigen into the arm of the person who is presumed to have it; they develop a reaction to it. If they develop the reaction, you are probably dealing with cat scratch disease. There is a very high degree of reliability, in fact, 95 percent confidence level in that test according to Dr. Hanson's own book.

He didn't do the cat scratch skin test. He said that he was going to do it, but he didn't do it. And he didn't do it not because it wasn't available, not because maybe it would transmit disease or something like that, but because he considered it unreliable when he had never done it, he never researched it, and the only book that he went to said that it was highly reliable.

Yet he told the Morrisons on several occasions that he was looking for it, he was trying to get it, planning on doing it, but he never did it. He never even tried to get it.

Finally, and most importantly, a node biopsy revealing histopathology consistent with cat scratch disease. That is under a microscope. You can't tell that it is a cat scratch disease 100 percent like you can with cancer, but there are certain characteristics that you see under the microscope. So if this was a typical case, three of these things had to exist. The only one that existed was the history of animal contact.

If it was an atypical case—which this clearly was, because it never was cat scratch disease—you need all four. Yet nothing was done, except an examination and a history; and the history wasn't even adequate. The thought process of the doctor wasn't very thorough. This is supposed to be a diagnostician who is going to be making a diagnosis. I think that even a lay person just looking at the check list can see that you can only check off one of these four things.

When I questioned Dr. Hanson under oath, he acknowledged that Shanna's symptoms should have caused him to put in his differential diagnosis, "Cancer, a malignancy in the lymph node."

In fact, he claims that he thought about that, that was the number-two thought in his mind after cat scratch fever. The only problem is that the only way to rule cancer in or to rule it out is to do the lymph node biopsy, which was never done. If the lymph node biopsy had been done or arranged for—because Dr. Hanson doesn't do them; you have to get a surgeon to do them—this diagnosis would have been made in September. . . . If he was thinking about cancer, he owed it to Shanna to do a biopsy to rule that in or rule it out.

Finally, Bergman noted how the doctor failed to act, even when the node became a huge mass, and became impatient with the plaintiff's expression of concern:

Now, I mentioned on September 20th that Dr. Hanson had said, "See in four to six weeks. Sooner if worse." Twenty-one days later, three weeks later Judy had Shanna back to Dr. Hanson's office. Dr. Hanson didn't even take the time or make the effort to write a note of what the situation was at that time. This is October 11th. The nurse wrote some things in. That's it. But Judy Morrison remembers some things about that visit. But the main thing is that Shanna was getting worse. She was expressing concern to Dr. Hanson.

. . . .

Judy said, "But I'm really worried about Shanna." Dr. Hanson got a little impatient with her on that day, and he said, "Mrs. Morrison, cat scratch fever just takes some time to work out. The symptoms are probably going to get worse before they get better. Just don't worry about it." He didn't even want to see Shanna again until she was better.

They didn't even arrange for another appointment. Notwithstanding that the node had gone from a tiny lymph node enlarged in July to a massive—he described it as "huge lymph node"—and into another region, no tests done.

Perlman pointed out that the defendant was one of the largest manufacturers of coal mining equipment, and that although it knew that the mining machine in question was defective, knew of its propensity to malfunction as it did, knew how to build a better electrical system, it still failed to warn the users of its machines that they would malfunction just the way they did.

Gibbons developed the deceased's noble character by noting that the plaintiff was a serviceman, serving his country, and that he was "one of the chosen few" who received the "highest of honors" from Oklahoma State University. He described how the deceased selected his jobs so that he could be near his wife and son. This was contrasted with the defendant airplane manufacturer who knowingly made planes that had a propensity to malfunction due to flight control jams and who was aware of some 29 previous mishaps due to flight control jams. Similarly, Gibbons pointed out how the manufacturer of the ejection seat knew of the defective design of its seat, and knew of mishaps involving the seat, but considered this design and potential for injury an acceptable risk, and failed to take steps to remedy the problem. He stated:

In this connection, we are going to also bring you a man named Russell Stanford, who works for our Federal Government, that has spent most of his entire professional career in the research and development of ejection seats. And he will offer certain expert opinions. Among others we will prove that McDonnell-Douglas knew of the defects in the inherent instabilities in their own seat that killed Harry Wahl and they did nothing. We will show by documents that they were warned back in 1977, and we have the documents right here blown up for you. In 1977 they were warned that their seat was inherently unstable and there was a major concern over it. And they did nothing to take that seat off the market. And that they knew what the state of the art was because McDonnell-Douglas actually came out with this Ace's 2 to replace it. But other manufacturers had come out for 20 years earlier with stabilization in the roll and the yaw areas. So Russell Stanford then will bring that type of proof.

After detailing the good character of the deceased, Block told the jury that he was killed, "not by the enemy, but by reason of defective ammunition." This illustrated the destructive effect of the defendant's negligence, and, in a sense, put the defendant's acts in the same category as the enemy in the war.

Habush created a negative image for the defendant by pointing out that it was a big, sophisticated corporation that was fully aware of the defects and dangers involved in its forklift, but that it refused to remedy the defect because the added cost might affect its marketability. Thus, it was suggested that the defendant placed profitability over the safety of its users:

> The evidence will tell you, Members of the Jury, that the Eaton Corporation is an international producer and seller of industrial machines such as this forklift, has hundreds of distributorships all over the world and sells all over the world, that they have been producing forklift trucks since 1923, that they have testing grounds and testing plants and locations, that they hire and retain competent expert engineers. That this particular model had a predecessor called the MR which looked essentially like it, was made in 1973, first design, and was sold from 1973 until 1985.
>
> We will show you, Members of the Jury, that we are dealing with a very sophisticated knowledgable manufacturer. And we will show you that they knew that operator protection on their forklift trucks was needed.
>
> We will show you that they either were aware or should have been aware of the hazards of rearward danger to the operator, that forklift accidents were quite common, and produced serious injuries, that workers could be injured and had been injured in similar type incidents from workers backing into racks, backing into shelving, backing into docks, and that this particular hazard was not addressed or answered at all on this particular model.
>
> You will hear evidence that in their committee meetings they considered providing protection to the rear of this particular model, but that they decided that it would require adding length and would affect its marketability.

In his gun case, Bergman compared his safety conscious plaintiff with the gun manufacturer that refused to attempt to remedy known hazards. He suggested that it was unfair for the manufacturer who made no effort to eliminate a known hazard to be critical of a safety conscious customer:

> Now they sit back and their evidence is going to criticize their customer, a person with a good safety record, good habits. They are blaming him. They are blaming the manufacturer of the holster, something wrong with the holster. They are blaming Alco Store who sold Paul the gun because the packet of instructions that they claim was in there wasn't in there when Paul got it home. And they accept no blame for themselves. You are going to hear a good deal of testimony in this case about what is known as safety

engineering principles. And that is a concept that we will have a very fine engineer named George Greene testify about, that in the design of a product you must eliminate, you must take all reasonable means necessary to eliminate the hazards that are inherent in the product. Reasonable means. And by hazards, we are talking about the potential for injury, serious injury or death. Until the manufacturer does its job of eliminating all these unnecessary hazards, it is not in a position to criticize anybody else who runs into the hazard that they created. So the issue in this case is whether the hazard that Colt knew about should have been designed out of the weapon. Whether there were reasonable means available to do that within the known state of the art in the firearms industry that would have absolutely protected Paul.

§6.12   That the Issues in the Case Are Simple

If the jurors believe the issues are complex, they have a tendency to think that the defendant should not be held liable, and certainly should not be assessed a large damage verdict. Thus, in those cases involving seemingly complex issues, these lawyers told the jurors that the issues in the case were simple.

After summarizing the collapse of the crane and introducing the parties, but before outlining his claims of negligence, Baldwin stated:

> So now, let me forewarn you and say that this case is really simple, and it won't become complicated, unless you allow it to become complicated. You're going to hear engineering terms and engineering theories, but simply put, it's not a complicated case, if you don't chase rabbits.

After Spence enumerated many instances of Kerr-McGee's careless conduct in the handling of plutonium, after explaining how Karen Silkwood was contaminated and damaged, and after explaining the defendant's contentions, Spence states, "Now, of course, the issues are simple, and I want you to know what the issues are, because you are going to have to sort through them throughout the course of the trial . . ."

In his gun malfunction case, in his introduction, Bergman took a complex case with relatively complex issues involving a manufacturer's duties, reconceptualized them simply to the single issue of how the plaintiff's injuries have affected the plaintiffs' lives, thus presupposing liability, and then told the jury that it was a simple matter:

> This case is really about the impact on the lives of Paul and Jannie that arose as a consequence of his injury. The injury has had a very heavy impact on the solidarity of their marriage and the fulfillment and satisfaction that they have in their lives. You see, as a result of the gunshot wound, Paul has been rendered impotent. It is what the doctors call an erectile impotence. Paul is not able to maintain the rigidity that is needed for intercourse. It is as simple as that. . . . Paul and Jannie are here to obtain compensation for the injuries and damages that they have sustained. It is as simple as that.

In his conclusion, Bergman returned to the theme of simplicity and stated, "So there is going to be nothing particularly complicated about the issues or the evidence in this case."

In his Hodgkin's disease case, just before outlining the issues, Bergman told the jury, "The issues are medical issues, but they are really not too complicated." In discussing the doctor's failure to properly diagnose the plaintiff's condition, Bergman stated, "I think that even a lay person just looking at the check list can see that you can only check off one of these four things." Finally, in his conclusion, before outlining the doctor's omissions, Bergman stated:

> I think that when you have heard the evidence in this case, there really isn't going to be any doubt at all that some of these things are just always considered basic.

Gibbons, in his conclusion, told the jury that although they would be talking about technical things, the case boiled down to be "quite a simple thing." He went on to concisely reconceptualize the seemingly complicated issues into very simple terms:

> . . . but it really boils down to be quite a simple thing, and that is that this airplane was defectively designed, and we will prove that because it allowed the flight controls to jam which necessitated ejection by an inherently unstable seat which in effect severed the spinal cord of Captain Wahl, when the seat was advertised to save your life.

After briefly describing the explosion of the howitzer shell, Block acknowledged that the jurors were probably thinking that they did not have any knowledge about munitions, but then told the jurors that it would be "clear as daylight once you analyze the case and once you hear the proof."

§6.13 Tone

In each case, the story the lawyer told was serious. These were the stories of tragedies. No humor was included because it has no place in such stories. As presented in the opening statements, these cases involved life and death struggles between heroic ordinary people against villains in order to overcome pain and undeserved injury. The lawyers wanted the jury to take them seriously, so they were serious. Corboy referred to the collision as a "tragic" occurrence. Spence spoke of "this very important case," and told the jury that the "case may ultimately be about the future survival of the American people." When discussing the jury's purpose and function, Spence told them that their job was "a terrible job, a terrible heavy job" of finding the truth, and that their job of evaluating the expert testimony was a "terrible responsibility."

In response to a sarcastic remark made by the opposing attorney, Welch responded, "He thinks this case is a funny case, but I don't." Welch referred to the "serious injuries" sustained by the plaintiff.

Block told the jury that the case emanated out of a "tragic war," was a "tragic occurrence," and referred to the "tragedy that befell these men." In beginning the opening on the damages portion of the trial, Block told the jury, "We are about to embark on a very important and responsible aspect, the second phase of this trial, to assess damages which were done to the survivors of Wendell Burns." In beginning his opening on behalf of the plaintiff Baird, Block told the jurors that their function "is a very important one." On behalf of the surviving wife, he told the jurors that she had suffered a "grievous and horrendous loss." In concluding his opening on behalf of the plaintiff Burns, he told the jury that "it's an important case."

In his conclusion, Gibbons told the jury, "But your job throughout the next week is a most important one."

Bergman set the tone for the story of his clients' heroic struggle by telling the jury, "I am personally honored to be able to be the Morrisons' representative and to be able to tell you what has happened to them, what has happened to Shanna." In his gun malfunction case, Bergman began by telling the jury, "This is a very serious and substantial case arising out of a gunshot wound that occurred to Paul Johnson on July 3, 1981." He told the jurors that the injury had a "very heavy impact on the solidarity" of the plaintiff's marriage.

§6.14 Creating Jury Purpose

In presenting their openings, the lawyers told the jury what its purpose and function would be in deciding the case. The jury purpose specified by the court in most cases was general and vague, such as to be fair and impartial, or to render justice. These lawyers went further and created and shaped the jury purpose. In his introduction, Spence suggested to the jurors that they should "try to become a part of" the case. In explaining the purpose of the litigation, Spence suggested that the jury's function would be to consider a money verdict:

> Now, the next thing I want to tell you about is the purpose of the litigation. I want to just come right up front with you about that. The purpose of this litigation has as its only ultimate goal in this lawsuit, in this courtroom, and that is a final money judgment. It is a case about money. That sounds kind of gross and crass, but that is what it is. It is true that the case is also about pain, and about death and fear, and terror, and panic. The case is about that. And, the case ultimately may be about the future survival of the American people. And, it's about damages, whether or not damages are sufficient in size to make Kerr-McGee, and other defendants, and other manufacturers, and other companies like them to perform their duties in the future in a way that American people can live and survive healthfully. And it is about preventing, ladies and gentlemen, the dastardly escape of plutonium particles ever again. And, although it is about all of those things, the bottom line is, it is about money, because unless there are sufficient exemplary damages, unless there are sufficient actual damages awarded by an understanding jury in a meaningful verdict, the case will have been about nothing.

After discussing the dangers of plutonium and the negligence of Kerr-McGee, Spence further defined the jury purpose as returning a money verdict in order to punish the defendant and keep the world safe:

> Well, of course, this case is one in which the law, because of its frailties—it seems powerful, you know, as I have a sense of awe in front of the law, and I have a sense of awe in your presence, in the presence of this court-room—but it is a frail institution because it is a human institution and it cannot return nine days to Karen Silkwood. It cannot remove the terror, cannot remove the cancer, and cannot change any of that, and has only the power, only the little small insignificant power, of returning a full money verdict. That is all the law can do, award damages for her nine days of terror and panic and award exemplary punitive damages to make an example for the world to see so that this will never happen again.

With respect to the evidence, Spence told the jury that its function would be to discover the truth:

> Now, why do we assert, ladies and gentlemen, in a public courtroom, cov-ered by the greatest press of this nation, that Kerr-McGee owes these sums of money? What are the facts? What is the suit based on? Well, the first thing you have to hear is that this case will become an incredible chal-lenge to discover what the truth really is. And, it is going to be an effort on your part to ferret out what those facts are. That is going to be the responsibility that you face and to solve a mystery, to solve a mystery. That will be your job.

In discussing the testimony of the expert witnesses, Spence asserted that the function of the jury would be to evaluate the credibility of the witnesses:

> Now, there is going to be some other kinds of evidence that you're going to be called upon to evaluate. You don't expect that the only people that are going to take the stand are experts that all agree. Experts don't all agree. And, you're going to be called upon to decide which expert to believe. That seems quite a terrible responsibility, because you will be listening to people of world reknowned positions, but you have to decide. And, some of you may feel that you are not qualified to decide, but the experience of the American judicial system has been that jurors are the best qualified to decide. That you will listen, and you will rely on your own common judgment, and your own common sense, and that your six minds, that aren't prejudiced or tampered with any preconception and pre-ideas, are the best qualified to see and cut through that maze. . . . But, one of the bottom line inquiries that you will be making under direc-tions from the Court will be to determine the credibility of the witnesses. That is, which witness is the most credible.

Baldwin first suggested to the jury that its function was to return a verdict against the defendant when he stated, "It was unreasonably dangerous, and you shouldn't have any trouble returning a verdict against the defendant, the Liebherr group." He then moved to the issue of damages and told the jury that its function was to assess damages against the defendant:

> Now to the question of damages. We expect to show that the damages in the case are substantial. . . . He made good money. He worked a lot of overtime, and had he worked out his life expectancy—had he been allowed or accorded that privilege, except for this unnecessary death, he would have earned more than a million dollars. I expect the Court will tell you that that's one element that you can consider in assessing damages is what he would have earned and contributed to his family. . . . And these damages are going to be substantial, and I hope you'll start thinking about them now, because it's going to be quite a job for you to come up with an adequate amount of damages in this case. . . . Then there's one other amount of damages that is intangible. You said on Monday that you could award damages for what I'm going to outline, and that's conscious pain and suffering. . . . It falls [sic] your lot to place a value on it.

Perlman told the jury that he would ask that the jury be fair, and that he knew that they would award fair and reasonable compensation.

Gibbons began his opening by suggesting that the jury's purpose was to find out why and how the plaintiff died:

> May it please the Court, ladies and gentlemen of the jury, and members of the defense: ladies and gentlemen, we are here today on behalf of he widow, Dianne Wahl, and minor son, Billy, to find out why Captain Harry Wahl died needlessly in the service of his country approximately 2 years ago right now. Your job is going to be to determine why, among other things, he had to bail out or eject from a crippled A10 fighter plane. . . . Your job will also be to determine why, when it was necessary for him to eject, that his spinal cord was severed in his neck during the parachute opening.

After Gibbons had thoroughly explained why the defendants were liable, he presupposed the liability issues and told the jury that its function would be to assess the various items of damage:

> And finally, we will bring you Dianne Wahl and her son Billy to testify about their losses, both monetary and otherwise, since the needless death of their husband and father. And also an economist by the name of Melissa Patterson who you will be called upon to award and assess damages pursuant to his Honor's instructions to you, and within the guidelines of those instructions. He will tell you what you can and cannot consider. But one of the things that he will tell you in all likelihood that you can consider will be the actual pecuniary losses to this family. And it is our burden of proof, if you will to reduce it to the present cash value because you are going to have to pass on a loss for the rest of their lives, since Harry Wahl is deceased.

Gibbons then shifted to the issue of punitive damages and forcefully told the jurors that it would be their duty to consider punitive damages in order to prevent this from happening to other servicemen:

> And then, ladies and gentlemen, as to the punitive damages that are sought in the case, and we might as well get it out on the table, His Honor will give you certain instructions about punitive damages in all reasonable likelihood, that if you find that these Defendants acted grossly, willfully and with wanton disregard to the rights of others, then you will be called upon to have the opportunity to assess punitive damages, in addition to the damages, the actual damages suffered by the Wahls. But punitive damages against them, to set an example so that this won't happen to any other serviceman. And this will be not only your opportunity but if the evidence warrants it, your duty.

In further discussing the need for punitive damages, Gibbons argued that the defendant had attempted to cover up the cause of the plaintiff's plane malfunction, and told the jury that its purpose would be, through a punitive damage award, to tell the defendants that they could not do what they had done:

> There will also be evidence that they tried to cover that up, and that is why we brought the suit for punitive damages in addition. They have tried to cover that up. They continue to do so. So you are going to be called upon not only to assess actual damages to the Wahls, but also to consider or at least have the opportunity to award punitive damages, to tell them this isn't the way that you can do.

Habush initially told the jury that its function was to sit on the case, judge the credibility of the witnesses, evaluate the evidence, and follow the law:

> You are, Members of the Jury, representatives of the community and competent to sit on this case, and competent to, as the Court has just instructed you, judge the credibility of the witnesses and evaluate the evidence and, of course follow the law.

Habush then told the jurors that their function would be to decide the issues of the case, and he outlined the issues. As he moved to the issue of damages, he told the jurors that they would be asked to award the various items of damages, such as past medical expenses and lost wages. Finally, he told the jury that he would ask it to return a fair and adequate award to the plaintiffs.

Block told the jurors that they were the conscious of the community and would have to make sure that the case was decided correctly. With regard to damages, in an attempt to argue that the jury must award all damages proved, Block told the jury on behalf of one plaintiff, "and that is the function for which you were sworn, to render full justice, not partial justice." In his opening on behalf of the other plaintiffs, Block told the jury:

> Now, your function is a very important one. You are here to evaluate damages so that Mr. Baird gets full and adequate compensation for each

and every injury he sustained and for the other damages such as loss of earning capacity and loss of earnings that the law allows.

Finally, Block told the jurors that their job was like that of bookkeeping, and that they must listen to all elements of damage and compensate the plaintiffs for all items of loss:

> Now, this case is almost like a cold bookkeeping operation. There is no other way, unfortunately. We don't have an eye-for-an-eye concept. We have to listen carefully to each item of loss that these people sustained, because at the end of the case, in his charge to you, Judge Cannella will tell you what you must compensate for if you find from the evidence that such compensation is warranted. . . .

Finally, Block told the jury that its function was to "do justice as you would have justice done for anyone who seeks a claim."

§6.15 Bases of Authority

In the course of the story, the lawyers established the basic premises from which they would argue. These were principles of law or principles in particular fields of expertise relevant to the trial, as well as the basic premises for deductive argument. These principles were woven into the narrative to demonstrate that the plaintiffs were entitled to favorable verdicts.

Spence invoked several bases of authority in proving his case. At times Spence relied upon the law. With respect to Kerr-McGee's responsibilities in handling plutonium, Spence told the jury that all of the evidence on the plaintiff's side would show that Kerr-McGee had the "legal and lawful responsibility" to keep its plant safe and to control plutonium such that people would not be hurt. His most important base of authority was the law of strict liability in tort. Spence stated:

> Now, yesterday His honor talked to you a little bit about the law that may be involved in this case—and that isn't my function, his Honor will instruct you on the law—but we talked something about, in the voir dire, absolute liability. It comes from the old common law where, you know, about the lion—somebody brought a lion in a cage—the lion, everybody knows, is a wild animal and dangerous—and without any negligence on the part of the man who had the lion in the cage, the lion got loose and clawed and hurt and ate and killed some people, and the lion owner said: "It wasn't our fault. We didn't turn him loose." And, the old common law says when you bring something dangerous, a dangerous instrumentality onto your property, and permit it to escape to the injury of others, it doesn't make any difference whether you are careful or not, you're liable—and that, we believe, will be the law in the case—except the lion is the plutonium particles, which are more dangerous, one small particle, than all the lions in the world. And, those lions, those dangerous particles,

escaped from Kerr-McGee, and that is sufficient for our recovery. We don't have to explain how it got from the plant to her apartment—and I'm glad of that—and I'm glad the law helps us—because I don't know how, I couldn't tell you, and if I tried to tell you, it would just be speculation. But, they can, I believe, tell you it was their plutonium, their plant. The evidence will be it was their control. It was their ballgame. It was their profit. And, they can tell you, I believe, where that plutonium is, how it got away, and where the forty pounds are. And, if they can't tell you how it got away, and if they can't solve that mystery, which is their obligation to tell us how the lion got out, then legally it makes no difference. But, factually and honestly the lips and the knowledge of Karen Silkwood remain sealed for eternity.

Whenever possible Spence invoked the judge as the authority with respect to the law. When talking about punitive damages, he stated:

They were negligent, ladies and gentlemen of the jury, and the evidence will show that not only they were negligent, but that there were some other things that they were that become the key words in this trial, and you will hear them from the Court relative to punitive damages.

One of Ring's bases of authority was expert witness testimony. The liability in Ring's case rested on proving that a spring in the brake press machine was defective. He told the jury that it would have to resolve a dispute as to why the spring malfunctioned and that an expert witness would be called to testify about the spring. In proving the plaintiff's damages, he told the jury:

You will have the benefit of the testimony of an economist who has taken the figures of his past earnings and computed what his future loss would be. And you will hear evidence about that economic loss; that is, the out-of-pocket loss itself, his past earnings, and future loss of earnings was—as I say, he was 19 years old at the time—somewhere around $400,000.00.

At one point Baldwin invoked the defendant's expert witness as his base of authority:

I think that you like I was will be surprised, if not alarmed to find out that this crane is so frail with design as to have absolutely no safety margin. That if an operator lifts a load like this one, well within the capacity, and for one reason or another lets that load slip six inches or even less and suddenly puts the brake on, that crane will collapse. Now, that's by design. It's hard for me to believe, but that's the testimony of their engineer.

With respect to liability, Block relied on experts as bases for authority when he first told the jurors that the cause of the shell explosion would be clear once they heard the proof, and then told the jurors that the proof would be made by expert testimony. He invoked the law as a base of authority when he told the jury that the plaintiffs were suing the defendant because they had "certain rights and obligations under the law." In his opening on damages, Block invoked the evidence as authority for his claims when he pledged that his claims would be supported by the evidence. At another point, he relied on medical records as a base of authority when he stated, "This is not lawyer's talk. The medical records, the VA records, will all show it." In arguing that the jury must compensate the plaintiffs for all items of damage, Block invoked the law:

> . . . but what the law also says in its wisdom is that there are certain items of damage to which they are entitled. If you can't compensate for grief and mental anguish, the law—and don't take it from me—the only person who can fitly and rightly give you the law in this courtroom is the Judge, Judge Cannella. . . . It's a family who is coming here on fault that's already established against the defendant, and they are entitled to each and every item of damage, no matter how large; because the law says that if the defendant casts a person into greater damage, they must compensate accordingly, dollar for dollar.

Gibbons relied on the evidence as a base of authority when he told the jury that the evidence and testimony would show that over 50 per cent of all of the planes in question, upon inspection, were found to have foreign object material in their flight controls. He invoked the defendants themselves as authority when he referred to their own records as proof for his claims. With respect to his claim that foreign object material caused flight control jams, he stated:

> And that is an acknowledged cause, even by Republic Fairchild in their own inter-office memoranda, from word they have received from the United States Air Force, including the word on the Wahl case, that it was a flight control jam.

He further stated that while Republic Fairchild made several design changes, by their own admission, there was still a problem of foreign object material jamming the controls. Finally, he noted that Republic's own records contained documents from the United States Air Force documenting that the deceased was required to eject from his plane due to flight control jam.

Gibbons invoked a test pilot as a base of authority for how the flight control jam occurred and required the deceased to eject. He told the jury that he would produce an expert witness who would tell the jury that ejection did not have to be a risky business. An economist was relied upon as authority for proof of lost income to the family as a result of the father's death. With respect to damages, Gibbons invoked the judge as authority and told the jurors:

> He will tell you what you can and cannot consider. But one of the things he will tell you in all likelihood that you can consider will be the actual pecuniary losses to this family.

Habush invoked the court and the law as the base of authority for his claims against the defendant:

We will show you, and the evidence will show you, and the Judge will instruct you, that a manufacturer in designing and manufacturing a machine, whether it's a forklift truck or a punch press or whatever it is, is the person who addresses the hazards, sees what hazards are associated with its use, and then tries to find a way to design into the machine safeguards, to reduce the possibility of injury to people who use it in a customary and proper fashion.

With respect to his loss of consortium claim, Habush told the jurors that the court would instruct them that spouses of injured people have a cause of action when their spouse is injured and they are deprived of their love, affection, and services. He referred to the plaintiff and other witnesses when he told the jury that the plaintiff and "others will testify" how the truck rolled away from the dock. With respect to the cause of the injury, Habush stated that the eyewitnesses would confirm that a portion of the dock intruded through the unprotected area of the forklift to crush the plaintiff's spine. He then relied on experts in this regard when he told the jury that he would present expert testimony in the form of biomechanical engineers and a neurosurgeon to prove that the cause of the plaintiff's injury was the intrusion of the dock plate into the unprotected area of the forklift. He also invoked the authority of experts when he told the jury that experts would tell the jury that the way the truck was parked made it more vulnerable to rolling away from the dock. With respect to the proper design of the forklift, a safety organization and safety standards were referred to when Habush told the jurors:

> We will show you that a safety organization recommended a rear post to protect the back of forklift operators using this type of forklift truck.
> We will show you that a recognized standard in an illustration recommended, by its illustration, better protection for the operators in the back.

Glaser told the jury he would rely on the defendant's own testimony and the medical records to substantiate his claims:

> She had swollen and painful joints, she has weakness and exhaustion constantly. She has severe pain in the back area, in the arm, in the leg. She has pain all over her body. And you'll see this document in the hospital record, not just her statement alone.

Perlman invoked newspapers and common experience when he told the jury, "From reading the newspapers, we all know that a machine malfunctioning in a coal mine, from personal experience, could mean instant disaster." He referred to expert witnesses in arguing damages:

> The medical testimony will be through doctors that will testify on video tape, plastic surgeons, a neurosurgeon, and a psychiatrist. And that testimony will be that because of these injuries, Henry will never work again, not in the coal mines, not anywhere else. He can't be cured.

In his gun case, Bergman suggested that commonly held knowledge supported his claims when he stated, "So exposed hammer firearms are well known to have this inherent hazard that must be controlled in the design." He again referred to personal and common sense experience when telling the jury that the plaintiff was not concerned when his gun fell out of his holster because the gun was not cocked. He stated:

> He watched it. And he remembers specifically saying to himself, that gun won't go off, the hammer is not cocked. He didn't even feel like he was in danger because of his experience and his common sense.

Bergman referred to the medical evidence in making his claims about the plaintiff's damages. He referred to safety engineering principles and an expert engineer's testimony in arguing that the manufacturer had a duty to eliminate the hazards that were inherent in the gun.

In his medical negligence case, Bergman invoked the authority of the medical literature generally when he stated:

> It was a small bump, a small lump, in the left axilla. And that is significant because an enlarged lymph node in the axilla within twelve to twenty-four hours after a cat bite cannot possibly be a cat scratch disease. Can't possibly be. There is nothing in the medical literature, nothing in the medical world, that would associate an enlarged lymph node that quickly after a cat bite with cat scratch disease.

He later reduced his claims to simple terms when he invoked common sense as a base of authority:

> The thought process of the doctor wasn't very thorough. This is supposed to be a diagnostician who is going to be making a diagnosis. I think that even a lay person just looking at the check list can see that you only check off one of these four things.

He continued this theme when he told the jury at the end of his opening:

> I think that when you have heard the evidence in this case, there really isn't going to be any doubt at all that some of these things are just always considered basic. If you are considering cancer, you do a biopsy. . . .

Bergman referred to the defendant doctor's own medical textbooks when he pointed out that while the emergency room doctor, within hours after her cat scratch, made a finding that the plaintiff had an enlarged node, and while the defendant doctor interpreted this node as evidence of cat scratch disease, the defendant's own medical text indicated that the disease usually manifested itself within two weeks after cat contact. Thus, the defendant's own text was used for support of the plaintiffs' claims that the defendant made an erroneous diagnosis. Finally, Bergman told the jury that expert testimony would be presented to the effect that the defendant doctor was negligent.

§6.16   Introducing Evidence and Concepts—Conditioning the Jury for Things to Come

Opening statements were used to introduce to the jury any important matters that would be involved in the trial. Jurors were conditioned for things to come. As already noted above, the lawyers used the opening statement to introduce the parties, damages, claims of liability, and bases of authority involved in the case. The lawyers introduced any key element in the trial and conditioned the jurors so they would be prepared for its introduction later in the trial. Certain aspects of the trial were highlighted. For example, Spence spent a great deal of time introducing plutonium and conditioning the jury to view it as a dangerous substance.

Ring pointed out that one dispute in the trial would be whether the brake spring broke due to defect or due to fatigue failure, and told the jury that they would be called upon to resolve the dispute. He also told them that the plaintiff's evidence would prove that the spring failed due to defect.

Corboy introduced the many medical terms that would come up in the testimony of the treatment of the plaintiff. He defined ventriculocisternosomy, foley catheter, neurogenic bladder, nasogastric tubes, tracheotomy, tenotomy, and many other medical terms that would follow in the trial. As well as illustrating the catastrophic injuries of the plaintiff, it no doubt helped the jury interpret the evidence when it came in.

Welch explained the nature of cervical discs and fusion surgery so that the jury could comprehend the nature and extent of the plaintiff's injuries.

Glaser was particularly adept at using analogies and examples to describe the plaintiff's female anatomy and illustrate what was done to her and how she was damaged. By introducing the jury to these terms and concepts in voir dire, the jurors were better able to assimilate and understand the evidence as it unfolded during the trial. Glaser first began by introducing and explaining such terms as "gynecology" and "pap smears." He then used examples to illustrate the plaintiff's involved female anatomy:

> You have the entrance to the uterus. Uterus, you're going to hear that word a lot. The uterus is the womb. That's where the egg fertilizes with the sperm, and that's where the baby—that's the baby's house during its fetal period. The entrance to the womb is known—well, of course, you go through the vagina and then you have the womb and the entrance to the womb, the front part of it is known as the cervix, c-e-r-v-i-x, that's like the neck to the womb, cervix, cervical, that means neck. And then you have the womb itself, and then there are two tubes coming out of the top upper part of the womb. And you have two ovaries on the end of the tubes. The tubes are known as the Fallopian tubes, and the ovary, of course, is the organ that produces the egg, and it also is very important hormonally. That you've got to understand, it produces hormones. One of them has to do with the sexual aspect and then there are other hormones that it produces, and it's important, these hormones are important in the balance of the body, the balance of the health of the body. You're

going to hear a lot about hormones in this case. It looks like a—when you look at a cow's head, you see the face and the horns, that's what it looks like in plain language.

Glaser went on the introduce and define such terms as "hysterectomy," "Salpingo oophorectomy," "intravenous pyelogram," "D&C," "sonogram," "laparotomy," and "diverticulitis." He again used an example to make diverticulitis understandable, saying:

> They also found Mekel's diverticulitis. Diverticulitis is more or less a congenital thing. A general surgeon was called in right at the time of the operation to take a look. The gynecologist found the adhesions and the general surgeon found the diverticulitis, that's congenital. Usually you're born with it, and what they are are outpouchings, best way I can describe it, it's the intestinal, I think it's the colon, the large valve. Best way to describe it, if you ever saw the inner tube of the tire with a bubble on it, that's diverticulitis. Those are diverticulums. They're generally, generally not symptomatic unless they're inflamed. Okay. At any rate, that was not apparently causing her problems before, she had it all her life, so that wasn't—and it was asymptomatic, without symptoms, which they usually are. That wasn't causing her problems after the operation.

Block introduced the law with respect to an assembler's duties:

> Why are we suing Day and Zimmerman, and I don't want to trespass on Judge Cannella's province, but in order to give you this outline, Day and Zimmerman, as an assembler, has certain duties, rights and obligations under the law and they are responsibilities to those for whom this product is intended, namely the servicemen in the field to make that product free from defects because if there is a defect, then what I just narrated will transpire as it did. Knowing that, the law casts upon them a burden to make a defect-free product. Also the law casts upon them a second burden, to use reasonable care in the assemblage.
>
> Now, we are suing on two bases. One, we are saying that under the law if they assemble this product with a defect in it, and if that defect was the cause of this accident, regardless of whether they use the best care in the world, as long as that product had a defect in it when it left their hands and that defect was a cause of the tragedy that befell these men, they are responsible, and on the second ground we are saying that they did not use reasonable care in the fabrication, in the testing, in the packaging and shipping of their product.

Habush introduced the concept of civil liberty and conditioned the jury to the fact that his case would not result in any criminal prosecution, and that the defendant's ability to do business would not be affected. This could have been expected to ease the fears of those jurors who felt that their verdict might adversely affect the defendant. He stated:

>   We all have our opinions of the court cases, sometimes shaped by television and what—we see or read about them so let me just, as a preliminary, remind you that this is a civil case. This is not a criminal prosecution. Nobody's licenses or ability to practice business is at a stake. No one is going to jail. Guilty or not guilty is not an issue.

He then introduced the concept of burden of proof by the preponderance of the evidence:

>   Moreover, unlike the old District Attorney in Perry Mason, Hamilton Berger, I don't have to prove anything to you beyond a reasonable doubt which is a criminal prosecutor's burden. But, rather, by the greater weight of the credible evidence.
>
>   If you have two scales of justice and one party's evidence seems to weigh with more persuasive power, that will be sufficient for us to have met our obligation to you.

Habush introduced the issues to the jury, and in so doing he subtly reconceptualized the trial into issues favorable to his presentation. By presenting the issues in a manner favorable to his case, the jury would tend to hear the evidence in terms of these issues:

>   In the course of this particular use, an incident occurred which has left Roger Schulz paralyzed. The issues that you will have to decide in this case are as follows:
>
>   Number 1: How was he hurt? That is, what happened?
>
>   Number 2: Since it's claimed that the truck that he was unloading at the time he was hurt rolled away from the dock, how did that happen? That is, did the truck driver of the Pre-Pac truck, who was backed up to the dock, fail to do something that he should have done? To secure his truck and prevent it from rolling away.
>
>   Number 3: Was the forklift truck that Roger was using unsafe? Was it reasonably manufactured and designed to prevent injury to users and operators? Did the manufacturer comply with common sense and address the probable hazards associated with its use?
>
>   Number 4: Was Roger careless with respect to how he took care of himself? That is, what did he do wrong if anything?
>
>   Number 5: Was there others who contributed to his injury as well?
>
>   And, finally, what's the extent of his injury? What is the extent of Mrs. Schulz's injury?

Habush then introduced such concepts as "pallets," "dock plate," and "wheel chocks."

Perlman used exhibits to introduce and explain the mining machine that caused the plaintiff's injury:

We'll also learn about a continuous mining machine, a Joy 15-CM continuous mining machine. From time to time, Your Honor, is it permissible for me to move to our exhibits?

THE COURT: Yes, sir, you may. If you want a pointer, there is a pointer right up here.

MR. PERLMAN: We'll learn about this 15-CM continuous mining machine that malfunctioned on May 15th, 1981. Some of you already know about, about it. For those of you that don't know about it, generally this, these are the cutting heads; they cut against the face of the coal. These are gathering chains, that when the coal is cut, carry it and put it onto this conveyor belt. This conveyor belt moves the coal down to here and this is the boom. And this boom then may dump the coal into a shuttle car and move it on out of the coal mine.

This particular continuous miner which was made in 1976 had a remote control station, which is a little box, and an operator would sit at that box and he would operate the controls on that remote control station.

He introduced such terms as "pillering" and "cribbing" in the following ways:

This machine had been used on the job to extract coal from this face. Its got the capability to do so at some four to eight tons per minute. On this particular day, or two days earlier, they had been pillaring. In other words, they had been removing the roof supports and mining the coal from those to go into another entry. Before you get through, for those of you who don't know all about the coal mine and pillaring, you will know all about that, so I won't go into any great detail about it. The next day they spent cribbing up the roof. In other words, they were putting blocks up because the roof had come down on the front end of this continuous mining machine. It sat down across the cutting heads, and they were cribbing up the roof with the boards cut longways and crossways so that the roof would not come down on the rest of the miner so that they could eventually back the miner out.

Gibbons was faced with presenting facts about a complicated fighter pilot that the jurors would not be familiar with. He, therefore, spent time in his opening explaining key terms, and thereby made a complicated mechanism fairly easy for the jurors to understand. With respect to foreign object material, he stated:

Foreign object material, ladies and gentlemen, you will hear a lot about it during the trial of the case, and it has to do with particles that have come from the cockpit or have been left in the white area, such as screwdrivers, bolts, drills, and such as that. And these are actually foreign object materials that the United States Air Force has found in over 60 per cent of every one of these A10 planes that are subject to jamming or causing a serious restriction of the flight controls.

He made the ejection system understandable by explaining key concepts:

Very generally, ladies and gentlemen, throughout most of this week you are going to hear testimony about this ejection system by McDonnell-Douglas. And to me as a lay person, very briefly, there is a D-ring between the pilot's thighs and when it is pulled the canopy jettisons off or back, if you will. Then a seat catapult rocket is fired to shoot the pilot up the guiderails, until he gets up right above where this canopy was to begin with, and then by the time he gets between there and here, the next sequence, what happened is a sustainer rocket is fired to further put him on up, and a STAPAC rocket is fired, located right here, to give stabilization in the pitch area. Now, very briefly you are going to hear terms throughout the trial of this case about pitch, roll, and yaw. And if I could just explain those very briefly, pitch is a forward and aft movement, and yaw is like when an automobile skids to the left or right. And roll is where the pilot rolls to one way or the other. Now, the only stabilization factor on this ejection seat had to do with the pitch. They actually intentionally designed it without any stabilization and yaw or roll.

Bergman began his gun case by explaining the workings of a Colt .45:

Now, what we are talking about, and I am referring to Exhibit 1 in this case, is a single-action revolver. It is the Colt Single Action-Revolver, the six shooter that I referred to on voir dire. It is called a revolver because it has a cylinder that turns. And that cylinder turns each time you cock the weapon so it revolves around a central point, and when the cylinder is lined up with the barrel, it is also in line with the hammer. It is a single action because you can't shoot it by pulling the trigger. You have to cock it and the hammer drops in one direction so it is a single action. A double action is a gun, as some of you know, where you pull the trigger and the hammer comes back and goes forward, so it is two actions with one pull of the trigger. It is different from a double action in some respects but is also the same as many double actions in many respects because it fits into a category of firearms called exposed hammer firearms. And exposed hammer, it is this component that delivers the force to the firing pin, and there is a little pin in here. The firing pin, which is awfully hard to see from there, but the firing pin is driven into the primer of the carriage and is detonated. The problem with the exposed hammer firearms, unless it is controlled, is that a blow to the hammer can drive the hammer into the firing pin and cause the gun to fire. So exposed hammer firearms are well known to have this inherent hazard that must be controlled in the design.

Bergman then describes the concept of foreseeability as it relates to gun use:

Guns can be dropped, they can be banged, many, many things can happen to a gun that are not necessarily negligence, that are foreseeable, and you will hear this term, foreseeable environment of use, because the manufacturer must consider the foreseeable environment in which its product is going to be used.

In his medical malpractice case, Bergman introduced key pieces of evidence. He told the jury about the emergency room physician's finding of an enlarged node one day after the cat scratch, which later should have caused the defendant doctor to rule out cat scratch disease:

> Now, during the visit to the emergency room the doctor made a finding which he didn't really know would be quite as significant as it is and as it was and as it could have been. He made the finding and wrote in the record, "A single, slightly tender lymph node in the left axilla."

He then explained the all-important concept of stating:

> Now you are going to hear testimony in this case about staging of Hodgkin's disease, the stages of Hodgkins' disease. There is a numerical classification system that is used: I, II, III, IV. I have got a diagram here. I'm not going to take time now to go through all of them -- in fact, I probably am going to take a moment to go through all of them.
>
> Stage I is involvement of a single lymph node region, like the axilla or the super clavicular region.
>
> II is involvement in two or more lymph node regions on the same side of the diaphragm, a couple of regions or more, or below; but limited to above or below.
>
> Stage III, involvement above and also below the diaphragm, which may also be accompanied by involvement in the spleen. That is given a III with a little "s."
>
> Finally, Stage IV, diffuse involvement of at least one extra lymphatic organ or tissue, like the liver. If it is there, it is considered Stage IV, or the lung, or some organ. And there is A or B attached. You can be I-A, I-B, II-B, constitutional symptoms, and they are listed here.
>
> The thing about staging is that the general understanding in the profession is that the higher the stage, the more extensive the disease, the worse the prognosis. Prognosis means your chances, your chance to be cured, what is going to happen, what kind of outcome.

§6.17 Enhancing Credibility

The lawyers used their opening statements to further develop the credibility of themselves, their clients, and their witnesses. They developed credibility for themselves and their clients by juxtaposing the good acts and aspects of their clients with the bad actions of the defendants by presenting themselves as the champions of justice and the defendants as subverters of justice and by linking themselves and their clients with the jurors.

§6.18   Juxtaposing the Good Acts of the Plaintiff with the Bad Acts of Defendant

As noted above in §6.08 the lawyers established the credibility of their clients by juxtaposing the good acts and aspects of their clients with the bad actions of the defendants. The plaintiffs were good and noble people, while the defendants were bad, careless people, committing acts in total disregard of the rights of the plaintiffs and the public.

Block described his clients as men who were "doing their duty as good soldiers." Wendell Burns was described as being like a chaplain in that his war buddies would come to him with their problems. Both plaintiffs were hard working men. He then juxtaposed the good plaintiffs and the negligent defendant. Block told the jury that the defendant was attempting to cover up the true cause of the explosion and that its negligence caused a "needless, senseless tragedy which could have been obviated by having a safe proper shell without any defects." At another point, he told the jury that Wendell Burns "was killed not by the enemy, but by reason of defective ammunition. . . ." In this way, he likened the defendant to the enemy.

Habush referred to his client as a "steady, loyal, hard working employee." By comparison, the defendant was described as a very big, very sophisticated, knowledgeable manufacturer with testing labs and competent experts, and either was or should have been aware of the hazards inherent in the design of its forklift. Habush suggested that the defendant was fully aware of the fact that users of the forklift would be injured, but that the defendant refused to act to correct the defect because it would affect the marketability of the forklifts.

After creating a positive image of the plaintiff, Perlman created a negative image of the defendant in the following way:

> The evidence will be that Joy Manufacturing Company, by their own advertising, is the largest manufacturer of coal mining equipment in this country, knew that these problems were there. They knew of malfunctions of continuous miners similar to this one. The proof will be that they knew the technology to create a better system for their electrical signals. The evidence will be that despite knowing that, they did not warn either the operator or the people in the vicinity of the miner that this machine could malfunction just the way that it did on that day.

Gibbons compared his noble serviceman with the defendant manufacturers who knowingly made products that could be expected to kill pilots such as the plaintiff. He noted that the manufacturer of the plane, prior to the plaintiff's death, was aware of at least 29 mishaps of flight conjams caused by foreign object material being in the planes. With respect to the manufacturer of the ejection seat, Gibbons told the jury that the manufacturer knew of the inherent instability of the seat and its propensity to kill or injure, but that it considered the danger an acceptable risk. He stated:

> And then we are going to prove during the trial of the case, ladies and gentlemen, as to McDonnell-Douglas who designed, manufactured and

sold this ESCAPAC seat, that they have known for some time that this very thing happens, but it is considered an acceptable risk.

Bergman told the jury how the defendant refused to eliminate the design defect in the gun that they knew had the propensity to injure users, and then attempted to place blame on the users and sellers of the gun when it malfunctioned and caused injury.

In his medical negligence case, Bergman compared the plaintiff's diligent efforts to get good treatment and to obtain a cure with the defendant's failure to properly obtain the plaintiff's history, failure to properly record the history given by the plaintiff in his chart, failure to keep good records, failure to conduct research, failure to advise plaintiffs of his diagnoses, failure to conduct appropriate tests, failure to be sensitive to the plaintiffs' concerns, the giving of false opinions, and his impatience with the plaintiffs' efforts to get appropriate care.

§6.19 Presenting Themselves as Champions of Justice and Defendants as Suberters of Justice

Current research demonstrates that if a listener perceives a speaker to be honest and to have the interests of the listener in mind, the speaker will be perceived as more trustworthy and hence, more credible.[11] It follows from this that, in the jury setting, if the jurors perceive that a lawyer is honest and interested in presenting the truth so that they can make a just decision, the lawyer will be perceived as credible. At the start of his opening, Spence presented his motives in the case honestly:

> Now, the next thing I want to tell you about is the purpose of this litigation. I want to just come right up front with you about that. The purpose of this litigation has as its only ultimate goal in this lawsuit, in this courtroom, and that is a final money judgment. It is a case about money. That sounds kind of gross and crass, but that is what it is. . . . And it is about preventing, ladies and gentlemen, the dastardly escape of plutonium particles ever again. And, although it is about all of those things, the bottom line is, it is about money, because unless there are sufficient exemplary damages, unless there are sufficient actual damages awarded by an understanding jury in a meaningful verdict, then it will have been about nothing.

When outlining his claims of liability against the defendant, Spence described the jury's purpose as one of discovering the truth with respect to those claims, ferreting out the facts, and solving the mystery. With respect to his role, Spence stated:

---

[11] C. Hovland, I Janis & H. Kelly, Communication and Persuasion 23-24, 34 (1953).

And, it will be our job to give you all the help that we can give you to solve it. And, I want to assure you at this time, each and everyone of you, that you can look to this table (indicating), and this side of the case, to present to you every available, reasonable, decent, honest fact that has any legal efficacy to you to help you solve that mystery, because it is your job, and it is a terrible job, a terrible [sic] heavy job on your part to find out where the truth is in accordance with the greatest weight of testimony, the preponderance of the evidence.

Spence then challenged the defendant to do the same:

It will be interesting for you to observe and to watch and to decide in your own mind as to whether or not you get the same kind of help from the other side.

With respect to the expert witnesses, Spence pledged to make them talk "straight" to the jury:

Now, in the process of this, ladies and gentlemen, my job is going to be to make these experts talk English to us so that we can all understand them. You know, they talk things that seem immeasurably complicated, but are unbelievably simple if you can cut through all the gobbledygook and malarkey and get to the actual substance and the bottom line, and that will be my function, and you will hear me admonish these experts to talk to us straight so that we can understand what they say.

Block associated himself with the law and justice by commenting that the law "in its wisdom casts the burden upon the assembler." In concluding his opening, Block asked for a "just decision." Further, Block committed to the jury that his claims about the good character of Wendell Burns would be borne out by the facts, when he stated, ". . . but I make this bond to you now, the evidence will bear out as to the sterling type of person Wendell Burns was. . . ." He then accused the defendant of attempting to cover up the "real cause of this accident." Thus, Block painted himself as the champion of justice and accused the defendant of attempting to mislead the jury away from justice.

Habush outlined the defendant's claims that the accident was caused by persons other than itself, and then told the jury that these claims were merely an attempt to shift blame to other people.

Gibbons, in discussing punitive damages, told the jury that the defendant was trying to cover up the cause of the accident.

But what we also have here are documents circulated among, they are called inter-office documents, where Republic Fairchild has found out and communicated with others that the United States Air Force concluded that this was a control jam, and we will produce those documents into Court and prove it up, that actually caused Captain Harry Wahl's plane to go down. There will also be evidence that they tried to cover that up, and that is why we brought the suit for punitive damages in addition. They have tried to cover that up. They continue to do so.

Bergman told the jury that the evidence would not bear out the gun manufacturer's claim that there was not a history of accidents with the gun in question.

§6.20 Linking Themselves and Their Clients with the Jurors

The lawyers developed their own credibility by linking themselves with the jury. In his article on lawyer credibility, Wells argues that jurors can be expected to like those litigants and lawyers perceived by the jurors as being similar to themselves.[12] Thus, the lawyer should establish credibility linking the case, the client, or himself or herself personally in interest with the jurors. Baldwin linked himself with the jury when he spoke to them in a way that suggested that they thought in the same way. He stated:

> I think that you like I was will be surprised if not alarmed to find out that this crane is so frail with design as to have absolutely no safety margin.

At another point he told the jury that it was difficult for a person "like you and me" to tell the difference between a reinforced and an unreinforced crane section.

When describing Karen Silkwood, Spence likened her to the jurors when he stated that she was a "plain ordinary human being like you and me."

Gibbons linked himself to the jurors by presenting himself as the common man. In the conclusion of his opening, when trying to convince the jury that while the case appeared complicated, it was really very simple, he presented himself in a down-to-earth manner when he stated:

> But your job throughout the next week is a most important one. We are going to be talking in terms of technical things which I never dreamed in my life, or in my most vivid imagination that I would have even the know-how to pronounce the words, but it really boils down to be a quite simple thing, and that is that this airplane was defectively designed . . .

Block linked himself with the jurors when, while discussing the workings of the howitzer, he told the jury, "I know you are wondering what am I talking about, those of you who have no idea of ordinance or munitions and when I first became involved in the case, I thought the same thing . . ." In this way, he linked himself with the jurors by expressing rapport and similarity with the jury. At many points in his openings, when addressing the jury, he referred to them as "we" in order to create a common bond. For example, in his introduction, he stated, "We are about to embark on a very important and responsible aspect, this second phase of the trial."

---

[12] *Lawyer Credibility,* Trial (July 1984), at 71.

§6.21 Presenting Their Clients and Witnesses as Experienced

Credibility studies indicate that one of the dimensions of credibility is that the speaker be perceived as expert.[13] When referring to their expert witnesses or their clients, when training or experience was an issue, the lawyers presented their witnesses and clients as expert, experienced, and trained. In order to counter any notion that the howitzer shell exploded due to the negligence of the plaintiffs, Block told the jury that they were "experienced men," who had been "trained in it and they had been firing rounds for six, seven months prior to this occurrence as a team." He referred to their expert witness as "a man of the highest eminence, the head of Rehabilitation Medicine for Bellevue Hospital."

Since Habush's client was driving a forklift at the time of his injury, and comparative negligence would be an issue, he told the jury that his client was experienced in using forklifts and in unloading various types of trucks.

Bergman described his expert witness physicians as persons of national prominence. It is interesting to note that he cites a lack of experience in testifying against other doctors as a source of credibility. He told the jury:

> Dr. Sullivan and Dr. Fuller will both be here to testify on these points. These are doctors, by the way, of national and international prominence. They are the doctors who treated Shanna. They are the ones, hand-on, who handled this case. They are the personal eyewitnesses to the facts. They are the only ones in a position to know the truth and the facts about the extent of Shanna Morrison's Hodgkin's disease, the reasons why it failed to respond.
>
> Neither of these doctors has ever testified against another physician in their years.

§6.22 Previewing Arguments

In his trial text, Mauet asserts that "arguments should be reserved for closings," and that they "are improper in opening statements."[14] However, these lawyers previewed all of the arguments that would be made during the trial. With respect to the construction of the crane, Baldwin argued the issue of who was at fault:

> Now, the Liebherr (Ireland) structural engineer, who has spent many, many pages doing figures on this has said in his disposition that this accident would not have occurred had not those sections been reversed. Now to me that means one of two things. Either Liebherr didn't tell Pecco how to erect that crane properly, or Pecco put it together wrong when they ought to have known better. And I think the answer to that question is

---

[13] Mc Croskey & Young, *Ethos and Credibility: The Construct and Its Measurement After Three Decades,* 32 Cent States Speech J 33 (1981).

[14] T. Manuet, Fundamentals of Trial Techniques 51 (1980).

obvious, because the facts in this case are undisputed that there's not one word in the Liebherr manual about how to erect those sections—the proper order for erecting them. There's not one scrap of paper that's gone from Liebherr to Pecco saying the proper order to erect them. It's undisputed that the Liebherr manual doesn't even refer to the word reinforced section. So, they fail [sic] to warn in that respect. That was one of the causes of this accident.

With respect to the plaintiff's medical needs, Corboy argued that with proper medical care, the plaintiff could live out a normal life expectancy:

> The evidence will show that somebody must be with him. As I indicated, his father and doctors decided that the potential for emergencies coming up is always going to be there. It is going to be there with Randy Block every day the rest of his life, however, with good medical care, the doctors—by the way, with whatever advances in medicine that come down the line and medicine is advancing day after day, week after week, month after month—as medicine advances, as the doctors supply him with care, his attending doctors, his attending doctors believe that with good fortune, with good medical care, staying in a hospital such as this, staying where he can get all of the advantages of an intensive care unit like that, staying in a hospital where he can get fed by the nurses, moved by his therapists, talked to by his speech therapist, have clean, healthy surroundings, live to have a normal life expectancy.
>
> These doctors, it will be shown, believe that life is sacred. These doctors believe that he will stay in that condition and if given proper medical care . . . in the future, these doctors believe he can live a normal life expectancy.

In the conclusion of his opening, Spence made the argument that if Kerr-McGee couldn't or refused to show how Karen Silkwood was contaminated, then the jury should return an $11 million dollar verdict:

> Now of course, the issues are simple, and I want you to know what the issues are, because you are going to have to sort through them during the course of this trial, but if they can show that, and convince a jury that she contaminated herself, they have to pay nothing. There is eleven and a half million dollars at stake on that determination. There is everything to gain and nothing to lose, because that is the only defense. There is no defense in fact, and there will be no evidence in this case that they took any substantial steps to try to stop the escape of that material. . . . And, so we will be asking Kerr-McGee, and the men in gray, to tell you, during the course of this trial, not only how that got out factually, to produce the witnesses that can say under oath how it occurred, not their arguments, not their accusations, but to produce evidence, not only as to how that got away, but how the forty pounds got away. And, it may be that you won't get any answers, and that all you get is the accusations against a woman whose lips are sealed by death, and who is helpless to defend

herself, and who everybody on behalf of Kerr-McGee knows is helpless to defend herself against those accusations. . . . But, they can, I believe, tell you it was their plutonium, their plant. The evidence will be it was their control. It was their ballgame. It was their profit. And, they can tell you, I believe, where that plutonium is, how it got away, and where the forty pounds are. And, if they can't tell you how it got away, and if they can't solve that mystery, which is their obligation to tell us how the lion got out, then legally it makes no difference. . . . And, maybe it will be the conclusion, after it is all over, that it's better to pay, for Kerr-McGee to pay the eleven million dollars, than it is to tell you what the facts are and where the forty pounds are, and how they got away.

Perlman concluded his opening on liability with a concise argument when he told the jury:

In conclusion, the evidence will be that there are many hazards in coal mining. Henry Shackleford had the right to expect a safe product in the coal mining environment. He didn't get one. And as a result of that, he suffered injuries. And Joy has not taken responsibility for that and that is why we are here.

In describing the workings of a howitzer shell, Block argued his claims:

First, let us describe what this 105 millimeter shell is all about. It has a cartridge case at the bottom. In that cartridge case there are bags of powder. On the top of the cartridge case is what is called the projectile. There is propellant powder, as I say, in the cartridge case and there is also an explosive charge in the upper portion called the projectile. That projectile bottom has to be intact and has to be perfect, has to be free of defects, has to be free from breaks because what could happen is, if the propellant in that bottom portion gets hot or cooks, it can, if the bottom of that upper portion of the projectile, the base of the projectile is not intact, you could have a flame from the heating of that bottom portion which would work itself way into that crack or the defect of the projectile and cause an explosion within the cannon and that is precisely what happened here as you will hear from the evidence and from the expert testimony.

Block went on to argue the law:

The law, we maintain, casts this obligation to protect these servicemen no matter whether or not the assembler knew the servicemen would use the product because you have fellows in the service, as Mr. Burns from Yakima, Washington, Mr. Baird from Boaz, Alabama, and knowing the product would come into contact with anyone who would use it for its intended purpose, the law in its wisdom casts the burden upon the assembler.

In his opening on damages, Block argued that his client was entitled to enormous sums of money:

> We will show you that this loss cannot be measured sympathetically, because the law does not allow us to do that; because the law says that if you had to pay for the grief and the sympathy of a family, the amounts would be incalculable, and no jury could really arrive at that figure; but what the law also says in its wisdom is that there are certain items of damage to which they are entitled. If you can't compensate for grief and mental anguish, the law—and don't take it from me—the only person who can fitly and rightly give you the law in this courtroom is Judge Cannella. We'll show that Wendell Burns had a life expectancy of approximately 49 years; and that he had a work expectancy of approximately 40-and-a-half years; and we will show that the amount of damage sustained by his survivors for the pecuniary loss alone of income over that period of time is really of great and enormous sums; and he is entitled to each and every item of damage; and that is the function for which you were sworn, to render full justice, not partial justice.
>
> . . . . .
>
> The wife has suffered a grievous and horrendous loss, far beyond any mere calculation of loss of earnings; the loss of society, companionship of her husband; and again, I will not belabor the point.

Glaser argued his claim that the plaintiff's reproductive system was unnecessarily removed:

> Now, all parts of the body have a purpose. And you don't remove parts of a body unless there's a reason to remove the part. I told you about the purposes of the womb and the purposes of the ovary. Well, she's in the hospital and they do certain tests. On the 8th—and by the way, I should mention another thing. In this case, you will find that the womb and the ovaries are not removed, according to good, sound, acceptable medical practice, unless there is a malignancy or cancer in either one of these organs, or unless there is a compression by the growth. Compression means pressure, interference by the growth on other organs with the abdominal cavity.
> If you have cancer or malignancy, yes. If you have compression or other organs, consider it. . . . The I.V.P. was done on the 8th, and it came back negative, clean. No cancer. We'll offer these records into evidence. No malignancy. Benign growth. And no compression of any of the other organs in the body.
> The next day on the 9th, they do what is known as a barium enema. . . . And the barium enema comes back, each on the same day, with a report negative for malignancy, benign growth, and no compression of any of the organs with the abdomen.
> They then do a D&C, which is a dilation and curretage. . . . They use a curet and they scrape and they take some tissue, examine it under the

microscope, which is a fine test for cancer. . . . Now they do not wait for the results of the D&C. You will find that they can do it separately, it's generally done separately, the D&C, separate from an incision, or they can, while the patient is on the operating table, send the tissue down to the laboratory and get an analysis whether or not it's cancerous. Instead of waiting for the results of the D&C, they do a hysterectomy and a Salpingo oohphorectomy, taking out the whole works. The whole reproductive system.

The tissue came back, yes. The—I mean the laboratory report on the tissue came back, yes. But, it came back after they removed the whole works. And what did the report say? Benign tumors. . . .

And so, without compression on any organs, the basis of all these tests, and without malignancy of the uterus or the ovaries, this operation wasn't necessary. It just doesn't make sense to do a test like the D&C and proceed with opening up the abdomen without determining the results. What was the sense in doing it if you're not going to get the results before you open the abdomen? Well, the case against Dr. Cavalli, is in performing unnecessary surgery, for whatever motive he had. . . .

In discussing damages, Glaser argued that, "Taking away the ovaries of a woman is like taking away the testicles of a man."

In presenting facts about the occurrence, Habush argued that the truck driver was negligent. In looking at his fact statement, it is clear that he went beyond a mere recitation of the facts and argued assumptions and conclusions:

Clearly, the evidence will show, Members of the Jury, that the truck rolled away and we believe the evidence will convince you that the truck had not been properly secured, that the driver of the truck had not blocked or chocked the tires of this truck as he is required to do so, and which signs in the docking area instructed to be done. That, clearly, the truck driver did not have his emergency break on or have the truck in gear or any combination of these things, because if he had, the truck wouldn't have rolled away.

Habush skillfully argued that the defendant was aware of the design defects in the forklift and set up an argument about the defendant's bad actions:

The evidence will tell you, Members of the Jury, that the Eaton Corporation is an international producer and seller of industrial machines such as this forklift, has hundreds of distributorships all over the world and sells all over the world, that they have been producing forklift trucks since 1923, that they have testing grounds and testing plants and locations, that they hire and retain competent expert engineers. That this particular model had a predecessor called the MR which looked essentially like it, was made in 1973, first design, and was sold from 1973 until 1985.

We will show you, Members of the Jury, that we are dealing with a very sophisticated, knowledgeable manufacturer. And we will show you that they knew that operator protection on their forklift trucks was needed.

We will show you that they either were aware or should have been aware of the hazards of rearward danger to the operator, that forklift accidents were quite common, and produced serious injuries, that workers could be injured and had been injured in similar type incidents from workers backing into racks, backing into shelving, backing into docks, and that this particular hazard was not addressed or answered at all on this particular model.

You will hear evidence that in their committee meetings they considered providing protection to the rear of this particular model, but that they decided that it would require adding length and would affect its marketability.

In anticipating the standard jury instruction that sympathy should not enter into their deliberations, Habush made an argument that subtly suggested that they should allow sympathy to enter into their deliberations:

You hear on jury selection requests that you avoid sympathy, and I urge that on you as well. I think you will hear and realize that you bring to a jury common sense, lifetime experiences.

You are not to have frontal lobotomies before you sit on a jury. You will be required to evaluate a person's loss and in that connection you use both your head and your heart.

Gibbons concluded his opening by arguing that the defendant had a duty to better design the ejection seat in question:

And although any ejection seat is a risky business, we expect to offer expert evidence that it doesn't have to be. It is like a fireman's safety net, like a fire extinguisher or any, any product that presupposes that an emergency has already occurred, but once that emergency occurs the customer, in this instance the United States Air Force officer, has a right to have a product designed that is not unreasonably risky or unreasonably dangerous, particularly one they knew that was that way.

Bergman began his opening by arguing that the case was about the impact of the gun injury on the lives of the plaintiffs. From an impression formation standpoint, this argument presupposed liability and shaped juror impression such that their initial thoughts would be to assume that liability was clear and the only issue was how much money to award. Bergman was confident in his approach when he stated:

Good morning, ladies and gentlemen. As I said yesterday, my name is Victor Bergman and I represent the plaintiffs in this case, Paul and Jannie Johnson, who are from Junction City, Kansas.

This is a very serious and substantial case arising out of a gunshot wound that occurred to Paul on July 3, 1981. The case is really about the impact on the lives of Paul and Jannie that arose as a consequence of his injury. The injury had a very heavy impact on the solidarity of their marriage and the fulfillment and satisfaction that they have in their lives. You see as a result of the gunshot wound, Paul has been rendered impotent. It is what the doctors call an erectile impotence. Paul is not able to maintain the rigidity that is needed for intercourse. It is as simple as that.

In attempting to establish the gun defect, Bergman used the plaintiff's extensive experience with guns to argue that the gun's design certainly involved hazards:

> The defendant, Colt Industries, could not have asked for a more ideal customer than Paul Johnson. I think you will be satisfied with that from the evidence. Paul is conscientious. He is safety conscious. He works in dangerous circumstances. He has been in the army, he has been in many hunting situations. And he has never had another accident besides this one. If this sort of thing can happen to Paul, I think it can happen to anybody by virtue of the hazard that is inherent in the particular gun that I am going to talk about.

Bergman then went on to construct the argument that the gun was defectively designed. Bergman first noted that the plaintiff had been taught that a gun should always be left uncocked, and if it was uncocked, it could not be fired. Bergman told the jury that the plaintiff followed this rule. In describing how the accident occurred, Bergman described the plaintiff's thinking when he realized the gun was falling out of the holster:

> When he changed his position, apparently the holster tilted backward, the gun slipped out, slid down this rock, which Paul estimates at about three and a half to four feet, and Paul looked at it, and he knew it had fallen out. He watched it. And he remembers specifically saying to himself, that gun won't go off, the hammer is not cocked. He didn't even feel like he was in danger because of his experience and his common sense. When the gun hit the base of the rock, it must have hit the hammer, the hammer must have hit a rock or something else that was down there and sure enough, the gun went off.
>
> . . . .
>
> Before this happened, Paul loaded the gun, the way he always did. They give you a cylinder with six openings for six bullets. It is a six shooter. So he loaded six. And he was careful to leave the hammer in the uncocked position because that is the way that he understood was the safest way to go. But we now know and Paul now knows that that is an extremely precarious and dangerous situation. Because in that particular configuration, the hammer is sitting on the firing pin and the firing pin is virtually in contact with the primer, and very little force exerted to the hammer will make that gun go off.
>
> . . . .
>
> Now, sometime after Paul was dismissed from the hospital, he retrieved his gun and holster which was brought over to his father's house by his

brother Gary, and Paul could not understand how this gun went off. He was telling a good friend of his named Ron McKenzie what happened, and he is also a member of the reserves, and Ron couldn't understand how it went off either. So they took the gun and went out in the back, in the country and loaded it up, put the hammer down. Paul took a hammer handle and wrapped it with cloth and tapped at the rear of the gun, and the gun went off. And as of that day, Paul was convinced that this is a dangerous gun and has never used it since.

But Paul still did not understand the inherent danger of the single action even up to that point. He suffered from the same misconception as many other people. And you are going to find out that many other people have been injured using the Colt and other guns of the exact configuration with the exact same problem. You will see in this case that a six shooter is really a five shooter, and that is what the defense is saying. If you assume that the six chambers are there to be loaded, and you load them, you are in danger. . . . If you load six, this gun is dangerous regardless of the hammer position, because there is nothing designed into this weapon that prevents the hammer from coming forward, given a drop or sufficiently stiff blow on the hammer. So if you have six bullets in there, you have a problem. The gun is set up for firing at that point.

Our evidence is going to be that there are numerous safety devices that are used on numerous exposed hammer weapons in this country that would have absolutely eliminated this possibility. They are simple, they are effective, they are proven, and they have no problems that go with them.

In arguing that Colt had a duty to eliminate the hazards present in the gun, Bergman argued:

> You are going to hear a good deal of testimony in this case about what is known as safety engineering principles. And that is a concept that we will have a very fine engineer named George Green testify about, that in the design of a product you must eliminate, you must take all reasonable means necessary to eliminate the hazards that are inherent in the product. Reasonable means. And by hazards, we are talking about the potential for injury, serious injury or death. Until the manufacturer does its job of eliminating all these unnecessary hazards, it is not in a position to criticize anybody else who runs into the hazard that they created.

In his medical negligence case, Bergman argued that the finding of an enlarged supraclavicular node should have alerted the defendant to a possibility of cancer:

> The reason that supraclavicular nodes are red lights flashing is that doctors always associate enlarged supraclavicular nodes with malignancy. All

of the medical literature says that. You will see that literature in this case, that it is malignant until proven otherwise. You do a biopsy, which is a removal of a node. You look at it under the microscope. You find out what you are dealing with with some assurance. If it is cancer, you know it.

§6.23   Refuting Defendant's Arguments

The lawyers acknowledged and refuted the defendant's contentions. Ring forewarned the jury about disputes in the evidence. The defendant contended that it did not sell the spring in question to the plaintiff's employer. Ring noted this contention and explained how the evidence would refute it. He first outlined how the defendant sold its parts and how the plaintiff's employer bought its parts. He then noted and refuted the defendant's contentions:

> I tell you this because you will hear some dispute in the evidence as to whether or not this is a Major spring. And I tell you what the evidence will show on it insofar as how the chain develops and how it traces to Major because the springs themselves are not such that they put any markings on them. So there is nothing on the spring to indicate it was manufactured by Major or ordered by Verson or that gives any marking. So they have—we have this chain of how it was done. And Verson, the evidence will show, ordered it from nobody else.

Ring then noted and refuted the defendant's contentions with respect to what caused the machine to malfunction:

> There will also be a dispute that you will be called on to resolve as to whether or not this was a fatigue failure, which you will hear from the experts is a failure through normal use in tension, or whether there was a defect in the manufacturing process of the spring. And the evidence will show, on the part of the plaintiff at least, that. . . . The reason it broke was a condition that was created in the course of manufacture of the particular spring.

Welch raised and refuted the defendant's contention that he was run off the road by a phantom driver:

> Then Mr. Hawk, who did have some injuries, some lacerations to his left hand and pain on the right shoulder, was taken to the Medical Center of Independence, and when asked there what happened, said, he thinks he blacked out while driving. But a week later, on 10/6/78 when he's filling out some report forms for his company, he decided that a phantom car crowded him. He said the traffic crowded him on the road.
>
> Now, when we asked him about this on his deposition, and we asked him to describe this phantom vehicle, he referred to it as a dark brown or maroon Chrysler. There will be some other statements that he gave. This is after, by the way, he came up with the story. There are some other statements that he gave where he described it as a black van, black van.

Okay. So that's about all I can tell you about the facts of the accident. There was nothing said, none of these eyewitnesses saw any phantom vehicle, anybody running off the road or anything like that. But those are the facts as we have discovered them through deposition.

Spence noted that the defendant would claim that it had no idea that Karen Silkwood was investigating its activities, but that the plaintiffs would present evidence to the contrary:

> Official after official of Kerr-McGee will testify under their oath that they didn't know that Karen Silkwood was out gathering information against them to go to the AEC, and to go to the New York Times. The evidence will be that there isn't a single person on the Kerr-McGee staff, from the testimony of their officials, that they didn't know that Karen Silkwood had documentary proof in her possession and was on her way to deliver that documentary information to Mr. Burnham of the New York Times on the night she died in an automobile accident. They'll say they didn't know she gathered that information. They'll deny it. The evidence will be, the fact will be that they need to deny it, because those documents are missing, including the X-rays of the doctored welds, the doctored X-rays. But, the final evidence in the case will come when one of their witnesses, who was actually listed as a witness in this case by them, and then suddenly and mysteriously dropped from their witness list, testifies and will testify that they knew she was gathering information, that everybody knew it, that they had been discussing it in their board meetings, in their daily meetings.

Spence acknowledged Kerr-McGee's contention that Karen Silkwood contaminated herself and stated:

> Well, ladies and gentlemen, excepting for the fact that now in this courtroom you will hear the accusations of Kerr-McGee and hear their lawyers in this case state and imply that she did it to herself—that is nothing new—those accusations have been made from the beginning—they were made during the period of time she was negotiating the contract—they were made by Kerr-McGee employers—they were made by management all along. . . . I warn you that there is nothing but the accusation and the supposition and the assumption and circumstances to suggest that. And their arguments—there will not be a single person who will testify that she took that plutonium and did it to herself and put the cancer and the dreaded disease in her lungs and into her body—there won't be a single witness that says that. The only person who will say it will be the arguments of counsel, from the lips of the counsel for Kerr-McGee.

Block refuted the defendant's contentions as to the cause of the explosion:

> Now we will show you that the other causes advanced by the defendant are mere sham, puffery and, if you will, a coverup for the real cause of

this accident, which was their defect in the base of that projectile which, ahead of time, caused a premature explosion in what was a needless, senseless tragedy which could have been obviated by having a safe, proper shell without any defects.

Apparently anticipating a claim by the defense that the plaintiff's experts were dishonest because their opinions differed from those of other experts, Habush argued that the jury can accept or reject expert opinion and that the jury should be suspicious of the defendant's claims of dishonesty:

> You will be hearing from a number of experts. Experts will be determined by the Court to be competent to give you opinion testimony, what they think, but you can take it or leave it, and you can accept or reject expert opinions if you don't buy it.
>
> The experts which you will hear are all competent, well-qualified prestigious people for both sides, and you will hear and realize that experts can differ in their opinions about how things happen and still be honest and still have integrity.
>
> I suggest you to be very suspicious of any attorney who suggests that because he or she doesn't agree with an expert, that means the expert is dishonest.

Habush noted and refuted the defendant's claim that the truck driver chocked his tires prior to the injury:

> There is going to be an issue as to whether or not the truck was chocked or not. Mr. Maldonado, the truck driver, has stated in a deposition that he did check the tires. There will be people who will testify that they didn't see any chocks near his tires.

Habush refuted the defendant's claim that the plaintiff was injured due to the force of the fall and not due to any design defect in the forklift, when he told the jury:

> Now as I indicated to you, we will present expert testimony of experts who recreate accidents. We will present biomechanical engineers, and a neurosurgon, Dr. Walsh, who is an expert in biomechanics of injuries, in addition to being a neurosurgeon, and they will tell you that this particular injury to Roger Schulz was caused by his spine being bent over and crushed by the intrusion of this dock plate, the dock into this operator's compartment.
>
> And my experts will tell you that had there been on this machine rear posts that went straight from the top to the bottom, as I will show you exist on other machines, that Roger Schulz would not be sitting in a wheelchair today, that had these posts been on this machine, he would not have been paralyzed in this accident.

They will use the X-rays of his injury and of his spine. They will use eyewitness statements. But they will believe—they will convince you that that is how the injury occurred and that it could have been prevented.

Habush also noted and refuted the defendant's claim that the plaintiff was negligent in using the forklift in question:

> I believe they will claim he should have been using a smaller one called a single bottom which you will see pictures of. It's kind of like a jack the worker walks behind and has forks on. It's not a stand-up or sit down. It's a smaller machine and they will claim that it was using this big machine that caused this truck to roll off the dock.
>
> You will hear evidence, members of the Jury, that Roger used this particular truck on other occasions going into these smaller trucks to unload and other employees did as well. You will hear evidence that he decided to use this particular machine because the truck appeared to be lower than the dock to him, and that this particular machine, the forks tilt down so he could get under that pallet whereas that other machine, he couldn't use it.
>
> And, finally, you will hear evidence that in any event, the pallets were at the end of the truck, that all he had to do was scoop them out and get them out and not have to drive into the truck at all.
>
> And that he sensed no hazard or no danger to himself unloading these pallets at the edge of the truck in this way.
>
> And I believe you will hear evidence from co-employees and others that on that specific type of operation, there wasn't anything wrong with him using this forklift truck to unload that particular delivery.
>
> And, finally, you will hear evidence that this particular truck was turned over to a co-employee that said, she is ready to go, just unload and that he, again, had reason to believe that everything was fine and that the truck was secure and that all he had to do was scoop it up.
>
> You will hear evidence that he had been using trucks like this for over twenty years and was an expert at it, that this was not a complicated operation, it was a very simple operation for him to do.

In order to refute the defendant's suggestions that alcohol may have been a factor in the plaintiff's impotence, Bergman stated:

> Now, you heard reference yesterday to alcohol, there were some questions about alcoholism. And I want to get into that in a minute. There were a couple of other things I will say about firearms and then I will get into alcohol because I think that is a nonissue in this case and I want to explain why. Prior to the service Paul had some but not a great deal of contact with firearms. He had gone hunting, he owned a rifle or two growing up, he has always lived in the country. But his first experience with a handgun was in the service. He was trained on a .45 automatic which is a different type of weapon, and also trained on an exposed hammer revolver which is a similar kind of weapon. It was a .38 caliber Smith

and Wesson Revolver. The basic difference is the Smith and Wesson is a double action, this is a single action and the calibers are different. Paul was drilled in the service in the basics of how to load, how to fire, how to take the gun apart, the rule of firing on the range. He was told several things that really he took with him out of the service. Always carry a gun with a hammer down. The only time that you cock the hammer is when you are ready to fire. The only time a gun is unsafe is when it is cocked. That pertained to the gun that he used in the service, obviously. When Paul got out of the service, he began to acquire a variety of firearms; trades, people who needed to sell them because they needed some money, or whatever. But the first new weapon that he acquired from the store, a purchase, was this gun. This Colt. The purchase was made May 22, 1974, from the Alco Store in Junction City, and Paul paid $75.87 including tax. The gun was manufactured by Colt in 1969 so it had been on the shelves of the Alco System for about five years. But it was new when Paul got it. Now I will get back to the circumstances of the purchase in a minute. I think a little bit more needs to be said.

I want to talk about Jannie a little bit because she is very much a part of this case, at least their relationship. Paul met Jannie at Randolph Air Force Base in San Antonio in the fall of 1968, shortly after he got back from Viet Nam. . . . It wasn't long before they got married. They had a nice big wedding on February 2, 1969. In less than a year after the Johnsons were married, Jannie left Paul and got a divorce. She refused to tolerate Paul's drinking habits. And those were his habits in 1969 and 1970. Jannie's father had been an alcoholic and she did not want to spend her life with a man who used alcohol to excess. So she left him and got a divorce. Within two weeks after the divorce, Paul convinced Jannie that drinking was not going to be a problem for him, that he set it aside, and they got remarried, I think two weeks after the divorce. They still celebrate their anniversary as of their original wedding date. They will be married, I think 16 years in February.

Now, Paul's drinking. The reason why Paul's drinking may be an issue in this case, we are not making it an issue, is that there is evidence in the medical literature that drinking can cause impotence. So I think there will be an attempt to convince you that Paul's impotence is not the result of the gunshot wound but rather the result of alcohol use. So let me tell you about the history of alcohol for Paul. He started drinking after he got in the service. And after the TET offensive drinking became a very serious problem for him. He was consuming several bottles of alcohol a day. I think the problem was under control when he got out of the service but he started drinking pretty heavily shortly after his marriage and that is why Jannie left him. Let me add that Paul has never had any contact with or use for any drugs of any kind. And there will be no evidence of that. After Paul convinced Jannie that drinking would not be a problem and after they got remarried, he has had no problems with drinking. He has—he is not a tee-totaler. He will drink socially, has drunk socially, but he has no reputation or history of or involvement with alcohol to anything that could be suggested to excess since 1970. I think he is a very ordinary—with regard to his drinking habits. In fact, in 1979, in addition to his regular job, Paul went back to K State University and at that time he stopped drinking altogether. I mean, he consumed no alcohol at all after 1979 up to the time of his injury, and if at all, very, very occasionally, and rarely, and since then I also believe right up to now that situation pertains.

So that issue is really a nonissue. I think you have to recognize it for what the evidence shows.

Bergman refuted the defendant's contention that there was not a history of accidents with respect to the gun in question such as to give rise to notice that additional precautions for the gun were necessary:

> You are going to hear evidence, I think, from the defense, that there is just not a history of accidents with this particular product to justify the implementation of a safety device. And I think that is going to be inconsistent with other evidence you hear, that from the inception of the design of many exposed hammer revolvers, manufacturers built in safety devices. They don't wait for a record of accidents to happen before they put in a safety device. Beyond that, in the course of our investigation in this case, we have made Colt admit to 18 separate instances in their own documented files of people injured using the Colt in ways that would have been prevented with the safety device that I am talking about. In fact, two of those people in their own files were killed. You are going to hear them say that everybody who uses this revolver knows only to carry five and carry an empty one under the hammer. It is just not consistent with what has been going on out there with regard to single-action revolvers.

In his medical negligence case, Bergman refuted the defendant's contention that other physicians who saw the plaintiff during the time in question should have done more:

> I believe that you will hear the suggestion made in the defense evidence in this case that there may have been some other physicians who saw Shanna along the way in that five-month period and perhaps they should have done more, perhaps they should have seen more, perhaps they should have treated the lymph node. But the fact is that the only physician who was asked to evaluate and treat the enlarged lymph node was Dr. Hanson. In fact, Dr. Hanson has admitted himself under oath when I asked him that as far as he knew, he was the physician and the only physician treating Shanna for this enlarged lymph node.

§6.24 Conclusion

In their opening statements, these lawyers became storytellers. The narratives became the cognitive schemata that organized these trials and guided juror perceptions. The central element in creating the narrative framework was transforming the case into a story, through the use of language and themes, to bring the events to life and to present the plaintiffs as heroes and the defendants as villians. Within the narrative structure, the lawyers also developed themes that organized the evidence and claims of liability, set a serious tone, defined jury purpose, specified their bases of authority, introduced key elements and key pieces of evidence, enhanced credibility, argued their central contentions, and refuted the central contentions of the defendants. The narrative structure integrated the evidence and law into a coherent whole that would guide and frame juror perception through the remainder of the trial.

Appendix 6-1
Opening Statement

THE COURT: Yes, sir.

MR. BALDWIN: Ladies and gentlemen of the Jury, as I have told you, I am Scott Baldwin, and I represent the Plaintiffs in this case, and I'm going to tell you what we expect to prove.

This case is one that involves what I determine the tragic and needless death of Kenneth Branch, as he was the operator of a crane that you know by now fell in Dallas, when he was working on One Dallas Centre. He was lifting two yards of cement, as he had done many times before, and importantly, the two yards of cement that he was lifting was well within the capacity of this crane. Suddenly and with no forewarning the crane collapsed. It crashed some twenty-seven stories below carrying Mr. Branch to his death. He made a noble effort to escape, but he didn't have time. That was denied him, and he went down with the crane and was killed in the wreckage of the super structure, if you please, of the crane, and leaves surviving his widow and his children, who are here before you today.

Now, this suit was brought originally against Liebherr(Ireland), Liebherr-America and Liebherr Crane Company. You'll see, as the case unfolds, that these are members of a worldwide syndicate of some twenty odd companies owned by a Mr. Hans Liebherr of Germany. And they largely were responsible for the manufacture and the sale of this crane, and I won't go into detail about that, except that you will receive it as the evidence unfolds.

And our contention against them is in the very simplest of terms that the crane was simply under designed. It was under strength, as you shall see.

Now, the Liebherr group after this suit was filed by us against them, sued American Pecco and Union Rebar, and if I could tell you in the simplest of terms that eliminate the legal mumbo-jumbo, they in effect said that we think you owe, or we think if we owe, you ought to share the burden of us having to pay, because we think you did something wrong, too. If we have to pay, number one, we want you to pay us what we had to pay, or number two, we want you to help us pay for this loss. And you will see that the way these companies fit in, Union Rebar was responsible for the jumping of the crane. American Pecco was responsible for the initial erection of the crane. It's quite a job to erect one of these cranes, and the Bateson people did not have this expertise. They're the general contractor. They hired it done, much as you would hire an electrician to come and fix a broken fixture in your home. They didn't have the expertise to do it. They hired American Pecco to do it. They did erect the crane and put it into service.

Now, with this brief explanation of the parts and how they line up, a general understanding of how the crane is set up and operates should be of some help to you. The crane comes in four sections, and you'll see it over here on the barest of outlines on the board, which is Plaintiffs' Exhibit No. 7. The bottom section there is what's referred to as the D section, like dog. Then there is another section called the A section, and another section on top of that called another A section, and you'll hear more about those in a moment. And then the section on top of that is called the C section, or the one that houses the cab. Now, these sections; though they were built to metric measurement, which will play an important part in this case before it's over with; are on the order of about twenty feet each.

Now, the crane is designed so that it can be housed in the building itself. A hole goes in the building that was being built in Dallas for the crane to operate, and incidentally, there were two on this building. There are building collars in frames to hold the crane in the building itself, and then it's jumped or climbed from floor to floor to floor. They build forward and move up. The obvious purpose now of the crane is to lift weights and materials and put it on the building.

Now, the operator sits high in the crane, and many times like the top of the podium is the top of the building, he's picking up loads way below on the ground and putting them maybe a floor below him. So, obviously, most of the time he can't even see the load he's picking up, and he has to depend on a flagman to tell him when to lift his load. And obviously, if he can't see the load, he doesn't have any control over how heavy the load is. So, with that in mind these cranes are built as they must be built. So that it is impossible to pick up a load more than its capacity, and they have some rather simple devices that you'll hear more about, that just simply shut the crane down, if it picks up more than its capacity, and it won't do it. So, it is important to remember here that the crane wasn't even trying to pick up more than its capacity. I think its capacity here—it was well within it—two yards of cement, some four thousand pounds below its rated capacity for that particular radius. The further out—you'll find out the further out you get on the boom, the less you can pick up.

So now, let me forewarn you and say that this case is really very simple, and it won't become complicated, unless you allow it to become complicated. You're going to hear engineering terms and engineering theories, but simply put, it's not a complicated case, if you don't chase rabbits.

Now, the law as it applies in this case we say is the law of strict liability, and that is a product that is unreasonably dangerous, is defective, and if that is a producing cause of the accident, then the Defendant is responsible in damages. We say the law of strict liability is that a product can be defective in this instance for more than one reason. It can be defective in design, which we allege it is, and I'll go more in detail in a moment. And it can be defective by reason of the fact that it does not have a proper warning, which you will hear more about in a moment.

So then we say that the major areas of defect—there are more than this, but I'm just going to cover the major ones with you—are as I alluded to previously. The design of the crane is simply under strength. I think that you like I was will be surprised, if not alarmed to find out that this crane is so frail with design as to have absolutely no safety margin. That if an operator lifts a load like this one, well within the capacity, and for one reason or another lets that load slip six inches or even less and suddenly puts the brake on, that crane will collapse. Now that's by design. It's hard for me to believe, but that's the testimony of their engineer.

Now, the A sections—as I told you we would talk more about them in a moment, and how they came into play. The Liebherr group made these A sections, which are the two middle sections in two different configurations or two different ways. One was what they call an A normal section. The other is what they call or refer to as an A reinforced section, and that means just simply what it sounds like. The reinforced section is reinforced. It has horizontal crossbars going across it to help withstand horizontal forces. It has three of them halfway up. Why it's not reinforced all the way up, I don't know. Why both of them are reinforced, I don't know, and I don't think there's a real good reason for it. And on the ones that's not reinforced there simply is no direct horizontal bracing, except on the bottom end and the top end. In other words, there's no horizontal bracing for the twenty odd feet.

Now, one thing is undisputed at this point in this case, and that's—if I may walk to the board—this crane had a reinforced section, and by the way, these things are difficult to—I say they're difficult to tell the difference to a person like you and me in a reinforced and unreinforced by looking at it. Now when this crane was assembled, it's not disputed but that the reinforced section, instead of being put on bottom or underneath this section up here—it has to go on top of the D section—remember that—because it has the hydraulic. Instead of being put on bottom where one might think it would be, because it's stronger, it was put on top. And that's important in this case. In other words, they were reversed. The order of the sections were reversed, so that you've got your reinforced section where it can't do much good—on top of the unreinforced section.

Now, the Liebherr(Ireland) structural engineer, who has spent many, many pages doing figures on this, has said in his deposition that this accident would not have occurred had not those sections been reversed. Now to me that means one of two things. Either Liebherr didn't tell Pecco how to erect that crane properly, or Pecco put it together wrong when they ought to have known better. And I think the answer to that question is obvious, because the facts in this case are undisputed that there's not one word in the Liebherr manual about how to erect those sections—the proper order for erecting them. There's not one scrap of paper that's gone from Liebherr to Pecco saying the proper order to erect them. It's undisputed that the Liebherr manual doesn't even refer to the word reinforced section. So, they fail to warn in that respect. That was one of the causes of this accident.

Now then, the next major cause is the welds, and I want to address that for a moment. How good the welding technique is on these welds may be debatable, but I simply say there was not enough welds. What happened is, as you would expect, a structure like this fails at the weakest place, and there is a section of a weld that you will see pictures of some twenty inches long where the weld just simply, as one witness put, came unzipped. And that's where she went when that weld came unzipped.

Then finally, this talk about the rollers. The rollers are supposed to hold the tower steady you might say in the column. Well, these rollers are put in by bolt and nut arrangement. There's some pictures of them showing—they're what they call lock nuts, and really they're a backup device. The rollers are screwed in by a bolt and nut device, and then there's a lock nut that goes on back of it, and you'll find out before this lawsuit is over that even though the lock nut may be backed off, the rollers can still be tight, because they're simply backing up the principal bolt that holds it. There's some pictures that show some loose bolts—lock nuts. Now whether they occurred after the accident when some—there will be some testimony that they were trying to do work on the crane to keep it from falling down the column. Whether they became loose during the accident or whether they were loose before the accident is debatable, but I say that the important thing to remember here is that even though the lock nuts might be loose, the rollers can still be tight, and there's not enough play in there anyway to cause it I don't think. And if this is so important that if those rollers were loose, and that's something that's predictable. Believe me, these cranes have to move in their column. They can't be rigid. Then a simple device like these other limit switches that we've talked about could have been put on there, so that if the rollers got loose, it would either flash a warning horn or flash something in the cab or simply shut the crane down like it does when it tries to pick up too big a load, but there was none.

Now then, there's some instructions to the crane about the use of cross bracing that a lot of people say should have been observed, and if cross bracing had been here or there, this might not have occurred. You wait until you see the socalled instructions on cross bracing, and I've not been able to understand it. They've got something in the manual about it, but I'm saying that certainly it doesn't rise to the dignity of a warning that if you don't put cross bracing here or there, this is going to happen. And if cross bracing is so critical, then the manufacturer like Liebherr ought to provide it, or at least they ought to warn people, and say look, you better put in this crane that we sold you, and they didn't.

So, in short we say there was no safety margin. There was no effort to warn about the order of putting the reinforced sections. There was no effort to warn about the cross bracing. And for these reasons, and the other reasons that will become evident in the trial, we say the crane was defective. It was unreasonably dangerous, and you shouldn't have any trouble returning a verdict against the Defendants, the Liebherr group.

Now to the question of damages. We expect to show that the damages in this case are substantial. Mr. Branch was a young man just starting out on his career as a crane operator, and I think by the time that this case is over, you're going to agree with this statement, that nobody as to this date, and nobody is going to say anything bad about Mr. Branch. He was a good operator. He was a dependable worker. He made good money. He made in the neighborhood of thirty thousand dollars a year. He worked a lot of overtime, and had he worked out his life expectancy—had he been allowed or accorded that privilege, except for this unnecessary death, he would have earned more than a million dollars. I expect the Court will tell you that that's one element that you can consider in assessing damages is what he would have earned and contributed to his family.

In addition to that, there is the element of loss of services that Mrs. Branch is entitled to damages for. What's it worth to have a husband around the house. The little things that he may do, like repairing a screen, painting the house. I won't go into detail, but that type thing has a value—a substantial value. And these damages are going to be substantial, and I hope you'll start thinking about them now, because it's going to be quite a job for you to come up with an adequate amount of damages in this case.

And then finally, the children. He's entitled to—they're entitled to receive care, nurture and guidance—money damages for that. I don't know how to put a value on it, but I think I can give you some suggestions and guidelines as the case progresses or in the argument.

Then there's one other amount of damages that is intangible. You said on Monday that you could award damages for what I'm going to outline, and that's conscious pain and suffering. Just a word about that, and I've completed what I have to say to you in opening statement.

Though some people criticize Mr. Branch for what he did, and say that, in effect, he should have gone down with the crane, when that man saw that he was doomed, he tried to get out of that crane, and he almost made it. Just a very few more seconds, and he would have been able to jump to a safe spot, but he didn't. That time was denied him. He went down with that and with inside the super structure of that crane knowing he was going to his certain death, and that took a horrible long amount of time. Now that's conscious pain and suffering, and we're seeking damages for it. It falls your lot to place a value on it.

So with that, that's briefly what the Plaintiff expects to prove.

Thank you.

THE COURT: Mr. Perry.

MR. PERRY: May it please the Court. Ladies and gentlemen, I want to introduce Mr. Bill Radford and Mr. Craig Eggleston, who are attorneys with the firm. I'm sure you're wondering who is sitting at the table, and Mr. Mike Wagner, who represents Bateson and was introduced to you before.

I am Frank Perry. I do represent Bateson Construction Company, and I have these observations about what we expect the proof will show. This case is fully developed. There are no lack of depositions to show you, witnesses to hear, both experts and fact witnesses.

So with that, listen carefully to the evidence that is presented in this particular case. We will start in the mornings at the time which we agree on, probably pretty early. We have a lot of testimony and a number of witnesses to present during this trial. And so with that I will introduce you to a person I have already introduced you to, Mr. Bob Gibbins, who will make the opening statement on behalf of Mrs. Wahl and her son.

Mr. Gibbins, you may proceed, sir.

MR. GIBBINS: May it please the Court, ladies and gentlemen of the jury, and members of the defense: ladies and gentlemen, we are here today on behalf of the widow, Dianne Wahl, and minor son, Billy, to find out why Captain Harry Wahl died needlessly in the service of his country approximately 2 years ago right now. Thus your job is going to be to determine why, among other things, he had to bail out or eject from a crippled A10 fighter plane. This is model replica of this fighter plane manufactured by one of the Defendants, Republic Fairchild in this case. Your job will also be to determine why, when it was necessary for him to eject, that his spinal cord was severed in his neck during the parachute opening.

Your job is also going to be to determine why, or if you will whether or not Captain Wahl's needless death, was caused or contributed to by the defective design of this airplane so that the flight controls became jammed. And then whether or not the ejection seat that was in there to save his life, and that is the purpose of an ejection seat, whether or not it was defectively designed in that during the process of the ejection, at chute opening or immediately prior thereto, his neck was literally yanked out of the socket, or whether they were both defectively designed products. And that is our contention in the case.

Now, this lawsuit then is brought against the Defendants, Republic Fairchild who manufactured, designed and manufactured, and actually sold the A10 fighter plane, as it has been known, the Thunderbolt 2, to one of its customers among others, the United States Air Force, and whether or not it was an unreasonably risky airplane as far as flight control jams or ejections were concerned. And it has also been brought against McDonnell-Douglas Corporation who was the designer and manufacturer of the ESCAPAC 1E9 ejection seat on the grounds that it was defectively designed because it is inherently dangerous and unstable, and mispositions the pilot, to set him up literally, even though he ejects within the design envelope, to have serious neck injuries and/or death.

Now, very briefly, a little background of what we expect to prove in this case.

Back on or about November 20th, 1979, the day that Captain Harry Wahl's head was literally yanked from the socket at C-3 and C-4, which the medical people, as you will see from the expert testimony, say is in the cervical spinal area, the day that his spinal cord was severed, the day that his collar bones were broken in, the day that his right arm was broken above the elbow, the day that his ribs were fractured, among other injuries, he was a healthy, young, approximately 34-year old United States Air Force officer who was planning on making a 20-year career out of the Air Force and to finishing that career. The evidence will also show that back when he was 17 years old he married his 17-year-old sweetheart, Dianne, that he then joined the United States Air Force as an enlisted man and that he was chosen by the United States Air Force to go to college. He was one of the chosen few. And that he did indeed go to college after serving several years as an enlisted man, and he graduated with highest of honors at Oklahoma State University through an Air Force program. He graduated as an electrical engineer. He was then sent to Officers' Training School, and you will find again that he was a distinguished graduate of Officers' Training School in San Antonio, Lackland Air Force base in approximately 1970. You will also hear evidence that this man, Harry Wahl, Captain Harry Wahl, had flown over 2000 hours of flying time. You will hear evidence that he had 535 actual combat hours of flying in Viet Namese war zone. You will also hear evidence that he was awarded with our nation's air medal with 7 oak leaf clusters for his service in the Viet Namese war zone, or Viet Nam as it was known. You will also hear evidence that he attended some 18 different United States Air Force schools to become a very skilled pilot in all respects. You will also hear evidence that even though he continued his career as an officer that Captain Harry Wahl attended night school and took extensive courses, and shortly before his tragic death he received a Masters of Business Administration Degree from Northern Colorado University, that he was looking forward to serving out his 20 years' retirement to go into the business world. And as a matter of fact on this very assignment in which he was killed, he had been sent to Davis Monthan Air

Force Base, the evidence will show he was given his choice of many many different assignments and that he actually put in on a United States Air Force document that he wanted this particular assignment because he thought it was in the best interests of his minor son to be close to him and his wife. And that was put in on the official documents that will be in evidence in this case, in July of 1979, as to why he wanted this particular assignment, to be close to his wife and son.

You will also hear evidence that eventually he was actually to become an instructor pilot with the A10. Now, the facts you will hear evidence of were that at approximately 2:30 p.m. on that particular date, November 20, 1979, Captain Harry Wahl, pursuant to the United States Air Force procedures, had been prebriefed on what was commonly known as a confidence maneuver. He had been prebriefed by a captain, now major, Rhett Butler of the United States Air Force. And in that prebriefing assignment he was given the necessary instructions on the confidence maneuver that was to take place. Major Butler was to serve as a chase pilot, to fly along at or near Captain Harry Wahl and guide him through a confidence maneuver. The evidence will show that during the recovery, and I might just transgress for one moment, the aircraft was to go up to approximately 19,000 feet, Major Butler was radioing to Captain Wahl, they were both captains at that time, pursuant to the prebriefed instructions to bring it back to idle at approximately 30 degrees. Then the nose came on up to approximately 70 degrees and approximately 21,000 feet, and then the plane was to fall through to approximately vertical, until it got to approximately 150 knots of air speed and then it was to begin the recovery. And the evidence will show by the now Major Butler that this was an excellent confidence maneuver, he said it was one of the best that he had ever seen. That Captain Wahl did a beautiful job until when Captain Wahl was trying to recover, the nose did not come all the way up. This being the horizon, this being 90 degrees down, this being 90 degrees up.

And, ladies and gentlemen, please bear with me, I have never flown an airplane myself. We have had to learn a great deal to bring this suit, to prepare it for trial, and I ask that you bear with me. As I understand it, this is 90 degrees up, this is 90 degrees down, and this is the horizon. That Captain Wahl could never get his nose quite up level. At that point Major Butler, then Captain Butler radioed to him and said nose up, nose up, get your nose up. The evidence will show that he got it up to approximately 5 degrees below the horizon but then the nose dipped down again to approximately 20 degrees. And at that point Captain Rhett Butler had to accellerate to catch up with him, and he was radioing on the FM radio, Fox Mike, and he got no response from Captain Wahl, and finally he said, "bail out, bail out". And he was going to say that three times, and during the second time he said "bail out, bail—" and at that point Captain Wahl ejected. And then immediately after he ejected the plane nose-dived and crashed. And Captain Wahl, who made the ejection, when he landed on the ground his spinal cord was severed, with the other injuries that I have mentioned, and he was pronounced dead at the scene by a witness, Colonel Peter Nash, whose testimony you will hear. And he is taken by video tape deposition in part, and in part by oral deposition.

Then why did this happen? Why was he not able to recover the aircraft? Why wasn't he able to control it and get the nose up? That is one of the issues you are going to have to determine. And at this point if we could have the blowup of the—we will be introducing into evidence, ladies and gentlemen, at the trial—

MR. COWLES: Now, if Your Honor please—

THE COURT: Just a moment.

MR. COWLES: We are going to have to object to showing the jury the exhibits until they have been introduced in evidence, please, sir.

THE COURT: I sustain.

MR. GIBBINS: Your Honor, this is merely to say what we are going to prove at the case.

THE COURT: Yes.

MR. GIBBINS: All right. Thank you.

We will prove, ladies and gentlemen, by Republic Fairchild documents, which we have exhibits blown up, and they will be introduced into evidence during the actual trial, that Republic Fairchild was actually aware of various mishaps that had been experienced, some 29 mishaps at least at that time, as recent, and these documents are dated January of 1981, that they were aware of some 29 mishaps or flight control jams caused by foreign object materials that had matriculated through to the white area. And if I may see that example of foreign object materials.

Foreign object materials, ladies and gentlemen, you will hear a lot about it during the trial of the case, and it has to do with particles that have come from the cockpit or have been left in the white area, such as screwdrivers, bolts, drills, and such as that. And these are actually foreign object materials that the United States Air Force has found in over 60 percent of every one of these A10 planes that are subject to jamming or causing a serious restriction of the flight controls.

THE COURT: Just a minute.

MR. COWLES: If Your Honor please, I don't want to object, but my goodness, he is again demonstrating things to the jury, testifying to the jury rather than making an explanation. We have got to object to this, please, sir.

THE COURT: Overrule. You understand what this is, this is what he thinks the testimony is going to show. Proceed.

MR. GIBBINS: And the testimony will show, and you may hold me to it, that way over 50 percent of every one of these planes that have been inspected by the United States Air Force have found foreign object material, that there are just minute clearances between the flight controls and actually where the pilot is able to control the airplane, and that if any of this foreign object material gets in there that is large enough, or a certain size, it can keep the pilot from being able to pull back on the stick. And that that is an acknowledged cause, even by Republic Fairchild in their own interoffice memoranda, from word they have received from the United States Air Force, including the word on the Wahl case, that it was a flight control jam. And so you are going to hear evidence then the remainder of this week how they are going to explain, after they became aware, even as recent as January of 1981, that the United States Air Force says the cause of Harry Wahl's A10 No. 76-0153 aircraft experienced this pitch control jam that he could not recover from and had to eject.

Now, we get to the ejection, and generally you are going to hear a lot of evidence about ejections. The ejection sequence, very generally, ladies and gentlemen, as advertised—turn this around for the Court too—as advertised by—

MR. MARONEY: Pardon me, Your Honor. I would like to rise and make the same objection, these matters have not been introduced into evidence. They can be described orally by the attorneys, but certainly not demonstrated, they have not been properly introduced.

THE COURT: I am going to overrule that. Just don't belabor the point, counsel.

MR. GIBBINS: Yes, sir. Very generally, ladies and gentlemen, throughout most of this week you are going to hear testimony about this ejection system by McDonnell-Douglas. And to me as a lay person, very briefly, there is a D-ring between the pilot's thighs and when it is pulled the canopy jettisons off or back, if you will. Then a seat catapult rocket is fired to shoot the pilot up the guiderails, until he gets up right above where this canopy was to begin with, and then by the time he gets between there and here, the next sequence, what happened is a sustainer rocket is fired to further put him on up, and a STAPAC rocket is fired, located right here, to give stabilization in the pitch area. Now, very briefly you are going to hear terms throughout the trial of this case about pitch, roll and yaw. And if I could just explain those very briefly, pitch is a forward and aft movement, and yaw is like when an automobile skids to the left or right. And roll is where the pilot rolls to one way or the other. Now, the only stabilization factor on this ejection seat had to do with the pitch. They actually intentionally designed it without any stabilization and yaw or roll. And we have, and we will prove that during this case, that as he is fired on up to here the harness that cinches him in, and a lap belt in his lap, are released and then at that point the man-seat separator rocket is fired, which spins away the seat that he was sitting in, and the harness having been previously released, and the pilot then comes on up here. And this is how it is advertised by McDonnell-Douglas. At this point a little external pilot chute comes out, that pulls out this main parachute pack, and here are your times, and then at this point, at the base of the main pilot—excuse me—main chute, parachute there are little ballistic scatter guns at the skirt that open up rapidly the chute. Full inflation occurs, and this is how they advertise it. That the pilot comes up, and gets into this position, and then drops down and everything is fine.

The facts in this case are going to show, ladies and gentlemen, that due to the fact that there was no stabilizing factors in either the yaw or the roll, that Captain Harry Wahl was yawing and pitching and rolling and tumbling, and that actually it didn't work as advertised because he was in effect facing the parachute. And then when it opened the abrupt opening shock of the parachute, after he had been mispositioned because their seat was inherently unstable, it literally yanked his neck apart. And then we are going to prove during the trial of the case, ladies and gentlemen, as to McDonnell-Douglas who designed, manufactured and sold this ESCAPAC seat, that they have known for some time that this very thing happens, but it is considered an acceptable risk. They literally designed it knowing that there was no stabilization in the roll or the yaw directions. And we are going to bring to you a Colonel Jerry Bowline, who approximately a year prior to Captain Wahl's tragic death, was appointed by a General to investigate another one of these mishaps with an ESCAPAC, and that he called upon the United States Air Force employee who was a biomechanical engineer, a Dr. Leon Kazarian, to say what would happen if you were going faster than this 200 knot speed that Colonel Gideon—that was the A10 crash a year prior that Colonel Bowline was called upon and appointed to investigate—and Gideon sustained certain injuries, and it was on film for the first time, the ejection, to allow everyone to see how you can become mispositioned for the opening shock of the parachute because there was no stabilization features designed into the seat, and roll and yaw. And we are going to prove to you that Colonel Bowline in his investigation of the Gideon ejection actually learned from Dr. Leon Kazarian, and it was in writing and it was submitted for McDonnell-Douglas to see, have access to, which they did, that Dr. Kazarian said if you get up to speeds higher than Gideon and get up in the range of so many more knots per hour, you are going to have a dislocation of the cervical vertebrae to the air crewman at C-3 and C-4 that could cause serious injury or death. Yet McDonnell-Douglas did nothing to design that risk out of this seat. And we will prove that other such events occurred of which they also had notice and they did nothing.

Now, ladies and gentlemen, in addition to that we will prove that shortly after Captain Wahl's tragic death, McDonnell-Douglas comes along and puts a new seat on the market, actually completes a retrofitting of the ESCAPAC 1E9 which killed Captain Wahl, they completed a retrofitting with another seat called an Ace's 2 that had a much safer record. And as far as I know no one has been killed with it yet because it had the stabilization features designed into it, to keep the pilot from rolling, tumbling, yawing. They did it with a simple device, among others, called a drogue chute, a little drogue chute that is attached to the Ace's 2 seat that slows the pilot down so that he doesn't tumble and roll and yaw, and also gives him stability, orthopedic support of the seat until the opening shock of the parachute. And then he doesn't experience the serious injuries and/or death.

In this connection we are going to also bring you a man named Russell Sanford, who works for our Federal Government, that has spent most of his entire professional career in the research and development of ejection seats. And he will offer certain expert opinions. Among others we will prove that McDonnell-Douglas knew of the defects in the inherent instabilities in their own seat that killed Harry Wahl and they did nothing. We will show by documents that they were warned back in 1977, and we have the documents right here blown up for you. In 1977 they were warned that their seat was inherently unstable and there was a major concern over it. And they did nothing to take that seat off the market. And that they knew what the state of the art was because McDonnell-Douglas actually came out with this Ace's 2 to replace it. But other manufacturers had come out for 20 years earlier with stabilization in the roll and the yaw areas. So Russell Sanford then will bring that type of proof.

And finally Mr. Sanford will also prove why it was technologically feasible for McDonnell-Douglas to come out with a stabilized ejection seat long before they did, long before the death of Captain Wahl. It was also economically practical. Then we will bring you Mr. Fred Hoerner, who is an Annapolis graduate, and a decorated war pilot, and now a test pilot for our government who will testify how this jam in the white area occurred that caused the plane to be out of control necessitating Captain Wahl's ejection.

And finally we will bring you Dianne Wahl and her son Billy to testify about their losses, both monetary and otherwise, since the needless death of their husband and father. And also an economist by the name of Melissa Patterson who you will be called upon to award and assess damages pursuant to His Honor's instructions to you, and within the guidelines of those instructions. He will tell you what you can and cannot consider. But one of the things that he will tell you in all likelihood that you can consider will be the actual pecuniary losses to this family. And it is our burden of proof, if you will, to reduce it to the present cash value because you are going to have to pass on a loss for the rest of their lives, since Harry Wahl is deceased. And the economist will establish how that loss, just from the loss of his career and the income from it, is in the range of $2,000,000.00 over the rest of his life, that these people have been deprived of.

And then, ladies and gentlemen, as to the punitive damages that are sought in the case, and we might as well get it out on the table, His Honor will give you certain instructions about punitive damages in all reasonable likelihood, that if you find that these Defendants acted grossly, willfully and with wanton disregard to the rights of others, then you will be called upon to have the opportunity to assess punitive damages, in addition to the damages, the actual damages suffered by the Wahl's. But punitive damages against them, to set an example so that this won't happen to any other serviceman. And this will be not only your opportunity but if the evidence warrants it, your duty. And we submit in this connection that you are going to hear from them about their good save rates and such as that. But we will prove to you that in addition to the ESCAPAC ejection seat that McDonnell-Douglas designed they actually sped it up a few years ago, they cut the time almost in half on the time delay to make the pilot get out faster and the chute open faster, which creates even more of a shock, the faster that he comes out. And what we will call upon you to do under the evidence in the case, is to look at the save rate before and look at it after they enhance the time to get a pilot out. Enhanced it with still no stabilization to keep the pilot in their advertised position so that he wouldn't get hurt or seriously injured.

Now, I might also point out to you that the proof in the case will be that McDonnell—excuse me—Republic Fairchild has come out with several design changes trying to seal up this white area to keep foreign object material from jamming these flight controls, but they still by their own admission have 10 percent approximately, 5 or 10 percent of that white area on these airplanes, the A10's, that are still subject to foreign object material matriculating from the cockpit into the white area and jamming the controls.

Now, I might point this out too, that normally the United States Air Force Safety Board, their findings are privileged by Government regulation and/or rule. There is also a Collateral Board, and you are going to hear that term in the next few days throughout those next few days, a Collateral Board is appointed and that is what we have to work with. But the conclusions and opinions of the people who testify before the Safety Board are not released by virtue of privilege. So what we have then, as the lawyers have been allowed to receive by the United States Government in Washington, under the Freedom of Information Act, is called a sanitized copy. That is findings but with no opinions or conclusions. But what we also have here are documents circulated among, they are called interoffice documents, where Republic Fairchild has found out and communicated with others that the United States Air Force concluded that this was a control jam, and we will produce those documents into Court and prove it up, that actually caused Captain Harry Wahl's plane to go down. There will also be evidence that they tried to cover that up, and that is why we brought the suit for punitive damages in addition. They have tried to cover that up. They continue to do so. So you are going to be called upon not only to assess actual damages to the Wahls, but also to consider or at least have the opportunity to award punitive damages, to tell them this isn't the way that you can do.

And so lastly we will also call, with the Court's permission, approximately two witnesses who knew Captain Harry Wahl during his lifetime and knew what kind of man he was, knew what kind of pilot he was, and knew the love and devotion that he had for his family, that they are now forever deprived of. So you be watching us closely, ladies and gentlemen, throughout the next 2 to 21/2 days, is what we calculated, our part of the proof would be with these witnesses.

And in the interest of time we might omit to call one or more, if it would be somewhat repetitious or overlapping with others, and we have been encouraged to move as fast as we can, and we want to do that, and at the same time still give our clients their day in Court. But your job throughout the next week is a most important one. We are going to be talking in terms of technical things which I never dreamed in my life, or in my most vivid imagination that I would have even the know-how to pronounce the words, but it really boils down to be a quite simple thing, and that is that this airplane was defectively designed, and we will prove that because it allowed the flight controls to jam which necessitated ejection by inherently unstable seat which in effect severed the spinal cord of Captain Wahl, when the seat was advertised to save your life. And although any ejection is a risky business, we expect to offer expert evidence that it doesn't have to be. It is like a fireman's safety net, like a fire extinguisher or any, any product that presupposes that an emergency has already occurred, but once that emergency occurs the customer, in this instance the United States Air Force officer, has a right to have a product designed that is not unreasonably risky or unreasonably dangerous, particularly one they knew that was that way.

Thank you very much, Your Honor.

7

Direct Examination

§7.01   Introduction

Four major types of witnesses were identified in the plaintiff's direct presentation of evidence: (1) plaintiffs or their representatives, (2) fact witnesses with respect to the occurrence, (3) fact witnesses with respect to damages, and (4) expert witnesses. Since these witnesses had different roles in the trial, they were all questioned differently. In what follows, I shall outline the techniques used for the questioning of each of these witnesses and demonstrate that the direct examination was used to present facts in support of the story line, personalize the plaintiffs, provide technical information, and enhance the credibility of the witnesses. The questions asked of all these witnesses were simple and direct, using simple, everyday language. The lawyers controlled the testimony of all of the witnesses by the use of leading or narrow questions calling for specific answers.

Modern trial texts admonish lawyers not to lead the witnesses on direct examination and suggest that leading questions diminish the impact of the testimony.[1] Procedurally, leading questions are prohibited on direct examination. Leading questions are questions in which the lawyer makes a statement and asks the witness to agree or disagree, or in which the lawyer suggests an interpretation of the evidence to the witness through the question. The rationale for prohibiting their use in the presentation of direct evidence is that, in direct examination, the plaintiff has the burden of proof, and, therefore, the witnesses should present facts as opposed to agreeing with answers or interpretations of the evidence suggested by the lawyer. In theory, the witness on direct examination should be presented with the use of open-ended questions calling for

---

[1] T. Mauet, Fundamentals of Trial Techniques 93 (1980).

narrative answers. In this way, witnesses are forced to testify as to what they actually know. Consistent with this theory, trial texts suggest that direct examination should elicit flowing, descriptive narratives that will paint pictures for the jury.[2] These suggestions stand in direct opposition to what these successful lawyers actually did in questioning their witnesses.

The direct examinations examined were those by Scott Baldwin, Melvin Block, Phil Corboy, Robert Gibbons, Herman Glaser, Robert Habush, Peter Perlman, Leonard Ring, Gerry Spence, and Lantz Welch. Scott Baldwin's case involved a product liability claim in which the plaintiff was severely injured while operating a tractor. A bale of hay fell off a front-end loader on the tractor, landing on the plaintiff and causing crippling injuries. The Block direct examinations involved the product liability claim against the manufacturer of an artillery shell that malfunctioned in a howitzer and injured two soldiers in combat during the Vietnam War. The Corboy examinations involved the automobile collision which left the plaintiff a spastic quadraplegic with locked-in syndrome. The Gibbons examinations involved the product liability claim for the negligent design of an ejection device that resulted in the death of a jet fighter pilot. The Glaser examinations were conducted in the medical negligence case involving the performance of an unnecessary hysterectomy. The Habush examinations involved the catastrophic injuries caused in an industrial accident involving a forklift. The Perlman examinations involved the mining accident in which an automatic mining machine malfunctioned and caused severe injury to a miner. The Ring examinations involved the malfunction of a machine brake press machine in which the operator's hands were severely crushed. The Spence examinations involved the trial of *Silkwood v. Kerr-McGee*[3] in which it was alleged that Karen Silkwood was negligently contaminated with plutonium. The Welch examinations involved the claims for damages and loss of consortium by the husband and wife stemming from an automobile collision.

§7.02 Plaintiffs or Their Representatives

The first major witness was the plaintiff or in the cases of decedents such as Karen Silkwood or Wendell Burns, their legal representative. Consistent with the narrative structure introduced in the opening statement, the role of the plaintiff was to tell his or her story to the jury.

§7.03 —Structure

The testimony of each plaintiff was presented in chronological order. First, the lawyer elicited background information about the plaintiff, the participants, and the instrumentalities involved in the trial. Second, testimony was elicited about how the injuries occurred. Third, testimony was elicited about the injuries and damages sustained by the plaintiff. Finally, direct examination of the

---

[2] T. Mauet, Fundamentals of Trial Techniques 89 (1980).

[3] No. 76-0888 (WD Okla, March 1979).

plaintiff was concluded with questions which summed up, repeated, and reinforced important points made previously.

§7.04 —Background Information

The first questions asked by each lawyer elicited background information about the plaintiff and his or her family. This questioning accomplished three purposes: it elicited background information that personalized the plaintiff, established the plaintiff's credibility, and established the plaintiff's good health prior to the injuries in question.

§7.05 —Use of Background Information to Personalize the Plaintiff

First, consistent with the story being developed, the background information allowed each plaintiff to present himself or herself as a human being that the jurors could begin to like and sympathize with. The background questioning personalized the plaintiff. For example, through questioning, Baldwin established that Larkin Foster was a simple man with a second grade education who had worked hard all his life to support his family. He started farm work with his father at age 13 and had done farm work all of his life. He married and had four children who still lived at home with him. His wife died after 20 years of marriage, leaving Mr. Foster to take care of the family. He worked hard for meager wages all of his life up to the time of the injury. With this information, Baldwin presented his client as a simple, hard-working man who was the sole support of his family. He became more than just a plaintiff presenting a claim; he became a likeable man who deserved justice. Baldwin questioned as follows:

BALDWIN: Would you give us your name, please?

PLAINTIFF: Larkin Alton Foster.

BALDWIN: Mr. Foster, there is a microphone, there.

PLAINTIFF: I have got the microphone, I forgot.

BALDWIN: Now speak up where everybody can hear. When were you born, Mr. Foster?

PLAINTIFF: 1925.

BALDWIN: Where?

PLAINTIFF: DeKalb.

BALDWIN: Mr. Foster, do you have a big family?

PLAINTIFF: I have got four kids.

BALDWIN: I am talking about when you were born.

PLAINTIFF: Yes, I got five brothers and a sister. I make the sixth one.

BALDWIN: How far did you get in school?

PLAINTIFF: Second grade.

BALDWIN: Second grade?

PLAINTIFF: Yes.

BALDWIN: Why did you leave school?

PLAINTIFF: To go to work.

BALDWIN: To help support your family?

PLAINTIFF: Yes, sir.

BALDWIN: And what is the first work you ever did?

PLAINTIFF: Farm work.

BALDWIN: How old were you when you first went to work?

PLAINTIFF: Well, I was making a regular hand at thirteen.

BALDWIN: Would it be fair to say, Mr. Foster, that you have done farm work all your life?

PLAINTIFF: Yes sir.

BALDWIN: You started out working with your Daddy and family?

PLAINTIFF: Yes, sir.

BALDWIN: Was that around DeKalb.

PLAINTIFF: Yes, sir.

BALDWIN: And have you done anything but farm work from then on down to now?

PLAINTIFF: No, sir.

BALDWIN: Are you married?

PLAINTIFF: I was. My wife is dead.

BALDWIN: Who did you marry?

PLAINTIFF: Dorothy Pearce.

BALDWIN: When?

PLAINTIFF: In '53.

BALDWIN: Do you have any children by that marriage?

PLAINTIFF: Yes, sir, four.

BALDWIN: Are they here in the courtroom?

PLAINTIFF: Yes, sir.

BALDWIN: Would you tell us their names and introduce them to the jury, please?

PLAINTIFF: One of them is Judy Nell.

BALDWIN: Which one is Judy Nell?

PLAINTIFF: Judy, get up.

BALDWIN: All right, go ahead.

PLAINTIFF: Leta, Jo and Nancy Larkin.

BALDWIN: Okay. Now they are all living at home with you?

PLAINTIFF: Yes, sir.

BALDWIN: And was this the only marriage that either you or your wife had?

PLAINTIFF: Yes, sir.

BALDWIN: Was she a devoted wife?

PLAINTIFF: Yes, sir.

BALDWIN: I believe you said she was dead?

PLAINTIFF: Yes, sir.

BALDWIN: When did she die?

PLAINTIFF: In '73, July 4th.

BALDWIN: Of '73?

PLAINTIFF: Yes, sir.

BALDWIN: And leave you with these children to raise?

PLAINTIFF: Yes, sir.

BALDWIN: Now, Mr. Foster, I notice you only have one eye. How did you lose your eye and when?

PLAINTIFF: I was 21, a chip hit me in it.

BALDWIN: Which eye did you lose?

PLAINTIFF: Left.

BALDWIN: Have you lost total sight of that eye?

PLAINTIFF: Yes, sir.

BALDWIN: When did you go to work for Mr. Crew?

PLAINTIFF: In '68, I believe.

BALDWIN: And where was that?

PLAINTIFF: At Old Salem.

BALDWIN: Near DeKalb?

PLAINTIFF: Yes, sir.

BALDWIN: What type of work were you doing for Mr. Crew?

PLAINTIFF: Well, seeing after cows and baling hay, keeping up fences.

BALDWIN: How many cattle did he have at that time, when you first went to work for him back in '68?

PLAINTIFF: About 200.

BALDWIN: And how many acres did he have?

PLAINTIFF: Twelve something, I don't know—

BALDWIN: 1200?

PLAINTIFF: Uh-huh.

BALDWIN: And do you remember what you were paid?

PLAINTIFF: I was paid sixty-five a week when I went there.

BALDWIN: And were you furnished a home?

PLAINTIFF: Yes, sir.

BALDWIN: And did you get other benefits?

PLAINTIFF: My light bill and pasture for a place for my cows and horse.

BALDWIN: Now you remember this accident that happened in October of 1973?

PLAINTIFF: Yes, sir.

BALDWIN: I believe it was October the 10th? And you were still working for Mr. Crew?

PLAINTIFF: Yes, sir.

BALDWIN: Have you worked continuously for him from the time you told us about—from 1968 down to the date of this accident?

PLAINTIFF: Yes, sir.

BALDWIN: Were you doing pretty much the same work?

PLAINTIFF: Yes, sir.

BALDWIN: How many acres does—does he still have 1200 acres?

PLAINTIFF: Yes, sir.

BALDWIN: The same 1200?

PLAINTIFF: Uh-huh.

BALDWIN: How many head of cattle was he running by then?

PLAINTIFF: 400.

BALDWIN: 400?

PLAINTIFF: Yes.

BALDWIN: In 1973?

PLAINTIFF: Yes, sir.

BALDWIN: And what were you being paid for that?

PLAINTIFF: $72.50 per week.

BALDWIN: And your home?

PLAINTIFF: Yes, and my lights and pasture for my cows.

BALDWIN: Now what kind of house is this, Mr. Foster?

PLAINTIFF: It is a four-room house.

BALDWIN: What do you mean when you say "four rooms?"

PLAINTIFF: Well, it has got four rooms and a bath.

BALDWIN: One bath?

PLAINTIFF: Yes.

BALDWIN: And how many bedrooms?

PLAINTIFF: Two bedrooms.

BALDWIN: All right, would it be fair to say that the rental on that type of house around there would be about a hundred dollars a month?

PLAINTIFF: Yes.

BALDWIN: All right, you are also keeping your cows there?

PLAINTIFF: Yes, sir.

BALDWIN: And your horse?

PLAINTIFF: Yes.

BALDWIN: And who else was working with Mr. Crew?

PLAINTIFF: Danny Garrett was working there when I got hurt.

BALDWIN: All right, and was your duties pretty much to look after the cattle?

PLAINTIFF: Yes.

BALDWIN: And mend the fences—you all raise hay out there?

PLAINTIFF: Yes.

BALDWIN: Help bale and store it?

PLAINTIFF: Yes.

Block questioned Wendell Burns' widow in a way that allowed her to personalize her relationship with her husband:

BLOCK: There came a time when you met Wendell?

PLAINTIFF: Yes.

BLOCK: Can you tell us how that came about?

PLAINTIFF: We were just with some friends and we just all got together and met, and we instantly liked each other and we just started dating constantly from then on.

BLOCK: And what were some of the things that you did?

PLAINTIFF: Well, he loved to hunt and fish. We went fishing a lot. I never dared to go hunting, but we just enjoyed being together. We'd go down and visit his mom a lot. He was working at the time that I did meet him, so we just usually had the evenings and there was another couple that we liked to double date with, and we'd go to the drive-in or the show or something, go bowling; something to occupy our time.

Block questioned the plaintiff Baird in a way that allowed him to personalize himself:

BLOCK: What is your full name?

WITNESS: Dorman LaVaughan Baird.

BLOCK: When were you born?

WITNESS: Etowah County in Boaz, Alabama.

BLOCK: With whom did you live?

WITNESS: I lived with my mother and father.

BLOCK: Was that on a farm?

WITNESS: Yes, sir.

BLOCK: What type of farm was that?

WITNESS: It was just a small farm. We had cotton, corn, pepper and other crops, hay, so forth.

BLOCK: Who lived on that farm with you?

WITNESS: It would be my mother and father and four brothers and three sisters.

BLOCK: Can you tell us what your education was, where you went to school?

WITNESS: I went to Center Point School, which was in DeKalb County, that was close to Boaz. I went to Sardis High School, which is also in right close to Boaz.

BLOCK: Up to what grade did you go?

WITNESS: I went to the tenth grade.

BLOCK: Can you tell us something about what your normal day was like as you were growing up on the farm?

WITNESS: Well, mostly we'd get up in the morning, go to school. We got out of school, we come home. In the spring of the year we would plow, work with the tractors, and then the fall time, we would gather the crop after we got out of school. We worked from the time we got out of school until dark each day that it was permitted by the weather, that we could work.

BLOCK: What did you do for recreation; were you involved in any sports, did you partake in anything?

WITNESS: We played on weekends and rainy days, when it was too wet to work, we'd play baseball, softball, football, basketball, horseback riding and just everything in the world of sports that we could think of to play.

BLOCK: Did you go hunting also?

WITNESS: Yes, sir.

BLOCK: As you grew up on the farm was that your sole occupation or did you take any other jobs?

WITNESS: After I got out of school and I went to work for this Boaz Service Station where I went in—first went in just as a helper, and then I went on to service manager and then I was service manager and mechanic, also while I was with them. And also I built mobile homes.

BLOCK: When you worked for this Boaz Service Station and you went up to the point of being service manager and mechanic, over what period of time did this take place?

WITNESS: I just started in and maybe I was there a couple of months and then I went to service manager because I was capable of doing a job and doing it very well. And then he told me, he says, "Well, this will be your full-time job,'' and then I done that job plus I was—started in mechanic work and I done both.

BLOCK: What sort of mechanic work did you do? Can you tell us, please, the types of jobs you did there?

WITNESS: Also I would rebuild carbureators, fuel pumps, minor tune-ups, some transmission work, which they—permitted, you know, that we could do. It wouldn't tie up our stalls too long at the station.

BLOCK: And you had this job, you say, for approximately six months?

WITNESS: Yes.

BLOCK: Can you tell us what you did when you worked for this mobile home company?

WITNESS: Yes, sir. I started out in the sheet metal department putting sheet metal or aluminum siding on mobile homes, and also putting roofs on them. I done that for, I'd say, three months or longer. Then I went into the cabinet department hanging cabinets, closets and set-ting up all the cabinets throughout the trailers, putting the bathrooms, the sinks, the overhead cabinets and all that in.

BLOCK: How long did you have that job?

WITNESS: I stayed with that job until, I guess, it was three or four months and then I was—I was on the road for a while doing service work which if something happened to the trailers, we would go and repair the trailers on the lot. The place where they was delivered to by the trucks.

BLOCK: Did you have any other jobs prior to your entering the service?

WITNESS: Yes, sir. I worked for—also worked for a poultry plant, poul-try processing, which consists of they cut and freeze and pack chickens where they are shipped. They are cut in parts and also they are packed whole, just the whole chicken, after they are dressed and everything, and we would pack them and ship them, load them on the trucks to be shipped out to different parts of the state.

BLOCK: What did you do particularly in that job?

WITNESS: I was a loader. I loaded on the truck in the shipping depart-ment and I also packed off of the land in the plant.

BLOCK: How long did you have that job?

WITNESS: I stayed with them maybe six or seven months, I don't know for sure.

BLOCK: Is there any reason why you left one job for the other?

WITNESS: Well, it mostly will be for better working conditions would be the reason why I would leave one job and go to another.

Similarly, Habush provided background information in order to personalize the plaintiff:

HABUSH: Will you state your name again for the record?

WITNESS: My name is Roger Schulz.

HABUSH: How old are you, Mr. Schulz?

WITNESS: I'm 49.

HABUSH: What is your birthdate?

WITNESS: April 3, 1937.

HABUSH: Where did you grow up?

WITNESS: In Milwaukee.

HABUSH: Where did you go to high school?

WITNESS: I went to Boys Tech. In Milwaukee.

HABUSH: Did you finish high school?

WITNESS: No, I went to the 11th grade.

HABUSH: And why did you quit high school?

WITNESS: I went into the service.

HABUSH: And what branch of the service did you go into?

WITNESS: In the army.

HABUSH: How were you doing in high school when you quit?

WITNESS: Average.

HABUSH: And did you work while you were in high school?

WITNESS: Yes, I did.

HABUSH: What kind of jobs did you—did you work at?

WITNESS: I worked at Kohl's Food Stores in Milwaukee. Part time.

HABUSH: What did you do for them?

WITNESS: Paper routes, paper corners. Sold papers on the corner.

HABUSH: What were your parents' names?

WITNESS: Marie and William.

HABUSH: Do you have any brothers and sisters?

WITNESS: Yes, I have three brothers.

HABUSH: And are your parents still alive?

WITNESS: My father died. About twelve years ago.

HABUSH: Where did you serve in the Army?

WITNESS: I served in California and Germany.

HABUSH: What did you do while you were in the Army?

WITNESS: I drove an ammunition truck in Germany and in California I was in ration breakdown. It's distributing foodstuffs to different companies.

HABUSH: And were you discharged honorably from the Army?

WITNESS: Yes, I was.

HABUSH: You were discharged in what year?

WITNESS: 1957.

HABUSH: What did you do then?

WITNESS: I—I had a couple of odd jobs when I got out of the service which lasted anywhere from two weeks to a month, and I finally started working for Kohl's again in Milwaukee.

HABUSH: What did you do for Kohl's when you started working for them?

WITNESS: I worked in the Delicatessen Department stocking the deli counters or deli coolers, cheeses and milk and ham.

. . . .

HABUSH: When were you married?

WITNESS: January 13, 1968.

HABUSH: Your wife is Beverly?

WITNESS: Yes.

HABUSH: And have you been married previously?

WITNESS: Yes, I was.

HABUSH: And did you have children from your prior marriage?

WITNESS: Yes.

HABUSH: What are their names and ages?

WITNESS: Craig is 25 and Amy is 23.

HABUSH: And you have been married to Beverly since January 13, 1968?

WITNESS: Yes.

HABUSH: Did she have children from her prior marriage?

WITNESS: Yes.

HABUSH: What are their names and ages?

WITNESS: Dean and Debbie. Debbie is 25 and Dean is 23.

HABUSH: So you'll be married 19 years this coming January?

WITNESS: Yes, sir.

HABUSH: So you practically raised both of those children?

WITNESS: Yes, I did.

HABUSH: Did you and Beverly have children of your own?

WITNESS: Yes, we have two.

HABUSH: And what are their ages?

WITNESS: Brian is 18 and Colleen is 16.

HABUSH: Had you and Beverly been continuously married since the time you got married?

WITNESS: Yes, we have.

HABUSH: Ever separate or anyone start any divorce proceedings?

WITNESS: No, we haven't.

HABUSH: How would you describe your relationship with all your children?

WITNESS: Very good.

HABUSH: With respect to your stepchildren, how would you describe your relationship?

WITNESS: They're exceptional kids.

HABUSH: And that's true today?

WITNESS: Yes, it is.

HABUSH: With respect to you and Beverly, nothing has changed with respect to your love and affection, either, has it?

WITNESS: I don't think so.

HABUSH: Is Beverly employed at the present time?

WITNESS: Yes, she is.

HABUSH: And where is she employed?

WITNESS: She works at Duerrwaechter Memorial Library in Germantown.

HABUSH: How long has she been employed there?

WITNESS: Ten years.

HABUSH: Do you know what she makes at the library?

WITNESS: Around $6 an hour.

HABUSH: And how many hours a week has she been putting in?

WITNESS: She works about 25 hours a week.

HABUSH: Prior to the accident, what type of activities did you like to do?

WITNESS: Well, we were definitely campers, or we did camping, snowmobiling, I had a motorcycle, did a lot of hiking, we participated in sports together.

HABUSH: Did you bowl?

WITNESS: Bev bowled and, yes, I bowled and we bowled together with other couples, also.

HABUSH: Were you in any bowling league?

WITNESS: Yes, I was.

HABUSH: How about baseball?

WITNESS: I played baseball for a church league.

HABUSH: Prior to the accident, how long did you play baseball for a church league?

WITNESS: Five years. And before that, I played baseball for Kohl's, a couple years after I started there.

HABUSH: Did you folks have a cottage up north you could go to?

WITNESS: Yes, we have.

HABUSH: Where is that place?

WITNESS: In the St. Germaine area.

HABUSH: When did you first acquire that?

WITNESS: We bought the property in 1971.

HABUSH: And had you started developing it, the cottage, prior to the day of the accident?

WITNESS: Yes.

HABUSH: How much work had been done prior to the accident?

WITNESS: The outside was done. We had—the stuff was done on the inside. I think we just got the water.

HABUSH: How would you describe your social life with respect to going out with friends and nonsport activities?

WITNESS: They're pretty good right now.

HABUSH: Did you have a lot of friends who go out often before the accident?

WITNESS: Yes, I did.

§7.06 —Use of Background Information to Establish the Plaintiff's Credibility

Second, the background information about the plaintiff provided facts about the plaintiff's good character, which the jury could use in forming inferences about the plaintiff's credibility. Welch elicited testimony about the plaintiff that demonstrated that he had been married for 28 years, had held the same job as a crane operator for 18 years, had high seniority among crane operators, had missed time from work only when he was injured, and had never made any other claims or been involved in any other lawsuits. The background facts established the plaintiff as a stable, dependable, hard-working man. The jurors could infer from this that the plaintiff was honest, and, therefore, believable in his claims for damages. Welch questioned as follows:

WELCH: Mr. Cooper, would you please state your name and address for the jury.

PLAINTIFF: Robert Floyd Cooper, 9802 East 77th Street, Raytown, Missouri.

WELCH: How long have you lived there, Mr. Cooper?

PLAINTIFF: Twenty-five years.

. . . .

WELCH: Are you married, and if so, what is your wife's name?

PLAINTIFF: Yes, I'm married. Ruth Eileen Cooper.

WELCH: How long have you all been married?

PLAINTIFF: Twenty-eight years.

WELCH: Do you and Mrs. Cooper have children?

PLAINTIFF: Yes. We have two: a girl, Julie, age 26; and a boy, Bruce, age 22.

WELCH: At the time of the collision we're here about, what was your business or occupation?

PLAINTIFF: I was a crane operator for Belger Cartage.

WELCH: How long had you been engaged as a crane operator with Belger Cartage?

PLAINTIFF: About 18 years.

WELCH: How long had you been interested in this profession of being a crane operator?

PLAINTIFF: Well, before I got involved in the Korean War, I was working for Brosnahan Construction Company. I was an oiler there.

WELCH: I'm sorry, Brosnahan?

PLAINTIFF: I was an oiler for Brosnahan. Then I went to work after I got out of the service for Belger Cartage as an oiler.

WELCH: How did you get to be a crane operator?

PLAINTIFF: Well, you work as an oiler for three or four years, and the operator teaches you to run the crane.

WELCH: Okay. Mr. Sherman Harlow was the oiler here today, and said he worked as an oiler for so many years and became a crane operator. He was an oiler for eight years. Why the difference?

PLAINTIFF: Well, I think he spent some time in the service and was away from it, but it can vary. Depends on the need of the company, too. You can learn and be qualified, but if they don't need an operator, they are not going to set you up.

WELCH: Is this what you call on-the-job training then?

PLAINTIFF: Yes, it is.

WELCH: Did you eventually graduate to the job of crane operator with the Belger Cartage Company?

PLAINTIFF: Yes, I did, in 1960.

WELCH: And did you continually operate cranes for Belger Cartage Company from that date until 1960, up until September 29th, 1978, the date of this auto collision?

PLAINTIFF: Yes, I did.

WELCH: What was your general condition of health before this automobile collision of September 29, 1978?

PLAINTIFF: Well, I'd have to say excellent, except for a few injuries I had while working at Belger.

WELCH: Let's tell us about some of those. What was the first one you remember?

PLAINTIFF: Well, in 1962, I got my arm and hand caught in the gear on a crane.

WELCH: All right. You got it caught in a crane gear. Could you be a little more specific about it?

PLAINTIFF: Well, that's a gear—it's a big bull gear, is what it's called. I got my arm and hand in there, and up to my elbow.

. . .

WELCH: With that damage to the right arm, were you able to get back to work for Belger as a crane operator?

PLAINTIFF: Yes. I went back to work and I worked full-time as a crane operator up until the collision.

. . .

WELCH: Did you suffer any other injuries there at Belger?

PLAINTIFF: Let's see. It was late '60s, I injured my right leg, and then in the early '70s, a board hit me in the forehead and I had to have that stitched.

WELCH: A timber hit you in the forehead and you had to get stitches?

PLAINTIFF: Yes, sir.

WELCH: Did you lose time from work for either of those injuries, either the right leg or being hit in the head by the timber.

PLAINTIFF: No, sir, I did not.

WELCH: Did you have any other injuries while you were there at Belger?

PLAINTIFF: Well, the year of the accident—

WELCH: You're talking about this accident?

PLAINTIFF: Yes, sir. In 1978, I injured my low back doing some lifting, and I hurt my ribs.

WELCH: Did you miss any time from work from either of those two incidents?

PLAINTIFF: I was off a week on account of my back, and I didn't lose any time on the ribs.

. . .

WELCH: Tell us what this means, being an operator and being an oiler. How does that relate to top seniority?

PLAINTIFF: Well, where do you want to start?

WELCH: First of all, let's start here. Based on some things that were said here earlier, do operators and oilers just switch off their jobs all the time?

PLAINTIFF: No. An operator is an operator. They don't bounce back and forth. Now, what I meant by seniority, the operators have seniority and the oilers have seniority.

WELCH: Let's talk about a crane operator. Do the crane operators of 18 years have seniority levels?

PLAINTIFF: Yes, they did.

WELCH: Since you've been there 18 years as an operator, before this automobile collision, where were you on the seniority level?

PLAINTIFF: I was number three.

WELCH: Number three out of how many?

PLAINTIFF: About twenty-five people.

Similarly, Block elicited background testimony from the widow of Wendell Burns that established his good character. Wendell Burns was portrayed as a talented, caring, sensitive, responsible individual:

BLOCK: You say he was working at the time. Where was he working?

PLAINTIFF: At Wapato Fruit Products in Wapato. He was a forklift driver.

BLOCK: Fruit products a big industry in Wapato?

PLAINTIFF: Right.

BLOCK: How old was he when he was operating the forklift?

PLAINTIFF: It was right out of high school, so he must have been 18.

BLOCK: For how long a period of time did he operate the forklift?

PLAINTIFF: Well, he worked in '67 and part of '68. Now, he might have been changed jobs, you know, occasionally, during this time. I would occasionally go down and have lunch with him and he was on the forklift at that time. He might have had similar other jobs, too, you know.

BLOCK: Do you know what he did with the money that he earned operating the forklift?

PLAINTIFF: Well, we were planning on getting married, so we saved quite a bit in savings, and then he did help his mother an awful lot. She didn't have any source of income at all at that time, and so he did contribute a lot to his mom to help her.

BLOCK: There came a time when you and Wendell decided to get married?

PLAINTIFF: Right.

BLOCK: When was that?

PLAINTIFF: We got married on July 6, 1968.

BLOCK: At that time, was there any discussion about future education of Wendell?

PLAINTIFF: Well, he expressed the desire to go to college when he got back. Now, I told him I would continue working; and I would work when he got back so he could, you know, further his education and get a degree in whatever he wanted to go into. He was very handy in electronics and, of course, architecture, too. He could have gone into that. He also had his band in high school. He could have easily gone into being a musician.

. . . .

BLOCK: Can you describe for us, please, the life you had with Wendell prior to the time he left for the Service?

PLAINTIFF: Well, it was kind of a relationship where you instantly meet someone and you like them. He was very warm, very friendly to everyone; and he always cared, he cared about people, and he always worried about people, whether or not they are getting along okay; worried a lot about his mother, whether or not she, you know, was going to get along okay.

If people had any problems, they could always go to him. He might not—could never solve all their problems, but at least, he had an ear that someone could go and talk to him, and he cared. He cared and worried a lot about us while he was in Service. He wrote every night, and I wrote him every night; and if he didn't get a letter from me every day, he wrote and was worrying about if something was wrong, if something was wrong with Stacy or me or his mother or my folks. He was the sort of person that you could depend on.

BLOCK: Prior to the time that he left for the Service, was he the type of person that would listen to problems or—

PLAINTIFF: Yes, he was. We made several decisions together. I never took it upon myself to just say, "Well, this is the way it is." We always decided things together. And even when he went into the Service, and we weren't even able to call each other and talk to each other on the phone, I always wrote him and asked him his opinion, and he would always tell me what he thought.

BLOCK: There came a time when you gave birth to Stacy?

PLAINTIFF: Yes, we met him in Hawaii on his R & R, the last week of July, and Stacy was four months old at the time, and we spent a week with him there.

BLOCK: Can you tell us what Wendell's attitude was? How he acted and what transpired during that week in Hawaii?

PLAINTIFF: Well, he was overjoyed to see his son. I think that was foremost in his mind besides me, and we didn't do an awful lot. We did everything together. We never left Stacy once. We always had him with us, and we had, you know, several opportunities to go out in the evening just by ourselves; but we always—would always have him with us, and he enjoyed being there with his son.

BLOCK: In the correspondence with Wendell, about Stacy, what generally was discussed in that correspondence?

PLAINTIFF: Well, he was concerned about, you know, his health. Was he healthy? What he was doing. He always wanted to know, well—is he laughing? Is he talking? Is he crawling? Things of this sort. He was just always curious about what was happening. If he was sick, he worried constantly until I wrote him and told him that he was well, and he wanted the best future for his son.

BLOCK: While he was in the Service, did Wendell contribute money home?

PLAINTIFF: Yes, he did. I had gotten an allotment, and he also sent extra money home.

BLOCK: When you say you received an allotment plus extra money home, can you explain that a bit?

PLAINTIFF: Well, I believe it was $130 a month allotment at the time. And then he would only keep what he needed for that month, like $25, $30, that he would need; this is, like, to buy soda pop or whatever. And he would send the rest of it home. He would alternate with me and then his mother. He tried to send some home to his mother every month or two, and if not, I would always check on her and make sure she had what she needed.

. . . .

BLOCK: Did you, in behalf of Wendell, receive any awards or decorations or citations?

PLAINTIFF: My husband received the Bronze Star as well as the Vietnam Campaign Badge, the Good Conduct Metal, and there were various other ones. I received the Bronze Star at ceremonies in Fort Lewis. It was in March of 1970.

BLOCK: Obviously, you also received a Purple Heart at that time?

PLAINTIFF: Yes.

BLOCK: Do you know when Wendell went from private to private first class?

PLAINTIFF: I believe he was in advanced, individual training when— and this was in Fort Sill, Oklahoma. This was before he went to Vietnam, that he was promoted.

BLOCK: Do you know when he made corporal?

PLAINTIFF: I believe it was about three or four months after he was in Vietnam he made corporal.

BLOCK: I show you these photographs, Mrs. Burns, and ask you what they depict, generally?

PLAINTIFF: Well, my husband loved to take pictures. He loved to take pictures of the men, and of the firing missions. What these pictures depict are the firing missions they were on, the guns; show them cleaning the gun, shows the men. I even have several pictures of the men after a firing mission. It just shows the men, and I know that they all got along well together.

. . . .

BLOCK: Mrs. Burns, did Wendell receive letters of commendation for his service work?

PLAINTIFF: Yes, he did.

. . . .

BLOCK: Mrs. Burns, I don't believe I asked you. Do you know what Wendell's marks were in high school?

PLAINTIFF: They were above average.

BLOCK: In work around the house, did he have any particular mechanical or electrical aptitudes?

PLAINTIFF: Yes, he did.

BLOCK: Can you describe the nature of the work he did?

PLAINTIFF: Well, he did a lot of wiring for his mom around the house, and anytime any of the small appliances broke down, he was always there ready to try to fix them. I had a problem with my TV once and he was able to fix that; he was very handy as far as household appliances went.

BLOCK: If you were to reflect back on your life with Wendell, how would you sum up his characteristics, his make-up, the type of person he was?

PLAINTIFF: He was a very beautiful person. He loved being alive, and he loved people. He loved being around them, doing things for people. He was very compassionate. He would help you in any way he could whenever he could, and if he was not able to help you, he would try to find some way or someone that could help you; and he never asked for more than what he ever had, even though he did have goals, and he had goals for me and he had goals for his son. And I know that if he had come back from Vietnam, I know that he would be doing very well today, because he was the type of person that had a goal and he would try to reach it, and he was not a quitter.

Habush established the plaintiff's credibility as an experienced forklift driver by detailing his experience as a dock worker. Since, at the time of the injury, Habush's client was involved in an activity that he had not had a lot of experience performing, it was necessary for Habush to establish the plaintiff's general experience in handling forklifts:

HABUSH: So for about 21 years you had worked at Kohl's warehouse?

WITNESS: Yes, I have.

HABUSH: What kind of warehouse is that?

WITNESS: It was a grocery warehouse.

HABUSH: And that would be shipping and receiving what type of goods?

WITNESS: All dry goods.

HABUSH: What were your duties in the grocery warehouse over the years?

WITNESS: Anything from—everything from selecting orders to driving forklift, single bottoms, double bottoms, riders, or sit down. Worked in a cheese cooler. I worked in a drug room. Just about everything Kohl's had to offer I—I did over there.

HABUSH: In the 21 years that you were in the grocery warehouse, did you have occasion to load and unload delivery trucks?

WITNESS: Yes, I did.

HABUSH: How frequent would that be part of your job?

WITNESS: About 6, 7 weeks out of the year I would be a receiving clerk.

HABUSH: You say 6 or 7 weeks out of the year?

WITNESS: Yes.

HABUSH: And when you say you were a receiving clerk, for whom or what warehouse?

WITNESS: For the drug room. That's in the same—same warehouse as—as the grocery, just a different part of the warehouse.

HABUSH: What types of vehicles did you use during that operation?

WITNESS: I would use dockers and single bottoms to unload trailers.

HABUSH: You used the word dockers. Is that something like the accident vehicle that we have been talking about?

WITNESS: Yes, it is.

HABUSH: What was the principal type of equipment that you used in the grocery warehouse during the 21 years?

WITNESS: I said I used—I used double bottoms and single bottoms and forklifts—they are called reach, reach forklifts.

.   .   .   .

HABUSH: This is what you did for 21 years?

WITNESS: Partly, yes.

HABUSH: Now, during the period of time, did you also have occasion to work part-time at the produce warehouse?

WITNESS: Yes, I did.

HABUSH: How often would you have a chance to do that?

WITNESS: My last year there was, I did Friday nights part time. I think we started about 6:30, 7:00. It was after working hours.

HABUSH: Was this overtime work?

WITNESS: Yes, it was overtime.

HABUSH: When you worked in the produce warehouse, what did you do, what kind of job did you have there?

WITNESS: We selected orders for the stores. Basically what I did in the grocery warehouses, I was picking produce rather than dry goods.

HABUSH: What do you mean by select orders?

WITNESS: Look at the order sheet, what the stores need, and we go up and down the aisles and select whatever we needed.

HABUSH: What type of equipment would you use when you were doing that?

WITNESS: Single bottoms and dockers. For picking orders, we use single bottoms.

HABUSH: Did you ever have occasion prior to June 8th, 1981 to load any vehicles at the produce warehouse during this part-time job?

WITNESS: Yes, I did.

HABUSH: And did you ever have any occasion to unload at the produce dock?

WITNESS: The only thing I unloaded there was empty pallets when we were assigned a trailer. There was always empty pallets in there and we'd pull them off first and empty the truck.

HABUSH: So prior to June 8th of 1981 when you started to work there full time, you had not ever unloaded a pallet with goods on it at the produce warehouse, am I right?

WITNESS: Correct.

HABUSH: What type of trucks had you unloaded at the grocery warehouse, going back to the grocery warehouse?

WITNESS: I unloaded—what kind of trucks?

HABUSH: Yes. Semis?

WITNESS: Semis and straight trucks, yes.

HABUSH: How many days, if you can recall, had you worked the produce dock prior to the day of the accident?

WITNESS: How many days prior?

HABUSH: Yeah, how many times would you estimate you had worked there before?

WITNESS: Ten to fifteen times on Friday nights.

. . . .

HABUSH: Had you had occasion prior to June 8th of 1981 to unload what has been called straight trucks with a docker?

WITNESS: Yes, I had.

HABUSH: Where did you have that experience?

WITNESS: I had that experience in the drug room.

. . . .

HABUSH: When you used a forklift truck or a docker like the one involved the day you were injured, had you ever had any trouble unloading a smaller truck or straight truck with it?

WITNESS: Never.

HABUSH: Did you consider yourself an experienced forklift operator on June 8th, 1981?

WITNESS: Yes, I do.

HABUSH: Had you ever had the opportunity prior to June 8th, 1981 to remove pallets from the back of a straight truck like you were attempting to do at the time you were hurt?

WITNESS: Yes, many a time.

HABUSH: Was that a complicated or a simple operation?

WITNESS: Very simple.

HABUSH: Why do you say that?

WITNESS: I had been doing that for 20 years, it's hard to explain, just the type of machinery you use, it's a scooping process. You go in with the machine and all you want to do is just grab the tip of the pallet, pull it back, drop it down, go up to it again and pull it back until you have got the pallets or pallet on a flat surface and then you can go in and grab the whole pallet then, but it's just a matter of just grabbing the tip of it and just keep pulling it back and pulling it back until you have it on a flat surface.

HABUSH: Have you had occasion prior to June 8th, 1981 to remove pallets that were located near the rear or the back of the truck and do what you just described?

WITNESS: Yes, sir.

HABUSH: How many occasions?

WITNESS: Gosh, many times. I couldn't tell you.

HABUSH: And have you used a docker or a forklift truck to do that?

WITNESS: Yes, I have.

§7.07   —Use of Background Information to Establish the Plaintiff's Good Health Prior to the Injury

Third, the background information about the plaintiff established his or her good health prior to the incident causing injuries, which was a necessary foundation for proving that the incident in question damaged the plaintiff. In all cases the lawyers elicited testimony outlining the plaintiff's good physical condition prior to the injury. This testimony would later be juxtaposed with testimony about injuries and damages.

In Habush's case, his client had suffered catastrophic injuries, and therefore, his testimony about prior good health was short:

HABUSH: Had you ever missed work due to any serious illness or serious injury before June 8th, 1981?

WITNESS: No.

HABUSH: Had you ever received any serious injury at work prior to 1981?

WITNESS: No.

HABUSH: Had you ever been laid off prior to 1981 at Kohl's?

WITNESS: Never.

HABUSH: On June 8th, 1981, what was your state of health?

WITNESS: Good.

HABUSH: Were you under the care of any doctor for any disease or injury or other condition on June 8th, 1981?

WITNESS: No.

However, in Glaser's case, the plaintiff's injuries and damages were not so obvious, and, therefore, he elicited detailed background information that allowed the plaintiff to stress her good health prior to the commission of medical malpractice:

GLASER: Beside that job, did you have a job at home?

PLAINTIFF: Oh, yes.

GLASER: What was that?

PLAINTIFF: Cooking, cleaning, washing, ironing, I mowed the backyard, I shoveled the snow, I could paint my house. I could do anything.

GLASER: Without a problem?

PLAINTIFF: Without a problem.

GLASER: Your kids were working?

PLAINTIFF: My kids were working.

GLASER: So they'd come home and—

PLAINTIFF: Dinner was ready for them.

GLASER: Who did the laundry in the house?

PLAINTIFF: I did.

GLASER: Could a lot of these tasks be done over the weekend?

PLAINTIFF: Yes.

GLASER: You didn't work weekends at the job?

PLAINTIFF: No, I had Saturday and Sundays free.

GLASER: How did you feel?

PLAINTIFF: Excellent health. No problems. Nothing.

GLASER: Did you indulge in any sports?

PLAINTIFF: Yes.

GLASER: What?

PLAINTIFF: My daughter and I jogged. We jogged two miles three times a week. I tried to play tennis a little, I couldn't play, but my daughters would and they take me along. I went dancing, I had a good social life.

GLASER: Any problems medically?

PLAINTIFF: No problems medically.

GLASER: How was your emotional state?

PLAINTIFF: Very good.

GLASER: Were you happy?

PLAINTIFF: Happy. Contented. Peace of mind.

GLASER: Active in the community?

PLAINTIFF: The block association.

GLASER: You go to church?

PLAINTIFF: Go to church.

GLASER: Did you enjoy jogging?

PLAINTIFF: I enjoyed it. I enjoyed life in general. Everything I enjoyed.

GLASER: Go on any trips?

PLAINTIFF: Yes, every summer.

GLASER: Where did you go?

PLAINTIFF: We traveled to South America, we went to Florida, we traveled to Bermuda, we went to all the islands.

GLASER: Cruises?

PLAINTIFF: Cruises.

GLASER: Did you enjoy that?

PLAINTIFF: Oh, I loved it. They treat you like royalty on the ships.

GLASER: How did you look physically at that time?

PLAINTIFF: I was a very attractive woman, not bragging.

GLASER: How about your medical history before that, before February 18 or 19—or before March 7 of '76, what was your medical history like? How many operations of any kind?

PLAINTIFF: I had a thyroidectomy.

GLASER: When was that?

PLAINTIFF: 1963.

GLASER: And were you on any medication after that for the thyroid?

PLAINTIFF: No.

GLASER: Okay. And you had two pregnancies?

PLAINTIFF: Two pregnancies.

GLASER: Two births?

PLAINTIFF: Two births.

GLASER: Those were two other hospitalizations, right?

PLAINTIFF: Yes.

GLASER: Any others.

PLAINTIFF: None other.

GLASER: You were 47?

PLAINTIFF: 47.

GLASER: How about medical treatment in the past?

PLAINTIFF: A cold, you know, simple cold, a virus.

GLASER: Any of these problems that you have today, did you have them then?

PLAINTIFF: None. I was free of everything.

GLASER: That arm problem, did you have it before?

PLAINTIFF: Never.

GLASER: You go to a psychiatrist before?

PLAINTIFF: No.

GLASER: Did you have any real deep melancholy before?

PLAINTIFF: No melancholy.

GLASER: Do you know what melancholy is?

PLAINTIFF: Yes, I know a mean melancholy all the time. I'm blue. Lord have mercy, please.

GLASER: Please try to control yourself. How about your menstrual periods, before March, before February of 1977?

PLAINTIFF: They were a little heavier, the flow. No extensive bleeding. None of that, no clots. As I got older, the flow became a little heavier. That's all.

GLASER: When was your last monthly period before February 4th, 1977?

PLAINTIFF: January, the beginning sometime.

GLASER: Were they regular?

PLAINTIFF: They were regular.

GLASER: Regular, okay. Did you ever have high blood pressure before?

PLAINTIFF: No.

GLASER: Headaches before?

PLAINTIFF: No.

GLASER: Flushes before?

PLAINTIFF: Never.

. . . .

GLASER: Did you have—ever bleed in between periods?

PLAINTIFF: Never, never, never.

. . . .

GLASER: At that time—by the way, what was the appearance of your abdomen, as you look at it?

PLAINTIFF: Slim. No stomach.

GLASER: Do you remember what you weighed approximately?

PLAINTIFF: About 135.

GLASER: And how tall are you?

PLAINTIFF: 5-5.

GLASER: And no—you never noticed any bulge?

PLAINTIFF: I had no bulge.

§7.08   —Background Information About Health— Establishing Credibility—Disclosing Any Prior Health Problems to the Jury

It is of note that the lawyers, in presenting background information, asked questions that volunteered any prior injuries or disabilities. As noted in the studies of juror credibility perceptions, jurors formed low credibility assessments of lawyers who failed to deal with the negative aspects of their cases and who allowed defense counsel the opportunity to expose the weakness.[4] The jurors perceived such lawyers as incompetent or dishonest. These lawyers avoided this pitfall and possibly enhanced their credibility by bringing out any prior health problems, thus projecting an image of honesty and fairness.

§7.09   —Background Information About the Instrumentalities or Things Involved in the Incident Causing Injury

The next type of background information elicited was information about the instrumentalities involved in the incident causing injury. For example, Ring asked questions about the machine in question, how it was operated, and how the plaintiff had operated it on previous occasions. Similarly, Baldwin elicited information about the tractor in question, including when and where it was purchased, instructions given by the seller about its operation, the type of overhead protection provided, the manner of operation, the use of accessories, and past maintenance. The jury was given general, descriptive information about the things involved in these cases.

Important information with respect to the issues of liability was embedded in this phase of the questioning. By way of background, the lawyers established that the plaintiffs were exercising due care and conducting themselves in appropriate ways. Baldwin asked his client about the nature of instructions given to him, his knowledge of the availability of safety accessories, his manner of operating the tractor, and his knowledge of any problems in operating the machine. By establishing the fact that the plaintiff was operating the machine the same way he had always operated it and in accordance with the instructions given him by the seller, the plaintiff established, by inference, that the machine must have malfunctioned due to defect. Baldwin questioned as follows:

---

[4] See §§3.14-3.20.

BALDWIN: Now this accident we are here about today occurred while you were driving a Ford tractor, is that right?

PLAINTIFF: Yes, sir.

BALDWIN: And what kind of a tractor was that, what model tractor was it?

PLAINTIFF: It was a 5000.

BALDWIN: 5000?

PLAINTIFF: Yeah, 5000.

BALDWIN: All right, had it been bought new?

PLAINTIFF: Yes, sir.

BALDWIN: When, how long before your injuries?

PLAINTIFF: I believe it was bought in June.

BALDWIN: In other words, in June or July of the year '73, the same year you got hurt?

PLAINTIFF: Yes, sir.

BALDWIN: And where was it bought, Mr. Foster?

PLAINTIFF: Mr. Hubert Meadows.

BALDWIN: Is that the Ford tractor dealer there in DeKalb?

PLAINTIFF: Yes, sir.

BALDWIN: Did you pick it up or was it delivered out there, what was the—

PLAINTIFF: I picked it up.

BALDWIN: You picked it up there?

PLAINTIFF: Yes, sir.

BALDWIN: Now when you picked this tractor up, did anybody there at Meadows Company give you any instructions about how to operate it?

PLAINTIFF: No, sir.

BALDWIN: Did it have a front-end loading device on it?

PLAINTIFF: Yes, sir.

BALDWIN: And was that the device that was put on there by Ford when they showed it?

PLAINTIFF: Yes.

BALDWIN: A hydraulic device that would pick things up?

PLAINTIFF: Uh-huh.

BALDWIN: Did anybody at Meadows or Ford at any time ever given you any instructions about what to do or what not to do about the front-end loader?

PLAINTIFF: No, sir.

BALDWIN: Did anybody at Meadows or for Ford ever tell you how to operate the levers that made it go up and down, or how to hook them up?

PLAINTIFF: No, sir.

BALDWIN: Now that tractor, front-end loader, did it have any kind of overhead protection on it?

PLAINTIFF: No, sir.

.   .   .   .

BALDWIN: Now, Mr. Foster, how did the levers operate on the tractor that caused the front-end device to go up and down?

PLAINTIFF: You push it forward to go up and pull it back to go down.

BALDWIN: And how did you—if you wanted to hook in the front loader with the hydraulic hoses that you had to hook up or not?

PLAINTIFF: Yes, sir.

BALDWIN: Was there one or two hoses?

PLAINTIFF: Two.

BALDWIN: Just describe how you hooked that up.

PLAINTIFF: Well, you put them in that thing and twist it and stick them in there.

BALDWIN: Just like any other hydraulic socket?

PLAINTIFF: Yes, sir.

BALDWIN: Did anybody give you any instructions about how to hook that up?

PLAINTIFF: No, sir.

BALDWIN: Was there any language on the tractor about one up or one down, or anything like that?

PLAINTIFF: No, sir.

BALDWIN: Any markings whatsoever?

PLAINTIFF: No, sir.

BALDWIN: Well, is it true, Mr. Foster, that depending upon how the hydraulic hookup was made that your levers may work one way one time and another way the other time?

PLAINTIFF: Yes, sir.

BALDWIN: Would you explain to the jury what you mean by that?

PLAINTIFF: Well, if you hook them up one way, you push it back, and it would come up and if you push it forward it would go down.

.   .   .   .

BALDWIN: Now where are the levers located?

PLAINTIFF: Right under the seat.

BALDWIN: Now you are sitting there in a wheelchair. If you could hold the microphone with the other and show the jury about where they would be seated, located, if you were on a tractor?

PLAINTIFF: Yeah, they would be right down under the seat, right there.

BALDWIN: About where you have got your hand?

PLAINTIFF: Yes, sir.

BALDWIN: Just below your hip there?

PLAINTIFF: Yes, sir.

BALDWIN: Would they be where you could see them sitting there like you are now?

PLAINTIFF: No, sir.

BALDWIN: You had to look down, didn't you?

PLAINTIFF: Yes, sir.

BALDWIN: And you are telling me now that depending on how those levers are hooked up, if you pushed them forward they might on one occasion raise the load?

PLAINTIFF: Yes.

BALDWIN: And if you pull them back, they would lower the load?

PLAINTIFF: Yes, sir.

BALDWIN: But if they were hooked up a different way, if you pushed them forward they might lower the load?

PLAINTIFF: Yes, sir, they would.

BALDWIN: And did that lead to confusion on your part?

PLAINTIFF: Yes, sir.

BALDWIN: And would that make it possible to where—depending on how they were hooked up, you might not know for sure which way that—if you push it forward it is going to come up or come down?

PLAINTIFF: That's right.

BALDWIN: Could that cause you to get the opposite results from what you wanted if you got in a tight spot?

PLAINTIFF: Yes, sir.

. . . .

BALDWIN: Now then, another feature of those levers—let's talk about that. If you push them—let's just say that—in other words, you looked up and you pushed it forward and it raised that load, if you pushed it in do they have a kind of feature on there if you pushed them forward then they will just kind of jump in and stay?

PLAINTIFF: Yes, sir.

BALDWIN: And if you push it forward and it jumps in and stays as we described, what will happen to the load then?

PLAINTIFF: It will keep coming up.

BALDWIN: It will keep coming up.

PLAINTIFF: Yes, sir.

BALDWIN: And in order to get it stopped, what do you have to do?

PLAINTIFF: You have to push it out.

· · · ·

BALDWIN: And, as an operator, state the facts of whether or not it is essential that you be able to see the load that you are lifting at all times.

PLAINTIFF: Yes, sir.

· · · ·

BALDWIN: And if for any reason you have to take your hand off, state the fact of whether or not you have to look down to find those levers in order to put your hand back on it?

PLAINTIFF: Yes, sir.

· · · ·

BALDWIN: And would that require you to take your hand off of—or your eyes, rather—off of what you are raising?

PLAINTIFF: Yes, sir.

BALDWIN: And had the levers been situated up on the front end of the tractor on your right side in a position so that you could reach them and see not only the levers but the load, would that have been a safer arrangement for you?

PLAINTIFF: Yes, sir.

· · · ·

BALDWIN: Now, have you had any trouble with these controls sticking before this accident?

PLAINTIFF: Yes, sir, it hung, it stuck or something, I don't know what.

BALDWIN: What would happen when it did this?

PLAINTIFF: It would keep coming up.

Block went into great detail with the plaintiff Baird in describing the howitzer and establishing that it was handled and fired properly:

BLOCK: Tell us a little bit about your training in the service.

WITNESS: Well, at first I went to Fort Benning, Georgia. I took basic training on small weapons and infantry training for eight weeks. Then I was shipped out from there to Lawton, Oklahoma, Fort Sill, where I took artillery training for approximately another eight weeks. And then after the training I went to Vietnam.

BLOCK: When you went to Vietnam, were you in any particular battery or battalion?

WITNESS: No. At that time I was training in jungle training in Vietnam after I got there for approximately two weeks and then I was assigned to a battery.

BLOCK: What battery was that?

WITNESS: It was the 1st Battalion, 14th Artillery in July.

BLOCK: What was the nature of the activity that unit was engaged in?

WITNESS: Sir?

BLOCK: What was the overall nature of the activity that that unit was engaged in?

WITNESS: Mostly in the jungle training we took prior to going into the field, mostly getting used to the country. Some of the things like bunker guard and things like that we were supposed to do. Then they sent us to the battery where we would be actually on the 105 howitzer.

BLOCK: How much training did you have with regard to the 105 howitzer prior to the time that you were actually assigned to that unit?

WITNESS: We went to school for approximately five or six weeks and then we was just on the job training with the gun for approximately two weeks.

BLOCK: When was that when you were assigned to that unit, was that Battery C?

WITNESS: Sir?

BLOCK: When you were finally assigned to a unit, that unit was Battery C, I take it?

WITNESS: Yes, sir.

.   .   .   .   .

BLOCK: Can you describe for us, please, Mr. Baird, what the members of the battery consist of, how many members there are and what their functions are?

WITNESS: Well, in artillery you have your gunner. You have your assistant gunner. You have a loader. You have a radio operator. You have ammo handlers and you are supposed to have a sergeant, A-5 or A-6 or above in charge of the gun over the men.

BLOCK: And when you were assigned to Battery C, what was your function?

WITNESS: I handled ammo when I first got there.

BLOCK: You were a what?

WITNESS: Handling ammo when I first got there.

BLOCK: Can you tell us what you did by handling the ammo, where did you take it from and what did you do with it?

WITNESS: We took the ammunition from the ammunition bunker near the gun. We were to fix the ammunition and hand it to the loader at that time that was loading the gun and then he would fire it.

BLOCK: Was this the 105 millimeter shell?

WITNESS: Yes, sir.

BLOCK: Can you describe for us, please, 105 millimeter shell?

WITNESS: Yes, sir. It has a cannister about, the cannister would be about that high. . . . It has seven powder charges in the cannister. There is a projectile and then there is a fuse on top of the projectile and you fix the fuse to the projectile and then set the projectile in the cannister and then you would have the fixed shape.

. . . .

BLOCK: Can you tell us, once the ammo is taken from the bunker or where the ammo is stored, what is done with it, to whom does the ammo handler give it?

WITNESS: After the ammo is brought from the ammunition bunker, which is located on the gun itself, just off to the side down in the ground, we would bring it out, check the ammunition, hand it to the loader and the loader would load the 105.

THE COURT: When it is in the bunker are all the pieces together, the cannister, the projectile and the fuse?

WITNESS: Yes, sir.

. . . .

BLOCK: Am I correct in understanding, then, that the cannister, the powder and the projectile come wrapped in a sealed box as one unit and there are two in such sealed boxes?

WITNESS: Yes, sir.

BLOCK: And the fuses come separately, right?

WITNESS: Yes, sir.

BLOCK: When they come in the sealed box, the unit, the entire shell, the cannister, the projectile and the powder in it, let's say nose of the projectile instead of the fuse, am I correct in stating there is a bolt which you remove and subsequently the men put in the fuse in place of the bolt?

WITNESS: Yes.

. . . .

BLOCK: You say that when it is all in the enclosed package it comes in, both the projectile and the cannister, it also comes with powder, bags of powder?

WITNESS: Yes, sir.

BLOCK: How many bags of powder does it come with?

WITNESS: Seven, sir.

. . . .

BLOCK: Once it is assembled—once you assemble it, what do you do with it?

WITNESS: On some occasions we will—when the ammunition was assembled we would put it in our ammunition bunker next to the gun and when some of the ammunition will be fixed we would carry it straight to the gun and bore it.

. . . .

BLOCK: On September 6, 1969, Mr. Baird, what duty or what function did you have within your battery?

WITNESS: On September 6, 1969 I was assistant gunner on gun No. 6.

. . . .

BLOCK: For how long a period of time were you assistant gunner prior to September 6th of 1969?

WITNESS: I had been assistant gunner approximately four to five months.

BLOCK: Did you go right from ammo handler to assistant gunner?

WITNESS: No, sir.

BLOCK: How long were you an ammo handler?

WITNESS: About maybe two to three weeks. Everybody would get a chance to get familiarized with the gun and then you could move, you would move up.

BLOCK: In other words, you weren't supposed to work on the gun until you were familiarized with it, correct?

WITNESS: Yes, sir.

BLOCK: Why is that?

WITNESS: It is a safety precaution, sir.

BLOCK: I beg pardon?

WITNESS: A safety precaution?

BLOCK: In other words, all men who worked on the gun had to take a certain amount of indoctrination of working in other functions before they could actually work on the gun itself; is that correct?

WITNESS: Yes, sir.

BLOCK: After you were an ammo handler for, what was it, three weeks, you say?

WITNESS: Yes, sir.

BLOCK: What function were you assigned to?

WITNESS: I was a radio telephone operator part time, sir.

BLOCK: Can you tell us what the duties and what purpose the radio telephone operator serves with respect to a crew such as you were on?

WITNESS: Yes, sir. The RTO had a data sheet, a piece of paper with the grids, azimuths and deflections and quadrants that we were shooting.

. . . .

BLOCK: So in other words, it was a slow process before people could actually work on the gun, they had to go through more or less an apprenticeship system, is that correct?

WITNESS: Yes, sir.

BLOCK: And watch and be with people who were more experienced in the gun crew?

WITNESS: Yes.

BLOCK: They didn't take like a green guy and put him on the gun right away, did they?

WITNESS: No, sir.

. . . .

BLOCK: What was the nature of the activity? What was the overall purpose of that gun crew's activity? Was it harassment?

WITNESS: The night of September, it was harassment.

. . . .

BLOCK: On September 6, 1969, had you as a crew been together for a long time?

WITNESS: Yes, sir.

BLOCK: For how long a period of time were the men together?

WITNESS: I don't understand.

BLOCK: Your unit, your gun crew, you say was together for a long period of time?

WITNESS: Yes.

BLOCK: For how long had you been working together?

WITNESS: Approximately five, anywhere from three to four months and then I had actually been on that one gun.

BLOCK: With the same people?

WITNESS: Yes, sir.

BLOCK: You were on this same howitzer, is that the gun?

WITNESS: Yes.

BLOCK: For several months. During that period of time did that gun ever malfunction in any way?

WITNESS: No, sir. Not to the best of my ability I don't think.

BLOCK: Did you ever have any trouble with any ammunition during that period of time?

WITNESS: No, sir.

§7.10 How the Injury Occurred

After presenting background information, the lawyers moved to eliciting testimony about how the injury occurred. The lawyers asked questions that allowed the plaintiffs to tell their story about how the incident in question occurred. The jurors were told in graphic detail how the plaintiffs were injured. For example, Welch questioned the plaintiff as follows:

WELCH: Let's turn to the automobile collision that brings us to the court this week. What was the date of that, for the record?

PLAINTIFF: That was September 29, 1978.

WELCH: Do you recall what time it occurred?

PLAINTIFF: Yes. It was 7:45 in the morning during rush hour traffic.

WELCH: What kind of car were you driving?

PLAINTIFF: 1973 Oldsmobile four-door.

WELCH: Was anyone with you?

PLAINTIFF: Sherman Harlow was my oiler. We were doing a job we'd been working on.

WELCH: Where was the car when this accident happened?

PLAINTIFF: It was on the hill on 23rd Street just east of 435.

WELCH: Tell us about the weather and light conditions that morning.

PLAINTIFF: Well, it was daylight and clear, and there was no problem with the weather.

WELCH: Tell us what the traffic was like that morning.

PLAINTIFF: Well, it was heavy rush hour traffic. The oncoming traffic was much heavier than the traffic in my line.

WELCH: Were you in a lane of traffic?

PLAINTIFF: No. There were cars ahead of me and cars behind me, but we weren't in any bumper-to-bumper traffic.

WELCH: What lane of traffic were you in?

PLAINTIFF: I was on the inside lane next to the median.

WELCH: Tell us about the speed limit there and what speed you were traveling.

PLAINTIFF: Speed limit is 55, and I was going something under that.

WELCH: What separated you two eastbound lanes from the two oncoming westbound lanes?

PLAINTIFF: A raised, concrete, paved median about the width of a driving lane.

WELCH: What was the first notice you had that there was danger of an accident?

PLAINTIFF: Well, when I saw this van coming down the median toward me.

WELCH: And what did you do?

PLAINTIFF: Well, I moved over to my right, clear to the outside lane. It's a good thing there wasn't a car there, and that allowed me to move over to the right.

WELCH: What happened next?

PLAINTIFF: Well, it looked like he was going to pass in front of me, and then all of a sudden he veered right into me, hit me almost head-on.

WELCH: Now, what portion—well, you've seen these photographs of your car that were put into evidence here, the damage along the left side?

PLAINTIFF: Yes.

WELCH: Is that the area where the van hit you?

PLAINTIFF: Yes. On the driver's side, on the front—left front corner.

WELCH: You said it looked like he was going to pass in front of you. Then what happened, please?

PLAINTIFF: Well, he turned really sharp, veered right into me. He could have gone the inside lane, or he could have passed in front of me, either way, but just all of a sudden at the last moment, he turned right into me.

WELCH: Okay. Mr. Cooper, how much time elapsed from the time you first saw this van coming towards your lane until the actual impact occurred?

PLAINTIFF: It seemed like just a split second. It could have been a second or two.

WELCH: Did you ever get your foot on the brakes before the impact?

PLAINTIFF: Yes, I did.

WELCH: Do you know what speed you were going at the time of the actual impact?

PLAINTIFF: No, I don't.

WELCH: What happened to you afterwards?

PLAINTIFF: Well, I felt the blood running down my face, and I knew I'd been cut; and then somebody stopped and helped get us out, and then helped get Harry out, and then helped me out of the car and laid me down on the pavement.

WELCH: What could you tell about your injuries at that time?

PLAINTIFF: Well, I hurt from the waist up, with most of the pain in my shoulder and base of my neck.

WELCH: Could you describe that pain to me, please?

PLAINTIFF: Well, it was very severe.

In presenting the plaintiff's account of how the howitzer exploded, Block presented the plaintiff's testimony in concise, yet effective terms:

BLOCK: On September 6, 1969, you say you had a harassing fire duty. When did you commence, when did you begin the harassing fire that night?

PLAINTIFF: It was approximately around 8:00 or 8:30 or 9:00 and I don't know exactly.

BLOCK: Can you tell us, please, were a certain amount of rounds to be fired before a certain time and a certain amount subsequent to a certain time?

PLAINTIFF: Yes, sir. There were 250 rounds to be fired before 12:00 o'clock and then after 12:00 o'clock there was additionally 250 rounds to be fired.

BLOCK: On that night did you fire the 250 rounds?

PLAINTIFF: Yes, sir.

BLOCK: And after you fired the 250 rounds, what did you do?

PLAINTIFF: We got our gun laid for a new azimuth into the direction we were going to shoot and then we were ready for the 250 rounds after 12:00 o'clock.

BLOCK: After 12:00 o'clock, tell us just what occurred.

PLAINTIFF: We was starting to shoot the 250 rounds and then all I seen was a ball of fire.

BLOCK: Before you saw the ball of fire, can you tell what was done with the ammo, what you did?

PLAINTIFF: I was the assistant gunner on the gun that night and then he was starting the 250 rounds after 12:00 and then the gun exploded. I tried to run but I couldn't go. I fell. I felt paralyzed. I won't say the reason why I couldn't move my leg. I raised up, I seen that I had lost my leg and I laid back down.

At this point, the lawyers also established and reinforced the fact that the plaintiffs were using due care and were operating the instrument in question in an appropriate manner. Welch asked questions about the nature of evasive action that the plaintiff attempted prior to the collision. Baldwin established that the malfunction happened so quickly that the plaintiff had no time to react to avoid injury.

§7.11   Nature and Extent of Damages

The descriptions of how the incident occurred led naturally to descriptions of the injuries and damages suffered by the plaintiffs. The lawyers asked questions that allowed the plaintiffs to tell the story of their injuries and damages.

§7.12   —Initial Injuries

The lawyers began with descriptions of how the plaintiffs were initially injured, including accounts of their initial pain and suffering. Ring asked this way:

RING: All right. Then what do you remember—do you remember anything with your hands caught in the machine?

PLAINTIFF: I remember it going, keep coming. I know it came down on me, kept coming down.

RING: It came down more than once?

PLAINTIFF: Yes.

RING: Do you know how many times?

PLAINTIFF: No, I don't.

RING: And then what were you doing?

PLAINTIFF: Screaming and hollering saying, "Oh, my God. Get me out." Someone to let—to get me out.

Similarly, Baldwin questioned:

BALDWIN: Now then, after this happened, what happened to you?

PLAINTIFF: Well, it broke my back.

BALDWIN: Did it knock you off the tractor or did you stay on the tractor?

PLAINTIFF: Yes, sir, I stayed on the tractor.

BALDWIN: Do you know where that bale of hay hit you?

PLAINTIFF: Well, it hit my shoulder and back there somehow, I don't know as how.

BALDWIN: All right, were you in pain?

PLAINTIFF: Yes.

. . . .

BALDWIN: What did the ambulance man do when he got there?

PLAINTIFF: He called Dr. Keller.

BALDWIN: Did Dr. Keller come?

PLAINTIFF: Yes, sir.

BALDWIN: Did you and him have any conversation?

PLAINTIFF: Not much, all I was wanting was a shot.

BALDWIN: Were you in awfully bad pain?

PLAINTIFF: Yes, sir.

. . . .

BALDWIN: Did you realize at that time that you couldn't use your feet or were paralyzed?

PLAINTIFF: Yes, sir.

BALDWIN: You knew it.

PLAINTIFF: Yes, sir.

BALDWIN: When did you know it?

PLAINTIFF: Right after it hit me.

. . . .

BALDWIN: Did Dr. Keller give you a shot?

PLAINTIFF: No, sir, he didn't have any with him.

BALDWIN: So did you get a shot or anything to relieve the pain for those two hours?

PLAINTIFF: No, sir.

Habush questioned in a way that allowed the plaintiff to graphically describe the seriousness of his condition initially after the accident:

HABUSH: What's the next thing you remember?

PLAINTIFF: I was laying someplace, evidently, on the dock. The paramedics were asking me if I could breathe and I said no and they stuck a tube in my chest. And he says, "Can you breathe now?" And I said no. And they stuck a tube underneath my arm and he said, "Can you breathe now?" And I says a little better. Then he said, "Can you move your legs?" And I said no. He says, "Do you wear contacts?" I said yes and he took my contacts out. That was it.

HABUSH: Do you remember whether you realized at that point in time that you were paralyzed?

PLAINTIFF: Yes, it certainly went through my mind.

Block questioned the plaintiff about his initial injuries:

BLOCK: Can you tell us what you remember happened next with respect to yourself and those around you?

WITNESS: After I seen the ball of fire come up in front of me, I thought we were being hit by enemy fire. I turned to start towards my M79 grenade launcher which was standing nearby and when I turned to run, I fell, and I felt paralyzed on my left side, which I wanted to see what happened, so I raised up and there was my leg cut off, which some of the other guys was on the gun had tried to keep me from raising up to see what happened to my leg, but I also seen my leg being off at that time.

BLOCK: Did you observe anything about the rest of the fellows at the gun crew?

WITNESS: I just—it was dark and they were shining lights around me and I just couldn't get, just a glimpse every once in a while of what was going on, but not enough to make anything out of it, no, sir.

BLOCK: Were you conscious or unconscious during this period of time?

WITNESS: I was fully conscious.

BLOCK: What did you feel with respect to parts of your body at that time?

WITNESS: I just—after I raised up and seen what had happened to me, I seen when I couldn't move my left leg, I was paralyzed, why, I raised up and I seen my leg is gone, and by that time there was a bunch of the guys from other guns and all was coming around and they was working with me, trying to stop the bleeding, and everything, and also they were talking to me, trying to keep me from going into shock, which I never did. And also the captain of the gun, he also talked with me while they was carrying me down to the chopper pad for the evacuation.

BLOCK: How long were you there before they took you from the spot by the gun?

WITNESS: Not very long. I couldn't say exactly, but minutes.

BLOCK: Were you—when you observed that your leg was off and that you were paralyzed or felt paralyzed, were you in the same spot where you were when the gun was—when your howitzer was loaded or were you in any different place?

WITNESS: I wouldn't know for sure, but I was in maybe two to three feet within where it was at.

BLOCK: When they took you from that place, by what means did they transport you?

WITNESS: Well, they put me on a stretcher there at the gun and carried me down to about where their captain's quarters were and put me on a truck and carried me about, I would say, 200 yards further to a helicopter pad which a chopper came in and picked me up and carried us to the hospital.

BLOCK: While you were in the chopper who was with you?

WITNESS: There was Edward Kaiser and Borgasano, Joseph Borgasano, Wendell Burns, and Fred C. Bryan, I believe.

.   .   .   .

BLOCK: Were they ministering to you or doing something to you? Was any medic there?

WITNESS: In the chopper?

BLOCK: Correct.

WITNESS: I think so. I wouldn't say for sure.

BLOCK: What did you observe about yourself and how did you feel at that time?

WITNESS: At that time whenever I was going to the hospital I seen the guys that wasn't as bad as you sitting in the chopper themselves. And also I was getting real weak, I done lost a lot of blood and I was getting sleepy and I was fighting, trying to stay conscious, you know, where I would not go to sleep.

BLOCK: Other than the left leg that was missing, did you observe where else you were bleeding from?

WITNESS: No, sir.

BLOCK: Where did they take you in the helicopter?

WITNESS: They took me, I believe, 51st Evacuation Hospital in Chu Lai.

BLOCK: What did they do for you there?

WITNESS: They gave me blood the first thing whenever I got there. And then they carried me into surgery and knocked me out and I don't know what they done that night until I woke up the next morning.

BLOCK: Do you know whether they were giving you intravenous in one arm or both arms at the time?

WITNESS: No, sir, I don't.

BLOCK: When they took you into surgery, did they tell you what they were going to do?

WITNESS: No, sir.

BLOCK: Did you know what they were going to do?

WITNESS: No, sir.

BLOCK: When did you come out of surgery?

WITNESS: It was some time in the morning. I don't know what time.

BLOCK: When you came out of surgery, how did you feel and what did you observe?

WITNESS: I felt real bad, rough, and then I found my face was burned and some of the boys that was on the gun with us that night came to me the next morning and told me—was telling me, you know, kind of what took place that night.

And I told them—I asked them, "My face is burned?" And they told me "Yes" and so they brought me a mirror and I seen it, and my face, my hair and all over my chest was just burned black. It was burned like—just like a piece of meat.

BLOCK: Were you casted in any way? Did you have a cast on?

WITNESS: Not at that time, no, sir.

BLOCK: How long did you stay in that hospital at Chu Lai?

WITNESS: I was left out, I believe, the following morning, going to Camranh Bay.

BLOCK: When you came out of the hospital, were you bandaged on any part of your body?

WITNESS: The stump part of my leg was bandaged and I didn't know anything about the other cuts or anything, I just know that my leg was gone and I was burned at that time.

§7.13   —Progression of the Injuries After the Accident

Following the initial accounts of the injury and pain and suffering, the lawyers asked questions that called for information about the course of medical care and treatment and the progression of the injury. Again, the lawyers, through their questioning, allowed the plaintiffs to tell their stories to the jury in a way that allowed the jury to experience their tribulations. Welch led the plaintiff through descriptions of his surgeries and his quest for relief from pain. With respect to his efforts to find relief from pain, the plaintiff told of electric stimulators, pain clinics, chiropractic treatments, acupuncture, and pain medication. Baldwin's client told of lying flat on his back for nine months, of the pain involved in the attempts at rehabilitation, and of his mental anguish upon learning that he would never walk again. Habush questioned the plaintiff about his fears and pains:

HABUSH: What was your state of mind during this period of time?

PLAINTIFF: Very confused and bitter. And I was worried about what am I going to do for the rest of my life, about a job, the kids, if Bev wouldn't accept me this way. A million things ran through my mind.

HABUSH: Did you have any pain while you were at Froedtert, physical pain?

PLAINTIFF: Yes, a lot.

HABUSH: Where was that?

PLAINTIFF: In my right leg and my back.

HABUSH: How frequent?

PLAINTIFF: Constantly.

HABUSH: How would you describe the pain, sharp, burning, dull?

PLAINTIFF: Sharp, like a blowtorch constantly in my legs. It's a medium type pain right now and then, but there's times, 20, 30, 40 times a day where the pain is so intense, it puts water in my mouth.

Block questioned the plaintiff Baird about his long course of treatment, great pain, and resulting physical disabilities:

BLOCK: And you say from there you went to Camranh Bay?

WITNESS: Yes.

BLOCK: What took place there?

WITNESS: It was just mostly a holding company until they could transfer us on to Japan. They done—they changed the bandages and stuff but I was on drugs at that time. I didn't know what they was doing because they was trying to keep the pain down because I was in a whole lot of pain.

BLOCK: Pain in any particular part of your body or all over?

WITNESS: Just all over. Because I was hurting all over from the burns and the wounds also.

BLOCK: How long were you at Camranh Bay waiting to go to Camp Zuma in Japan?

WITNESS: Maybe two days, I don't know for sure.

BLOCK: What did they do for you there at Camranh Bay?

WITNESS: Just changing the bandages and keep giving me blood. I don't know.

BLOCK: Were any of the wounds running?

WITNESS: I don't know. I wasn't at that time able to raise up. The wounds were bandaged. I didn't look to see, you know, if they were bleeding or anything.

BLOCK: When you got to Camp Zuma, how did you get from Camranh Bay to Camp Zuma?

WITNESS: By plane.

BLOCK: When you got to Camp Zuma, what did they do for you there?

WITNESS: Well, I first went to an Air Force Hospital, which they also changed the bandages and were still giving me blood at the time and I waited over there until I was transferred into Camp Zuma which whenever I got there they changed the bandages and started work with the burns and everything on my hands and all trying to doctor all them up. Then they had done surgery on me and after they done the surgery and brought me back to my bed, that night I had a real bad dream about the explosion and everything and I jumped up out of bed. I was coming up, and whenever I did, I also broke all the stitches, which then was in my right leg, that they had put in there—I didn't know at the time that they was in.

BLOCK: When they did surgery, do you know on what portion of your body they did the surgery?

WITNESS: They done something to the stump of the leg and then they put the stitches in the right leg.

BLOCK: In the other leg?

WITNESS: Yes.

BLOCK: Do you know where they put the stitches in the right leg?

WITNESS: They was just put all the way up, you know, in the right leg. They had it bandaged all over and I couldn't tell anything about it but I knew that my leg was cut because that was the only time that I had noticed it after I had been in the hospital?

BLOCK: I see. You have a scar there, right?

WITNESS: Yes, sir.

BLOCK: Do you know how long the scar is?

WITNESS: I'd say about 12 inches.

BLOCK: Where in the right leg did you say it was?

WITNESS: It is in the upper part of my right thigh.

. . . .

BLOCK: What else did they do for you at Camp Zuma?

WITNESS: After they had done surgery and changed the bandages and everything, whatever they done when I was in surgery, they brought me back and I had the bad dream and got up that night and started bleeding again. Then the next morning they come in there and found all the blood so they carried me back to surgery then and they put me in a full length body cast from here all the way down.

. . . .

BLOCK: What else did they do for you?

WITNESS: Well, I stayed there, I don't know how long. They were still giving me blood and then I stayed there until I was transferred back to the States.

. . . .

BLOCK: When you got to Augusta, Georgia, where did you go?

WITNESS: I went to the Fort Gordon Army Hospital.

BLOCK: How did you feel when you got to the Fort Gordon Army Hospital?

WITNESS: I wasn't in any pain because they had—I was drugged up again, which I wasn't—if I was hurting, I didn't feel anything because I had took shots for the flight and I just didn't feel anything. I was so up on those pills and everything to keep the pain down, I wasn't realizing the pain at that time.

BLOCK: When you got into Fort Gordon, what did they do for you?

WITNESS: They just assigned me to a ward that day and assigned doctors to me. Then the next day they started taking the body cast off itself.

. . . .

BLOCK: Were you in a stretcher all the time since you were injured at Chu Lai?

WITNESS: I was on a stretcher until we got to the hospital. Then they would take us off the stretchers and put us in hospital beds and then when they go to move us again we were back on the stretchers again.

BLOCK: I see. So you were on your back or on your stomach all the time.

WITNESS: I was on my back all the time.

BLOCK: On your back. Go on, please tell us what took place at Fort Gordon.

WITNESS: About the morning or two after they carried us to the place, they call the cast room where they put casts on broke bones and take them off with instruments, and they cut the body cast off, the top part, and I was still laying in the bottom part. And this doctor he lifted me up and took me out of it, which I had not been out of it in a good while, and you know, he started changing the bandages which he had untaped and jerked the bandage off. He said that I wouldn't have much pain that way, which I fainted about three times whenever he jerked the bandage off—

BLOCK: You fainted?

WITNESS: —my stump. Yes, sir.

BLOCK: And how long were you in that body cast?

WITNESS: I wouldn't have the least idea. I was somewhere about a week or longer in a body cast.

BLOCK: When they took the body cast off, what took place next?

WITNESS: They changed the bandages and finally carried me back to the room and they just mostly checked me every day and doctored the burns on my face and hands and neck and all, and then kept the wounds and everything cleaned out and kept my right leg in a cast.

. . . .

BLOCK: Mr. Baird, would you please continue to tell us what took place at Fort Gordon Army Hospital?

WITNESS: After I was—kept the bandages dressed and everything daily, sometimes two or three times a day, and then until the wound was clean enough to—that they went in and pulled the skin over the stump and covered it itself and closed the right leg with stitches except maybe for about an inch, which they left open for the drainage and then later closed it with a butterfly bandage.

BLOCK: Where did they leave that half inch open, at what portion?

WITNESS: About halfway between—in the scar, which scar is about 12 inches, they left it right in the middle.

BLOCK: At the bottom?

WITNESS: No, sir, it was in the side.

BLOCK: All right. I see. Were they giving you any medicines or drugs at the hospital at the time?

WITNESS: After the surgery, after they—well, the whole time I was in Augusta, before the surgery and after, also I was taking Darvons and also shots.

BLOCK: How was your temperature during this time?

WITNESS: After the surgery my temperature went extremely high, they said, because of the infection. I was out of my head for maybe a day or so. I don't know exactly how long after the surgery.

BLOCK: After the surgery, you were taken back to your ward, I take it?

WITNESS: I was taken back to the ward or maybe after the recovery room I went back to the ward I was normally in.

BLOCK: What did you observe about yourself after the surgery, what did you see?

WITNESS: All I seen was just they had a whole bunch of bandages on my stomach, and my right leg was bandaged also, and they put my right leg back in a cast to prevent me from bending my leg and pulling the scar back open and busting it back open again.

· · · ·

BLOCK: After they put that cast on, what else did they do for you at the hospital?

WITNESS: Mostly just stayed in the ward and they kept changing the bandages and saying—until they took the stitches out of my stump, and also out of my right leg, and they took me to—took me down, was going to put me in a whirlpool bath and when they got me down there was when I asked, my foot was broke because the guy picked me up and told me to stand up and when I did, pain went through my leg and foot and when I fell down, he caught me. When I went ahead in the whirlpool bath, and when he carried me back to the room, he told me he wouldn't put me back in the whirlpool any more because there was something wrong with my foot and they x-rayed my foot and found that it was broke.

BLOCK: After they x-rayed your foot, and they found it was broke, what did they do?

WITNESS: I was put back in cast again on my right leg and stayed in bed.

. . . .

BLOCK: During this four or five months, were you given painkillers all the time?

WITNESS: Just about the whole time that I was down there except for the time—after I got up and the pain had quit and all I could tell that—well, they told me all the time I was down there, they said "You can't get addicted to these drugs," so after they told me that, I tried, you know, to bear the pain as much as I could and come off these shots hoping that I wouldn't get addicted to them because I know myself what drugs will do. And I didn't want to be messed up with them so I beared the pain most I could and didn't take any more of the pain-killers.

BLOCK: Were you out of bed at any time during these four or five months?

WITNESS: Maybe at the last—whenever I was in the hospital, before I went to the holding company, I got up and then they put me in a wheelchair.

. . . .

BLOCK: At what point were you able to stand?

WITNESS: I had been there, I guess, maybe four months before I was able to stand.

. . . .

BLOCK: And they fitted you and then there came a time when you got your artificial leg.

WITNESS: Yes, sir.

BLOCK: Tell us how they trained you to utilize that artificial leg.

WITNESS: Well, they would just carry us in these rooms where they had two handrails down the side and we would put the leg on and they would show us how to use—they had mirrors at the end to show you whether you were walking right or how to handle it, the leg itself.

BLOCK: How did it feel?

WITNESS: It hurt.

BLOCK: Were you able to use that artificial leg?

WITNESS: No, sir.

BLOCK: In what way were you not able to use it?

WITNESS: The artificial leg itself didn't fit right. It didn't feel right itself and it also had—the knee in it didn't lock and whenever I would make a step and all it would fold up under me and cause me to fall.

BLOCK: How long did you have that artificial leg?

WITNESS: How long did I keep it?

BLOCK: Correct?

WITNESS: Let's see. Well, I had a new one made, I believe it was in— about the last part of 1970.

. . . .

BLOCK: By the way, did they do anything to your scrotum in any of these hospitals?

WITNESS: They did but I don't remember which one.

BLOCK: Do you know what they did?

WITNESS: No, sir, not—right before I was to get out of the hospital and go in this holding company in Augusta, a doctor—they mentioned it to me that I had some, you know, surgery down there to a testicle.

. . . .

BLOCK: What do you observe there now?

WITNESS: Well, mostly the testicle is cut into, which they told me that it would dry up, which it still to me hasn't dried up completely.

BLOCK: Is it the same size as the other one?

WITNESS: No, sir. It is a lot smaller.

BLOCK: Do you observe any scar or wound there?

WITNESS: Yes, sir.

BLOCK: What do you observe?

WITNESS: I've got a scar on the bag itself.

BLOCK: Are there stitches there do you know?

WITNESS: I don't know, sir.

BLOCK: At the time you were discharged from Fort Gordon, tell us how you felt with respect to the various parts of your body.

WITNESS: After I got in this holding company—well, they processed my papers to be discharged and I was still in some pain, which they told me that I would have some pain for a while, which I have—still have the pain itself and have had ever since I had been out. They told me that—in my stump that the nerves would die in the stump within three years, and the nerves to me they are still there because I have pains still in my foot. I could still feel my knee. I hurt whenever—it feels like my foot is hurting, it feels like my toes draw and I take a cramp in the muscle part of my leg which it ain't even there and it is a lot of pain to it at night. There ain't no way to relieve the pain to it at night. There ain't no way to relieve the pain. You just have to take it until it feels like it turns loose itself, then it will kind of get easy.

But this happens pretty often and they told me that after I lost my leg, they said, "Well, you won't have any pain in there after maybe three years, them nerves will die and they still feel to me like they are very much there.

. . . .

BLOCK: Mr. Baird, there is an aspect of this case that I obviously told you we would be talking about, and that is your relationship with your wife Barbara. Have you been ever able to complete or consummate sexual intercourse with your wife Barbara?

WITNESS: No, sir.

BLOCK: As best you can, can you tell us what happens?

WITNESS: Well, whenever you get ready, you know, to have intercourse and everything like that, you just lose everything you've got and I can't ever go through with it. About the only way that I can raise an erection is by masturbating, that's all.

BLOCK: You say that the only way you can raise an erection is by masturbation. Does that take long?

WITNESS: Yes.

BLOCK: I know you don't like to talk about this, but when you raise the erection, is it a firm erection?

WITNESS: No, sir.

BLOCK: When you raise it as best you can, what then happens?

WITNESS: It just goes. I just lose everything. You don't have any—it just goes down. I can't stay up.

BLOCK: Did you try to make entry into your wife?

WITNESS: Yes, sir.

BLOCK: What happens?

WITNESS: It just goes away.

. . . .

BLOCK: How do you feel when you try and you can't make entry into your wife?

WITNESS: I don't know, it is a feeling, you can't hardly describe. You are just down, you don't—you just don't feel that much of a person, much of a man at all.

The lawyers elicited descriptions of the depressing, painful trials and tribulations experienced by the plaintiffs in attempting to rehabilitate themselves from their injuries. For example, Habush questioned the plaintiff about bowel training:

HABUSH: Did they give you any bowel training as to how to evacuate your bowels?

PLAINTIFF: Yes.

HABUSH: What did they train you to do?

PLAINTIFF: Well, first of all, they did it for me about the first three months. I'd lay in bed and they'd put a suppository up your rectum, then they would take, what I did was, what they taught me, to sit on the pot, it's got a raised toilet seat with a side entry and you have to put a suppository up yourself, use nonsterile gloves, sit on a pot for an hour and wait for it to work. And hopefully—if it doesn't come out—hopefully, it comes out. Or if it doesn't come out, then you have to put gel on your finger, stimulate your—there's sphincter muscles in there. And if you stimulate them, you'll open up and hopefully your bowels will drop.

From descriptions of the injury and pain, the lawyers moved to questions that elicited descriptions of the limitations imposed on the plaintiffs by virtue of their injuries. These descriptions were contrasted with the previous background descriptions of good health. For example, Baldwin asked:

BALDWIN: Do you know of any kind of work that you can do in your condition, Mr. Foster?

PLAINTIFF: No, sir.

BALDWIN: You farmed all your life?

PLAINTIFF: Yes, sir.

BALDWIN: You have got to be a strong man to farm don't you?

PLAINTIFF: Yes.

BALDWIN: Were you strong and able-bodied before this accident happened, with the exception of losing your eye?

PLAINTIFF: Yes, sir.

§7.14   Concluding Questions

The lawyers concluded the direct questioning of the plaintiffs and their representatives with questions that summed up, repeated, and reinforced important points made previously. For example, in completing his direct examination, after his questions about damages, Baldwin returned to a previously covered area and asked:

BALDWIN: And when you lifted this—started to lift this bale, did you have any idea it was going to fall on you?

PLAINTIFF: No, sir.

BALDWIN: Now, did anyone from Ford ever warn you or were there any decals or signs on that tractor warning you about not using this or that implement to lift?

PLAINTIFF: No, sir.

§7.15   Use of Language

The language used in the direct questioning of the plaintiffs was simple and to the point. There was no effort to embellish or use complex or figurative language. This selection of language was understandable given the backgrounds of the plaintiffs. Baldwin's client had terminated his education after the second grade in order to support his family, and had spent his entire life doing farm work. Similarly, the other plaintiffs were ordinary, everyday people, and, therefore, the lawyers used ordinary, everyday language to communicate with them.

§7.16 Form of Questions

In examining their witnesses, these lawyers almost exclusively used leading questions or narrow questions calling for specific narrow answers. Rarely did the lawyers ask open-ended questions, and rarely did the lawyers ask questions calling for narrative answers. An examination of the backgrounds of the plaintiffs reveals the reason for this strategy. All of these plaintiffs were working people with moderate to low education with no prior court or public speaking experience. Thus, they could have been expected to be nervous and ill at ease sitting on the witness stand talking to the jury. Thus, the lawyers literally led the witnesses through their testimony. For example, Spence questioned Bill Silkwood, the legal representative for Karen Silkwood, as follows:

SPENCE: Good morning, Mr. Silkwood.

SILKWOOD: Good morning.

SPENCE: How are you doing today?

SILKWOOD: A little nervous.

SPENCE: Okay. I take it that you haven't made a life of sitting on the witness stand and testifying to the jury, is that correct?

SILKWOOD: No, sir.

SPENCE: You do something else, as a matter of fact, for a living, don't you, Bill?

SILKWOOD: Yes, I am a painter.

SPENCE: And it has been pretty hard for you to sit here in the courtroom, hasn't it?

SILKWOOD: Yes, it has been.

. . . .

SPENCE: Now, Mr. Silkwood, I'm not going to ask you very many questions about Karen, for several reasons, the main reason is that you asked me not to, isn't that correct?

SILKWOOD: That is correct.

SPENCE: And I guess that is because you have some difficulty in talking about it?

SILKWOOD: Yes, I do.

SPENCE: And, Mr. Silkwood, you find it difficult to talk about that subject?

SILKWOOD: Yes, I do.

SPENCE: Would you tell the jury just a little bit of something about your background. I think we can know something about Karen Silkwood by knowing about her parents. Where were you born and raised?

SILKWOOD: I was born in Oklahoma.

.   .   .   .

SPENCE: And before the war was over, was Karen born?

SILKWOOD: Yes. She was born in '46.

SPENCE: Where was she born?

SILKWOOD: Longview, Texas.

SPENCE: Was that while you were still in the Service?

SILKWOOD: Yes.

SPENCE: And Mama was there waiting for you to come home?

SILKWOOD: Yes.

SPENCE: Did you get off when she was born, so that you could see the birth of your first child?

SILKWOOD: Yes. I had a furlough. I got down there the day before she was born.

SPENCE: And then she was born, and that is your first baby?

SILKWOOD: Yes, that is correct.

SPENCE: All right, Mr. Silkwood. After the war you say you started doing mostly labor?

SILKWOOD: Yes.

SPENCE: What kind of labor did you do?

SILKWOOD: Bricklayer's helper. Cement finisher. Worked in lumber yards for awhile.

SPENCE: Whatever you could do to support your family?

SILKWOOD: That is true.

In discussing important issues, such as warnings and instructions for the tractor and how the tractor operated, Baldwin used exclusively narrow questions and leading questions. He interrogated as follows:

BALDWIN: Did anybody give you any instructions about how to hook that up?

PLAINTIFF: No.

BALDWIN: Was there any language on the tractor about one up or one down, or anything like that?

PLAINTIFF: No, sir.

BALDWIN: Any markings whatsoever?

PLAINTIFF: No, sir.

BALDWIN: Well, is it true, Mr. Foster, that depending upon how the hydraulic hookup was made that your levers may work one way one time and another way the other time?

PLAINTIFF: Yes, sir.

. . . .

BALDWIN: And if you pull them back, they would lower the load?

PLAINTIFF: Yes, sir.

BALDWIN: But if they were hooked up a different way, if you pushed them forward they might lower the load?

PLAINTIFF: Yes, sir they would.

BALDWIN: And did that lead to confusion on your part?

PLAINTIFF: Yes, sir.

BALDWIN: And would that make it possible to where—depending on how they were hooked up, you might not know for sure which way that—if you push it forward it is going to come up or come down?

PLAINTIFF: That's right.

BALDWIN: Could that cause you to get the opposite results from what you wanted if you got in a tight spot?

PLAINTIFF: Yes, sir.

§7.17   Fact Witnesses with Respect to the Occurrence—Structure and Background

Included in this category were lay witnesses who offered eyewitness testimony about how the incident in question occurred. The testimony of these witnesses focused on the facts of the occurrence. Their testimony was presented chronologically, beginning with background information about themselves and the instrumentality in question, followed by accounts of how the incident occurred.

The background information elicited from these witnesses focused on background information about the witnesses relative to credibility, their relationship to the plaintiff, how they came to be involved as a witness, and descriptive information about the instrumentalities involved in the accident.

§7.18   —Credibility

When necessary or possible, the lawyers elicited background information that established the witnesses' believability. For example, Ring established that the employee in question had worked for the plaintiff's employer for 35 years, which would support an argument that the employee was a stable, honest person.

Gibbons called the pilot who witnessed the decedent's plane go down in order to establish that the plane went down due to mechanical malfunction as opposed to pilot error. Since this proof was a critical part of his case, Gibbons elicited a great deal of background information designed to establish the witness's credibility:

GIBBONS: Tell the Court and jury your full name, please, sir.

WITNESS: My name is Michael Rhett Butler.

GIBBONS: What is your occupation or profession?

WITNESS: I'm a Major, pilot in the United States Air Force.

GIBBONS: Where do you live?

WITNESS: I presently live in North Highlands next to McClellan Air Force Base, Sacramento, California.

GIBBONS: What is your age?

WITNESS: I'm 35.

GIBBONS: Are you a married man

WITNESS: Yes, sir.

GIBBONS: Where were you born and raised?

WITNESS: Oak Park, Illinois and I was raised throughout the world. My father was in the service.

GIBBONS: All right. In what branch of the service, please, sir?

WITNESS: United States Air Force.

GIBBONS: So you grew up in the military?

WITNESS: That's correct, sir.

GIBBONS: Now, when did you enter the United States Air Force?

WITNESS: In 19—February 1969, I believe.

GIBBONS: Have you been continuously in the United States Air Force since that time?

WITNESS: That is correct sir.

GIBBONS: What does your formal education consist of, please, sir?

WITNESS: I have an Associate of Arts degree in Physics and Electronics and a Bachelor of Arts degree in Industrial Arts.

GIBBONS: And from where did you obtain those degrees, which institutions?

WITNESS: Two-year junior college in Santa Maria for the double A and Cal State, Los Angeles. That was a state college then. It's now a state university for the BA.

GIBBONS: When did you obtain those degrees, please, sir?

WITNESS: 1966 and 1968, respectively.

GIBBONS: And when did you enter the United States Air Force?

WITNESS: Again, sir, active duty February of 1969.

GIBBONS: '69?

WITNESS: Yes, sir.

GIBBONS: Upon entering, what did you do?

WITNESS: I went to officer training school, sir.

GIBBONS: And where was that located?

WITNESS: In the Medina Annex in San Antonio, Texas, Lackland Air Force Base.

GIBBONS: Did you graduate?

WITNESS: Yes, sir.

GIBBONS: And then did you undertake pilot's training?

WITNESS: I did, sir.

GIBBONS: Where did you do that?

WITNESS: Laredo Air Force Base, Texas.

GIBBONS: How long was your pilot training in the United States Air Force?

WITNESS: 53 weeks.

GIBBONS: Approximately how many total hours of flying time do you have to your credit at this time, Major Butler?

WITNESS: Very close to 4,000, sir.

GIBBONS: Have you ever flown any combat missions?

WITNESS: Yes, sir.

GIBBONS: And approximately how many combat missions have you flown?

WITNESS: Approximately 670.

GIBBONS: Approximately how many hours of combat flying time do you have?

WITNESS: 1,577, sir.

GIBBONS: And where did you fly all those various individual combat missions and combat flying hours?

WITNESS: For the first eight months in the Republic of Vietnam with the night corps. And for the rest of the near two-year tenure, I'm not at liberty to say for classified information, sir.

GIBBONS: In order that the jury can evaluate your background to some degree, would you tell us, have you received any decorations while you have been in the United States Air Force?

WITNESS: Yes, sir, I have.

GIBBONS: Approximately how many personal decorations have you received?

WITNESS: Approximately 30, sir.

GIBBONS: Now, tell us, if you will, briefly what some of those individual decorations are for, please, sir, some of those 30?

WITNESS: For action in combat and combat flying.

GIBBONS: And what are some of those decorations?

WITNESS: Three Distinguished Flying Crosses, 26 Air Medals and one Air Force Commendation which was for peacetime operations.

GIBBONS: Have you received any Presidential Unit Citations?

WITNESS: I have been with two units that have received the Presidential Citation, sir.

GIBBONS: Now, you mentioned the Air Force Commendation Medal. What was that for, please?

WITNESS: That was for my work at Davis-Monthan Air Force Base as the Officer-in-Charge of FCF Section attached to Quality Maintenance, 354th Tactical Fighter Wing—

GIBBONS: Involving what airplanes?

WITNESS: Excuse me. Involving the 355th Tactical Fighter Wing.

GIBBONS: Involving what airplane?

WITNESS: The A-10, sir.

. . . .

GIBBONS: Is that the plane that you received the Air Force Commendation Medal for while you were in the Davis-Monthan?

WITNESS: Yes, sir, I was flying an A-10 aircraft at that time.

GIBBONS: What other types of aircraft, if any, were you responsible for at Davis-Monthan?

WITNESS: Just the A-10, sir.

GIBBONS: All right. Now, in addition to the decorations you received in the United States Air Force, did you receive any decorations by the Vietnamese Government?

WITNESS: A Vietnamese Gallantry Cross, sir.

GIBBONS: Did that have any Palms?

WITNESS: Yes, sir, one.

GIBBONS: Now, what does that represent, please, sir?

WITNESS: Generally, sir, for again, action in combat, sir.

GIBBONS: And what is your current position at this time?

WITNESS: I am presently flying at McClellan Air Force Base, Sacramento Air Logistics Command as the chief A-10 pilot, STAN/EVAL flight examiner and instructor pilot for Air Force Logistical Command.

GIBBONS: How long have you been there?

WITNESS: Since April 15, 1980.

GIBBONS: What are you primary duties at McClellan Air Force Base?

WITNESS: Primarily, sir, to fly production A-10 aircraft and production A-10 that are brought to the depot, which is McClellan, and certain technical changes. And work is done to the aircraft, depot level modifications, requiring a great deal of work. And after they are put back together, I fly them to see if they have—if they are airworthy to fly.

. . . .

GIBBONS: All right. Now, when did you come to McClellan Air Force Base in Northern California?

WITNESS: It was April 15 of 1980, sir.

GIBBONS: And where were you stationed before that?

WITNESS: Davis-Monthan Air Force Base, Tuscon, Arizona, sir.

GIBBONS: During what period of time were you stationed at Davis-Monthan Air Force Base?

WITNESS: I believe it was May-June time frame of 1978 through April of 1980.

GIBBONS: All right. And what was your position while you were stationed there, please, sir?

WITNESS: First I checked out in the aircraft and then I went through instructor's school.

GIBBONS: In the A-10?

WITNESS: Yes, to become an A-10 instructor. I flew as a squadron IP and I was a flight commander.

GIBBONS: I'm going to butt in and ask you what is a squadron IP?

WITNESS: A squadron instructor pilot. They had instructing squadrons down there and at the time it was the only A-10 instructing unit until they opened up the two new squadrons at which time I became fully assigned under what they call permanent change of assignment without leaving the station to become the Officer-in-Charge of the functional check flight section, loosely called flight test, under the maintenance there of the wing and I was attached as a squadron pilot to the 358th squadron.

GIBBONS: For the A-10?

WITNESS: Yes, sir.

GIBBONS: Now, at that time were you—what was your rank?

WITNESS: I was a Captain, sir.

GIBBONS: And when were you promoted to Major?

WITNESS: I was selected about May of this year and I just put the rank on 1 December, sir.

GIBBONS: December 1 of this year?

WITNESS: Yes, sir.

GIBBONS: Did you have occasion during that period of time from May 1978 until April of 1980 while you were at Davis-Monthan to fly the A-10?

WITNESS: Yes, sir.

GIBBONS: Approximately how many hours have you flown in an A-10?

WITNESS: I keep hesitating to look. Approximately 700, sir, is a good guess.

GIBBONS: Would that be a minimum or maximum, conservative or liberal?

WITNESS: It would be in the ball park, sir. I haven't looked lately.

GIBBONS: And tell me, if you will, were you instructor pilot of the A-10 at the time that Captain Harry Wahl met his untimely death?

WITNESS: I was commander of an A-10, yes, sir.

GIBBONS: Were you actually his instructor at that time?

WITNESS: Yes, sir.

§7.19   —Descriptions of the Instrumentalities or Scene Involved in the Accident

When possible, the lawyers called witnesses other than the plaintiffs to describe the things involved in the incidents in question. These witnesses provided background information about the relevant instrumentalities involved in the accident or the scene of the accident. For example, Ring called a fellow employee to explain the actual operation of a brake press machine:

RING: What does it do? You depress the pedal; what does that cause to happen on the machine?

WITNESS: It throws the clutch.

RING: When the clutch is thrown in, what happens?

WITNESS: The press starts to turn.

RING: Does it activate the ram in a downward position?

WITNESS: That's right.

RING: When the ram goes down, what happens next?

WITNESS: Well, as long as you have your foot on the pedal, it's going to go.

RING: All right. Well, assume then you take your foot off the pedal. What happens to the ram then?

WITNESS: The machine stops; the ram stops.

RING: Does that disengage the clutch?

WITNESS: Right.

RING: And by disengaging the clutch, the ram goes up?

WITNESS: The clutch.

RING: All right. And you take your foot off the pedal, and it disengages the clutch?

WITNESS: Right.

RING: What happens to the machine next?

WITNESS: It simply stops. As long as you have your foot on the pedal, the machine will go; you take your foot off the pedal, the machine stops.

RING: Does it stop when the ram is in the downward position?

WITNESS: No, it just—the ram goes up and down as long as you have your foot on the pedal.

RING: When you take your foot off the pedal—

WITNESS: It will keep going as long as you have your foot on the pedal, whether it's electrical or mechanical. It's not a punch press where you hit it once and it goes down and up. With a brake, when you have your foot on the pedal, whether it's electrical or mechanical, it will keep going until you take your foot off or your hand off the button.

RING: Okay. Is the function of a brake spring the same in both a mechanical pedal and an electrical switch?

WITNESS: Yes.

. . . .

RING: We are talking about the clutch only. When you let go of the switch in an air-activated device, the clutch disengages; but it doesn't disengage instantaneously?

WITNESS: Yes, it does.

RING: It disengages instantly?

WITNESS: Yes.

RING: What lets the air out? Does it go out in a psss sound?

WITNESS: There is a device that lets the air out. It has a sound.

RING: So, when you lift up on the button, the device would go "psss?"

WITNESS: Right.

RING: And you hear that each time you take your hand off?

WITNESS: Right.

RING: In the mechanical foot pedal type then, you would not have that sound?

WITNESS: No, you wouldn't.

RING: Is there a difference in the speed of the ram as it goes up and down in the electrical air system and the mechanical foot system as a result of the difference in the engaging of the clutch?

WITNESS: No, there wouldn't be.

RING: What I am trying to figure out is how, during the period of time that the air is still compressed but is being released, that moving disc has jumped away from the other disc. How does that happen instantly?

WITNESS: It does.

RING: It does. All right.

WITNESS: I presume that would be your difference between the mechanical pedal and the electrical pedal, where you could actually— with a mechanical pedal you could ease it in.

RING: So that you could engage it more slowly?

WITNESS: Where it would go a little.

RING: When you are trying to touch the machine, as you showed with a piece of paper? When you are trying to touch the ram to the piece?

WITNESS: Right.

RING: You use the mechanical foot pedal and don't depress it all the way?

WITNESS: Right.

. . . .

RING: Is there a flywheel type of mechanism on these press brakes that keeps the inertia going, the clutch going, so that the power is not diminished by the engaging of the clutch?

WITNESS: There is a flywheel.

RING: And the purpose of the flywheel is to keep the momentum of the power source going rather than having it die down each time you engage the clutch?

WITNESS: Right.

RING: Is the flywheel turned directly by the power source, or is it turned through a gear system?

WITNESS: A belt.

. . . .

RING: On this particular machine, when the operator would engage the double-run buttons, by engaging the buttons, what activity would begin when the operator engaged the buttons?

WITNESS: Well, it would push in the clutch for the press to go.

RING: Would this engage the clutch?

WITNESS: Yes.

RING: When he pushed it in, would that engage the clutch?

WITNESS: Yes, it would.

RING: And by engaging the clutch, what would that accomplish?

WITNESS: That would make the ram go up and down.

RING: Would it come up automatically?

WITNESS: No, it wouldn't.

RING: What would have to be done in order to bring the ram up after it had come down and made the mold?

WITNESS: He would have to hold his hands on the buttons.

RING: Would he continually keep his hands on the buttons throughout the complete operation?

WITNESS: That's right.

RING: If he took his hands off the buttons when the ram was down on the die, would the ram stay down?

WITNESS: If he took his hands off the buttons, the press would stop.

§7.20   —How the Injury Occurred

The lawyers elicited facts from these witnesses about how the injury occurred, the condition of the instrumentality after the injury, and observations of injury. For example, Ring elicited the witness's account of how the machine in question behaved during normal operation, how he was drawn to the plaintiff's injury upon hearing the plaintiff's screams of pain, and the continuing operation of the machine after he had attempted to shut it off. Ring elicited information about how the machine was operating differently at the time of the accident than it had on past occasions, and how his examination of the machine revealed a broken spring.

Similarly, Block elicited testimony from an eyewitness about how the howitzer explosion occurred, and the condition of the plaintiff immediately afterwards:

> BLOCK: Continue, please, tell us what you observed, what you heard. Everything your senses told you about this accident that you can recollect.
>
> WITNESS: During that time lapse—I'm trying to think. It's been so long. I know—the reason why I know of the time lapse is because at that particular point we were going to swap positions on the gun because so many rounds had fired and what happens is like again, safety is involved, whereas a guy is constantly in that one position, he may make an error, whereas he is doing that same thing and he feels so confident that he is doing the same thing, there is chance of error, so what we usually do is in some type of break we usually change positions on the gun and at that particular time, waiting for—you see, my job, duty, was all over.
>
> The round was in the tube so I was going to swap my position with Mr. Baird and the new loader was going to take my position inside the turret of the gun and I stepped out and I was all set to take over Mr. Baird's job and he said, "Let's wait until this round is fired."
>
> The next thing I knew was, all I saw was an explosion and red, and fire, and I got hit in the leg and I got thrown 25, 30 feet from the spot I was in and all I heard was a scream and a yell and somebody yelling about a leg and I thought we got hit. I thought it was the enemy hitting us. I don't know, everybody like more or less ran over to Alabama because his leg was bleeding. We didn't want him to fully know what had happened to his leg because it wasn't something pretty to see. We were trying to keep his head down and he wanted to see it. We were putting tourniquets and stuffing rags in his leg, tried to stop the bleeding.
>
> · · · ·
>
> BLOCK: You told us that you observed the condition of the men after the explosion. What did you do then?

WITNESS: I was screaming because I was hit in the leg myself. I tried to help Alabama and Doc, which was the doctor at the time, came over and he more or less took care of what was going on.

Then from that position there I crawled over to see where Mr. Burns was and Mr. Burns was up—he was lying face down in a puddle. It was by the crew. A couple of guys rolled him over and tried to revive him and started to give him mouth to mouth resuscitation. All I know, I was hysterical. I was nervous and there was things happening and guys screaming and we just didn't really know what had gone on.

The next thing I realized, there was a chopper coming in, which is a helicopter to pick us up and they evacuated us to a hospital. When I hit the hospital bed I was knocked out and I didn't come to until the next morning.

Habush questioned an eyewitness about his account of how the forklift accident occurred:

HABUSH: Did you have occasion to witness an incident in which a forklift truck driven by Roger Schulz went off the dock and he injured himself?

WITNESS: Yes, sir.

HABUSH: How was your attention drawn to the incident just before it happened?

WITNESS: I had to stop as I came out of the cooler, because I had to wait for him to go into the truck. Because he was blocking the aisle to the trailer that I was going to load.

HABUSH: Did you see Roger Schulz operating the forklift truck then?

WITNESS: Yes, sir.

HABUSH: And what type of forklift was he operating?

WITNESS: A Yale.

HABUSH: I show you what has been marked as Exhibit 5-C. And is this a picture of the Yale forklift truck that he was operating?

WITNESS: Yes, sir.

HABUSH: Had you operated this yourself?

WITNESS: Yes, I have.

HABUSH: What did you see Mr. Schulz doing when you first saw him?

WITNESS: He was on the Yale starting to go into the truck.

HABUSH: Were you able to see the metal ramp that he was traveling on just before he went into the truck?

WITNESS: Yes, sir.

HABUSH: What were you able to observe about the relative level of the truck and the dock itself?

WITNESS: They're just about level, even.

HABUSH: Did you watch Mr. Schulz going into the truck?

WITNESS: Yes, sir.

HABUSH: What did you see him do with the truck itself before the truck started rolling away? What did you observe him doing?

WITNESS: He was going in to pick up a pallet of potatoes.

HABUSH: Did you see the pallet of the potatoes on the truck?

WITNESS: Yes.

HABUSH: Could you tell us how close to the rear edge of the truck the pallets appeared to be?

WITNESS: About a foot inside.

HABUSH: Can you tell us whether or not you saw the forks of the fork-lift truck actually go into the pallet?

WITNESS: Yes, sir.

HABUSH: Can you tell us what you observed about that?

WITNESS: I observed that they were just about going in when the truck started moving forward.

HABUSH: Do you recall where about the front wheels of Roger's forklift truck was at the time the truck started moving forward?

WITNESS: On the lip of the straight job.

HABUSH: Where would that be with respect to the outer edge of the truck?

WITNESS: That would be extended out, depending, about eight to ten inches. They have got a lip on the straight job trucks.

HABUSH: When you say the straight job trucks, you're talking about that truck we showed Mr. Maldonado, a Pre-Pac truck?

WITNESS: Yes, sir, a straight job.

HABUSH: When you observed the truck starting to move forward, did you observe anything about the truck with respect to whether it went higher or lower or stayed the same?

WITNESS: It went lower.

HABUSH: And I'm talking about the straight truck, the delivery truck.

WITNESS: Right, it went lower.

HABUSH: What did you see happen to Roger's forklift truck?

WITNESS: It started tilting backwards and going down into the pit.

HABUSH: Did you observe this from the time it started going backwards until the time it hit the floor?

WITNESS: Yes, sir.

HABUSH: Could you tell us what you observed about Roger? Did he stay inside the forklift operator's space?

WITNESS: Yes.

HABUSH: Could you tell us whether or not he fell out of the forklift truck?

WITNESS: No, he did not.

HABUSH: Did you watch this accident sequence happen?

WITNESS: Yes.

HABUSH: What did you observe about Roger's back and the dock itself as he went down?

WITNESS: He was pressed up against the dock as he was going down in the Yale.

HABUSH: What did you observe as to whether or not or what happened with respect to the edge of the dock as it touched the forklift truck, when it first touched the forklift?

WITNESS: When it first touched the forklift truck, it slid up and hit his back.

HABUSH: Where did you see the dock hit his back? Did you see it hit what portion of his back or where on his back?

WITNESS: Lower back up.

HABUSH: Did you observe the forklift truck kind of sliding down the dock?

WITNESS: Yes.

HABUSH: What did it appear like to you?

WITNESS: It appeared like he was being crushed.

HABUSH: What did his body look like it was doing as it was being crushed?

WITNESS: He just started slumping.

HABUSH: Did you see the forklift when it hit the bottom of the dock?

WITNESS: Yes, sir.

HABUSH: And how did that appear?

WITNESS: Just fell and landed stationary.

HABUSH: Was Roger still in the forklift truck?

WITNESS: Yes, he was. He was slumped over unconscious.

HABUSH: At any time did you see Roger's rear end come out of the back of the forklift truck and bounce on the dock itself?

WITNESS: No, I didn't.

HABUSH: Are you certain of that?

WITNESS: I'm pretty certain of that.

.   .   .   .

HABUSH: Lou, did you observe the—you said you observed the forklift truck that Mr. Schulz was using. Had you seen that dock or that type of forklift truck being used to unload straight trucks or smaller trucks before?

WITNESS: Straight trucks like his, but not no smaller ones.

HABUSH: Pardon me?

WITNESS: Straight trucks like Pre-Pac's.

HABUSH: That's what I mean.

WITNESS: Right, I seen it being used.

HABUSH: Had you personally seen it done on occasion?

WITNESS: Yes.

HABUSH: And with respect to the operation that Roger was doing, that's attempting to get the forks under the pallets at the end of the truck, did that strike you as anything unusual?

WITNESS: No.

HABUSH: Had you seen other employees at Kohl's do similar unloading operations with a docker on the ramp in a truck about the size of the Pre-Pac truck before?

WITNESS: Yes.

HABUSH: Had you personally done it?

WITNESS: Yes.

Gibbons presented the story of the pilot who saw the plaintiff's aircraft go down. Throughout the story, in an effort to prove the ejection was not required by the deceased pilot's error, Gibbons elicited opinions to the effect that the deceased followed proper flight procedure and executed proper flight maneuvers:

GIBBONS: Did you have a briefing with Captain Harry Wahl prior to that confidence maneuver in which he met his death?

WITNESS: Yes, sir.

GIBBONS: And what is a briefing?

WITNESS: A briefing is where the instructor and the student sit down and cover all of the items to be covered in the flight in detail. And I instruct with the techniques, the way he's supposed to do it, the mechanical requirements plus the actual technique of how he's supposed to accomplish the maneuver, the sequence they are going to be done.

. . . .

GIBBONS: I'll ask you to state whether or not you followed those briefing guides?

WITNESS: Yes, sir.

GIBBONS: What is rest criteria?

WITNESS: We're speaking of crew rest, sir. It's a 12-hour period from shutdown of engines until reporting to squadron for your next mission. It's minimum required time including four hours of recreation and eight hours of rest.

GIBBONS: Tell us whether or not Captain Wahl had met the rest—crew rest criteria.

WITNESS: To the best of my knowledge, yes sir.

GIBBONS: Had you met it?

WITNESS: Yes, sir.

GIBBONS: I will ask you did you make any observations of Captain Wahl's physical condition at the time of his briefing and prior to take-off?

WITNESS: Yes, sir.

GIBBONS: Could you tell us what you recall about that?

WITNESS: He seemed alert and ready to fly.

.   .   .   .

GIBBONS: And you began the specific confidence maneuver approximately what time?

WITNESS: 10 minutes of 3:00 p.m.

GIBBONS: Now, what was your role to be during this flight, please, Major Butler?

WITNESS: I would give him the lead and as the—in command of the flight, I would chase.

GIBBONS: Would you also instruct?

WITNESS: Oh, yes, sir.

GIBBONS: All right. And where were you to be as far as close or non-close to him during this maneuver?

WITNESS: I would be a little bit further away than during other maneuvers. However, I would be, as they say, padlocked where I would have a visual on him at all times.

.   .   .   .

GIBBONS: Now, did you observe whether or not there was an ejection by Captain Harry Wahl and a crash of his A-10 aircraft?

WITNESS: Yes, sir, I did.

GIBBONS: Can you explain to us and please take the A-10 model, if it would be of assistance to you and/or the jury, what your observations were as you and Captain Wahl went through the confidence maneuver. First, what altitude were you at and what were your instructions and just trace the flight path, if you will, up to the point of ejection with the model airplane?

WITNESS: All right, sir. We were at approximately 19,000—a little over 19,000 MSL which is above mean sea level. The area we were directly over was approximately 4,000 to 4,500 feet to the ground.

.   .   .   .

GIBBONS: Go ahead.

WITNESS: We lined up for the maneuver. He was then in the lead and I went back to his rear right quarter, approximately 600 to 1,000 feet away in chase . . . at which time I began to talk to him and we rehashed quickly some of the fine points of what the confidence maneuver was going to be. Specifically that everything was locked and stowed.

. . . .

GIBBONS: And did he roger back as to whether or not he was secure in the seat?

WITNESS: Yes, he acknowledged me. I think he said "Roger" or "Yeah."

GIBBONS: All right. And would that mean both lap belt and shoulder harness?

WITNESS: I would assume so, yes, sir.

GIBBONS: All right. Please continue with your—after you got that acknowledgement, what happened next?

WITNESS: Okay, sir. Then I also mentioned about the throttles. And this maneuver is such that prior to passing 45 degrees of positive pitch—here he is straight and level, wings level flight—now, that's about 45 degrees and that's 90.

Prior to passing that 45 degrees, his throttles were to be in the idle position, both throttles. I told him that he would call me prior to that 45 degrees, tell me his throttles were on idle or I would abort his maneuver.

. . . .

GIBBONS: All right. Did he acknowledge where his throttles were?

WITNESS: As we pressed on into the maneuver, he did, sir.

GIBBONS: All right. And at what degree was his airplane toward the horizon or above the horizon, if you will, when he put his throttles back to idle?

WITNESS: As he began his maneuver, the nose started to come up and I reminded him, I said, "Throttles." He says, "Throttles coming to idle. Idle." And that was approximately 30 degrees of pitch.

GIBBONS: All right. What happened next then?

WITNESS: He continued the maneuver.

GIBBONS: All right. And please go through the maneuver, if you will, Major.

WITNESS: There was a new limit on the confidence maneuver in that we used to go to 90 degrees or a very healthy pitch up. There was a restriction that you would not go beyond 80 degrees. He pulled the nose up, throttles at idle, and got to approximately 70 degrees nose high was my estimation.

At this time I was in a spiral, starting to turn around him, and at this point his airspeed would bleed off. He got to that pitch and I said, "What do you have?" Not that he should respond but for him to look out and see what he had, estimate his own, check his attitude indicator to see how it felt.

Also, from the briefing, he was to monitor the stick, which I also mentioned. Monitoring a stick is when you move the aircraft to go in this direction and it's in transit. You're pulling back on the stick so that the elevators move so that the nose will go up, at which time he hit the attained degree he thought was about 80, which was actually about 70 at which time he neutralized the controls. It's almost the same thing as if you're flying straight and level here except you're running out of airspeed going up in this direction.

. . . .

GIBBONS: Your observations that you saw and observed and where you were?

WITNESS: Okay. If you can picture that we're talking about several miles. Okay. He began the maneuver and I got him up to the 70 degrees or he got up to the 70 degrees at which time I was turning back in front of him at a higher rate of speed.

He got to the apex and after I had also told him, "What do you have? Check your attitude" type of thing. "Check airspeed." Then the aircraft, as it ran down to essentially zero knots, it began to fall off on the tail slightly. And then the nose fell through and I said, "Let it fall through."

All the time he's not making any control movements with the stick. And the aircraft fell through straight ahead and the nose came down not quite to the vertical. He never went past the vertical on 90 degrees straight down negative pitch attitude. He never quite went past the vertical, just fell straight down in kind of a hammerhead and came down.

The only thing that I saw of any motion whatsoever as he passed, the right wing dipped about five or 10 degrees, just very light dip. And that was the only roll or yaw I saw in the whole maneuver.

I said, "Good maneuver." It was excellent. It was classical. And I said, "Check—"

. . . .

GIBBONS: Now, go on through from the apex down. What happened?

WITNESS: Okay. He got his nose down. He was picking up airspeed about that time and I had cut—as his nose had dropped through, I cut behind him and I turned again coming around the outside. I was in a very tight spiral because the conditions were excellent. I said, "Check 150" which means check for 150 knots on the airspeed indicator. At that time he looks down.

If you try to pull on the stick before 150 knots, you'll get what they call a secondary stall and the aircraft won't recover. It will stall or shake on you. You need enough flying airspeed and instead of using engines to get the power to get you going, you just use gravity. It falls down till you get 150 knots and at that point you start pulling back on the stick to recover.

GIBBONS: Pulling back on the stick like I'm doing?

WITNESS: That's correct, straight back to make the elevators go up.

GIBBONS: And what happened, based upon what you observed?

WITNESS: What happened was that he pulled the nose up and then stabilized approximately 15 degrees below straight and level flight.

GIBBONS: What did you do then? Where were you and what did you do?

WITNESS: I was coming around him and I said "Hey Harry, get your nose up. We want to stay up here" because we wanted to use the altitude for some more maneuvers that required this altitude. And I saw a positive nose-up motion and it came not quite to wings level straight and level flight. It was only momentary. So I passed around behind him—oh, I also said, "Get your nose up. We want to stay up here. Acknowledge." What I'm saying there is I want him to start responding, acknowledging my radio calls. The nose did not come up. However, there was no response. At this time I was trying to get—trying to pull up so I could get back towards the chase position, and I noted that the nose transition smoothly down to approximately 20 degrees nose low.

GIBBONS: So what did you do at that point?

WITNESS: At that time I tried calling him again on FM, frequency modulated radio which has a discrete frequency which we can talk airplane-to-airplane without bothering anybody else. I called several times on FM. At that time I kicked a rudder which will get the nose to come down from where I was flying, unloaded the aircraft. In other words, I released the G forces which is an acceleration type maneuver and went full to mill power. At the time his nose went down to about 20 degrees, nose low. He started to accelerate away from me.

. . . .

GIBBONS: What did you do then?

WITNESS: At that point I turned in and dropped down into a chase position which was actually now a tail chase position. And I estimated approximately 3,000. It turned out that when we finally measured the wings and I checked the mills, it was actually about 3,500 feet and I was sitting above him about 1,000, 2,000 feet. 3,500 feet in trail about half a nautical mile, a little more, and I was paralleling his flight path and trying to figure out why he was in a steady state 20-degree dive, as straight as an arrow.

I called him several times. How many times, I don't remember now, UHF and VHF. UHF was a common frequency for the area. It's like AM-FM radio in your car and you have the option of talking on either one. He continued to accelerate away.

At that point we were starting to get close to—closer to the ground. As you get lower, if you look outside an airplane window you'll notice that the horizon tends to move a little faster when you get lower to the ground. I picked it up in my peripheral vision. I noticed we were getting lower and I thought, "We're going to have to get him out."

There was no radio communication. The last communication I heard was, "Throttles coming to idle. Idle," back up as he initiated the maneuver. I'm in a tail chase with the aircraft, and as I was watching the aircraft, getting ready to bail him out because 2,000 feet is the controlled bail-out altitude . . . I could barely see the top of the airplane, the top of the engines and top of the wing from my vantage point.

. . . .

GIBBONS: So what did you do, Major Butler?

WITNESS: I watched the airplane for a second and I noticed that the nose dipped. It began to dip beyond 20 degrees . . . I saw the nose start to dip and I saw the two dots like the nose was going down further and I noticed the transition even lower.

. . . .

GIBBONS: After you saw the nacelles, what did you do?

WITNESS: At that point, I'm uniform, very forcefully said, "Bail out. Bail out. Bail out." Just about that fast.

GIBBONS: And what happened?

WITNESS: I got the "bail out bail," and there was a puff of white smoke, and at that point the nose rapidly started to nose down. And the puff of white smoke—I said, "It can't be." Just—I saw smoke. It couldn't have hit the ground and then the belly of the airplane—and then I padlocked on the smoke. In other words, it was "bail out bail" and then just rapidly increased its rate to go nose low.

GIBBONS: And what happened to the aircraft—well, was that when Captain Wahl ejected?

WITNESS: That was, it turned out to be, when Captain Wahl ejected the white smoke.

GIBBONS: All right.

WITNESS: I thought I saw an orange and black dot come out, but I could not be sure.

§7.21 —Concluding Questions

The lawyers concluded their testimony with questions that summed up, repeated, and reinforced important points. For example, Ring concluded his examination of the plaintiff's coworker by eliciting questions that demonstrated that when the worker set up the machine and tested it two days before the injury, the machine functioned properly and that the ram action on the machine stopped when the operator took his hands off the buttons of the machine. This testimony stood in contrast with testimony of the improper functioning of the machine on the day of the injury.

§7.22   —Use of Language

The lawyers again used simple, direct language. The occurrence witnesses were all lay witnesses or co-employees who happened to be at the scene of the occurrence. Therefore, the lawyers spoke in simple, everyday language.

§7.23   —Form of Questions

The lawyers questioned these witnesses in much the same manner as they questioned the plaintiffs. Fewer leading questions were asked, probably because they were neutral witnesses rather than their own clients. However, the questions were narrow questions calling for specific answers. The witnesses were led through the testimony in a step-by-step fashion with few questions calling for descriptive, narrative answers. For example, Ring questioned the coworker as follows:

> RING: Did the machine operate properly during that test cycle?
>
> WITNESS: Yes, it did.
>
> RING: As a part of the operation, do you make sure that you can stop the ram at any point that you want to? Did you make that kind of test?
>
> WITNESS: I have to.
>
> RING: And that includes half-way down and half-way up and three-quarters of the way down at the bottom?
>
> WITNESS: That's right.
>
> RING: You made all these tests?
>
> WITNESS: Yes.
>
> RING: And they all worked?
>
> WITNESS: Yes.
>
> RING: And each time you then made the test, did you do it by releasing the buttons to stop the machine?
>
> WITNESS: Yes, I did.

§7.24   Fact Witnesses with Respect to Injuries and Damages

These witnesses were nonexperts called to elicit testimony about the nature and extent of the plaintiff's damages. They included family members and coworkers.

§7.25   —Structure

The testimony of these witnesses focused on the facts of the plaintiff's injuries and damages. Their testimony was presented chronologically, beginning with background information about themselves followed by descriptions of how the injury damaged the plaintiff.

§7.26 —Background

The background information elicited from these witnesses focused on their relationship to the plaintiff and descriptive information about the plaintiff's physical condition prior to the accident. The information about the plaintiff's prior good health was used to contrast the plaintiff's prior good condition with the resulting injuries. For example, Spence established that Karen Silkwood's mother and sisters had grown up with her and had knowledge of her prior mental and physical condition. He then asked questions that elicited testimony about Karen Silkwood's healthy prior mental and physical condition. Spence used two types of questions to elicit this information. Initially, he propounded questions that asked for general statements about her past conditions, such as "was she healthy," "was she affectionate," and "how did she do in school." These general questions were followed up with questions that called for anecdotal descriptions that provided specific illustrations of her health, affection, intelligence, and popularity. In questioning Karen Silkwood's mother, Spence asked:

SPENCE: Okay. In the course of her growing up and going to school, did she show some special talent in certain areas?

WITNESS: Yes. She was always very smart in chemistry, biology, and math. That was her best subjects in school.

SPENCE: All right. And did she—show well did she do well in school?

WITNESS: She did so well that they put her in an accelerated class. She had an advanced chemistry class with 32 boys. There were two more girls that started out in the advanced class, but if you didn't keep your grades up to a certain average you couldn't stay in the accelerated class, and Karen was the only girl in the class with 32 boys. And, I talked to her teacher about that because I really didn't care for her being in the class with just boys, but the teacher assured me that Karen could keep up with her lab work and chemistry work just as well as any of the boys, and that as long as she could do that that they would not take her out of the accelerated class.

SPENCE: I guess that kind of shows that the women are as smart as men, doesn't?

WITNESS: Sometimes; yes sir.

SPENCE: And, Mrs. Silkwood, that class was an advanced chemistry class, wasn't it?

WITNESS: Yes, sir.

SPENCE: Did she have a special relationship with that teacher there?

WITNESS: Yes. She babysat for him. And then later on when they had their first little daughter they named her after Karen.

Glaser called the plaintiff's daughter to testify about the plaintiff's condition prior to the unnecessary hysterectomy:

GLASER: What were the relations between your parents like, before the surgery?

WITNESS: They were a very loving couple, warm, they loved each other. There was a lot of warmth. You could look at them and feel it. They really cared for each other.

GLASER: And what was your mother like before, in appearance, before this surgery?

WITNESS: Well, people thought she was my sister when we went places. She was thin, she had a nice figure, an attractive woman. Her skin was in very good condition, like mine. She was just a real attractive, physically active person—physically attractive person.

GLASER: Just before the surgery, did you notice any bump on her abdomen?

WITNESS: Not at all, she had an excellent figure.

GLASER: And was she productive?

WITNESS: Very productive.

GLASER: Briefly, what did she do? Very briefly.

WITNESS: Active. We went to all kinds of places. We went to dances.

GLASER: Did she dance?

WITNESS: She danced.

GLASER: Did she live to dance?

WITNESS: She did, yes.

GLASER: Go ahead.

WITNESS: She even when—my—we even went jogging three times a week.

GLASER: She participated?

WITNESS: She participated in that. We—some nights we went out to dinner after work. We were always going places. We went on many cruises, about seven or eight cruises.

. . . .

GLASER: Mother looked, well on those cruises and—

WITNESS: Oh, she really was an attractive women.

GLASER: She had a good time?

WITNESS: A good time. A lot of joy, a lot of laughter, just having a fantastic time, enjoying ourselves.

. . . .

GLASER: What was your mother's condition of health before the hysterectomy?

WITNESS: She was an attractive person. She was full of energy, she was never tired. She would clean the house, cook. She did everything, the laundry, she would mow the grass, she would shovel snow. She was always doing something. We went out. Her social life was very full, people came over, she cooked, entertained.

Glaser presented the testimony of a friend of the plaintiff's daughter to demonstrate the plaintiff's good health prior to her injury:

GLASER: Mrs. Ross, are you a friend of Mrs. Lewis?

WITNESS: I'm a friend of her daughter, yes.

GLASER: Her daughter. And you now live in Texas?

WITNESS: Yes, I do.

GLASER: When did you move down there?

WITNESS: 1979.

GLASER: And before you moved down to Texas, did you know the Lewis family?

WITNESS: Yes, I did.

GLASER: Did you socialize with them before?

WITNESS: Yes, I did.

GLASER: And frequently?

WITNESS: Yes.

GLASER: Visit their home?

WITNESS: Yes.

GLASER: They visited you?

WITNESS: Yes, they did.

GLASER: How far away did you live?

WITNESS: Walking distance, about five blocks.

GLASER: And did you get to know the family?

WITNESS: Yes, I did.

GLASER: And just tell us you—the occasions that you'd meet Mrs. Lewis.

WITNESS: Mrs. Lewis quite frequently would participate in community functions that I was a part of, my sorority would sponsor charitable activities and she would participate with them. She would sell tickets, she would buy a ticket for luncheons. My church would give dances, boat rides. She would come to the dances and dance and just have a good time.

GLASER: I see. And did you visit the home, their home?

WITNESS: Yes, I did.

GLASER: Did you eat dinner at their home?

WITNESS: Yes.

GLASER: And who would cook, by the way?

WITNESS: Mrs. Lewis.

GLASER: Is she a good cook?

WITNESS: You can see, yes.

. . . .

GLASER: Before Misericordia Hospital.

WITNESS: She was very attractive, radiant. She had a look of life to her, very—she had a very active, energetic look.

GLASER: What about her personality?

WITNESS: She was very independent. I mean she was a housewife, a mother, she maintained the responsibility and the role of a mother. Self-reliant. Independent is the word, basically very independent.

GLASER: How did she walk?

WITNESS: Like I walk, very normally—I mean well.

GLASER: And did she seem to be a happy person?

WITNESS: Yes.

§7.27   —Nature and Extent of Damages

The lawyers elicited facts from these witnesses about how the plaintiff had been injured and damaged, and how their lives had been changed. The lawyers asked questions that elicited both general information about their damages and specific anecdotal descriptions of how the injuries had affected them. The general descriptions were necessary to describe the plaintiffs' damages, but consistent with the storytelling structure, specific anecdotes of how the plaintiffs' lives had been changed were more dramatic and illustrative of the plaintiffs' plight. For example, Spence asked Karen Silkwood's sister to tell the jury about phone calls she received from Karen Silkwood prior to her death:

SPENCE: Now, relative to those last phone calls in October, would you tell the ladies and gentlemen of the jury what those telephone calls were about?

WITNESS: She was scared. She asked me to come and visit her—

SPENCE: And what time of the day would you receive them?

WITNESS: At night, or in the late evening.

SPENCE: All right. Now, what did she say to you?

WITNESS: Well, she was scared, very scared. She was very hysterical, upset, and she wouldn't tell me anything over the phone. She just told me something was happening to her.

SPENCE: Now, when she said to you that "something was happening to her," and you said she was hysterical—

WITNESS: Yes, sir.

SPENCE: —was that the way your sister ordinarily was?

WITNESS: Never.

SPENCE: And what was she—how do you—you say hysterical. What made you come to the conclusion—what was she doing to make you think she was hysterical?

WITNESS: Crying. She couldn't get the words out—some women would get upset and they start crying in such a way that they can't express theirselves to tell someone exactly what they are trying to say.

· · · ·

SPENCE: I see. In November, the first part of November, just a few days before her death, did you have a telephone conversation in which she discussed with you any of her fears?

WITNESS: Yes.

SPENCE: What did she day?

WITNESS: She told me that she only had five years to live—that she was going to die.

Habush presented the testimony of the plaintiff's wife to explain how the injury had dramatically altered their lives:

HABUSH: At Froedtert when he became more alert how would you describe how he was reacting to what was going on?

WITNESS: He cried a lot. I thought we were carrying on an intelligent conversation, but in questioning him later I realized that he remembered very little of the months that he was at Froedtert. He just was on a lot of medication. He was in a lot of pain. He cried a lot. I guess he knew I was there, but he didn't remember it.

HABUSH: When was it that you first found out that Roger would be paralyzed permanently?

WITNESS: The day after his back surgery on my birthday, June 26th.

HABUSH: Did you discuss that with Roger afterwards, or had he been told by the doctor, or didn't you remember?

WITNESS: I don't remember.

HABUSH: When he went from Froedtert over to VA, what particularly seemed to bother him the most attitude-wise?

WITNESS: He was concerned that I would leave him. He didn't know what the children were going to say. He didn't know what he was going to do.

HABUSH: Were you able to determine why he was so concerned about you leaving him?

WITNESS: At Froedtert Hospital one of the nurses had told me that the divorce rate for a marriage like ours was eighty-five percent, and I was out to prove them wrong.

HABUSH: Did he have any continuing concerns at Veterans?

WITNESS: Yes.

HABUSH: And how did he express that? Why was he concerned?

WITNESS: He was just so terribly frustrated at Froedtert. He was with people in chairs and he saw how they coped, and he coped, and he just didn't think he was able to.

HABUSH: Was it difficult when you got him home?

WITNESS: About the end of September as part of his rehab they allowed him to come home on weekends, and I would pick him up on a Saturday morning and I would take him home on a Sunday night. This was to get him used to coming home and to get him accustomed to things.

It proved to be extremely exhausting for both of us. Roger felt insecure at home because he was used to the attention and the security of the hospital. I, of course, didn't know what to do because I didn't have the proper equipment at home. For example, at night when he was supposed to be turned every four hours I had to take a slip sheet and turn him myself. I don't have the strength to turn him. And so I would drop him off on a Sunday evening thinking how are we ever going to manage?

HABUSH: You have subsequently, of course? He now has his trapeze?

WITNESS: Yes.

HABUSH: And you work that out?

WITNESS: Right.

HABUSH: At VA he did receive some training in self-care and driving the van and everything like that?

WITNESS: Right.

HABUSH: During the first year or two were you doing some things or had to do some things that he used to do around the house?

WITNESS: Pretty much all of it.

HABUSH: And were you able to observe how this affected him?

WITNESS: He had very little self-worth because he couldn't do anything.

HABUSH: How was he with respect to going out in public during the first year?

WITNESS: When he was discharged October 31st, that winter was just beginning to set in. He had no transportation, so if we went anywhere I drove and he transferred into the passenger seat of my car. When he got his van he still felt a little apprehensive about going out especially in the wintertime.

HABUSH: The van has made a big difference?

WITNESS: Yes, very big difference.

HABUSH: Able to get out?

WITNESS: Right.

HABUSH: How did you finally get him out of the house to start seeing people again and going to restaurants and stuff? How did you work that miracle?

WITNESS: I guess I pushed and prodded and cajoled and nagged to go to a movie, to go out to a restaurant, and before we did I would always call and make reservations and tell them that one in our party was in a wheelchair and would they please seat us at a table that wouldn't interrupt anyone else while they were eating and find out if it was accessible.

HABUSH: Did you have some disappointments in that regard?

WITNESS: We had some disappointments. We also had some positive experiences, but one of the disappointments was one of the restaurants I had called had said, yes, they were accessible, and when we got there there were six steps. I had to go in and two bartenders came out and carried Roger in. This happened to be on our anniversary.

HABUSH: What does he do around the house or been able to do around the house the last couple of years?

WITNESS: He has learned to cook.

HABUSH: How does he do that?

WITNESS: Pretty good. He does a limited amount of housework. Most of all he really helped with the kids. Our youngest just turned sixteen this summer and has her driver's license, so Roger's chauffeuring jobs pretty much have been taken care of.

HABUSH: With respect to his self-consciousness or lack of it in going out, has that gotten better as the years have gone on?

WITNESS: Yes, it has been a gradual process.

HABUSH: How would you describe his attitude today as compared to a couple of years ago?

WITNESS: Well, I think he has made remarkable strides.

HABUSH: Have you and Roger been able to have any kind of normal sexual relationship since the accident?

WITNESS: No.

HABUSH: Does it appear to concern him and bother him that you are able to observe?

WITNESS: Yes.

HABUSH: How about you? Have you been able to adjust to that?

WITNESS: It was a terrible loss for us, but it wasn't the only reason that I married him. And it is probably different for a man than it is for a woman. It bothers him a lot.

HABUSH: And your love for him today?

WITNESS: Is the same.

HABUSH: And will be forever?

WITNESS: I didn't marry him just for his body; I married him for other things.

After having the family friend testify as to the plaintiff's good condition prior to the surgery, Glaser elicited testimony about the plaintiff's bad condition after the surgery:

GLASER: Within several months after March of 1977, what did you notice about her?

WITNESS: Well, she was in bed most of the time.

GLASER: What did you notice about her face?

WITNESS: The radiancy was gone. She was not independent anymore. It's like the role sort of reversed, she became dependent on her family. She just had a loss of life, she just looked very listless and—

GLASER: Okay. Now, you were in New York until when?

WITNESS: 1979.

GLASER: When in 1979?

WITNESS: May.

GLASER: And thereafter, you went to Houston, right?

WITNESS: Yes.

GLASER: And did you visit New York from time to time?

WITNESS: Well, I still have a family here.

GLASER: How many times a year do you visit?

WITNESS: About four times a year.

GLASER: And have you visited the Lewises on each visit?

WITNESS: Every—as often as I can when I come to New York.

GLASER: And up until today, what have you noticed about Mrs. Lewis?

WITNESS: She seemed to have deteriorated from the times that I've seen her. She just seemed to deteriorate.

GLASER: All of the things that you found within several months, are they better or worse or the same?

WITNESS: They appear worse to me.

GLASER: No further questions.

§7.28   —Use of Language

The lawyers again used simple language. These witnesses were all relatives, friends, or co-employees who happened to be involved with the plaintiffs. Therefore, the lawyers spoke in everyday language.

§7.29 —Form of Questions

As with the plaintiffs and the occurrence witnesses, the lawyers used predominantly narrow or leading questions calling for specific responses. Again, the witnesses were led through the testimony in a specific step-by-step fashion with few questions calling for descriptive, narrative answers.

§7.30 Expert Witnesses

Expert witnesses are useful, since they are allowed, by virtue of their training and experience, to go beyond observation and render expert opinions about issues such as causation and the nature and extent of damages. Testifying for the plaintiffs in these trials were medical, economic, engineering, and scientific expert witnesses who testified about the causes of injuries, the nature and extent of injuries, the value of economic losses and future medical expenses, and the causes of machine malfunctions.

§7.31 —Structure

The testimony of these witnesses focused either on the cause of the injury or the nature and extent of damages. Their testimony was presented chronologically, beginning with background information about themselves and their experience with the matters involved in the lawsuit, followed by their opinions on causation or damages.

§7.32 —Background

The background information elicited from these experts was used to enhance their credibility. In some cases, the experts were involved in the cases before the lawyers were hired, such as treating physicians. However, most of the experts were hired by the lawyers to provide key testimony about causation and damages. Thus, one of the rhetorical problems in presenting the testimony of these witnesses was to establish their credibility and avoid their being perceived as "hired guns." The lawyers used the background information to establish their credibility.

Studies indicate that credibility assessments are made by listeners based on the extent to which the speaker appears to exhibit the dimensions of expertness, trustworthiness, and dynamism.[5] Expertness is the extent to which the witness appears to be competent,[6] intelligent, authoritative, trained, experi-

---

[5] Delia, *A Constructivist Analysis of the Concept of Credibility,* 62 QJ Speech 361 (1976).

[6] McCroskey & Young, *Ethos and Credibility: The Construct and Its Measurement After Three Decades,* 32 Cent States Speech J 33 (1981).

enced, skilled, informed,[7] professional,[8] and a source of valid information.[9] Trustworthiness is the extent to which the witness appears to be honest, just, open-minded, friendly,[10] well-mannered, warm,[11] fair, loyal to listeners, and a reliable source of information.[12] Dynamism is the extent to which a witness appears aggressive rather than meek, emphatic rather than hesitant, bold rather than timid, active rather than passive, and energetic rather than tired.[13] The lawyers asked questions that elicited background information that supported projections of these dimensions. The witnesses' education, training, and experience were presented in order to establish these dimensions.

§7.33 —Background Information Used to Establish Expertness

In *Silkwood,* for example, Spence used background information to establish a witness's expertness. The issues in the case were whether Karen Silkwood had been contaminated by plutonium, whether this contamination caused her injury, and whether Kerr-McGee was negligent in its handling of plutonium. Therefore, the case required expert testimony in the areas of nuclear chemistry and medicine. Spence based his case in large part on the testimony of Dr. John W. Gofman. In eliciting background information, Spence established that the witness had a Ph.D. in nuclear chemistry and a Doctor of Medicine degree. Thus, the witness demonstrated training, skill, and experience in both of the required areas of expertise. Spence further established that after his Ph.D. studies, Dr. Gofman was recruited to work with two other scientists to research and discover the chemical properties of plutonium. In the course of these studies, Dr. Gofman developed the procedures for isolating plutonium, patented these procedures, and then gave the patents to the United States government because of his patriotic involvement in the war effort. After helping isolate and produce plutonium for use in creating the atomic bomb, Gofman went into the practice of medicine to study the effects of radiation on the human body. This background information obviously established the witness's expertness in both areas.

Similarly, Habush asked many background questions that allowed his expert to establish his credibility as an expert. Habush first elicited information about the doctor's education in order to establish his qualifications. Then he elicited information about his experience with spinal injuries that further established

---

[7] Berlo, Lemert & Mertz, *Dimensions for Evaluating the Acceptability of Message Sources,* 33 Pub Opinion Q, 563, 575 (1969-1970).

[8] Schweitzer & Ginzberg, *Factors of Communicator Credibility,* in Problems in Social Psychology 94, 99, McGraw-Hill C. Bachman & P. Secord eds (1966).

[9] C. Hovland, I. Janis & H. Kelley, Communication and Persuasion 20 (1953).

[10] Berlo, Lemert & Mertz, *supra* note 7, at 574-75.

[11] Schweitzer & Ginzberg, *supra* note 8, at 98.

[12] C. Hovland, I. Janis & H. Kelley, *supra* note 9, at 23-24, 34.

[13] Berlo, Lemert & Mertz, *supra* note 7, at 574.

his expertness. As noted in §7.32 above, expertness is one of the elements of the expert dimension of credibility. It can be argued that once a witness's educational and training qualifications are established, experience in the particular field further enhances and strengthens credibility. Habush followed this formula, first establishing education and then detailing experience:

HABUSH: Are you a medical doctor, sir?

WITNESS: Yes, I am.

HABUSH: And are you licensed and are your credentials on file with the proper authorities in the state and county in which you practice?

WITNESS: Yes, sir.

HABUSH: Where did you receive your medical school training, Dr. Walsh?

WITNESS: My medical school training was carried out at the Medical College of Wisconsin, formerly Marquette.

HABUSH: And when did you graduate medical school?

WITNESS: I graduated from medical school in June of 1973.

HABUSH: And after you graduated from medical school, did you have any additional training?

WITNESS: Yes, sir, I did.

HABUSH: And what's that?

WITNESS: I served a surgical internship at the Milwaukee County Medical Complex and affiliated hospitals the year after graduation. Subsequently a residency in neurologic surgery, which was completed in July of 19, or June of 1978.

HABUSH: And after you finished your neurological residency, what did you then do?

WITNESS: I took a position as an Assistant Professor of Neurologic Surgery at the Medical College of Wisconsin and its affiliated hospitals, and enrolled as a graduate student and ultimately received a Ph.D. degree in 1984.

HABUSH: And what did you receive your Ph.D. degree in?

WITNESS: My Ph.D. thesis was entitled "Anatomic Correlates Physiological and Spinal Cord Injury in Feline Model."

HABUSH: That sounds like a mouthful. You want to tell us in regular language what that is?

WITNESS: It certainly is a mouthful. It related to mechanisms of injury to the spinal cord in an experimental model.

HABUSH: So this is something that you did as part of your doctorate thesis, the mechanism of injury?

WITNESS: Yes, sir, of the spinal cord.

·   ·   ·   ·

HABUSH: Now, have you been practicing neurosurgical medicine since you completed your training?

WITNESS: Yes, I have.

HABUSH: And where?

WITNESS: At the Medical College of Wisconsin and its affiliated hospitals. I have staff privileges at the Wood, V.A., now the Zablocki V.A. Hospital. As well as the Froedtert Hospital and courtesy privileges at Elmbrook Hospital and I am, I believe the title is consultant, at the Sacred Heart Rehabilitation Hospital.

HABUSH: What type of conditions do you see and treat as neurosurgeon?

WITNESS: As a neurosurgeon, I see a number of conditions affecting the brain, spinal cord, and the peripheral nerves, tumors, trauma, injury, degenerative diseases, any and all of a number of situations which affect the brain, the spinal cord, the peripheral nerves or the bone which enclose the brain and spinal cord.

HABUSH: And in your training did you have any particular contact with paralyzed spinal cord injured?

WITNESS: Yes, I did, I dealt with a number of individuals with spinal cord injury during the course of my training in the first two years in which I served as an assistant professor at the Medical College in the Department of Neurosurgery. After completing my formal residency I was a Fellow of the American, of the Paralyzed Veterans of America.

HABUSH: Where did you do that work?

WITNESS: That work was carried out at the Medical College as well.

HABUSH: You presently have a teaching position?

WITNESS: Yes, sir, I do.

HABUSH: And that's with the Medical College of Wisconsin?

WITNESS: Yes, it is.

HABUSH: And who do you teach?

WITNESS: I teach a number of groups, medical students and graduate level physicians who, some of whom are in a residency program leading to recognition in neurosurgery. Or they may be in our service for a short period of time who are training to become general surgeons or other surgical specialists.

HABUSH: You said that you were board certified as a neurological surgeon?

WITNESS: Yes, sir.

HABUSH: And any specialized organizations?

WITNESS: Yes, sir, I am a member of a number of organizations.

HABUSH: And in connection with your practice, do you have any supervisory or committee chairmanships affecting the hospitals that you are associated with?

WITNESS: Yes, I have a number of committees. I chaired several committees in the past several years. Currently a member of the Institutional Research Committee at the Froedtert Hospital. There are a number of committees I don't necessarily recall until I find out I am late for a meeting.

HABUSH: Dr. Walsh, are you presently involved in any investigation programs on behalf of the National Institute for Occupational Safety and Health?

WITNESS: Yes, I am the principal investigator of a National Institute of Occupational Safety and Health funded study on back problems, back pain in the industry.

HABUSH: Is that going on at the present time?

WITNESS: Yes, it is, sir.

HABUSH: Who is it being funded by?

WITNESS: It's funded by the National Institute of Occupational Safety and Health.

HABUSH: Dr. Walsh, have you published a number of articles, have you not?

WITNESS: Yes, sir.

HABUSH: And in you C.V., which has been marked and which is before us, you list 35 on the first part?

WITNESS: Yes, sir.

HABUSH: There are some abstracts that you have done. What are abstracts?

WITNESS: Abstracts are brief resumes of literature or of investigations which are distributed to individuals who may be attending a meeting. These are a summary of the study that was then discussed in a forum.

HABUSH: Now, you indicated that in your Ph.D. thesis, you did a study involving injury mechanisms, is that correct?

WITNESS: Yes, sir.

HABUSH: Define for the Court and jury what you mean by injury mechanisms or mechanisms of injury.

WITNESS: To define the injury, one has to begin with defining trauma and for the purposes of scientific investigations, trauma, I think, is best considered energy transferred to a biologic system. Any form of energy which acts on the system, including mechanical energy as is often the case in such things as automobile accidents or other injury constitutes any form of energy such as that, constitutes a potential mechanism for injury to the organism.

If the organism receives sufficient input of energy, it may not be able to continue to function normally and injury may occur. Mechanisms of injuries are the specific biomechanical, bioengineering structural or functional changes that occur in the tissue as a result of too much energy input to the tissue.

HABUSH: In connection with that, you study what happens to various parts of the body by virtue of types of forces that are exerted on it?

WITNESS: Yes, sir. For the thesis, the primary area of interest was the spinal cord.

HABUSH: The cord itself, including the structures that the cord goes through?

WITNESS: For the bulk of the thesis, simply address the bulk of the thesis was addressed to the spinal cord, the supporting studies which were carried out, part of the thesis were included, interest in the spinal column, as well.

HABUSH: Now, Dr. Walsh, since your original paper, have you continued your interest in mechanism of injury or injury mechanisms?

WITNESS: Yes, sir, I have.

HABUSH: And in some of the articles that you described, did you specifically, either yourself or in participation of others, write about that very subject?

WITNESS: Yes, sir.

HABUSH: Approximately how many published articles have you written on that subject?

WITNESS: Either on my own or in collaboration, I believe there are probably five or six of these articles directed toward mechanisms of spinal injury.

HABUSH: Could you read the article that you wrote, No. 7 on your publication list?

WITNESS: This was one I co-authored with Dr. Larson, Sanchez, Ewing, Thomas, Weiss, Berger, Myklebust, Cusick and Saltzberg, "Experimental Methods for Evaluating Spinal Cord Injury During Impact Acceleration."

HABUSH: And what does that mean?

WITNESS: I described the techniques employed to permit us to evaluate the structure and function of the spinal cord during acceleration in a model system. The organism of the animal was accelerated within a chair, which was subjected to impact so that over a matter of seconds, extensive forces were delivered and were able to track, so to speak, the electrical and functional status of the nervous system.

HABUSH: In connection with this interest in the mechanism of injury, did you participate in it and become familiar with experiments on models in which various types of forces are applied to parts of the human body and then you observe what happens to them?

WITNESS: Yes, sir.

HABUSH: Is that fairly common in the practice of injury mechanism and biomedical, as you have called it?

WITNESS: Yes, sir.

HABUSH: In connection with your interest in the subject, in addition to your practice as a neurosurgeon, have you involved yourself in consultations in which you were asked to investigate in connection with litigation cases what type of mechanism caused what type of injury?

WITNESS: Yes, sir, I have.

HABUSH: Approximately how many times?

WITNESS: Probably between four and six, I don't recall which of them I was simply asked to give a deposition and which went to trial.

HABUSH: Now you and I have never had a case together, prior to this case, am I correct?

WITNESS: Not so far as I know, sir.

HABUSH: Now, Dr. Walsh, these consultations, are they involved in the spinal cord injuries or that area?

WITNESS: Yes.

HABUSH: Did you have occasion, Dr. Walsh, to see as a patient Roger Schulz?

WITNESS: Yes, sir, I did.

§7.34 —Background Information Used to Establish Trustworthiness

Background information was also used to established witnesses' trustworthiness. The background with respect to Spence's expert set out in §7.33 above also established trustworthiness because Dr. Gofman's past actions had demonstrated his loyalty to the government and his willingness to put the interests of his country ahead of his personal interest. As a witness, he could be expected to put the interests of justice ahead of his personal interest. Spence went on to outline the important positions Dr. Gofman had held in universities, government projects, and private industry, as well as the awards he had received from his peer groups. This information bolstered not only his expertness but also his trustworthiness because, by implication, only an honest, trustworthy person would be given such positions and honors. Recognition by his peers demonstrated that the witness was a source of both valid and reliable information. Spence went on to elicit information that demonstrated experience with cancer caused by radiation and facilities like Kerr-McGee. By the time Spence finished his background questions, the witness had established himself as expert and trustworthy in the fields in question. Spence concluded his background questions by asking the doctor if he felt that he was qualified to testify to the jury on the questions of the adequacy of the controls that took place at the Kerr-McGee plant, the general background and the dangerousness of plutonium, and the general problems of plutonium, radiation, and lung cancer, to which the doctor replied, "It is my opinion that I am so qualified."

Habush established through questioning that the doctor had not had any cases with Habush before, which dispelled any notion that the witness was a "hired gun" used by Habush in his cases. Habush also established that the doctor had actually seen the plaintiff as a patient, as opposed to seeing the patient on a referral by his lawyer.

With respect to his engineering expert, Habush established his credibility by demonstrating that he had been hired in the past by large corporations as well as the defense firms involved in the case. This established that the expert was not simply a plaintiff's expert, but was respected and utilized by defendants and large corporations as well as plaintiffs. Habush also disclosed that the expert had done work for him in the past, thus preventing the defendant from bringing this out on cross-examination and diffusing any claim that the witness was biased in favor of Mr. Habush's client. He questioned as follows:

HABUSH: How long, Dr. Richardson, have you been doing consulting?

WITNESS: Oh, I have been doing consulting in one form or another during the past 28 years while I have been in the Milwaukee area.

HABUSH: Twenty-eight years?

WITNESS: Yes.

HABUSH: And have you done that consulting in litigative matters for companies?

WITNESS: Yes, sir.

HABUSH: Could you give us an example of some of the companies that you have done litigation consulting for?

WITNESS: Briggs and Stratton, Teledyne, Wisconsin Motors, Bucyrus Erie, the ones that come to mind. There are other companies that I've worked for, defense cases where I was working on behalf of a company, but I was brought into it by an insurance company or by an attorney.

HABUSH: Have you done consulting work on cases for my law firm before?

WITNESS: Yes.

HABUSH: Over a period of how many years?

WITNESS: Probably more than ten.

HABUSH: All right. Approximately how many cases have you and I or someone in my office worked on with you? Do you have an approximate recollection?

WITNESS: I guess more than 50.

HABUSH: Have you had occasion to do consulting work on litigation files for Terry's former firm, Borgelt Powell?

WITNESS: Yes.

HABUSH: Over how many years?

WITNESS: Probably over roughly the same time span.

HABUSH: Do you remember roughly how many cases?

WITNESS: Maybe ten or less.

HABUSH: Have you had occasion to do litigating consulting for Mr. Daily or Mr. Gonring's firm on litigative matters?

WITNESS: Yes.

HABUSH: On how many cases, probably, if you recall?

WITNESS: One case comes to mind where I worked with the firm and then I've worked for Briggs and Stratton on defense cases, and I believe they represented Briggs and Stratton as the local counsel here.

HABUSH: Have you had occasion to work on a case, for instance, where Mr. Daily was involved?

WITNESS: I believe he was involved in one case. It involved a machine tool.

HABUSH: Have you had occasion to be asked by attorneys around the country to help them with products liability cases?

WITNESS: Yes, sir.

Dynamism was established by background questioning in that the witnesses established themselves as distinguished, energetic individuals. Dr. Gofman's research was a bold project at the time, and it was clear from his work that he had led an active life in the areas of research and medicine. Similarly, Baldwin elicited testimony from his consulting engineer that demonstrated that he had studied physics with a Nobel prize winner, had worked on the Manhattan Project during World War II, had been a past Director of Reliability for the Boeing Corporation, and had published over 100 papers dealing with engineering.

§7.35 —Preparation

When appropriate, the witnesses were asked what they had done to prepare themselves for their investigation and testimony. This further demonstrated the expert dimension of credibility. The experts established their competence by establishing that they had done all necessary and appropriate homework. Baldwin's expert engineer was asked actually to investigate the machine malfunction, as opposed simply to reviewing documents and depositions. In establishing that his expert had done his homework, Baldwin asked:

BALDWIN: Now, at my request, have you had an investigation of an accident involving Mr. Larkin Foster?

WITNESS: Yes, sir.

BALDWIN: What have you done to prepare yourself?

WITNESS: Well, first, I sought to find out what happened and I did this by reading the various depositions—of Mr. Foster himself, Mr.

Crew, and Mr. Sewell, Mr. Greene—then looking at photographs. Then I went out and saw the actual tractor involved and had it operated, recognized the hydraulic controls were—they were different, so I watch the operation, sat in the seat and pretended I was the operator, to study what happened. Next I tried to find out all I could about how the Ford Company went about developing this product and putting it on the market. So in the answers to interrogatories I tried to—did they do the things that a prudent management group would do to assure the safety in a tractor system.

BALDWIN: All right, sir, and have you conferred with Mr. Foster too?

WITNESS: Yes, sir, I have conferred with Mr. Foster directly and also I sought to study the instructions that the Ford Company had given to the users to see whether they had given the communications I thought should be done.

Similarly Perlman established that his expert witness had viewed all relevant documents:

PERLMAN: Okay. Mr. Bowman let me ask you whether at my request you have performed a safety evaluation or an engineering analysis of the 15 CM 1 continuous miner in this case.

WITNESS: Yes, sir, I have.

PERLMAN: And what, look at your notes there and tell the jury what documents you have reviewed and what have you looked at.

WITNESS: I started off reviewing Mr. Shackleford and Mr. Webb's statements and depositions. I also reviewed Mr. Campbell's deposition, Mr. McDowell's, Mr. Kendrick's, Mr. Minn's, Mr. Ritchie's, Mr. Green's, Mr. Ordakowski's, Mr. Hurt's, also reviewed several patents to apply to remote control machinery. I also looked at remote control stations similar to the one that you see over here. I reviewed and looked at a hydraulic assembly that was representative of one that was in the miner, continuous miner at the time of the accident. I also looked at a, the cable that was between the multi, or the remote control station and the miner at the time of the accident, and reviewed the group of relays that were in the machine at the time of the accident.

PERLMAN: Have you reviewed the blueprints and specifications that Joy Manufacturing Company has furnished that show the way that all of these electric circuitries are made up?

WITNESS: Yes, sir. Joy supplied at my request, supplied a set of schematics describing the implementation or the design of the remote control station, the demultiplexer in the machine, and also supplied schematics for the hydraulic control system or hydraulic system in the machine and a bill of materials of all the parts or the prints.

§7.36 Cause of Injury, Negligence, Nature and Extent of Damages

The lawyers elicited opinions from these witnesses about how the injury occurred, whether the machines were safe or defective, whether the defendants were negligent, and the nature and extent of damages. In order to get to these opinions, the lawyers all established by way of background, as noted above, that the witnesses were qualified to render the opinions and that they had done the necessary groundwork to support the formation of expert opinions. A series of questions was then asked to elicit the expert opinions. As a rule, before the opinions were rendered, the witnesses were asked to explain terms and concepts. After the opinions were rendered, the witnesses were asked to elaborate upon and justify the opinions. Baldwin took the simplest approach when he questioned as follows:

> BALDWIN: Did you come to any conclusions about this tractor or this front-end loader system here?
>
> WITNESS: Yes, sir.
>
> BALDWIN: And what is your basic conclusion that you reached?
>
> WITNESS: Well, first, on the nature of the accident, and the general cause of the accident, and then I went on to the specific design features that contributed to converting this incident into an accident. Then I reached some conclusions on the management of the development program.
>
> BALDWIN: All right, sir, let's take the tractor system itself. The front-end loader, did you reach a conclusion as to whether it was safe or unsafe—and tell us why?

Baldwin went on to ask whether the witness found anything about the arms of the machine that contributed to the accident, whether the accident was predictable, whether the design deficiencies could have been remedied, whether warnings were adequate, whether there were methods of giving adequate warnings, whether Ford acted in a prudent manner in designing and marketing the tractor, and whether there was anything unsafe about the attachment being used on the tractor.

After establishing that his expert was competent to testify on the matters in issue, Spence established that the witness would testify only to those facts and opinions about which experts in his field were in agreement. He then moved to questions about the witness's expert opinions. In connection with the claims of strict liability, Spence asked whether the doctor had an opinion as to whether or not plutonium was "uniquely hazardous." In asking whether the doctor had an opinion as to the negligence of Kerr-McGee in connection with its failure to instruct its employees about the dangers of plutonium, Spence asked:

> SPENCE: Doctor, I was about to talk with you about negligence and getting your opinion relative to negligence. That is a legal term that

has a very simple meaning. It simply means the failure to use due care. Now, do you have an opinion, doctor, as to whether or not a company who failed to adequately instruct its employees relative to the dangers of radiation from plutonium would be negligent?

WITNESS: I have an opinion.

SPENCE: And, what is your opinion?

WITNESS: My opinion is that that is clearly and unequivocally negligence.

Spence went on to ask for the doctor's opinions as to the negligence of Kerr-McGee in the handling of plutonium and the contamination of Karen Silkwood.

Ring used a formal hypothetical question and asked the consulting engineer to assume numerous facts, including the state of the machine prior to the injury, the facts of how the plaintiff was operating the machine on the day in question, the facts of how the machine operated when it malfunctioned, the facts of the expert's inspection of the machine after the injury, the facts set out in the diagrams and specifications for the machines. He then asked the witness, assuming all of those facts to be true, whether he had "an opinion based on a reasonable degree of engineering certainty to what caused the ram to come down at the time the young man put his hands in to retrieve the piece of metal?"

An issue in Corboy's case was the amount of money that would be allowed for future medical care. Corboy argued that only with substantial medical care would the plaintiff have a normal life expectancy. Corboy elicited the doctor's opinion based on a reasonable degree of medical and surgical certainty:

CORBOY: Doctor, specifically, do you have an opinion within a reasonable degree of medical and surgical certainty, that if he continues to get the care that he is receiving in Columbus Hospital with the team effort supplying him with assistance and with the hospital care available to him if he needs it on an emergency basis, as to whether or not Randy Block has a normal life expectancy?

WITNESS: Yes, he should have a normal life expectancy.

. . . .

CORBOY: If he were taken out of this environment at Columbus Hospital and put in a nursing home, what in your opinion would be his life expectancy?

WITNESS: Well, his life expectancy is absolutely directly proportional to the care that's given to him.

After laying the foundation for his expert's qualifications, Gibbons asked his expert witness what his role was as an expert in the case. He then asked a series of expert opinions with respect to the defects in the ejection seat in question. He started with questions asking for a general opinion on the cause of the decedent's death, and then as the testimony progressed, asked more specific questions about more specific causes of the malfunction. After each opinion was rendered, Gibbons asked the witness to define terms, and elaborate:

GIBBONS: All right, sir. Now, what was your specific role as far as being retained as a consulting expert in this case, please sir?

WITNESS: My role was to investigate the circumstances of Captain Wahl's accident with particular emphasis on the effects, if any, that the aircrew escape system installed in the A-10 aircraft, which is the Escapac, the Douglas Escapac 1E-9 ejection seat, and to the best of my ability and from the facts provided to me in various documents, to attempt to determine whether or not Captain Wahl's use of the ejection seat predisposed him to his untimely death.

GIBBONS: And when were you so retained?

WITNESS: To the best of my recollection, in March of this year.

GIBBONS: Based on approximately 19 or 20 years of testing and evaluating various ejection systems, as well as your expertise in the area of ejection systems, do you have an opinion, in reasonable scientific probabilities, as to the cause of death of Captain Harry Wahl as it relates to the Escapac 1E-9? First, do you have an opinion?

WITNESS: Yes, sir, I have.

GIBBONS: What is that opinion?

WITNESS: It is my expert opinion that Captain Wahl died as a result of his body being randomly mispositioned subsequent to seat/man separation and just prior and during the instant of parachute separation.

GIBBONS: And what do you mean, if you will, by random or gross mispositioning, Mr. Sanford?

WITNESS: By random mispositioning, I am referring to the uncontrolled placing of his body in free space without consideration for the attitude that his body is in at the moment of parachute operation.

GIBBONS: And why, in your expert opinion, based upon a reasonable scientific probability, was he grossly mispositioned or randomly mispositioned during this process? First, do you have an opinion?

WITNESS: Yes, sir, I do.

GIBBONS: What is that opinion?

WITNESS: The mispositioning of Captain Wahl's body was a direct consequence of several features of the Escapac 1E-9 seat. And I should say that it isn't limited just to the 1E-9 seat. It has appeared to me over a period of years that the conditions that Captain Wahl found himself in could be duplicated in a number of Escapac escape systems.

The short timing sequence from the time Captain Wahl pulled the ejection seat control to the time he found himself out of the seat predisposed him to the lack of any orthopedic support in his ejection seat. It caused him to be oriented in such a manner—in fact, according to Navy Aeromedical Laboratory parameters, he was in the worst possible position for parachute opening. There was no capability for Captain

Wahl to have the forces related to the opening of his parachute transmitted into his seat rather than into his body.

GIBBONS: All right. So then, are there primarily two bases, if you will, for that gross or random mispositioning; that being, number one, a shortened or enhanced timing? Is that number one?

WITNESS: Yes, sir.

GIBBONS: And did you also say number two, a lack of any stabilization?

WITNESS: I omitted the lack of any stabilization system, other than a device known as a Stapac vernier rockedt pitch stabilization system. And if I could have the model of the ejection seat.

GIBBONS: Would this model aid or assist you in trying to explain that to the jury?

WITNESS: I certainly hope so, for the benefit of the jury.

GIBBONS: What do you mean by—you have explained up to a point, enhanced or what we will refer to as the timing of the ejection system. But what do you mean by lack of stabilization?

WITNESS: As I previously mentioned, the Escapac 1E-9 ejection seat has what is called by Douglas a Stapac vernier rocket pitch stabilization system mounted underneath the bottom of the seat bucket which acts in conjunction with the burning of the rocket motor which, in turn, provides the propulsive force to get the man out of the aircraft. The pitch stabilization system controls, to a certain degree, the pitching motion about the lateral axis of the seat. There is no stabilization system to stabilize the seat in either the yaw or roll or a coupling of yaw and roll, sometimes referred to as tumbling.

GIBBONS: All right. What can be the consequence of that lack of stabilization, please, in yaw and roll and/or tumbling?

WITNESS: The consequences can be, essentially, what got Captain Wahl into trouble during his ejection.

. . . .

GIBBONS: All right. Now, tell us, if you will, you have explained the enhanced timing on the 1E-9 and also the lack of yaw and roll stabilization which permits randoming mispositioning. Tell us, if you will, based on your approximately 20 years of testing and evaluation of various type ejection seats and/or systems, as well as your general expertise in the area of escape systems, do you have an opinion, in reasonable scientific probabilities, as to whether or not the technology or state of the art, if you will, was available prior to 1979 to eliminate or design out those problems that you have just pointed out? First, do you have an opinion?

WITNESS: Yes, sir, I do.

GIBBONS: What is that opinion?

WITNESS: My opinion is that, based on my knowledge of other escape systems, that the technology was readily available.

. . . .

GIBBONS: All right. Thank you. Based upon your familiarity with ejection systems, your testing and evaluation over approximately 20 years as an expert in this area, do you have an opinion, in reasonable scientific probabilities, for the jury as to whether or not those design features of the Escapac 1E-9, which Captain Wahl met his untimely death in—those design features being, number one, a lack of yaw, roll stabilization and, number two, enhancing the time between initiation and seat/man separation—do you have an opinion, based on those factors, whether or not those two conditions constitute design defects? First, do you have an opinion?

WITNESS: Yes, sir, I do.

GIBBONS: And tell us what that opinion is.

WITNESS: My opinion with regard to the features you have just enumerated is that by incorporation of just those features alone, the aircrewman was predisposed to major and possibly fatal injury under certain conditions of their use.

GIBBONS: All right. Do you consider those, in your professional opinion and expertise, design defects?

WITNESS: I would say they would be lacking in essential qualities, and I believe that's Webster's definition of design—or a deficiency.

GIBBONS: Do you have an opinion, based upon those same qualifications, in reasonable scientific probabilities, as to whether or not those design defects constitute and expose the aircrewman to inherent hazards and/or dangers or unreasonable dangers? First, do you have an opinion?

WITNESS: Yes, sir.

GIBBONS: What is that opinion?

WITNESS: They do.

. . . .

GIBBONS: Based on your expertise in the field of testing and evaluating ejection systems, in reconstructing these mishaps of aircrewmen in ejection seats, do you have an opinion, in reasonable scientific probabilities, as to specifically what is wrong with the design of the McDonnell Douglas 1E-9 seat or what are the specific defects, in your opinion? First, do you have an opinion?

WITNESS: Yes, sir.

GIBBONS: Would you tell the jury what your opinion is?

WITNESS: The design deficiencies, in my opinion, with regard to the Escapac 1E-9 seat relate, first of all to the lack of any type of seat stabilizing drogue parachute which would either dampen out or serve to eliminate the perturbations, as we call them, in yaw and roll. The reduced seat/man timing—seat/man separation timing which denies the ejectee, the pilot using the seat, the support of the seat during the deceleration phase of his ejection when he's slowing down, and also the fact that in throwing him out of the seat in about a half a second, you deny him the support of the seat during his parachute opening which, in effect, would serve to diminish some of the forces that his body sees during parachute opening and transmit them instead to the seat. The final thing being, of course, the fact that he is thrown out randomly and allowed him to tumble, as you saw in the film. And at that point in time, he approaches the most critical part of the ejection scenario; that being the parachute opening.

GIBBONS: And are those design defects that you classified as unreasonably dangerous?

WITNESS: Yes, sir.

. . . .

GIBBONS: All right. Now, tell us, if you will, based upon that same expertise and the testing and qualification, how do those design defects relate to the death of Captain Wahl? First, do you have an opinion?

WITNESS: Yes, sir.

. . . .

GIBBONS: Now, and is that your opinion, then based upon a reasonable scientific probability, as to the cause of Captain Wahl's death based on or how it relates to the design defects or inherent dangers that you spoke of?

WITNESS: With respect to the random positioning at that end of the scenario, yes, sir.

GIBBONS: All right. Now, I want to ask you to assume that it is in evidence in this case, pursuant to the Aircraft Accident Investigation Report obtained under the Freedom of Information Act, that the lap belt on Captain Wahl was adjusted tighter on one side than the other; that is, that there was excess webbing of approximately 4.5 inches on the left and approximately 6.5 inches on the right. Will you make that assumption?

WITNESS: Yes, sir.

GIBBONS: Based on your expertise in testing and evaluating ejection seats and reconstructing these incidents, do you have an opinion, in reasonable scientific probabilities, as to whether or not the excess webbing that I have asked you to assume had any part in causing the death of Captain Wahl? First, do you have an opinion?

WITNESS: Yes, I do.

GIBBONS: What is that opinion?

WITNESS: My opinion is that it probably had little or no effect for a number of reasons.

GIBBONS: All right. I would like to ask you what is the basis of your opinion?

WITNESS: The basis of my opinion is, from my own personal knowledge and my background as a pilot, I know, for example, that on frequent occasions, for one reason or another, I would adjust my own lap belt so it would be slightly off center. In other words, the buckle would be displaced to one side or another. There would, of course be—more of an excess of belt on one side than on the other, but that wouldn't mean that the belt was loose.

.   .   .   .

GIBBONS: All right. Now, I want to ask you to further assume that it is or will be in evidence, please, sir, that Captain Wahl had one hand on the control stick, fighting a jam or restriction, as that term is known, in the pitch axis at or immediately preceding when he pulled the D-ring or ejection handle to eject. Will you make that assumption?

WITNESS: Yes, sir.

GIBBONS: I would ask you to further assume, as your familiarity bears out with the autopsy report, that he suffered a fracture of the right humerus above the elbow. Will you make that further assumption?

WITNESS: Yes, sir.

GIBBONS: Now, do you have an opinion, in reasonable scientific probabilities, based upon your some 20 years' experience in this area, as to whether or not the fact that he might not have had both hands on the D-ring—whether or not that caused or contributed to his death in any shape, form or fashion? First, do you have an opinion?

WITNESS: Yes, I do.

GIBBONS: What is that opinion?

WITNESS: I don't think it contributed in any way to his death.

.   .   .   .

GIBBONS: Now, based on your review and reconstruction, as well as the Aircraft Accident Investigation Report, do you have an opinion, please, sir, based upon reasonable scientific probability, as to whether or not Captain Wahl ejected within the design envelope? First, do you have an opinion as to whether or not he ejected within the advertised design envelope of McDonell Douglas?

WITNESS: Yes, sir, I have.

GIBBONS: What is that opinion?

WITNESS: I'm convinced that he ejected well within the design envelope of the 1E-9 ejection seat.

GIBBONS: And tell us, if you will, also based upon that same expertise as a qualification, as well as your reconstruction of Captain Wahl's bailout sequence as shown on the chart and your expertise in this area, do you have an opinion, in reasonable scientific probabilities, as to whether or not Captain Wahl would be here today if this seat did not have these design defects at the time and on the occasion in question? First, do you have an opinion?

WITNESS: Yes, sir, I do.

GIBBONS: What is that opinion?

WITNESS: I'm convinced that he would be here today.

GIBBONS: Now, it's been suggested and I'm prompted to ask you is—does an ejection have to be a "risky," quote, unquote, business? First, do you have an opinion based upon your years of expertise?

WITNESS: Yes, sir.

GIBBONS: What is that opinion?

WITNESS: There is little, if any risk involved if the seat or escape system is intelligently designed.

GIBBONS: All right. And are we talking about properly designed as recommended since '63 and '59?

WITNESS: Yes, sir.

GIBBONS: Now, on the film you mentioned a ballistic spreader gun. And without taking the time to go into that, I think you explained it briefly on the film. Based upon those same qualifications and areas of expertise, do you have an opinion, in reasonable scientific probabilities, as to whether or not the ballistic spreader gun played any major or significant role in the death of Captain Wahl? First, do you have an opinion?

WITNESS: Yes, sir, I do.

GIBBONS: What is that opinion?

WITNESS: I don't feel that the spreader gun played any significant part, inasmuch as it was used in conjunction with an external pilot chute.

GIBBONS: All right. Is there any other basis for that opinion other than that? In other words, would—do you have an opinion as to whether or not, in reasonable scientific probability, he would have been killed with or without a ballistic spreader gun? First, do you have an opinion?

WITNESS: Yes, sir.

GIBBONS: And what is that opinion?

WITNESS: I don't think it would have made any difference whether he had the spreader gun incorporated or not.

GIBBONS: Is that because of this lack of stabilization and enhanced timing defects?

WITNESS: My opinion is based primarily on an Air Force study that was done some years ago at the National Parachute Test Range wherein it was determined that the spreader gun, when used in conjunction with this particular external pilot chute, mitigated the abrupt opening force that was then suspected about the spreader gun. And he did have the external pilot chute incorporated on this chute.

GIBBONS: Lastly, Mr. Sanford, has there been any pressure exerted on you directly or indirectly by McDonnell Douglas not to appear here today?

WITNESS:　Yes, sir.

GIBBONS:　I'll pass this witness.

§7.37　Use of Language

The language used in questioning the expert witnesses was simple, yet technical. On one hand, the lawyers did not want to confuse or lose the jury in technical jargon. On the other hand, these witnesses were experts and the lawyers allowed them to demonstrate their command of the technical material in question. Therefore, the lawyers asked their questions in simple, straightforward terms. In most cases, the witnesses were allowed to testify in technical terms, with the lawyers then following up with questions that elicited explanation of the technical terms in everyday language.

The lawyers enhanced their personal credibility in questioning the witnesses in that they demonstrated knowledge and command of the technical terms and material being discussed by the witnesses. Consistent with the credibility dimensions, the lawyers demonstrated competence, training, and preparation in the presentation of these witnesses.

§7.38　Form of Questions

In questioning the experts, the lawyers asked fewer leading questions and more open-ended questions calling for narrative answers. These witnesses were professionals who were used to addressing groups of people and had probably testified many times before in similar cases. Thus, they knew their "scripts" and were in a position to give narrative answers comfortably. The lawyers "turned them loose" and allowed them to give lengthy answers. With respect to plutonium, Spence asked Dr. Gofman:

> Doctor, as a person who has been referred to many times as the Father of Plutonium, I wish you would tell the ladies and gentleman of the jury, first of all, just what is plutonium?

However, the lawyers continued to lead their witnesses. The lawyers followed the rule that the only questions asked are questions to which the answers are known. The majority of their questions were narrow, specific questions calling for specific responses. The lawyers exerted control over their witnesses at all times. If the witnesses began to stray from the desired path, the lawyers interrupted and asked questions that led them back to the desired train of thought. The lawyers never appeared to be surprised by the answers they received.

§7.39　Conclusion

In their direct presentation of evidence, the plaintiffs used four major types of witnesses: (1) plaintiffs or their representatives, (2) fact witnesses with respect to the occurrence, (3) fact witnesses with respect to damages, and (4) expert witnesses. All of these witnesses presented facts in support of the story line. The witnesses filled in the story about how and why the plaintiffs were injured, and about the nature and extent of the plaintiffs' damages. The plaintiffs or their representatives told of how the plaintiffs were injured and damaged. The fact witnesses added supporting and reinforcing testimony about how the plaintiffs were injured and damaged. The expert witnesses explained technical causation and damage issues. The lawyers elicited background information from the witnesses that personalized them and enhanced their credibility.

The lawyers used language that was simple and direct and could be easily understood by both the witnesses and jurors. The form of questioning ranged from narrow questions calling for specific narrow answers to leading questions. Due to their training and experience, the experts were given more latitude than lay witnesses to provide narrative answers. However, in all cases, the lawyers controlled the testimony of the witnesses by their use of narrow questions. In all cases, the lawyers knew exactly where they were going with their evidence, and their witnesses were led step by step through their testimony.

8

Cross-Examination

§8.01   Introduction

In the following, I will demonstrate that successful lawyers for the plaintiff used cross-examination to achieve three purposes: (1) to destroy the credibility of the witness, (2) to controvert arguments or facts presented previously by the witness or by the defense, and (3) to elicit facts in support of the plaintiff's case. I will further demonstrate that the basic strategies used in the questioning were designed to control all aspects of the witnesses' testimony.

The cross-examinations examined were those by Scott Baldwin, Melvin Block, Phil Corboy, Robert Gibbons, Herman Glaser, Robert Habush, Peter Perlman, Leonard Ring, Gerry Spence, and Lantz Welch. As the reader will recall, Scott Baldwin's case involved the product liability claim in which the plaintiff was severely injured while operating a tractor. A bale of hay fell off a front-end loader on the tractor, landing on the plaintiff and causing crippling injuries. The Block cross-examinations involved the product liability claim against the manufacturer of the artillery shell that malfunctioned in the howitzer and injured two soldiers in combat during the Vietnam War. The Corboy examinations involved the automobile collision which left the plaintiff a spastic quadraplegic with locked-in syndrome. The Gibbons examinations involved the product liability claim for the negligent design of the ejection device that resulted in the death of the jet fighter pilot. The Glaser examinations were conducted in the medical negligence case involving the performance of the unnecessary hysterectomy. The Habush examinations involved the catastrophic injuries caused in the industrial accident involving the forklift. The Perlman case involved the mining accident in which the automatic mining machine malfunctioned and caused severe injury to the miner. The Ring examinations involved the malfunction of the machine brake press machine in which the operator's hands were severely crushed. The Spence examinations involved the trial of *Silkwood v Kerr-McGee*,[1] in which it was alleged that Karen Silkwood was negligently contaminated with plutonium. The Welch examinations involved the claims for damages and loss of consortium by the husband and wife stemming from an automobile collision.

§8.02 Destroying Credibility

As noted previously, the three dimensions by which listeners judge credibility are expertness, trustworthiness, and dynamism.[2] The lawyers undermined the credibility of the defendants' witnesses by attacking their expertness and trustworthiness.

§8.03 Attacking Expertness

The lawyers attacked the expertness of the witnesses in two ways. First, they questioned the training and experience of the witnesses, and second, they questioned the validity of the witnesses' testimony.

§8.04 —Training and Experience

In each instance in which an expert witness testified during direct examination, the defense lawyer elicited background information about the witness's qualifications and training in order to qualify the witness as an expert and in order to bolster the witness's credibility. In each instance on cross-examination, the plaintiff's lawyer questioned the qualifications and training of the witness in order to undermine credibility. For example, in Baldwin's case,

---

[1] No. 76-0888 (WD Okla, March 1979).

[2] Delia, *A Constructivist Analysis of the Concept of Credibility*, 62 QJ Speech 361 (1976).

the defendant presented an engineer to offer testimony in support of the defendant's contentions. Baldwin first established that the witness was an employee of the defendant Ford Motor Company and was designated by the defendant as the employee at Ford who knew the most about the design and manufacture of the tractor system in question. He then damaged the credibility of both Ford and the witness by demonstrating that the "engineer" was not a licensed engineer and could not practice engineering in the state of Texas, where the case was being tried, or in his home state. Baldwin questioned as follows:

BALDWIN: All right. Now let's go back to the beginning. You have heard in this lawsuit—I asked Ford to furnish me with the man that knew the most about the design and the manufacturing of this tractor system, and you showed up, is that correct?

WITNESS: Well, I may have been a substitute for the man that knew the most, I don't know.

BALDWIN: Well, I may have been a substitute for the man that knew the most, I don't know.

WITNESS: I think they did.

BALDWIN: In all due modesty to you, I will give you a chance to advertise.

WITNESS: Thank you.

BALDWIN: And I have asked some questions since then and each time they were referred back to you as the man that knows the most about the design and manufacture of this tractor by Ford—Ford Motor Company, one of the largest corporations in the country, or the world, I guess, is that right?

WITNESS: Yes.

.   .   .   .

BALDWIN: All right. Now you are the man who knows the most about Ford tractor design. Are you a licensed engineer?

WITNESS: I am a graduate engineer.

BALDWIN: I asked you a licensed engineer.

WITNESS: No, sir.

BALDWIN: You couldn't even practice engineering in Texas, could you?

WITNESS: I don't—

BALDWIN: In something as a licensed engineer?

WITNESS: I don't know what the requirements in Texas are.

BALDWIN: Well, the requirements are that they be licensed, like they are in your state where you come from.

WITNESS: Then I couldn't practice in Texas.

BALDWIN: You couldn't practice there either, where you live?

WITNESS: No, sir, I have got my hands full where I am.

BALDWIN: But you can't practice as a licensed engineer, can you?

WITNESS: That may be right, I have never investigated that.

Similarly, Spence established that Kerr-McGee's manager of operations, who testified on direct examination that Kerr-McGee ran a safe operation, had had no experience or training with respect to radiation, other than a six-day seminar, prior to going to work for Kerr-McGee. Spence did a skillful job of setting up the witness by establishing that his decisions were a product of his training and experience, and that he had no training and experience relating to operation he was running. In the process, Spence also established the credibility of his expert witness, Dr. Gofman. He cross-examined as follows:

SPENCE: Well, Mr. Dunn, I'm Gerry Spence for the plaintiff here. You and I haven't had a chance to talk about this case, or haven't even met each other before, have we?

WITNESS: Not that I know of.

SPENCE: Okay, I guess what the bottom line of your testimony is is that you were out there running the plant, that it was a good safe operation, and that everything was okay—that is about what it comes down to, isn't it?

WITNESS: We didn't run a perfect plant there. We tried to.

SPENCE: I know, but ultimately that is what you're saying, is that it was a good operation, and a safe operation, and that is what you want us to think, isn't it?

WITNESS: I think that is fair.

SPENCE: Okay, Now, just a few things about you and the reason I'm asking you these questions about your own background and the background of some of these other folks, Mr. Dunn, is just to determine what your specific educational qualifications were and your background for the job that you had, because you, as a man out there, you had to make judgments from time to time, didn't you?

WITNESS: Yes. I had a very competent staff to discuss things with.

SPENCE: But, you had to make judgments yourself, didn't you?

WITNESS: Yes, sir.

SPENCE: And those judgments came as a result of—you used what you had to make them—you used your experience, and your education just like the rest of us do?

WITNESS: Yes.

SPENCE: What did you write your Master's Degree in—just for my curiosity?

WITNESS: Heat transfer.

SPENCE: Involving what?

WITNESS: Well, the coefficient of heat transfer between a boiling film and a flat plate.

SPENCE: A boiling film?

WITNESS: Yes.

SPENCE: What would that be relative to "a boiling film?"

WITNESS: Well, evaporators and—

SPENCE: Evaporators in what kind of industry or function?

WITNESS: Well, they had evaporators in the chemical industry, and sugar industry—any place you have to remove water.

SPENCE: Like when you take sugar beets, or sugar pulp, and the transfer of heat in a factory like that?

WITNESS: That is right.

SPENCE: I see.

WITNESS: Of course, we also had a small evaporator at the plutonium plant.

SPENCE: Uh huh. Your degrees were back there in 1930 and '31. Did you go back for any refresher courses—back to any university?

WITNESS: I went back to UCLA for a six-day course in nuclear energy.

SPENCE: I think you misspoke yourself—I thought I heard you say that—I wrote it down—and I'm sure it must have been a mistake—you said that in 1967 you went to UCLA for a five to six year radiation course—you meant a six-day course, didn't you?

WITNESS: I didn't say five or six years—I don't believe.

SPENCE: Yes, you did. You misspoke yourself. You didn't mean to say that, did you?

WITNESS: No. It was a five or six-day course.

SPENCE: Five or six days. And I think I've got a copy here of the five or six-day course you took. Could we just mark that as an exhibit, and we'll just introduce it into evidence? I hand you what has been marked Plaintiff's Exhibit 284, and I will ask you if this is the certificate that you got for that six-day course?

WITNESS: Yes sir, it is.

SPENCE: Now, other than that six-day course, did you have any special training in any university in radiation which would qualify you to operate and be in control and charge of this plant?

WITNESS: Not in any other university.

SPENCE: I offer into evidence Plaintiff's Exhibit 284.

DEFENSE COUNSEL: No objection.

THE COURT: It will be admitted.

SPENCE: It was called a one-week executive review of the atomic energy field, wasn't it?

WITNESS: Yes. And one of the lecturers was a Mr. Gofman.

SPENCE: Thank you for bringing that up. That was the next question I was going to ask you. One of the men who lectured for that course was Doctor Gofman, wasn't it?

WITNESS: Yes.

SPENCE: What did you think of his lectures—did you like them?

WITNESS: Well, at that time I thought quite well at that time he hadn't developed some of his later theories—he wasn't talking about hot particles in those days.

SPENCE: Well, I don't know—he didn't talk about hot particles in these days, either—and didn't talk about hot particles to the jury, that I recall. He said he didn't believe in the hot particle theory. But, did you think that Doctor Gofman knew what he was talking about?

WITNESS: Yes. He was arguing for the reduction at that time of the exposure, which was about three times what it is at the present time.

SPENCE: My question to you—listen to me, Mr. Dunn. Did you think he was a qualified man?

WITNESS: Well, he sounded all right to me, if that is what you mean?

SPENCE: No. You can't have it both ways. You can't tell the jury, you know, that you got this big course in radiation, but then when I ask you about the people that taught you that, you can't say that you didn't think they were any good. Do you think that you got good instruction?

WITNESS: At that time I considered whether he might be a consultant for another plant we were operating, but the occasion never arose to use him.

SPENCE: That is one of the points I was wanting to raise. You did know of the existence of Doctor Gofman as an expert in the field, didn't you?

WITNESS: Yes, sir. He was presented as an expert in the field.

SPENCE: And by the University of California.

WITNESS: At that time.

SPENCE: Did you ever call upon Doctor Gofman at any time to help you consider the standards of radiation that you established out there for your workers—did you ever call on him?

WITNESS: No, I never called on him.

SPENCE: Do you know anybody in your organization who did?

WITNESS: No, I don't.

SPENCE: Now, prior to the time that you came to Kerr-McGee—and you just sort of came in with the Potash Company—the Potask Company was absorbed by Kerr-McGee, so you came with it—that is how you came here, isn't it?

WITNESS: Yes, sir.

SPENCE: Prior to that time you came to Kerr-McGee had you ever run a plutonium plant?

WITNESS: No, sir.

SPENCE: Had you ever designed one?

WITNESS: No, sir.

SPENCE: Had you ever been in one?

WITNESS: No, I hadn't.

. . . .

SPENCE: Now, the man who preceded you out there, I think you said the plant was in operation, the man that had your position was a man by the name of Dr. Fryar, wasn't it?

WITNESS: Yes, sir.

SPENCE: And he was a PhD, wasn't he?

WITNESS: Yes, sir.

SPENCE: And he had some special nuclear material experience, didn't he?

WITNESS: Yes.

SPENCE: And so you, Mr. Dunn, took the place of a PhD who had special nuclear material experience, when in fact you, from your own experience, had none whatever when you took over that job, isn't that true?

WITNESS: I had a very competent staff, though.

SPENCE: I understand, but you had none whatsoever—it is like me not being a lawyer, but I have competent staff to take over a trial, or me, a competent administrator, to take over an operation, although I have competent doctors under me—you had no specific nuclear material experience at all, had you?

WITNESS: I had considerable chemical experience, about 36 years of it, and it was a chemical plant primarily.

SPENCE: I understand, but my question was: You had no special nuclear material experience, had you?

WITNESS: The six-day course—

SPENCE: The six-day course?

WITNESS: —and the operation of a rare-earth thorium operation for about eight years.

SPENCE: That rare earth was thorium, wasn't it?

WITNESS: Yes, sir.

Corboy was faced with a physician who was called to testify that the plaintiff would have a reduced life expectancy and did not require hospitalization in an acute care medical institution. Corboy attacked the expertise of the witness by undermining the witness's experience and training and by establishing that the witness had never treated a person with the plaintiff's condition of locked-in syndrome, thereby suggesting that the doctor's testimony was based on conjecture rather than actual experience:

CORBOY: Now, what is an assistant clinical professor, which is, I believe, is what you said you were?

WITNESS: Right. The University of Illinois has two ranking systems. The starting out professors are assistant professors; you then have associate professors; and you then have full professors. You move up in rank, depending on the amount of duties, the amount of teaching responsibilities one has at the University; also, you move up in rank, depending on how long you've been there.

The clinical assistant professor is a category that teachers, such as myself, have, where we are not necessarily at the University of Illinois, we are not teaching at the medical school, but we have teaching responsibilities to medical students out at the outlying hospitals. We are primarily in clinical practice. We are not primarily just teaching. The clinical designation points out that. The assistant professors are predominately just teachers.

CORBOY: How long have you been an assistant—

WITNESS: —clinical professor?

CORBOY: Yes, sir.

WITNESS: 1974 or '75, it was right in there. I was part of Northwestern between '72 and '74, and I switched, due to my responsibilities at Lutheran General, at approximately that time.

CORBOY: Whatever your responsibilities are, you've been an assistant for either a decade or almost a decade?

WITNESS: I probably will be for the next 20 years.

CORBOY: So that when you say you are an assistant clinical professor at the University of Illinois, it means you teach people at Lutheran General Hospital?

WITNESS: Yes, I do.

CORBOY: You do not teach people at the University of Illinois?

WITNESS: No, I don't; just from there.

. . . .

CORBOY: Doctor, as an assistant clinical professor, you get paid by the University of Illinois?

WITNESS: No, I don't.

CORBOY: Have you ever gotten paid by the University of Illinois in the last decade that you've been an assistant clinical professor?

WITNESS: No.

. . . .

CORBOY: You've mentioned you've done some writing?

WITNESS: Yes.

. . . .

CORBOY: Thank you. That is the article that you wrote on toxic encephalopathy?

. . . .

WITNESS: Correct.

CORBOY: The other article you said you wrote—by the way, did that article on toxic encephalopathy with seizures secondary to ingestion of an explosive material, composition C-4, have anything to do with locked-in syndrome?

WITNESS: No.

. . . .

CORBOY: All right, sir. There is an article you mentioned that you wrote with a fellow by the name of Andre J. Ognibene.

WITNESS: Yes.

. . . .

CORBOY: And that had nothing to do with locked-in syndrome, did it?

WITNESS: No.

CORBOY: The next article I think you wrote, it looks rather lengthy, it is from the proceedings in the lengthy seminar in neurology; it is written by four fellows. It is written by Rudolph Maier, W. Bruce Ketel, Thomas Mathews, and Ruitson Ouyang?

WITNESS: Right.

CORBOY: And this article is an article of review of cerebral edema, and I take it we are right back to the absence of the bibliography, it is ten pages long?

WITNESS: Correct.

CORBOY: And all four of you wrote the article?

WITNESS: My part was on the treatment.

CORBOY: Let's go to the part where it says "treatment." Could you go to that part where it says "treatment?"

WITNESS: The last three pages.

CORBOY: The last three pages, all right. And that has nothing to do with locked-in syndrome?

WITNESS: Not the locked-in syndrome part, no.

. . . .

CORBOY: So, in this case you were retained not as a consultant and referred to a patient by another doctor in another discipline, but you were retained to examine John Randolph Block by somebody else?

WITNESS: Correct.

CORBOY: And who retained you?

WITNESS: Mr. Johnson.

CORBOY: And you, of course, pursuant to the responsibilities that you have between you and Mr. Johnson, and I don't mean to suggest improperly or discourteously or anything else, and I am certainly not going to ask you the amount, but are you getting paid?

WITNESS: Yes, I am.

CORBOY: Doctor, in this particular case when you were involved in the preparation for the trial of this case you had to determine what your experience and your exposure and actual on-th-job work was with locked-in syndrome victims who have become victims of the locked-in syndrome by way of trauma, did you not, sir?

WITNESS: Yes, I did.

CORBOY: And you determined that in your practice you had never treated anybody who had ever suffered a closed head injury, traumatic, resulting in locked-in syndrome?

WITNESS: Resulting in that syndrome. It's a very rare syndrome, correct.

CORBOY: Whether it be rare or whether it be general you have not had the opportunity—what year did you get out of medical school, sir?

WITNESS: 1966.

CORBOY: You have not had the opportunity in the 18 years since you have gotten out of medical school to treat this rare condition called locked-in syndrome resulting from trauma?

WITNESS: Correct.

CORBOY: I take it then by the same token that you have never testified in Court at any time in your life before or after you were employed by Mr. Johnson in a case involving a spastic quadraplegic with brain stem injury resulting in locked-in syndrome.

WITNESS: No, I have not.

Glaser demonstrated that while the defendant's medical expert was offering opinions in the area of gynecology, he was not a specialist in that field. Glaser further demonstrated that the witness was not Board Certified in any field, thus, challenging the witness's training and experience:

GLASER: Doctor, you are an endocrinologist, right?

WITNESS: I am, sir.

GLASER: Were you certified by the American Board in that area?

WITNESS: I am not.

GLASER: Am I correct in saying that each speciality has different classifications, they're all part of the American Boards, there's an American Board of Gynecology and Obstetrics, American Board of Internal Medicine, there's an American Board of Pathology, etcetera, right?

WITNESS: There are.

GLASER: And am I correct in saying that the function of the Boards is essentially to separate the self-styled specialists from those that are truly certified by the Boards, correct? That's the essential purpose?

WITNESS: I am not a self-styled—

GLASER: I didn't ask you if you were.

WITNESS: The Boards are set up for people who need this type of specialization. I'm a member of the American Obstetrician and Gynecology.

GLASER: I didn't ask you that. Will you answer the question?

THE COURT: Just answer the question.

WITNESS: Would you state the question again?

GLASER: One of the reasons for setting up the American Boards is to separate the self-styled from those who are truly certified by the American Boards, correct?

WITNESS: It may be, I don't know.

GLASER: Okay. You're not a gynecologist, right, sir?

WITNESS: What do you mean by that?

GLASER: Are you a specialist in gynecology as well?

WITNESS: I'm a member of Obstetrics and Gynecology, that gives me that speciality.

GLASER: Sir, is that a Board—

THE COURT: Just a minute. Now, Doctor and counselor, let's cut out the screaming and let's cut out the arguing. And, Doctor, you have to answer the questions.

GLASER: Do you claim to be a specialist in gynecology?

WITNESS: I'm a specialist in endocrinology.

GLASER: Okay. Now, will you answer the question? Do you claim to be a specialist—

WITNESS: If you talk loud, let me know, I'll turn down my hearing aid. If you talk softly, keep your voice moderately so I can hear well.

GLASER: I'll try.

WITNESS: Thank you.

GLASER: Now, will you answer the question?

WITNESS: What was it?

GLASER: You said you're a specialist in—

WITNESS: I said I'm a specialist in endocrinology.

GLASER: I mean in endocrinology. When I asked you the question, are you a specialist in gynecology, you answered, "I'm a specialist in endocrinology," correct?

WITNESS: I did.

GLASER: I take it that means you are not a specialist in gynecology?

WITNESS: No, sir, that's not so.

GLASER: Okay. Have you ever been certified by the American Board as a duly qualified gynecologist? That ought to take a yes or a no, right?

WITNESS: I'm not a duly qualified specialist.

§8.05   —Validity of Assumptions

The lawyers further attacked the credibility of the witnesses by challenging the validity of the assumptions on which their testimony was based. The lawyers established that the witnesses had not done their homework and taken into account all relevant information in arriving at their conclusions, that their conclusions were not based on accurate information, or that their opinions were biased.

In attempting to establish that the defendant's doctor was a "hired gun," Corboy established that the doctor had not talked with any of the physicians associated with the plaintiff's care and treatment, thus suggesting that the doctor had not done his homework and did not have enough information upon which to base his opinions:

CORBOY: And one of the reasons you as a neurologist are a consultant is because, and I don't mean this is any derogatory fashion at all, but these fellas from other disciplines give you business?

WITNESS: People in the other disciplines that find that their patients have a neurological question or problem refer them for analysis of that problem, diagnosis, and treatment.

CORBOY: Is that the same as giving you business?

WITNESS: It's business.

CORBOY: And by business, and there is nothing wrong with having business, you get paid?

WITNESS: I get paid for consultations, yes.

CORBOY: And ordinarily when you are consulted and are consulted for the purposes of the consultation the neurosurgeon that sends a patient to you, or the opthalmologist, or the obstetrician, or the otolaryngologist, or the emergency surgeon, or the general practitioner—by the way, there is now a specialization called general family practice, is there not?

WITNESS: Yes, there is.

CORBOY: So that even those folks who do everything are now specialized?

WITNESS: There are boards—

CORBOY: Capability of being specialized?

WITNESS: Capable, yes, sir.

CORBOY: Thank you, sir. Now when you get a patient by way of consultation who pays you, the doctor that referred you the case or the patient?

WITNESS: The patient.

CORBOY: So that there is a direct line then between you and the patient and the fellow that refers you to the case is responsible for his portion of the case and you are responsible for your portion of the case?

WITNESS: Correct.

CORBOY: And if a physiatrist, say, sent a patient to you you would be the consultant in the case and ordinarily you would refer back to, or at least talk with the physiatrist who sent you the case?

WITNESS: Whenever I see anyone in consultation I either talk or send a letter back, or both, to the referring physician.

CORBOY: All right, sir. In this case did you talk with Dr. Shawn Mullan?

WITNESS: No, I did not.

CORBOY: Did you talk to Dr. Vinad Sahgal?

WITNESS: I have talked to Dr. Sahgal. He and I trained together at Northwestern. We were together at the Venice meeting in Venice last May. We did not discuss this case.

CORBOY: I will try the question the other way then. Did you talk to Dr. Sahgal about this case?

WITNESS: No, I did not.

CORBOY: Did you talk to Dr. Speer?

WITNESS: No.

CORBOY: Did you talk to Dr. Laros?

WITNESS: No.

CORBOY: Incidentally, any time I say "talk to" I mean about this case, okay?

WITNESS: I agree.

CORBOY: Thank you. Did you talk to Dr. Grimm?

WITNESS: No.

CORBOY: Dr. Grimm is the psychologist at Rehabilitation Institute, remember?

WITNESS: I don't know who he is, no.

CORBOY: Did you talk to Dr. Matz?

WITNESS: My understanding in reviewing a case like this is I am not supposed to talk to any of these people.

CORBOY: Whether that's your understanding or not, Doctor, I will ask the questions. Please.

WITNESS: That's my understanding.

CORBOY: Did you talk to Dr. Matz?

WITNESS: No.

CORBOY: Talk you talk to Dr. Spiegler?

WITNESS: No, I have not.

CORBOY: Did you talk to Dr. Shroudt?

WITNESS: No.

CORBOY: Talk to Dr. Godfred?

WITNESS: No.

CORBOY: Talk to Dr. Dordal?

WITNESS: Talk to Dr. Reese?

WITNESS: No.

CORBOY: Have you ever introduced yourself to Dr. George Block:

WITNESS: No, I have not.

CORBOY: So, in this case you were retained not as a consultant and referred to a patient by another doctor in another discipline, but you were retained to examine John Randolph Block by somebody else?

WITNESS: Correct.

CORBOY: And who retained you?

WITNESS: Mr. Johnson.

CORBOY: And you, of course, pursuant to the responsibilities that you have between you and Mr. Johnson, and I don't mean to suggest improperly or discourteously or anything else, and I am certainly not going to ask you the amount, but are you getting paid?

WITNESS: Yes, I am.

CORBOY: And you are getting paid not by a patient, but by a lawyer.

WITNESS: Yes, I am.

In *Silkwood,* the defense presented a physician who testified that based on tests performed prior to Karen Silkwood's death and during her autopsy, it could not be conclusively established that she suffered any damage, or would have suffered any damage had she lived, from radiation poisoning. The doctor's opinions were based in part on his examination of Karen Silkwood, and in part on models and formulas used for determining and computing the amounts of plutonium contamination existing in the human body and the amount of contamination necessary to damage human tissue. Spence attacked the validity of his testimony by first establishing that there were many reputable experts in the field of medicine and nuclear chemistry who disputed the witness's opinions on the subjects in question. He then challenged the doctor's methods of arriving at his opinion by establishing that cigarette smokers were more easily damaged by plutonium contamination, and that the doctor did not take a history from Karen Silkwood when he examined her, and did not account for her cigarette smoking in his model for arriving at her possible tissue damage. With this questioning, Spence established that the doctor's calculations, results, and opinions were based on inadequate information and, therefore, were invalid. Spence first established that other experts disagreed with the witness's conclusions:

SPENCE: Dr. Voelz, you are the same Dr. Voelz the other experts, I
guess, have been telling us about, and now you are here in the flesh
and blood. Well, doctor, somebody isn't coming out with it quite right,
and I guess we're going to have to find out why, because you say that
as far as Karen Silkwood was concerned, she had a chance like five out
of 10,000 of getting cancer, and Dr. Gofman says, as you know now,
that had she lived she was guaranteed to die of lung cancer. Now, that
is quite a difference in testimony, isn't it?

WITNESS: It certainly is; yes.

SPENCE: And, you are under oath, aren't you doctor?

WITNESS: Yes, I am.

SPENCE: And you have been in this business quite some time. And,
I want to ask you: Do you recognize the fact that there is indeed respectable, quite a body of respectable authority in this country that don't
agree with your conclusions?

WITNESS: I recognize that there is controversy in this area.

SPENCE: And, do you recognize that some of these people say you are
wrong—not only are you wrong, but you are "dead wrong?"

WITNESS: That is their opinion.

SPENCE: Yes. And, you have given your opinion, and we have heard
the opinions of others. Now, I want to find out about that. Are you
aware of the fact that there are at least, that I can count of on two of
my hands, at least eight people who have criticized the current standards that you now claim are just okay?

WITNESS: That is a very small number out of hundreds that have
approved it.

SPENCE: I'm only talking about—I'm talking about eight persons who
have—who are respected authorities, who have published on this matter. There are hundreds, thousands, who perhaps disagree with the
standards, but I'm talking about the respectable top echelon people.
For example, do you know that Karl Morgan agrees with the standard?

WITNESS: Yes, I do.

SPENCE: He was on the standard forming committee, wasn't he?

WITNESS: Yes, he has been on committees.

SPENCE: And, he says the standard—and testified to the ladies and gentlemen of the jury—should be reduced some 460, or eight times—are
you aware of that fact?

WITNESS: No, I am not. It is 200—

SPENCE: Well,—

WITNESS: Or, 240.

SPENCE: Are you aware of what he testified here?

WITNESS: No, I am not, but his papers, his writings, it is 240. And,
then in another place it is 200.

SPENCE: I understand. And he has explained that to the ladies and gentlemen of the jury, and his final conclusion was in this case, relative to those standards, some 400 times. There are others that—

WITNESS: And, he's wrong.

SPENCE: Pardon?

WITNESS: He's wrong.

SPENCE: Well, doctor, you know, I think you and I are going to get along just fine if you answer my questions.

WITNESS: I will try.

SPENCE: Now, you see, you had a full opportunity—I sat here for a day and a half and didn't interrupt your testimony—gave you a chance to lay it all out, didn't I?

WITNESS: Yes, you did.

SPENCE: Now, I'm going to see if I can't get you to be fair and answer my questions. You are aware of the fact that other noted authorities believe those standards should be reduced from 100 to 1,000 times?

WITNESS: I am aware of the controversy.

SPENCE: Are you aware of the position taken on that by Carl J. Johnson, who has made a study at Rocky Flats?

WITNESS: I am aware of it.

SPENCE: Have you read his articles?

WITNESS: I have read some of them. I don't know about all of them.

SPENCE: Have you read the article by Dr. John Edsall in which he claims the standards should be reduced?

WITNESS: Yes, I have read that article.

SPENCE: Have you read the article of Dr. David Meyer claiming the standards should be reduced?

WITNESS: I have not read David Meyer's.

SPENCE: Are you acquainted with Dr. Helen Caldicott claiming that the standards should be reduced?

WITNESS: I don't know her personally, but I am aware of her opinions.

SPENCE: Have you read her book called Nuclear Madness?

WITNESS: Yes.

SPENCE: Are you acquainted with the facts she claims, based upon all of the data gathered, that the standards are ridiculous?

WITNESS: That is her opinion.

SPENCE: Yes. Now, aren't you aware of the fact that the NRC itself has spoken through one Robert Minogue, in a newspaper letter to another noted scientist, and that the NRC itself has said that there has got to be some adjustment of those standards downward—aren't you aware of that fact?

WITNESS: I am aware that the standards are under review all the time by committees and scientific bodies.

Spence then challenged the assumptions upon which the witness based some of his conclusions:

SPENCE: When you walked up to the ladies and gentlemen of the jury and gave figures like 65 additional cancers, instead of 0.02—and you gave some other figures here based, I think you said, on a model, is that correct?

WITNESS: That is correct.

SPENCE: Model. Now, I don't think you ever told the ladies and gentlemen of the jury what was wrong with that model, and maybe this would be a good time for you to tell the ladies and gentlemen of the jury, in your own words what is wrong with the model.

DEFENSE COUNSEL: Object to the form of the question, your Honor. It makes no sense at all.

SPENCE: I'm asking him what was wrong with the model.

THE COURT: Well, overruled. I don't—I'm in the learning stage here myself—maybe your next objection will be okay. If the question is not familiar to the doctor, why that is another matter.

WITNESS: I indicated nothing wrong with the model. I said there were variations in people as compared to the results of calculations by the model. But the model represents an average situation. And I don't know anything that is wrong, or a better model by a scientific committee—and ICRP-19.

SPENCE: Let me ask you this question: Did you ever take the time to read the article of May 14, 1975, by Dr. Gofman, in which he tells you what is wrong with the model?

WITNESS: Is that the one that is published?

SPENCE: It is the one that I have in my hand—it appears to be published to me. But, I want to know: Have you read it?

WITNESS: I would like to know where it was published.

SPENCE: I will give it to you. Take a look at it.

WITNESS: It is published by the Committee for Nuclear Responsibility, it says here.

SPENCE: Yes. Have you ever read that?

WITNESS: Yes, I have.

SPENCE: When did you read that last? Did you read it before you came up here to tell the ladies and gentlemen of the jury about your calculations?

WITNESS: I read it in 1975 sometime, when I got a copy of it.

SPENCE: You are aware of the fact that your model makes certain assumptions, aren't you?

WITNESS: Yes.

SPENCE: And, you are aware of the fact that the model is totally based on the assumption of normally functioning epithelieum of the bronchial system, isn't that true?

WITNESS: I don't know that that is in the assumption.

. . . .

SPENCE: Okay, I guess, after I have listened to you read that, it didn't make much sense, but it in substance is saying that smokers, as you smoke the cilia that pushes the material out of the lungs, including plutonium, is destroyed by smoking, isn't that true?

WITNESS: Some fraction of it.

SPENCE: And, it is called a "serious loss of ciliary presence in cigarette smokers," isn't that true?

WITNESS: That is what it says.

SPENCE: Yes. And, it is a cilia that you say, you know, brought up a percentage of plutonium—what percentage did you say was brought up out of the lungs in the first 500 days?

WITNESS: In the model?

SPENCE: Yes.

WITNESS: I said half of it.

SPENCE: Yes. Thank you.

WITNESS: Half of 60 percent, which is 30 percent.

. . . .

SPENCE: Now, Dr. Voelz, you gave this jury a series of figures on the board yesterday. I want to go back to those because there is such a divergence in the bottom line in this so-called numbers business between what you have said and what Dr. Gofman and Dr. Martell and Dr. Morgan have said. Relative to those figures, isn't it true that you did not plug in any specific factor for the fact that Karen Silkwood was a heavy smoker?

WITNESS: That is not true.

SPENCE: All right. I have asked you, and I'm going to give you a chance to listen to this again, because I think it is true: Isn't it true that you did not plug in a specific factor for the proposition that Karen Silkwood was a heavy smoker?

WITNESS: That was not a specific factor.

SPENCE: Thank you. So what I have just said is true, isn't it?

WITNESS: That is true.

SPENCE: And, are you aware of the fact that Dr. Morgan, and Dr. Voelz (sic), both, took the position in this—Strike that. Dr. Morgan and Dr. Gofman both took the position in this case that a factor of at least ten would have to be used—that is, you would have to multiply it by ten because of the fact that she had plutonium in a lung that was already exposed to heavy smoking—are you aware of that fact?

DEFENSE COUNSEL: Object to the form of the question. Dr. Morgan gave no such testimony. In fact, the jury will recall the calculation that Dr. Morgan put on the board, which is vastly different.

SPENCE: Oh, come on—let's not have a speech.

THE COURT: I don't know what is the jury's recollection. Overruled. I don't recall the precise matter myself.

SPENCE: Let's just zoom into the issue: Dr. Gofman has published on that subject. You have read his publications, haven't you?

WITNESS: One.

SPENCE: Dr. Auer—What's his name?

WITNESS: Auerbach.

SPENCE: Dr. Auerbach has also published on the subject of smokers, and smoking dogs?

WITNESS: Right.

SPENCE: And, so I'm asking you if you aren't aware of the fact that Dr. Gofman, in making his publications, and in doing his deed, says that this model isn't right, that you have to plug in a factor of ten for a heavy smoker, because the cilia isn't pumping out the plutonium that you say is pumped out in the model lung, isn't that what Dr. Gofman says?

WITNESS: That is what Dr. Gofman says.

SPENCE: Now, you recognize, do you not, that studies have shown that the ciliary function of a heavy smoker's lung is reduced by 33 to 36 percent—you are aware of that, aren't you?

WITNESS: Is that Dr. Gofman's recitation of Dr. Auerbach?

SPENCE: Are you aware of those studies?

WITNESS: Yes. But, it is wrong on Dr. Gofman's article. And you have the article—I can show you—

SPENCE: Listen to my question, doctor. You're an intelligent man—

DEFENSE COUNSEL: Just a moment. Your Honor, the witness is not being permitted to fully respond.

SPENCE: The witness is not even trying to answer the question. He's trying to argue.

THE COURT: Let's get the question first, and then maybe he can incorporate it in his answer, if it is appropriate.

DEFENSE COUNSEL: He didn't get an answer to the last question— that is my objection.

THE COURT: Well, I don't think he had the question out.

SPENCE: Thank you, Judge. Doctor, aren't you aware of the fact that heavy smokers don't have as good a ciliary function as non-smokers?

WITNESS: Yes, I certainly am.

SPENCE: That is an established medical fact, isn't it?

WITNESS: I believe so. There are some controversies in some articles, but, yes, I accept that.

SPENCE: You do accept that?

WITNESS: Yes, I accept that.

SPENCE: And, do you accept the proposition that you were telling the jury in this case, that a percentage of this plutonium in the figures that you made was taken out of the lung through ciliary action?

WITNESS: Yes.

SPENCE: Now, could you tell me, doctor, what factor was placed on the model that you used for smokers?

WITNESS: Yes, I will be glad to. There is a whole section in report 19 of ICRP that I used that described the discussions on smoking and the committee considered in their model, and why they felt the human data that was used included smokers and non-smokers in the data. It was an average. So that the actual data that was incorporated in that model did not just include data from non-smokers—it included smokers' data as an average—not as a specific factor.

SPENCE: If you were using a non-smoker—if Karen Silkwood had been a non-smoker—you would have included data in a smoker's lung. If she was a heavy smoker, you'd use an average smoker. That is all a numbers game, isn't it? That has no specific reference to Karen Silkwood as she exactly was, isn't that true?

WITNESS: In these kind of numbers, using averages of population is the best you can do.

SPENCE: I didn't ask you that. Read the question to the witness. I will ask if you can't answer the question as I put it to you fairly. (Question was read back).

WITNESS: The question is: "That is a numbers game, isn't it?" And the answer is yes.

SPENCE: Thank you.

Block demonstrated that although the defendant's expert rehabilitation specialist claimed that the plaintiff could be rehabilitated from 100 percent disability to full-time employment, the witness was not familiar with the employment opportunities in the area of the country in which the plaintiff resided, thus questioning the basis of the witness's assumptions and conclusions:

BLOCK: We are dealing with a relatively unsophisticated person when we talk about Dorman Baird, are we not?

WITNESS: Yes.

BLOCK: A farm boy.

WITNESS: He is from Alabama. I didn't know if that—

BLOCK: Do you know what town in Alabama or what village?

WITNESS: No.

BLOCK: Boaz, Alabama. Do you know the population of Boaz, Alabama?

WITNESS   No, I don't.

BLOCK: Do you know what types of occupations they have available in Boaz, Alabama?

WITNESS: I'm not familiar with the employment situation in Alabama for anybody.

BLOCK: For any type of person, regardless of their bodily integrity or mental equilibrium?

WITNESS: Exactly.

. . . .

BLOCK: Well, that's assuming that there is constructive work that can be done, isn't that so?

WITNESS: That's economics and sociology.

BLOCK: And that's not your field?

WITNESS: That' right.

BLOCK: So the employment market, we agree is not your field?

WITNESS: A disabled worker can find work in many areas and a person who is trained for a skill will find work probably more easily than an able-bodied person who is unskilled.

BLOCK: Assuming jobs are available?

WITNESS: Of course assuming there are jobs available.

§8.06   —Trustworthiness

The trustworthiness of the witnesses was questioned by demonstrating that they were biased and prejudiced, were influenced by unsavory motives, had testified inconsistently, had testified falsely, or had behaved dishonestly.

Glaser began the cross-examination of one medical expert by eliciting testimony to the effect that the witness was acquainted with the defendant and that the two had attended staff meetings at the same hospital for some 20 years. This suggested a personal relationship with the defendant and a potential for bias:

GLASER: Okay. You, of course, know Dr. Cavalli, right?

WITNESS: Dr. Cavalli?

GLASER: Yes.

WITNESS: Yes, I know Dr. Cavalli.

GLASER: He's on the same staff?

WITNESS: He is, indeed.

GLASER: At Misericordia Hospital?

WITNESS: Misericordia Hospital.

GLASER: You're in the pathology department, he's in the gynecology department?

WITNESS: Right.

GLASER: You've seen him at the hospital, right?

WITNESS: Sure.

GLASER: Many times?

WITNESS: Sure. I've been at the hospital twenty years.

GLASER: And he's been at that hospital for a similar period, right?

WITNESS: I don't know, but I would say about that, sure.

GLASER: You meet him at staff meetings.

WITNESS: I do.

Ring suggested bias and prejudice on the part of the defendant's expert engineer by demonstrating that his business consisted primarily of testifying in civil trials as opposed to "real" engineering work, thereby creating the characterization of a "hired gun:"

RING: Mr. Barnett, this business of yours, Triodyne, is a consulting business, right?

WITNESS: Yes.

RING: One of the main parts of that business is to work on cases in litigation, isn't that right?

WITNESS: Yes, sir. About 90 per cent of our work.

RING: So that you hold yourself, as we call it, as an expert witness?

WITNESS: Yes.

RING: To testify in cases in court?

WITNESS: Yes.

RING: On various kinds of machines?

WITNESS: That's correct.

Similarly, Corboy established that the defendant's doctor was hired and paid by the defendant's lawyer, and did not have a doctor-patient relationship with the plaintiff.

Spence established that the defendant's expert testifying on behalf of Kerr-McGee was previously called in by Kerr-McGee to examine Karen Silkwood prior to her death and to perform the autopsy after her death, thereby suggesting that he was always an agent of the defendant Kerr-McGee and not a neutral expert. Spence then established that, although the Kerr-McGee team had an opportunity to have Karen Silkwood's remains examined by an independent group, they chose not to. He cross-examined as follows:

SPENCE: Isn't it true that Kerr-McGee, the very people who now hire you in this case, were the ones who tried and did get you involved in this?

WITNESS: Do I know that?

SPENCE: Yes.

WITNESS: Ho, I don't know that.

SPENCE: Can you deny that?

WITNESS: No, I can't deny it, either.

SPENCE: Well, the same old people showed up after her death as were involved in this matter prior to her death—you were there, Doctor _____ was there, isn't that true?

WITNESS: At the post-mortem examination?

SPENCE: Yes.

WITNESS: Yes.

SPENCE: And by this time a former Kerr-McGee employee, by the name of _____—who was also a witness for Kerr-McGee in this case—was there—that is true, isn't it?

WITNESS: That is true.

SPENCE: So it would be fair to say that the whole Kerr-McGee team that appeared in this case was there at the autopsy before the case was even heard of, isn't that true?

. . . .

SPENCE: During the period of time that all of this was being done, when you and Dr. Sternhagen were together in Los Alamos, when you and Dr. Sternhagen and Valentine were there at the autopsy, whenever you were dealing with Karen Silkwood as a live person, or as a dead person, at any time, was any independent person or medical person available and called in to represent the Silkwood interests in this matter?

WITNESS: No.

SPENCE: Did you ever make an attempt to divide the samples so that some independent agency could run a duplicate test to make sure that what you did was indeed fair and just?

WITNESS: No sir, we did not.

Baldwin established, through the defendant's expert engineer, that both the engineer and Ford Motor Company were motivated by profit in designing and selling an unsafe tractor. Baldwin established that the plaintiff's use of the tractor and the plaintiff's accident were foreseeable by Ford in the design and marketing of the tractor. He then elicited testimony from the witness that the tractor could have been equipped with safety devices that would have prevented the plaintiff's injury, but that the safety devices were not used because they would have increased the cost of the tractor and would have prevented the tractor from being sold competitively in the open market. Thus, by establishing that, in the past, Ford and the expert had put money interests ahead of consumer safety interests, Baldwin demonstrated a lack of loyalty to consumer protection and undermined the witness's trustworthiness on consumer issues at the trial. Baldwin first established Ford's position that the safety devices could have been supplied, but that the cost would create a problem with competition with other manufacturers:

BALDWIN: Can't you very simply protect against both contingencies, rollover protection and operator protection?

WITNESS: The cheapest protection is the rollover protection.

BALDWIN: Would you answer my question?

WITNESS: What was the question again?

BALDWIN: I said you can very easily design one thing that would protect both things from happening, the rollover protection and f-o-p—

WITNESS: You can do the whole package, yes, that's right.

BALDWIN: All right. Now the reason you told me on your deposition that you didn't furnish it was because you couldn't compete, isn't that right?

WITNESS: It would be a non-competitive practice.

BALDWIN: That means that you wouldn't—you couldn't sell as many tractors with it as you could without it?

WITNESS: Yes, sir, that would be it.

BALDWIN: And, therefore, you wouldn't make as much money?

WITNESS: That's right.

BALDWIN: It is a profit thing, isn't it.

WITNESS: Well, I assume that that's part of doing business.

BALDWIN: Is doing profit. So what you have on one hand here is one of your design considerations—isn't it—that you balance off your market ability with your safety?

WITNESS: No, I don't think that's a true statement.

BALDWIN: Is it not safer with this protection?

WITNESS: There is many people that do not require this device at all.

BALDWIN: Now, would you mind answering my question?

WITNESS: Is it safer with or without—

BALDWIN: Is that tractor safer or—

WITNESS: Yes, sir, it would be safer with it.

BALDWIN: All right, and safety is one consideration, isn't it?

WITNESS: That's right, and that's why we make it available.

BALDWIN: All right, safety has a design consideration and you said it certainly would be safer if you provided it, didn't you?

WITNESS: Yes.

BALDWIN: But the reason you didn't provide it is because of market-ability, is that right?

WITNESS: Marketability, that's right.

Baldwin then established that it was foreseeable that farmers would be using the tractor in the way that plaintiff was using it at the time of his injury:

BALDWIN: Now, another consideration when you design a product is the risk involved, isn't it?

WITNESS: Uh huh.

BALDWIN: In other words, if somebody is going to get hurt?

WITNESS: Uh huh.

BALDWIN: And cannot design—you know this as a design engineer—is that you balance off the risk versus safety?

WITNESS: Uh huh.

BALDWIN: IOs that right?

WITNESS: (No response)

BALDWIN: That is a sound engineering principle?

WITNESS: There is a balance there, yes, sir.

BALDWIN: Sir?

WITNESS: There would be a balance there.

BALDWIN: Al right.

WITNESS: Function certainly is on this list.

BALDWIN: Now then, let me ask you, sir: you know when you design this product that farmers are famous for being jacks-of-all-trades, don't you?

WITNESS: I am seeing it demonstrated here.

BALDWIN: Well, you knew it before that, didn't you?

WITNESS: Well, I have seen lots of attachments on the back end; I haven't seen front-end loaders.

BALDWIN: Well, would you answer my question? Don't you know that farmers are jacks-of-all-trades?

WITNESS: I think that would be generally agreed, yes.

BALDWIN: And that's something that you anticipate when you design?

WITNESS: We didn't anticipate this.

BALDWIN: Would you answer my question, Mr. Sewell?

WITNESS: Yes.

BALDWIN: All right, isn't that something that you, as a design engineer, anticipate that farmers are going to use that bucket for practically every contrivance a man can come up with?

WITNESS: Well, yes, they are using it for about everything that comes along, I guess.

BALDWIN: Well, I will refresh your memory, sir. Do you remember your deposition being taken?

WITNESS: Yes, sir.

BALDWIN: When I asked you if you knew that farmers were famous for being jacks-of-all-trades, you answered "Yes."

WITNESS: Well, they are famous for improvising and you answered "yes."

WITNESS: Yes, sir.

BALDWIN: And you know when you made these that when you made these tractors—you know that they are going to use these bucket devices for all sorts of things, whether it is manure, gravel, rocks, practically everything imaginable that they are going to be lifting, and for practically anything they want to move, they are going to move it. You know that—you knew that when you designed it, didn't you?

WITNESS: Uh huh.

BALDWIN: Sir?

WITNESS: Yes, sir, I have to say that.

BALDWIN: And you knew and you know when you designed that tractor that they were going to put all kinds of implements on the front of it, anywhere from an implement that John Deere would make to the implement that the village blacksmith would make, you knew that, didn't you—For, we are not saying you—I am talking about Ford?

WITNESS: Yes.

BALDWIN: Ford knew that. As a matter of fact, that's one of your market objectives, isn't it, to have the front-end device so that you can put many implements on it and make it more marketable?

WITNESS: Our market objective is to provide a loader and all the necessary attachments to do the farmer's job, that is right.

BALDWIN: You design it so that they can put all kinds of implements on the front of that loader, isn't that right?

WITNESS: That is right, our implements.

BALDWIN: All right, we will come to that. But you know they are going to put implements that scoop, lift and one of your objectives in your design is to provide—fix it to where they can put more of these implements on it so that they will have more uses for it, isn't that right?

WITNESS: Flexibility.

BALDWIN: Flexibility?

WITNESS: Yes.

BALDWIN: And, again, that comes back to marketability, doesn't it?

WITNESS: Yes, sir.

Similarly, Spence established bias and prejudice on the part of the defendant's doctor by demonstrating that he had worked in private industry and government funded jobs all of his work life, and that those jobs depended on his proving plutonium to be safe for use by humans. Spence thereby suggested that the doctor's calculations and testimony about how much plutonium contamination a human could stand without permanent injury were motivated by greed rather than an interest in human safety:

SPENCE: Who were your employers?

WITNESS: Well, recently the University of California, the last ten years. And, prior to that it would have been the Atomic Energy Commission.

SPENCE: Have you ever testified for any private industry before?

WITNESS: No, I never have.

SPENCE: Did you ever testify for Gulf Oil Company?

WITNESS: No, I never have.

SPENCE: Are you a consultant for Gulf?

WITNESS: Yes, I am.

SPENCE: Do you get paid by them?

WITNESS: I haven't—we had a daily fee when we met, but that's—

SPENCE: Are you a consultant for Kerr-McGee?

WITNESS: No. Well, I am in this case.

SPENCE: Yes. You are a consultant for Kerr-McGee in this case, and you work for the—who is your employer?

WITNESS: University of California.

SPENCE: And, this is funded, the University, I think, you said by the United States government, is that correct?

WITNESS: That is correct.

SPENCE: All right. Now, doctor, I want to ask you some more questions about that latch-up.

WITNESS: By "latch-up" are you talking about Kerr-McGee and the University of California?

SPENCE: No. I want you to, first of all, tell me—I'm going to put your name up here: Dr. V-o-e-l-z. Dr. Voelz. Now, you are from the standpoint of the medical aspects, the head of the whole sheebang out there to LASL, aren't you?

WITNESS: The Health Division.

SPENCE: I want you to tell me the departments that are under you.

WITNESS: There are twelve.

. . . .

SPENCE: Now, each one of these people have a department head?

WITNESS: That is correct.

SPENCE: And they ultimately report to you?

WITNESS: Correct.

SPENCE: Now, let me ask you a question: Are there any more areas that you supervise, or that you have control or input in, other than these?

WITNESS: No. These are the—

SPENCE: This is all?

WITNESS: As far as I—

SPENCE: All right. Now, Dr. Voelz, are each one of these supported by government money, each one of these deals?

WITNESS: Yes.

SPENCE: Now, Dr. Voelz, we've heard some testimony here from Kerr-McGee about one of their men by the name of Valentine, who they criticize for "building an empire." Do you know Mr. Valentine?

WITNESS: Yes I know Mr. Valentine.

SPENCE: Now, this government money, all of these things that we're talking about here, have to do more or less with the problems of radiation, don't they—nuclear industry?

WITNESS: Not all of them, but for the most part.

SPENCE: And, who is your boss?

WITNESS: I report to the director.

SPENCE: Director who?

WITNESS: Director of LASL.

SPENCE: Director of LASL. Now, is this, all this government money, coming from the NRC or the ERDA?

WITNESS: It is now DOE, Department of Energy.

SPENCE: Well—

WITNESS: ERDA became the Department of Energy.

SPENCE: So it is coming from ERDA.

WITNESS: Well, it is now called DOE, Department of Energy.

SPENCE: All through this trial we heard it referred to as ERDA, and that's the same as DOE?

WITNESS: At the time that the case went on, it was all AEC.

SPENCE: This is the promotion end of nuclear energy we've heard— would you agree with that?

WITNESS: Are you talking about now, or at the time—

SPENCE: I'm talking about ERDA, that ERDA, or which is now the Department of Energy, is the promotional end of the governmental, you deal with the AEC, is that right?

WITNESS: I never quite heard it explained that way, but I would say research and development end; yes.

SPENCE: Research and development. "Development" and "promotion" mean about the same, don't they?

WITNESS: No, not to me.

SPENCE: And, you've got to have research to get either promotion or develment, don't you?

WITNESS: Yes.

SPENCE: And, so when people say that, you know-wouldn't you say there's an interest in ERDA and has been continuously all along, to forward the nuclear energy business in the country?

WITNESS: They are interested in nuclear as one energy source.

SPENCE: And, you're the head of this whole sheebang, all this below you, aren't you?

WITNESS: That is right.

SPENCE: What would happen if all of this government money got taken away, and the people kind of got upset about exposures, and standards, and numbers games, and words, and things like that—would that affect your—would that affect your, you know, your empire at all?

DEFENSE COUNSEL: Well, just a moment, Dr. Voelz. Your Honor, I object to the question as argumentative, improper, speculation.

THE COURT: Sustained, as to form.

SPENCE: Let me ask this question: What would happen to all of this business that is going on here under you, if we take the government money away?

DEFENSE COUNSEL: Well, I renew my objection. Improper as to form, your Honor, and speculative.

THE COURT: Sustained. One of those, again, I think the answer is obvious.

SPENCE: All right.

. . . .

SPENCE: Do you think that—let me go into your background a little further, if I can—I have notes here a long time ago—it's getting late in the day, and I see from my kind of slopping around here that I'm getting a little tired—and maybe you are too. Did I understand you correctly that your first opportunity to get into industrial medicine came from the AEC?

WITNESS: That is correct.

SPENCE: That is the AEC educated you in that area, or paid for your education?

WITNESS: Yes. And they granted me a fellowship.

SPENCE: And, then you went directly to Los Alamos?

WITNESS: After the first year. I went to Los Alamos for the second year.

SPENCE: Then you trained at Los Alamos, and you were a sort of a child of Los Alamos, a prodigy of that area, weren't you?

WITNESS: I worked there, yes.

SPENCE: And, you worked for the government, or through government funded programs all of your life, from the day you got out of medical school, isn't that true?

WITNESS: For the vast majority.

In questioning a defense expert on ejection seats, Gibbons attacked his trustworthiness by demonstrating that the expert was also involved in the promotion and sales of A10 airplanes, and that, as such, his job was to warrant the planes as safe. In this way, Gibbons established the expert as "just another car salesman:"

GIBBONS: All right. Now, let's talk about that. First, this film that you showed, that is a sales type film to try to make more money for Republic Fairchild, isn't it?

WITNESS: Of course.

GIBBONS: And that is your job, isn't it?

WITNESS: Yes, sir.

GIBBONS: Ever since you left the United States Air Force that is what you have been doing for them?

WITNESS: That's right.

GIBBONS: Going around all over the country and in foreign countries with your advertisement, your promotions to try to sell more of these A10s?

WITNESS: Yes, sir.

GIBBONS: And what is the cost of one of these A10s?

WITNESS: In the year 1982 dollar, about $9,000,000.00.

GIBBONS: All right. Of course, the more you sell the more money your company and you make, isn't that right?

WITNESS: Well, it would be true if—

GIBBONS: That's right, isn't it?

WITNESS: I know the company makes more. I don't know if I will make any more on it.

Gibbons then went on the demonstrate that the witness was testifying in an evasive manner by showing that although the witness attempted to downplay flight control jam mishaps and attempted to deny deaths due to flight control jam, it had been determined that one of the witness's friends had died as a result of a flight control jam. This evasiveness damaged the witness's trustworthiness:

GIBBONS: Thank you. And likewise it is also true that—I made a couple of notes about the film, having seen it with the jury for the first time, and there was a lot of talk here on the film pertaining to specifically about flight controls, wasn't there?

WITNESS: Yes, sir.

GIBBONS: How easy it operates with flight controls.

WITNESS: I don't believe it said it answered, or that it said it operates easily with the flight controls.

GIBBONS: It talks about how efficient they work, did it not?

WITNESS: It had three different flight control systems.

GIBBONS: Nothing was said about flight control jams.

WITNESS: No, sir.

GIBBONS: Now, you said that you are the Republic man, and you claim to have, as I understand your testimony, and please correct me if I'm wrong, only heard of four flight control mishaps, is that right?

WITNESS: No. I think what I said was that I have heard that there were 6 accidents which may have involved flight controls.

GIBBONS: As a matter of fact, there has even been deaths caused from known flight control jams in the white area, hasn't there?

WITNESS: No, sir there have not.

GIBBONS: Didn't one of your friends, Colonel Thompson, get killed?

WITNESS: He did.

GIBBONS: And you participated in a wake for him, didn't you?

WITNESS: I certainly did.

GIBBONS: And you told his widow, Mrs. Thompson, that it was a flight control jam in the white area?

WITNESS: I did not.

GIBBONS: Let me ask you this—approaching the witness, Your Honor.

THE COURT: All right.

GIBBONS: How many flight control mishaps do you say have occurred because of jams?

WITNESS: None.

GIBBONS: Okay. No flight control jams or restrictions have occurred that you are aware of during your entire career with Republic Fairchild?

WITNESS: I didn't say that, sir.

GIBBONS: Well, let me ask the question again. Maybe I put it poorly. How many A10 flight control mishaps are you aware of?

WITNESS: 27. I beg your pardon. Is that flight control mishaps?

GIBBONS: Right.

WITNESS: I am aware that, I believe there are 6 Class A mishaps that have had probable cause or possible cause being cited as flight control problems.

GIBBONS: Well, were you aware that—and, of course, the Air Force Accident Safety Investigation Board, that is all privileged, isn't it?

WITNESS: Yes, sir.

GIBBONS: Are you aware that they found, and your company knows, that the Board found that a flight control jam caused Colonel Thompson's death?

WITNESS: No, sir. I'm not.

GIBBONS: Let me show you a document.

.   .   .   .

GIBBONS: Right here, this is a Republic Fairchild document, even the signal of your company from New York is on there, right?

WITNESS: Yes, sir.

GIBBONS: And that is to T. R. Drummond. You know him, don't you?

WITNESS: Yes, sir.

GIBBONS: Even look at all the copies sent to all these folks. And Mr. Townsend, whose deposition we read very late last night, I might add at about 10:00 o'clock, he is the man that designed these flight controls in the white area, isn't he?

WITNESS: Yes, sir.

GIBBONS: All right. Let's go down here. Fairchild Republic personnel, Mssrs. Dick Johnston, do you know him?

WITNESS: Yes, sir.

GIBBONS: Ed Shance, do you know him?

WITNESS: No.

GIBBONS: And Hank Anderson, do you know him?

WITNESS: Yes.

GIBBONS: Arrived at Bentwaters, that is England and where Colonel Thompson was killed.

WITNESS: Yes.

GIBBONS: On Tuesday to aid the Accident Board members with the investigation of subject aircraft. Now, the subject aircraft is 77-0253, and that was your buddy's wasn't it?

WITNESS: That's correct.

GIBBONS: All right. And Fairchild Republic is coming over there to aid the Safety Board, right?

WITNESS: That is what it says.

GIBBONS: All right. They were released by the Board President, Colonel Cater, on Friday, 20th of July and returned to the United States on Saturday, 21st of July. Did I read that correctly?

WITNESS: Yes.

GIBBONS: Although their efforts were appreciated by the Board members, they were unable to override the evidence on hand, that is the switch setting, warning light and eyewitness testimony that an aircraft problem existed which caused the aircraft to become uncontrollable and depart flight. The Board is firmly convinced in their own minds that a flight control jam caused the accident. This aircraft had a previous white area foreign object damage inspection at Davis Monthan Air Force Base prior to arriving at this station. Did I read that correctly?

WITNESS: Yes, sir.

GIBBONS: So at least Fairchild Republic, these people, Mr. Townsend whose deposition I read, they weren't able to override the Board who was "firmly convinced that a flight control jam" killed your buddy, isn't that right?

WITNESS: That is what that says, yes, sir.

Glaser damaged one of the defendant's medical expert's trustworthiness by challenging the witness's willingness to answer questions in a straightforward manner, and by not allowing the witness to be evasive. As noted above, the witness attempted to characterize himself as a specialist in gynecology and attempted to state that he had completely reviewed the plaintiff's medical chart. In each instance, Glaser continued to question the witness until he was forced to admit that he was not a specialist in gynecology and that he had not actually completely reviewed the plaintiff's chart. This caused the witness to project low credibility with respect to trustworthiness. As the testimony progressed, the witness continued to try to be evasive by refusing to answer yes or no questions in a straight forward fashion. Glaser insisted that the witness respond and asked the court to require the witness to respond. The court advised the witness either to answer questions with a yes or no answer or state that he could not answer with a yes or no. Rather than cooperate, the witness refused to answer obvious yes or no answers. Glaser forced the witness to answer or to refuse to answer, thus demonstrating the witness's unwillingness to be candid. Examples are as follows:

GLASER: One of the signs of functioning of the ovaries, am I correct, you said on direct exam, is the existence of menstrual periods on the part of the patient, right, sir?

WITNESS: I did not say—one of the signs of estrogen secretion can be a menstrual period, but it can be inadequate though. It can occur.

GLASER: Sir, one of the signs can be?

WITNESS: Yes, one of the signs can be, but it can be also—

GLASER: I didn't ask you about others.

THE COURT: Doctor, we're going to get through a lot faster if you just answer the questions.

WITNESS: Sometimes I have to answer with an explanation.

THE COURT: If you can't answer the question with a yes or no, say so, but where it can be answered, do that, otherwise we'll be here all day and maybe tomorrow all day.

· · · ·

GLASER: Were you interested in reviewing the hospital records, what her medical history was in connection with all of these items before the hysterectomy and the bilateral salpingo oophorectomy? Were you interested in that Doctor? Yes or no?

WITNESS: Only with an explanation.

GLASER: You can't answer that?

WITNESS: I can't, no.

.   .   .   .

GLASER: Without going into every record, am I correct in saying since you read the hospital records that every single record says that all of her complaints began after the hysterectomy and the oophorectomy? You agree with that?

WITNESS: I would have to qualify my answer, counselor.

GLASER: Can you answer that one yes or no?

WITNESS: I said I would have to qualify my answer, counselor.

GLASER: Okay. Well, my question is did you read that in every single record?

WITNESS: They meant when she came into the hospital.

GLASER: Sir, can't you answer that?

WITNESS: I don't know whether she had these before she went to the hospital. These are years after, she's been on estrogen therapy, that's why I want to qualify the answer.

GLASER: I move to strike it out.

THE COURT: Strike it out. Doctor—

WITNESS: I want to qualify it.

THE COURT: Then if you can't, just don't answer it.

WITNESS: Okay.

GLASER: Now, my question simply is, and tell us if you can answer this yes or no—

WITNESS: I can't.

Glaser also damaged the above witness's credibility by demonstrating that the witness was rendering opinions without any understanding of the facts of the case. Glaser used this approach to challenge the validity of the expert's opinions as demonstrated in §8.05, but it also damaged the witness's trustworthiness. For example, Glaser demonstrated that while the doctor was claiming that the defendant's removal of the plaintiff's ovaries had no effect on the plaintiff, the doctor had no knowledge of the plaintiff's prior medical history, or her physical or mental condition. By demonstrating that the witness rendered opinions based on an inadequate review of the plaintiff's medical records the night before trial, and had little or no knowledge of the plaintiff's condition prior to the removal of her ovaries, Glaser damaged the witness's projections of trustworthiness. For example, at one point Glaser asked:

GLASER: Do you know, sir, whether or not she had flashes, nervousness, numbness of the fingers, depression, insomnia and irritability before the operation?

WITNESS: No, I don't know.

Finally, Glaser further damaged the trustworthiness of the defendant's medical expert by demonstrating that the witness was unreliable. Although the witness was testifying that it was proper to remove the plaintiff's ovaries in the absence of any pelvic disease, in an effort to prevent future disease, particularly due to her age, Glaser elicited on cross-examination that the witness had previously expressed a conflicting opinion in the Journal of the American Medical Association to the effect that the ovaries should be retained in the absence of pelvic disease, and that routine bilateral oophorectomies should not be performed just because of age.

Perlman attacked the validity of one of the defendant's expert's opinions by demonstrating that his opinions were formed the night before the trial based on discussions with the defense lawyer. This attack also damaged the trustworthiness of the witness's testimony because it suggested that the witness was simply advancing positions spoon-fed to him by the defense attorneys. Perlman questioned as follows:

PERLMAN: You met at a session with Mr. McDowell and Mr. Minns, who was here yesterday, and some other experts and some lawyers in Pittsburgh, or in Franklin, Pennsylvania, on November 6th, 1984, didn't you, sir?

DEFENSE COUNSEL: Your Honor, I don't believe this is proper cross-examination. It's not something that I went into.

THE COURT: Well, overruled. You may go into that.

PERLMAN: Is that right, sir?

WITNESS: Yes.

PERLMAN: And it was at that time that you for the very first time gave any opinion relating a wire that was a naked wire or nicked wire, that was the first time that you gave any opinion that that had anything to do with this malfunction, wasn't it, sir?

WITNESS: That's right.

PEARLMAN: And you didn't look at any pictures at that time, did you?

WITNESS: At that time, I did not, that's right.

PEARLMAN: And you simply heard the discussion by these people, by Mr. Campbell and by Mr. Minns and all of these other people, and based on what they said, you formed an opinion that that was the wire that caused the problem; is that right, sir?

WITNESS: I, I, I believe I qualified that and said that if the picture would indicate that existed, that is a likely candidate, yes.

PERLMAN: Before that day, you didn't have an opinion.

WITNESS: That's right.

PERLMAN: Yet you were going to testify in this case as an expert witness and you didn't have any opinion?

WITNESS: I'm—I don't know about an expert witness. I, that term, that expression was never made to me.

PERLMAN: Isn't that what you are? You have been hired to testify as an expert witness?

WITNESS: No, sir, I have not been hired.

PERLMAN: What is your opinion that you have here then? Is that the opinion of a layperson?

WITNESS: Well, that's an opinion of a person who is familiar with the inner workings of that part of the equipment.

PERLMAN: Isn't it fair to say that the system that you and your company designed is being challenged in this case and that's one of the reasons you are here?

WITNESS: That, that's fair, I would say.

PERLMAN: At the meeting in Franklin, Pennsylvania, on November 6th, did Mr. Minns tell you that he thought it was water contamination within the system?

WITNESS: No, sir, I don't believe he told me that.

PERLMAN: Have you discussed with Mr. McDowell his testimony here yesterday?

WITNESS: No, I really didn't.

PERLMAN: You haven't discussed with him what he told this jury here yesterday?

WITNESS: Not—no, I have no idea what he told the jury. We have discussed, obviously, the, you know, various points, but I have no idea what he told the jury, no.

PERLMAN: Did you have dinner with him last night?

WITNESS: Yes.

PERLMAN: You mean you can't remember?

WITNESS: No, no, I had to think because one meal we did have, but it wasn't dinner. Yes, I did have dinner with him last night.

PERLMAN: Did you have breakfast with him this morning?

WITNESS: No, I did not.

PERLMAN: What about his attorney?

WITNESS: Did I have breakfast?

PERLMAN: Did you have dinner or breakfast with either one?

WITNESS: No, I did not.

PERLMAN: Did you discuss this thing with him, this circumstance or these events or the malfunction or whatever happened here with Mr. McDowell either at dinner or after dinner or before dinner last night?

WITNESS: We discussed some points about the abrasion or nick or whatever, yes.

. . . .

PERLMAN: That problem with connection number 29, the first time you ever mentioned that in either your deposition or in court was just a few minutes ago, wasn't it?

WITNESS: The first time I ever mentioned the number 29, yes. But it's not the first time I mentioned the second fault, no.

One element of the trustworthiness dimension is the perceived reliability of the speaker.[3] Thus, credibility can be weakened by demonstrating that a witness has testified inconsistently over time. Whenever possible, the lawyers pointed out those important inconsistencies between deposition testimony and testimony from the stand. For example, in Baldwin's case, as demonstrated above, the witness testified that in the design and manufacture of the tractor, he and Ford did not anticipate the plaintiff's use of a certain implement. Baldwin used the witness's deposition to demonstrate that the witness had previously testified differently, to the effect that he and Ford, in designing the tractor, realized that farmers were jacks-of-all-trades and were famous for improvising.

§8.07   Controverting Defense Arguments or Positions

The lawyers used cross-examination to controvert defense positions and arguments. In Ring's case, one witness for the defendant manufacturer testified that the manufacturer shifted its design of the machine to use a compression spring rather than a tension spring because the compression spring was a better design. In cross-examining the defendant's expert engineer, Ring elicited the opinion that a compression spring was not better than a tension spring, and that the shift in design was not as good as with the tension spring. Ring used one of the defendant's witnesses to controvert the testimony of another witness:

RING: I see. But you think a compression spring is a bad design for the spring with a treadle?

WITNESS: It is not as good as a tension spring. It is not a bad design, just not as good as the tension spring.

RING: The truth of the matter is that compression springs are the kind of springs you should use on that press brake, whether it is the foot treadle or the modified version, isn't that true?

---

[3] C. Hovland, I. Janis, H. Kelley, Communication and Persuasion 23-24, 34 (1953).

WITNESS: That is absolutely incorrect.

RING: Is that right?

WITNESS: That's right.

RING: So that if Verson shifted in 1967 from a tension spring to a compression spring for that model press, they shifted to an unsafe design, is that it?

WITNESS: To a design which is not as good as the tension spring.

Similarly, while the position of the defendant was that it did not add protective accessories to the tractor because the additional cost would prevent it from being competitive in the open market, Baldwin established on cross-examination of the defendant's representative that the tractor was sold competitively in England where the protective accessory was placed on the tractor as standard equipment due to regulation:

BALDWIN: Now you said you do compete in England?

WITNESS: Yes.

BALDWIN: And, if I understand your testimony, it comes down to that you didn't furnish this cab protection because you can't compete in the market, the marketability is the reason, as you put it, you can't be competitive, is that right, is that what you told us?

WITNESS: We compete in England, I said that.

BALDWIN: You are competitive in England, aren't you?

WITNESS: Everybody has to put it on their tractor.

BALDWIN: My question is: You are competitive in England, aren't you?

WITNESS: Yes, sir, we are.

BALDWIN: And you have to put it on your tractors in England, don't you?

WITNESS: Yes.

BALDWIN: And you do it?

WITNESS: Yes, sir.

BALDWIN: And you do make a profit over there, don't you? You don't show a loss?

WITNESS: Doing pretty good right now, sir, yes, sir.

When a Kerr-McGee official admitted that he had a duty to advise employees of the dangers of radiation contamination and claimed on direct examination that he had so advised the employees, Spence read through the warnings with the official and established that the warnings never advised the employees that cancer was a hazard of radiation contamination, thus controverting the position that full warnings had been given. Spence first forced the witness to admit that employees should be warned of the dangers of lung cancer, and then established that the warnings actually given did not warn of lung cancer. Spence further established that, not only were the warnings unintelligible to the 18 to 19-year-old farm boys they were designed to protect, but that Kerr-McGee's own manager did not understand them:

SPENCE: Thank you. Now, I want to ask you this: In view of the fact that you think that the hazard, the major hazard is inhalation of those alpha particles that cause cancer—do you think that a responsible operator of a plant would make sure that, first of all, that major danger, that major problem, be made known to his workers?

WITNESS: It was made known—

SPENCE: Wait a minute. I'm not asking you whether it was made known. I'm asking you: Do you think it should be made known?

WITNESS: Yes.

SPENCE: Now, why do you think it should be made known?

WITNESS: So that we would know the hazards of the material they are dealing with.

SPENCE: Do you think it is important for workers to have a clearcut, unquestioned, open, notorious understanding of the fact that plutonium particles, when inhaled, will cause cancer—do you think that is important?

WITNESS: I think it is important.

SPENCE: Do you think, from a health standpoint—we've been talking about awards—we've been talking about citations—we've been talking about hours of accident-free work—do you think that the most important thing that you could do in a safety program for your people would be to tell them clearly that inhaling plutonium may cause cancer?

WITNESS: That was done.

SPENCE: I didn't ask you if it was done. Do you think that is the most important thing you could do?

WITNESS: You said it was the most important.

SPENCE: Yes. And that is what I'm asking you—do you?

WITNESS: Plutonium has—if it gets under the skin, if it is ingested it is a hazard.

SPENCE: Wait a minute. I think you said the most important hazard, the most difficult, and most frightening hazard was the inhaling of it, so I'm talking about the most important hazard, and I'm asking you: Do you think that is the most important thing a safety program could do, would be to inform the employees clearly of that hazard?

WITNESS: To give them a clear understanding of the hazardous material they are working with; yes sir.

SPENCE: Thank you. Would you show me Defendants' Exhibit 5, please, Mr. Clerk? Now, you, of course, would be in charge of seeing that that information, that is that plutonium ingested into the lungs may cause cancer—you would be in charge of seeing that that information was clearly delivered to your employees—that would be part of your job as a manager, wouldn't it?

. . . .

SPENCE: Now, Defendants' Exhibit 5 is a nice safety—is a nice manual made by your people about plutonium safety. Have you ever seen that before?

WITNESS: Yes, sir.

SPENCE: You think it is a pretty good manual?

WITNESS: Yes, I thought it was.

SPENCE: You though it was fair to your employees?

WITNESS: Well, I understood that this was what was presented to the employees, with certain films, and other things.

SPENCE: Did you think the manual was fair?

WITNESS: Yes.

SPENCE: Have you read it?

WITNESS: Yes, I have.

SPENCE: And, you're telling the ladies and gentlemen of the jury that this is the kind of manual that you approved on behalf of your company—I guess that is your testimony, isn't it? That is your testimony?

WITNESS: That was written in 1969—and this was a part of the instructions; yes.

SPENCE: Now, I want to read you just the matter that is the most important, that we have agreed, namely, the inhalation of plutonium. I want to read to you from the manual:

"The problem of lung absorption, retention and elimination of inhaled materials is complex, since the various factors are dependent on particle size of the material inhaled, solubility, particle density, rate of respiration of the individual, etc. Although it is not possible at present to determine quantitatively what happens to inhaled plutonium under all specific conditions of exposure, it is possible on the basis of animal experiments to make some broad generalizations.

If 100 radioactive particles of optimum size for lung retention are inhaled, about 25 are immediately exhaled without depositing in the lungs. Of the 75 particles that remain in the lungs 50 are deposited in the bronchial tree and removed in a few hours to a few days by ciliary action and swallowed. Of the remaining 25 particles which were deposited in the alveolar sacs, about 10 (10 per cent of the originally inhaled dose) are rather rapidly absorbed into the circulating blood and deposited predominantly in the skeleton. The remaining 15 particles may be phagocytized—"

Let me get some help from you on this word. What does that word mean, or say? (indicating) First of all, what is the word?

WITNESS: Looks like "phagocytized" to me.

SPENCE: What does that mean?

WITNESS: I don't know.

SPENCE: Me neither. But, of course, those 18 and 19-year-old farm boys out there would know the meaning of the word, so—

WITNESS: Well, this spoke from a different—

SPENCE: Well, let's go ahead. It says: (Reading)
"—deposited in the lymph nodes, or eliminated up the bronchial tree and swallowed, the time of removal being on the order of 150 to 200 days."
What are the lymph nodes—do you know?

WITNESS: Well, there are several around the body.

SPENCE: Where are they?

WITNESS: Where are they?

SPENCE: Do you know anything else about them?

WITNESS: No. I'm not a doctor.

SPENCE: Well, of course, this wasn't written for doctors—it was written for 18 and 19-year-old farm boys.

WITNESS: It was presented by health physicists in different terms.

SPENCE: Well, let's go on: (Reading)
"Experimental data on animals—"
Now, these were given to them to take home—you haven't heard all the testimony—but they took these home with them.
(Reading) "Experimental data on animals, at least in so far as plutonium oxide is concerned, suggest that 10 per cent absorption may be a conservative upper limit. Absorption may actually be more nearly 1 per cent. Nevertheless, the data do suggest that inhalation is the principal potential route of entry of plutonium into the body. Experiments on animals show also that some of the inhaled material may accumulate in the pulmonary lymph nodes from which the elimination rate is slow, resulting several days later in a higher concentration in the nodes than in the lungs proper."
Just a question now: Do you think that that is the kind of information that you wanted to give to your employees in a manual that would fully, and fairly, and honestly, and completely advise them of the danger that exists in inhaling plutonium?

WITNESS: If that were the only thing, it would be difficult to say they had been fully advised.

Perlman used the defendant's expert to controvert their argument that the mining machine did not malfunction. The defendant was arguing that the mining machine malfunctioned due to a wire that became nicked as opposed to an inherent defect in the machine itself. Perlman questioned as follows:

PERLMAN: Mr. Ritchie, in the operation of this machine, even with the short, even if the wire had been nicked and even if the wire had touched the top of the lid, even if all of that had happened, is it your testimony that the operator could have stopped the boom swing?

WITNESS: Yes, sir.

PERLMAN: And if he had not been able to stop the boom swing, that would have been, that's a malfunction of the system, isn't it?

WITNESS: If he had not been able to stop the boom swing, that would be a malfunction, yes, sir.

PERLMAN: And if, in fact, the operator said he tried to stop the boom swing, but he couldn't, and that would be a malfunction in the system—

DEFENSE COUNSEL: Your Honor, I want to object as that not being the testimony of the witness.

THE COURT: Overruled. If it's not, the jury will disregard it, however. He can couch the question.

WITNESS: Can you state the question again?

PERLMAN: If the operator said he tried to stop the boom swing once he saw it starting but he couldn't, then the system malfunctioned?

WITNESS: I would have to know what measures he took to stop it before I could answer that question.

PERLMAN: Suppose he tried to reverse the lever that the swing was controlled by.

WITNESS: That would be one method to stop it.

PERLMAN: And if it didn't work that would be a malfunction?

WITNESS: That would be a malfunction. But there are other methods.

PERLMAN: Well, that's one method, and if it didn't work, it's a malfunction.

WITNESS: That particular function, that particular method would have malfunctioned, that's right.

The defense in Glaser's case called a pathologist who attempted to justify the defendant's unnecessary surgery in two ways. First, the pathologist asserted that his examination of the slides indicated submucous fibroid tumors and pronounced atrophy of the ovary, therefore supporting the argument that the plaintiff had the potential of developing cancer had her ovaries been left in, and for this reason, the surgery was justified. Secondly, he testified that his microscopic examination of the slides of the specimens of the plaintiff's ovaries, cervix, fallopian tubes, and uterus indicated that the plaintiff was already in a menopausal condition at the time of the removal of her reproductive system by the defendant, and further, that when the ovaries are removed, a woman can be maintained on estrogen without any adverse effects. This testimony was an attempt to convince the jury that the unnecessary removal of the plaintiff's reproductive system did not cause her problems in that she was already in a menopausal state, and that she would have experienced all of these problems in the near future, in the normal course of events, regardless of the surgery. This testimony was all based on the expert's review of slides of specimens of the plaintiff's tissue some seven years after they were removed from the plaintiff. Further, these conclusions were not made by any of the pathologists or physicians who were treating the plaintiff at the time of her surgery and were not noted in the pathology report. Glaser elicited testimony from the witness to controvert these claims. He established that most of this witness's assertions were not supported by the findings of the pathologist who actually examined the plaintiff's organs after removal, and that the evidence did not support a finding of submucosal tumors or atrophied ovaries. He further established that the plaintiff's medical history prior to the unnecessary surgery indicated that she was not in a menopausal state prior to the surgery, and that estrogen therapy had adverse effects. He questioned as follows in demonstrating that the pathology report described subserosal tumors rather than submucosal tumors:

> GLASER: Dr. Belsky, the man who got the tissue here, he's a pathologist, right, sir?
>
> WITNESS: Correct.
>
> GLASER: Do you know him?
>
> WITNESS: No.
>
> GLASER: And he was called into this case so that this lady could be helped, right, sir, in one way or another, by his analysis of the tissue, right, sir?
>
> WITNESS: I think that's true.
>
> GLASER: This report was not issued as an incident to the court proceeding, this report was issued in a hospital where a lady came for care and where the purpose was to help her, right?
>
> WITNESS: That's correct.
>
> GLASER: The pathologist got the tissue in two parts, according to the record, right?
>
> WITNESS: Yes.
>
> GLASER: And the first part were the curettings and the second part was a—consists of a uterus with cervix, both fallopian tubes and both ovaries attached. That was the whole reproductive system, in fact. He got that one whole mass, right, according to his report?
>
> WITNESS: That's correct.
>
> GLASER: And he reported—he reported several large subserosal lesions, right.
>
> WITNESS: Yes.
>
> .   .   .   .
>
> GLASER: And on the second part he says there are several large subserosal lesions. That's the kind, right?

WITNESS: Yes.

GLASER: Okay. Am I correct in saying that the report, the pathology report does not say submucosal lesions? Can you answer that one yes or no without—

WITNESS: These words are not in the report.

GLASER: Okay. The word subserosal is in the report a number of times, right?

WITNESS: That's right.

GLASER: He reports saying subserosal lesions, right?

WITNESS: That's correct.

GLASER: And what he reports is intramural lesions that project or push into the cavity, right, sir?

WITNESS: Yes.

GLASER: He does not say I find submucosal lesions in this case, can you answer that yes or no?

WITNESS: No, he does not.

With respect to the ovaries, he established:

GLASER: I think you testified that atrophy should be obvious to the operator. Atrophy consistent with what your opinion was as to the extent of atrophy should be obvious to the operator, right?

WITNESS: Yes.

GLASER: And he reported, the report dictated by him and signed by him, that the ovaries—I want to use the exact language, if you please— that the ovaries on both sides were normal.

WITNESS: That doesn't exclude atrophy.

GLASER: Sir, please, would you answer that one yes or no, sir?

WITNESS: Normal for her age, yes.

GLASER: Sir, I didn't ask you whether it was normal for her age. I asked you if he reported that the specimen included fibroid uterus, normal tubes and ovaries on both sides. Did he report that?

WITNESS: Yes, he did.

He then established that the evidence indicated that the plaintiff was not in a menopausal state at the time of her surgery:

GLASER: If Dr. Cavalli testified that menopause is when a woman hasn't had a period for a year, would you agree with that?

WITNESS: That's a reasonable definition, yes.

GLASER: Okay. And were you told when the last monthly period was, yes or no?

WITNESS: Yes.

GLASER: And when was it?

WITNESS: it was approximately five or six weeks before the operation, I believe.

Finally, he established that estrogen therapy can have adverse effects:

GLASER: Right. And it's important for the body, for the—to have a hormone balance, endocrine balance, right, sir?

WITNESS: Yes.

GLASER: All sorts of complaints can come from hormonal imbalance, correct?

WITNESS: That's correct.

GLASER: And when you remove the ovaries, you can bring about a hormonal imbalance, right?

WITNESS: That's correct.

. . . .

GLASER: Okay. When ovaries are removed, you have to substitute it with estrogen, a drug, right?

WITNESS: That's correct.

. . . .

GLASER: Well, estrogens have side effects, correct?

WITNESS: That's correct.

. . . .

GLASER: Well, do you agree with the statement in the PDR, estrogens may cause excessive fluid to be retained in the body?

WITNESS: I think that's a reasonable statement, yes.

GLASER: Okay. Do you agree that estrogen can produce severe headaches, dizziness, faintness or changes in vision?

WITNESS: I think that's possible, yes.

. . . .

GLASER: Do you agree that estrogen can elevate the blood pressure?

WITNESS: Yes.

. . . .

GLASER: Okay. Do you agree that it changes the libido, sex drive, can be a side effect of Provera?

WITNESS: Yes.

GLASER: That changes in appetite, headache, nervousness, dizziness, fatigue, backache, can all be side effects of Provera?

WITNESS: Yes.

§8.08 Eliciting Facts in Support of Plaintiff's Case

The lawyers never missed an opportunity to use the defendants' witnesses to establish facts in support of their cases. Although these witnesses were opposing, and frequently hostile witnesses, the lawyers used them to provide facts and corroborate opinions of the plaintiffs' witnesses. There were areas of agreement among the witnesses, and the lawyers exploited the areas.

Corboy used the defense doctor to establish his damages. He brought out testimony that proved that his client was a permanent quadriplegic who would never work again, and who would never be able to enjoy such things as a normal sex life. He obtained an acknowledgement from the defense doctor that the plaintiff was entitled to optimal medical care, that the plaintiff was receiving optimal care in the acute care facility, and that optimal care was directly related to the experience of the available medical staff:

> CORBOY: Thank you. Let's see if we can reach some areas of complete agreement. John Randolph Block is a spastic quadriplegic who is, for all intents and purposes, paralyzed below the eye area, except that, now, as you know, now that you've looked at the records, he can move his head to the left and he can move his head to the right?
>
> WITNESS: Slightly to the left and slightly to the right.
>
> CORBOY: And you say it is slightly?
>
> WITNESS: I don't know that it is as far—
>
> . . . .
>
> CORBOY: Doctor, when you examined John Randolph Block on the second day of February, 1983, he was what you call a severe spastic quadriplegic, was he not?
>
> WITNESS: Yes, he was.
>
> CORBOY: Just so we have no questions and no doubts about this, this gentleman will never be able to work again, will he?
>
> WITNESS: No, he will not.
>
> CORBOY: Just so we have absolutely no doubts about this—and I am hesitant about it, but I'm going to ask you anyhow—there is no question. He can never involve in sexual activity?
>
> WITNESS: He can never be involved in normal sexual activity. Now, erection, ejaculation are reflex acts. With the proper partner, with the proper stimulation, it is conceivable he could have an erection, that he could have intercourse, that he could have an ejaculation; it is questionable there as to how much he might feel, how much of an enjoyment it might be, but physiologically, it could happen, but it would not be a normal experience.
>
> . . . .
>
> CORBOY: His quadriplegic condition is completely permanent, is it not, doctor?
>
> WITNESS: Yes, it is.

In an effort to maximize the plaintiff's damage award, Corboy argued throughout the trial that the plaintiff would need optimal medical care for the rest of his life. That is, rather than allowing the jury to be convinced that the plaintiff could be warehoused in a nursing home at a minimal cost, Corboy argued that the plaintiff required optimal care that could only be supplied by certified physicians and therapists, and that the plaintiff was entitled to a jury verdict that would pay for this optimal care. He used the defendant's expert to establish this contention. Corboy established that optimal care was directly related to the experience of the available medical staff. He then obtained an acknowledgement from the defense doctor that the plaintiff was entitled to optimal medical care, that the plaintiff was receiving optimal care in the acute care facility, and that the plaintiff would require optimal care for the rest of his life.

> CORBOY: Sir, in your way of defining and your way of supplying us with definition, what does the term "optimal care" mean?
>
> WITNESS: As good a care as possible.
>
>   . . . .
>
> CORBOY: So in looking for whatever system of treatment for whatever therapies are available, for whatever emergencies occur, for whatever medical needs Randy Block is going to need for whatever the rest of his life is, as you sit there, he is entitled to as good as possible care available?
>
> WITNESS: Yes.
>
> CORBOY: And that is which is as good as possible available, is available in the City of Chicago today?
>
> WITNESS: Yes.
>
>   . . . .
>
> CORBOY: Doctor, we were talking yesterday I think about matters as optimal care that certain hospitals, certainly accredited hospitals, doctors are restricted in the type of activities and procedures they can engage in, are they not, sir?
>
> WITNESS: Some hospitals, yes.
>
> CORBOY: Most good hospitals?
>
> WITNESS: Most good hospitals. It's what we call credentialling.
>
> CORBOY: Let's even go further. Most good hospitals in Chicago?
>
> WITNESS: Yes.
>
> CORBOY: And that is in order to assure optimal care to the patient?
>
> WITNESS: Yes.
>
>   . . . .
>
> CORBOY: In any event optimal care subsequent to the operation would require he be in the IC unit, the intensive care unit of the neurosurgical ward wherever the operation was performed?
>
> WITNESS: He had optimal care at Billings Hospital, yes.

CORBOY: He had optimal care at Rehabilitation too, didn't he?

WITNESS: I believe so, yes.

CORBOY: He had optimal care at Columbus?

WITNESS: I believe so, yes.

CORBOY: He is receiving optimal care right now?

WITNESS: Yes, sir, he is.

. . . .

CORBOY: And, Doctor, you are familiar, are you not, with the principle in medicine of avoidable complications and avoidable factors?

WITNESS: Yes.

CORBOY: And I guess that's the fancy way of saying identifying the risks and then attempting medical care to avoid them?

WITNESS: As best as possible.

CORBOY: And in John Randolph Block's case identifying th risks and doing the very best to avoid them entitles him to optimal care?

WITNESS: Yes, it does.

CORBOY: And sometimes that optimal care will be very, very expensive.

WITNESS: I assume so.

CORBOY: Are you aware there are over $900,000 worth of medical expenses already in this case?

WITNESS: No, I was not aware until you mentioned it.

CORBOY: That's a sizable amount of money, isn't it?

CORBOY: In any event, in this concept of avoidance and identification this also applies to avoiding complications in head injury cases resulting from brain stem injury with the flow of, or the delineation of, locked-in syndrome?

WITNESS: Agreed.

CORBOY: And identifying those complications of locked-in syndrome from the trauma of brain stem injury requires constant vigilance?

WITNESS: Yes.

CORBOY: And that constant vigilance requires optimal care?

WITNESS: At this time yes.

CORBOY: Required it all the way from the time he was in the ambulance at Copely Memorial Hospital?

WITNESS: Yes, it has. Right through to now.

CORBOY: Right up to now?

WITNESS: Correct.

CORBOY: That optimal care is not going to stop tomorrow, is it?

WITNESS: Should not.

CORBOY: He is entitled to optimal care the rest of his life, isn't he?

WITNESS: Yes, he is.

Baldwin used the defense engineer to establish the plaintiff's claims that the injury was foreseeable, that the defendant was aware that farmers improvised with the use of implements on the tractors, that the defendant encouraged the use of different implements on the tractor, that the plaintiff's use of the tractor created a death trap, and that although foreseeable, the defendant placed no warnings on the tractor or in the operator's manual. For example, Balwin questioned as follows in eliciting the opinions that the use of the tractor created a death trap and that the defendant placed no warnings on the tractor or in the operator's manual:

BALDWIN: All right, sir. Now, as I understand the crux of what you have told Mr. Smith, is that any time you get a load like that, that high with that type of device, that you are going to have a catastrophe?

WITNESS: With this type of attachment, yes.

BALDWIN: Yes, isn't that right?

WITNESS: Yes.

BALDWIN: Isn't that something you can easily foresee and you can easily know?

WITNESS: No, sir.

BALDWIN: That you can have a catastrophe if you get a load like that?

WITNESS: We, sitting up there in Detroit, cannot see this happening on some farm in Texas.

BALDWIN: Well, let's say that you in Detroit could foresee an attachment like that and a 2500-pound load up here above the foreman—you will know that that's going to fall and that would be a catastrophe. I think that's what you told Mr. Smith.

WITNESS: Well, I say if you get 2500-pound loads above the farmer, and it does fall, it is going to be a catastrophe.

BALDWIN: It is your position, as I understand it, if you get a load like that up there that high with that kind of attachment, you are going to have a death trap, as Mr. Smith put it?

WITNESS: With this particular attachment here?

BALDWIN: Yes, with that particular attachment.

WITNESS: Yes, that is right.

BALDWIN: All right. Now then, would you look in your literature—the owner's manual—your operator's manual—any of these brochures that you have—or any literature that you have and point to me one line that says just what you said: "Look out, you are going to have a dangerous situation if you put this kind of attachment . . ."

WITNESS: No sir, it is not in there.

BALDWIN: It is not there, is it?

WITNESS:No, sir.

BALDWIN: There is not any decal on the tractor that says that is there?

WITNESS: There wouldn't be one on the tractor, no, that would have to be a part of the loader.

BALDWIN: You can't—well, is there one on the loader?

WITNESS: No, sir.

BALDWIN: You can't point to a single place where any such warning was given to a man like Mr. Crew or Mr. Foster, can you?

WITNESS: A warning that a 1500-pound weight above your head—watch out—watch out it doesn't fall on you?

BALDWIN: Yes, with this kind of attachment.

WITNESS: No, sir, it doesn't say that.

BALDWIN: But that is something you know about, in design, isn't it? You just told us it is going to happen.

WITNESS: With this attachment it could happen, yes, sir.

BALDWIN: All right.

WITNESS: And did happen.

Block's questions of one of the defendant's medical experts established the plaintiff's total disability:

BLOCK: Doctor, we are agreed, are we not, from your testimony, that Dorman Baird is 100% disabled from the time of this traumatic accident in Vietnam to the present time?

WITNESS: That is correct.

BLOCK: We are talking both about physically and employment-wise?

WITNESS: That is correct.

Block's final questions of this witness established the credibility of the plaintiff's rehabilitation specialist:

BLOCK: Do you know of the rehabilitation departments in the Bellevue Hospital here in Manhattan and Beckman-Downtown Hospital in Manhattan?

WITNESS: Yes, I do.

BLOCK: Do they have excellent departments of rehabilitation?

WITNESS: Perfectly fine departments.

BLOCK: And are you familiar with Dr. Bruce Grynbaum?

WITNESS: Yes, I am.

BLOCK: An outstanding man in the field?

WITNESS: Yes, I know him personally.

Gibbons began his cross-examination of the defendant's ejection seat expert by establishing that the plaintiff had acted appropriately in the emergency preceding his death, thus establishing that the plane had not gone down as a result of pilot error:

> GIBBONS: Mr. Stitzel, as I understand it he did everything right, Captain Wahl, just what you just said to Mr. Cowles, he did everything right.
>
> THE COURT: Is that a question? Did he do everything right?
>
> GIBBONS: Yes, sir. I understood you to say that. Is that correct?
>
> WITNESS: I think when he got into an emergency situation that he did everything right.
>
> GIBBONS: And yet he was still killed?
>
> WITNESS: That's correct.

Gibbons further established through this same witness that there had been many documented flight control restrictions in the white area that had caused problems:

> GIBBONS: And you are aware, as I understand, without going into and getting into the numbers game, you know, do you not, Mr. Stitzel, that there have been flight control jams in the white area on these A10s?
>
> WITNESS: There have been flight control restrictions in the white area.
>
> GIBBONS: All right. Restrictions that some pilots recovered from, they were lucky enough to shake it out, is that right?
>
> WITNESS: As far as I know all the restrictions in the white area have been recovered, sir.
>
> GIBBONS: Except what I just read to you. That was two of them the Safety Board found, your buddy Colonel Thompson and Captain Wahl, but the ones you know of they were able to recover, isn't that right?
>
> WITNESS: Yes.
>
> GIBBONS: New, and it is true that when they experienced the ones you know of, when they experienced jams or restrictions, and they were fortunate enough to recover by shaking violently at their control stick, when they got on the ground the white area had foreign objects that were definitely confirmed that had restricted or jammed at least temporarily the flight controls, isn't that correct?
>
> WITNESS: Yes, sir.

Glaser established facts to support his case whenever possible:

> GLASER: If Dr. Cavalli testified in court there that hormonal imbalance can produce many symptoms, including pain all over the body, would you agree with that?

WITNESS: They can produce symptoms, yes.

GLASER: Including psychiatric symptoms, right, sir?

WITNESS: Yes, sir.

GLASER: The—to a patient with psychiatric symptoms, genuine psychiatric symptoms, the pains and the aches and the complaints are very real to them, isn't that true? That's fundamental in medicine, isn't it?

WITNESS: Yes.

GLASER: And sometimes more difficult to treat than an organic injury, correct, sir?

WITNESS: Yes.

. . . .

GLASER: Okay. All right, now, Dr. Cavalli, and Dr. Crumb, a pathologist, testified that you can have a surgical menopause by removing the ovaries. Do you agree with that?

WITNESS: If the ovaries are actively functioning, depending upon the activity of the functions of the ovaries, yes, that can happen.

GLASER: They also testified that a surgical menopause can precipitate all of the symptoms of menopause in a pre-menopausal patient. Do you agree with that?

WITNESS: It can, yes, sir.

GLASER: And menopause can bring on physical complaints as well as psychosomatic complaints or emotional complaints, am I correct?

WITNESS: Yes. sir.

GLASER: And these complaints can be very real to the patient, right, the emotional complaints?

WITNESS: They can be.

GLASER: And they range from neurosis to psychosis, correct?

WITNESS: They can.

In questioning a pathologist called by the defense, Glaser used the witness to establish that the defendant had performed an unnecessary surgery that was contraindicated by the available information and without waiting for any of the pathology reports, all of which would have shown the plaintiff to be cancer free. In so doing, he established that the pathology reports were reliable in diagnosing cancer and attempting to determine the necessity of surgery, that the doctor had failed to utilize or wait for the results of these tests, and finally that when the test reports came back, they were negative for cancer:

GLASER: And a D and C is an important test, correct?

WITNESS: That's correct.

GLASER: And the decision as to whether or not to do a hysterectomy depends largely upon the findings with regard to the curettings, right?

WITNESS: It may. Not necessarily.

GLASER: Okay, it may. It may, right?

WITNESS: It depends on what the currettings show.

GLASER: Sir, it may, is that right?

WITNESS: It may.

GLASER: Okay. You have been given curettings of a D and C while a patient is on the operating table, right, sir?

WITNESS: That's correct.

GLASER: And lab—you and your laboratory department while a patient is under anesthesia and the tissue is sent to you, you examine it, analyze it and immediately send the report back to the surgeon, right?

WITNESS: No, not necessarily. Depends on whether they request a rapid diagnosis.

GLASER: They can have it, right?

WITNESS: If they want it.

GLASER: Okay. Do you know if that was done here?

WITNESS: There's no record that it was.

GLASER: Isn't it a good practice for a surgeon upon a—doing a D and C to wait for the laboratory report on the cutterings before he opens the belly?

WITNESS: It is not a strict practice, no.

GLASER: Is that a good practice?

WITNESS: It's up to the judgement of the—

GLASER: Sir, will you answer it?

WITNESS: I cannot answer the question.

GLASER: You can't. Well, then, say so. An examination of curettings by the pathologist can reveal whether the curettings or the tissue is cancerous or not, right, sir?

WITNESS: That's correct.

GLASER: And if it were cancerous, that would be a good reason for going into the belly, right sir?

WITNESS: I can't answer that question. I don't think that's an appropriate question.

GLASER: Well, that would be one reason to go into the belly and do a hysterectomy or an oophorectomy, if the curettings showed cancer, right?

WITNESS: Usually they don't do it, they wait and re-evaluate the patient. You mean frozen section, I'm sorry. You mean a frozen section?

GLASER: A frozen section.

WITNESS: That would usually be—usually a reason for stopping the procedure and re-evaluating the patient.

GLASER: Forget about a frozen section. Was a frozen section done here?

WITNESS: I didn't see a record of one.

GLASER: Okay. A D and C was done?

WITNESS: Right, that's correct.

GLASER: One of the reasons for a D and C is to determine whether or not the patient has lesions that are cancerous, right, sir?

WITNESS: That's correct.

GLASER: So that before you open up the belly, you'd like to know if the lesions are cancerous or not, correct, sir?

WITNESS: That's correct.

DEFENSE COUNSEL: May I object to this, your Honor? It's not related to this case at all.

THE COURT: Overruled.

GLASER: Since the surgeon here did not wait for the result of the pathologist—pathology analysis, he opened up the belly without knowing whether the curettings are cancerous or benign, correct, sir?

WITNESS: That's correct.

GLASER: Okay. The curettings came back non-cancerous—withdrawn. The report on the curettings came back after the operation with the report benign, right, sir?

WITNESS: They were benign, yes.

. . . .

GLASER: And the cervix, there was nothing wrong with the cervix, right?

WITNESS: That's correct.

GLASER: Did you ask about whether or not the patient had pap smears before the operation

WITNESS: No.

GLASER: Did you ask?

WITNESS: No.

GLASER: The pap smear would tell whether or not there was cancer of the cervix, right?

WITNESS: It might. It's one of the best techniques.

GLASER: Yes. And before you did a hysterectomy, you'd want to know about the condition of the cervix from the point of view of malignancy or nonmalignancy, right?

WITNESS: Yes.

GLASER: And you didn't ask whether pap smears were done and if they were done, what the results were? You didn't ask that?

WITNESS: No, I did not.

GLASER: Did you ask if IVPs were done?

WITNESS: No, I did not.

GLASER: Did you ask if barium enemas were done?

WITNESS: No.

GLASER: Is that an important test to determine whether or not organs are being impinged upon or interfered with or compressed by fibroid tumors?

WITNESS: Yes, it is one of the tests which may be useful for that.

GLASER: Okay. Did you ask, "Did you do it" and what the results were?

WITNESS: Did I ask about the results?

GLASER: Yes.

WITNESS: I did not ask directly, no.

GLASER: And the same with the barium enema insofar as interference with the intestional organs that are concerned, right?

WITNESS: No, that's not correct, I did not.

GLASER: You didn't ask it?

WITNESS: No.

GLASER: Well, Doctor, these tests have a purpose. You put the patients through them prior to cutting into the belly so's to help you know whether or not you should go in, right?

WITNESS: As a clinician, yes.

GLASER: Did you know that in this case all of those tests were negative and he still went in? Did you know that?

WITNESS: I saw the reports and I did see that they were negative, yes, when I read the reports and the charts. Both the IVP and the barium enema were negative.

GLASER: And the tissue report that can be on a D and C, that would be—could be another assistance to a surgeon as to whether or not to do a hysterectomy, right?

WITNESS: As a general statement, yes.

GLASER: Yes. And you know he didn't wait for the pathology report from the pathologist before he opened her belly, right, sir?

WITNESS: He didn't request one so, therefore, he could not wait for one.

GLASER: He had requested one?

WITNESS: He did not request one, therefore, he cannot wait for one.

GLASER: He could have requested one, right, sir?

WITNESS: That's correct.

§8.09   Strategies for Questioning

The lawyers' cross-examination strategies were aimed at controlling the testimony of the witnesses. The role of these witnesses was to prove the defendant's case and to damage the plaintiff's case. If the lawyers ventured into areas that were damaging to the defendant, the witnesses became evasive in their answers and the lawyers had to pin them down and pry the answers out of them. If the lawyers allowed them the opportunity to expound, the witnesses attempted to justify their positions. Therefore, the lawyers had to use strategies that controlled the witnesses' testimony.

§8.10   —Leading Questions

Whenever possible, the lawyers used leading questions to control the witnesses. As noted previously in the discussion of direct examination, in asking leading questions, the lawyer suggests an answer and asks for the witness's agreement, or suggests an interpretation of the evidence to the witness. That is, the lawyer makes a statement of fact and asks the witness to agree, or asks a question that suggests an interpretation of the evidence. This is effective because it controls the witness and allows the plaintiff's lawyer the opportunity to testify. A few examples of leading questions are set out below. An examination of the questioning set out in the other sections in this chapter will demonstrate that almost all of the cross-examinations consisted of leading questions.

Corboy led the defense doctor when questioning him about the plaintiff's medical condition:

> CORBOY: Doctor when you examined John Randolph Block on the second day of February, 1983, he was what you call a severe spastic quadriplegic, was he not?
>
> WITNESS: Yes, he was.
>
> CORBOY: Just so we have no questions and no doubts about this, this gentleman will never be able to work again, will he?
>
> WITNESS: No, he will not.

Ring led the witness in his cross-examination of how the machine functioned:

> RING: All right. I will go back. When the ram has completed its downward movement and is now on the way up; and it reaches the top of the stroke?
>
> WITNESS: Yes.
>
> RING: And at that point it has its greatest energy?
>
> WITNESS: Right. Its greatest potential energy.
>
> RING: And if the spring were to break then, as the operator is removing his hand from the palm buttons, the ram will come down?
>
> WITNESS: Yes.

Spence used leading questions throughout his cross-examination. In controverting the defendant's argument that there is no proof that plutonium causes lung cancer, Spence questioned as follows:

> SPENCE: Now, I want to talk to you about your recognition of certain proofs that have been developing, and knowledge that has been developing in population studies around the country about plutonium. First of all, when somebody says that it has never been proven that plutonium causes a single case of cancer, that is just a word game, isn't it— because we know that plutonium causes cancer, don't we?
>
> WITNESS: Yes, we do.
>
> SPENCE: And, so when people have been standing under their oaths—or sitting under their oaths in this case—and testifying to the ladies and gentlemen of the jury that there has never been a single case of plutonium radiation proven to cause cancer, that misleads the jury, doesn't it?
>
> WITNESS: It may.
>
> SPENCE: Yes. Because, as you have already stated, we know that plutonium causes cancer—it is just that twenty years later we can't prove that a particular exposure caused that particular cancer—that is the problem, isn't it?
>
> WITNESS: That is the problem.

§8.11   —Admonition of Witnesses

When the witnesses became evasive or attempted to explain rather than answer the leading questions, the lawyers cut off the explanations and directly admonished the witnesses to answer the questions or asked the judge to admonish the witness. When Baldwin began to get evasive answers he directly confronted the witness:

> BALDWIN: Now then, let me ask you, sir: you know when you design these products that farmers are famous for being jacks-of-all-trades, don't you?
>
> WITNESS: I am seeing it demonstrated here, yes.
>
> BALDWIN: Well, you knew it before that, didn't you?
>
> WITNESS: Well, I have seen lots of attachments on the back end, I haven't seen front-end loaders.
>
> BALDWIN: Well, would you answer my question? Don't you know that farmers are jacks-of-all-trades?
>
> WITNESS: I think that would be generally agreed, yes.
>
> BALDWIN: And that's something that you anticipate when you design?
>
> WITNESS: We didn't anticipate this.
>
> BALDWIN: Woud you answer my question, Mr._____?

WITNESS: Yes.

Gibbons interrupted the defendant's expert who was attempting to evade his question and insisted that the witness respond to the question:

GIBBONS: Now, you would agree with me then that if you switched to manual reversion you should be able to recover on your flight controls unless they were jammed?

WITNESS: And again that is a function of—

GIBBONS: Do you agree with me, Mr. Stitzel?

WITNESS: I agree, yes, sir.

Glaser was faced with cross-examining several medical experts. Many times medical experts attempt to joust with opposing lawyers and try to evade straightforward answers with narratives or by simply dismissing the questions. Glaser, when faced with a witness who attempted to avoid direct answers to his questions, tenaciously insisted on obtaining answers to his questions. Glaser's success in this approach damaged the expert's credibility on both the expertness and trustworthiness dimensions. An example of Glaser's approach is as follow:

GLASER: When did you first meet with Mr. DeMaggio for the first time?

WITNESS: I met with him last night in my home.

GLASER: And where is that?

WITNESS: 100 West 57th Street.

GLASER: And what were you shown at that time?

WITNESS: He showed me the chart which we reviewed now.

GLASER: How many hours did you spend with him?

WITNESS: About an hour and a half or so.

GLASER: Now, you've referred to certain portions of those charts, right?

WITNESS: I'm sorry, sir?

GLASER: You've referred in your testimony to certain portions of the chart, correct?

WITNESS: I did, sir.

GLASER: Were those portions pointed out to you by counsel during your discussion?

WITNESS: I reviewed all the charts and went through the part I could read. Certain parts.

GLASER: Sir, will you answer the question, please? Did he point out certain portions of the chart, yes or no?

WITNESS: Yes, he did.

GLASER: Okay. Did you read, sir,—withdrawn. You say you spent about an hour and a half with him?

WITNESS: An hour and a half or two.

GLASER: And part of that conversation had to do with the discussion of this case, right, without looking at the charts?

WITNESS: Small part, yes.

GLASER: And are you telling us that during a period of approximately an hour and a half to two hours you read every line in those charts?

WITNESS: I never said that.

GLASER: Did you read the entire chart, except for what you couldn't read?

WITNESS: More or less.

GLASER: More or less. Now, will you answer the question? I want to know if you read every line that you could read in those charts?

WITNESS: Every line that I could read in the charts to the best of my knowledge.

GLASER: To the best of your knowledge. It happened last night. Don't you know?

WITNESS: I haven't gone—I don't know whether these charts have other material in them, the charts he showed me did.

GLASER: Sir, you have been referred to a number of charts here. Are those the charts that you read last night?

WITNESS: I think I read copies of the charts.

GLASER: All right, copies of those charts.

WITNESS: Right, yes.

GLASER: And are you telling us that with regard to all of these hospital records you read every line except, during an hour and a half or two, except that part which you couldn't make out?

WITNESS: I didn't read the nurses' records, no. I didn't read the extraneous records, I read the pertinent parts.

GLASER: What do you call extraneous in a hospital record?

WITNESS: I'm talking about nurses' records and things of that type.

GLASER: Oh, nurses' notes are—what was the phrase you used?

WITNESS: They're other—

GLASER: Extraneous. Are they extraneous?

WITNESS: Well, I read the parts concerned with what the physicians had to say about the patient.

GLASER: Sir, you said nurses' notes are extraneous. I take it you meant that they're immaterial, is that what you're saying?

WITNESS: No, sir, I never said that.

GLASER: They're extraneous?

WITNESS: Right, but not immaterial.

GLASER: Does that mean they don't matter?

WITNESS: They do matter.

.   .   .   .

GLASER: What else didn't you read?

WITNESS: I read—certain of the orders were written for drug medications, I could not, I skimmed over those.

GLASER: You skimmed over the orders, I see. What else?

WITNESS: I read very carefully all the doctors' notes, all the laboratory reports that I could decipher, all the X-ray reports and the summaries that were present in each one of the charts when they were legible.

GLASER: Summaries are typed out, mostly?

WITNESS: Some of them were not.

GLASER: Okay. You read all the physical examinations, sir?

WITNESS: I went through those, yes.

GLASER: Well, did you read them, I asked you?

WITNESS: Well, that's what I meant by reading them. I went through them.

GLASER: That called for a yes, right?

WITNESS: Yes.

GLASER: You did all of this in an hour and a half, two hours, which included a discussion of the case, right?

WITNESS: Yes, sir.

§8.12 —Narrow Questions

When the witnesses became evasive or refused to answer the leading questions, the lawyers moved to a series a very narrow questions calling for specific answers. The lawyers broke the testimony down into discrete items and moved through the testimony bit by bit in an effort to pin the witnesses down and avoid explanations.

After obtaining an acknowledgement from the defendant's doctor that the plaintiff was entitled to and required optimal medical care, Corboy attempted to elicit testimony to the effect that optimal care was more expensive than less than optimal care. This testimony was to be used to bolster Corboy's claim that the plaintiff required a substantial verdict to pay for medical care. The witness became evasive and answered "not necessarily." After attempting to get an affirmation from the witness, Corboy went through a long series of questions in which he identified a specialty such as orthopedics and established that in the case of a broken bone, you would get better care from an orthopedic surgeon as opposed to a general practitioner, and that the orthopedic surgeon would cost more than a general practitioner. After moving bit by bit through the various specialities, Corboy finally received the acknowledgement that, as a rule, the specialists who provide optimal care were more expensive.

When Spence asked the Kerr-McGee representative to tell the jury the major hazard of plutonium to human life, the witness became evasive by using vague terminology. Spence responded with a series of narrow questions:

> SPENCE: Now, would you tell the ladies and gentlemen of the jury what you considered to be the major hazard of plutonium to human life?
>
> WITNESS: Well, I think its major hazard is when it is breathed in and not exhaled from the body.
>
> SPENCE: And what is that hazard?
>
> WITNESS: It is the alpha particles acting on the tissue and over a period of time causing a deterioration of the tissue.
>
> SPENCE: I haven't heard the word yet. I've asked you three times about it: What is the major hazard of breathing plutonium particles?
>
> . . . .
>
> SPENCE: What do we call that?
>
> WITNESS: Well, it's sometimes called a malignancy.
>
> SPENCE: I haven't heard the word yet. What do ordinary folks call it?
>
> WITNESS: Well, now, I imagine it is what they talk about when they talk about cigarettes—cancer.

When Spence asked the witness whether he had advised the Kerr-McGee workers that cancer was a hazard of plutonium contamination, the witness became evasive and gave answers that were not responsive to the questions. Spence again moved through the questioning bit by bit, establishing through the use of the plant manual that the employees had never been told that plutonium contamination would cause cancer. At times he interrupted the witness to tell him that he didn't ask the question to which the witness was responding, and re-asked his question and stayed with it until he obtained the desired response.

§8.13   —Depositions and Exhibits

The lawyers used the pretrial discovery process to take depositions and gather as much evidence as possible in order to pin the witnesses down on cross-examination. In those cases in which the witnesses attempted to evade answers, the lawyers used deposition answers given previously to pin them down and get straight answers. In other cases, the lawyers used exhibits, such as company manuals, to obtain answers. Baldwin used the owners' operator's manual to establish that the defendant had failed to warn tractor users of the dangers involved in its operation, and Spence used the Kerr-McGee plant manual to contradict the manager's testimony that he warned employees that cancer was a hazard of plutonium contamination. Gibbons used records of flight inquiry boards to cross-examine witnesses about the causes of aircraft malfunction. As noted above, after one witness claimed that he was not aware of any deaths due to flight control jams, Gibbons cross-examined the witness with a flight board inquiry report that concluded that one of the witness's friends had died in a plane that crashed due to flight control jam.

Perlman used a deposition to pin down an expert witness on the issue of whether the machine in question had failed to work properly when it was originally tested. He questioned as follows:

PERLMAN: Yoyu recognize that when you make these machines, these boxes, that they have a potential to fail, don't you?

WITNESS: Yes, I do.

PERLMAN: And, in fact, when you, when this machine, this very one that was on this continuous miner was being tested, it didn't work properly then, did it?

WITNESS: I'm not sure I understand.

PERLMAN: Do you remember giving your deposition?

WITNESS: Well, I, I remember giving a deposition. I don't remember every detail.

PERLMAN: I just, I asked you if you remember giving your deposition. That is a simple question.

WITNESS: Yes, I do.

PERLMAN: November 7th.

WITNESS: Yes.

PERLMAN: At the offices of Joy Manufacturing Company in Pennsylvania in Pittsburgh?

WITNESS: Yes.

PERLMAN: Let me read to you the question and answer and see if you recall this question. "What are you going to testify—"

DEFENSE COUNSEL: Reference, please.

PERLMAN: Page 27. (Reading from the deposition) "What are you going to testify to that your testing of this component when it came to you showed?" Answer: "You mean functional will you?" Question: "Yes." Answer: "Okay. I will testify that the unit functioned in a normal manner and would have passed the tests with one exception." Question: "What is that?" Answer: "That was that in an abnormal situation of holding a function on for an approximate three minute period, that that function would continue after the command was released." Question: "That is not a normal part of its operation, that's abnormal." Answer: "Yes, sir, that's abnormal."

WITNESS: Yes, sir, I remember that.

PERLMAN: So when you tested it it was not working properly then, was it?

WITNESS: I didn't know what you were referring to, but, yes, you are right.

§8.14   —Development of a Few Strong Points

The lawyers limited their cross-examinations to establishing a few basic points. The witnesses were, in most cases, advocates, and, therefore, the lawyers could not have expected to get a lot of help from them. In each case they knew in advance the important points that they should cover for each witness. They did not cross-examine the witnesses on every matter that they testified about on direct examination, but only on the points that were critical to their cases, or on which they could be expected to obtain concessions. The lawyers did not lose the interest of the jury by spending time on irrelevant matters.

For example, Corboy spent his time on cross-examination of the defendant's doctor establishing four basic points: that the doctor had no experience treating patients with the same injuries the plaintiff had, that his opinions with respect to the plaintiff's life expectancy were speculative and not based on experience, that optimal medical care would be found in hospitals with experienced and highly trained medical personnel, and that optimal medical care was more expensive than care that was less than optimal.

Similarly, Baldwin's questioning of the defendant's expert engineer was spent primarily on establishing foreseeability, failure to warn, that protection could have been built into the tractor, and that protection was not built in due to the profit motive.

Block, in questioning the defendant's rehabilitation specialist, established three points. First, he established that the plaintiff was 100 per cent disabled at the time of trial; second, he established that the witness was not familiar with the employment situation in the area where the plaintiff resided, thus questioning the basis of the witness's assumptions; and, finally, he established through the witness that the plaintiff's rehabilitation specialist was respected in his field.

§8.15   —Adherence to the Laws of Primacy and Recency

As a rule, the lawyers opened and closed their cross-examinations with their most important points. The law of primacy holds that first impressions are the most lasting, while the law of recency holds that the most recent impressions are the most lasting.[4] Assuming some merit to both "laws," the jurors' first and last impressions of the cross-examination would be the most lasting. The lawyers capitalized on these "laws" and opened and closed their examinations with their strongest points. The weaker material was buried in the middle of the examination. Baldwin began his cross-examination by establishing that the tractor was dangerous:

> BALDWIN: Mr. _____, to pick up where Mr. _____ left off, I believe
> you said something about if you picked that bale of hay up with that

---

[4] For primacy effect, see Lund, *The Psychology of Belief: IV. The Law of Primacy in Persuasion,* 20 J Abnormal Psychology 236-49 (1925); for recency effect, see Anderson, *Test of a Model for Opinion Change,* 59 J Abnormal & Soc Psychology 371-81 (1959).

sort of arrangement and get it above the operator's head, you have got a very dangerous situation?

WITNESS: Yes, sir, with this attachment.

Baldwin closed his cross-examination by establishing that Ford had accepted the risks inherent in the design of the tractor:

BALDWIN: Now a hay-loader, you are just as dead, if you are killed by a hay-loader, as if you are from something else, aren't you?

WITNESS: That's right.

BALDWIN: And that's an acceptable risk that Ford undertook?

WITNESS: Yes, sir, I guess you would have to say that.

Gibbons began his cross-examination of one of the defendant's experts by establishing that the deceased pilot had handled his plane appropriately:

GIBBONS: Mr. Stitzel, as I understand it he did everything right, Captain Wahl, just what you just said to Mr. Cowles, he did everything right.

THE COURT: Is that a question? Did he do everything right?

GIBBONS: Yes, sir. I understood you to say that. Is that correct?

WITNESS: I think when he got into an emergency situation that he did everything right.

GIBBONS: And yet he was still killed?

WITNESS: That's correct.

Block began his cross-examination of the defendant's rehabilitation expert by establishing that the plaintiff, as of the date of the trial, was still 100 per cent disabled. He closed his cross-examination of the same witness by eliciting testimony to the effect that he was acquainted with the plaintiff's rehabilitation expert and that he was respected in his field. In questioning a mechanical engineer who purported to offer opinions as to the cause of a gun malfunction, Block began by establishing that when the expert completed his examination, he did not know the cause of the explosion.

Glaser closed the cross-examination of one of the defendant's experts with a knockout punch. The expert had expressed an opinion that the oophorectomy or removal of the plaintiff's ovaries was proper even though she had no pelvic disease or cancer and even though the pathology reports showed the ovaries to be relatively normal. Although the plaintiff suffered serious adverse effects from this procedure, the expert maintained his position that the removal was proper. In closing, Glaser forced the witness to admit that in a previousy published article, he had referred to women with removed ovaries as "castrated women." He questioned as follows:

GLASER: And, Doctor, just one last question. In this article, you referred to these whose ovaries were removed as castrated women, right?

WITNESS: May I see what I wrote, please?

GLASER: Here.

WITNESS: Thank you. Yes, castrated and oophorectomy are the same.

THE COURT: Would you read it, sir?

WITNESS: Yes, of course. Of necessity one would anticipate a—I'm sorry, it—may I go back? Of necessity one would anticipate a relatively longer and possibly more difficult time in treating these castrated women.

THE COURT: Is that still your opinion as of 1977, sir?

WITNESS: I would not say that in '77.

GLASER: At any rate, the term castration is a medical term synonymous with removal of ovaries, right?

WITNESS: With oophorectomies, right.

GLASER: No further questions.

Baldwin began his cross-examination of the defendant's expert engineer by establishing that the tractor as used created a dangerous situation, and that Ford could have protected the operator against such a situation:

BALDWIN: Mr. Sewell, to pick up where Mr. Smith left off, I believe you said something about if you picked that bale of hay up with that sort of arrangement and got it above the operator's head, you have got a very dangerous situation?

WITNESS: Yes, sir, with this attachment.

BALDWIN: With that attachment?

WITNESS: That's right.

BALDWIN: And I believe I heard you say earlier—your words were: "We can protect the operator."

WITNESS: Yes, sir.

BALDWIN: And if it had been the design and intent of Ford to protect that operator from a falling object such as the one you have in front of you there and that you have described, it could have been achieved, couldn't it?

WITNESS: Uh huh. If this had been our test run, he would have been protected.

BALDWIN: My question was: If it had been the design and intent of Ford to provide protection for that operator against the very event that you have just described, it could have been achieved, couldn't it?

WITNESS: Yes.

§8.16   Strategic Use of Language

The lawyers used language strategically to control the testimony of the witnesses. The lawyers phrased their questions using words that had persuasive impact that would affect juror impression formation. Baldwin, in describing the defendant, referred to Ford as "one of the largest corporations in the country, or the world." The language suggested and emphasized the wealth of the corporation and detracted from the defendant's argument that it hadn't put safety devices on the tractor due to the cost. Spence, is referring to the defendant doctor's possible loss of government funded jobs, asked if that would affect the doctor's "empire," suggesting the doctor's vested interests in the government programs.

§8.17   Conclusion

Substantively, successful lawyers for the plaintiff used cross-examination to achieve three purposes: (1) to destroy the credibility of the witness, (2) to controvert arguments or facts presented previously by the witness or by the defense, and (3) to elicit facts in support of the plaintiff's case. Since the witnesses were at best adverse and at worst hostile, the lawyers used questioning strategies that allowed them to control the testimony. The testimony was controlled by the use of leading questions, the use of admonitions to the witnesses to answer questions directly, the use of narrow questions calling for specific answers, the use of depositions and exhibits, developing a few strong points, adherence to the laws of primacy and recency, and the strategic use of language to shape juror impression formation.

9

Closing Statement

§9.01   Introduction

As would be expected, the lawyers all devoted a certain amount of time in their closing statements to arguing and highlighting the facts and the law involved in each case. However, these lawyers all moved beyond simple, logical argumentation to higher levels of appeals directed toward affecting the impression formation processes of the jurors. This chapter will analyze structure used by these lawyers to affect juror impression formation.

In the opening statement, the lawyers for the plaintiff developed a narrative or storytelling structure in order to create the cognitive scheme that would guide the jurors' perceptions throughout the trial. Similarly, the defendants developed competing narratives. Each narrative or story contained different sets of facts, interpretations of the law, and witness credibility assessments. Each side of the case claimed that its narrative represented the "correct" view of reality. The jurors' function was to resolve this conflict. In closing statements, the lawyers were faced with the problem of resolving which competing view of reality should be accepted. Thus, the lawyers were faced with the rhetorical problem of constructing a coherent whole out of the evidence and the law such that they could convince the jurors that their version of the facts was the "true" and "correct" version. Further, in constructing this coherent whole, the lawyers were faced with bringing home to jurors such abstract, subjective, nonobservable concepts and conditions as negligence, damages, pain, and suffering. Finally, although the judges' instructions delineated the juries' purposes, as described by the judges, these purposes were generalized and vague, such as to render "fair and impartial justice." The lawyers were faced with defining "fair and impartial justice" and with further refining the juries' purposes.

In what follows, I shall demonstrate that successful lawyers for the plaintiff surmounted these rhetorical problems by further utilizing and refining the narrative or storytelling structure created in the opening statement. The narrative structure, through the use of themes and language, integrated the evidence, created meaning for abstract concepts, and created jury purpose.

The closings analyzed were those by Scott Baldwin, Victor Bergman, Melvin Block, Phil Corboy, Robert Gibbons, Herman Glaser, Robert Habush, Leonard Ring, Gerry Spence, Peter Perlman, and Lance Welch.

§9.02   Structure

The structure of these closing statements was geared to the process of creating meaning. The lawyers had a short period of time to prevail upon jurors presented with competing and conflicting views of reality. They integrated the material from the trial into a coherent whole that was a vivid human drama with which the jurors could identify. In order to create this meaning, the lawyers again became storytellers.

§9.03 Tone

In the role of storyteller, the lawyers became tragic playwrights. In all cases, the lawyers presented the plaintiffs as people who had suffered great losses and were in need of great compensation. The lawyers wanted the jurors to take the plaintiffs' claims for damages seriously, and, therefore, they approached their tasks seriously. The lawyers all stressed to the juries the importance of the cases and the jurors' roles in the cases.

In discussing his role in the trial, Spence conveyed a serious tone to the jury:

> It's the most important case of my career. I'm standing here talking to you now about the most important things that I have ever said in my life. And, I have a sense that I have spent a lifetime, fifty years, to be exact, preparing somehow for this moment with you. And, so, I'm proud to be here with you, and I'm awed, and I'm a little frightened, and I know that's hard for you to believe because I don't look frightened. But, I've been frightened from time to time throughout this trial. I've learned how to cover that up pretty well, but I can remember when Dr. Voelz got on the stand, and after we listened to his testimony we got together, Jim and I and Art, and we sat down and said: "Have we spent two-and-a-half months here, and are we going to lose it all at this spot? It all depends on your ability to turn the coin over, and show the truth and what's on the other side of that matter—can you do it?" I hope you think I did it— that we did it together.
>
> And, what I am setting out to do here today is frightening to me. I hope I have the intelligence, the insight, and the spirit, and the ability, and just the plain old guts to get to you what I have to get to you.
>
> What I need to do here is to have you understand what needs to be understood. And, I think I'll get some help from you. You know, my greatest fear has always been—and the way to deal with fear is to talk about it—I always tell my kids that: "If you're afraid, talk about it." My greatest fear in my whole life has been that when I would get to this important case—whatever it was—I would stand here in front of the jury and be called upon to make my final argument and suddenly, you know, I'd just open my mouth and nothing would come out. I'd just sort of stand there and maybe just wet my pants, or something. But I feel the juices—they're going, and I'm going to be alright.

At the outset of his closing on damages for Dorman Baird, Block characterized the case as important, saying:

> At the outset, I want to thank you because I venture to say when you were selected and questioned by Judge Cannella you had no idea that you were going to be ultimately sitting in a case of this magnitude, of this devastation, and it is devastation.

In his case involving the negligent design of the gun, Bergman told the jury:

I want to personally thank Paul and Jannie for entrusting this matter to me. It is an opportunity for a lawyer to try a case like this that has importance, I feel, beyond just the parties in the case, and I am grateful for that opportunity.

In all cases, the jurors were told that they held the key to the plaintiffs' futures and happiness, and this was cast as a serious burden. Corboy told the jury that its job was a "terrible, tremendous responsibility." Similarly, in the introduction to his closing argument, Baldwin told the jury:

> You are about to receive your responsibility in this case and I daresay it is as awesome a responsibility as you will ever bear for your entire life, because you will decide the future of this man, the future of his family. It is now up to you. I know that when you go into the jury room you will accept that duty with the gravity that it deserves.

In his case involving improper delivery of a child, Bergman stated:

> Let's not lose sight of why we're here. There really is only one reason why we're here, and that's because on the day of his birth, the day that was supposed to have been a day of joy, a day of awakening, Brent Olsen was horribly injured, permanently injured. We're here because Brent Olsen has never had a normal day in his life and never will, and that's the only reason why we're here and I've been honored and somewhat overwhelmed at times with the opportunity and the responsibility to represent Brent. A lawyer could not ask for a more deserving client, a less blameless client. A lawyer wouldn't and couldn't have or ask for a heavier responsibility. This may be the most important job that I'll ever do, representing Brent, and a boy like Brent could not ask for finer parents than the good Lord gave Brent Olsen.

In his case involving the failure to timely diagnose Hodgkin's disease, Bergman told the jury:

> I am sure that you noticed it in the jury selection process; I have several fears. I don't think that I have ever had a job this important. I don't think that I've ever had a responsibility that has felt this heavy, and I hope that I don't again, very frankly. But, you know, the acceptance of responsibility and doing the job the best that you can—sometimes I know that I may have been pretty intense about it—is part of being a professional person and taking on a professional responsibility. I think that is one of the things that we have been hoping to emphasize in this case.
>
> The deep fear that I have had has to do with whether or not our evidence was going to fall on deaf ears or closed minds. I feel the need to mention that again, because when you represent a plaintiff in a medical malpractice case against a physician in 1987, you have got a heavy burden. Your only hope is that it doesn't become an impossible burden.

At the end of his closing on the liability portion, Block described the handling of his case as a great burden that he was passing on to the jury:

> But basically the decision is yours to make. Whether with the millions of dollars of equipment that are turned out by armaments plants, and ultimately utilized in battle, and perhaps ultimately millions and millions left strewn on the battle field, all that cost wasted, whether among that ruin, among that tragic event is meant to be left also a woman's husband and the manhood, the better part of the manhood of another man, simply because of sloppy manufacturing and assembly procedures, it is up to you to say, yea or nay. Yours is a great responsibility, I don't envy it. The lawyers in this case on behalf of the plaintiff have had this burden for many, many years. It is now being shifted to your shoulders. I know they are waiting with bated breath and will be waiting for your decision.

In the conclusion of his closing on damages for Dorman Baird, Block again noted the burden of holding the plaintiff's future in his hands and told the jurors that this burden would be passed on to them:

> Now, I've had this case with Mr. Roberts from Alabama, Benny Roberts, a fine lawyer, for six years. It has not been an easy case, it is a responsibility and it is a burden. You try cases, people's futures are in your hands, you try to treat the case with the respect it deserves, all in the cause of justice.
>
> After these six years, I don't relish the job that you are going to have to perform because that burden in a few minutes is going to be passed to you.

Perlman told the jurors that their task was "an awesome responsibility that you have, because your decision today must play a major part in the future of this young man."

In closing, Glaser told the jury:

> I've carried the ball to the best of my ability. It's been a great responsibility representing Mrs. Lewis, and now I transfer the ball to you, and let justice be done. Thank you.

§9.04 Themes

Various themes were used to integrate the mass of evidence that had been presented during the trial, and to shape the jury purpose. Through the development of these themes, facts were argued, credibility was established or destroyed, appeals were made to justice, and jurors were invited to take part in a ritual of rectifying wrongs and of reintegrating the injured party into the community and reaffirming certain fundamental values of community life.

§9.05   —The Defendant Was Negligent

As in the opening statements and during the presentation of evidence in direct and cross-examination, the lawyers continued to argue that the evidence clearly proved that the defendants were negligent, and that due to this negligence, the plaintiffs had been seriously damaged. First, the facts with respect to negligence were reviewed and analyzed, and arguments were made about what testimony had been believable and what the evidence had established. Once negligence was established, the same process was repeated for damages. One of the key guidelines for accepting or rejecting testimony was the credibility of the witnesses. The relevant laws and jury instructions were analyzed and applied to the evidence to demonstrate the defendants' negligence. As in the opening statements, the lawyers continued to refute the defendants' arguments. As a rule, the lawyers led with their strengths, refused the defendants' claims in the middle of their summations, and closed with their strengths.

§9.06   —Credibility: Plaintiff's v Defendant's Witnesses

As noted above, one of the key guidelines for accepting or rejecting testimony was the credibility of the witnesses. The lawyers argued that the plaintiffs' witnesses were believable while the defendants' witnesses were not. For example, Baldwin suggested that the defendant's expert witness was not believable because he testified that Ford had not put a safety device on the tractor due to the prohibitive cost, when in reality a cost of $300 was clearly not prohibitive.

Spence argued that the plaintiff's witnesses were not paid witnesses and had no reason to lie, while the defendant's witnesses were all paid witnesses motivated to prove to the world that plutonium was safe. He asserted that the defendant's manager should be disbelieved because he had testified that a human could breathe a pollen-sized particle of plutonium without harm, when the experts all agreed that a pollen-sized piece of plutonium was lethal.

Corboy demonstrated that the defendant's doctor was not believable because his testimony conflicted with his own published articles.

Habush argued that the defendant's key expert witness testified deceptively because of his desire to mislead the jury:

> Who is Mr. Olsen? From 1969 to 1983 he was in charge of product safety. He claims to know all about dealer modification requests. He claims he knows about the network with respect to accidents. He's worked on 450 lawsuits. He's done extensive work in connection with this lawsuit, strategizing, preparing witnesses, working with the lawyers.
>
> Now having that in mind, let me remind you of what he told you under oath. It would take a major modification of the forklift truck to put on rear guard posts prior to 1976. He never saw an overhead guard like that at Evans or the one which I just held up from California. The Waukesha guard he said would not even comply with ANSI Standards. There was,

he said, no type of guard in existence for our accident model, where an owner could put rear posts on the machine to make it safer. He said there was no print in existence, no blueprint that would describe rear posts, and on the day of the last day of the trial, before he knew that I had discovered the part number for this guard, he stood up in front of you in this court and proceeded to tell you why a straight post was no good and why the post they had was strong because of the gusset and told you that a post that went from top to bottom would not comply with ANSI Standards, would not be safe. You couldn't use it. Why? Because at that time he wanted you to believe that this guard which was known as the Evans guard was no good, that it was some cockamamee scheme that some dealer dreamed up and made in his back shop, that it was dangerous because he was worried that you folks would like their guard and this thing should have been on the machine. And so he had to tell you that a great guard was unsafe and proceeded to do so with this exhibit.

But that afternoon he was given the part number and before the trial ended, up it came, the blueprints. And lo and behold, what do the blueprints show? A straight guard with two rear posts, not square, round, and posts that go into—not any machine—our accident machine. And blueprints which are dated November 30, 1972, a year before our accident machine is produced. And blueprints that show the guard mounted on the back with the two brackets, and blueprints which describe it as a drive-in rack overhead—drive-in rack overhead guard.

And so we had a page from a Yale book dated March of '84 which described that guard, drive-in rack 26 inches wide, March of '84 and I asked him, can we assume if it's in here that it must be safe, that it must comply with standards, and he had to admit, of course, that it would.

Members of the Jury, here's where the common sense comes in. You ask yourselves why, why would he be so concerned about that guard being discovered? Because, as I told you, he knew that it was available on our machine. It was an option. He knew it should have been standard. He knew that it would increase operator protection. He knew that it would have prevented this injury. He knows it.

And I ask you, think of common sense. Can you believe that this man with all his experience, all his involvement, all his contact with Eaton, as an employee and a litigative consultant, that he did not know this existed? That he was surprised? That a lawyer from Milwaukee, Wisconsin, had to find a blueprint he couldn't find? With all their technology and their computers in their Parts Department, when he knew I was looking for it? Come on. He knew it was there all along. And in this trial, day after day, question after question, he denied it, he denied it, he denied it.

Because they know that you can say to them, look, we're not asking you to redesign the whole machine. We are not saying you had to do '85 designs in '76. But for goodness sakes, if you had two lousy posts, two posts that were available, that could go on the machine, Members of the Jury, is this a major redesign of the machine? Is this adding eight inches?

Do you have to be a design engineer to know that this is safer than the one they put out that Roger was using at the time of the accident?

He admits that himself. This would have done it.

Habush then contrasted the negative credibility of the defendant's witnesses with the positive credibility of the plaintiff's witnesses:

You saw Dr. Walsh. Dr. Walsh has—has no interest in the lawsuit. He was the treating neurosurgeon. When he made his observations in the hospital record, he wasn't thinking of coming to court and trying to explain accident mechanism to you.

He also happens to be experienced in accident mechanism so he was able to testify in that respect. But the man is truly an impartial independent witness.

. . . .

Members of the Jury, Dr. Walsh was the treating neurosurgeon. When he was treating this man, he wasn't hired by anybody to testify in the trial.

Perlman, responding to the defendant's attack on his expert witnesses, bolstered the credibility of the witnesses by highlighting their backgrounds:

They make light of the experts that we brought in to you. One of the electrical engineers, Mr. Bowman, who is not a typewriter man, he is a very skilled electrical engineer. He formerly worked at the research department of the University of Kentucky bioengineering laboratory. The other witness was a research director for the United States Bureau of Mines.

Perlman then attacked the credibility of the defendant's witnesses by demonstrating that they had testified inaccurately:

They knew how to do it, they just didn't do it. They didn't design a system where the operator can override the boss.

Again, Mr. Hurst said he thought they did. He said it was designed so that the operator could override the movement of the boom. I said, is that what you meant, Mr. Hurst? Well, that's what I meant, but that's not exactly the way it worked.

I said, what about the warning signal, Mr. Hurst? You said that it had a red warning signal. And this was what was said. Adequate redundancy was built in and a red warning signal was clearly visible. I said, Mr. Hurst, come over here and show us where that red warning signal was to the operator. He said, well, I meant the red switch there.

That's not a warning signal, that's a circuit breaker switch. And it's not even an adequate circuit breaker.

Finally, Perlman suggested that the defendant's witnesses changed their testimony in an effort to mislead the jury:

Their experts under oath changed their testimony. They said one thing and they came in here and said, well, we were all wrong about that, it's the naked wire. What made him see the light all of a sudden three weeks before the trial when they had all of this evidence all along? Were they really wanting to find out the cause or were they wanting to find out what they might be able to sell to this jury?

A major part of Gibbons' closing was to contrast the impartiality of his witnesses with the partiality of the defendant's witnesses. With respect to one of the plaintiff's witnesses, Gibbons stated:

Now, Captain Wahl in the ejection process, the ejection seat that was designed as a last effort to save his life, executed the ejection according to Major Rhett Butler, now Major Butler. He said he followed everything according to proper procedures. And bear in mind now that Major Rhett Butler is no hired witness. He is no hired expert. He is no designer of the ESCAPAC seat. He is no designer or salesman of the airplane, but he said in his expert opinion that it was no pilot error, and Captain Wahl ejected according to proper United States Air Force procedures.

With respect to one of the defendant's witnesses, Gibbons stated:

The only thing that I recall that he really brought you were, number one, a salesman, Mr. Stitzel, who sells these $9,000,000.00 airplanes and prepared a videotape for you showing how they bomb Russian tanks, playing dramatic music and goes right along with the theme, wartime.

With respect to the defendant's witness who testified in his deposition that he was unaware of the cause of a previous crash involving a personal friend, Gibbons stated:

Ladies and gentlemen, this was taken June 28, 1981. And Mr. Townsend, the man that designed those flight controls tells you that he didn't know what caused it. Now, look right here.

. . . . .

And then, ladies and gentlemen, more significantly, and remember I take his deposition in June of '81 and, listen, he doesn't know the cause of Colonel Thompson's crash, and listen to this. Right here, this message came back, and there is Mr. Townsend's name underlined, and it was to Drummond, and listen, just listen to this. "Accident investigation on aircraft 770253, Colonel Thompson", and it says "Although their efforts—" and right here he testifies that he went to England and didn't know the cause, "Although their efforts, the Board President, Safety Board released that report and although their efforts were appreciated", and it says, "Dick Townsend, Shance, Henderson arrived at Bentwaters in England, and although their efforts were appreciated by the Board members, they were unable to override the evidence on hand, and the Board is firmly convinced in their own minds that a flight control jam caused the accident and killed Colonel Thompson." And he said that he didn't know anything about it in his deposition, and he knew enough to go over there, ladies and gentlemen, with these other Republic Fairchild people and try to override the Board, the Safety Board of the official safety privileged report that said the cause of it, Colonel Thompson's death, was a flight control jam. And yet he swore right here under oath he didn't know anything about it.

.   .   .   .

Now, the significance of that, ladies and gentlemen, we have read Mr. Townsend's deposition to you that we took, the man designed these flight controls, and the man that has had experience in knowing what is wrong with this white area, and they didn't bring him down here for you to put him on that witness stand and have him give any expert opinions. And that ought to tell you something.

So what did they bring you? They brought you two salesmen. One of them a salesman of their $9,000,000.00 airplane, and the other a customer relations man. Both Republic Fairchild employees, both have a job to sell these airplanes, and as the statement was made to put that propaganda on you about how war, kill Russian tanks. Don't stop a battleship to save a sailor, and if you get caught up in war, then, ladies and gentlemen, that is what the defense wants you to do in this case. They want to run statistics by you, all kind of statistics. And I was never good at statistics. But I know that Harry Wahl, this man right here, was more than a statistic. We were allowed to introduce one picture into evidence, and he was more, and should be more than a statistic. But what did these two pilot salesmen try to tell you? They had to go with an unheard of theory to try to avoid responsibility in this case. They had to try to convince this jury that there was a double engine flameout. A double engine flameout, to avoid a flight control jam that they know, and they have known since last January of 1981, according to these reports, is what killed Colonel Thompson and is what killed Captain Wahl, and they have known it, but they had to come in here with a charade, ladies and gentlemen, and try to tell you it was a double engine flameout. And each one of the pilots, each one of them on cross-examination—I wasn't afraid of hearsay—normally a lawyer is a fool if he says what have you heard. Well, I am a fool anyway, but I wasn't afraid. And I said have you ever heard of a double engine flameout in a confidence maneuver, and they knew I had them because there has never even been one heard of. So their whole theory has to fall, ladies and gentlemen of the jury. Their whole theory, their whole theory, and Mr. Shawler had to admit that because if you want to believe their theory, here is what you have got to believe. It is one fantasy stacked upon another. First you have got to believe that Captain Wahl had a loose lap belt, and you have got to ignore the air crewman who sat there and saw him tighten it, whose deposition was read. And then number two you have to ignore the prebriefing assignment that Major Rhett Butler gave him and said hey, I am going to radio you and ask if everything is secure, if you are in that seat secure, and that means your lap belt tight and your shoulder harness locked. Remember Major Rhett Butler testifying to that? It is in his sworn testimony. And Captain Butler, Captain at that time, and he has since been promoted notwithstanding they would like you to believe that he told Captain Wahl the wrong way to do a confidence maneuver, and notwithstanding that he was cleared, the official Board found that he did nothing wrong. We are talking about Major Rhett Butler. A man that had three distinguished flying crosses and fought for your country and mine. And they would try to tell you that he told Captain Harry Wahl to execute this confidence maneuver in a wrong manner and that is why he experienced this double engine flameout. Ladies and gentlemen, don't buy it. Don't buy it.

Finally, Gibbons contrasted the witnesses when he told the jury:

> Now, it is like Fred Hoerner, the other expert on the airplane that we brought in here to you. An Annapolis graduate, if you will remember Mr. Hoerner. An honest man, really a teacher, if you will. He said to you ladies and gentlemen of the jury, why wouldn't he be at or near idle? In other words if he, if his control stick was jammed, what is he supposed to do, give it, and get to the ground faster and crash faster, and give them all the power? Certainly when Captain Wahl recognized that control stick was stuck and jammed and he was fighting for everything he was worth, even to the point that it broke his right hand, it broke his hand, he was holding onto that stick so tight, he obviously pulled his throttles back to at or near idle. Because the ground was coming up so fast, he didn't even eject until he was within 2500 feet of the ground, ladies and gentlemen. So these former United States Air Force pilots, now Republic Fairchild salesmen, stack one fantasy upon another. And I ask you, which is more probable, a disinterested witness like Major Rhett Butler who served for our country and was right there on the spot?

Block contrasted the lack of credibility of the defendant's witnesses with the credibility of the plaintiff's witnesses when arguing damages for Dorman Baird:

> In fact, Dr. Ruskin admits that the castration is normal for a person having traumatic neurosis, which Dr. Ruskin himself says emanates and was caused by this event, trauma, an accident, by this event.
> And he says that, yes, he is 100% disabled to date. And then he tried to, this armaments manufacturer, tries to show, well, perhaps he is not telling the truth. He says he was in the hospital, Fort Gordon, Georgia, for six days—six months, but he went home on leave.
> Don't you think candor would compel someone to say what you heard, that he was taken by a brother, a sister-in-law and in back of a car with crutches.
> Mother sends a boy away to service. He has to lay down in the back of a car. She sees him again on crutches. That's not brought out. No, he's hop, skipping and jumping back home to Boaz, Alabama.
> I think that the most experienced, the most qualified witness that we brought here was Dr. Bruce Grynbaum, a man whom International Development sent to Vietnam itself to examine, to evaluate, to analyze the reha-

bilitation facilities, a man who is Director of Rehabilitation Medicine right here across the street from the courthouse, almost, of Beekman-Downtown Hospital, Director of Rehabilitation Medicine of Bellevue, Director of Rehabilitation for the Sidney Hillman Health Center, for the AFL-CIO, former Director of Rehabilitation Medicine for the City of New York and the Department of Health, and I can't—the Urban Coalition, international awards, organizations and volumes and papers all over the world in presentations, a man without peer, and he tells us something that we all know: As much as he didn't like to say it because this is the time when you have got to say it, that a person can be so far gone that you can go through the motions, you can make a facade of things, but we live in a real world and sometimes as much as you would like, yes, as much as Dr. Ruskin perhaps might hope, it just won't work. A person is just too far gone.

And what did Dr. Grynbaum come to in his conclusion: "It is my opinion the patient is fully disabled from any type of occupation."

Glaser began his attack on the credibility of the defendant's witnesses by noting that the defendant did not call any medical experts who were qualified as gynecologists, even though the case was a gynecological case. This attack suggested that the experts lacked training and qualifications for their opinions:

Now, you've heard all the testimony, there's no sense in going over it really. I'm not going to comment on the—it's fresh in your minds, you heard it within the last week and ten days, I'm not going to comment on each witness, we'll spend a day on that. But, did it ever occur to you that they did not produce a gynecologist in a gynecological case? I don't believe it. Can you believe it? We're dealing with a specialty of gynecology. Should this operation have been performed or not, and not one single gynecologist is brought in by the defendant. They bring in Dr. Kupperman, an endocrinologist. Did you hear his testimony, unbelievable testimony? Was he a gynecologist? No.

Glaser damaged the credibility of the defendant's key expert by demonstrating that he rendered opinions in his testimony that were contrary to opinions expressed previously in published works:

So, 19—Oh, I asked him, "Did you say this in the article?" The article, you remember his statement? His words, his words, and he said something Dr. So and So, I forget his name, do you know Dr. So and So, never heard of him. In his article, I said I agree with Dr. Randall, I agree with—in the article, he says I agree with Dr. Randall and he cites a book by Dr. Randall, we strongly urge—that's the language that he used—we strongly urge not removing ovaries unless there's good reason. First the doctor said, well, he was talking about young women. Later on I showed him another part of the article where it says this also goes for women who are older. Now he's stuck. What's his comeback? "I wrote that article in 1959." Doctor—and this article was published in the Journal of the American Medical Association, a very prestigious magazine, for doctors to treat their patients, to help them make the right diagnosis and do the right surgery, etcetera. I said, "Doctor, when did you change your mind?" He said he changed his mind after the '59 article. "When did you change your mind?" He mentioned a period up to 1960. I think it was '55 to '60, up to '60, 1960, between two periods up to '60. Okay, Doctor. On direct examination, I was fortunate, I was very fortunate, counsel produced these three beautiful books to impress you. Nicely bound, nice color. I said, "Doctor, do you agree with this statement in your own book published in 1963, which is after 1960?" Well, same statement, right. Who was he kidding? What are they trying to do to this poor lady? For what, to deprive her of her right to sit on that witness stand under oath and to make such statements, all to deprive this lady of her rights? This is not a game.

Bergman contrasted the impartiality of the plaintiff's witnesses with the speculative nature of the testimony of the defendant's witnesses:

Imagine two busy and important physicians from M.D. Anderson, Dr. Sullivan and Dr. Fuller, who came here to testify for no pay, no personal gain, against another physician. Doctors do not like to testify against other physicians. In fact, Dr. Sullivan and Dr. Fuller have never testified against another physician in their years.

The reason that they did it is because they knew, they know firsthand, they know what the significance of the negligence was to Shanna, and they were appalled when they saw her, and they were outraged. That is honest, obvious outrage. I'd place myself in their care sooner than I would any of the other doctors that I've seen in this case.

The same thing goes for Dr. Carrithers. We showed the videotape of Dr. Carrithers the first morning of trial. There was nothing in this for him. He testified, I think that he said, "after a lot of soul searching." It is not something that he wanted to do. He was very reluctant to do it, but he is an honorable man. He knew that there was a wrong done here. When called upon, he had to step forward.

Who stood up to defend Dr. Hanson's diagnosis? Think about it. The diagnosis? Nobody. Nobody.

And the very people that he vouched for as experts, Dr. Lacher and Dr. Jenkins, couldn't defend his conduct. The most remarkable moment in the trial for me was when Dr. Lacher said that he didn't even know that was in issue, he thought that was a given, that there was negligence in failing to make the diagnosis. And I said, "You mean that he missed the diagnosis? He was negligent?" The answer: "Yes." "You agree that he blew it badly?" "I agree to that."

. . .

Dr. Jenkins acknowledged that the adult data fairly applies to Shanna Morrison initially. I probably should have left it right there. Then he backed off and, for some reason, he said, "It doesn't," and that, "Because there is no scientific data" that would allow him to make that leap from the adult Hodgkin's population to the adolescent Hodgkin's population. He needs scientific data before he can have an opinion.

Then he proceeded to admit that his theory is based upon total speculation. Total speculation. He has suggested that there are some people in some labs working on whether or not his theory may have some validity. If you recall, in order to establish this genetic resistance theory that we talked about, you have to have the cell, and then you have got to culture the cell and expose it to treatments and see that it is resistant. None of that has been done.

Now, I don't think that it is fair for somebody in the position of a party to have to respond to a theory that has no basis in science just because somebody is willing to come in and say it. Dr. Lacher and Dr. Jenkins certainly may have qualifications. I don't want to be crude about this, but I think that when it comes to them, it is, "Have resume, will travel." I think that is fairly applicable to them.

Dr. Lacher has been paid $15,000 for his short appearance here. Dr. Jenkins, by my calculations, depending on what time he got home, was going to get somewhere between $8,000 and $10,000 for coming in here and speculating for you.

They are here to do what they can for another member of the fraternity is what it comes down to. They want to be paid handsomely to do it.

§9.07 —Credibility: Plaintiff v Defendant

The plaintiffs continued their theme of the good and noble plaintiffs juxtaposed against the bad defendants. Thus, the lawyers set up a conflict between good and evil, and in society, good must be rewarded and evil punished. The jury process with its verdict became a ritual whereby the plaintiffs were rewarded for their good ethos, the defendants were punished for their bad ethos, and the evil spirits were driven out. The jurors were invited to participate in this ritual by rendering a verdict that would reward good and punish evil.

Two kinds of credibility were addressed. The first was the negative credibility of the defendants in committing the negligent acts. Baldwin demonstrated that the plaintiff was a humble man who had worked hard all of his life to support his family. He then characterized the defendant's bad actions:

About the only thing I can say about Ford Motor Company in that regard is that they selectively kill people, they selectively cripple people. Why not give the farmer that same protection? Why, oh, why? And you know every time in this case that they have had a choice involving profit or safety, they have taken profit.

"Mr. Sewell, don't you have to balance off marketability—or profit— that is marketability—to sell more tractors to make more profit—against safety?"

Answer: Yes.

Question: And in this case, Mr. Sewell, didn't Ford choose profits?
Answer: Yes.

I was surprised he admitted that.

"And, Mr. Sewell, don't you know that we are dealing with a dangerous instrument here, that eight hundred to a thousand people a year are killed—don't you know that Ford's own figures show that one out of six thousand—for every six thousand tractors, there is one fatality."

And Mr. Sewell said: "Well, when you balance that off against safety—the risk against safety . . ."

What did he say: "One death for every six thousand tractors is an acceptable risk."

That's the judgment Ford made, somebody in management, and yet there is about six thousand tractors in this area isn't there? And Mr. Foster, you are an acceptable risk to Ford. It is just as though they made a booklet and put his name on it.

Now that attitude of this company is incredible. It is hard to believe in 1977, in the United States of America, we can have one of our leading companies with that kind of attitude.

Spence demonstrated Karen Silkwood's dedication to informing her fellow workers and the world about Kerr-McGee's mishandling of plutonium. He told the jury that she "cared" about people and that she was a "heroine." He then pointed out how the defendant Kerr-McGee had lied to the public, covered up plutonium contaminations, and had failed to advise employees that plutonium could cause cancer. Spence told the jury that this behavior was "encouraged and countenanced" by those who were regulating Kerr-McGee. In each instance he asked the jurors whether they approved of that behavior and invited them to punish the defendant's action with their verdict.

Habush attacked the character of the defendant by arguing that the defendant was able to manufacture a forklift with appropriate guards, but failed to do so because of economic considerations:

> And listen to this. He said it was technologically and economically feasible for them to have produced a forklift truck with an overhead protective device that would have afforded protection, that would have prevented the injury in this type of dock fall.
>
> But do you remember why he said he didn't do it? Because it would require a major redesign of the forklift truck. It would require eight inches, he said, to add to the machine.
>
> The last question in this trial I asked him, if the jury concludes that our witnesses' accounts are accurate and that Dr. Walsh and Dr. Roberts' account of how this accident happened are accurate, would these rear posts have prevented Roger Schulz's injury, and his answer was yes.
>
> · · · ·
>
> What are we dealing with? Years of—of conduct. You're dealing with a corporation that is a leader, has technological expertise, international networks, knowledge of hazards, refusal to respond to the hazards, questionable forgetfulness at best, had lots of time to prevent this injury.

Habush juxtaposed the bad character of the defendant with the good character of the plaintiff and his wife:

> So here is a perfectly relying, innocent man who has no reason to believe that this is going to happen to him, no prior experience, and it happens.
>
> . . . .
>
> Roger Schulz, a worker just trying to do his job on one given day, not knowing of any dangers or hazards, against this company that had all this time to do something and did nothing. And had all the expertise in the world to have done something to avoid this and did nothing.
>
> . . . .
>
> By any standard, Roger and Beverly had an ideal life. Roger had 21 years on the job. He was well respected. He was well liked. He loved his work. He went for overtime as much as he could. And it was steady employment. No time off for illness or—or injury. He was just the kind of person that was just there everyday. I mean, he was a perfect example of a loyal, hard-working person.
>
> They had obviously a happy marriage. They shared a great many common interests, camping, and sports. They had a wonderful relationship, as he did with his stepchildren and their two children.
>
> . . . .
>
> I suggest to you that it takes one heck of a solid citizen not to get knocked on your rear end with that kind of news. And while he was in the hospital they had to teach him to dress all over, teach him how to go from a bed to a wheelchair, from a wheelchair to a bed, a wheelchair to a car, a car to a wheelchair, from the floor to the wheelchair. How to take care of himself. And he learned good.
>
> Don't you remember Bev saying in the hospital how someone said, well, 85 percent of these marriages fail. And you remember her say, well we're going to prove them wrong. And she has.
>
> . . . .
>
> I want you to believe something else. I want you to believe that Roger Schulz is not going to quit. I want you to believe that he has come back as far as he can come back in attitude. I want you to believe that he's going to be gainfully employed. And that he's not going to sit away somewhere in a corner feeling sorry for himself. And whatever you do with respect to damages in this case, I want you to believe that.

Glaser noted the good qualities of the plaintiff and then advised the jury that the defendant had taken away the plaintiff's most prized possession, her health. With respect to the good qualifies of the plaintiff's family, he stated:

> You heard the testimony from Beverly—and by the way, you've had a chance to see a couple of members of that family on the stand; fine, uprighteous, fine people. This gal has three college degrees, three Master's degrees—not that you have to go to college to be a fine person, don't get me wrong, but it's a credit to her family of modest means to bring

up two children like this. Three master's, she's taking her doctorate. That's pretty good. And you heard—and these are gracious people, they're gracious people.

Gibbons compared the good qualities of the plaintiff with the bad actions of the defendant in bringing about the plaintiff's death. With respect to the deceased, Gibbons stated:

> He could have gone to Europe, he could have gone to England, the Riviera, anywhere there was an Air Force base and he wanted that little boy right there to have a shot at going to college and to be with that woman and provide for them. This is where your actual damages are. He chose out of any assignment in the world to be right there with those two people, and he put it, and it is in evidence, his last request for his wife and son.

With respect to the defendants, Gibbons stated:

> Because he didn't deserve to die. He had been in Vietnam in the war zone. He got killed, they killed him better than if a Viet Cong bullet would have gotten him.

Block set up the comparison between good and evil when he discussed the defendant's state of mind in committing its negligent acts:

> They are trying to get out from under. The same way they denied it was their ammunition in the first place, because the most expendable commodity is the soldier in the field. He is the poor guy at the end of all this. They are so involved in their business of turning out multiples and multiples of units that the human being becomes a cipher, becomes another digit and another unit to them. And this is what this case is all about. Every case, every issue resolves itself to one fundamental issue really: those who are concerned about human welfare and those who are callous about it; those who are involved in it, and those who are indifferent to it; those who forget what it was when you are at the bottom of the line, and those who feel for those.
>
> But I don't want the case decided on anything but the logic and the persuasion of the arguments, but this is what fundamentally this case is all about, because if people weren't interested in dollars and profits here you'd have more adequate inspection, you'd have ultrasonics and you'd have x-rays. You heard the whole thing. Well, it would cost more money, it would take more time. Well, let them take more time. Let them spend more money if it saves one life, one leg, one husband, one father.

With respect to the character of the plaintiff Wendell Burns, Block told the jury:

> You heard the type of person he was. Inconceivable. During my association with this case, when I heard of the attributes, of the type of life he

lived, he didn't smoke, didn't drink, except for an occasional beer, didn't swear, was a take-charge guy. Captain Starr says that of all of the men he had under him, Wendell Burns was in the top one per cent; that he, as a non-commissioned officer, would have been his next gun crew chief; that they didn't have corporals any more; that he was a non-commissioned officer inside of a short time—he went from private to PFC to corporal.

You heard Dorman Baird say how the men looked up to him; how they came to him with their problems. Yes, Mr. Brumbelow, he was mature and old beyond his years. You heard his boyhood friend, Mr. Quantrille, say how he always helped out. You heard the sister and other witnesses testify as a kid how he chopped wood, how he wrapped it up, how he sold it; how, when his father died, he was the man of the house; how he contributed to his mother.

. . . .

And this was a fellow who was devoted, who was loyal. You see his attitude toward his sick mother. He was a person that very rarely you see around, where mothers don't have to call up, you know, "Why didn't you call me this week?" or, "When are you coming over?" He was there with his wife, with his mother. He was a close person, who had a sense of ties, and a sense of obligation. That was Wendell Burns.

And you can bet your bottom dollar that even with work-life expectancy, the type of person Wendell Burns was, he wouldn't say to his wife, "Well, my work-life expectancy is now over. I am not going to support you any more." He was a kid who was always working. He would have worked, had he lived, I venture to say and suggest, beyond his work-life expectancy. I suggest that with his attributes, with his get-up-and-go, with his skills, he would have gone to college. I suggest that even if he did not go on to college—let's assume that—with the type of character, the type of motivation he had, he would have made far beyond what the average high school graduate in the United States made, because we know from Professor Berenson, these figures were based on those without special skills; and we know the type of person that Wendell Burns was; and I represent, nobody said one thing to the contrary about his character.

So when we speak of Wendell Burns, we don't speak of the average. We speak of, really, the top one per cent, because in Vietnam, under Captain Starr, you had soldiers and servicemen drawn from all over the United States; and in time of tension, in a time of strife, in a time of leadership, Wendell Burns was judged to be in the top one per cent.

Bergman compared the good qualities of the plaintiff with the bad actions of the defendant in bringing about her problems and in how he responded to them:

Shanna is a fighter. She is an inspirational person. Her friends love her. I don't know whether it was good to call them as witnesses or not, but one thing was clear, they can't talk about her without crying. They miss her.

Even Dr. Hanson said that Shanna was a very personable, intelligent, mature 13-year-old. He had no trouble relating to her in his office.

Shanna was and still is Daddy's girl. Shanna is very lucky to have a mother who is as dedicated to her, and always has been, as Judy.

This is the child, this is the person, who was entrusted to the care of Dr. Hanson and she is the person who was treated so casually, despite symptoms that Dr. Carrithers and the literature and the other doctors all said "strike fear into the heart of doctors;" supraclavicular nodes.

There has been a major wrong done, a major wrong done to one of our children. It is not acceptable to deny responsibility. It is not acceptable to say that, "It doesn't matter. Let's just forget it."

. . . .

There was casual follow-up care and very lazy documentation. I suggest that the documentation in this case reflects the general attention and attentiveness that Shanna got from Dr. Hanson. He wouldn't even face her and deliver the bad news, and he attempted to cover this up. That, I think, became clear yesterday afternoon when you saw his discharge summary. He tried to smooth this thing over.

A significant part of Bergman's other closing was highlighting the bad actions of the defendant in causing catastrophic injuries to the plaintiff and then failing to investigate the cause of the injuries and in failing to in any way discuss the injuries with the plaintiff's family. Bergman began by describing the plaintiff and telling the jury that he could not ask for a "more deserving, a less blameless client." He then went through the facts, highlighting the defendant's bad behavior:

Humana did not provide skilled nurses who were competent to do the job that was entrusted to them. They didn't do anything to train their nurses, putting a book behind the nurses' station with a couple of manuals from the manufacturer, and hoping that some of these part-time nurses would read it when they got around to it, is not training and that's the evidence in this case and that's not acceptable.

Linda Carter testified on my examination of her that she hadn't read that book in several years prior to this incident . . . Sharon Johnson, the other nurse, entrusted daily with the responsibility for people who are about to have babies and those babies, said that her knowledge of monitoring, her ability to recognize abnormalities was vague. That's the word, "vague," on November 11, 1979. In 1982, when I took Linda Carter's deposition, that's two and a half years after this all happened, she still didn't understand the basics, the fundamentals of fetal monitoring. She didn't know what late decelerations were or how to recognize them or what caused them. She didn't know what variable decelerations were. She didn't know that variable decelerations are the most common pattern associated with fetal distress, and instead of treating them, like the book says, she watches them. What did she learn those two and a half years, not a thing, and that is the most alarming and outrageous part of this case in my opinion. They didn't learn a thing.

Nobody seems to care. Nobody has acknowledged one ounce of responsibility. You heard the denial. "We deny that we are negligent, and we deny we caused the damages." . . . They've never even bothered to ask question number one, internally, in the—within, about this situation, and they continue to work there. These nurses continued to work there until recently. Nobody even questioned them. Nobody ever retrained them . . .

You would think that when a baby is transferred to Children's Mercy Hospital continuously seizuring with the kind of Apgar scores that Brent Olsen had, somebody might be interested in finding out what happened, but nobody has ever asked a question, and that is totally offensive . . .

"Now we don't care. We really don't care, who is responsible for the pediatrician not being there. I mean, we just don't care." The pediatrician wasn't there. That's up to them to find out. In fact, that's exactly the reason why some questions should have been asked. Let's nail it down on the day it happens. "Why wasn't the pediatrician here for forty-five minutes after the call was made, presumably? Where did our system break down? What went wrong? How could we be sure that it won't happen again? That there won't be more Brent Olsens." They don't care. They just don't care.

The second level was the negative credibility of the defendants in handling the litigation. Welch told the jury that the plaintiffs were the "kindest and most honest and nicest people" he had ever served. He pointed out how the defendants had exposed the plaintiffs' personal lives, run them through an obstacle course, and made fun of them during the trial. He then invited the jurors to judge those acts:

> You know, after their lawsuit was filed, and when things like this happen, your life becomes somewhat of an open book. The Coopers have been deprived of their privacy. They have had to expose their most personal lives to you, the jury, and to the public, in order to achieve their rights. And this has been an awful obstacle course, some of which you have seen here in these four days, that this fine family has been run through. And it all happened because they were victimized by this corporation and their corporate driver. There has been some fun made of them and their case during this week, and you're going to have to decide if you approve of this.

Habush first criticized the defendant for attempting to create an accident scenario that would fit their theory of how the collision occurred:

> They tried like the dickens during the whole trial to recreate an accident scenario that would fit their theory. They tried like the dickens to create an accident scenario that had the truck going frontwards, not backwards, that would discredit the eyewitnesses, that would discredit the treating doctor. Why? Because they are interested in anatomy? No. Because they knew darn well that if they could convince anybody of that, they would

be safe from the fact that they neglected to put common, ordinary safety devices on this forklift truck.

. . . .

They can't live with Dr. Walsh's explanation, folks. They can't live with it because they know that if this man was crushed, as we say he was, those posts or posts like them would have prevented it. So they got to have them coming out. They got to have him bouncing on his rear end. They have got to have him have a burst fracture. It's baloney. He didn't have it. And that's why they are trying so hard to prove it.

Habush then suggested that the defendant's bad character was made evident by its attempts to deny the existence of blueprints that demonstrated a feasible safeguard for the forklift in question:

I suggest to you that the best evidence, the best evidence of their guilt in this respect is their attempt to keep from you the truth about the overhead posts by those blueprints.

. . . .

As you recall, questions that were put to Mr. Olsen during the course of the testimony, we had been trying to get blueprints since the beginning of the trial. And an order of the Court had gone out requesting these blueprints, and it wasn't until the last day of the trial that providence shined upon us and the blueprints came forth.

But that doesn't explain why all that testimony went on before, and I'm not going to repeat it for you, but on my opening part of my final, I read statement after statement by Mr. Olsen denying its existence, denying the prints existed, denying that there were rear posts, denying that there were round posts, denying all that stuff.

I'd be embarrassed too.

The fact of the matter is it was in existence and they knew it. And the only reason we didn't see it is because it stuck in their throat like a bone. They couldn't spit it out and they couldn't swallow it because, Members of the Jury, that was in existence since 1972. It permitted ingress and exit. It didn't hamper visibility. It didn't require major modifications. It would, in the words of Mr. Olsen, have limited his injuries. It could have been made standard.

In responding to the defendant's assertion that the year-and-one-half delay in filing the claim after the malpractice was committed was evidence that the case was without merit, Glaser noted that this argument was simply an effort of the defense attorney to confuse the issues of the case. He went on to note the attempted manipulations on the part of the defendant during the trial:

Now, counsel said something about, I don't know, architecture. He manipulates some words like that. Look at how the theories have changed in the case on the defense. First there was bleeding, remember his opening statement? He said she was bleeding. When on cross-examination it developed that there was no bleeding in between periods, and there was no bleeding when she came into the doctor's office, and there was no bleeding on admission at the hospital and no bleeding for the two days before the operation, now they take another, submucosal, and we'll talk about that in a moment. There's been a change of theories in this case.

Gibbons criticized the defendant for its decision to call in biased witnesses who presented self-serving testimony, and for refusing to produce those witnesses who would tell the truth and present damaging testimony. He began by reminding the jury that the defendant claimed in its opening statement that it would prove that the accident in question was not caused by foreign object material in the white area. He then reviewed the testimony and argued that the defendant's key witnesses were employees of the defendant involved in sales of the planes and whose normal jobs were to convince prospective buyers of the planes that they were good products. Gibbons pointed out that the employees of the defendant who were actually involved in the design of the plane and who had given damaging testimony in their depositions were not called by the defendant, but rather were presented to the jury by way of deposition by the plaintiff's attorney. Gibbons noted that the defendant brought in two salesmen with a "charade" and "one fantasy stacked upon another" in an effort to convince the jury to deny the plaintiff's claim. Finally, Gibbons suggested that the defendant was attempting to divert the jury's attention from the true facts when he told the jury, "They are just trying to get you lost with this double engine flameout theory." With respect to one of these witnesses, Gibbons stated:

> Now, why do they do it? One little Republic Fairchild document came to light. For cost, to save cost they chose the 1-E-9. And the reason is they knew that Aces 2 was coming out. And Mr. Sustarsic, one of their witnesses, one of our witnesses, they didn't bring Mr. Sustarsic down here, McDonnell didn't. I took his deposition and I am the one that introduced it into evidence, ladies and gentlemen. And I think again it is like Mr. Townsend, keep in mind they didn't bring him down here.

Finally, Gibbons told the jury that the defendants knew all along that the plane and ejection seat in question were dangerous and defective, and yet they required the plaintiff and her little boy to needlessly relive the tragedy of Captain Wahl's death in order to prove what the defendant already knew.

In his closing on liability, Block criticized the defendant for claiming at the outset of the trial that it did not know that the ammunition in question was its ammunition when he told the jury:

> At the outset of this case, and you may remember it but I took it down, because I knew the statement was not so, and also there was a bit of colloquy during the trial, the statement was made by the defendant in his opening to you, "We don't know that it is our ammunition."
>
> Now, at this late date, during the summation, having realized that we have not gotten in the government records, see, they were hoping we

wouldn't get them in, they come up and say, "Well, now that Mr. Wilcox took the stand and testified that it was our lot number, of course we admit that it is our ammunition."

Do you believe—and this goes through the whole web of the case, because there is something out of the order going on here—do you think for one moment that the first time the defendant knew its lot number was involved in this case was when Mr. Wilcox took the stand? Didn't they speak to him earlier? Didn't they have access to the same government reports? Didn't they have access to Picatinny Arsenal which tested the lot numbers? Didn't they come in with a whole panoply of witnesses, half of Texarkana, Arkansas, almost—Texas—with papers and details about this lot number?

Why did they refuse to admit it at the outset? Because they hoped by some flaw in our evidence, you could not pin it on them.

But that is not to the merits of the case, but is just a certain way of thinking about a lawsuit, and maybe they are afraid of something, as they should be.

In his closing on damages for Dorman Baird, Block criticized the defendant's attempts to appeal to the regionalism of the New York jurors in judging an Alabama plaintiff:

And I don't pretend to be the oldest practitioner nor the most experienced practitioner. I have tried a few cases in my time. But I have never heard such an overt, such a blatant argument to chauvinism. We are all God's children. What difference does it make if Dorman Baird comes from Alabama or comes from New York or comes from Topeka, Kansas? He is a human being and as a great American playwright once said "Attention must be paid."

Perlman advised the jury at the outset of his closing that the reason he and his client were in the courtroom at that moment was that the defendant "has not accepted the responsibility" for its negligent acts and was simply trying to shift the blame to other persons:

So what's their defense? First, they say blame Golden Glow because of the maintenance. They went out and tried, they went out of business shortly after this thing happened. They are not on trial here. There is not one shred of evidence that what caused this thing to malfunction had anything to do with Golden Glow.

Next, they blame the exposed wire. If it meant anything to them, if it meant anything to them, who was there and helping the inspector find out what caused it? That's why they were there. There was an investigation. If it meant anything to Mr. Campbell, it wasn't in his logbook. It wasn't in his records. And he held it in his hand. They come down ten months later, Mr. McDowell and all of them, and they went over there to see what caused it. What's the most obvious thing you look for if you are Joy? You are going to find something that would take you off the hook.

What would they look for? Some change in the product that would relieve them, some alteration, some defect, some exposed wire that would cause a short. They didn't find any. Under oath—Mr. McDowell in October of 1983, he had been here, he took all of these pictures—I asked him, what caused it? I don't have a good idea, he said. And I had to read it to him and cross-examine him about it.

. . . .

They began the trial by saying the demultiplexer was the same, in his opening statement. The proof in this case was it was not. Then they changed the proof and they said, well, if the demultiplexer wasn't the same, then the wire that came out of it was the same. Well, wouldn't it make sense, if they were changing the demultiplexer, that they would have so many people, so many people would have to have looked right at that wire that they want to blame?

The next defense is to blame the witness. No matter what the cause, he and he alone was to suffer the consequences. And they ask you to turn your back on him.

§9.08 —Credibility: The Pursuit of Justice

A closely related theme was that the plaintiffs and their lawyers were engaged in the pursuit of justice, while the defendants sought to subvert justice. The jury's purpose as enunciated by the judge was to do justice. Thus, the plaintiffs' lawyers enhanced their credibility by becoming the champions of justice. They aligned themselves with the pursuit of justice, which linked them and their clients to the positive aspects of the justice system. In all cases, the lawyers told the jurors that they and their clients wanted justice. On the other hand, the lawyers demonstrated that the defendants or their lawyers were trying to keep the jury from doing justice by withholding evidence, distorting evidence, prejudicing the jury, and diverting the jury's attention from the task at hand. The defendants and their lawyers were debunked as guides to truth and justice.

For example, Spence demonstrated how the defendant's witness withheld evidence, distorted the truth, and in some cases, lied. He asserted that the defendant's lawyers attempted to mislead the jury, while he presented the "honest" issues. He argued that the defendant's defenses were slanderous creations of the defense lawyer that were not supported by any competent evidence. He argued that the defense lawyer "points his finger at everybody, and anything that shows the truth, and anything that uncovers the truth of Kerr-McGee, of his client, is 'despicable.'" He then asked the jurors:

What does that all mean to you? How does it feel to be honorable men and women, with families and children—how does it feel to be dealt with like that and to have accusation after accusation like that made in a court of law before all of these people, and have those men in gray expect you to believe that?

Spence repeatedly asked the jurors to judge the defendant's efforts to subert justice.

Bergman continually aligned his claims with a theme of justice when he told the jury:

> The Olsens are indeed grateful for your participation in this trial. They've put a lot of faith, great faith, in your commitment that you made at the beginning of the trial to follow the law, to pay attention to the facts, and it's in that way that we have gained some confidence, as we have gone along, that justice in fact will be done.
>
> . . . .
>
> Terri and Bob are not here on behalf of Brent for your sympathy. They are not here out of any vindictiveness or hostility or malice or ill will. They are here because they have an obligation to their child, and they have demonstrated that commitment, and I think you've seen that, as we've gone through the evidence, and part of that commitment is to get him justice which he is entitled to.
>
> . . . .
>
> The heavy responsibility that I was talking about a minute ago, I'm very happy to say, is about to pass from me to you, and that's the responsibility to see to it that justice is done, complete justice is done for Brent Olsen.
>
> . . . .
>
> I would hope, and I know that you'll be guided by the facts of this case. You'll be guided by the law and you'll be guided by your sense of what is right and what is just and what needs to be done, and again, I want to thank you on behalf of Brent and his family and Mr. Johnson and myself. Thank you very much.

Bergman characterized the defense as attempting to cover up the facts in the case and to induce the jury to disregard jury instructions:

> . . . and I expect that there'll be considerable smoke tossed at you in closing arguments of the defense lawyers, and that started at the beginning of the case.
>
> . . . .
>
> Now, he told you ten minutes for a well designed reason because after ten minutes, there was no paracervical block, bradycardia. So he kind of looks like he cares, and he's responsible, but he's out of there before the damage, before the obvious damage, is done and somehow, you're supposed to exculpate him on the basis of that. That's just another coverup, and this, they've tried to cover up what has happened since the day it happened.

With respect to the defendant's suggestion that the jury should not return a large verdict for the plaintiff because, due the physical state of the plaintiff, the money would not do him any good, Bergman responded that the defense was attempting to induce the jury to disregard the judge's jury instructions:

> Now, Brent Olsen is a human being. He is a citizen of the State of Kansas, and he has the same rights as any other person, whether he can use the

money or not, and I suspect that by the time Brent Olsen lives out his life, there'll be use for that money for his benefit, but whether or not he can, he is entitled to have you consider each and every element of his damages and to ask you not to do that, I think, is—and that's the objection I made, is to ask you to disregard the Court's instructions. I think that would add insult on injury to walk out of here and leave Brent sitting here uncompensated because his injuries are so bad, that maybe he can't use the money. That is callous, and that is wrong, and that is just an extension of the attitude that the hospital and Humana has had since the day this all happened. They really don't care. They want to walk out of here with as little damage to themselves as possible, and without any concern for Brent, and that's wrong. There is a continuing coverup of what happened at the hospital; it is very clear to me.

Glaser began his opening by reaffirming his belief in the justice system:

Your Honor, Mr. Foreman, ladies and gentlemen of the jury. I want to thank you for your kind attention. You've come from all walks of life, you've given of your time and been away from your work, and you've done it to do justice between the parties in this case and the jury system is a great system and I want you to know that we all appreciate it.

Glaser accused the defendant of attempting to subvert justice in arguing that the plaintiff's gesture of sending the doctor a card before she became aware of the malpractice was evidence upon which to base a defendant's verdict:

Well, let's talk about that thank you card. . . . Well, not everybody does it, but it's a nice thing when you—somebody tells you something like that, and you're grateful. They found out later on they weren't so grateful, naturally, when all the fuss—and by the way, it does in fact—and by the way, it doesn't take a day to get all the facts. It took them some time to retain us, it took some time, and it took us probably, to get all these records, probably took us another six months to a year to get all the records and to analyze them and to get an opinion. Or to get opinions, whatever it is. So, don't blame those people for being gracious, really. And we're not going to decide this case on a card, a thank you card. That would be absurd, would be a great miscarriage of justice, wouldn't it be? That's nonsense. A plant and a card, like that wipes out all he did.

Perlman used the symbols of justice to explain the concept to the jury:

You have all seen the Statue of Justice, I'm sure. It's got a blindfold across the eyes. It can't see. It treats people the same way, whether they are human beings, corporations, whatever they might be, the lowest to the highest. It also has in one hand, it has the scales of justice. In the other hand the statue carries a sword. The Scales of Justice are fairness and justice, and the sword is punishment. And when you retire and you consider this case, you will have both of those, because you will be carrying the sword and you will be carrying the Scales of Justice. And when you consider punitive damages, think about the things that you can't compensate for in any other way. You can't compensate for what this little girl, Shelly, has being a nurse, and she was and still is a loving wife.

In criticizing the defendant for claiming at the outset of the case that it did not know that the ammunition in question was its ammunition, when in fact the defendant knew all along that it was its ammunition, Block told the jury that the lawsuit was not a game, but was an endeavor to do justice:

> Now there is a certain thing of putting cards on the table. A lawsuit is not a game; a lawsuit is really a serious endeavor to do justice and things should be brought out immediately and admitted readily before there is no need for taking up a jury's time unless there is an ulterior motive.

In closing his argument on damages, Block appealed to the jury to do justice:

> All I ask you is not to consign Dorman Baird to ask heaven what has been denied him here on earth. He is here for compensation for each and every injury. And the fact that he is from Alabama makes no difference.
>
> You know there was a play written a few years ago that won a Pulitzer Prize, called "All My Sons," and it involved a manufacturer who put out defective airplane engines, and they failed and people, GIs, got killed. And it didn't faze the manufacturer until one day his son in the service was flying and it was equipped with a defective engine that his father had built in his plant and he, too, died, and hence the father's realization of what became the title of the play, "All My Sons."
>
> So when we speak of Dorman Baird, we all have to take a broad concept of justice that everyone who seeks redress in a courtroom, essentially all my sons, all my brothers, all my sisters, so don't let an appeal to sectionalism faze you. The only appeal and the right appeal is to justice.

§9.09 —The Plaintiff Is not Looking for Sympathy

Closely related to the theme involving the pursuit of justice is the theme that the plaintiff is not looking for sympathy. The lawyers told the jury that the plaintiffs were seeking justice or monetary compensation rather than sympathy. As a practical matter, the lawyers may have been concerned that the jurors would feel sympathy, but would return little or no money as compensation, and, therefore, the jurors were told directly that the plaintiff was not seeking sympathy or that sympathy would be of no help to the plaintiff. Further, by telling the jury that they were not looking for sympathy, the lawyers were reinforcing their position as seekers of justice. For example, Welch told the jurors that the plaintiffs did not want sympathy because they had already received that from their friends and neighbors and at home. Rather, he continued, the plaintiffs wanted justice, which was then defined as a money verdict for the plaintiffs. He told the jurors that "the real question that you're going to have to be called upon to decide, I think, is the matter of damages."

Bergman told the jurors that his clients were not in court on behalf of their son "for sympathy," but rather, were there because they felt a "commitment to get him the justice which he is entitled to." In his case involving the failure to diagnose Hodgkin's disease, Bergman told the jury:

> We are not asking for sympathy. We have not played for sympathy. This case is sympathetic. We have not tried to play on sympathy. Who needs to? I mean, the facts speak for themselves. The injury is horrendous.

Perlman told the jury that the time for sympathy was past and that the plaintiff was seeking justice:

> And we are not here asking for sympathy. That figure has been mentioned to you. We haven't mentioned it once. Sympathy and the time for that is passed three and a half years ago with the flowers in the hospital and the wet pillows and all of those things, and the cards and friends. In this courtroom nobody has to get in here and beg and pray for justice. And that's all we ask. Not charity, but justice, based on the evidence. Be true to your oath.

§9.10 —The Issues are Simple and the Jury is Competent

As in opening, the lawyers continued their assertion that the issues in the case were simple. There had been technical expert testimony, and the lawyers did not want the jurors to become lost in technical jargon, or to shy away from the issues because they appeared complex. Therefore, they all argued that the issues of negligence and damages were simple and that the jury was competent to hear and decide the case. For example, Ring told the jury that although the case appeared complicated, and although the lawyers attempted to make the case appear complex, that "very frankly, when you separate the wheat from the chaff in this case, it really is a very simple case."

Baldwin conceptualized the issues in the case concisely and told the jury that the case was simple:

> It is just like I told you Monday morning, it comes down to a really very simple case. His Honor will charge you, when we finish, what the law is and you will have to follow it, because you are an officer of the Court now and you are obligated to follow the law. He will use a lot of technical legal terms, but essentially he will tell you this: that if the tractor was unreasonably dangerous and was defective when it left the hands of Ford Motor Company and caused Mr. Foster's tragedy, then Ford Motor Company is responsible for damages. It is just that simple.

Glaser noted that the defense lawyer's job was to make the case appear complicated and then reassured the jurors that they should not be concerned about the fact that the case involved medical or surgical issues because it was really a simple case of unnecessary surgery:

It's really a simple case. I told you, do you remember, when you were selected, don't be worried, don't be concerned about the medicine or the surgery in the case, that by the time you are ready to go into that room and deliberate, you will have all of the medical facts at your fingertips and you will understand the case thoroughly, because it's not a complicated case, it's a very simple case of unnecessary surgery.

.   .   .   .

What is this case all about, really? I can reduce it for you in one line, that's how simple it is. The lady, forty-seven years of age, in her premenopausal state—that means she's still having periods, she has not reached her change in life, in plain language—in good health, active and living a full and complete life. She goes to Dr. Cavalli for a vaginal cyst and after two office visits, she ends up in a hospital and she is castrated. That's not my word, castrated, you heard it used by the doctors. You heard it used, or written, by Dr. Kupperman. That's what this case is about. It's that simple.

Perlman boiled the issues of his case down to whether or not the machine in question was safe:

This is not a complicated case. You have heard a lot of complicating terms about multiplexers and demultiplexers and cable connections and wiring and all this kind of thing, but it's a very, very simple case. It comes down to this. Was this continuous miner unsafe or unreliably dangerous due to any defect or any hazard in either the design or the way it was made or in the mechanics of it, in the way that it functioned? If either of those are true, Joy is responsible. All you need is one. And the record and the testimony in this case is that you didn't have one, but you had many. You had so many that Mr. Milby didn't even talk about any of them in his closing argument, and he's their lawyer.

This case is really about inadequate safety for coal miners. Did it have adequate safety? It did not.

The lawyers wanted the jurors to have the confidence necessary to do the tasks asked of them. Returning huge verdicts against large corporations was not something the average juror was used to doing. Thus, the lawyers told the jurors that they were fully competent to hear and decide the issues involved in the lawsuit. Corboy told the jurors that the system had been tested and that it worked with jurors brought together as they had been brought together in his case, and that the jurors were competent to decide the case.

Spence told the jurors that he had confidence in their abilities to hear the evidence and cut through the "garbage":

You've been here two-and-a-half months listening to testimony. "How does it fit in?" "What does it mean?" Now, the judge has told you that we know something about what's going to happen under the law because he's told us what the instructions are essentially going to be. So, when I tell you that I think instructions are going to be this, that's just because

I really do know because I've already read them, and the judge is always able to surprise us, and maybe change some, but basically we know both sides of what the law is. The law isn't any different now than it was when the case started. But you've wondered how all this evidence fits in, and what the legal principles are that you have to follow, and so I want—and they are simple—I'll tell you this—they've got to be simple or most lawyers that I know couldn't learn them. Now, just listen to that. Now, I want to tell you something else, before we get started—you need to hear this: You may feel a little insecure. You may be sitting here just like me, not knowing whether you're up to doing this in a case full of number crunching statistics, and scientific data, and conflicting evidence. Well, let me tell you what: You are beautifully constituted to make this decision, and the law has proven that over and over again. Experts are just experts, all tied up with their numbers and their word games. But, you know, Abraham Lincoln once said: "You can fool part of the people part of the time, but you can't fool all of the people all the time." And, a jury, with the composition of this jury of people from all walks of life, with all kinds of experience, comes together as the common composite mind, and you bring with you all of your common sense. And, if there's one thing that I've tried to do through this trial—and I hope you have seen it with me—is that we are dealing with the most complex issue maybe in the world. But, I am bringing to you—I have hoped—common sense, and that's how it will be decided, and I have seen it done successfully, beautifully, almost like magic, case after case, and, it's because jurors can do that. Because they can cut through all of the garbage that experts, and lawyers, and legalists like to lay down—they can cut through it all with their common sense, is what has permitted mankind to survive, and what has permitted the judicial system to survive to this day.

And, so I want you to know that you are beautifully suited, I think— forgive me for saying it, but I think hand-chosen, specially chosen, for the joint combination talent and experience that you have that makes you a composite body.

Habush told the jurors that they were competent to evaluate the conduct of the defendant:

> You are, members of the jury, competent to sit on this case and competent to evaluate the conduct of the parties. Yes, you are even competent to evaluate the conduct of the Eaton Corporation, the manufacturer, and there is nothing that precludes your ability to do so.
>
> You bring to this jury common sense, and the experiences of your life. And sometimes common sense will make and have more influence on what you do and decide than anything you've heard.
>
> You bring to this jury your experience of life and although I agree that your decision should not be dictated by passion or by emotion, the law does not require you to leave your hearts at home either. And when we are talking about damages, in particular, that's a subject that you all have

to draw upon your personal experiences to assist you in arriving at a just verdict.

In the rebuttal part of his closing, Bergman told the jurors that he would rely on their intelligence and memories, and, therefore, would not respond to everything said by the defendant:

> I want to say first at the conclusion of Mr. Larson's closing argument, I was rather infuriated. I was totally offended. I wanted to respond to everything that he'd said and then we had a break, and I was reminded by my partner that I should rely on the jury's intelligence, on their memories. They were here. They heard the evidence, and you don't have to respond to every single thing, and since there is no way to respond, you know, I am going to rely on that.

§9.11 —Rectifying Wrongs

Due to the defendants' negligence, the plaintiffs lost or were deprived of something that caused them to be separated from their communities or families in some important way. That is, the plaintiffs were damaged and lost some important part of their lives such as their ability to work, to be good husbands and fathers, or to simply enjoy life. The lawyers recast the jury process into a ritual of reintegration, arguing that only a verdict for the plaintiffs would in some way restore them to their former positions and make them whole. The issue became one of separation and reintegration, and the jurors were invited to participate in the ritual and help reintegrate the plaintiffs and make them whole. The ritual took the form of a specific human drama in each case.

In setting up the process by which the jury can "right a wrong," the lawyers many times began by telling the jury that the plaintiff would prefer to have his or her health back rather than money, but that the plaintiff cannot regain his or her health, the jury cannot restore health, but rather, the jury can simply award money, which is the only way that these wrongs can be rectified.

Welch argued that his clients' lives had been shattered, and that Robert Cooper had been deprived of his right to work and earn a living for his family. He recast the issues so that rendering a verdict for the plaintiffs became the reintegrative act of making the plaintiffs whole and helping them down the road of life. In his conclusion, Welch stated:

> Now, I think you know from listening to the Coopers and listening to the evidence that they have been robbed of the pleasures of their lives, and all they have left is survival. And that is what they are doing, they are surviving, and they are getting along, because the pleasure's been taken. They impaired his most important right, and that is his right to live his own life in his own quiet, undemanding, unassuming way. And that must be reckoned with. And you must come to grips with that.
>
> Now, the Coopers are not here to demand anything. They are not demanding people. They are asking for your help to try to obtain some

justice, so they want me to ask you to bring in a verdict that's sanctioned by your conscience and rationalized by your reasoning. That's all they really want.

Corboy's client was a helpless quadriplegic who needed health care for the rest of his life. Corboy presented testimony to the effect that with acute care, his client would live out a normal life expectancy. The cost of acute care for the rest of the plaintiff's life was astronomical. The defense, in order to avoid a huge verdict, presented testimony that the plaintiff would have a shortened life expectancy, and, therefore, the jury should return a verdict for medical care for only a few years. In recasting the issues into the ritual of reintegration, Corboy argued that the plaintiff had been deprived of his health, and could not live out his normal life expectancy unless he was placed in an acute care hospital. Therefore, the plaintiff was in need of a substantial verdict to pay for acute care, and only such a verdict would give the plaintiff a normal life expectancy. Corboy argued this way:

> But remember, when you walk in there and I don't know why you got thrown into this case any more than I know why Randy Block got hit, but you have to make the decision how long is John Randolph Block going to live. And then when you make that decision, you decide what type of optimal care he is entitled to. And you put a dollar figure on it. . . . But the responsibility and the vicissitudes of the world casts its shadow upon people at times. Sometimes, they have to make decisions which affect people's lives for the rest of their lives. In this case, twelve people from twelve different walks of life are going to remember the evidence in this lawsuit, and they are going to have to say John Randolph Block is going to either live this long or this long. . . . He's got a shot at it. It is your job to fund it and let the chips fall where they may and make the decision what type of optimal care and for how long is John Randolph Block entitled to it.

Baldwin's client was rendered a cripple, prevented from working, and in need of regular hospital care. The defense argued not only that were they not negligent, but that the plaintiff's claims were excessive. Baldwin transformed the issue into a reintegration ritual and invited the jurors to participate in the ritual in a way that would be pleasing to them. He first defined the issue by asking the jurors:

> Should Larkin Foster be sentenced to second-class treatment at the hands of this defendant, when if he gets first-class treatment he will have the opportunity to live a normal life?

Next, in arguing that the jury should return a verdict for the medical expense suggested by the plaintiff rather than the defendant, Baldwin stated:

> I submit that this is a reasonable figure, that it ought not be reduced, it ought not be compromised, that he ought not be sentenced to second-class treatment, that his life is at stake, and if he gets the best medical

care—that's what you can do, that's the one thing you can do. You can't give him back his legs, you can't give him his body functions that he has lost, you can't give him back his ability to walk, to work, to support his family, but the one thing that you can do is to see that he gets first-class medical treatment.

Baldwin then argued that the plaintiff had been deprived of hope and the pleasures of his life and invited the jury to participate in the ritual of reintegration by rendering a verdict that would restore the plaintiff to a decent lifestyle, and would allow the jurors to feel good about their part in the process:

> In this case there is no hope. The cold cruel facts are that Larkin Foster will never walk again. He will never play with his children again by running. He will never work again. Now what is that worth to a man? You gentlemen on the jury will appreciate this—if somebody asks you what is the possession that you prize the most, I believe right up on top of the list would be my ability to work and to provide the things of pleasure to the people I love.
>
> This has been taken, it is gone, and all you can do is what the Court tells you you must award, money damages for pain. So, I am going to close by saying that that, to me, is not an unrealistic figure, that the $2,500,000.00 is a figure that you would tell Ford Motor Company: "If you are going to put this kind of machine on the market, you are going to respond in full damages, and you are not going to selectively hurt people in the country—and, yes, you have accepted the risk of Larkin Foster, but you are going to respond in damages as the law says you should."
>
> And when you have returned a verdict in that amount, I say that you can be proud, you can say to yourself and your neighbors: "I was proud to have been a part of that, because I made a little part—ever so small—to see that the life of Larkin Foster was a little bit more comfortable and that he got the things he needed by way of medical care and treatment and I did what little bit I could to ease his comfort, and to see that he lived as near as possible a normal life." And I trust that you will unhesitatingly do this, and I thank you.

In *Silkwood,* there were many separation-reintegration issues. Karen Silkwood's children were deprived of their mother, and a verdict for the plaintiff would provide compensation for this loss. Karen Silkwood was slandered, and a verdict for the plaintiff would clear her name. The defendant Kerr-McGee had lied to the public, covered up its negligent actions, and placed society in danger from plutonium contamination. The defendant had escaped responsibility for its actions and had deprived society of honesty, safety, and accountability. A verdict for the plaintiff, punishing the defendant, was recast as forcing the defendant to be honest and careful in the future, returning society to a position of safety, and holding the defendant accountable for its actions. Spence continually asked the jurors whether they approved of the defendant's actions and invited them to punish and correct them by returning a verdict

for the plaintiff. For example, on the issue of lying about the effects of plutonium, he asked:

> Can you put your stamp of approval on that kind of conduct? Or, are you
> outraged? Do you feel the outrage inside of your humanness, that people
> would say that not only to thousands of workers, but under their solemn
> oaths in this courtroom to every one of you—every one of you they said
> that to—and they didn't look out blindly, you know, out over this court-
> room—they looked into your eyes and said it under their oaths that "plu-
> tonium didn't cause cancer," right down to Dr. Bottomly, and the word
> games they played with you. How does it make you feel? These are the
> people, the men in gray, that called those witnesses to testify to that. . . .
> Can you buy that? Can you permit that to happen? Can you put your
> stamp of approval on that? Can you pass the buck? Are you saying, "It
> ain't up to us. It ain't up to us?" Let me tell you something: There are
> only six of you in this world—there aren't any others like you—there will
> never be another time when there are six people like you, ever, ever, ever.
> There will never be another courtroom with a Judge like that one with
> the fortitude and decency and patience to let this case come to you ever
> again. The buck stops here—there's no other place for this buck to stop.
> There isn't any other time.

In his case involving the failure to timely diagnose Hodgkin's disease,
Bergman noted the pain and suffering experienced by the plaintiff in the past
and the pain and suffering she would no doubt experience in the future. He
reminded the jury that there was a cloud hanging over the plaintiff, and as such,
she should be made financially secure so that she could enjoy whatever life
she had left and take advantage of any medical possibilities available to her:

> Shanna is not dead. Shanna is a fighter. There is a cloud, a very big, black
> cloud over her future. And when she dies, she is going to go hard, but
> she could be here for a long time. Let's hope she is.
> She should be in a financial position for the rest of her days where she
> can take advantage of any possible breakthrough, any possible thing that
> will help her, no matter where in the world that it is, no matter how expen-
> sive it is, without having to worry or put any more financial pressure on
> her family. I think she should be financially wealthy. I think that she should
> be able to live for the rest of her life with the sense that, if she is nothing
> else, she is independently wealthy—if she can fell good about that—she
> can do whatever she wants to for whomever she wants. She should have
> that. And that is part of the point of this case.

Glaser told the jury that the defendant had taken away the plaintiff's most
prized possession, her health. He then detailed her damages and losses, noting
that she had been castrated, made barren, and had her sexual desires
destroyed. He acknowledged that the jury could not give her back her health,
but said that it could do the next best thing, which was to compensate her for
her damages:

What is the value, be conservative, what's the value of a womb and ovaries to a woman—and I do have to tell you about the psychological effects of being castrated, man or woman? Loss of womb, tubes and ovaries. What is the value? I know we can't—listen, we can't give her back those organs, we can't give her back her health. But society says let's do the next best thing, let's try to compensate her as well as we can in damages. That's a civilized way of thinking and doing things. What is that loss of those organs? What's the value of that?

Perlman told the jury that its award of monetary compensation would replace what was taken from the plaintiff and would allow him to live through the humiliation and loss of pride brought on by his injuries:

And the term used by Mr. Milby, they are asking you to give. We are not asking you to give anything. This is evidence of what he has lost and what he will lose. You are not giving him the wages or the wage he would lose. You are replacing what he would have earned except for the fact that that boom malfunctioned. Otherwise, he would be the one that would have to suffer the loss. And you have decided that it wasn't his fault and it was their fault.

. . . .

And are we being fair? The next element is pain and suffering. That's the—the Court tells you, that's physical and mental. And we are talking about three and a half years in the past, forty-six years in the future, fifty years. And the figure that we have asked for is not millions of dollars like they tell you. For the total amount of his life, fifty years, we ask for $750,000 pain and suffering, present and future.

Now, what does that mean? That's separate from what he would have earned and what he would have lost in his earnings, because you can't restore his sight by his verdict, you can't restore his taste or his smell, you can't take away his epilepsy, the grand mal seizures, you can't take the wires out of his face or restore his balance and coordination, you can't restore his ability to read and write, you can't give him back the brain damage that—where his face hung precariously off his skull. Of the five senses that the Lord gave him, he suffered damage to almost all of them, and has lost almost three totally. His dad said it best. He said he's a twelve-year old boy in a man's body. If you could restore and replace all of these things and say, Henry, we'll give you a choice, we'll give them all back to you and you won't have to suffer all these things, but you come over here and you decide. Do you want all those things back or do you want $750,000? He would say I don't want a nickel, I want to be back like I was. But you can't do that.

It took him twenty-four years to be a coal miner and to be proud of what he was doing and to be supporting his family. It took that long (counsel makes snapping noise) for that boom to destroy it all.

. . . .

And that's what all of the evidence in this case is, that he has got all of these problems, they are permanent, he can't ever quit. And if you were just to say $100 is fair, that would be in the millions of dollars. We are not asking for that. We are asking for $750,000, past, present, and future pain and suffering, to go through the humiliation, the indignity, the loss of pride, the disfigurement. I can't go on enough to tell you about that.

. . . .

The question is, how much does it take to get the attention of the biggest coal equipment manufacturing company in the world? If one of those machines sold for $500,000, is two of those too much?

When you think about this question, think about how much power you have in this courtroom as you sit here and as you retire in a few minutes. As much as you will ever have in your lifetime. When you go to the polls on election day, you are one of thousands. When you go to a school board meeting, you are one of maybe hundreds. When you sit here, you are one of six. And your verdict will send a message far beyond the corners of this courtroom that you want to right a wrong, for the sake of the future, so other coal miners won't go through this kind of experience.

. . . .

In short, your verdict will determine the quality of life for Henry. You will give him back some sense of self-respect and some pride, independence, some manhood. You will give him a fighting chance.

Block recast the "righting wrongs" ritual into a burial for Wendell Burns when he told the jury that in the American justice system they could not go by "an eye for an eye," but rather, they could give only monetary compensation, and that fair compensation would put the deceased to rest with dignity:

We don't go by "An eye for an eye; a tooth for a tooth." You can't go down to Day & Zimmerman and say, "Give us one of your officers. We are going to put you in a similar situation." That's not the way you do it in an American courtroom. So when I say, "The loss of pecuniary income from the wages alone, is the smallest part of the case," I say it based upon knowledge of what a father is in the community, a husband or a wife is in the community. Those are the real losses in the case, and the wife is entitled not only to the lost income, but to certain other items that were not mentioned to Mr. Brumbelow.

She's entitled to the protection, the care, the guidance, a companionship throughout her lifetime.

. . . .

This is—perhaps, other than on some Fourth of July, maybe, in Yakima—will be the last time Wendell Burns will be spoken of in a public place. It's our job, really, to put him to rest with dignity; to give his family what justice requires, and justice being all the elements that the law allows in full measure, in full measure, because the award must be commensurate with the loss sustained; and this was a very, very great person, young person, but great person.

Habush wove the theme of making the plaintiff whole again throughout his closing when he told the jury:

. . . And the law states that if you are injured by the negligence or wrongful conduct of another, the law tries to make you whole.

Now you and I both know that with respect to making you whole in a physical sense that that's not possible. Trying to make you whole in an economic sense is not always possible either, but it asks you to award damages which in a sense is your expression of what you think the seriousness of the injury was. And it's done in a—very unusual way.

· · · ·

When we talk about loss of enjoyment of life, you bring your—common sense again and your human experience to the courtroom. And you look at what this couple had before, and you compare it to what they have now. Look at what Roger was able to enjoy before and what he is able to enjoy now.

· · · ·

And remember, folks, that Roger is not a computer specialist. He was not a C.P.A. He was a physical, working person. He did not have a high school degree, dropped out of high school to join the Army. His whole life has been what? His whole life has been working as a forklift operator.

· · · ·

His future earning capacity has been taken away from him as if someone just took the next egg out of the cookie jar, and that also is a separate item of damages, separate from the medical, because what we are talking about is replacing earning capacity in the future, putting it in a separate fund, and out of that, they live off it.

· · · ·

And I think for future pain and suffering, for the twenty-five years left in his life, hopefully, that he's entitled to the same. In other words, I think that for the loss of dignity, the humiliation, the embarrassment, the body functions, the devastation to his life, that he's entitled to a total for past and future pain and suffering of two million dollars.

§9.12   Jury Purpose

Woven into the stories were several themes that functioned to create jury purpose. Although the judge had instructed the jury that its function was to render fair and impartial justice, this was an abstraction subject to interpretation. As in their opening statements, the lawyers took an active role in interpreting and shaping jury purpose.

§9.13   —To Judge the Evidence

One of the themes designed to shape jury purpose was that the jurors' role was to judge the evidence. The jurors had been presented with conflicting views of reality during the trial, and in their closing statements, the lawyers argued and analyzed the conflicting evidence. The lawyers told the jurors that one of their functions was to resolve this conflict by judging the evidence. For example, Ring told the jury:

Again, just as the opening statement, what we say is not the evidence. We try as best we can to talk about the evidence, but you are the sole judges of the evidence and it is your recollection and your views that, in the final analysis, count.

Corboy told the jurors that one of their functions was to find the facts, and that it would be up to them to resolve any discrepancy in the facts:

And you folks are going to go in there, and you are going to have the responsibility which is two-fold, finding the facts, which we agree to most of them, and then applying the law that this wonderful court is going to supply you.

· · · ·

I don't think you have to spend much time in there, but the discrepancies that did exist or might have existed have come down to your responsibility in making ultimate decisions.

· · · ·

Now, you've heard all of the economists talk. You've heard the fellow that testifies for the plaintiffs and the defendants and he decides which way he's going to go when he comes into court.
You've heard Dr. Linke, and Dr. Linke uses the one percent differential.
If that's the wrong differential, you decide what the right one is. That's what you're here for.

Bergman suggested to the jurors that they would be responsible for finding the true facts when he stated:

I just can't respond to every falsity that was stated right here about what the data shows, what it doesn't show, who said what. I'll have to rely on your memories for that. All that I can say is that this is a very important moment in Shanna's life, and I am sure that you know that. All that we'll be doing is just waiting anxiously to hear what your verdict is. Thank you.

§9.14 —To Judge The Parties and Their Actions

The lawyers told the jurors that their function was to judge the actions of the parties by their verdict. After having compared the good actions of the plaintiffs with the bad actions of the defendants, the jury was asked to judge those actions. For example, Welch told the jurors that their function was to judge one of their "fellow citizens."

Judging the actions of the defendants was an important theme for Spence. He continually pointed out the bad actions of the defendant and asked the jurors how they felt about them. He argued that the jurors should hold the defendant accountable for its actions. He invited them to let their verdict be the judge of those actions. Spence began pointing out the bad actions of the defendant. He characterized the actions of Kerr-McGee in covering up its handling of plutonium and the effects on its employees as the "big lie." He characterized the defense theory as the "big lie." He then continually asked the jurors if they were going to approve of these actions:

Documented doctored X-rays. . . . There has been an effort to try to cover this business and to confuse by saying there weren't X-rays, or these weren't this, or weren't that, or weren't this kind of X-rays or they weren't that kind of X-rays or trying to confuse where they were, and all that. The truth of it is that they were doctored X-rays that dealt with the quality control of those pins, and Hammock said, "We were shipping them."

. . . And the question is whether you are going to put your stamp of approval on that with a verdict for the defendants, or some piddling little ten million dollar verdict for the plaintiff.

. . . .

. . . How does it feel to be honorable men and women, with families, and children—how does it feel to be dealt with like that and to have accusation after accusation like that made in a court of law before all of these people, and have those men in gray expect you to believe that?

. . . .

. . . How about when people slander you like this in the most important case in the world, and base their defense on it? Now stop and think about what I just said. How about it when the slander is in the most important case of this century—maybe of this nation's history—and all the defense is a slander? What about that—how do you feel? How does it make you feel? How do you feel about the kind of corporation that tells Mr. Paul this is what he has to do?

. . . .

Now, let me ask you this question: When we walk out of here I ain't going to be able to say another word, and you're going to have to make some decisions, and they are not going to be made just about Karen Silkwood, and not just about those people at that plant, but people involved in this industry, and the public that is exposed to this industry. That is a frightening obligation. You need to trust somebody. You need not to get involved in mud springs. If you get in there you are lost forever. If you get down in there and start dealing with the number crunches, and this exhibit and that exhibit, and all the other junk, you get into mud springs. But, you don't need to. You need to trust somebody. Who are you going to trust? Are you going to trust Kerr-McGee? Are you going to leave your kids to them? Do you feel safe in that? Are you going to leave your children and your futures to those people, the men in gray? Do you feel safe about that? I'm not saying they are bad men—I'm saying: Are you going to leave it on those arguments? Do they satisfy you? Can you do it? Is your verdict going to say something about the number crunching game—that it's got to stop? Is it going to be heard from here around the world? Can you do it? Do you have the power? Are you afraid? If you are, I don't blame you, because I'm afraid, too. I'm afraid that I haven't the power for you to hear me. I'm afraid that somehow I can't explain my knowledge and my feelings that are in my guts to you. I wish

I had the magic to put what I feel in my gut and stomach into the pit of every one of you.

. . . .

How do you like Dr. Voelz standing up here and telling you that these standards are safe? And, on cross-examination he admits to you there isn't any safe level, and he knows it. How does that make you feel? How does it make you feel to have had witness after witness, Mr. Valentine, Mr. Untnage, the nice old man Norwood, come up here under their oaths and tell you there hasn't been a single evidence of cancer proved? How does that make you feel? You know why he told you that? He told you that because he wanted you to believe that it was safe—that plutonium doesn't cause cancer. That is what he said. That is what they told those workers. Can you put your stamp of approval on that kind of conduct? Or, are you outraged? Do you feel the outrage inside your humanness, that people would say that not only to thousands of workers, but under their solemn oaths in this courtroom to every one of you-every one of you they said that to—and they didn't look out blindly, you know, out over this courtroom—they looked into your eyes and said it under their oaths that "plutonium didn't cause cancer," right down to Mr. Bottomly, and word games they played with you. How does it make you feel? These are the people, the men in gray, that called those witnesses to testify to that.

And finally, their witness Dr. Voelz had to admit it: Yes, we know it causes all kinds of cancer. Yes, we know it causes cancer of the gonads. Yes, we know it causes lung cancer. Yes, the model is for people who don't have asthma. Give me only little child, one little child, that's got asthma—and how many do you know that has asthma—one little child exposed to the model level may have in fact received scores or maybe hundreds of times of the same amount of exposure than a child without asthma. Can you buy that? Can you permit that to happen? Can you put your stamp of approval on that?

In telling the jurors that their purpose was to judge their peers, Baldwin stated:

You are about to receive your responsibility in this case and I daresay it is as awesome a responsibility as you will ever bear for your entire life, because you will decide the future of this man, the future of his family. It is now up to you. I know that when you go into the jury room you accept that duty with the gravity it deserves. And I know, I have confidence that you are compassionate for your fellow man, that you will discharge it in a manner that you are proud of, and that you can hold your head up high and say, "I was proud to be a part of it."

Perlman told the jury that the parties were in court because the defendant had not accepted responsibility for its actions. With respect to punitive damages, Perlman told the jurors that it was up to them to decide whether the defendant was fair in its actions:

And the Court tells you, in addition to that, the Court will tell you in its instructions that there is a question about whether or not their conduct, Joy's conduct was grossly negligent. And that's, if you believe that, it was grossly negligent, then you can decide to award punitive damages. And the reason for that is that if somebody like a corporation shows a reckless disregard or an indifference, then it's up to a jury to decide, we don't think that you were fair, we don't think that you were careful, we think that you were reckless and we think punitive damages should be awarded, not only to punish you, but to deter you from doing it again and to deter others that do the same thing from doing it.

Habush told the jurors that they were competent to evaluate the conduct of the defendant. With respect to determining the issue of negligence, Habush told the jurors that they would be asked to "compare the parties."

Block told the jury that the case came down to one fundamental issue: "Those who are concerned about human welfare and those who are callous about it; those who forget what it was when you are at the bottom of the line, and those who feel for those." He then told the jurors that it was up to them to say whether they approved of the defendant's actions:

Now it is up to you, really. You are going to say whether what they did here you put your stamp of approval on, on this testing that they did in this case of one in 50, of testing without ultra-sonics, without x-rays. You know they say, "Well, the government approved it." Well, the government has approved a lot of things, many wrong, many degrading, in its long history. That doesn't make it right this time. And they are asking you, saying, "Put your stamp of approval on this testing, so we can do it some more, so we know what we are doing is right, so we can say a jury told us it was all right."

. . . .

But basically the decision is yours to make. Whether with the millions of dollars of equipment that are turned out by armaments plants, and ultimately utilized in battle, and perhaps ultimately millions and millions left strewn on the battle field, all that cost wasted, whether among that ruin, among that tragic event is meant to be left also a woman's husband and the manhood, the better part of the manhood of another man, simply because of sloppy manufacturing and assembly procedures, it is up to you to say, yea or nay.

Gibbons told the jurors that they had the opportunity to pass on whether the actions of the defendant were dangerous and whether the deceased's death was needless:

So all of their efforts, even to this good day, have not been effective to keep foreign object material out of the white area from jamming controls. So all they can do is create this theme, they revert back to this theme. You are going to hear all the great things about the A-10, and I don't question that, ladies and gentlemen. I was a foot soldier, not a pilot, and

I respect airplanes and I respect pilots. But don't forget, don't forget the people we send out in peacetime to train, to protect us in wartime, do we sweep them under the carpet? I ask you, you are going to have the opportunity to pass on it. Is what happened an unreasonably dangerous thing? Was it a needless death? These are questions, ladies and gentlemen, that must go through your minds, and during your deliberations I ask you to consider them. And don't get off on this war thing.

§9.15   —To Send a Message to the Defendant: Deter Future Actions

Many times, after the lawyers asked the jury to judge the actions of the parties, they went one step further and asked the jury to send a message to the defendants in the form of a substantial verdict that would deter the defendants and others like them from committing similar acts in the future. This request was made in all cases in which punitive damages were claimed and in some cases in which no punitive damages were claimed.

Gibbons told the jurors that they needed to send a message to the defendant in order to stop the needless deaths of servicemen and make government contractors take safety into consideration when building airplanes:

> How many near misses does it take? That is going to be up to you when it comes to exemplary or punitive damages. You have got to take them the message, ladies and gentlemen. If they can spend millions on advertisement, and if they can spend millions to sell that kind of a product and get $9,000,000.00 a pop for it, and you know ironically enough that is just the amount that this lawsuit that we brought, we sought $5,000,000.00 in actual damages, and I will discuss those briefly in a minute, and we sought $4,000,000.00 in punitive damages, as I recall . . . I am tired, you are tired, we all have jobs to do. . . . How many more misses, ladies and gentlemen? It is going to be up to you.
>
> . . . .
>
> Think about it. If their own man, Mr. Sustarsic, knew that they put out a Model T, waiting on a Cadillac, something is wrong somewhere, ladies and gentlemen.
>
> And again, take the message to them.
>
> . . . .
>
> Because they knew what was wrong with that aircraft, ladies and gentlemen, and they have known since January of this year that the official safety board said a flight control jam probably in the white area is what killed Captain Wahl. Yet they have taken us, this widow and this little boy, through replaying all this tragedy to make us prove it when they knew it. And I say, you bet I say take them the message. And I don't know where else he heard it. Maybe he has had other messages that he ignored.
>
> I ask you, don't ignore this, ladies and gentlemen. The security of this country depends upon proper—when these, if these people are going to let these big military contracts for all these millions of dollars, make them

do it right. Make them do it safely, make them care about the poor air crewmen.

We are right, stay with us. Hold with us and do send a message. Not just a message to McDonnell-Douglas in Los Angeles or Republic Fairchild in New York, but to all these government contractors. When our servicemen are going out there putting their lives in that equipment sold to the cheapest bidder, make them take safety into consideration.

In this closing on liability, Perlman stressed that a verdict for punitive damages would deter not only the defendant, but also other manufacturers like the defendant:

And then the Court tells you, in addition to that, the Court will tell you in its instructions that there is a question about whether or not their conduct, Joy's conduct, was grossly negligent. And that's, if you believe that it was grossly negligent, then you can decide to award punitive damages. And the reason for that is that if somebody like a corporation shows a reckless disregard or an indifference, then it's up to a jury to decide, we don't think that you were fair, we don't think that you were careful, we think that you were reckless and we think punitive damages should be awarded, not only to punish you, but to deter you from doing it again and to deter others that do the same thing from doing it.

. . . . .

Ladies and gentlemen, if you answer that they were in reckless disregard, in a short time maybe somebody else won't have to be carried out on a stretcher like him. A lot can be done for mine safety, and you, by your verdict, can say we are the conscience of this Court and of this community. We have done our part. Now, Joy, you go out and do yours.

In his closing on damages, Perlman told the jury that it's verdict would protect other miners in the future:

And your verdict will send a message far beyond the corners of this courtroom that you want to right a wrong, for the sake of the future, so other coal miners won't go through this kind of experience.

Baldwin told the jurors that there was something they could do to compensate the plaintiff and to protect others like him:

Now there is something you can do about that, and it is going to be up to people like you and I to do something about it. And I submit to you that you can say to Ford Motor Company: "If you are going to have that attitude and you are going to say to Mr. Foster: 'You are an acceptable risk,' then you are going to have to accept that risk." They have accepted it and you can say to them: "Ford Motor Company, you are going to respond in full damages," and maybe two years from now somebody like Mr. Foster won't be hurt.

I say that $2,500,000.00 is a reasonable figure in this, and I am going to tell you why in more detail in a minute.

. . . .

So, I am going to close by saying that that, to me, is not an unrealistic figure, that the $2,000,000.00 is a figure that would tell Ford Motor Company: "If you are going to put this kind of machine on the market, you are going to respond in full damages, and you are not going to selectively hurt people in the country—and, yes, you have accepted the risk of Larking Foster, but you are going to respond in damages as the law says you should."

In his gun case, Bergman told the jury that it should act as the conscience and protector of the community to deter future negligent actions by the defendant:

You are going to be instructed by the Court that in certain circumstances our society feels that a lawsuit is significant beyond the parties to the case, for the benefit of society, for the protection of our community as a whole. That is, cases where you find a defendant has acted in reckless disregard or complete indifference to the probable consequences of its actions. And when you find that that occurs, then you, as a jury, have the responsibility to assess damages in addition to the compensation that the parties are entitled to. And I think this is one of those cases. I think there is a reckless indifference, a casting out into the world of something that is very dangerous and not attaching to that any safeguards at all except the ability to always blame the guy that runs into the problem. And that if you find that to be the case, you are to award an additional amount as punitive damages in such sum as you believe will punish the defendant and deter others from like conduct. That is the important part of that.

I suggest to you if they have sold a million of these guns that it would not be unreasonable to assess them a dollar a gun in punitive damages, and cause them to get the word to all the people who have those guns out there about how dangerous this is.

The reason that I think we have a punitive situation is based on Mr. Brown's testimony. They accept no responsibility, they have done nothing, made no effort to find out how many people have this understanding that Paul has about the gun. They have made no efforts to find out how many people are getting the instructions, although they are not getting all the warranty cards out. They haven't made an effort to find out how many accidents happen. They don't keep responsible records. That is not a responsible thing for a firearms manufacturer to do.

I think you have to make two statements. One is to Colt. I think there really is an emergency about this. The jury serves a function, not only to find the facts for the parties in the case, but to serve as the protector and conscience of the community. In this regard, I think there is an awful lot to be done by this jury in this case that will have an impact beyond the case. The Johnsons have lost something very precious, very important, that has great value to them, that can never be replaced, and their lives have been changed dramatically by what's happened to them, and that is going on into the future. And they have placed their trust in this community to place a value on that, and they will accept what you tell them about the value of their loss. They are the ones who are going to have to live with that statement. Not Colt.

And a second statement has to be made to Colt and to the firearms industry, that, you know, let's not sell guns in 1969, the year we sent men to the moon, that don't have safety devices and that don't have any information with them, in a positive kind of way, so people can avoid getting hurt. As they pointed out, it is not just Paul that can be hurt. Even if they have an irresponsible user, somebody who throws the gun on the ground, it is other people who can get hurt, too, those people who didn't even use the firearm.

.   .   .   .

I think there are very significant damages in this case. I think you have been shown clearly there is absolutely no concern at all for the safety of the users of these guns. For the future safety of the users of these guns. They sit back smugly satisfied. And when enough is enough, let's say that this is enough. I think that is the message they should get. Enough is enough. Let's put some safety devices on these guns. Let's alert the people who have them to what the problem is.

In his case involving negligence in the delivery of a child, Bergman told the jurors that their verdict would send a message to the hospital that it needed to provide better training for its nurses:

The only remaining question is whether punitive damages are warranted in this case, and you were given some instructions by the Court on punitive damages, and I think it's important in talking about this to understand why the law in its wisdom provides for this concept of punitive damages. There's really two reasons, and they're in the instruction. To punish the Defendant, and to deter others from like conduct, those are two separate reasons, and I think some punishment is definitely warranted here for their reckless indifference to what happened, their reckless indifference to the consequences—the tragic consequences, to a family who's been living in our community for the last five years, they don't want to know. They don't want to hear about it, but I think even more important is how punitive damages fit into our concept of the world that we live in.

You, as the jury, put on a little bit different hat when you talk about punitive damages. You become the conscience of the community. You become the people who set the minimum standards below which nobody is going to be allowed to fall. When practices that need change are not changed, there is a need to set an example. There is a need to protect other people in our community against this kind of thing from happening. There is a need to be sure that it doesn't happen at Suburban or any of the other eighty, ninety Humana hospitals, or at any of the other hospitals in our community. There's a need to get a message from you, as representatives of our community, to these people who just—which don't want to hear. They haven't heard yet.

The message is train your nurses. You vouch for those nurses when they're in those delivery rooms. That's intensive care nursing. You'd better be sure that they're skilled and they're competent and that they're evaluated. Monitor your physicians. Yeah, you've tried to delegate that responsibility to some local physicians. I think Dr. McGuire said he's just a figurehead. Monitor the people who are practicing at your hospital. Make sure that they're not using drugs that are not recommended. Review your charts. When people come "belly up" in your swimming pool, find out why. I don't think these things are complicated at all. These are the most basic things that you could ask of a health care provider. Say you're sorry when you know you've done something wrong. Do the right thing. Accept the responsibility. Improve yourself, improve your methods, learn from your mistakes.

· · · ·

I think when you want to make your business the provision of health care, that comes with a very heavy responsibility. People who come into your hospital don't have the first idea of what's going on. They don't know whether the nurses are skilled or not. They completely entrust themselves to the hands of the people who are providing the care, and those people who provide the care have to be required to take that responsibility seriously, and the vehicle that we have, the only vehicle that I'm aware of for doing that, is punitive damages. So, you have your work cut out for you, ladies and gentlemen.

You've got to—you've got to do justice for Brent Olsen, and think that's a must, both in determining the amount of his damages and percentages of fault that's attributable to the various defendants, but you have also got to fulfill your responsibility to the community. The community is interested in this case. You've got to make a statement about what this community will tolerate and what it will not tolerate in connection with our health care.

In cases that did not involve punitive damages, the lawyers told the jury that its verdict would send a message to the defendants that they would be held accountable for their actions or that they would have to stop their improper activities. In his case involving the failure to diagnose Hodgkin's disease, Bergman told the jury that its verdict should be a message to professional people:

You know the amount that we are asking, five million. That is for compensation in an amount that will tell Dr. Hanson, "You blew it badly. You can't cover it up. We are not going to sweep it under the rug for you. It is not going to be overlooked. Sorry." An amount that tells Shanna, "We place a high value on your life. We are not going to disregard your losses. We are not going to discount your losses." An amount that will tell all of the professional people in our community, "When you hold yourself out as a hot-shot expert and you take our money and you accept the responsibility for the lives of our children, we consider that important and heavy, and you are going to be a hundred per cent accountable when you are negligent and someone is tragically injured."

Glaser told the jury that its verdict would send a message to the the medical community to the effect that unnecessary surgeries would not be tolerated:

Okay, that's the case. Is this the kind of surgery we want in our community? I'll use the words of Mr. DeMaggio, "you put an end to it," that's what he said. No more of these unnecessary surgeries. You send the message loud and clear that this community will not tolerate unnecessary surgery.

§9.16　—To Render Justice

As noted in §9.08, the pursuit of justice was a theme in all of the cases. This theme was extended to jury purpose, and in all cases the lawyers told the jurors that their function was to render justice. The lawyers suggested that if the jury did not do justice in their case, then the entire system of justice failed. In this way, the jurors were encouraged to follow the law and behave as good jurors. Corboy produced testimony that the plaintiff would live a normal life expectancy, would need acute medical care to maintain his life during this expectancy, and that the medical expense in question would cost millions of dollars. The judge instructed the jury that it must return a verdict to pay for whatever medical care the evidence proved was necessary for the plaintiff's care and treatment. Corboy was afraid that some jurors might shy away from this astronomical verdict. Therefore, he first alluded to the American system of justice and how important it was to a free society. He then told the jurors that they were duty-bound to do justice, and that doing justice required that they follow the law as explained by the judge. If they followed the law, he reasoned, the system would work.

A review of the example in §9.08 will provide illustrations as to how this theme also functioned as jury purpose.

§9.17　—To Return Money Damages

Once it was established that the jury was required to do justice, the lawyers defined justice as returning a money verdict for the plaintiff. In determining their verdict, the jurors were told that they would have to consider injuries, damages, pain, and suffering. Three subpurposes were imbedded within the general purpose of returning money damages. First, the various items of damages were outlined, and the jurors were told that they must consider all elements of damage. Second, the lawyers told the jurors that nothing could bring back the health that the plaintiffs had lost, and that only a money verdict could compensate the plaintiffs for their losses. Third, the lawyers told the jurors that this time was the only time that the plaintiff would ever get to come before a jury and ask for damages, and, therefore, the jury had to return a verdict that represented full and complete compensation for all elements of damage, past, present, and future.

§9.18 —Itemization of the Various Elements

In discussing damages, the lawyers itemized the various elements of damage, and the jurors were told that under the law the plaintiff was entitled to these various damages, and that the jurors should consider each element of damages. The jurors were told that the consideration of these elements of damages was not discretionary, but, rather, the law required them to consider and award these damages if the evidence warranted it. Each element of damages was itemized and discussed.

Perlman told the jury that consideration of the elements of damages was mandatory under the law and he concisely itemized each element of damage:

> The question is, is it a just verdict? And when we go through these elements of damages, and the Court tells you with regard to each of the first elements, it's not a question of whether or not you may do it, but simply that you must do it. It says you shall do it. And unless there is evidence to the contrary, by your oath and by what are the principles of this Court and the system of justice, you have got to find it. The medical expenses, the proof in this case is clear to date, they are $13,000 and some dollars. And the Court tells you what that is. And in the future—and as we go through these, I want to show you how reasonable we are trying to be. There is no inflation here, no exageration. The future is $8,208. That's based on what Dr. Weitzel said, four visits a year, $180, for his life expectancy.
>
> The lost wages. The evidence on that, had he worked the full year of 1981, he would have made $19,240. So he lost six and a half months. That's $11,223. At a five per cent increase, which the vocational expert testified was what was fair and what was reasonable and what the United States Department of Labor used, would be $20,202. You see, as you go up from year to year, it's really not that much. For 1983, would have been $21,000. For '84, it would have been $22,000. So your loss as of today, he had those, would be $74,000. You keep doing that for sixty-five years, and then you come to $2,534.616. That's the proof. And there is not one shred of evidence that that's not the loss that's been suffered in this case.
>
> . . . . .
>
> And are we being fair? The next element is pain and suffering. That's the—the Court tells you, that's physical and mental. And we are talking about three and a half years in the past, forty-six years in the future, fifty years. And the figure that we have asked for is not millions of dollars like they tell you. For the total amount of his life, fifty years, we ask for $750,000, pain and suffering, present and future.

Block told the jury that justice demanded that the jury compensate the plaintiff for all elements of damage:

> It is not what Dorman Baird asks, it is what justice demands in this case. Justice says he is to be compensated for each and every injury he sustained, for his past suffering, for his future suffering, for the permanency of his injuries, for his mental anguish, for his psychological, neurological damage, and because we come to great sums of great magnitude, don't give them a medal.
>
> .   .   .   .
>
> He will tell you that you are to compensate him fairly and adequately for his personal injuries and for his pain and suffering, past and future, and permanent.

Block then itemized the plaintiff's general damages, a few examples of which are as follows:

> Now, let us get down to the injuries. And you must remember, as Dr. Grynbaum said, that these injuries in and of themselves, as devastating, and we heard the word here before, as catastrophic, as the injuries are that this man suffered, in their totality they are far worse because a person is a whole person, he just doesn't lose a leg, you just don't damage a scrotum, you just don't damage another leg. It just doesn't affect that part; it affects you as a human being.
>
> .   .   .   .
>
> Dorman Baird's injuries are as follows: 1. Amputation of the left lower extremity with approximately a three-inch stump, with several revisions and debridements.
>
> .   .   .   .
>
> And because he has phantom pain, and Dr. Ruskin himself admits that because of the nerve pathways, that's a real phenomenon, and in that lower left extremity he has pain in and of itself that is going to last him for the rest of his days. And because of the short stump it is unstable, and you see the way he walks, not with a simple limp, but with a marked limp. And though they may have plastic-type prosthetic devices, and for what we used to call a wooden leg, it is not the warm flesh and blood of what Dorman Baird was born with.
>
> .   .   .   .
>
> He had a scrotum that was torn open and part of a testicle torn off. In fact, the scrotum and the spermatic cord, the testicle and spermatic cord were hanging from the scrotum extruded right there in the hospital record and they had to do an operation on him and the remaining part of the testicle dried up and atrophied. . . .This farm boy, three doctors in the hospital record, in the Army, say loss of procreative power. What they meant by that apparently no doctor who testified here really knows, but one thing we all know, that all doctors, who testified here say he's impotent and it came about because of the accident. To achieve an erec-

tion solely by masturbation and it falls down when you try to penetrate, is that a damage to a man?

. . . .

An eardrum blown open, tympanic membrane. Bilateral hearing loss, high, low neurosensory.

. . . .

Right foot, the good foot, the only foot, God forbid something should happen to that foot. The good foot, fractures of every toe of the metatarsals with overriding. The bones didn't grow back right, they didn't heal right. And fracture of the navicular in the ankle.

. . . .

Deep scar of the right thigh needing a debridement in an operation in the hospital record.

Multiple small fragment wounds over the upper extremities.

Burns of face, head, chest areas.

Drain wounds of blood and pus.

Now, justice requires, in my estimation, and I want to show you this, and I repeat, this is only a guideline, it is not evidence—you are free to accept it, you are free to reject it—but I feel as a human being, no matter where he lives he is entitled to the following:

For the loss of the leg, that includes the loss of his ability to engage in such activities as sports, to get around; for the phantom pain, for the pain in the stump; for his limp, $1 million.

. . . .

For the depression, the traumatic neurosis, the loss of confidence, for the damaged scrotum and testicle, and nightmares, lack of concentration, headaches and dizziness, $1 million.

For the disabled right leg, for the ruptured eardrum, for the loss of hearing, for the fractured navicular bone in the ankle, $500,000.

For the pain and suffering in the future and mental anguish for the remainder of his days, and remember he will suffer pain and have the mental anguish and these disabilities far greater in time than his work expectancy, for a person's life expectancy obviously is greater than their work expectancy, $1 million.

For his pain and suffering to present, for his hospitalizations, for his operations, for his shock at the battlefield, having blood running out of his leg and other parts of his body, for that period of time when he hovered between life and death, as you will see in the hospital record, for those times when pus and blood was oozing from his wounds throughout that time, for the several operations and debridements to the time of trial, from the date of accident to the time of trial, $500,000.00.

So you see I say that that alone comes to $1 million, and you can see very readily why the defendant wants to make short shrift of your time here and hope that you don't give this case the kind of attention and deliberation it deserves.

And then you see that's general damages, and the reasons it is general damages is because there is another category called special damages.

General damages are more or less universal in application. Everybody
sustains this type of general damages, the injuries, the pain and suffering
in the past, the pain and suffering in the future.

People in Boaz, Alabama suffer it, people in the Bronx suffer from this
type when they are in accidents, people in Westchester, people in Manhattan, people in Rockland.

So everybody suffers from general damages. It makes no difference
where you come from, your sex, your race, your creed, your nationality.

Finally, Block explained and itemized the special damages for the jury:

There's another type of damages called special damages and that's
where they want to turn the case, put in a smokescreen, so you are blinded
from the enormity of the damage of general damages sustained by the
plaintiff.

Now, the special damages here are what the individual suffers due to
his own unique situation in life such as loss of earnings, future loss of
earning capacity. They are not the same thing. Here you have heard the
various findings concerning Dorman Baird's loss of earnings in the past,
and his future earning capacity. And they try to make out that a fellow,
you know, who had three odd jobs really not more than six months, where
he was earning maybe no more than 53 bucks tops is going to earn that
the rest of his life.

Well, sure he earned that, and that you should take into consideration,
but you should also take in the expectations and the probabilities; was
he going to do that all his life? Did he take that job maybe, those jobs
maybe because he was, let's say, drifting because he knew he was going
into the Service? He was an able-bodied fellow at that time; he knew how
to drive a truck.

So, we have had various computations made and they come up with
anywhere from maybe the earnings before and the earnings after from
about $250,000 to $500,000.

Bergman reminded the jurors that the judge had instructed them that they
must provide reasonable compensation for the various elements of damage:

Now, you were just instructed that you must provide reasonable compensation for each of the five elements that the Judge talked about, pain and
suffering, past, present and future; disability, past, present, and future;
the reasonable expenses of medical care, which there's an exhibit on, both
past, present and future, and the reasonable value of the services that
have been provided to Brent in the future, plus the loss of income that
Brent is reasonably certain to lose.

§9.19 —You Cannot Restore the Plaintiff's Health

In order to get money, the lawyers had to convince the jurors that a money
verdict was the only thing they could do to help the plaintiffs. They advised

the jury that the plaintiff would rather have his health back instead of money, but that the jury could not restore the plaintiff's health, and, under our system, a money verdict was the only way to compensate or help the plaintiff. For example, Baldwin told the jury:

> You can't give him back his legs, you can't give him back his body functions that he has lost, you can't give him back his ability to walk, to work, and support his family, but the one thing that you can do is to see that he gets first class medical treatment.
>
> .   .   .   .
>
> That has been taken, it is gone, and all you can do is what the Court tells you you must award, money damages for pain.

With respect to lost wages, Perlman told the jurors that they could not take away the plaintiff's physical problems, they could not restore his health, and that the plaintiff would prefer his health rather than money, but that the jury could not restore his health:

> Now, what does that mean? That's separate from what he would have earned and what he would have lost in his earnings, because you can't restore his sight by your verdict, you can't restore his taste or his smell, you can't take away his epilepsy, the grand mal seizures, you can't take the wires out of his face or restore his balance and coordination, you can't restore his ability to read and write, you can't give him back the brain damage—where his face hung precariously off his skull. . . . If you could restore and replace all of these things and say, Henry, we'll give you a choice, we'll give them all back to you and you won't have to suffer all these things, but you come over here and you decide. Do you want all these things back or do you want $750,000? He would say I don't want a nickel, I want to be back like I was. But you can't do that.

Glasser told the jurors that they could not give the plaintiff back her lost organs or her lost health, and, therefore, the only thing they could do was to compensate her as well as they could in damages.

Welch told the jury that if the plaintiff had a choice, he would not have traded his health for $2 million:

> Now, I will tell you something. You know Bob Cooper is not a very articulate man, okay, but I will tell you that if he could stand up here and talk to you, he wouldn't trade his health and his happiness for two million dollars. He wouldn't take—you couldn't give him enough to make the trade. And that's the way he and his wife feel, but, of course, you don't have that power. All you can do is compensate. And that's the way it is in our society.

Block expressed the plaintiff's preference to have his health rather than money in the following way:

> You know, there is an old saying—some of you have been around long
> enough to have heard it and to know it—"Rockefeller can keep his mil-
> lions, give me my good health." That's what this case is all about.
>
> · · · ·
>
> If you had a time machine and you put Dorman Baird in that time
> machine and said to him, "Dorman, Mr. Baird, we are going to press a
> button, we are going to put you back in time to before September 6, 1969,
> and you are going to be made whole again," he would say, I am quite
> certain, "Keep it."
>
> But that's impossible. We can't do it. We don't have those time
> machines. We can only do what a civilized society does.

Bergman told the jury that the American system of justice was imperfect in
that juries could not restore the plaintiffs' health, but, rather, could only place
a value on the loss:

> If this kind of tragedy can happen to Paul Johnson, it can happen to any-
> body. And I think that is very important. Paul and Jannie are entitled to
> absolutely all the consideration that any two citizens of this state would
> be entitled to. They are prepared to have you tell them what the monetary
> value is of the loss that they have sustained. And unfortunately, you know,
> that is the imperfect method that we have of doing civil justice in this
> country. If people want justice, they have to come to court, and the only
> measure that exists is monetary compensation.
>
> We can't return Paul's manhood to him. But we do have to tell him
> the value that we place on that manhood. We have to tell Jannie the value
> of her loss. And that is a difficult thing to do, and, frankly, I am glad that's
> your part of the job.

§9.20 —This is the Plaintiff's Only Chance to Ask for Damages

The lawyers told the jurors that the plaintiff could not come back into court
periodically and ask for future damages, or damages that had accrued since
the last trial, and, therefore, it was necessary for the jury to award all of the
plaintiff's future damages. For example, with respect to lost wages, Perlman
told the jury:

> And I submit to you, ladies and gentlemen, that that should not be
> reduced one cent. And why is that? Because that's the proof. That's the
> evidence. That's what he would have earned except for this injury. The
> only difference is that he would have earned it a year at a time. And you
> can't do that in the courtroom. This jury only sits one time. And you can't
> come back every year in December and say, what would you have earned
> this year, Henry, if you had been able to work? Because that's what he
> would have earned for forty-six years. The doctors and the occupational
> experts say he will never work. And there is not any question about that.

. . . .

These are just a few things. Most of all, he will never be able to come back here and look at each one of you in the eye like I am doing and say, I wish you could go back to that day, that Christmas week. I wish you could change, I wish you could think about all of the things that I had facing me, because when you heard that case some years ago, you didn't realize what I had to do and what I had facing me.

. . . .

. . . He has lived three and a half years waiting for this day. And your decision will have to last for the next forty-six years.

In his case involving the failure to timely diagnose Hodgkin's disease, Bergman told the jury that the plaintiffs had only one opportunity to make a recovery of damages:

And that is a concept I would like for you to keep in mind as you go deliberate. Because one of the things the Judge will tell you is that the damages in the case are not only the damages to now but the damages on into the future. A person has only one opportunity to make a recovery for all of the damages, and that opportunity for the Johnsons comes now, so they are not able to come back in 10, 20, 30 years, and confer about whether a complete justice was done today, but rather, it has to be done today. This is the only opportunity.

In his birth defect case, Bergman told the jury that the plaintiff had only one chance to obtain full compensation:

Brent has only one chance. That is it. He's not allowed to come back in ten or twenty or thirty years and you're not allowed to ask, "Did we give enough?" you know, "Did we do our job, correctly? Is it working out for you?" This is it. This is the only opportunity he has.

§9.21   Reminding Jurors of Their Voir Dire Commitments

During voir dire, the jurors made certain public promises on relevant issues, and in the closings, the lawyers reminded them of their commitments, and argued that they were bound to follow them. These commitments were then linked with the jurors' duty to render justice. The public commitments, linked with the commitment to justice, could have been expected to deter jurors from publicly going against these commitments during jury deliberations. For example, Corboy's case was dependent on the jurors following the law that provided that the plaintiff was entitled to any fair and reasonable medical expense that was necessary to sustain his life. Therefore, Corboy reminded the jurors of their commitment to follow the law, and then reminded them of their voir dire commitments that they believed in the concept that life was sacred:

And I was just not lawyer talking, I don't think, when I started at this end and went all the way through each panel of four and asked each and every one of you, do you agree with the phrase that life is sacred no matter what? Those that gave tentative answers, those that were hesitant, in the exercise of my right as a lawyer, I asked this Court to excuse them and they were excused. So that the thirteen that are remaining are those that gave their word that they believe that life is sacred no matter what.

There are times when a man or a woman should be allowed to go on to whatever men and women go to according to our own beliefs; but there are other times when the decision is made to save them. Once that decision is made, the thirteen of you have agreed that life is sacred.

If the jurors had been persuaded to follow the law that the plaintiff was entitled to any fair and reasonable medical expense necessary to care for and treat his condition, and to follow their voir dire commitment that life was sacred, Corboy could expect to receive a substantial verdict.

Baldwin invoked the voir dire commitment that the jurors would place a dollar figure on pain and suffering.

Spence invoked the jurors' voir dire commitment that they would be willing to return a verdict for $10 million, and stated, "Would you write a check for ten million dollars if you think it was the right thing to do? You all said it wouldn't bother you."

Bergman reminded the jurors that they had all promised to be open-minded and receptive to the evidence in the case:

> The deep fear that I have had has to do with whether or not our evidence was going to fall on deaf ears or closed minds. I feel the need to mention that again, because when you represent a plaintiff in a medical malpractice case against a physician in 1987, you have got a heavy burden. Your only hope is that it doesn't become an impossible burden.
>
> I think that we are all inclined to be understanding and forgiving of doctors because our lives are in their hands and we really want to believe and hope that they are not going to drop the ball on it. So we hold the plaintiff in a case like this to a heavy burden. That is why I spent so much time during jury selection asking all of you if you would search your souls and your backgrounds and start out this case fair and even and open-minded and receptive to the evidence that was going to be presented to you.
>
> You all, under oath, were committed to that, that you would be open-minded, follow the law that the Court instructed you on—and now you have heard what the law is—and hold Shanna Morrison only to that burden of proof that the law imposes upon her. And I think that, as you heard, I think that in relation to the evidence in this case, that is really not a very heavy burden.
>
> You also committed yourselves to placing a value on each item of damages that the Court instructed you that the law recognizes, if there was evidence on it. Now, you have heard what those are. We have trusted and relied on the fact that you will all do all of those things.

In his case involving negligent delivery, Bergman reminded the jurors that they had promised to provide fair compensation for all elements of damage:

> I want to ask you all to recall October 15th, the first day of the trial, when we selected the jury, and I asked a lot of questions and I hope, as we've gone through this process, you saw why some of these questions were asked, but I asked whether you would follow the law in all respects, whether you would be willing to provide full and fair compensation for Brent, for all of his damages, according to the Court's instructions, and whether you would be willing to put a monetary value on the intangible losses, the irreplaceable losses, the pain, suffering, disability, and disfigurement that Brent is entitled to be compensated for, and you all stated under oath that you'd be willing to do that and you took an oath, even following that, that you would follow the Court's instructions and follow the evidence in that regard, and we took a leap of faith and we believed that it was the correct thing to do, and we trusted that you will follow those instructions and compensate Brent for all of his damages.

§9.22 Strategic Use of Language

Within the storytelling structure, the lawyers were involved in creating meaning for the persons, places, and things in their stories. They used words and labels to describe and to create dramatic impact. They used examples, analogies, allusions, and metaphors to create presence, and to describe and illustrate abstract concepts, such as negligence, pain, and suffering.

§9.23 —Use of Words and Labels to Describe and to Create Dramatic Impact

The lawyers used words and labels to infuse their cases and the responsibilities of the jurors with drama in order to gain juror attention. These were not just personal injury cases, but life and death struggles in which the plaintiffs' futures hung in the balance, dependent upon the jury verdict. For example, Spence told the jury that the *Silkwood* case was the most important case in the history of Oklahoma.

The lawyers selected words and labels to create meaning and dramatic impact for the people and things involved in the trial. Welch labeled the jurors "helpers" and the plaintiffs "humble, unassuming people." He told the jury that the defendant "knowingly and cunningly" brought in certain medical records to try to take advantage of the plaintiff. Corboy reminded the jurors of the doctor's description of the plaintiff's injury as the most "agonizing, disastrous, physical problem." He argued that to stop supplying the plaintiff with optimal medical care would be "murder." Ring described the plaintiff's deformed hand as a "claw." Baldwin referred to the plaintiff's "little family." He characterized the plaintiff as a "hopeless cripple," and his injury as a "tragedy." Spence called the defendant's lawyers the "men in gray," and called Kerr-

McGee's plutonium contamination of its workers "the most dastardly crime in the history of man." In describing the defendant's key witness, Spence stated:

> Here is a man who was bred and fed and led by the AEC. Bred and fed and led. He was suckled at the breast of government. That is where he came from. He was the infamous child of that bureaucracy. He was struck blind by his own power and his own shine, and he was struck deaf from having listened too long to the deadly sounds of number crunching.

In referring to the motivation of the defendant Kerr-McGee, Spence used words and labels to create emphasis and impact:

> You know, I was amazed to hear that Kerr-McGee has eleven thousand employees—eleven thousand employees. That's more than most of the towns in the state that I live in—that it is in 35 states—well, I guarantee that corporation does not speak "south;" it doesn't speak "Okie;" it doesn't speak "western;" it doesn't speak "New York." And it is in five states—or in five countries. It doesn't speak any foreign language. It speaks one language universally. It speaks the language of money. That is the only language that it speaks—the only language that it understands, and that is why the case becomes what it is. That is why we have to talk back to that corporation in money.

Spence linked himself in interest with the jury by continually referring to himself and the jury as "we." By linking himself in interest with the jury, he enhanced his credibility. He noted that "we've spent a season here together," and that although the trial had been tough on the jurors and himself, "We made it through this matter together." In telling the jury that the case depended on the jury's being able to see the truth, he stated:

> I can remember when Dr. Voelz got on the stand, and after we listened to his testimony we got together, Jim and I and Art, and we sat down and said: "Have we spent two-and-a-half months here, and are we going to lose it all at this spot? It all depends on your ability to turn the coin over, and show the truth and what's on the other side of that matter—can you do it?" I hope you think I did it—that we did it together.

Glaser referred to the unnecessary surgery performed on the plaintiff as "castration," and the plaintiff's damages as "horrendous."

Gibbons used labels to refer to the manner of the plaintiff's death at the hands of the defendant:

> Because he didn't deserve to die. He had been in Vietnam in the war zone. He got killed; they killed him better than if a Viet Cong bullet would have gotten him.

Bergman described the plaintiff's future damages and medical expenses as "scary," "overwhelming," and "chilling." With respect to the plaintiff's disability, Bergman told the jury that if others' injuries were "catastrophic," the plaintiff's injuries were "worse." With respect to the cause of the plaintiff's birth defects, Bergman told the jury, "God made Brent what he was at four o'clock in the afternoon, and these Defendants made Brent what he was at 6:01 in the evening." In attempting to make the jury understand that although the plaintiff was a cute looking five-year-old at the time of the trial, the plaintiff's parents would have to care for him for the rest of his life, Bergman painted a picture with words when he told the jury:

> He's going to grow up. He's not going to remain 5 forever. His six-month-old brother in some respects is more advanced than he is. Little children smaller than him look at him as a baby. He's not a baby. He's a 5-year-old child. He should be in kindergarten. He should be out playing soccer. He should be doing all of those things, and he will be a man. Whether he'll have the mental capacity of a man is another question. He will be a man. He will be five feet eight, six feet tall, who knows, and that will be a very, very sad and pathetic sight, but he will be here, and maybe you won't have to deal with Brent, but he will have a world that he lives in, and people that he relates to, and as he grows up, I think his understanding of what's going on around him will get better, but he's going to always have these limitations, and that, that's what upsets me so much, the thought, the chilling thought, of what lies in store. You know, to change a—the diapers of a 40-year-old, eight times a day, after you've already done it for forty years, is a depressing thought and that's what lies in store here, and I just don't think that the defendants ought to be allowed to keep running away from this thing to keep trying to put it out of their sight, to keep trying to down play it.

§9.24 —Use of Examples and Figurative Language to Create Meaning

After initially discussing the facts and the law, the lawyers turned to the use of examples, allusions, analogies, and metaphors to create meaning and support their arguments about the facts and the law.

As in all rhetoric, examples are of limited probative force because they simply present a single instance of the phenomenon. However, as persuaders have recognized for centuries, they have great psychological power because they invite identification and they prompt inferential leaps from a single vivid case to a generalization. In *Silkwood*, Spence used the example of harvester ants to illustrate the devious way in which Kerr-McGee exposed its employees to plutonium contamination. According to the example, in Wyoming, ecologists attempted to kill off the harvester ants. However, the ants were smart, and every time they realized they were being poisoned or threatened, they reacted in some way to protect and save themselves. Finally, someone developed a poison with a delayed reaction that would not work on the ants until they had all been exposed to the poison, and before they had a chance to react and save themselves, the ants died. By use of this example, Spence illustrated how Kerr-

McGee treated its employees like bugs, and by not educating its employees about the dangers of plutonium, deprived them of the opportunity to protect and save themselves.

Analogies are extended examples that compare two or more things. They are used for evaluation and prediction, and if differences are taken into account and enough cases are compared, they can be sound bases for conclusions. However, psychologically, such comparisons move audiences from the familiar and the known to the unfamiliar and the unknown, permitting generalizations and allowing them to feel confident about judgments they make in areas outside their own experiences. For example, in arguing that a $70 million verdict was a fair verdict, Spence analogized the amount to a normal pay period for an ordinary person:

> And I realized, finally, that this was a corporation of immense propor-
> tions, that I didn't really understand before. This is a corporation that
> earned daily over five million dollars a day. And, that seventy million dol-
> lars would represent like fourteen days—not quite fourteen days of
> work—two weeks—a payday—a pay period for most folks.

Metaphors are figurative analogies, comparing items not obviously alike in terms of some principle of similarity. In the words of rhetorical theorist Kenneth Burke, a metaphor is a "device for seeing something in terms of something else. It brings out the thisness of a that and a thatness of a this . . . metaphor tells us something about one character as considered from the point of view of another character."[1] For example, Spence used the metaphor of the caged lion to illustrate the concept of strict liability in tort. Strict liability in tort provides that if a producer places a dangerous substance in the stream of commerce, and the substance injures someone, the producer is liable for the injuries without a showing of negligence, because the substance was inherently dangerous. Spence used the story of the caged lion, out of which the common law doctrine of strict liability arose, to illustrate the principle metaphorically. According to the story, a lion escaped from its cage and attacked someone. The owner of the lion was held liable for the injuries even though the injured party could not prove the escape was caused by the owner, because the lion was an inherently dangerous animal. Plutonium was compared to the lion, and Spence argued, "If the lion got away, Kerr-McGee has to pay. It's that simple— it's the law." In refuting Kerr-McGee's contentions that the plaintiffs could not show how Karen Silkwood was contaminated, Spence returned to the metaphor and argued that even if no one knew how the lion got away or the owner said he had done everything in his power to keep the lion caged, it didn't matter. The owner had to pay because it was his lion. Spence stated:

> Well, we talked about "strict liability" at the outset, and you'll hear the
> Court tell you about "strict liability" and it simply means: "If the lion
> got away, Kerr-McGee has to pay." It's that simple—that's the law. "If

[1] K. Burke, A Grammar Of Motives 503-04 (1945).

the lion got away, Kerr-McGee has to pay." You remember what I told you in the opening statement about strict liability? It came out of the Old English common law. Some guy brought an old lion on his ground, and he put it in a cage—and lions are dangerous—and through no fault of his own—the lion got away. Nobody knew how—like in this case, "Nobody knew how." And, the lion went out and he ate up some people—and they sued the man. And they said, you know: "Pay. It was your lion, and he got away." And, the man says: "But I did everything in my power—I had a good cage—had a good lock on the door—I did everything that I could—I had security—I had trained people watching the lion—and it isn't my fault that he got away." Why should you punish him? They said: "We have to punish him—we have to punish you—you have to pay." You have to pay because it was your lion—unless the person who was hurt let the lion out himself. That's the only defense in this case: Unless in this case Karen Silkwood was the one who intentionally took the pluto-nium out, and "let the lion out," that is the only defense, and that is why we have heard so much about it.

Strict liability: "If the lion gets away, Kerr-McGee has to pay," unless Karen Silkwood let the lion loose. What do we have to prove? Strict lia-bility. Now, can you see what that is? The lion gets away. We have to do that. It's already admitted. It's admitted in the evidence. They admit it was their plutonium. They admit it's in Karen Silkwood's apartment. It got away. And, we have to prove that Karen Silkwood was damaged. That's all we have to prove. Our case has been proved long ago, and I'm not going to labor you with the facts that prove that. It's almost an admit-ted fact, that it got away, and that she was damaged.

Does Silkwood prove how the lion got away? You remember this—Mr. Paul walking up to you and saying, at the beginning of the trial: "Well, listen, it's important to find out how the lion got away." Well, it is impor-tant, because they have to prove how—but we don't. And the Court will instruct you on that. As a matter of fact, I think you will hear the Court say exactly this, and listen to the instruction: It is unnecessary for you to decide how plutonium escaped from the plant—unnecessary to decide how plutonium escaped from the plant—how it entered her apart-ment—or how it caused her contamination, since it is a stipulated fact—stipulated between the parties—that the plutonium in Silkwood's apart-ment was from the defendant's plant. So the question is: "Who has to prove how the lion got away?" "They have to prove it." They have to prove that Karen Silkwood carried it out. If they can't prove that by a preponderance of the evidence, they've lost. Kerr-McGee has to prove that. Why? Well, it's obvious. It's their lion—not Karen Silkwood's lion. It's the law. It's that simple.

So, if the lion got away and Kerr-McGee can't prove how, then Kerr-McGee has to pay—Kerr-McGee loses—and the verdict is for the Silk-woods. It's that simple.

Allusions are comparisons made through references to a common body of cultural knowledge, such as well-known television programs, movies, the Bible, or great works of literature. Once again, the speaker who makes such an allusion can call up a whole host of associations, including intense feelings, through a very brief reference. In his introduction, Spence created dramatic impact for the role of the jurors when he alluded to the framing of the Constitution and compared the task of the jurors with the task of the writers of the Constitution:

> I have asked my friends, during the recess—and they are here, I asked my father, my mother, my close friends for strength to do this. I hope that you have been able to do that for yourselves, and that you can, with each other, call upon your own strength and from your own sources, because this is the last time that we, as living, breathing humans, will talk together about this subject. And it is the last time that anybody will speak for Karen Silkwood. And, when your verdict comes out, it will be the last time that anybody will have the opportunity that you have, and so it is important that we have the strength and the power to do what we need.
>
> You know, history has always at crucial times reached down into the masses and picked ordinary people and gave ordinary people extraordinary power. That is the way it has always been in history, and I have no reason to believe that it is any different now.
>
> Ladies and gentlemen of the jury, two hundred years ago, a little over, there were a group of people meeting in a dingy little room—nothing nearly as pretentious and beautiful as this one—meeting in a little town they called Philadelphia. And it was a hot summer—they didn't have air conditioning. And, one was named George, and one was named John, and one was named Thomas—ordinary folks. They knew each other like you know each other. Nobody seemed to understand the importance of what they were doing. . . . And, they didn't really probably have a presence and a knowledge that what they were doing was going to be historical, but what came out of that, as you know, was our Constitution, which guaranteed this trial today. They probably weren't aware of their presence, and I doubt if any of you, or I, can really be aware of my presence or your presence to somehow know, or to comprehend, how important what we are doing. I just don't think that any of us have been prepared to realize that. And yet somehow you were chosen in this case, and I trust that selection, I trust you, and I trust the power that you have, and I trust the methodology by which you took your seats in this case.

The lawyers in these cases used devices such as these throughout their cases, but most particularly in their closing statements. In the opening statement and the presentation of the evidence, the lawyers were primarily concerned with getting the facts to the jury. In the closing statements, the lawyers initially reviewed the facts, and then moved to the use of examples and figurative language to create a general interpretive framework and make the events come alive and the experiences of the plaintiffs vivid and compelling for the jurors. In some cases, the meaning was created on a conscious level of thought with the use of obvious comparisons. Sometimes, as with the use of metaphors, the associations and comparisons occurred on a subconscious level, creating subconscious meaning. The lawyers used the figures of speech to create dramatic impact, prove and argue negligence, and prove and argue damages.

Ring alluded to Abraham Lincoln, and compared the defendant's defenses to mudslinging:

> The deflated angle theory is another. The treadle spring is another. You know, in Lincoln's time he used to say—and there's an old story that, you know, if the facts are against you, young man, argue the law. If the law is against you, argue the facts. If they're both against you, just throw mud. So there is a lot of mudslinging. Dirty it up all things so everything is confused, so that there is one big morass when all we've got is a simple broken spring.

Similarly, Spence alluded to legal history when he characterized the defendant's actions as inviting the jury down into mud springs in order to confuse them:

> One of my favorite—I guess my favorite jurists—and one you know very well, has an old saying he has told us many times: He says if you want to clear up the water, you've got to get the hogs out of the spring. And, if you can't get the hogs out of the spring, I guarantee you can't clear up the water. And, I will guarantee you one thing, that during the course of this trial you have observed a process by which you have been invited over and over again to get down into the mud springs where you can't see—where you can't understand—where things are all muddy. And I want you to know that getting jurors confused is not a proper part of jurisprudence—and getting people down in the mud springs is not the way to try a case.

The lawyers used figures of speech to create meaning for relevant legal concepts. The courts instructed the jurors to return all "fair and reasonable" damages. However, "fair and reasonable" are subjective terms. Corboy used examples and analogies to create meaning for these terms:

> Now, the damages in this lawsuit, the Court will tell you, shall be fair and shall be reasonable. Long before you became officers of the Court, the word fair did not mean in the middle. The word fair did not mean half. The word fair didn't mean mediocre.
>
> You know he is a fair pitcher. That's not what we are talking about. He is a fair basketball player, but he can't make free throws. That's not what we are talking about. He can go to the left, but he can't go to the right. That's not what we are talking about.
>
> .   .   .   .
>
> We are talking about fairness meaning justice. And half justice is worse than no justice. So if you say to yourself, well this is a case where a car was running down the highway and somebody bumped into the rear of the car and there was $180,000.00 damage to the rear of the bumper but that farmer had no right being out on that highway in the first place; he

should have been tilling his corn and instead of giving him $180,000.00, we gave him $90,000.00, that wouldn't be fair. It might be in the middle. It might be medium, but it wouldn't be justice. It would be half justice.

. . . .

The term reasonable, reasonable doesn't mean you wait for an ad in the Sun-Times or the Tribune for a holiday sale to go buy a scarf right after Christmas and there is a reasonable sale and you go down to the basement of one of the stores and, instead of paying six bucks, you pay three. That's a sale.

That's not reason. Reason means using your intellect. So fair and reasonable means using justice and your intellect, your own intellect and your own experiences in life in arriving at the verdict.

Similarly, Baldwin used analogy to argue that his damage verdict request was reasonable:

There is no such thing as a large or small verdict. If anybody in the jury room says, "Look, I think we ought to give him the two and a half million dollars," and somebody else says, "Wait a minute, that's too much money, that's more money than I have heard of for this or that," I hope one of you will say, "Wait a minute, you should not discuss whether it is a large amount," because it isn't proper, and here is why it isn't proper: There is no such thing as a large verdict.

Now, take this as an illustrastion: Suppose they burn up my yellow pad over there. It is worth thirty-five cents. Suppose I came in and had you as a jury and you gave me a dollar. That would be a large verdict, wouldn't it? It would be too much, it would be more than it is worth.

Suppose, on the other hand, you gave me a dime. That would be a small verdict, wouldn't it? It wouldn't be enough.

But, if you gave me thirty-five cents, that would be a just verdict, and that's what Larkin Foster is entitled to in this case, and it is not a question of whether it is large or small, or what it might cost the Ford stockholders—a penny a share or a mil of a share is more likely—the question is: Is it a just verdict?

In his conclusion, Spence told a story that had an embedded metaphor. Throughout the trial, Spence argued that Kerr-McGee was responsible for the plutonium, and, therefore, it was its responsibility to explain how Karen Silkwood became contaminated. Kerr-McGee countered by arguing that it should not be held liable because the plaintiffs could not prove how Karen Silkwood became contaminated. The story was told as follows:

I'm going to tell you a story, a simple story, about a wise old man—I think he would have looked like Dr. Gofman—and a smart aleck young boy who wanted to show up the wise old man for a fool. The boy's plan was this: He found a little bird in the forest and captured the little bird. And, he had the idea he would go to the wise old man with the bird in his hand and say: "Wise old man, what have I got in my hand?" And the wise old man would say: "Well, you have a bird, my son." And, he would say: "Wise old man, is the bird alive, or is it dead?" And, the old man knew if he said, "It is dead," the little boy would open up his hand and the bird would fly away. Or if he said "It is alive," then the boy would take the bird in his hand and crunch it and crunch it, and crunch the life out of it, and then open his hand and say: "See, it is dead." And, so the boy went up to the wise old man and said: "Wise old man, what do I have in my hand?" The old man said, "Why, it is a bird, my son." He said, "Wise old man, is it alive, or is it dead?" And the wise old man said: "The bird is in your hands, my son."

Spence thanked the jury and concluded his closing with the story. He did not explain the story or its moral. The moral metaphorically embedded in the story was the proposition that the young man had control over the life or death of the bird and could trick the old man into attempting to explain something that was under the control of the young man. The wise old man refused to be seduced by simply acknowledging that the young man had control of the bird. This was analogous to Spence's position that Kerr-McGee had control of the plutonium and could trick both the plaintiff and the jury by seducing them into trying to prove how Karen Silkwood was contaminated. Spence argued that the plaintiff had to prove only that the plutonium was in the defendant's control, and it then became the defendant's responsibility to explain how the contamination occurred. The message to the jury contained in the story was that the jury should not be concerned with how the plaintiff became contaminated, because that was Kerr-McGee's responsibility, and since the defendant had not given such an explanation, the verdict should be rendered for the plaintiff. Some of the jurors no doubt figured out the story on a conscious level, but for those who did not, the story, through the metaphor, conveyed subconscious meaning.

Gibbons used the analogy of a smoking gun in a murder case to explain the concept of circumstantial evidence:

> And His Honor will most likely instruct you in that respect, and we used to have a saying when I broke in trying lawsuits of what circumstantial evidence is, the importance of it. It has the same weight. Direct evidence is what you see or what you touch, or what you actually see, I guess. And circumstantial evidence is the inference to be drawn from what you see and what you have. For instance, if you run up to a street corner, there is a dead man laying there and another one standing over him with a smoking gun, you can draw the inference by circumstantial evidence that that man killed him if it was still smoking. I say to you, they are still smoking over there in that white area, still having the same tragedies, and near misses, and how many near misses, we have got stacks of them in the documents.

In explaining why the defendant nurses were guilty of "total and reckless disregard" for the safety of the plaintiff, and, hence, liable for punitive damages, and in arguing that the defendant hospital should have investigated the incident in question, Bergman used the analogy of a lifeguard:

> I likened Linda Carter's role in this situation to a lifeguard. She's there. The Labor Room is in her pool, and there's only two people she needs to worry about, Terri Olsen and Brent Olsen, and right before her eyes, somebody is drowning, is going down, and is screaming for help. What does she do, nothing, nothing. Nobody lifted a finger. You would think that when somebody comes "belly up" in your pool, you would ask some questions about why. You would think that when a baby is transferred to Children's Mercy Hospital continuously seizuring with the kind of Apgar scores that Brent Olsen had, somebody might be interested in finding out what happened, but nobody has ever asked a question, and that is totally offensive. That is totally unacceptable.

Pain, suffering, grief, and disability are subjective concepts. It can be argued that the amount of any verdict in a personal injury case is dependent on the extent to which the plaintiff's lawyer is able to convey to the jury the nature and effect of pain, suffering, grief, and disability. In arguing damages, the lawyers used these figures of speech to create presence and meaning. With respect to pain generally, Welch used an allusion when he stated, "On the subject of pain, I guess you know history is replete with people who have been in great pain and have asked for death in lieu of pain." In describing the plaintiff's pain, Welch used the meetaphor of a prison and the analogy of a ticking clock:

> Now, Bob Cooper is in a daily prison encapsulated by pain. That's his daily life. . . . I'm sure that nothing breaks the human being in body and soul so much as constant, irretractable pain. . . . It's not pleasant to hear about the suffering of other people. . . . That's the next twenty-four years we're talking about. Now that's a big segment, twenty-four years, and pain is not measured by the calendar. It's measured by the clock, because when you're victimized by pain, that's how you endure it, by each tick of the clock.

Corboy described the plaintiff's injuries by listing a series of examples of things that the plaintiff could not do, such as talk, walk, joke, eat, stretch, go to a football game, control his bladder, control his bowels, have sex, brush his teeth, or laugh. He told the jury that the plaintiff had no freedom in that he could not go anywhere he wanted or be alone and contemplate and watch rivers. He then gave examples of what the plaintiff could do, such as wish he was well, agonize, yearn to be with women, feel pain, and experience fear.

Spence used the analogy of punishing a child to articulate his claim for damages based on two weeks of Kerr-McGee's profit, and argued that if a child had lied about something that had to do with the life and death of a brother or sister, it would not be unreasonable to punish the child by taking away two weeks' pay. Analogously, Spence argued that taking two weeks of Kerr-McGee's profits was not an unreasonable way to punish Kerr-McGee for lying to its employees:

If the defendants are grossly or wantonly negligent—listen to this language in the Court's instructions—you may allow exemplary or punitive damages, and you may consider the financial worth. I didn't bring that out to try to have you be prejudiced against a large corporations—I brought that out because what is fair punishment for one isn't for another. It is fair punishment to take a paper boy who makes five dollars a week, and it might be fair punishment to take away five dollars from him for not coming home when he was supposed to, or to lie, if he lied. If one of your children lied about something—one of your children lied about something that had to do with the life and health of a brother or sister, and he covered it up, and he lied about it, and he said that the brother and the sister were safe when he knew that he had exposed them to death—I suppose that you might not find it unreasonable to hold him responsible for two weeks, two piddling weeks, allowance in bucks, and leave fifty weeks left for him.

Similarly, Bergman used an analogy to argue the amount of money the defendant hospital should pay in punitive damages:

I think a key thing to look at is the cash assets. There are some questions asked about cash assets. How much money do they have in their pockets in cash right now, 261 million dollars, a quarter of a billion dollars in cash. Now let me use this analogy. If I wrongfully and recklessly injured somebody else and didn't care about it, and you thought that some punishment was warranted, and you took me to the police station and I had $260 in my pocket, if you fine me $10, that might not be enough. Now, that is the equivalent of a company that's got 260 billion—million dollars in its pocket, being fined $10 million. Let me go at it another way. Talk about net worth, 760 some odd million dollars, if my net worth—if I was lucky enough to accumulate after the payment of all my debts and mortgages and everything else, $75,000, and I did something this wrong and I caused this kind of destruction to another human being and you thought I should be punished and you fined me $1,000, I would probably feel like I was getting off pretty easy. That is the equivalent of a ten million dollar punitive damage verdict against Humana when their net worth is $768,000,000.

Bergman used the contract of baseball player George Brett as an example of worth in order to decide what the plaintiff's damages were worth when he told them, "You are the only people who can give Brent and his family the message that you think the things that he's lost are worth something. That you think his life is worth as much as George Brett's baseball contract or a day of Humana's profits, because it is."

In his case involving the failure to diagnose Hodgkin's disease, Bergman used the analogy of the value of art objects in order to argue the plaintiff's worth:

The Morrisons are little people. This is probably what is in the back of the mind. The big justice is for the big people, but the little justice is for the little people. Maybe that is what is in the back of Mr. Saunders' mind. Maybe that is what he is relying on. I am not embarrassed to stand and say that $5 million is what Shanna Morrison's damages are worth. In fact, I would be embarrassed to ask for anything less. Think about that. You have to put a value on it. You have to step forward for Shanna Morrison.

What is really appropriate? We are constantly hearing of these masterpieces. I could go on and on and give you all sorts of examples. The masterpieces that hang in the museums. There was one sold, a Van Gogh, fifteen flowers in a pot, forty million dollars. There are scores and scores of examples of that, and if I walked into a museum with a knife and I slashed one of those masterpieces, everybody would say, "What an awful thing that is, a terrible thing, outrageous, irreparable damage," I should go to jail, I should pay for it.

Well, isn't Shanna a masterpiece? Isn't she much more of a masterpiece than any painting that hangs in any museum or any horse that runs in the Kentucky Derby or as much a masterpiece as any athlete that makes a couple of a million dollars a year? That is why I think that when you put a value on the sum total of a life of a 13-year-old girl who hasn't really had a chance to live that life, and now a 16-year-old girl, that is not unreasonable at all. It shouldn't just be the big justice for the big people and the little justice for the little people.

In my mind, Shanna Morrison is a big person. She is a hero. She is an inspirational person. Her story should be known. I know that she has been an inspiration at M.D. Anderson to many other patients. She is a strong, courageous girl who did nothing wrong, who was just simply let down.

Glaser used an allusion to refer to the plaintiff's loss of health:

What is good health worth to us? Isn't it the most prized possession? Only recently on the New Year's, how many of us said, "A Happy New Year," and the response was, "And a healthy one, too." Well, they took this lady's health away. They took her most prized possession away.

Glazer used the analogy of a barren fruit tree to describe the plaintiff after having been castrated:

They made a fruit tree barren, that's what they did. And when they castrated her, they brought about hormonal imbalance and they reduced— and they destroyed her sexual drives.

In attempting to explain to the jury the impact of the plaintiff's loss of her sexuality, Glaser alluded to a commonly held belief about the place of sex in a marriage:

And the loss of sex drive. You heard her say she had a happy marriage before, good sex life. Very important in marriage you'll please excuse me, I must get a little—go into some personal kinds of thing now, but it's very important in marriage. Marriages that don't have a full sex life suffer from it. Brings on nervousness of the couples, irritation, irritability with each other. I hate to say it, but you'll forgive me, you've heard it said, many an argument between man and wife is settled in bed. No more for Mrs. Lewis.

In dramatizing the worth of the plaintiff's pain, suffering, and disability, Perlman used an analogy:

And what's fair for that pain and that mental anguish that he has got and he will always have? Let's say he had a newspaper, an ad in the newspaper, a job description. It said: Wanted, person who wants to work for $100.00 a day. Job description: There are no forms, there are no hours, there are no supervisors, there are no responsibilities. You don't have any duties. All you have got to do to earn your $100.00 is to give up one eye, give up your sense of smell and taste, have your face wired up, have seizures that you never know when they are going to come, lose your ability to coordinate and walk and support your family. And you can't quit, because it's permanent. You keep getting the $100.00 per day, as long as you have all of those problems, and you can't ever resign.

And that's what all of the evidence in this case is, that he has got all of these problems, they are permanent, he can't ever quit. And if you were just to say $100.00 is fair, that would be in the millions of dollars. We are not asking for that. We are asking for $750,000.00 past, present, and future pain and suffering, to go through the humiliation, the indignity, the loss of pride, the disfigurement. I can't go on enough to tell you about that.

In order to allow the jury to grasp the full extent of the plaintiff's disability, Perlman listed a series of examples that would convey an understandable impression of the loss:

When you think about this country and the great things we have, the right to life and liberty and the pursuit of happiness that he was guaranteed, think about the things he won't enjoy. He will never hear his wife, Shelly, say, have you had a hard day in the mines today, Henry? He will never hear his little girl say, hey Dad, how about driving me to school or helping me with my homework? He will never hear his children ask him to read them bedtime stories. He will never hear anybody ask him how the steak dinner was. He will never smell bacon frying in the frying pan. He will never again feel proud about the remodeling job he did of his own house. He will never earn a day's pay for a day's work. He will never go out just for a long walk or for a drive in the country. He will never sit at Christmas at the head of the table with a sense of pride that he provided it with his wages that he earned in the mine. He'll always wonder when the next seizure is going to be. What's going to happen if I lose my good eye? How am I going to be able to face these new people I'm going to meet? How does this scar look? What happens if something happens to Shelly? Who is going to take care of me? Will I be the community freak again?

Block used the example of the value of a racehorse and the cost of the space program to illustrate the value of the plaintiff's damages:

Now, let me give you some guidelines because the injuries here are monumental, they are permanent, and what I say to you as a lawyer is not evidence, but I ask for Dorman Baird what I would ask for any other human being; in this day and age when millions are paid for racehorses, when they put a man in space and they have all the safety features and programs of a nation spending billions of dollars to make sure that one, two or three people come back to earth safely, are we going to be so callous to say that a human being who in the course of service to his country damaged not by his own fault but by defective ammunition deserves less?

Habush used a religious allusion to describe the human reaction to pain when he said, "Pain, of course, needs no explanation. An old prophet once said, 'People have asked for death, but no one has ever asked for pain.' " To illustrate the plaintiff's loss, Habaush used examples of activities the plaintiff used to engage to create an image of an active, physical man before the injury. This image was dramatic in its comparison to his damaged condition:

He was a physical man. Not only was his work physical, but his extracurricular activities were physical. He loved bowling. He played baseball for the church. He loved to hike and camp. He loved to be outdoors. And he looked forward, as Bev did, to a life together, with job security, a life together after the kids were grown up and out, out of the house.

Habush gave further examples of things the plaintiff could not do that brought home to the jurors the full extent of the plaintiff's loss:

You're going to have to evaluate past and future pain and suffering. We've talked a little bit about the past. Let me just suggest some things to you.
He never again will be able to enjoy the ultimate gift of love with respect to sex with Bev. He will never again enjoy standing up straight and erect. He's not going to enjoy walking. Whether it's down the street or through some woods. He never will have the pleasure of walking down the aisle with one of his daughters. Or romping around and rolling around with grandchildren.
He never again will be anonymous in a crowd, you know? Where he can just melt away. He always will have the rest of his life a cloud of ill feeling and ill health. He always will be taking pills several times a day

and do procedures several times a week, and he always will have pain and a reminder the rest of his life.

And he never again will enjoy the pleasure of twirling around his best girl and hugging her close on a dance floor. Now we all take those things so for granted. We never even think about it.

But I suggest to you this is staggering, and as Dr. Walsh said to you, of all the injuries other than death and brain damage where you're just wiped out, there isn't any more devastating to a human being than a spinal injury because they have all their sensitivities and mental faculties and they know what they have lost. So what would be fair and adequate?

Habush then used an analogy to the value of a racehorse to argue the value of the plaintiff's loss:

You know, if this man was Seattle Slew or some racehorse which was worth ten million dollars and some fool ran the horse over and destroyed the horse, I would bring in—in a racehorse appraiser and say, well, this horse had a ten million dollar value and this person wiped out that horse and that's what you should pay, and you would probably have an easy time, say, well, that's what the horse was worth.

Or if the man was a work of art that had a market value of 5 million dollars, and some fool ruined the work of art, I would bring in an art appraiser. An art appraiser would say, this painting is worth 5 million dollars, this person ruined it, pay up. And you would have—you won't have any trouble there.

But, Members of the Jury, there are no appraisers for human beings. There is no one I can bring into this court to tell you what this man's injury is worth.

With respect to the plaintiff's wife, Habush used a Biblical allusion to characterize her goodness:

Let's talk for a moment about the marriage. The marriage is a rock. It will, without any question in my mind, survive. I think there should be a special place in heaven for Beverly Schulz because I think that she has been singularly responsible for him doing as well as he has done.

Habush metaphorically reconceptualized the plaintiff's loss of sexuality from simply the loss of a physical activity to the loss of his ability to express his love for his wife when he told the jury:

I don't mean to exaggerate or minimize the role of sex in a marriage. Some people feel it's very important. Some people don't. It's a very personal thing. But, clearly with respect to Roger, he's been deprived of being able to show in the ultimate way his love for Bev. And I don't think it requires an awful lot of statement that this is a staggering loss.

§9.25   Conclusion

In their closing statements, the lawyers were faced with the task of integrating the evidence into a coherent whole. During the trial, the jurors had been presented with competing views of reality, and in their closing statements, the lawyers had to resolve the conflicts in the evidence and persuade the jurors that their version of the facts was the "correct" version. In so doing, the lawyers were required to prove abstract, subjective, nonobservable concepts and conditions, such as negligence, damages, pain, and suffering. Although the judges' instruction delineated jury purpose, those purposes were generalized and vague, and the lawyers were faced with further defining and refining jury purpose.

The lawyers surmounted these rhetorical problems with the use of a narrative structure that integrated the evidence, created meaning, and shaped jury purpose through the use of themes and the strategic use of language.

Appendix 9-1
Closing Argument to the Jury

MR. BERGMAN: May it please the Court. Good morning again, ladies and gentlemen. On behalf of the Morrison family, I want to thank you in all sincerity for your service. Remembering back to two weeks ago, the jury selection process, there were a lot of people who either could not or did not want to devote this kind of time at this time of the year to hearing the difficult, grueling kind of a case which this has been. We really do appreciate it.

We felt good in the sense that—and there has been a lot of comment on it—that you have all been attentive and listened. That's the first thing that you hope for is that at least people will listen to your evidence as it comes in. So we are very grateful for that.

I am sure that you noticed that Shanna and Ken Morrison are not here. The evidence, if you recall, was that Shanna was probably going to be going in for some additional chemotherapy. That is where she is. The methotrexate, which is what they were intending to start, is what is going on right now. She regrets and I regret that she can't be here. She's here on the other end of the phone and very excited about having her day in court. I am just sorry that she can't be here to hear this.

I am sure that you noticed it in the jury selection process; I have several fears. I don't think that I have ever had a job this important. I don't think that I've ever had a responsibility that has felt this heavy, and I hope that I don't again, very frankly. But, you know, the acceptance of responsibility and doing the job the best that you can— sometimes I know that I may have been pretty intense about it—is part of being a professional person and taking on a professional responsibility. I think that is one of the things that we have been hoping to emphasize in this case.

The deep fear that I have had has to do with whether or not our evidence was going to fall on deaf ears or closed minds. I feel the need to mention that again, because when you represent a plaintiff in a medical malpractice case against a physician in 1987, you have got a heavy burden. Your only hope is that it doesn't become an impossible burden.

I think that we are all inclined to be understanding and forgiving of doctors because our lives are in their hands and we really want to believe and hope that they are not going to drop the ball on it. So we hold the plaintiff in a case like this to a heavy burden. That is why I spent so much time during jury selection asking all of you if you would search your souls and your backgrounds and start out this case fair and even- and open-minded and receptive to the evidence that was going to be presented to you.

You all, under oath, were committed to that, that you would be open-minded, follow the law that the Court instructed you on—and now you have heard what the law is—and hold Shanna Morrison only to that burden of proof that the law imposes on her. And I think that, as you heard, I think that in relation to the evidence in this case, that is really not a very heavy burden.

You also committed yourselves to placing a value on each item of damages that the Court instructed you that the law recognizes, if there was evidence on it. Now, you have heard what those are. We have trusted and relied on the fact that you will all do all of those things.

On the burden of proof, the Court read you Instruction 8. You'll have this, "The party that has the burden of proof must persuade you that his claim is more probably true than not true," more probably true than not true, to tip the scale. If the weight of the evidence is in your favor, you have satisfied the burden of proof.

There is another instruction that is the essence of this case. It is the basis upon which we have proceeded in this case. That is Instruction No. 17. I hope that you can take a very close look at it in determining whether the failure to properly and timely diagnose the plaintiff's disease caused or contributed to cause the plaintiff's injuries. You must determine whether the misdiagnosis reduced Shanna Morrison's chance for survival, or cure; reduced her chance.

I told you at the beginning, there is no way that we can prove that, had the diagnosis been made in September, that Shanna would definitely have been cured. It is impossible to prove because the loss of the opportunity to prove that is why we are here. She didn't have that chance. So the real question is whether her chances were appreciably reduced. The word "appreciably" is key. "Appreciably" is capable of being perceived or measured. Was there a perceptable or a measurable prejudice to her chance for cure or for survival? That is all that we have to prove. That is our burden of proof.

Now, I don't know whether you all agree with that, that should or should not be our burden of proof. But that is what we have to prove, that is what we have proven in this case. Let me put that in real human terms.

I was really appalled at one point in the trial when I was asking Dr. Jenkin, and he was talking about how the results at M.D. Anderson for children are so good. We talked about the mediastinal children versus the non-mediastinal group. And he thought that the results were pretty good either way; after all, it was 97 percent for the non-mediastinal involvement and still 88 percent with mediastinal involvement.

What does that mean? Why is that appalling to put it that way? He admitted this. It means that if 100 people present themselves in Dr. Hanson's office, September 6, 1983, and they are diagnosed properly on that day, that 97 of them will live and 3 will die. It also means that if the same group of 100 people present themselves in Dr. Hanson's office on September 6, 1983, and treated as Shanna Morrison was, 88 will live and 12 will die.

Now, I think that is an appreciable reduction in some people's chances. If we are going to use the statistics, and unfortunately, although I don't like to make a statistic of my client, we have some pretty strong, heavy, statistical information that has been presented to you. I think that is all that we can fall back on in this case. That is what it means for there to be an appreciable reduction in a person's chance. It is really not fair to the 9, the extra people who die. "You are still in the 88 percent group, and that's pretty good." I think that is, in essence, what is happening here.

There was a lot of evidence about Shanna. Shanna was described by Mrs. Claire—who I thought was a lovely lady, the school nurse—as a beautiful person inside and out.

Shanna is a fighter. She is an inspirational person. Her friends love her. I don't know whether it was good to call them as witnesses or not, but one thing was clear, they can't talk about her without crying. They miss her.

Even Dr. Hanson said that Shanna was a very personable, intelligent, mature 13-year-old. He had no trouble relating to her in his office.

Shanna was and still is Daddy's girl. Shanna is very lucky to have a mother who is as dedicated to her, and always has been, as Judy.

This is the child, this is the person, who was entrusted to the care of Dr. Hanson and she is the person who was treated so casually, despite symptoms that Dr. Carrithers and the literature and the other doctors all said "strike fear into the heart of doctors," supraclavicular nodes.

There has been a major wrong done, a major wrong done to one of our children. It is not acceptable to deny responsibility. It is not acceptable to say that, "It doesn't matter. Let's just forget it."

If it doesn't matter in this case where there is such clear evidence of the dramatic change in a person's condition with regard to cancer, then it will never matter in any case. If this case isn't the case where you can prove to people that a person's opportunity for cure is compromised, then there is no Hodgkin's disease victim who could ever have a complaint that any doctor prejudiced them by delay. Then it becomes open season on Hodgkin's disease victims.

You know, I have thought about this many times. I think that fate intervened on behalf of Shanna when that cat bit her. There was a reason that the cat bit her. The cat bit her to get her to that emergency room the next day. When that doctor found that node that Dr. Hanson just doesn't seem to accept was there, fate intervened on her behalf. Her mother intervened on her behalf when she took her, five weeks later, to the right doctor at the right time. She had all of that going for her.

The specialist. Dr. Hanson is a specialist, and I think that you are going to hear that "since the Morrisons didn't know that he was an oncologist, maybe we shouldn't hold him to the standard of care of an oncologist." Well, he's an oncologist. He has accepted that he should be held to that standard of care. His care was—well, there is even an instruction that you have gotten, "A physician who holds himself out as a specialist in a particular field must use the skill and knowledge as a specialist in that field." That is the standard of care that applies to Dr. Hanson, even as a Board certified internal medicine specialist. He is a diagnostician. That is his job.

If Shanna's case was a question on a first-year medical school examination, Dr. Hanson would fail. Think about that. Set out these facts to a person who is supposed to be a diagnostician and see what the medical clues are. He fails.

His care was sloppy. His records are incomplete. Nobody else, none of the doctors—you have all of the records, Dr. Liu, Dr. Brewer, the first-year medical student who took the history and the physical at St. Luke's Hospital—they all picked up on the fact that the node was enlarged within one day after the cat bite. That is very significant, that from day one it could not have been cat scratch disease.

Dr. Hanson didn't listen to what he was being told. I mean, Dr. Korasco's blood work is in his record for a reason. It is not just there by accident. It was there because Judy Morrison was trying to tell him that Shanna's problems preceded the cat bite.

Dr. Hanson misread his own x-ray. He admits that. He takes money to do x-rays and to read them. Dr. Fuller is the only person who testified—Dr. Fuller, who is qualified, by the way, in radiology, I think, if you will see her curriculum vitae—is the only person who commented on the x-ray, that there is an abnormality in the mediastinum that should have been seen. There wasn't one witness who the defendant brought in to contradict that except Dr. Hanson.

Now, if that is not correct testimony, that it was there from the beginning, if there is another reason why he should have made the diagnosis, shouldn't there have been one witness that the defense brought in? Even Dr. Jenkin? Look at his curriculum vitae. He's a radiologist, lots of training in radiology. If that's wrong, they should have put some witness up there to say so.

The diagnosis in this case was made without a medical basis. We don't even get to the question of medical judgment. If you are going to be a "cookbook doctor," at least follow the recipe. If you don't know anything about cat scratch disease and all that you learn is from the book that you go to, at least follow the recipe. Give your patient the benefit of that at least.

There was casual follow-up care and very lazy documentation. I suggest that the documentation in this case reflects the general attention and attentiveness that Shanna got from Dr. Hanson. He wouldn't even face her and deliver the bad news, and he attempted to cover this up. That, I think, became clear yesterday afternoon when you saw his discharge summary. He tried to smooth this thing over.

I am not sure that I proved to you that Dr. Brewer was set up to do what he did, but I think that there is something to that, when Dr. Brewer—and I just want to say it because my clients want me to say it; that they are disgusted with Dr. Brewer—when Dr. Brewer looked Ken Morrison in the eye and said, "we know that it is cat scratch disease," and when Ken Morrison left Dr. Brewer's office, he was relieved and satisfied that that was what it was.

Dr. Hanson didn't even attempt to explain why that record read that way, why the change was made. Obviously he is going to leave it to his lawyer to explain that to you. But on what we call the rehabilitation testimony, when Mr. Saunders put him on, there was not one question asked about it, not one explanation offered. The only explanation that he offered was that he was copying from the history and the physical that was in the medical records, which had been changed, which certainly didn't reflect many of the things in his discharge summary. As I think that I said, the reason that he did that, he knew if he was negligent, it made a big difference, he knew that Shanna Morrison was compromised.

Imagine two busy and important physicians from M.D. Anderson, Dr. Sullivan and Dr. Fuller, who came here to testify for no pay, no personal gain, against another physician. Doctors do not like to testify against other physicians. In fact, Dr. Sullivan and Dr. Fuller have never testified against another physician in their years.

The reason that they did it is because they knew, they know firsthand, they know what the significance of the negligence was to Shanna, and they were appalled when they saw her, and they were outraged. That is honest, obvious outrage. I'd place myself in their care sooner than I would any of the other doctors that I've seen in this case.

The same thing goes for Dr. Carrithers. We showed the video tape of Dr. Carrithers the first morning of trial. There was nothing in this for him. He testified, I think that he said, "after a lot of soul searching." It is not something that he wanted to do. He was very reluctant to do it, but he is an honorable man. He knew that there was a wrong done here. When called upon, he had to step forward.

Who stood up to defend Dr. Hanson's diagnosis? Think about it. The diagnosis? Nobody. Nobody.

And the very people that he vouched for as experts, Dr. Lacher and Dr. Jenkin, couldn't defend his conduct. The most remarkable moment in the trial for me was when Dr. Lacher said that he didn't even know that was in issue, he thought that was a given, that there was negligence in failing to make the diagnosis. And I said, "You mean that he missed the diagnosis? He was negligent?"

The answer: "Yes".

"You agree that he blew it badly?"

"I agree to that."

He said that the nodes were never explained on any medical basis until the biopsy was done—that's a true statement—and that Dr. Hanson should have arranged for the biopsy at the first visit. Now, that's his own witness that he vouched for.

Dr. Jenkin, he has never seen a case of cat scratch disease, but he knows that if you have got enlarged nodes within twelve or twenty-four hours of a cat bite, that can't be cat scratch disease. He knows that. He expects other doctors to know that, all doctors, not just oncologists. And he would have expected Dr. Hanson to consider cancer as a first possibility and rule it in or rule it out.

Dr. Brewer testified or wrote a report that this is not inconsistent. It could be consistent and compatible with cat scratch disease, but he never really stepped up and was asked directly, "Do you think that Dr. Hanson satisfied the standard of care that applied to him in making that diagnosis?" He never testified to that. He testified that he has never used the cat scratch antigen. Why? Because it is "impossible to find." And I thought that it was rather revealing of what he was here to do when I asked him, "Have you ever tried?" And he said, "No."

We know now that in his own hospital all that he had to do was call the virology laboratory and there were two people there that knew very well that they had it right over at Children's Mercy Hospital. Most revealing of all, as soon as he got the history from Shanna of the cat, of the node enlarged the day after the cat bite, he knew that it was not compatible with cat scratch disease.

The textbooks that Dr. Hanson referred to, Cecil's, which is written by Margolith and Harrison, the textbooks testified against him.

Even Dr. Korasco. And I had no idea why Frank Saunders read her deposition because I asked her that question at the end, whether the standards of care that applied on September 6th called for a biopsy, and she said yes.

It is not possible to produce more evidence than that. If you are going to hold us to a higher standard than that, then we never had a chance to begin with. At least Dr. Hanson should be required to produce one objective, competent witness to defend his diagnosis. He has not done that.

You would just expect in these circumstances that he would admit, "I blew it. I am sorry. I am sorry," and then defend the case on the basis that it didn't make a difference, because that's the second line of defense. But he has known, just as Dr. Sullivan has known and Dr. Fuller has known, that it made all the difference in the world. That's why he can't admit that.

Dr. Sullivan knew it the day that she first saw Shanna—that is Exhibit 45—when she wrote in her record, "Because of the extent of the disease, the treatment sequence is not final at this time pending information to patient's sensitivity to chemotherapy."

Five days later she wrote a letter to Dr. Saffo, the referring doctor, which says, "Therapy in Shanna's case posed real problems because of the extent of the abdominal, axillary and supraclavicular disease." And she testified she should have also put in there "pelvic." She said, "We are, of course, very concerned about this girl because of the extent of the disease and hope that she can be managed successfully." That is day one.

For Shanna, the delay was the difference between a 90-plus percent chance for cure, very optimistic chance, and the very grim reality expressed by Dr. Sullivan that, "We are concerned about this girl because of the extent of her disease." It is the difference between the quality of life and the length of life which is normal, which is equal to the general population, according to Dr. Lacher, and that is true. An existence where Shanna has been dragged from one torture chamber to another for the rest of her days, from one disappointment to the next, where a beautiful human being is just wasted away by the toxic poisons that she has got to put into her body to stay alive.

Now, did the delay appreciably reduce her chance for survival or cure? If common sense and the honest impression of her doctors isn't enough, right in the record, let's start with Dr. Hanson's testimony.

He admitted a couple of key things. "With Hodgkin's disease it is generally accepted that a patient is better off when the diagnosis is made early and the treatment is started early." "A patient who is diagnosed and properly treated has an appreciably better opportunity for cure and recovery than that same patient in a more advanced stage." I used the word "appreciably" when I asked that question on purpose because I knew what the law is in this case, and he agreed to that.

Now, at trial—"that's for adults." He didn't say that at his deposition. That was a general statement that applied to Hodgkin's disease in the context of this case.

Dr. Sullivan and Dr. Fuller. Dr. Fuller in all of her years has never seen the extent and the bulk of tumor in a Hodgkin's disease patient that Shanna had when she came down to M.D. Anderson, except for one patient from Guatemala. That was her testimony. And the bulkiest areas, which is really significant, I think, were the precise areas that they couldn't get rid of with the chemotherapy and the radiation treatment. That is not a coincidence.

The massive pelvic involvement that Shanna had has never been seen by Dr. Jenkin, at least in terms of the 110 patients which he originally told us were all of the patients that he has had and that he has reported on. He tried to back up on me and he said that it was in a five-year period, and I pulled out the articles and it is in a ten-year period. In 110 patients, none of them had disease in the pelvis. He has no comparability to make a judgment about.

I thought that the most significant admission that those two doctors made was that the treating doctors are in a much better position to make judgments on these issues than Dr. Lacher and Dr. Jenkin; Dr. Lacher, who never even bothered to read the record. Right there, the case should be over and we should be talking about the damages. But there is more.

The data. There are no studies, I will acknowledge to you, there are no studies of a pediatric population of patients to determine whether tumor bulk has prognostic significance except the mediastinal bulk. Of course, as you might expect, it does have significance. In pediatric patients, even in the mediastinum, even today. But the reason why there are no other studies anywhere of pediatric patients with regard to the bulk, Dr. Sullivan explained, people bring their kids into the doctor before things get out of hand. Adults tend to let things go as to themselves. There are also more adults who have had Hodgkin's disease.

But every time, everywhere, every place that the issue of the prognostic significance of tumor bulk has been studied, the answer has been, unequivocally, it has the most significance to outcome, to cure, to survival, much more than "appreciably." I am not going to go over the numbers today, but much more than appreciably. The difference between a 90 percent chance and a 45 percent chance; nobody is entitled to rob a person of that kind of a chance.

Dr. Sullivan, Dr. Fuller, and Dr. Lacher all agreed that the adult data is fairly applicable to Shanna Morrison's case. Dr. Lacher acknowledged that three or four times. He had no quarrel with it. He said, "Yes. That is the data. I accept that." The only person who didn't agree that it was Dr. Jenkin.

On Dr. Lacher, he also finally admitted that the only known explanation that he had for Shanna's failure of treatment was tumor bulk. That is the only known explanation. Anything else in his opinion is conjecture, but he has seen patients who just do not do well in Stage I, II or III. We don't deny that. There are patients where the explanation may not exist. This is a patient where there is a very complete, very satisfactory, very logical explanation.

Dr. Jenkin acknowledged that the adult data fairly applies to Shanna Morrison initially. I probably should have left it right there. Then he backed off and, for some reason, he said, "It doesn't," and that, "because there is no scientific data" that would allow him to make that leap from the adult Hodgkin's population to the adolescent Hodgkin's population. He needs scientific data before he can have an opinion.

Then he proceeded to admit that his theory is based upon total speculation. Total speculation. He has suggested that there are some people in some labs working on whether or not his theory may have some validity. If you recall, in order to establish this genetic resistance theory that he talked about, you have to have the cell, and then you have got to culture the cell and expose it to treatments and see that it is resistant. None of that has been done.

Now, I don't think that it is fair for somebody in the position of a party to have to respond to a theory that has no basis in science just because somebody is willing to come in and say it. Dr. Lacher and Dr. Jenkin certainly may have qualifications. I don't want to be crude about this, but I think that when it comes down to them, it is, "Have resume, will travel." I think that is fairly applicable to them.

Dr. Lacher has been paid $15,000 for his short appearance here. Dr. Jenkin, by my calculations, depending on what time that he got home, was going to get somewhere between $8,000 and $10,000 for coming in here and speculating for you.

They are here to do what they can for another member of the fraternity is what it comes down to. They want to be paid handsomely to do it. They couldn't even agree with each other. Dr. Lacher does not accept Dr. Jenkin's genetic resistance theory. You hadn't heard it yet. But the question was asked, I asked whether there was any other explanation for the failure of treatment that he knew of. And he said, "No." So I don't know what more Shanna Morrison could present to you to tip the scale that probably her tumor bulk is why she isn't cured, why she is considered a terminal patient. I think that we have to be fair with her. We cannot impose an impossible burden on her. We can't impose an impossible burden on ourselves when we come into Court with a legitimate claim.

The M.D. Anderson doctors saw Shanna with their own eyes. They were appalled. They tried to treat her; they couldn't. They saw her response and they knew why the treatment failed. They weren't paid. Their opinions are honest, they are logical, they are based upon data. They are consistent with data, and that's all that we can do. Again, I think if that isn't enough, we were doomed from the start.

I wish that I could turn back the clock to September 6th, 1983, and have the diagnosis made. Shanna would love to take her chances with that small bit of tumor that was in her body. She would love to have that chance. We can't do that.

For me, I would love for there to be a way for Dr. Hanson to know and to experience somehow the pain and the hardship that Shanna has been through, but that won't happen. Maybe that seems harsh, and

I am sorry. We would even have had some satisfaction in this case if we could have just had a sincere apology, just a sincere apology, maybe just an acknowledgement of some fault, that something was done wrong. We weren't even able to accomplish that.

And this case, unfortunately, because this case is not going to have an impact on Dr. Hanson's practice or license—it is not what this is about—his practice goes on. That is just the reality of the world. There is only one way for Shanna Morrison to get any satisfaction in this case. That's in the form of your verdict.

You know the amount that we are asking, five million. That is for compensation in an amount that will tell Dr. Hanson, "You blew it badly. You can't cover it up. We are not going to sweep it under the rug for you. It is not going to be overlooked. Sorry." An amount that tells Shanna, "We place a high value on your life. We are not going to disregard your losses. We are not going to discount your losses." An amount that will tell all of the professional people in our community, "When you hold yourself out as a hot-shot expert and you take our money and you accept the responsibility for the lives of our children, we consider that important and heavy, and you are going to be a hundred percent accountable when you are negligent and someone is tragically injured."

I am concerned about detachment in this case. I have had to try, and I have tried, you just naturally have to try to detach your emotions from this horrible experience or you just can't go on and talk about it and deal with it. And I am sure that the natural response of the jury is to do the same thing.

You have got to be the finders of fact. You can't be emotionally involved as you are hearing the evidence. When it comes time to considering the damages, when you get to that point, then your job is to try to understand. Then the job is to try to empathize, to try to figure yourself what are the damages that we are compensating for, what has really happened here?

We are not asking for sympathy. We have not played for sympathy. This case is sympathetic. We have not tried to play on sympathy. Who needs to? I mean the facts speak for themselves. The injury is horrendous.

You heard the instruction on the damages, and I have listed the various categories that are considered in damages, and they are expressed in longer terms, but these are the things that you are committed to putting a dollar value on. Some of these are lumped together, but they are different concepts: pain and suffering, disabilities, disfigurement, mental anguish—these are all different concepts—loss of time, future earnings. Just take Shanna Morrison's life expectancy that the Court has given you. Allow a satisfactory, reasonable factor for the earnings that she won't have and multiply that yourself. That is a huge loss. She is entitled to be compensated for that in this case. Again, maybe it is something that you don't really agree with, but she is entitled. That's what the law says.

The reasonable value of the services that have been provided by her family, put a reasonable value on it. I am not even going to try to suggest one to you, but there has been an awful lot of services, including giving blood every couple of days for the last however many months. Enjoyment of life. Medical and related expenses. The stipulated evidence is that it is $293,000, not including anything that has happened since March. That is stipulated. That is a starting point.

You know, it is easy to say—I gave it a little thought; let me remind you of a few things. Ten major surgeries; the herpes, the isolation that goes with that; the sores down her throat to her stomach; the shake-and-bake treatments, remember those? eighteen days of shaking and then cooking; the hemorrhagic cystitis, which is very painful and still a problem; the nausea—which this is all constant—nausea, vomiting; fatigue; her heart problems; nerve damage to the extremities so she can't really write too well, she can't walk very well; she has been wasted, physically wasted, by the treatment that she didn't need; loss of enjoyment of life.

There are life experiences that she is never going to have. She thinks about that. She can't complete her education. She can't have the college experience that she looked forward to. She can't really have friendships. She can't have a meaningful relationship with a boy. She won't be able to get married and have children. She just can't even have fun. That's loss of enjoyment of life.

I am not going to stand here and do more of this because that really is part of your job. You have got to try to come to grips with it. You've got to try to empathize. You've got to try to understand what the damages are in each of these categories and put a reasonable value on it.

It is easy to say that money can't replace those things. That's true. I am not arguing with that. But it is not the point. The point is that each of you searched your hearts and answered as honestly as you could, and you said that you would attempt to put a reasonable value on those things. You are not permitted to say at this point, "What is the use?" because there is a use. There is a point. It makes a big difference.

Shanna is not dead. Shanna is a fighter. There is a cloud, a very big, black cloud over her future. And when she dies, she is going to go hard, but she could be here for a long time. Let's hope that she is.

She should be in a financial position for the rest of her days where she can take advantage of any possible break-through, any possible thing that will help her, no matter where in the world that it is, no matter how expensive that it is, without having to worry or put any more financial pressure on her family. I think that she should be financially wealthy. I think that she should be able to live for the rest of her life with the sense that, if she is nothing else, she is independently wealthy—if she can feel good about that—she can do whatever she wants to for whomever she wants. She should have that. And that is part of the point of this case.

She should know that you care about her. She should know that you put a large value on the things that she has lost. I try to think what must really go through her mind? She is a smart, perceptive, sensitive person. She doesn't complain. She cries sometimes, but she doesn't complain. She gets worried when she knows that her friends are worried about her. She doesn't like them to be worried about her.

She probably knows about as well as anybody on earth what hell is like. She probably knows that. She has got more insight to that than anybody that I know. She has lived an existence since 1983 of fear, pain, hopes that are dashed, bitter disappointments. She has had to hug her loved ones and go into, really, a chamber of horrors, that bubble, not knowing whether she would ever touch them again. That isn't easy, and Hodgkin's patients shouldn't have to do that.

She has lived in the world of hospitals. It has been much harder for her to accept that because of the knowledge that she has that it didn't have to be that way. It shouldn't have been that way, no matter what Frank Saunders or Dr. Lacher or Jenkin are paid to say.

Shanna Morrison is going to go to her grave knowing that it made a difference and Judi and Ken are going to hurt for the rest of their lives knowing that it made a difference. And I hope that you people realize and believe that it made a difference and that your verdict reflects that. I'm sorry to get emotional.

(Mr. Saunders' closing argument has been deleted.)

MR. BERGMAN: A lot has been said. I kind of feel like, when we are dealing with the facts and the evidence at this point, after hearing Mr. Saunders, that it is sort of like trying to swat at a silverfish. He kept saying, "I may—" one thing that he said, I wrote it down because I think that it really is true—"I may sound like I am, but I am really not."

You know, where do you start when you believe that the evidence has been misstated throughout closing argument? I glanced over. My senior partner is over there. I remember one instance where I was so upset after hearing the closing argument of another lawyer, and I had my opportunity to go again, he just settled me down and he said, "Look, the jury was here. They heard the evidence. You have got to give them some credit and rely on their memories." I've always tried to remember that. There is no way that I can try to respond to everything that I think was said that was wrong, but there are a few things that definitely need a response.

This animal in the tree. You know, this is not a game. This is not a newspaper hieroglyphic. This is life and death. When a doctor accepts that responsibility and he holds himself out as a diagnostician, that's his job. He is paid to look for the animal in the tree, to look at the clues, sort them out, to use the tools that are available and to get at the diagnosis. He is supposed to establish a diagnosis, not guess. As Dr. Hanson said, "Guessing isn't judgment." You have got to fulfill some diagnostic criteria before you can casually disregard what should be recognized as a possibility of cancer.

You know, there is no magic. It doesn't take a doctor to know that when you are looking at bulges and bumps that you should be worried about cancer, tumors. So, you know, this idea that the issue is whether he can be excused isn't the issue at all. The issue is whether there was any testimony that he offered that said that he fulfilled the standard of care that applied to him. He did not offer any testimony. Regardless of what Mr. Saunders says about that. There is no witness who defended the diagnosis in this case.

The constant reference to Dr. Sullivan and Fuller's testimony and their writings. One of the principal exhibits in this case is the chart that is Table 5. It is Table 5 from Dr. Fuller's article that Mr. Saunders was referring to. It is the table that isolates III-1, III-2, III-3. It shows that when you are looking at the III-3, the extensive disease into the pelvis, your chances for a cure go down to 47 percent, not even a probability of cure at that point. That is what her paper says.

This reference to Desser and Stein, and the idea that findings in the abdomen are not significant statistically when we use the Desser and the Stein classification system; that's true, the Desser and the Stein classification system is III-1, III-2. It includes the abdomen and the pelvis. When you break out the sub-set, the population of patients that have the disease down into the pelvis, there is that dramatic difference.

So we are not here to talk about Desser and Stein's criteria. Even Desser and Stein, the article—and I confronted Dr. Jenkin with it— shows that there is a significant decrease in the prognosis even with the disease in the pelvis. All that Dr. Fuller's article says is that, "We do just as well when we look at our results based upon that criteria as they do." But the point of that article is that we want to look at a further sub-set of patients.

The thing about Dr. Sullivan and Fuller, it is a little different than some of the other articles that we have been referring to. We don't have to refer to the articles; we had Dr. Fuller and Dr. Sullivan. We heard what they had to say, what their opinions are. You may be able to pull a sentence out of an article and confront them with it, but they kept answering, "Shanna is not in this category of patients. She was a unique patient. Her bulk was massive. She doesn't compare with the other groups. We have a specific reason why she failed. We know what it is. We didn't develop that opinion because we were distressed," as though they are supposedly portrayed as some elderly women who are just distressed and are looking for some sort of person to blame.

These are the doctors that have been through the wars. They have seen everything. Dr. Sullivan was distressed on day one. She put it in writing on day one. So they didn't develop some opinion and look for somebody to blame later on. They were distressed, all right; they are distressed that that this happened to Shanna.

Just so many things that I wrote down. The idea that Dr. Jenkin has only seen 110 patients. Frankly, I think that is true. I think that his entire patient population is included in those articles, and the fact is that he has never seen a female patient with disease in the pelvis. I think that is the fact. He wouldn't admit that. Now he has got other unreported patients that he was telling us about.

That Dr. Sullivan has only seen 122 patients is not true either. She said that is a series of patients who went through laparotomy in a given number of years. She testified, I think, that she has seen many more hundreds of patients than that.

The idea that the only bulk that any of the articles refer to as having any significance is the mediastinum; that is false. That is not the evidence. We refer to the data at Stanford where they looked at the spleen and there were five nodules or less in the spleen. That was one category of patients; more than five nodules was the other. He found that the most statistically significant factor as to prognosis is the number of nodules in the spleen, and Shanna has twelve. She is off the scale.

The article by the group, the MAZA group in Italy, which Dr. Jenkin, he didn't know the article, he knew the group in Balogna, Italy, that looked at whether there were masses in the pelvis greater than three centimeters. The other group was less than three centimeters. They also looked at the spleen data, more than five, less than five. They came to the same conclusion, that the single-most statistically significant prognostic factor for Hodgkin's disease was the amount of tumor bulk in the spleen and the size of the tumor bulk in the pelvis.

Now, we can't forget those things. That is scientific data that is in evidence. One thing that was remarkable to me, I am glad for it, and it makes your job, I think, a lot easier, is that there has been no issue taken with the amount of money that we are suggesting is appropriate.

Parties are compelled—this is an adversary proceeding, we each present our side, we each present what we think **is** a reasonable position to you—a party is compelled, if he doesn't agree with a position on an issue, to make that known, to say to you what he thinks is appropriate. And there has been no comment on that. That really does, I think, make the job very easy.

It is up to you. It is whatever you think is appropriate, but I did a little thinking. Because I know that $5 million is a lot of money, I have tried to explain some of my rationale to you. This is 1987. This case encompasses the last almost 4 years for Shanna. However long that the rest of her life is, don't forget that. This case is not only for what has happened up to now but what will happen in the future.

I decided, well, let's give Dr. Hanson credit for the first year of treatment because he didn't cause the Hodgkin's disease, and Shanna, the testimony was six months, but let's give him credit for a year. Then let's take Dr. Lacher's view of his importance and value of $250 an hour, twenty-four hours a day, and determine what that comes to.

That's 818 days times 24 hours times $250 comes out to $4,908,000. You know, that is just playing with numbers. I realize that. But the point is, where do we put our value in our society? What do we put the value on? What is really reasonable to compensate a person for having to live like Shanna has had to live life versus sitting in the lap of luxury in a Central Park office, reviewing some records, or sleeping at the Alameda Plaza, or wherever that it was, and having the clock run. I just think that there is that evidence in the case. It is something that you ought to think about. There are many individuals in this society that earn that amount of money in a year.

Now, maybe Shanna would never have earned that amount of money in a year, probably not. We are talking about the value of the totality of her existence, which has probably been cut drastically short. That is what we are really talking about. We value race horses at millions of dollars, arbitragers walk away with millions of dollars for doing nothing.

The Morrisons are little people. This is probably what is in the back of the mind. The big justice is for the big people, but the little justice is for the little people. Maybe that is what is in the back of Mr. Saunders' mind. Maybe that is what he is relying on. I am not embarrassed to stand and say that $5 million is what Shanna Morrison's damages are worth. In fact, I would be embarrassed to ask for anything less. Think about that. You have to put a value on it. You have to step forward for Shanna Morrison.

What is really appropriate? We are constantly hearing of these masterpieces. I could go on and on and give you all sorts of examples. The masterpieces that hang in the museums. There was one sold, a Van Gough, fifteen flowers in a pot, forty million dollars. There are scores and scores of examples of that, and if I walked into a museum with a knife and I slashed one of those masterpieces, everybody would say, "What an awful thing that is, a terrible thing, outrageous, irreparable damage," I should go to jail, I should pay for it.

Well, isn't Shanna a masterpiece? Isn't she much more of a masterpiece than any painting that hangs in any museum or any horse that runs in the Kentucky derby or as much a masterpiece as any athlete that makes a couple of a million dollars a year? That is why I think that when you put a value on the sum total of a life of a 13-year-old girl who hasn't really had a chance to live that life, and now a 16-year-old girl, that is not unreasonable at all. It shouldn't just be the big justice for the big people and the little justice for the little people.

In my mind, Shanna Morrison is a big person. She is a hero. She is an inspirational person. Her story should be known. I know that she has been an inspiration at M.D. Anderson to many other patients. She is a strong, courageous girl who did nothing wrong, who was just simply let down.

As I said before, Mr. Saunders can stand here all day, but it made a difference. It made a drastic, big difference. There is no person alive who would feel or believe that the difference between her situation in September versus February didn't make a difference. It doesn't make sense. It is not reality. It is not consistent with what happens in any cancer, including Hodgkin's disease.

I just can't respond to every falsity that was stated right here about what the data shows, what it doesn't show, who said what. I'll have to rely on your memories for that. All that I can say is that this is a very important moment in Shanna's life, and I am sure that you know that. All that we'll be doing is just waiting anxiously to hear what your verdict is.

Thank you.

10

A Structure For Successful Trial Technique

§10.01   The Structure for Successful Trial Technique

Plaintiffs face common rhetorical problems in civil jury trials. The plaintiff and defendant present conflicting views of reality, and the jury is ultimately required to resolve those claims. Thus, the overall rhetorical problem is one of helping the jurors resolve this conflict in favor of the plaintiff's view.

In persuading the jury that their version of reality is "correct," lawyers for the plaintiff are faced with the problem of presenting the case in such a way that the mass of evidence is made meaningful to the jurors. In many cases, the evidence is massive to the jurors. In many cases, the evidence is massive and complex. The lawyers have to integrate and present the evidence in such a way that the jurors do not become confused or misled in hearing and deciding the case. The lawyers have to create schemata to guide the process through which jurors form impressions of the plaintiffs, the defendants, the witnesses, and the lawyers who represent them.

During the trial, each side of the case claims that its witnesses are credible, while the other side's witnesses are not. Since the jurors do not know the lawyers, litigants, or witnesses involved in the case, the credibility of each is in issue. Therefore, lawyers have to demonstrate to the jury that their witnesses are believable.

In order to win, lawyers must prove that the defendants are negligent, and that the plaintiffs have suffered injuries and damages. Negligence, pain, and suffering are abstract, subjective concepts, and the outcome of cases depends on the lawyers' ability to present the evidence and arguements in such a way that the jury can appreciate and understand these abstract, subjective concepts.

Finally, although the jury is instructed by the court that its purpose is to do justice and to render a fair and impartial verdict, this definition of purpose is vague. The concepts of justice, fairness, and impartiality are open to interpretation, and the way the concepts are interpreted will determine the outcome of the case. Therefore, lawyers for the plaintiff are faced with defining and refining jury purpose.

The prominence of these problems differs in each segment of the trial. The ostensible purpose of voir dire is to get at juror attitudes and beliefs so that meaningful jury selection can occur. Although lawyers seek this information, they are also involved in resolving the competing views of reality. Since initial impressions may influence the impressions jurors form throughout the trial, the lawyers must begin to shape jurors' impressions in voir dire. The passive lawyer may lose his or her case before the opening statement begins. Thus, while probing juror background and attitudes, the lawyers begin the process of resolving the competing claims of reality and credibility, proving their cases, and shaping jury purpose. Since the ostensible purpose of voir dire is to discover background information about jurors and juror attitudes, and since this segment of the trial is prescribed and limited by the court, the persuasive maneuvers have to be handled subtly.

In the opening statement, the lawyers create the schemata that will guide impressions jurors make throughout the trial. Here the lawyers are faced with the problem of previewing the trial and putting the case together in such a way that subsequent evidence will be meaningful.

During direct examination, lawyers are involved in proving their cases and establishing the credibility of their witnesses. Many of the witnesses are inexperienced in presenting themselves before groups of people and some have limited communication abilities. Therefore, the lawyers must pattern their questioning in a way that allows the witnesses to present all relevant and important information. Since unintentional errors in testimony can prove fatal to the cases, lawyers must pattern their questions in a way that allows them to guide the witnesses' testimony.

During cross-examination, lawyers are faced with the defendant's witnesses, who have repesented the competing view of reality. In order to win their cases, the lawyers must controvert either the credibility or the testimony of these witnesses.

In closing statements, lawyers are faced with the problem of integrating the evidence and law into a coherent whole. In order to win their cases, they must create a framework that gives meaning to the evidence, present abstract concepts, such as negligence, pain, and suffering, in a way that the jury can appreciate and understand, and shape jury purpose.

This study demonstrates that successful lawyers for the plaintiff approach and surmount the rhetorical problems inherent in civil jury trials in similar ways. These common responses to the rhetorical problems may be viewed as a structure for successful trial technique.

In their overall approach to the trial, successful lawyers take an active role in the impression formation process. They do not take the jury as constituted, nor do they take jury purpose as given by the judge. They begin molding the jury and the jury purpose from the outset of the trial. They do not accept the setting of the trial itself as given, but, rather, they create the purpose of the trial consistent with the needs of the plaintiff's case. They do not accept the jurors as people with rigid schemata for impression formation, but rather, they create frameworks that will influence the jurors' perceptions throughtout the trial. Most importantly, they do not accept the parties, lawyers, witnesses, facts, or law as things with set, commonly understood meanings. Rather, they create meaning for all of the people and things involved in the trial. If some aspect of the case is incompatible with the plaintiff's case, the lawyers attempt to transform it symbolically in such a way that it becomes compatible. In short, successful lawyers for the plaintiff use language and symbols to create the reality of the trial and to guide juror impression formation.

In the specific segments of the trials, the lawyers use various techniques to accomplish these goals. During voir dire, it is clear that they are looking beyond the jury selection process to the trial itself. They use voir dire to begin shaping the impression formation process of the jurors. These lawyers take an active role in using voir dire to shape juror perception and jury purpose. As well as skillfully gathering background information about jurors in order to eliminate those biased against their clients, themselves, or their case, they (1) set the tone for the trial, (2) introduce concepts and evidence and condition the jurors for things to follow in the trial, (3) obtain public comitments favorable to their cases from jurors, (4) use language that creates connotations favorable to their clients, their witnesses, and other relevant facets of their case, (5) rehearse the arguments they will use in the trial, (6) refute opposition arguments, (7) enhance their credibility, and (8) create jury purpose. By the time voir dire is completed, the lawyers have previewed the entire trial for the jurors and have created a favorable atmosphere for the plaintiff's case.

In their opening statements, successful lawyers for the plaintiff become storytellers. They develop a narrative structure to create the cognitive schemata that guides the perceptions of the jurors throughout the trial. The central element in creating such a framework is transforming the case into a story, through the use of language and themes, to make the events come alive and to present the plaintiffs as heroes and the defendants as villains. In the course of telling the story, the lawyers also develop themes that organize the evidence and claims of liability, set a serious tone, define jury purpose, specify their bases of authority, introduce key concepts and key pieces of evidence, enhance credibility, lay out the central arguments in their cases, and refute the central contentions of the defendant. The "story" becomes the cognitive schemata that organizes the trial and shapes juror perception. The storytelling structure integrates the trial into a coherent whole that will guide juror perception through the remainder of the trial.

In their direct presentation of evidence, witnesses are used to present facts in support of the story line. The witnesses fill in the story about how and why the plaintiffs were injured and about the nature and extent of the plaintiffs' damages. The lawyers elicit background information from the witnesses that personalizes them and enhances their credibility. The lawyers use language that is simple and direct and can be easily understood by both the witnesses and jurors. The form of questioning ranges from narrow questions calling for specific answers to leading questions. Due to their training and experience, experts are given more latitude than lay witnesses to provide narrative answers. However, in all cases, the lawyers control the testimony of the witnesses by their use of narrow questions. In all cases, the lawyers know exactly where they are going with their evidence, and their witnesses are led step by step through their testimony.

Successful lawyers for the plaintiff use cross-examination to achieve three purposes: (1) to destroy the credibility of the witness, (2) to controvert arguments or facts presented previously by the witness or by the defense, and (3) to elicit facts in support of the plaintiff's case. Since the witnesses are at best adverse and at worst hostile, the lawyers use questioning strategies that allow them to control the testimony. The testimony is controlled by the use of leading questions, the use of admonitions to the witnesses to answer questions directly, the use of depositions and exhibits, developing a few strong points, adherence to the laws of primacy and recency, and the strategic use of language to shape juror impression formation.

In their closing statements, the lawyers pull the case together into a coherent whole with the use of a storytelling structure that integrates the evidence, creates meaning, and shapes jury purpose through the use of themes and the strategic use of language.

§10.02 Implications

For these lawyers, the trial is viewed as a whole, with the parts being interrelated. During the course of the trial, through use of a narrative structure integrating themes essential to the plaintiff's case, vivid language, and persuasive strategies, the "facts" and "evidence" are reframed and reconstituted in such a way that they lead the jury to a verdict for the plaintiffs. The lawyers create the context which gives rise to meanings favorable to their cases.

The fact that, within the trial setting, meaning and the context for meaning are ambiguous and open to interpretation highlights the nature of trying jury cases. Concepts such as negligence and justice have no real meaning in the abstract. They begin to have concrete meaning only when applied in real situations in interaction with the judge, jury, lawyers, and litigants. As a rule, the defendants and skilled lawyers who are willing to do whatever is necessary to create meaning favorable to their cases. Thus, in order to be successful, the lawyers for the plaintiff must take an active role in the process of creating meaning. It is clear that these successful lawyers for the plaintiff have adapted their behavior to conform to the demands of the rhetorical forum within which they operate.

A further implication is that strategies and techniques of highly successful lawyers trying particularly difficult civil suits differ in significant ways from the advice given lawyers in standard trial texts. First, the entire trial must be viewed as a whole, as opposed to separate parts that can be studied and prepared separately. For example, commitments elicited in voir dire will be strategically invoked in the closing statement, and, therefore, the voir dire must be prepared with the closing statement in mind. Similarly, the narrative structure serves as the framework for guiding jurors' impressions throughout the trial. Second, voir dire must be used for more than gathering evidence about juror backgrounds and attitudes. It may be used productively to preview the trial and create a favorable atmosphere for the plaintiff's case. Third, the opening statement may be used to do more than simply laying out the facts. It must be used to create the framework that will guide juror perceptions throughout the trial. Major arguments must be previewed in the opening and the central arguments of the defendant must be refuted. Fourth, in direct examination, the form of the questions must be designed to conform to the style and experience of the particular witnesses involved in the case. If witnesses are nervous, inexperienced, or inarticulate, leading questions must be used to elicit their testimony. Open-ended questions asking for narrative answers could be disastrous. Finally, in closing, and throughout the trial, lawyers must be prepared to use language to create meaning for the people, concepts, and things involved in the trial. Facts, legal concepts, and jury purpose have ambiguous meanings for jurors, and lawyers must be prepared to use language to create meaning favorable to their clients and cases.

Index

A

ARGUMENT
Common sense §§2.17, 3.13
Cross-examination, controverting
 defense arguments in §8.07
Opening statement
–refuting defendant's arguments
 §6.24
–rehearsing arguments §6.23
Voir dire. See VOIR DIRE

ATTITUDES AND BELIEFS
Voir dire. See VOIR DIRE

AUTHORITARIAN PERSONALITY
Background §§4.12-4.16
Jury selection basis §§4.10-4.16
Plaintiff vs. defendant §4.15

AUTHORITY, BASES OF
Opening statement §6.16

B

BALDWIN, SCOTT
Biographical information §1.04
Cases studied, description of
 §1.04

BERGMAN, VICTOR
Biographical information §1.04

BERGMAN, VICTOR, *continued*
Cases studied, description of
 §1.04

BLOCK, MELVIN
Biographical information §1.04
Cases studied, description of
 §1.04

C

CLOSING STATEMENT
Generally §§9.01, 9.25
Jury purpose
–generally §9.12
–itemization of damages §9.18
–judging evidence §9.13
–judging parties and their actions
 §9.14
–money damages, returning
 §§9.17-9.20
–plaintiff's health, inability to
 restore §9.19
–rendering justice §9.16
–sending message to defendants:
 deter future actions §9.15
Language, strategic use of §9.22
–examples and figurative language
 to create meaning §9.24

529